RENAISSANCE ENGLAND'S CHIEF RABBI: JOHN SELDEN

A detail from John Selden's letter to Ben Jonson (printed in full in the Appendix) of 28 February 1616 (dated 1615). MS Selden supra 108, fo. 64r; reproduced by kind permission of the Bodleian Library, Oxford.

Renaissance England's Chief Rabbi: John Selden

JASON P. ROSENBLATT

OXFORD
UNIVERSITY PRESS

OXFORD
UNIVERSITY PRESS

Great Clarendon Street, Oxford OX2 6DP

Oxford University Press is a department of the University of Oxford.
It furthers the University's objective of excellence in research, scholarship,
and education by publishing worldwide in

Oxford New York

Auckland Cape Town Dar es Salaam Hong Kong Karachi
Kuala Lumpur Madrid Melbourne Mexico City Nairobi
New Delhi Shanghai Taipei Toronto

With offices in

Argentina Austria Brazil Chile Czech Republic France Greece
Guatemala Hungary Italy Japan Poland Portugal Singapore
South Korea Switzerland Thailand Turkey Ukraine Vietnam

Oxford is a registered trade mark of Oxford University Press
in the UK and in certain other countries

Published in the United States
by Oxford University Press Inc., New York

British Library Cataloguing in Publication Data

Data available

Library of Congress Cataloguing in Publication Data

Rosenblatt, Jason Philip, 1941–
Renaissance England's Chief Rabbi :
John Selden / Jason P. Rosenblatt.
p. cm.
Includes bibliographical references and index.
1. Selden, John, 1584–1654—Influence.
2. Great Britain—Intellectual life—17th century.
3. Jewish learning and scholarship—England—History—17th century.
4. Judaism—England—History—17th century. I. Title.
BM755.S385R67 2006   828′.409—dc22   2005024539

Typeset by SPI Publisher Services, Pondicherry, India
Printed in Great Britain
on acid-free paper by
Biddles Ltd., King's Lynn, Norfolk

ISBN 0–19–928613–2   978–0–19–928613–3

1 3 5 7 9 10 8 6 4 2

for Zipporah

Contents

Acknowledgements   viii

Introduction   1

1. *Hamlet*, Henry, *Epicoene*, and Hebraica: Marriage Questions   14

2. Selden, Jonson, and the Rabbis on Cross-Dressing and
   Bisexual Gods   54

3. Selden and Milton on Gods and Angels   74

4. Samson's Sacrifice   93

5. Andrew Marvell, Samuel Parker, and the Rabbis on Zealots and
   Proselytes   112

6. Natural Law and Noachide Precepts: Grotius, Selden, Milton,
   and Barbeyrac   135

7. Selden's *De Jure Naturali . . . Juxta Disciplinam Ebraeorum*
   and Religious Toleration   158

8. Selden and Stubbe on Idolatry, Blasphemy, and the
   Passion Narrative   182

9. Culverwel on Selden's Rabbinica: The Limits of a
   Liberal's Toleration   202

10. Selden's Rabbis in the Court of Common Pleas   226

11. Selden on Excommunication   244

Conclusion   259

Appendix: Selden's Letter to Jonson, edited by
Jason P. Rosenblatt and Winfried Schleiner   279

Select Bibliography   291
Index   305

Acknowledgements

APPROACHING John Selden, with his vast network of patrons, friends, clients, and correspondents, one begins at last to understand the crucial importance of intellectual communities where knowledge is shared rather than hoarded. Like one of Selden's objects of benevolence, whose poverty he often relieved, I have been lucky to have received substantial help. My first debt is to Professor G. J. Toomer, who knows more about Selden than anyone in the world. His meticulousness is exceeded only by his generosity, and he shared information from his forthcoming intellectual biography of Selden and submitted extensive corrections and additions to almost every chapter, even though we had never met.

It gives me great pleasure to thank Winfried Schleiner for permission to include as an appendix Selden's letter to Ben Jonson, which we co-edited for *English Literary Renaissance*, 29 (1999). Winfried and I have been friends since graduate school as students of Barbara Kiefer Lewalski, who continues to be my best teacher, though her genius for taming whirlwinds, evident in her scholarship, is not teachable.

It is a boost to the spirit that Oxford University Press is publishing this book. Selden studied at Hart Hall, later Hertford College, and the Selden End of Duke Humfrey's Library at the Bodleian was built to accommodate the eight thousand volumes donated by his executors. Approval of the book by the Delegates of the Press virtually coincided with the 350th anniversary of his death, 30 November 2004. Andrew McNeillie, Senior Commissioning Editor, Literature, has been hospitable and encouraging ever since my first tentative enquiry. More recently Tom Perridge, Assistant Commissioning Editor, has shown the same welcoming spirit. The first anonymous reader for the Press, sensitive and practical, suggested valuable improvements in organization and presentation, while the second reader, immensely learned, exposed errors. With exemplary patience and skill, Jacqueline Baker, Production Editor, and Veronica Ions, copy editor, have turned script into book.

Work on this book would never have begun without access to the resources of the Folger Shakespeare Library, nor would it have been completed without the gift of time in the form of a Folger/NEH Fellowship. The years have not blunted the privilege and pleasure of reading at the Folger, with its courteous and efficient library staff, led by Betsy Walsh. Thanks to Gail Kern Paster, Director; Richard Kuhta, Librarian; and Georgianna Ziegler, Reference Librarian and problem solver.

Georgetown is a Jesuit university that strongly supports the teaching and scholarship of an observant Jew who teaches the poetry of heretical Protestants. Gerald M. Mara, Executive Associate Dean of the Graduate School, and Jane

Dammen McAuliffe, Dean of the College, deserve particular thanks. Among friends of many years in the Georgetown English Department, James Slevin and Penn Szittya have set an impossibly high standard as scholars and human beings. I am also lucky to count as friends Paul Betz, Michael Ragussis, Joseph C. Sitterson, Jr., and Kathy Temple, and saddened to recall the loss of Roland Flint, Keith Fort, and Thomas F. Walsh.

The Wednesday seminars I attended on Christian Hebraism during 1999-2000 at the University of Pennsylvania's Center for Advanced Judaic Studies helped to give shape to this project. David Ruderman and his staff made my treks from DC to Philadelphia the highlight of the week. Chanita Goodblatt invited me to lecture on Selden's rabbinic thought in May 2003 at Ben-Gurion University of the Negev. Meirav Jones and Yoram Hazony did the same at the Shalem Center in Jerusalem in August 2004. I have needed and received a lot of help with this project, and each of the names listed alphabetically deserves a separate paragraph: Sharon Achinstein, Noah Dauber, Matt Goldish, Achsah Guibbory, Dina and Amnon Haramati, James Holstun, Daniel Lasker, Tod Linafelt, Charles Manekin, Jodean Marks, David Norbrook, Annabel Patterson, Gary Remer, Yael and Raphael Rosenblatt, Gordon Schochet, Alexander Sens, Noah Shavrick, Harvey Shoolman, Nathaniel Stogdill, and Laetitita Yeandle. I can't leave out the members of a weekly Talmud study class that has been meeting for twenty-three years: Zachary Dyckman, Harvey Nathan, Jack Rutner, Avram Weisberger, and Mel Zeltser. Nor can I fail to acknowledge the work of two scholars I have never met, Richard Tuck and J. P. Sommerville.

Parts of Chapter 1 are transplanted from 'Aspects of the Incest Problem in *Hamlet*', *Shakespeare Quarterly*, 29 (1978), and most of Chapter 4 appeared as an essay in Amy Boesky and Mary Thomas Crane, eds., *Form and Reform in Renaissance England: Essays in Honor of Barbara Kiefer Lewalski* (University of Delaware Press, 2000). An earlier version of Chapter 7 was published in Allison P. Coudert and Jeffrey S. Shoulson, eds., *Hebraica Veritas? Christian Hebraists and the Study of Judaism in Early Modern Europe* (University of Pennsylvania Press, 2004). The Appendix first appeared in Jason P. Rosenblatt and Winfried Schleiner, 'John Selden's Letter to Ben Jonson on Cross-Dressing and Bisexual Gods [with text]', *English Literary Renaissance*, 29 (1999), 44–74. I am grateful for permission to reprint.

I want to close by remembering my own chief rabbi, my late father, Morris D. Rosenblatt, who served as rabbi of Annapolis, Maryland, for almost forty years. My mother, Esther, who seeks peace and pursues it, recently celebrated sixty years of service to that community. Noah, Colleen, and Tehila Rosenblatt-Farrell are a source of constant joy, and Judy and Gary Rosenblatt are best friends as well as family. All I can say in a sentence about the dedicatee, Zipporah, is that I was put on this earth to love her.

Introduction

Rabbi Selden

In a series of letters written in the summer of 1629, Peter Paul Rubens expresses his distress at learning 'that poor Selden is a prisoner of state for having spoken too freely in the last assembly of the English Parliament'. John Selden's troubles always resulted from his standing on principle—in this case, as Rubens put it, for 'provoking the anger of an indignant king' by helping to promulgate the Petition of Right—but Rubens still laments a great scholar's sacrifice of a life of contemplation for one of action. Perhaps Selden, a titanic intellect, reminded Rubens of his own great Prometheus, only with his insides gnawed at by the eagle of quotidian public responsibility. Rubens knows Selden as the author of an important comparatist historico-philological study of the gods condemned in the Hebrew Bible, *De Diis Syris* (1617), and he laments his abandonment of his studies and his immersion 'in the turbulence of politics, which seems to me a profession so alien to his noble genius and most profound learning, that he must not blame fortune' for his imprisonment with other parliamentarians. In a letter to Nicolas-Claude Fabri Peiresc, who had introduced him to Selden, Rubens repeats his wish that Selden had kept himself 'within the boundaries of the *vita contemplativa* without mixing in these public disorders'.[1]

It is true that Selden (1584–1654) would involve himself in the *vita activa*, enjoying a long career as practitioner of the law and adviser to the wealthy and powerful as well as membership in parliaments during and beyond the Civil War. As burgess for Oxford University in turbulent times, he would help to protect and preserve universities, scholarship, and scholars—among them Meric Casaubon, Edward Pococke, Thomas Greaves, and Gerard Langbaine. Despite Selden's accomplishments in the worlds of law and politics, Rubens need not have

---

[1] *The Letters of Peter Paul Rubens*, ed. Ruth Saunders Magurn (Evanston: Northwestern University Press, 1955), 332; *Correspondance de Rubens et documents épistolaires concernant sa vie et ses œuvres*, ed. Charles Ruelens and Max Rooses (Antwerp: Veuve de Backer, 1887–1909), v. 148, 152. I owe these references to Peter N. Miller's *Peiresc's Europe: Learning and Virtue in the Seventeenth Century* (New Haven and London: Yale University Press, 2000), 100–1, 203–4. Miller also quotes an observation by Peiresc, in a letter to Hugo Grotius, that as a result of his imprisonment 'le pauvre mons.' Seldenus' would no longer be contributing to the study of antiquity (p. 204 n. 140).

worried. His first expression of 'grand desplaisir' at hearing of Selden's fate is dated 21 July 1629. Only seventeen days earlier, on 4 July, Selden wrote a letter from prison to Sir Robert Cotton that would change the course of his life and deepen the quality of his scholarship:

Noble Sir,

Your favors are alwaies so great and ready upon all occasions to me that I take upon me the confidence to trouble you in all kinds. I have much time here before me, and there is in Westminster Library the Talmud of Babylon in divers great volumes. If it be a thing to be obtained, I would beseech you to borow them (for the Library is not yet so setled as that books may not be lent if the founder will,) of my Lord of Lincoln [note: Bishop Williams founded the Library], and so get me the use of them. But I would not be so unmannerly as to ask them if they be in that state that they may not conveniently be lent, the consideration wherof I leave wholly to your favour and judgement.
And I am ever
Your most affectionate
  And acknowledging frende
·   and servant,
        J. Selden[2]

De Diis, the work that Rubens praised, which demonstrates Selden's early proficiency in rabbinic scholarship, is less mature than the six works, some of them immense, that add to that scholarship remarkable competence in the Babylonian-Aramaic texts of the Talmud: *De Successionibus ad Leges Ebraeorum in Bona Defunctorum* (1631), which covers every phase of the Jewish law of inheritance; *De Successione in Pontificatum Ebraeorum* (1636), on succession in the Hebrew priesthood; *De Jure Naturali et Gentium juxta Disciplinam Ebraeorum* (1640), which conceives of the imperatives of natural law in terms of the rabbinic Noachide laws or *praecepta Noachidarum*, divine voluntary universal laws of perpetual obligation; *De Anno Civili* (1644), a lucid and methodical account of the Jewish calendar and its principles as well as a treatise on the doctrines and practices of the Karaite sect; *Uxor Ebraica seu De Nuptiis et Divortiis Veterum Ebraeorum* (1646), a thorough survey of the Jewish law of marriage and divorce and of the status of the married woman under Jewish law; and the massive *De Synedriis*, in three books (1650, 1653, 1655, the last, incomplete and published posthumously), a study of Jewish assemblies, including the Sanhedrin, with parallels from Roman and canon law.

Rubens did not count on Selden's voracious intellectual appetite, which allowed him to begin his talmudic study, as he drily put it, 'while enjoying in abundance the tranquil leisure of prison'.[3] For the remaining twenty-five years of his life, from 1629 to 1654, Selden studied the Westminster Abbey Library's copy

---

[2] BL, Cott. MS Julius C. III. fo. 18b, cited in *Original Letters of Eminent Literary Men of the Sixteenth, Seventeenth, and Eighteenth Centuries*, ed. Sir Henry Ellis (London: Camden Society, 1843), 142–3. This is the first of many references supplied by Professor G. J. Toomer.
[3] Selden, *De Successionibus*, 1: 'dum tranquillo Carceris abundauimus Otio'.

of the Babylonian Talmud, a combination of the first and second editions published in Venice by Daniel Bomberg (1520–3, 1526–39), forty-four tractates, approximately two and a half million words on 5,894 folio pages, unadorned by either vowel points or punctuation.[4] The main subject of this book is the cultural influence of rabbinic and especially talmudic scholarship on some early modern British poets and intellectuals as mediated principally by Selden, the most learned person in England in the seventeenth century. His immense, neglected rabbinical works contain magnificent Hebrew scholarship that respects, to an extent remarkable for the times, the self-understanding of Judaic exegesis.

An example of that neglect appears in a translation of a passage from the *De Doctrina Christiana* by John Milton, who revered Selden, and who will appear in subsequent chapters of this book, even in some of those devoted principally to other figures. Milton, writing on divorce in one of the non-Pauline chapters of his theological treatise, follows 'Selden, [who] demonstrated particularly well in his *Uxor Hebraea*, with the help of numerous Rabbinical texts [or testimonies], [that] the word *fornication*, if it is considered in the light of the idiom of oriental languages, does not mean only adultery.' In the still definitive Columbia University Press edition of *The Works of John Milton* (1931–8), Charles Sumner (1790–1874), Bishop of Winchester, translating '*multis Rabbinorum testimoniis*', elides the phrase's central term so that it becomes only 'numerous testimonies'.[5] Since the Columbia Milton editors rely on Bishop Sumner's translation, the elision could serve as a synecdoche of the effacement of seventeenth-century rabbinical scholarship in the writings of literary figures such as Ben Jonson and Andrew Marvell as well as Milton and of philosophers ranging from Hobbes and Locke to Vico. We can measure the falling off in quality of Hebrew learning in England after the seventeenth century when we recall that the Bishop of Winchester during Selden's lifetime and Milton's was the incomparable Lancelot Andrewes, justly renowned for his great learning and eloquence, and the only bishop who read with pleasure Selden's controversial *Historie of Tithes* (1618) and supported him in the bitter aftermath of its publication.

The work of restoring what neglect has effaced continues. In late September 2004 Professor Daniel Lasker discovered in the Osborne collection of the Beinecke Library at Yale University a beautifully written Hebrew letter to Selden,

---

[4] Although the Bomberg editions of the Talmud are usually bound in twelve volumes, the Westminster Library Talmud, now in the possession of the Valmadonna Trust, in London, is bound in nine volumes.

[5] John Milton, *De Doctrina Christiana*, in *The Works of John Milton*, gen. ed. Frank Allen Patterson (New York: Columbia University Press, 1931–8), xv. 171. For evidence that the effacement continues, see Paul R. Sellin, 'The Reference to John Milton's *Tetrachordon* in *De Doctrina Christiana*', *Studies in English Literature*, 37 (1997), 137–49. Professor Sellin, displaying meticulous Latin scholarship, takes to task scholars who rely on translation and examines single words in the passage at some length, but never mentions Sumner's deletion of 'Rabbinorum'. Indeed, in the section of *De Doctrina* in question, he prefers Sumner's translation over that of John Carey in the Yale edition of Milton's prose, even though Carey restores the word 'Rabbinical'.

dated 29 September 1641, by the Christian Hebraist Joannes Stephanus Rittangel. The catalogue, ignoring the author's family name and noting only his given names, attributes the letter to a 'John Stevens' and places it incorrectly in the 'S' file (shelf mark OSB Mss. File S, folder 14513). Filled with lavish praise of Selden in the Levantine style, including twenty-nine quotations from the Hebrew Bible, the letter asks for his help in publishing Karaite literature. Of all the titles bestowed upon Selden—including lofty master, genius, wonder of our generation, skilled in Arabic, Hebrew, Syriac, and Aramaic—perhaps the most interesting is the one reserved in rabbinic literature for the most distinguished scholars, 'Seldenus [ר[ב] הר[ב] [ורנו]מ', *morenu ha'rav rav Seldenus*, 'our honoured teacher and rabbi, Rabbi Selden'. Rittangel is sufficiently Judeophilic to use 'rabbi' in its original honorific sense, as a title of respect given by the Jews to a doctor of the law, and not in the contemptuous sense of Jesus' denunciation of the hypocritical Pharisees who love the title and of his admonition, 'be not ye called Rabbi' (Matt. 23: 8). And although Selden is not Jewish, the title is not misplaced. Between the expulsion of the Jews by Edward I in 1290 and the first visit to England, in 1655, a year after Selden's death, by Rabbi Menasseh ben Israel, lobbyist for their readmission, Selden would have been the most learned rabbinic scholar in the country—more learned than any member of the tiny Spanish and Portuguese community living in London during his lifetime. Christian rabbi by default, Selden's title marks the inferiority of Jewish scholarship in England when compared to that on the Continent, due in part to the long expulsion. Working alone rather than as the member of a community of rabbinic scholars, Selden can make sense of the Babylonian-Aramaic talmudic texts, itself a remarkable accomplishment. He can hardly be expected to reach a level of scholarship comparable to that of the rabbinic sources he cites.

In his letter Rittangel also refers to Selden 'בשבת הגזית' *b'shevet ha'gazit*, 'sitting in the [chamber of] hewn stones', where the Sanhedrin sat, a reference to Selden as a member of Parliament, 'among the distinguished gathering', who has the ear of the king. (Selden himself connected Parliament with the great Sanhedrin as early as 1618 in his *Historie of Tithes*.[6]) Although Rittangel's letter assumes a close relationship between Selden and the king, less than four months after its composition, on 17 January 1642, Selden would be appointed to a committee to examine Charles I's violation of the privileges of Parliament and to petition the king for the payment of damages to Pym, Hampden, and others unjustly accused of treason.

The letter is a curiosity—one non-Jew writing to another, from 'Cantabrigia עיר וישיבה המהוללה', 'the city and exalted *yeshiva* of Cambridge'—that is,

---

[6] Selden, *Historie of Tithes* (1618), 18, on the 'great *Sanedrim*, or Court of seventie Elders (that is, *the greatest Court*, that determined also, as a Parliament, of matters of State).' Selden discusses the chamber of hewn stones at great length in his *De Synedriis, Opera Omnia*, ed. David Wilkins (1726), i.1552 ff., esp. 1563. The question of whether the Sanhedrin could try capital cases once it abandoned the chamber relates to matters of Jewish responsibility for the crucifixion of Jesus.

from Cambridge University—about matters of Torah, but it also raises questions about appropriation. The only hint in the long letter that Rittangel is not Jewish appears in a single sentence, contrasting the Karaites, whose 'delight was solely for the Torah of the Lord' [Ps. 1: 2], with the mistaken interpretations of 'the Pharisees', 'the vipers' (the name given to the Pharisees in the New Testament). Among the Karaite texts Rittangel wants to publish is 'an honorable composition . . . against the entire Talmud'. Rittangel is a true Christian Hebraist, whose published works express dogmas, typological and tropological scriptural hermeneutics, and conversionary motives. Selden is interested in Karaite laws and customs, but he is also a partisan of the oral law. Long before his intensive talmudic researches, in his *Historie of Tithes*, he offers unqualified praise of the Pharisees for their piety and generosity in their tithes and offerings.[7] In his coolly analytical historical approach to the laws and institutions of the Jews, he eschews dogma. He wants neither to convert nor refute the rabbis, whom he calls 'Magistri', and Christology is absent from his scholarship.

I hope to demonstrate in a later chapter the positive effect of Selden's scholarship on the question of Jewish resettlement in England after their long exile. But a more indeterminate matter is whether Selden serves as proxy for the rabbis he admires or whether he appropriates rabbinic scholarship. Most of his learned readers refer to 'our [that is, our English] Selden,' an equal of the foreigners Scaliger, Grotius, and Salmasius. But however benign his own intentions toward ancient Pharisees and contemporary Jews, 'our Selden' may be as much of a rabbi as most learned English Christians want. A scholar such as Nathanael Culverwel, like many others in mid-seventeenth-century England, seems to regard Selden's scholarship as a national and natural resource, whose endless bounty can be plundered with impunity. It is as if Selden were a primary rather than secondary source of rabbinic scholarship. Reading *De Jure* on Rashi, Ibn Ezra, Kimhi, or Maimonides becomes the equivalent of reading the *Biblia Rabbinica* or the *Guide of the Perplexed*. Milton refers in the *Areopagitica* to 'the chief of learned men reputed in this Land, Mr. *Selden*', and it is hardly coincidental that in *Doctrine and Discipline of Divorce*, where he reserves his most lavish praise for *De Jure Naturali et Gentium*, 'that noble volume written by our learned *Selden, Of the law of nature & of Nations*', he cites Maimonides, Kimhi, 'two other Rabbies who glosse the text' of Judges 19: 2, and Levi Ben Gershom.[8]

The naval commander and diplomat Sir Kenelm Digby writes to Lord Conway on 23 February 1644, from aboard a vessel, expressing concern for the safe arrival of his letter, which is indeed torn and water-damaged. But the captain

[7] Selden, *Historie of Tithes*, 19–21.

[8] John Milton, *Areopagitica*, in *The Complete Prose Works of John Milton*, gen. ed. Don M. Wolfe (New Haven: Yale University Press, 1953–82), ii.549; *Doctrine and Discipline of Divorce*, ii.350, 335–6, 257. Parenthetic volume and page references to this Yale edition of Milton's Prose, abbreviated as *YP*, are to this edition.

'assureth me that if he be not drowned, he will deliver this safe; which casualty, himselfe feareth little; for he sayth that God (who is iust) will certainly be so iust to him as to lett him dye the death he deserveth: which the learned Rabbies (and Mr. Selden upon them) do interpret, Hanging'.⁹ One expects Digby, not a talmudist but much rather a friend of poets, to quote any one of Gonzalo's lines from the opening scene of Shakespeare's *The Tempest*: 'I have great comfort from this fellow. Me thinks he hath no drowning mark upon him; his complexion is perfect gallows.' 'I'll warrant him for drowning, though the ship were no stronger than a nutshell and as leaky as an unstanched wench.' 'He'll be hanged yet, | Though every drop of water swear against it | And gape at wid'st to glut him.'¹⁰ Who could imagine that for someone like Digby the first thing to come to mind would be neither the familiar proverb 'He that was born to be hanged will never be drowned' nor lines from the bard but a talmudic discussion on the death penalties of the *beth din* or Jewish court in *De Jure Naturali et Gentium juxta Disciplinam Ebraeorum*, published four years earlier. 'Our Selden' belongs to Englishmen like Digby, and the rabbis belong to Selden.

The classical republican political theorist James Harrington provides numerous examples from Jewish history to support his Erastian position, some from the Bible but others, especially the most arcane, from Selden's *De Synedriis*. The power of the Sanhedrin as a civil body, the model for Parliament, includes rule over all matters civil and ecclesiastical, extending even so far as punishing a guilty king or high priest. In *The Prerogatives of Popular Government*, Harrington derives much support from Selden's rabbis for the position that *chirotonia*, election by show of hands, rather than *chirothesia*, being ordained by the laying on of hands, accords with scripture: 'in this therefore I shall follow Selden, the ablest Talmudist of our age or of any'.¹¹ But Harrington, mixing rabbinic authors and titles indiscriminately, as if he cannot distinguish among them, concedes his ignorance and his debt with refreshing honesty. He will be happy if he simply gets the names straight:

All ordination of magistrates, as of the senators, or elders of the Sanhedrim, of the judges, or elders of inferior courts, of the judge or *suffes* [chief magistrate] of Israel, of the king, of the priests, of the Levites, whether with the ballot or *viva voce*, was performed by the *chirotonia* or suffrage of the people. In this (especially if you admit the authority of the Jewish lawyers and divines called the Talmudists) the Scriptures will be clear, but their

---

⁹ *The Correspondence of Anne, Viscountess Conway, Henry More, and their Friends, 1642–1684*, ed. Marjorie Hope Nicolson (New Haven: Yale University Press, 1930), 26.

¹⁰ William Shakespeare, *The Norton Shakespeare Based on the Oxford Edition*, gen. ed. Stephen Greenblatt (New York and London: W. W. Norton, 1997), 3056–57 (1.1.25–7, 41–3, 52–4). Unless otherwise noted, parenthetic act, scene, and line references to Shakespeare are to this edition. Double-numbered lineation such as 18.9–18.10 indicates Second Quarto material included in Norton but relegated to the appendix in the Oxford edition.

¹¹ James Harrington, *The Prerogatives of Popular Government*, bk. II, in *The Political Works of James Harrington*, ed. J. G. A. Pocock (Cambridge: Cambridge University Press, 1977), 531.

names are hard; wherefore not to make my discourse more rough than I need, I shall here set them together. The authors or writings I use by way of paraphrase upon the Scripture are the Gemara Babylonia, Midbar Rabba, Sepher Siphri, Sepher Tanchuma, Solomon Jarchius, Chiskuny, Abarbinel, Ajin Israel, Pesiktha Zoertha, these and many more being for the election of the Sanhedrim by ballot. I might have spoken them more briefly, for the truth is in all that is Talmudical, I am assisted by Selden, Grotius, and their quotations out of the rabbis, having in this learning so little skill that, if I miscalled none of them, I showed you a good part of my acquaintance with them.[12]

J. G. A. Pocock, Harrington's editor, comments that he 'was not indulging in false modesty. He appears to have relied solely on Selden'—in fact, exclusively on *De Synedriis*. Harrington defensively claims not to be 'wedded' to 'Selden, whom sometimes I follow and sometimes I leave', borrowing his scholarship but using his own reason. Even so, Harrington's derivative comparisons provide a point of entry into Selden's synthesizing imagination and the sheer pleasure he takes in ancient polysemous texts that have over the course of centuries been subjected to vastly divergent interpretations. Harrington's somewhat fanciful assertion that the lottery by which Moses chose the seventy elders—that is, the first 'senate or Sanhedrim'—'was of the nature of the ballot at this day in Venice', provokes a droll reminder to the modern reader by Pocock: 'how elaborate are the interpretations of the scriptural text by which Harrington arrives at this picture of the Venetian ballot being carried out in the wilderness'—interpretations supplied exclusively by Selden in *De Synedriis* (II.iv).[13]

The chapters that follow continue to consider the complex question of appropriation or proxy in Selden's rabbinic scholarship and the related problem of simultaneous prejudice against Jews and surprising value attached to their exegeses. They also consider various other topics: gender issues, which connect Henry VIII's divorce, *Hamlet*, Ben Jonson's *Epicoene*, and Hebraica; rabbinic thought in the important natural-law work of Hugo Grotius, *De Jure Belli ac Pacis libri tres* (1625); the positive influence of Selden's own great work *De Jure Naturali et Gentium juxta Disciplinam Ebraeorum* on religious toleration in England, and of his *De Diis Syris* (1st edn. 1617; 2nd edn., used by Milton, 1629) on the conception of idolatry in *Paradise Lost*; and an unironic Hebraic reading of *Samson Agonistes*. The new Yale edition of Andrew Marvell's prose inspires a chapter on the intermittent but fierce talmudic exchanges between Samuel Parker, future Bishop of Oxford, and Marvell. A chapter devoted to the Cambridge Platonist Nathanael Culverwel's critique of Selden's thought throws into relief three of the most important ideas of *De Jure* and in the process of doing so reveals the limits of a seventeenth-century liberal's religious toleration. A legal decision written fifteen years after Selden's death by his disciple Sir John Vaughan, Chief Justice of the Court of Common Pleas, constitutes one of the

---

[12] Ibid. 519–20.   [13] Ibid. 522 n. 1.

purest expressions of Selden's thought as a lawyer, political theorist, and Hebraist. Separate chapters are devoted to Selden's approach to two topics of capital importance: the Passion of Christ and excommunication. The Appendix consists of an extraordinary letter from Selden to his dear friend Ben Jonson on the subjects of cross-dressing and the bisexuality of the pagan gods (Selden supra 108 Bodl L.). In the letter, which I have co-edited with Professor Winfried Schleiner, Selden adopts an explicitly Maimonidean reading 'of the holy text usually brought against the counterfeiting of sexes by apparell', namely Deuteronomy 22: 5. Jonson, like Shakespeare, was writing for a transvestite English theatre in which men took women's parts, and his friend provides him with an elegant Maimonidean loophole. The rabbinic material adduced by Selden about gendered or ungendered forms of worship of deities imagined male, female, or both male and female bears on issues that have become pressing in twenty-first century forms of Jewish and Christian worship, of which the aim of a gender-neutral language in speaking of God is the best-known example.

John Selden contributes important ideas to all of those topics, although he appears late in the first chapter, to weigh in on the subject of Henry VIII's attempt to marry Anne Boleyn, which took place before he was born. Selden's opinion derives from a manuscript of *Riti Ebraica*, by the Venetian rabbi Leone da Modena, with whom he corresponded. Each owned and admired the other's scholarly productions. Modena's *Riti Ebraica*, translated into many languages, presents Judaism sympathetically to a Christian audience, and Selden draws on it in both *De Successione* and *Uxor Ebraica*. One would hope that an intellectual atmosphere that fosters a relationship between the cosmopolitan and politically powerful Selden and the learned Venetian rabbi might have contributed at least indirectly to the eventual readmission of the Jews into England. *De Jure* contributed directly to it.

It seems appropriate to begin with Henry, since his solicitation of rabbinic opinion on his great matter was the first important introduction of post-biblical Hebraica into English culture. The Babylonian Talmud that he imported into England to support his position, formerly in the Royal Library, is at present in the British Library. At the heart of the opening chapter—and in all those that follow—is rabbinic interpretation, often divergent, applied by Selden and various Christian Hebraists to biblical verses, phrases, and individual words in both the Hebrew and Greek Bibles. And this chapter introduces consideration of the irony, contradiction, and double vision inherent in Christian Hebraism, which extends into seventeenth-century Britain. When Joseph Mede, a champion of apocalyptic millenarianism, responds sympathetically to Henry Finch's tolerationist argument in *The Calling of the Jewes* (1621), he confesses that it accords with his own long-held view: 'God forgive me if it be a sin, but I have thought so many a day.' Mede's asking God to forgive him for not condemning the Jews is the contrite version of Huck Finn's defiant decision to tear up the letter that would have betrayed Jim the runaway slave: 'All right, then, I'll *go* to hell.' In both cases the generous heart overcomes the condemning conscience, but not without a struggle that reveals the depth of prejudice in the culture at large.

Scholars have documented the pervasiveness of Judaeophobia in Renaissance English culture—in poems, plays, broadsides, travel diaries, chronicles, sermons, political tracts, confessions of faith, legal texts, parliamentary debates, and biblical commentaries. Exhaustive as some of these studies have been, there are inevitably some omissions, particularly of writings strikingly less Judaeophobic than those that are generally cited. They are precious precisely because they are uncommon, like the courageous few who throughout history have refused to be swallowed up by the mob. In the midst of an age of prejudice, John Selden transmitted an uncommonly generous view of Judaism. The book explores a fairly wide range of provocative post-biblical Hebraic ideas that served as the foundation of his thought.

ENGLAND'S OSIRIS

Despite its range of topics, there is much about Selden's achievement and cultural influence that the book either omits or mentions only in passing, which is why his name follows rather than precedes the colon in the title. These include his 'Illustrations' to Michael Drayton's poem *Poly-Olbion*; *Titles of Honor*; important studies of English legal history, such as his notes on Fortescue and Hengham and the *Dissertatio ad Fletam*; the content of *The Historie of Tithes* and the controversy surrounding its publication; works on English medieval history, including *Eadmer* and his contributions to *Matthew Paris* and Twysden's *Decem Scriptores*; his edition of *Marmora Arundelliana*; his *Mare Clausum* in the context of Anglo-Dutch commercial rivalry; and his edition of the Arabic text of *Eutychius*. Although the book takes some account of Christian Hebraists with whom there is a clear English connection (Hooker, Grotius, Lightfoot, Pufendorf, Barbeyrac), it omits important Continental scholars such as Johannes Reuchlin, Pico della Mirandola, Sebastian Münster, Konrad Pellikan, Wolfgang Capito, Santi Pagnini, Cardinal Egidio da Viterbo, Paul Fagius, the Buxtorfs, and a host of others, as well as Jewish converts to Christianity such as Felix Patensis and Alfonso de Zamora.

The book even leaves open the question whether Selden is in fact a Christian Hebraist as that title is generally understood. After all, he rejects the biblical ten commandments as part of a civil law intended only for the Jews, while he accepts the universality of the rabbinic Noachide laws. Identifying natural law with a universal divine voluntary law of perpetual obligation, Selden follows the Talmud, which for him records a set of doctrines far older than classical antiquity. As Richard Tuck and J. P. Sommerville have demonstrated, natural law as conceived by Selden consists not of innate rational principles that are intuitively obvious but of specific divine pronouncements uttered by God at a point in historical time.[14] In *De Jure's* 847 folio pages, Selden discusses the rabbinic identification of natural law with the divinely pronounced Adamic and Noachide laws, the *praecepta Noachidarum,* considered by rabbinic tradition as the minimal moral duties enjoined upon all of humankind. *De Jure* consists of seven books, corresponding to the seven commandments promulgated by God to the children of Noah—hence, to all of humankind: the prohibitions of blasphemy, idolatry, homicide, robbery, unchastity (incest, adultery, bestiality), and eating a limb torn from a living animal, and the positive order to establish a civil judicial system in order to enforce these laws.

A surprisingly large number of early modern thinkers, representing a wide variety of religious and political points of view, accept the validity of this non-biblically rabbinic idea, sometimes for very different reasons. Discussions of Noachide law appear in the work of Richard Hooker, Hugo Grotius, Isaac Newton, Henry Burton, John Lightfoot, Henry Stubbe, Jeremy Taylor, James Harrington, Edward Stillingfleet, John Toland, Samuel Pufendorf, and Lancelot Addison (father of Joseph Addison). Except for Hooker and Grotius, who wrote before Selden, each of the persons listed above refers, respectfully and sometimes reverentially, to Selden's *De Jure*. Theoretically, the discovery of shared moral rules in the natural, pre-civil state of humankind would provide a basis for relationships among human beings anywhere in the world. This is in part what makes the works by Grotius and Selden pioneering contributions to international relations. Historians warn us that no absolute correlation exists between a Christian scholar's knowledge and admiration of rabbinic scholarship and his attitude toward contemporary Jewish persons. Yet the history of the religious toleration of Jews is incomplete without acknowledgement of the impact of the idea, disseminated by great humanists such as Grotius and Selden, that the rabbinic Noachide precepts are a universal, perpetually binding law issuing from the will of God.

Returning to the problem of the book's omissions, one might suggest that even the best work on Selden (for example, David Ogg on the *Dissertatio ad Fletam,* Tuck, Sommerville, and Paul Christianson on his political theory, David Berkowitz on his Parliamentary career) is necessarily incomplete. The chapters that follow, then, constitute only an incomplete study of Selden's rabbinic scholarship, which takes up most of the six immense folio volumes of the *Opera Omnia*. Selden's long-neglected achievements in that sphere should both augment our general perception of him as a legal historian and philologist and reveal the

---

[14] See Richard Tuck, *Natural Rights Theories: Their Origin and Development* (Cambridge: Cambridge University Press, 1979), 82–100; J. P. Sommerville, 'John Selden, The Law of Nature, and the Origins of Government', *Historical Journal,* 27 (1984), 437–47. In the course of a uniformly excellent survey of the topic, Sommerville corrects Tuck by pointing out that for Selden six of the 'Noachide' laws go back not merely to a point in time after the Flood but all the way back to Eden—the seventh, the prohibition against eating the limb of a living animal, would have been irrelevant to our vegetarian first parents in paradise.

integrity of his scholarship. A single example, which will be elaborated in a later chapter, is Selden's radical interpretation of the common law of England as a limited law of nature, which integrates political philosophy, a passionate commitment to the common law, rabbinic scholarship, and *realpolitik*. The view that Noachide law was original and universal, and that it was supplemented by civil laws that have the same force within a specific nation as natural laws, dovetails in Selden's mind with the view that the original natural law evolves for his own countrymen into the English common law, the highest legal authority, from which there is no appeal. As early as the *Notes on Fortescue* (1616), explaining how different and mutable laws of nations issued from the same universal and immutable law of nature, he called the common law of England a limited law of nature:

> But in truth, and to speak without perverse affectation, all laws in generall are originally equally ancient. All were grounded upon nature, and no nation was, that out of it, took not their grounds; and nature being the same in all, the beginning of all laws must be the same.... [A]lthough the law of nature be truly said immutable yet it is as true, that it is limitable, and limited law of nature is the law now used in every state. All the same may be affirmed of our *British* laws, or *English*, or other whatsoever. But the divers opinions of interpreters proceeding from the weakness of man's reason, and the several conveniences of divers states, have made those limitations, which the law hath suffered, very different.[15]

Years later, Selden will assimilate this view of the common law as a limited law of nature to the Noachide precept of *dinim* (*de Judiciis*), a religious injunction to 'install judges and legal authorities in every district'. For Selden, whose torah is law, the English common law has an added status as a natural law ordained by God, a parallel to the Mosaic law as the civil law of the Jews. There could then be no appeal to a higher law or to general principles outside of the law. Alan Cromartie is entirely persuasive when he notes that Selden's passionate commitment to the common law gave him an advantage 'in coping with the tactics of the crown'—particularly, with the king's attempt to appeal 'outside the common law to an inalienable prerogative'.[16]

The foundation of Selden's theistic approach to the common law is the discussion of the *Leges Noachidarum* in tractate *Sanhedrin* (56a–b), which he quotes in its entirety in *De Jure*. Selden includes the Talmud's elaborate inference of these universal laws from seven key words in Genesis 2: 16. The hermeneutic principle of *gezerah shawah* permits one to infer a rule from the use in two different verses of a common scriptural expression. Selden's knowledge that the Bible uses the word *Elohim* to refer to judges as well as to God is not remarkable. But he also knows the text of *Sanhedrin* in which Rabbi Yitzhak derives the injunction to establish civil lawcourts specifically from the word *Elohim* in

---

[15] Selden, *Opera Omnia*, ed. David Wilkins (1726), iii.1891.

[16] Alan Cromartie, *Sir Matthew Hale (1609–1676)* (Cambridge: Cambridge University Press, 1995), 31.

Genesis 2: 16, supplying as his parallel proof-text Genesis 22: 7: 'And the master of the house shall be brought to the judges [*Elohim*].'[17]

Sir Edward Fry's brief life of Selden in the *Dictionary of National Biography* (*DNB*), an admirable work of its kind, pays elegant lip-service to his subject's 'oriental' researches: 'Their author's familiarity with rabbinical literature was such as has been acquired by few non-Israelite scholars.' But Fry, who devotes four paragraphs to the content and reception of the *Historie of Tithes*, crowds the six talmudic books, the work of twenty-five years, into a short list before hurrying on to a topic 'of more general interest than rabbinical law'. In fragmenting Selden's achievements and concentrating on what interests him—the life of 'John Selden, jurist'—Fry, like all of us who write about Selden, must limit himself to the contexts that he recognizes. Although it may be dangerous to flirt, as Selden himself does, with the myth of a prelapsarian unified sensibility beyond our reach, it is tempting to speculate that we can only reconstruct partially, and with the distortion that accompanies emphasis on our own limited preferences, what Selden experienced with comprehensiveness and integrity.

Selden can justly be called England's Osiris, if we keep in mind the famous passage in Milton's *Areopagitica* that compares the body of truth to the body of Osiris, 'torn into a thousand peeces, and scatter'd . . . to the four winds. From that time ever since, the sad friends of Truth, such as durst appear, imitating the carefull search that *Isis* made for the mangl'd body of *Osiris*, went up and down gathering up limb by limb still as they could find them' (*YP*, 2: 549). The figure is evocative for various reasons: the cross-cultural implications of the story of an Egyptian god, found in Plutarch's *Moralia* and adapted by Milton, an English Puritan; the mastery of Eastern learning by the young Selden, who writes brilliantly of Osiris in his great work of cultural anthropology and comparative religion, *De Diis Syris*; and even the images of scattering and gathering, diaspora and ingathering, that suggest the Jews' dispersion and the controversy over their readmission in the 1650s. (The image of the scattered limbs of Osiris is said to have found its way into some Jewish cabbalistic texts as a figure of exile.[18] Certainly it resonates with a central cabbalistic concept, *shevirat ha'kelim*, the shattering of the vessels and the subsequent attempt to gather the sparks of holiness that escaped. It resembles as well the midrash that recounts how Moses, while the escaping Israelites were plundering Egyptian gold and jewellery, searched for the bones of Joseph in the Nile to carry on the journey to the land of Israel.) Osiris for Milton is the body of truth. For most English intellectuals in mid-seventeenth-century, Selden, a Christian, embodies rabbinic thought; and even today no one has been able to see him whole. Like his seventeenth-century

---

[17] See Selden, *De Jure Naturali et Gentium juxta Disciplinam Ebraeorum* (1640), 1.10, p.124, and 7.5, p. 805: '*Gem. Bab. ad. tit.* Sanhed. *cap*.7. *fol.* 56b.' This usage of *Elohim* to mean *judges* is unique to the Book of the Covenant, though it is frequent elsewhere, most notably in Psalms.

[18] See on this point Jeffrey S. Shoulson, *Milton and the Rabbis: Hebraism, Hellenism, & Christianity* (New York: Columbia University Press, 2001), 279 n. 79.

contemporaries who appear in these chapters, the few who study him are slowly gathering up limb by limb as we can find them. Eighty years ago, David Ogg described him accurately as one who stands out alone in a century of greatness, 'seeking not fame but truth in an erudition more vast than was ever garnered by any other human mind'.[19] And even Ogg, concentrating on Selden as a historian of the laws and constitutional institutions of England, has not a word to say about the six rabbinical works that constitute his most mature scholarship.

[19] Selden, *Ad Fletam Dissertatio*, ed. David Ogg (Cambridge: Cambridge University Press, 1925), p. lxvi.

1

Hamlet, Henry, *Epicoene*, and Hebraica: Marriage Questions

The still more or less current status of some non-theological interpretations of the incest prohibition in *Hamlet* attests to the ingenuity with which guilt can be assigned. Sophisticated ethical systems are always interesting, and critical emphasis has shifted accordingly from Claudius's sinfulness in marrying his murdered brother's widow to Hamlet's more obscurely sullied nature. Sigmund Freud's first reference to the Oedipus complex, in a letter of 1897 to Wilhelm Fliess, traces Hamlet's delay to his 'passion for his mother'.[1] Ernest Jones, developing his master's insight, stresses Hamlet's incestuous desire to supplant his father in his mother's affection: Hamlet's hatred of Claudius thereby becomes 'the jealous detestation of one evil-doer towards his successful fellow'.[2] This conception of incest in *Hamlet* has found its way into many psychoanalytic readings as well as into films by Olivier (1948), Zeffirelli (1990), and Branagh (1996), seen by millions, featuring closet scenes charged with sexual tension.[3]

J. Dover Wilson refers to scripture in adducing evidence of Hamlet's 'sullied flesh', but even he misapplies the relevant verse. The Prince 'is wishing that his "sullied flesh" might melt as snow does. For his blood is tainted, his very flesh corrupted, by what his mother has done, since he is bone of her bone and flesh of her flesh.'[4] The verse Wilson quotes actually refers, of course, to the relation of wife to husband rather than to that of son to mother: 'Then the man said, This now is bone of my bones, and flesh of my flesh. She shalbe called woman, because she was taken out of man. Therefore shal man leave his father and his mother, and shal cleave to his wife, and they shalbe one flesh' (Genesis 2: 23–4; see also

[1] Sigmund Freud, *The Origins of Psychoanalysis*, ed. Marie Bonaparte, Anna Freud, and Ernst Kris (New York: Basic Books, 1954), 224.
[2] Ernest Jones, *Hamlet and Oedipus* (1949; repr. Garden City, NY: Doubleday, 1954), 99.
[3] For a history of psychoanalytic criticism of *Hamlet*, see Norman Holland, *Psychoanalysis and Shakespeare* (New York: McGraw-Hill, 1966), 163–206. See also Janet Adelman, *Suffocating Mothers: Fantasies of Maternal Origin in Shakespeare's Plays, "Hamlet" to "The Tempest"* (London and New York: Routledge, 1992); and the useful survey by William Kerrigan in *Hamlet's Perfection* (Baltimore and London: Johns Hopkins University Press, 1994), 1–33.
[4] *What Happens in Hamlet* (Cambridge: Cambridge University Press, 1937), 42.

Matthew 19: 4–6 and Mark 10: 6–8).[5] Hamlet is so familiar with these verses that he can sport with them at the King's expense. He correctly applies them to the conjugal relation when he bids farewell to Claudius as his 'dear mother':

KING. Thy loving father, Hamlet.
HAMLET. My mother. Father and mother is man and wife, man and wife is one flesh, and so, my mother. (4.3.52–4)

Alluding to the indissoluble bond between Gertrude and the murdered King Hamlet, Hamlet's reply is calculated to discomfit a man who has ignored the impediment of affinity in the first degree collateral by taking his brother's wife. In the fourth century, St Basil, relying on these verses, had condemned marriage between a brother-in-law and a sister-in-law.[6] Twelve centuries later, Nicholas Harpsfield handled the argument that 'he that marrieth his brother's wife taketh his brother's flesh and blood to marriage, the which thing plainly is against the law of nature; for seeing the husband and wife be one flesh and blood, truly he that taketh his brother's wife taketh also the flesh and blood of his brother.'[7]

Aside from carrying the logic of incest to its conclusion by fusing Claudius, Gertrude, and his dead father, Hamlet reminds the King of the very basis of affinity. As Calvin notes in the *Institutes,* 'man and woman are made one flesh only by carnal copulation.'[8] By the eighth century carnal intercourse (*unitas carnis*) had replaced the marital contract in establishing identity of relationship between oneself and the relatives of one's spouse, thus putting affinity on a plane with consanguinity.[9]

Hamlet's reply to his 'uncle-father' suggests that a traditional conception of incest need not lack ingenuity, particularly if it draws on the special resources available to an obsessed mind. At the end of the play, when the Prince, in a final, terrible pun on 'union', dispatches the 'incestuous, murd'rous, damnèd Dane' to seek his union with Gertrude in the hereafter (5.2.267–9), he gives full expression to an outrage first registered in the low tones of the opening aside. 'A little more than kin, and less than kind!' (1.2.65)—Hamlet's first words, in their binary aspect, ingeniously parody the antitheses of Claudius's first speech; they

[5] Unless otherwise noted, all parenthetic biblical references in the text are to the Geneva Bible (1560). For Shakespeare's use of this translation in *Hamlet,* see Naseeb Shaheen, *Biblical References in Shakespeare's Plays* (Newark, Del.: University of Delaware Press, 1999), 536.

[6] See 'Affinity', in *New Catholic Encyclopedia* (New York: McGraw-Hill, 1967); 'Affinité', in *Dictionnaire de Droit Canonique,* i. cols. 264–85; and 'Affinità', in *Enciclopedia Cattolica,* i. cols. 366–8.

[7] *A Treatise on the Pretended Divorce Between Henry VIII and Catherine of Aragon* [1556], ed. Nicholas Pocock (Westminster: Camden Society, 1878), 98.

[8] *Institutes of the Christian Religion* (IV. xix. 37), ed. John T. McNeill and Ford Lewis Battles (Philadelphia: Westminster Press, 1960), ii. 1484.

[9] For canon law on questions of affinity and consanguinity, see ch. 7 of J. J. Scarisbrick's magisterial biography *Henry VIII* (Berkeley and Los Angeles: University of California Press, 1968), 163–97, to which this chapter is heavily indebted. See also the entries, cited in n. 6, on 'Affinity', 'Affinité', and 'Affinità'.

also declare an absolute spiritual opposition to the King, whose trespass has obscured familial identities once clear and firmly fixed.

I

Hamlet's argument against Claudius rests on a text in Leviticus: 'Thou shal not discover the shame of thy brothers wife: for it is thy brothers shame' (Lev. 18: 16; see also 20: 21). The act of uncovering that convicts Claudius of incest engrosses Hamlet's attention: the flash of 'incestuous sheets' (1.2.157) and the image of the King 'in th'incestuous pleasure of his bed' (3.3.90) expand in the closet scene to the duration of an act, performed 'In the rank sweat of an enseamèd bed' (3.4.82).

Though Claudius may be 'as shrewd and relentless at catechizing himself as he is at manipulating others',[10] he *never* adverts to the sin of incest. Even during the prayer scene (3.3), when he frankly acknowledges responsibility for the sins attendant upon a brother's murder, he remains silent on the question of incest. His silence may derive, not from shame that prevents him from facing a peculiarly offensive act, but rather from a conviction that in this instance, at least, his behaviour was unexceptionable. For *Hamlet*, no less than *Richard II*, 'sets the word itself against the word'.

The scriptural passage opposed to Hamlet's central text and associated with Claudius is from Deuteronomy:

When brethren dwell together, and one of them dieth without children, the wife of the deceased shall not marry to another; but his brother shall take her, and raise up seed for his brother. And the first son he shall have of her he shall call by his name: that his name be not abolished out of Israel. (Deut. 25. 5–6)[11]

A galaxy of authorities, both Christian and Jewish, was available to sanction a man's marriage to a deceased brother's relict. The ironies and contradictions resulting from Christian dependence on Jewish learning are reserved for Sections VII and VIII of this chapter. Among Christian interpreters, St Augustine refers to this tradition as a way of resolving an apparent contradiction in scripture, by which St Joseph is identified first as the son of Jacob (Matthew 1: 16), then as the son of Heli (Luke 3: 23). Earlier, Augustine had implied that Heli was the adoptive father: 'The Law, however, also adopted the children of the deceased by ordering that a brother marry the wife of his childless, deceased brother and raise up seed for his deceased brother.'[12] Renaissance expositors likewise insisted

---

[10] Harry Levin, *The Question of Hamlet* (New York: Oxford University Press, 1959), 33.

[11] This is the Douai–Rheims translation (1582, 1609).

[12] St Augustine, *Retractationum, Patrologia Latina* (Paris: J.-P. Migne, 1877), xxxii. 633: 'Lex autem filios etiam mortuis adoptabat, jubens ut fratris defuncto semen ex eadem frater uxorem, et fratri defuncto semen ex eadem suscitaret.'

that a brother 'in so doing, did no wrong, *sed officium praestabat defuncto fratri,* but did performe a good office to his deceased brother'. They observed that 'the law doth not only permit a widow to marie againe: but if her husband died before he had any children, it commanded the next kinsman that was living and free to marie her, that he might raise up seed to his brother deceased.' They were careful to note, however, that 'when God commanded to doe this, he willed them not to doe this to satisfie lust . . . but onely that the elder brother might be a tipe of Jesus Christ, who should never wante a seede in the Church.'[13] On the authority of Deuteronomy, then, Renaissance theologians insisted that 'the brother not only might, but then was bound to marie his brothers wife.'[14]

Hamlet's very existence, of course, keeps the relationship of Claudius and Gertrude within the scope of the Levitical prohibition. Only a childless widow might remarry; thus, the marriage of Gertrude and Claudius, in addition to denying the dead King any claims upon his widow, insults the living prince by ignoring his birth, which should have blocked the union. I will return to this point, which is of some importance in explaining Hamlet's depression. Meanwhile, we should note Shakespeare's mastery in portraying Claudius, from the very start, as a caricature of the virtuous brother of Deuteronomy.

The true levirate marriage is a secondary union, an extension of an existing marriage. By virtue of the moral bonds between brothers, it exists to preserve the individual identity of one brother beyond his normal lifespan by the sacrifice of at least part of the individuality of the other.[15] This kind of self-sacrifice is rejected by Onan, who is slain by God for his refusal to raise up seed to his dead brother Er (Genesis 38). In Deuteronomy (25: 7–10), less severe punishments were provided for refusals such as Onan's, perhaps in recognition of a brother's natural reluctance to give up the right to found a family of his own.

Claudius's marriage to Gertrude, far from the true levirate relationship described in Deuteronomy, is an example of widow-inheritance, a very different, and more primitive, kinship institution, in which the identity of the deceased is supplanted by that of the successor. King Hamlet's life, crown, and queen are taken by Claudius, who has violated every token of his brother's identity. Yet these two spiritually opposed kinship institutions are superficially similar. The features they share include the principle of equivalence of siblings (because one brother replaces another),[16] and the non-equivalence of *genitor* and *pater.* Where

---

[13] *Seriatim*: Cardinal Cajetan, cited in Andrew Willet's *Hexapla in Leviticum* (London, 1631), 425; William Gouge, *Of Domesticall Duties* (London, 1622), 186; John Weemse, *An Exposition of the Ceremoniall Lawes of Moses* (London, 1632), 195.

[14] Note on Mark 12: 19 ff., in *The New Testament,* tr. the English college then resident in Rheims (Antwerp: D. Veruliet, 1600), 121.

[15] R. G. Abrahams, 'Some Aspects of Levirate', in *The Character of Kinship,* ed. Jack Goody (Cambridge: Cambridge University Press, 1973), 167.

[16] Alfred Reginald Radcliffe-Brown, Introduction, in *African Kinship and Marriage,* ed. Daryll Forde and A. R. Radcliffe-Brown (London: Oxford University Press, 1950), p. 64. Abrahams, cited above, treats the difficulties faced by social anthropologists who try to discriminate between widow-

a legal fiction in Deuteronomy counts the son of the *levir* as the descendant of the dead elder brother, this fiction operates in reverse in the case of widow-inheritance and makes the surviving brother the 'owner' of the children begotten by the brother now deceased.[17]

If Claudius can 'smile and smile', it is partly because blurred distinctions between two superficially similar institutions afford him, if not a true refuge, at least a role to play. A Tudor audience's knowledge of the true levirate would have been sharpened by the controversy surrounding the marriage and subsequent divorce of Henry VIII and Catherine, the childless widow of Henry's brother Prince Arthur. All of us know that Claudius is a sham, but this more specialized knowledge might help us to see more clearly what type of sham he is. We know that Claudius's marriage to Gertrude is

> such a deed...
> As from the body of contraction plucks
> The very soul, and sweet religion makes
> A rhapsody of words.   (3.4.44–7)

I would like to suggest, more specifically, that the King's role is a travesty of the *levir*'s. The validity of his marriage to Gertrude actually depends on the absolute severance of the earlier marital union by death and obliteration of all his brother's claims. Yet Claudius opens the play's second scene by pretending that he keeps those claims alive. Far from remaining silent on the matter of his brother's death and his own recent nuptials (for even the true levirate links a funeral with a wedding), he refers to 'our dear brother's death' (1.2.l), 'our late dear brother's death' (1.2.19), and 'our most valiant brother' (1.2.25). Gertrude's equivocal status, similar to that of the sister-in-law/wife of Deuteronomy, is forthrightly acknowledged: 'our sometime sister, now our queen' (1.2.8). Even the figure of freshness Claudius suggests in his opening words ('Though yet... | The memory be green' [1.2.1–2]) is biblical; see Jeremiah 17: 7–8 and Hosea 14: 8.

In taking the Queen as his wife, Claudius also takes Denmark, the estate Gertrude holds in jointure (1.2.9). He prefers to dwell on his role as protector of the land won from King Fortinbras by 'our most valiant brother' (1.2.17–25). Reminding us that one of the most important conditions attached to the levirate bond is that 'the inheritance must be preserved, and kept' for the dead brother's son,[18] Claudius says:

> We pray you throw to earth
> This unprevailing woe, and think of us

---

inheritance and the true levirate. He sees 'an element of paradox in this situation, where such different institutions are said to be demonstrative of a single principle' (p. 166).

[17] S. R. Driver, *Deuteronomy: The International Critical Commentary,* gen. eds. S. R. Driver, Alfred Plummer, and C. A. Briggs (Edinburgh: T. & T. Clark, 1895), 281–4.

[18] Willet, *Hexapla in Leviticum,* 425.

> As of a father; for let the world take note
> You are the most immediate to our throne,
> And with no less nobility of love
> Than that which dearest father bears his son
> Do I impart towards you.   (1.2.106–12)

This solemn proclamation of Hamlet as heir must have seemed to the court at Elsinore a 'confirmation of the inheritance' of the dead brother's estate.[19] It is clear, for example, that Rosencrantz can scarcely credit Hamlet's complaint that he lacks advancement: 'How can that be, when you have the voice of the king himself for your succession in Denmark?' (3.2.312–13). Yet the condition of the levirate bond that the inheritance be preserved is designed to prevent family property from being broken up and passing into strange hands. Its purpose is to protect a son who is at the time of the marriage unborn. Hamlet, however, already exists and he is of age. Claudius is thus in reality 'preserving' an inheritance that he has stolen.

Since the only clear exception to the Levitical prohibition is the case of marriage with a widow whose husband has died without offspring, the presence of Hamlet in the second scene is utterly destructive of Claudius's status as *levir*. Yet Claudius sounds unperturbed. In his treatment of Hamlet in this scene, he seems to be exploiting the principle of the non-equivalence of *genitor* and *pater* that is common to both the true levirate and widow-inheritance. As Nicholas Harpsfield notes, a principal reason for the levirate marriage 'was that the brother deceased might continue his name and family by his brother's child (which should be counted not his brother's but his own), and that he might avoid the shame and infamy wherewith they were noted ... in the old law which had no children.'[20] In Deuteronomy's statement that 'he shall call [the child] by his name' (Deut. 25: 6), 'his' refers to the dead brother. The child is to 'be counted and called the seed of the dead man, not of the living'.[21]

Claudius's determination to play paterfamilias with Hamlet goes beyond the common custom whereby an adoptive father refers to a stepson as a son. The King's inheritance of the empire and the Queen involves collateral ownership of the son. Claudius thus attempts to exploit the legal fiction of widow-inheritance that makes Hamlet his son. His rhetoric, however, is furnished by the conventions of the true levirate. His first words to the Prince remind us of Deuteronomy 25: 6: 'But now, my cousin Hamlet, and my son—'(1.2.64). For Hamlet this is one more example of Claudius's obscene unification of a natural duality—of what Stephen Booth calls 'the excessively lubricated rhetoric by which Claudius

---

[19] Harpsfield, *A Treatise on the Pretended Divorce*, 87.

[20] Ibid. 145. See also Sir James George Frazer, *Totemism and Exogamy* (London: Macmillan, 1910), i. 502.

[21] Henry Ainsworth, *Annotations Upon the Fifth Booke of Moses, called Deuteronomy* (1619; repr. London, 1639), 114.

makes unnatural connections between moral contraries'.[22] Claudius, who would like to see things differently, does not sound ashamed to be Hamlet's 'uncle-father' (2.2.358). Indeed, he concludes his conversation with the Prince by placing an additional stress on the already complicated relationship: 'Our chiefest courtier, cousin, and our son' (1.2.117).

The relationship of father to son has been defined in this scene by Polonius and Laertes. The son requests leave to return to France, and the father grants it. Now Claudius, in a 31-line lecture on fathers and sons (1.2.87–117), acts like a father by refusing to grant Hamlet leave to return to Wittenberg. Hamlet rejects this sham by proclaiming obedience to his mother: 'I shall in all my best obey *you,* madam' (1.2.120; my italics).

Giving the dead a 'name' is a subsidiary element of the levirate institution, based on Deuteronomy 25: 6. In his explication of the verse, John Weemse considers the question of giving the name of the dead man to the child begotten by his living brother: 'For Deut. 25. 6. the words in the originall are these: *Primogenitus quem pepererit stabit super nomen fratris sui, shall succeed in the name of the brother.* Therefore it may seeme they were called after the elder brothers name.'[23] In a figural reading of this passage, influenced by Origen, Augustine, and Ambrose, among others, Henry Ainsworth identifies the dead brother as Christ and his living sons as Christians, who bear his name: 'For the church of *Israel* was his wife … who bare him no children by the Law. … But the Apostles (his brethren, Joh. 20.17) by the immortall seed of the Gospel, begat children unto him not that they should be called by any mans name, 1 Cor. 1.12.13 but to carry the name of Christ.'[24]

The coincidence of an identical name for his dead brother and his dead brother's seed ('Hamlet our dear brother', 'my cousin Hamlet, and my son') contributes to making Claudius's situation superficially similar to the *levir*'s. Of course a moment's thought reveals the true face behind the King's temporary and imperfect disguise. His own name, in fact, suggests incest and manipulation, for the Roman Emperor Claudius married his niece Agrippina, an act considered incestuous according to Roman law, to which he created an exception.

[22] 'On the Value of *Hamlet*', in *Reinterpretations of Elizabethan Drama*, ed. Norman Rabkin, Selected Papers of the English Institute (New York and London: Columbia University Press, 1969), 149.

[23] *An Exposition of the Lawes of Moses* (London, 1632), 121. See also the anonymous 16th-c. tract 'A Glasse of the Truthe', in *Records of the Reformation: The Divorce 1527–1533*, ed. Nicholas Pocock (Oxford: Clarendon Press, 1870), ii. 391.

[24] *Annotations Upon … Deuteronomy,* 115. See also Harpsfield, *Treatise on the Pretended Divorce,* 142; Martin Luther, *Lectures on Deuteronomy,* in *Works,* ed. Jaroslav Pelikan (St Louis: Concordia, 1960). Luther allegorizes the text of Deuteronomy, identifying the widow with the 'synagog', the deceased brother with Christ, and the *levir* with the Christian community that teaches in Christ's name: 'thus, although we teach people, we teach only in the name of Christ, and children born by the Word shall not be called Pauline or Apollonian or Petrine but only Christian' (p. 250).

The levirate, presupposed in patriarchal times and institutionalized in Deuteronomy,[25] is the only law in the Pentateuch in which the punishment consists of public degradation. The man who refuses to marry his sister-in-law has silenced his brother; hence the law speaks metaphorically of an Israelite's name being wiped out. Claudius, of course, is a fratricide who has the audacity to rely on the law of fraternal succession in order to supplant his brother. And when he succeeds in his plot against young Hamlet, he blots out his brother's name, just as he has earlier blotted out his brother's life.

The true levirate is an exception to the Levitical prohibition. The Bible 'forbiddeth such commixtions for lust, but for the succession of mankind [it] commandeth.'[26] Like other social institutions and ritual activities, the levirate appears in this light as a denial of the power of death. The common birth of brothers is the principal base in nature for the institution. By subverting the levirate institution, Claudius allies himself with the power of death. The solitary human organism born at a particular time and place is the biological base for his position, which opposes continuity: 'Thou know'st 'tis common—all that lives must die' (1.2.72); 'you must know your father lost a father; | That father lost, lost his' (1.2.89–90). Little did King Hamlet know that his marriage with Gertrude more nearly resembled a primitive sort of adelphic polyandry than a Christian institution. Similarly, behind the rhetoric of the levirate lies the reality of incest, the violation of Leviticus 18, a 'decalogical' code forbidding the promiscuous unions practised among the Canaanites.[27]

II

Our knowledge of the conflict between verses in Leviticus and verses in Deuteronomy and their respective commentaries sets the stage for a deeper understanding of the conflict between Hamlet and Claudius in the play. The clash may be as private as a duel in a lady's chamber:

> QUEEN. Hamlet, thou hast thy father much offended.
> HAMLET. Mother, you have my father much offended.   (3.4.9–10)

But that the scale of the conflict is larger is dramatized by Claudius's strategically placed reminder of the court's participation in his marriage decision:

> Nor have we herein barred
> Your better wisdoms, which have freely gone
> With this affair along. For all, our thanks.   (1.2.14–16)

[25] John Diodati, *Pious and Learned Annotations upon the Holy Bible* (London, 1651), Deut. 25: 5: 'this thing was in use before Moses time by some ancient custome ordained by God, and passed over from father to son, Gen. xxxviii. 8: but here it is established by the written law.'

[26] Willet, *Hexapla in Leviticum,* 510.

[27] Martin Noth, *Leviticus: A Commentary* (London: SCM, 1965), 134.

Later, the private domestic conflict expands beyond even national boundaries, encompassing the entire universe. Hamlet tells Gertrude:

> Heaven's face doth glow,
> Yea, this solidity and compound mass
> With tristful visage, as against the doom,
> Is thought-sick at the act.   (3.4.47–50)

Hamlet's capacity to weight personal conflict with the gravity of universal implication distinguishes it from its sources. Political and religious implications of incest are absent from Saxo's *Historiae Danicae* and Belleforest's *Histoires tragiques.* In these versions of the Hamlet story, incest is a general term of abuse, always coupled with fratricide to emphasize unnatural villainy. Though the term is used dyslogistically in *Hamlet* ('that incestuous, that adulterate beast'; 'thou incestuous, murd'rous, damnèd Dane'), it is also seen as a specific offence: marriage to a deceased brother's widow. In moments of uncontrollable rage, Hamlet emphasizes this offence directly: 'married with mine uncle, my father's brother' (1.2.151–2); 'You are the queen, your husband's brother's wife' (3.4.15; see also line 28). In moments when his rage is kept under control, Hamlet names the offence more indirectly, noting that it imposes on his family a hyphenated set of unnatural mixed relations: 'my uncle-father and aunt-mother' (2.2.358).

But if incest in *Hamlet* is a specific, particular offence, it is also symbolic of a more general religious and political corruption. Hamlet's opening soliloquy suggests that the incest of the King and the Queen is emblematic of goodness in thrall to evil, of the state in thrall to a usurper. The Ghost warns that the kingdom is polluted:

> Let not the royal bed of Denmark be
> A couch for luxury and damnèd incest.   (1.5.82–3)

III

An allusion in *Der Bestrafte Bruder-mord* (lost MS 1710, publication 1781) hints at some of the larger implications of incest in *Hamlet.* In that play's closet scene, Gertrude, her heart wrung by Hamlet, complains:

Had I not taken in marriage my brother-in-law, I should not have robbed my son of the crown of Denmark. But what can be done about things that are done? Nothing, they must stay as they are. *Had not the Pope allowed such a marriage,* it would never have happened. [my italics][28]

Gertrude's reference to a papal dispensation from the impediment of affinity in the first degree collateral might remind us of the 'great matter' of King Henry

[28] *Fratricide Punished,* 3.6, in *Narrative and Dramatic Sources of Shakespeare,* ed. Geoffrey Bullough (New York: Columbia University Press, 1973), vii. 145–6.

VIII, which furnished Shakespeare with the plot of his last history play. For at certain moments in *Hamlet* the imagined world of the play seems to shade into the real world of Shakespeare's England.[29]

Henry VIII's decision to divorce Catherine of Aragon and marry Anne Boleyn had generated a conflict international in scope and warlike in intensity. Henry rested his case on the fact that Catherine, his wife of eighteen years, was the widow of his deceased brother, Prince Arthur, who had died in 1502 at the age of 15. In the eyes of the English people, the divorce struggle pitted Henry against Emperor Charles V and the Pope (for Julius had originally granted the bull of dispensation that permitted the marriage, and Clement VII now defended that decision). By implication, however, the struggle also amassed other polarities: Anne and Catherine, their respective daughters Elizabeth I and Mary I, England and Spain, Protestantism and Catholicism. Of special interest here is the extent to which these oppositions were brought into focus by the apparent conflict between Leviticus and Deuteronomy. Henry's decision was authorized primarily by the text of Leviticus, which he interpreted as a divine prohibition the Pope was not permitted to set aside. Henry's many learned enemies in England and on the Continent based their counter-offensive on the verses in Deuteronomy treating levirate marriage.

In that quarrel, a great deal depended on the translation of *Ah* (*frater* in the Vulgate) as 'brother' in the Hebrew and Vulgate texts of both Leviticus and Deuteronomy. Tudor history would invite Claudius's alliance with the unacceptable (but correct) Douai translation of Deuteronomy 25: 5: 'his [the deceased brother's] brother shall take her [the wife of the deceased].' Hamlet's (and Shakespeare's) Protestant Bibles, however—the Coverdale (1535), the Geneva (1560), and the Bishops' (1568)—all distorted this verse into compliance with a Henrician emphasis on the unacceptability of the levirate.[30] These Bibles interpreted 'brother' in the strict sense in Leviticus, while they took it to mean *cognatus*, a relative, in Deuteronomy. For them, the crucial phrase in

---

[29] For other examples of such shading in *Hamlet*, see E. A. J. Honigmann, 'The Politics in *Hamlet* and "The World of the Play"', in *Hamlet*, ed. John Russell Brown and Bernard Harris, *Stratford-upon-Avon Studies*, 5, (London: Edward Arnold, 1963), 129–47; and William Empson, '*Hamlet* When New', *Sewanee Review*, 61 (1953), 18 ff.

[30] William Tyndale's correct translation of the verse in Deuteronomy is an admirable exception: 'the wyfe of the dead shall not be geven out unto a straunger: but hir brotherlawe shall goo in unto her and take her to wife' (*Five Books of Moses called The Pentateuch*, 1530). Indeed, Tyndale's exegetical integrity enforces a position of moderation on the question of Henry VIII's divorce. Given the tenor of his exposé of prelatical abuse in his earliest known work, *The Practice of Prelates* (1530), one would expect Tyndale to defend the divorce on the grounds of the Levitical prohibition. Yet even in this anti-Catholic polemic, he contends at some length that the terms of the levirate marriage in Deuteronomy should protect Catherine's status as the King's lawful wife. He notes that the texts in Leviticus and Deuteronomy 'seem contrary, the one forbidding, the other commanding, a man to take his brother's wife'; he concludes that the levirate 'is not a permission, but a flat commandment'. See Henry Walter's Parker Society edition of *The Practice of Prelates* (Cambridge: Cambridge University Press, 1849), 323–7.

Deuteronomy read: 'his [the deceased man's] kinsman shall go in unto her [the widow], and take her to wife, and do the kinsmans office to her.' A note on this verse in the Geneva Bible explains the substitution of 'kinsman' for the literally correct 'brother': 'Because the Ebrewe worde signifieth not the natural brother, & the worde, that signifieth a brother, is taken also for a kinseman: it semeth that it is not ment that the natural brother shuld mary his brothers wife, but some other of the kinred, that was in that degre which might mary'.

The Geneva gloss's political bias becomes clear when it is compared with the relevant text of a partisan sixteenth-century English tract on the divorce. The form of the anonymous 'Glasse of the Truthe' is that of a Socratic dialogue between a lawyer and a divine, with the divine speaking for Henry (and the author). Here they consider the word 'brother':

THE LAWYER. Why, I pray you, is there more mystery of that word in the Deuteronomyke than in the Levityke?

THE DIVINE. Yea, forsooth; for in the Levityke it can nor may be taken for other than for the very brother, the text being judge itself. But by the Deuteronomyke, as many taketh it, is meant the next of the blood after the degrees prohibite; though he be but kinsman.[31]

The divine adds that 'the taking of this word' in Deuteronomy is 'so highly entreated in many other works . . . that it were but a loss of time to commune any more of it'.[32]

If 'kin' and 'brother' are politically charged terms, then Hamlet's first words, addressed to the audience, may help us to establish a context for the conflict that will follow. Claudius, playing the *levir,* emphasizing relation, calls Hamlet his cousin and his son—with cousin a term 'frequently applied to a nephew' (*OED*), as in 'where is my cousin, your son?' (*Much Ado About Nothing* (1.2.1). Hamlet's aside—'A little more than kin, and less than kind'—may be construed as alluding to the version of Deuteronomy that he (and the audience) accepts, where a kinsman may marry a man's widow but a brother may not.

A brief excursus into Henry's great matter, ending with Shakespeare's own treatment of the subject in *The Life of King Henry VIII,* will perhaps help us to understand some of the problems raised in *Hamlet* by a marriage that admits impediments.

---

[31] 'A Glasse of the Truthe', in *Records of the Reformation*, ii. 393–4.

[32] Ibid. 394. See also John Calvin, *Commentaries on the Four Last Books of Moses,* tr. C. W. Bingham (1850; repr. Grand Rapids: Eerdmans, 1950), iii. 177. For the Catholic position, see John Fisher, *De Causa Matrimonii Serenissimi regis Angliae liber* (Alcalá, 1530), fos. 7 ff. Fisher cites the following authorities who understand that the Deuteronomic precept applies to a real brother: Origen, Hesychius of Alexandria, John of Damascus, Chrysostom, Eusebius, Raoul de Flaix, Maimonides, Nicholas of Lyre, Alphonsus, Jerome, Hilary, and Africanus.

IV

Formulations of Henry's urgent problem in terms of contrasting scriptural verses abound in the sixteenth century.[33] Pressing for divorce, Henry put his case to universities at home and abroad ('all famous colleges, | Almost, in Christendom', *Henry VIII* [or *All is True*] 3.2.66–7). Though he managed to get favourable replies, the one hard place in their various determinations was 'the dispensation by the law of Deuteronomie, of stirring up the brothers seed'.[34]

Under political pressure, what would otherwise be only an interesting theological crux became a vexed question, and the note of urgency we find in many of the sixteenth-century tracts is one we associate with polemic rather than with exegesis. The adherents of Leviticus 18: 16 could exploit two fears that plagued Englishmen: Catholicism and the influence of Spanish power. Boundaries between religion and politics were so fluid that it is impossible to tell whether or not Thomas Beard was deliberately punning when he attributed the marriage of Henry and Catherine to the desire 'to have this Spanish affinitie continued'.[35] In any event, his subsequent comments on the 'unfortunat marriage', 'unjustly dispensed withall by the Pope', indicate his displeasure with both the incestuous union and the alliance with Spain.

Many partisans were able to fuse personal, religious, and political sentiments—to see the events neatly—as in the quip that 'the King divorced from Lady *Katharine*, and from the Pope, both at the same time';[36] or, as in the claim of the Roman Catholic Cardinal Jean de Lorraine that 'the perverse interpretation of this chapter [Leviticus 18] was *Fundamentum schismatis Anglicani*: the very foundation of the schisme of England.'[37]

Some of the participants in the divorce dispute, conscious of mixed attitudes, achieve an admirable degree of control in their writings. Recognizing that each side's arguments are determined as much by political as by moral considerations, they treat dissenting opinions with a tolerance bred of sophistication. Thus Hugh

---

[33] See contemporary formulations by Juan Luis Vives, *Apologia sive Confutatio* ... (1531); 'A Glasse of the Truthe', in *Records of the Reformation*, ii. 391; Harpsfield, *Treatise on the Pretended Divorce*, 37. Scarisbrick, *Henry VIII*, 163–97, cites many additional contemporary sources. Among the church fathers who treat the problem, see St Augustine, *Questionum in Heptateuchum, Patrologia Latina*, xxxiv. 705; St John Chrysostom, *De non iterando conjugio, Patrologia Graeca*, xlviii. 609–20; Tertullian, *Treatises on Marriage and Remarriage* (Westminster, Md.: Newman Press, 1951), 84.

[34] Raphael Holinshed, *Chronicles of England, Scotland, and Ireland* (1587; repr. London: J. Johnson, 1808), iii. 771. See the 'Determinations of diverse universities ... ,' 767–72.

[35] Thomas Beard, *The Theatre of Gods Judgements* (London, 1597), 329. In his commentary on Leviticus 18, Gervase Babington forces the laws against sexual contamination into a nationalist context. He sees the French, Italians, Spanish, and Turks as modern equivalents of the Canaanites. See his *Comfortable Notes upon the Five Bookes of Moses*, in *Works* (London, 1622), 393.

[36] John Foxe, *Actes and Monuments* (1563; repr. London: Stationers' Company, 1684), ii. 276.

[37] Jean de Lorraine, cited (and disputed) by Willet, *Hexapla in Leviticum*, 447. See also Lorin's *Commentarii in Leviticum* (Lyons: H. Cardon, 1619), 546 ff.

Latimer notes the extent to which shifting political currents have influenced interpretations of the crucial biblical verses: 'Yea, men think that my lord himself [Dr John Stokesley, Bishop of London] hath thought in times past, that by God's law a man might marry his brother's wife, which now both dare think and say contrary; and yet this his boldness might have chanced, in pope Julius's days, to stand him either in a fire, or else in a fagot.'[38] Bishop Latimer himself accepts the validity of the Levitical prohibition; but he emphasizes his fellowship with those who disagree with him, and he laments the 'dissension in a Christian congregation' caused by extremist views.[39]

When Shakespeare treated the matter of Henry's divorce directly, in *The Life of King Henry the Eighth*, he dramatized the modulation of received opinion into compassionate generosity. By 1613, the contradictory attitudes toward the divorce given full treatment in the play would probably have been conventional. They are striking nonetheless. Shakespeare's Katherine, a foreigner and a Roman Catholic, solicits our sympathy throughout the play. Against the Latinizing Wolsey, she appears as a plain-speaking Englishwoman (3.1.41–5). Here, as in *Hamlet*, the conflict of biblical verses is at least strongly implied. For Henry the question is 'Whether our daughter were legitimate, | Respecting this our marriage with the dowager, | Sometimes our brother's wife' (2.4.176–8).[40]

In this play, the conflict between verses in Leviticus and Deuteronomy is subordinated to still another conflict relevant to *Hamlet*. Like the marriage of Gertrude in *Der Bestrafte Bruder-mord*, Katherine's marriage to Henry was dispensed by the Pope from the impediment of affinity in the first degree collateral. Katherine thus refuses to be bound by the Church of England and submits her case to the Church of Rome. She tells the various English bishops and cardinals:

> I do refuse you for my judge, and here,
> Before you all, appeal unto the Pope,
> To bring my whole cause 'fore his holiness
> And to be judged by him.   (2.4.116–19)

A question vehemently debated by Protestants and Catholics was the dispensability of God's word in Leviticus. The reformation leaders held that the Levitical prohibition was fixed for all time by divine law, that no dispensation could validate Henry's marriage to his dead brother's widow, and that in general the

[38] Hugh Latimer, *Sermons and Remains*, ed. George Elwes Corrie, Parker Society (Cambridge: Cambridge University Press, 1845), 340.

[39] Ibid. 341.

[40] It should at least be noted that ever since 1850, when James Spedding published his essay 'Who Wrote Shakespeare's *Henry VIII*?' in the *Gentleman's Magazine*, editors have speculated that Shakespeare co-authored this play with John Fletcher. See the survey of opinions on shared composition in Jay Halio's introduction to *King Henry VIII, or All is True* (Oxford: Oxford University Press, 1999), 19 ff. See also Stanley Wells, *Shakespeare: A Life in Drama* (New York: Norton, 1995), 381: 'the authors worked closely enough together to achieve at least a superficial unity of tone for most of the play.'

practice of papal dispensations was motivated by the desire for profit.[41] The Parliamentary 'Act concerning the King's succession' (1533) declared that the Pope could not dispense from the impediment of marriage with a deceased brother's widow.

The Protestant Andrew Willet, in *Synopsis Papismi* (1594), sets down the starkly opposed doctrines of 'Protestant' and 'Papist'. He holds, with Calvinist opinion definitely accepted by the Church of England, that the Levitical law forbidding the marriage is 'natural and perpetual': 'We may affirm that it is utterly unlawful for any Christian man to marry within the degrees prohibited: neither can any human power dispense with such marriages, but the equity of that law being grounded upon nature is in force for ever.'[42]

Opposing Catholics, as Willet notes, held that the Levitical law was in large measure judicial and therefore dispensable. The opinions of two great Catholics, John Fisher, Bishop of Rochester, and the Dominican jurist Francisco de Vitoria, hold special interest, since they can be applied to the case of Claudius. Fisher considers the question of marriage with a dead brother's wife *who has had children by him*, and concludes that in such a case a papal dispensation is possible, valid, and licit. *A fortiori*, he says, such a dispensation is even easier in the case of a dead brother's childless widow.[43] Vitoria holds that in the absence of human law, marriage with such a widow is lawful, whether she be childless or not.[44] One of the reasons given to support the dispensability of the Levitical prohibition is the absolute severance of the marital union by death.[45]

Though the fate of Shakespeare's Katherine is bound up in these doctrinal matters, mechanistic duality is complicated in the play by human feeling. Katherine, in her patience, has been compared favourably with Hermione in *The Winter's Tale*.[46] Indeed, a virtually allegorical servant named Patience attends Katherine: 'Patience, be near me still, and set me lower' (4.2.76); 'Softly, gentle Patience' (4.2.82); 'Nay, Patience, | You must not leave me yet' (4.2.166–7). This bearing of such emphasis in a Protestant play might have reminded the audience of a long narrative poem on the divorce, *The History of Grisild the Second*, written by Queen Mary's chaplain William Forrest, which identifies Catherine with the eponymous heroine.[47]

[41] See George Hayward Joyce, SJ, *Christian Marriage: An Historical and Doctrinal Study* (London and New York: Sheed and Ward, 1933), 527 ff.

[42] Andrew Willet, *Synopsis in Papismi* (London, 1594), 755.

[43] *De Causa*, fo. 38v. See also Harpsfield, who cites John Bacon on this point, in *Treatise on the Pretended Divorce*, 21.

[44] *De Matrimonia* [1531], *Relecciones Teologicas*, ed. Luis G. Alonso Getino (Madrid, 1934), ii. 440–504.

[45] Fisher, *De Causa*, fo. 37v; Harpsfield, *Treatise on the Pretended Divorce*, 99–100.

[46] *King Henry VIII*, ed. R. A. Foakes, Arden Edition (Cambridge, Mass.: Harvard University Press, 1957), 80 n.

[47] William Forrest, *The History of Grisild the Second: A Narrative, in Verse, of the Divorce of Queen Katharine of Aragon*, ed. W. D. Macray (London: Whittingham and Wilkins, 1875).

The only way that Shakespeare can balance sympathy for Katherine with unequivocal acceptance of the divorce is by emphasizing Henry's sincere concern for the next generation. Katherine's failure to produce an heir would have weighed powerfully with Shakespeare's audience:

> ...her male issue
> Or died where they were made, or shortly after
> This world had aired them. Hence I took a thought
> This was a judgement on me that my kingdom,
> Well worthy the best heir o'th' world, should not
> Be gladded in't by me.   (2.4.188–93)

Henry's distress in the play is generated by concern for his children—for those who died in the womb or shortly after birth, and for his daughter Mary, whose marriage to the Duke of Orleans was impeded by the question of her legitimacy.

In Shakespeare's *Henry VIII*, the child Elizabeth, symbol of England's future, purifies the union of Henry and Anne Boleyn. The play concludes with the pageantry of Elizabeth's christening and with Cranmer's prophecy, filled with biblical images and phrases. Frank Kermode has properly noted that Katherine's tragedy 'must not be allowed to detract from the pleasure the auditors are expected to feel at the end of the play, which is of course related to the happy dynastic progress of English history since that birth, a progress which might have been very different if Henry had not put away Katherine.'[48]

That the birth of Elizabeth transforms an otherwise sinful union into a virtuous one is confirmed by Andrew Willet in his commentary on Leviticus 18. Willet repeats the most vicious slanders against Henry, including his purported involvement with Anne Boleyn's mother. He relishes the ribald counsel of Francis Bryan, Henry's Vicar of Hell, and rehearses the accusation that Henry 'had first carnall knowledge of the mother and then of the daughter; and that he made his owne bastard daughter his wife'. Then, abruptly, he rejects all the scandals: 'The renowned fame, and prosperous raygne of the issue of this Marriage, our late most noble Soveraigne, Queene *Elizabeth*, doth cleare this suspition, and stop Papists slaunderous mouthes.'[49]

V

The figure of Elizabeth affords us a convenient opportunity to return from the court of Henry VIII to the court at Elsinore, though in returning we relinquish absolute distinctions between the world of history and the world of a play. Elizabeth's silent, powerful presence connects the history play that celebrates

---

[48] Frank Kermode, 'What is Shakespeare's *Henry VIII* About?' *Durham University Journal,* NS 9 (1947–8), 54.

[49] Willet, *Hexapla in Leviticum,* 447–9.

her birth to the more fictive drama written for an audience she rules. Critics of *Hamlet* have observed that an audience being asked to convict Claudius and Gertrude of incest is at the same time being asked to remember the circumstances of Elizabeth's birth and to take the Henrician side in the scriptural controversy. On the question of incest, Bertram Joseph notes, 'The subjects of Elizabeth were likely to have been very much alive to it, for she owed her throne and her legitimacy to her father's belated insistence on the sinfulness of his union with Catherine of Aragon, his dead brother's widow.'[50]

One royal brother marrying another brother's widow is the single strong likeness in the cases of Henry and Claudius. The differences may be more important. Henry dissolves a marriage of almost twenty years on the suspicion of incest ('no Marriage . . . but rather an incestuous and detestable Adultery, as the Act of Parliament doth term it').[51] This suspicion depends on a perhaps overly rigorous interpretation of the Levitical prohibition. Claudius, on the other hand, marries in defiance of even the most permissive interpretation of either Leviticus or Deuteronomy. More important, Henry's stated motive for dissolving the union is concern for a child yet unborn, symbol of England's line. By contrast, Claudius and Gertrude, posting with 'dexterity to incestuous sheets', have in effect denied Hamlet's very existence.

Elizabeth's birth is the ultimate vindication of Henry's decision to divorce Catherine, and it turns the questionable union with Anne Boleyn into a virtuous one. Hamlet's birth is a diriment impediment to Gertrude's remarriage (one that renders a marriage null and void from the beginning), and it turns what would otherwise have been a virtuous union (at least according to Deuteronomy) into an incestuous one. The true levirate requires that the widow be childless. Hamlet's existence has thus freed Gertrude from the obligation to marry Claudius, but she has not chosen freedom. Where a Freudian, Oedipal view of incest presumes Hamlet's envy of his father, a scriptural view of the incest prohibition might posit instead a relationship of concord between father and son, both of whom require from Gertrude the loyalty that would confirm their existence. The union of Gertrude and Claudius confirms instead the death of love, and it constitutes an insult to Hamlet, who might as well never have been born.

Gertrude might have been innocent of the sin of incest had Hamlet never been born, and it is tempting to suggest that this fact cuts both ways. Certainly before Act 5, Scene 2, in which Hamlet interprets his rescue, and thus his continued existence, as a sign of Divine Providence, he can be heard complaining against the

---

[50] *Conscience and the King* (London: Chatto & Windus, 1953), 46. A lucid explanation of the incest prohibition appears in Joseph Quincy Adams's edition of *Hamlet* (Cambridge, Mass.: Riverside, 1929), 199, 278–9. See also Richmond Noble, *Shakespeare's Biblical Knowledge*, 205; John W. Draper, *The Hamlet of Shakespeare's Audience* (Durham, NC: Duke University Press, 1938), 114; Richard Flatter, *Hamlet's Father* (London: Heinemann, 1949), 26.

[51] Foxe, *Actes and Monuments*, ii. 277.

limitations imposed by fate on human will. Sometimes these complaints focus upon the problem of '*birth, wherein [men] are not guilty,* | *Since nature cannot choose his origin*' (1.4.18.9–18.10). Many of the death-wish passages in the play express Hamlet's desire never to have been born: 'O cursèd spite | That ever I was born....' (1.5.189–90); '...it were better my mother had not borne me' (3.1.124–5). Laertes speaks truer than he knows when he says of Hamlet: 'his will is not his own, | For he himself is subject to his birth' (1.3.17–18).

It is difficult to refrain from developing the point that existence is indeed problematic for Hamlet—that he feels tainted, even before the Ghost has appeared to him, because Gertrude's incestuous guilt is somehow involved with his birth. Some of the play's best critics have, after all, remarked on its ability to contain contradictory systems of value, and on the Prince's extraordinary self-consciousness, his habit of considering all sides of a problem. Nor is it surprising that the play has been subjected to such a large share of existential cant: Hamlet encounters his existence as gratuitous; he feels *de trop*; he stands in for superfluous twenty-first-century humanity. Finally, in Hamlet's trenchant identification of his mother in the closet scene, the accusation of incest and the wish never to have been born are uttered in the same breath:

> You are the Queen, your husband's brother's wife.
> And—would you were not so—you are my mother.   (3.4.15–16)

Yet this idea accords too well with the anachronistic modern tendency to see Hamlet in the closet scene as somehow, like old Norway, 'impotent and bedrid'. To be sexually impotent yet confined to (and obsessed with) the bed is like being unable to assassinate the King yet confined to his court. Such a view, emphasizing Hamlet's helplessness, would obscure the truth: it is not Hamlet's birth that has made the marriage incestuous; rather, it is the action of Gertrude and Claudius in marrying.

VI

Our knowledge of the sixteenth-century conflict between Protestants and Catholics over the dispensability of the text in Leviticus helps us better to understand Hamlet's absolute allegiance to the word. Claudius, in the prayer scene, acknowledges his own 'shuffling' (3.3.61), recognizes his failure to circumvent divine law, and comes close to entering into a deeper awareness of the inwardness of true renovation, before falling silent and finally confessing failure. His case has merit only in this corrupt world, where power and wealth buy out the law (3.3.57–60). For Hamlet, of course, God's Levitical prohibition against incest is absolute, fixed for all time, and indispensable by any worldly authority. The 'better wisdoms' of Denmark, 'which have freely gone | With this affair along' (1.2.15–16), are merely a sign that 'shuffling' and temporizing are general in the state.

It is interesting to remember in this connection that belief in the absolute severance of the marital union by death supports the Catholic position of dispensability. We have already seen that Claudius, from the start, relies on the power of death to break King Hamlet's hold on Gertrude. Nicholas Harpsfield affirms the Pope's right to dispense from the Levitical prohibition and brands as untruth the Protestant idea that the wife is the flesh of her dead husband:

This unity is to be counted while the husband and wife do live and no longer, for as long as they live the wife's privie member is accounted his according to the saying of St. Paule. The woman hath no power of her owne body, but the husband.... Now the husband being dead, it is no longer his member, and therefore no discovering of his foulness, but it is now the foulness of him that hath married her.[52]

Hamlet, of course, considers the marital bond that makes Gertrude and King Hamlet one flesh to be indissoluble, even by death (4.3.53–4). One imagines that he would oppose any second marriage, holding that 'a good widowe ought to suppose, that her husbande is not utterly dead, but liveth, both with life of his soule, which is the very life, and beside with her remembraunce. For our freends live with us ... if the lively image of them be imprinted in our harts.... And if we forget them, then they die towards us.'[53]

His father's namesake, Hamlet embodies the act of memory that keeps the old King alive; he reminds us constantly that such memory is an ethical imperative. This is what animates his appeal to Gertrude's conscience in the closet scene. Earlier, he has relied on the tenacity of memory to maintain and strengthen his resolve to avenge his father's death (1.5.95 ff.). One can imagine the pain with which Hamlet hears the player-king complain, perhaps in a line that Hamlet has 'set down' and inserted himself, that 'Purpose is but the slave to memory' (3.2.170). We can well understand, even without recourse to a sixteenth-century controversy, why Hamlet must remember. Yet this specific debate on the dispensability of the incest prohibition provides doctrinal justification for both remembering and not remembering. Hamlet and Claudius thus stand even more starkly opposed to one another.

It has not been my purpose to belittle earlier interpretations of incest in *Hamlet*. Jones's study of the workings of repressed desire on Hamlet's 'unconscious' continues to be valuable—though Claude Lévi-Strauss's definition of incest as 'the overvaluation of kinship' is droll in a public-relations sense that Claudius himself would have appreciated. I have only sought to suggest that a theologically orthodox interpretation of the incest prohibition can lead to increased understanding of the play. Conflicting scriptural passages, together with their commentaries, help to identify Claudius's role as a travesty of the *levir's*

---

[52] *Treatise on the Pretended Divorce*, 99.
[53] Juan Luis Vives, *The Instruction of a Christian Woman*, tr. Richard Hyrde (1529; repr. London, 1592), 424.

role. They also help to explain the intensity of Hamlet's antipathy toward his 'uncle-father and aunt-mother'.

VII

Where the preceding sections of this chapter have attended to differences between Roman Catholics and Protestants over marriage questions, the next two sections, more relevant to the book as a whole than to *Hamlet,* concentrate on Henry VIII's soliciting of opinion on his 'great matter' from Italian scholars proficient in both biblical Hebrew and post-biblical rabbinic thought.[54] The topic, unsurprisingly, lends itself to ironies and to the double vision inherent in Christian Hebraism, which, at least in sixteenth-century England, often appropriates the Hebrew Bible and its language, while it lays claim to the racial, national, and religious privileges befitting the true Children of Israel. According to Robert Wakefield, the first official university lecturer in Hebrew at Cambridge (*c.* 1523) and 'the first [early modern English Christian] Hebraist worthy of the name', the 'Jews do not have a particular language for common use, since their vernacular language, which had disappeared, belongs to us.'[55] In sixteenth-century England, the view that the Jews are racially distinct and have never been grafted onto the stock of other people combines with the view that only Christians are the true Israel. In Paul's metaphor (Romans 11: 17–24), only the latter, engrafted in Christ, become the olive tree, including root and branch, while the Jews are the branches broken off. Paul's distinction between the children of faith and the children of loins, 'the children of the flesh' and 'the children of promise' (Romans 9), has been used for millennia to disenfranchise the Jews from the promise of salvation.

However serious their differences, Henry VIII and Charles V share in these appropriations and distinctions. Scholars have documented the pervasiveness of Judaeophobia in sixteenth-century English culture—in poems, plays, broadsides, travel diaries, chronicles, sermons, political tracts, confessions of faith, legal texts, parliamentary debates, and biblical commentaries.[56] And Charles V's maternal

---

[54] This section owes a great deal to the chapters on 'The Canon Law of Divorce' and 'The Struggle for the Divorce' in Scarisbrick's *Henry VIII,* 163–240, and to 'The Jewish Advocates of Henry VIII's Divorce', in David S. Katz, *The Jews in the History of England 1485–1850* (Oxford, Clarendon Press, 1996), 15–48. Both Scarisbrick and Katz have pointed the way to relevant primary sources.

[55] Robert Wakefield, *On the Three Languages* (London, 1524), ed. and tr. G. Lloyd Jones (Binghamton, NY: Medieval and Renaissance Texts and Studies, 1989), 178; cited by James Shapiro in *Shakespeare and the Jews* (New York: Columbia University Press, 1996), 41. Shapiro (p. 41) also cites Andrew Borde, who maintains that 'the Hebrew spoken by modern-day Jews was as unlike the "true Hebrew tongue" as "barbarous" Latin was from true Latin' (Borde, *The Fyrst Boke of the Introduction of Knowledge* (*c.*1560), 221. On Wakefield's competence in Hebrew, see G. Lloyd Jones, *The Discovery of Hebrew in Tudor England: A Third Language* (Manchester: Manchester University Press, 1983), 180–4.

[56] Most recently, James Shapiro, in *Shakespeare and the Jews, passim.*

grandparents, Ferdinand and Isabella, presided over bloody persecutions of the Jews before expelling them from Spain in 1492, in what has been called 'the culminating tragedy of medieval Jewish history'.[57] What *is* surprising, then, is the importance to the principals on both sides of the divorce—and especially on the Henrician side—of Jewish thought and religious practice. Equally surprising is the unexamined assumption by the king's best biographer that such importance is self-evident. J. J. Scarisbrick notes the indefatigable efforts by Henry's agents to solicit favourable opinions:

They sent home copies of valuable texts in Latin, Greek, and Hebrew.... They argued with Scripture scholars, Hebrew scholars, canonists, doctors of medicine, rabbis, friars, laymen. They held formal sessions at universities, and, where successful, despatched homewards the so-called 'determinations' thereof. They gathered lists of signatories, collected copies of rare letters of Fathers and rabbinical writings. They even sent home from Venice two Hebrew scholars...

After citing rabbinical opinion that seems to favour Henry's case, Scarisbrick points to the 'lamentable mishap' of two levirate marriages taking place, in Rome and Bologna, in 1530, and concludes: 'Between them they discredited the royal case more effectively than could a score of learned treatises and university determinations.'[58]

David S. Katz goes even further, while portraying Henry as the victim mainly of bad timing. Although the pope had annulled the marriages of other monarchs in similar circumstances, after the imperial sack of Rome in 1527, he was for seven months a prisoner of Charles V in Castel Sant' Angelo. And unfortunately for someone basing his case on the prohibitions of the Hebrew Bible and 'current Jewish practice', 'it was just at this moment that Italian Jews were reconsidering the entire issue of levirate marriage, and the result of their rabbinical rulings would leave Henry's case in ruins, with no hope other than an unequivocal declaration of royal supremacy in the English reformation.'[59] This seems to attribute the creation of English Protestantism to a few mostly anonymous Italian Jews!

Why should Henry or his agents care what the Jews think about his great matter? Tudor anxiety regarding Jews to a degree radically incommensurate with their tiny number and powerlessness creates terrible myths about them that strip them even of their simple human dignity. As early as the 1490s, Henry VII had assured the Spanish ambassador that he would punish soundly any immigrant Jews found in his realms.[60] And yet, in a letter to Charles V, Eustace Chapuys, the

[57] Cecil Roth, *A History of the Jews in England*, 3rd edn. (Oxford: Clarendon Press, 1985), 90.

[58] Scarisbrick, *Henry VIII*, 256–7.

[59] Katz, *The Jews in the History of England*, 15. He also points out (p. 41 n. 60) that there was only one levirate marriage in 1530, in Rome.

[60] *Calendar of ... State Papers ... Relating to the Negotiations between England and Spain*, i, ed. G. A. Bergenroth (London: Longman, 1862), 164; hereafter cited as *State Papers Spanish*.

Imperial ambassador in England (Shakespeare's gallantly sympathetic Lord Caputius in *King Henry the Eighth*) speculates that the purpose of a letter sent by Henry to Rome without informing the papal Nuncio may be

to bring over here an old Jew, now at Rome, who says he can prove incontrovertibly that the King's marriage was unlawful.... [I have] advised Messire [Miguel] Mai [the emperor's agent] of this, so that should the Jew be a man of such learning and parts as to inspire confidence, he [Mai] may prevail on the Pope to stop his coming [to England], at least until his arguments have been heard, so that the bishop of Rochester may be prepared to refute them.[61]

Why should the powerful invest the powerless with such authority, and why should the powerless be so feared?

The role of Jews, Jewish converts to Christianity, and Christian Hebraists in the divorce offers a convenient point of entry into the situation's omnipresent ironies and contradictions. Nothing is what it seems. In fact, Marco Raphael, the Jew to whom Chapuys's letter refers, is not Jewish but rather a convert to Christianity, although we cannot even be certain whether or not Chapuys believes in his conversion. One transcript of a letter to Charles, written after Raphael's arrival in England, reads: 'le dit juif que se dist estre pieça baptizé soubs ombre de charité vouldroit semer telle dragee iudaique' (The said Jew, who pretends to have been baptized some time ago, would now under the cloak of charity spread his Judaizing doctrines).[62] 'Se dit' could be 'said he was' or, introducing more doubt, 'claimed to be', and a second transcript of the same letter, which substitutes 'indaignee' (not to be condescended to?) for 'iudaique', makes Chapuys seem at least to allow for the possibility of conversion.[63] Posted to England, the imperial ambassador Chapuys wrote mostly in French, spoke not a word of English, and used Latin to communicate with Henry's courtiers. Chapuys's national identity and the subject matter and textual instability of his letter might remind us of the sixteenth-century classifications that destabilize the notion of a fixed Jewish identity: New Christian, Converso, and Marrano, under the Spanish Inquisition; Judaizer, false Jew (Christian masquerading as Jew), and counterfeit Christian in early modern England.

The preceding six sections of this chapter have taken a Henrician stance and, in accord with Tudor myth, endorse a teleological reading of Elizabeth's reign. The effect if not the purpose of examining the Jewish material is to turn from reassuring myth to perplexing history, whose meaning depends in part on who is writing it. Chapuys, opposing the divorce, writes dismissively of the Jews, but

---

[61] *State Papers Spanish,* iv. ed. Pascual de Gayangos (London: Longman, 1879), 1. 460, p. 761: 15 October 1530.

[62] Ibid. 2, p. 45: 31 January 1531.

[63] 'The said Jew, who says he has been some time ago baptised, under colour of charity *vouldroit semer telle dragee indaignee.*' *Letters and Papers, Foreign and Domestic, of the Reign of Henry VIII,* ed. J. S. Brewer (London: Longman, 1876), v. 31–2, no. 70: 31 January 1531.

Henry's agents write about them as if they were Christians or, at times, as if they themselves were Jews. A typical letter from Richard Croke, a Cambridge humanist who had taught King Henry Greek, to Stokesley, presents Jewish opinion, based on the most basic literal reading of the verses in Leviticus and Deuteronomy, as if it were the most learned scholarship. Croke reports on information supplied by his chief interpreter of the Jews, Francesco Giorgi, Venetian theologian, Hebraist, and Christian cabbalist:

The Jews tell [Giorgi] that the law of Deuteronomy has not been kept since the fall of Jerusalem, and, what Stokesley was very desirous to have confirmed, that it is not intended to be kept, except where it is allowed by the Levitical law, and they do not consider it obligatory except where causes and circumstances expressly urge it, and not even then is it absolutely obligatory. They say that it was always an alternative, either to marry the brother's widow, *vel pati discalciationem* [*or else to endure the removal of the sandal*—see Deut. 25: 9–10]. Has letters on this point from two Jews—one a physician and the other a convert to Christianity. Will send them, with a copy of the book of Francis George, by the first messenger, and also the writings of anyone else whom he thinks learned enough to consult.[64]

This information is either incorrect or so noncommittal as to be useless. Many rabbinic authorities in the post-talmudic period (the Sura *geonim*) and in the later, rabbinic period (Alfasi, Maimonides, Joseph Caro) regarded levirate marriage as an obligation. Cabbalistic scholars held that 'levirate marriage is very beneficial for the souls of the dead', and the custom was practised until recently among the Jews of Spain and in North Africa from Morocco to Egypt.[65] What Croke describes as learned opinion is nothing more than the most basic reconciliation of the two sets of biblical verses—namely that the prohibition applies except 'when [marriage] is allowed', that is, when the brother has died without issue. By allowing *halizah*, the ceremony of loosening the shoe that releases the *levir* from his obligation (Deut. 25: 7–10), described in more detail than the levirate institution itself, the Bible indicates that the levirate is not 'absolutely obligatory'. The surviving brother can marry or else suffer being unshod (*discalceatus* in the Vulgate on 25: 10).

This opinion may be rudimentary, but its refreshing straightforwardness distinguishes it from various hermeneutic contortions, especially on Henry's side, that invent differences where there are none. Henry's absolute adherence to the law in Leviticus may be seen as symbolic of the Reformation's ranking of scripture over *ecclesia*. One can hardly say *sola scriptura*, since the Henrician side took liberties with the text, starting with the contrived distinction, already noted,

[64] *State Papers, Spanish*, iv. 1.563, p. 869: 6 July 1530. Croke, like his adversary Chapuys, persists in referring to the Christian convert 'Mark Raphael' as 'a learned Jew [who] has written most plainly on our side, and offers to defend his writings, which are in Hebrew' (*Letters and Papers*, iv. 3. 2749, no. 6156: 29 January 1530.

[65] See the full entry on 'levirate marriage and *halizah*' in *Encyclopedia Judaica* (Jerusalem: Keter, 1972).

between *frater germanus* and *cognatus,* despite the identical word for brother (*Ah* in Hebrew, *frater* in the Vulgate) in both Leviticus and Deuteronomy. The Christian Hebraist Robert Wakefield undertook to defend Henry by referring to 'the best learned and most excellent authors of the interpreters of the Hebrews', assuring the king that support for his action would be forthcoming from rabbinic sources. In order to make the curse of Leviticus 20: 21 ('they will be without children') apply to Henry, who has a surviving daughter, Wakefield mistranslates the Hebrew *aririm,* which in both the Bible and in post-biblical rabbinic texts always means childless (lit., 'barren', 'stripped'), as 'without sons'.[66]

Although the Hebrew Bible makes no division among its laws, St Thomas Aquinas classified them as moral, ceremonial, and judicial. Henry's advocates saw the ceremonial and judicial laws as abrogated, but they still accepted the authority of the moral law. This allowed them to see the law in Leviticus as moral and perpetual, that in Deuteronomy as ceremonial and temporary. Luther held that Christians should follow even the Bible's moral law only in so far as it accords with universal natural law, so the Henrician side could base its case on the prohibition's accord with such a law, dismissing the levirate as merely a special case, applicable only to the Jews. Hence, although Henry's printed book, the *Assertio Septem Sacramentorum* (1521), attacked Luther's *De Captivitate Babylonica* (1520), and Luther himself would not affirm that the laws of either biblical text were still binding on the Christian conscience, German reformers, as well as those in Zurich and Basel, could support the divorce.[67] Conversely, though Tyndale's heterodoxy lay in the idea that scripture opposed the teaching of the Catholic Church, especially its oral tradition, and that scripture is as much antecedent to the church as a parent is to a child, he could argue in favour of levirate marriage because in this case the plain sense of scripture and the ruling of the church were in accord.

We have already noted indeterminate textuality in a letter expressing contempt for a doctrine spread by a 'Jew' under the cover of charity. The rest of Chapuys's letter to his emperor identifies the doctrine and raises a number of curious issues. 'The Jew sent for by the king' [most likely, Marco Raphael] advised him

not to impugn the Queen's marriage, but that the King might take another wife—which advice is not to the King's taste, as it would be too infamous to attempt such a course. I believe his ground is that though the King's marriage with the Queen is legitimate, the issue must be reputed those of his brother, and it would be unreasonable that he should be precluded from having issue for himself. The Jewish law also permits him to take another wife.[68]

---

[66] David S. Katz makes this point in *The History of the Jews in England,* 21–2.

[67] See on this point Guy Bedouelle, 'The Consultations of the Universities and Scholars Concerning the "Great Matter" of King Henry VIII', in *The Bible in the Sixteenth Century,* ed. David C. Steinmetz (Durham, NC, and London: Duke University Press, 1990), 29–30.

[68] *Letters and Papers,* v. 31–2, no. 70: 31 January 1531.

According to Chapuys, Henry finds the idea 'so extravagant and absurd that he has openly declared to the Jew himself that this will not do, and *that he must devise some other means of getting him out of the difficulty, for that he would never adopt, indeed would rather die than resort to said expedient,* as it would be an infamous and blameable act for him to have two wives at the same time.[69]

Despite his protestations, Henry had already endorsed the idea of bigamy in a letter that he signed twice, at the beginning and at the end. He addressed his ambassadors Sir Francis Bryan and Peter Vannes, asking that they communicate their charge to Sir Gregory da Casale, English ambassador at Rome:

the ambassadors must secretly retain the best advocates whom they can find in Rome, by secret rewards and conven[tion], and must learn from them whether, if the Queen can be induced to enter into . . . religion, the Pope may, *ex plenitudine potestatis,* dispense with the King to proceed to a second marriage, with legitimation of the children; and, although it is a thing that the Pope perhaps cannot do in accordance with the divine and human laws already written, using his ordinary power, whether he may do it of his mere and absolute power, as a thing in which he may dispense above the law. Furthermore . . . if they find that the Pope will not dispense with the King to proceed *ad secunda vota* while the Queen is alive in religion, but that she will still be reputed as his wife, they shall inquire whether the Pope will dispense with [the King] to h[ave *duas] uxores,* making the children of the second marriage legitimate as well as those of the first; whereof some great reasons and precedents, especially of the Old Testament, appear.[70]

The latter expedient, undoubtedly supported by a roster of patriarchal biblical polygamists, turns out to be one of the least malignant of Henry's dirty tricks, at least in so far as it leaves poor Catherine alone. A more intrusive stratagem consists of trying to persuade Catherine to become a nun, thus freeing Henry to marry Anne. Lorenzo Campeggio, Bishop of Salisbury, and Wolsey meet with her and advise her that for the good of the kingdom

and in order also to remove any difficulties as to the succession to the crown of England, [the Pope] thought the best expedient to be adopted was that she should profess in some religious community and take vows of perpetual chastity. That since Her Highness had already reached the third and last period of natural life . . . she would thus put a seal to all the good actions of her life, and could besides prevent by such religious profession the many and incalculable evils likely to arise from such matrimonial discord.[71]

Behind the flattery lies 'Get thee to a nunnery' and 'at your age | The heyday in the blood is tame'. Caught as she is in a world of deception, where nothing is what it seems, Catherine's reply, exemplary in its loyalty and self-possession,

---

[69] *State Papers, Spanish,* iv. 2, p. 45: 31 January 1531; cited by Katz, *The Jews in the History of England,* 44.

[70] *Letters and Papers,* iv. 2158, pt. 2, letter no. 4977: 27 November 1528.

[71] A letter from Don Iñigo de Mendoza, particularly entrusted with the management of Catherine's affairs in England, to Charles V. *State Papers, Spanish,* ii ed. G. A. Bergenroth, 2, p. 845: 18 November 1528.

seems profoundly uncomprehending. Assuming that the idea originates with Wolsey, she tells Campeggio:

She had always held the Pope's dispensation to be valid, and her conscience was as tranquil as it would have been troubled had she suspected that the King was doing for her sake a thing so much against his conscience and honour. [Wolsey, the Legate] must know for certain that all attempts to make her take the veil in a convent would prove vain, as she would defend to the last the soul and the honour of her husband and herself. He [the Legate] might write to the Pope that such was her determination.[72]

Catherine professes concern for Henry's honour, as if he has not been pressing for a divorce, and as if the couple were united in being accused groundlessly rather than that her husband has initiated groundless accusations.

An insidious variation of the nunnery ploy, anticipating Catherine's reluctance, involves convincing her to enter religion and take the vow of chastity on condition that Henry do so as well, with the understanding that the Pope will then 'dispense with him for the said promise or vow, discharging him clearly of the same', and proceed to let him take a second wife.[73] Yet another gambit involves telling Pope Clement, with appropriate indignation, that the document containing Julius II's original dispensation is a forgery: 'nothing can be a higher indignity than that so noble a prince should be frustrated of his expectation by the falsehood of one most wicked person forging the Pope's breve.'[74]

Perhaps the worst indignity of all is Catherine's interrogation by the Archbishop of Canterbury and the Bishop of London, together with 'two more persons of distinction'. The first question put to her,

which they said had been put forward by the adverse party (*parte contraria*), [is] namely, whether it was true that she had attempted the King's life, in order to have herself and her daughter the Princess married at her will. Her answer was ... that she could not imagine that such an abominable accusation could come from the King her lord, for he knew well that she prized his life more than her own, and that, therefore, there was no need for her to answer such a question.[75]

Henry and his agents ring cruel changes on Bertram's observation in *All's Well That Ends Well*: 'all impediments in fancy's course | Are motives of more fancy' (5.3.216–17). In his desire for Anne, Henry ingeniously devises ways to overcome all impediments between them by exaggerating all impediments between him and Catherine. When he instructs his envoys to use 'dexterity' in proposing bigamy before the Pope, it is 'to the more cautele ['precaution', but also 'a crafty device, artifice, stratagem; a trick, sleight, deceit' (*OED*)], and to show that nothing shall be pretermitted on the King's behalf which man's wit can excogitate

[72] *State Papers, Spanish*, ii. 2. 843.
[73] *Letters and Papers*, iv. 2158.
[74] Ibid. 2159.
[75] *State Papers, Spanish*, ii. 2. 845.

or devise, for lack of one thing to devise another.'[76] The contrast between Henry's brutality and Catherine's composure exposes as pure myth Henry's professed reluctance to divorce Catherine and his desire to ascertain the truth about the papal dispensation, 'that his conscience might be quieted, and this kingdom have a legitimate heir when his days should be over'.[77] Similarly, the absence of either a male heir to the throne or of generational continuity even after Henry divorces Catherine and marries Anne compromises the Tudor myth endorsed earlier in the chapter of Elizabeth's apotheosis and glorified dynastic standing. Adding to the confusion is a fact both simple and strange: that the arguments put forward not by his enemies but rather by Henry himself and his friends connect him to Claudius as a king who has violated God's law by marrying the wrong woman.

VIII

David S. Katz has supplied the names of Italian Jews who participated in the controversy over Henry's divorce, including Elijah Menahem Halfan on Henry's side and Jacob Mantino on the side of the Pope.[78] The Jewish arguments noted in the state papers, such as the case for bigamy, are not impressive, perhaps because those hostile to the king cite them. Two elegant and devastating treatises against the divorce by Thomas de Vio, Cardinal Cajetan, contain far more impressive Hebraic scholarship. Cajetan's philological skill, applied to the verses in question, bears out his claim: 'I have made the effort to obtain an exact translation of the text from the original Hebrew.'[79] Cajetan relied on Jews to help him with his translation and commentary on the Psalter (1527) and for the commentary on the Hebrew Bible he was working on in 1530.[80] He proves that both Leviticus and Deuteronomy refer to brothers, adding: 'It is strange that anyone should doubt that this law refers to blood-brothers, since in the Gospel the Sadducees bore witness to this meaning when they presented to Christ the case of the wife of the seven brothers according to the law of Moses [Matthew 22: 23–33].'[81] He also quotes directly from the document of dispensation from Pope Julius, which, expressing an ardent desire for 'peace and harmony between nations', provides yet another justification for the marriage between Henry and Catherine not available to ordinary citizens. What appears to be Cajetan's most

---

[76] *Letters and Papers*, iv. 2. 2161, letter no. 4978.

[77] *State Papers, Spanish*, ii. 2. 845.

[78] See Katz, *The Jews in the History of England*, 24–41.

[79] Cajetan, 'The King's Marriage', a letter to Clement dated 13 March 1530, in *Cajetan Responds: A Reader in Reformation Controversy*, ed. Jared Wicks, SJ (Washington, DC: Catholic University of America Press, 1978), 178.

[80] Guy Bedouelle, 'The Consultations of the Universities and Scholars Concerning the "Great Matter" of King Henry VIII', in *The Bible in the Sixteenth Century*, ed. David C. Steinmetz (Durham, NC, and London: Duke University Press, 1990), 33. See also *Cajetan Responds*, 285 n.

[81] *Cajetan Responds*, 179.

original hermeneutic principle—that when we find a general law, such as the Levitical prohibition, followed by a specific law, such as levirate marriage, we follow the specific—accords with the rabbinic principle of *k'lall u'prat* (general followed by specific) contained in Rabbi Yishmael's hermeneutic rules, which are part of the daily Jewish liturgy.

If it is noteworthy that some Christians treat Jews as if their pronouncements were as authoritative as those of Christians, then it is even more remarkable that some Italian Jews maintain an elaborate fiction allowing them to treat Christians as if they were Jews. Various state papers mention the Jews of Venice and Padua. Rodrigo Niño writes to Charles from Venice about Bishop Stokesley: 'All his negociations here, since his return [from Padua], have been conducted with the Jews about whom I wrote to your Majesty, and with a certain prior of St. John and Paul of the Order of St. Dominic.'[82] In another letter he complains that 'prothonotary Casale, the English resident ambassador at this Court', along with 'Ricardo, the solicitor, went about getting the opinions of Padua and of all this territory and with all the Jews here and at Bologna (*y con quantos judios aqui y en Boloža ay*). The first thing they tell them is that both the Pope and the Emperor are very glad that the affair is to be disputed, and that after that their King will grant them more favours than they can wish for.'[83] Niño is contemptuous of Casale's unscrupulousness and of the Jews' gullibility and ignorance of the facts. He knows that the Pope 'had positively forbidden such discussions of the matter' of Henry's divorce, and that becomes the decisive argument that he uses in persuading the Prior of St John and Paul to retract any opinions favourable to Henry.[84]

It is at least worth mentioning that, despite the many vicissitudes resulting from the policies of Charles V toward Jewish subjects in the crown's Italian possessions, Jewish religious and cultural life flourished during this period. Great scholars who might, if asked, have offered definitive interpretations of the texts relating to Henry's divorce include Obadiah Sforno (*c.*1470–1550), renowned for his commentary on the Pentateuch. In Rome, under Cardinal Grimani's recommendation, he taught Hebrew to the Christian humanist Johannes Reuchlin. Like Sforno, the Hebrew philologist Elijah Levita (*c.*1469–1549) taught some of the leading Christian humanists of the time, and they taught him Greek and Latin. Regarding *halakha* (the legal tradition of normative Judaism), the important yeshiva of Padua was led by Meir ben Isaac Katzenellenbogen (1473–1565), one of the greatest Italian rabbis and *halakhists* of his time. He was recognized as the *av beth din* (head of the rabbinical court) of the Republic of Venice. He completed a book written by his father-in-law, Abraham Minz, *Seder*

---

[82] *State Papers, Spanish,* iv. 1. 869, no. 563: 6 July 1530.

[83] Ibid. 552, no. 317: 25 May 1530. See also Richard Croke to Henry, *Letters and Papers,* iv. 3. 2723, no. 6105: 27 December 1529: 'will treat with the Jews as Stokesley advised.'

[84] *State Papers, Spanish,* iv. 1. 869.

Gittin va-Halizah (a study of divorce and of the levir's release ceremony), published in Venice in 1553. As we shall see, neither they nor any of the lesser lights that we know were solicited by both sides provided the simple *halakhic* answer to the question of Henry's divorce.

A reference to Maimonides in *Censurae academiarum,* the Henrician determinations of the universities of Italy and France, highlights the irony. The report accepts Maimonides' defence of a lax position on affinity when the world was young and needed to be populated and a more rigorist position in contemporary times. It also cites his explanation for the strongest deterrents for incest, death by a court of law and the threat of being cut off: in the majority of cases of prohibited unions the females 'are constantly in the company of the male of the house and . . . they are easy of access for him and can be easily controlled by him—there being no difficulty in making them come into his presence.'[85] According to the determination:

whan mankinde was increased and multiplied/there were many mo persons excepte by Moses lawe/whiche began evin at that time to restrayne and refrayne mans concupiscence and luste. wherfore (as sayth Rabbi Moses) al those persones be excepte from mariage/ whiche be wonte to dwell to gether in one house. For seinge it must nedes be, that they/ whiche come of one parentes, or of one father and mother, bothe men & women indifferently, company to gether of long tyme in one house, plainly they shuld have great provocacion & stirringe to flesshly luste/if it were not forbidden, that there shulde be no suche medley betwene those persons.[86]

Maimonides is the most illustrious figure in Judaism in the post-talmudic era and the greatest of all codifiers of the Torah, but the rigorist position on incest expressed in both the *Guide* and the *Mishneh Torah* applies only to Jews. Christians, like other non-Jews, are bound only by the seven Noachide laws: universal commandments whose observance guarantees them a share in the world to come. Maimonides is very clear on the point that there are only six illicit relations forbidden to a Gentile: his mother (even if she is not his father's wife), his father's wife (even if she is not his mother, and even after his father's death), a married woman, his maternal sister, a male, and an animal.[87] Any Jew familiar with rabbinic thought would have been able to tell Henry that neither the prohibition against marrying a brother's wife nor the commandment to marry his brother's childless widow applies to him. It is no small irony that in this instance radical antinomianism converges with the most rigorous application of rabbinic law. Luther and Maimonides come together in the argument that the regulations of Leviticus and Deuteronomy are not binding on the Christian

---

[85] Moses Maimonides, *Guide of the Perplexed,* bk. 3, ch. 49, tr. Shlomo Pines (Chicago: University of Chicago Press, 1963), 606.

[86] *The Determinations of the moste famous and mooste excellent universities of Italy and Fraunce,* in *The Divorce Tracts of Henry VIII* [1531], ed. Edward Surtz, SJ, and Virginia Murphy (Angers: Moreana, 1988), 141.

[87] Maimonides, *Mishneh Torah, Hilkhot Melakhim,* ch. 9, *halakha* 5.

conscience. Perhaps the silence of the Italian Jews on this point has something to do with courtesy in the face of persecution, even as hinted in the letter by Niño, that with a favourable answer 'their King will grant them . . . favours'.

In its discussions, at least, the Talmud is not monolithic on the question of the prohibition of incest for non-Jews. A famous passage interprets the repetition of the word i*sh* (a man) in Leviticus 18: 6, translated as 'None [lit., 'no man man', the repeated word functioning as an intensive] shal come nere to anie of the kinred of his flesh to uncover her shame': 'our rabbis taught . . . why does scripture say, "a man, a man"? To include gentiles, who are prohibited from engaging in forbidden sexual relations just as Jews are.'[88] For Christians, incest as fornication violates the thrice-repeated Apostolic Decree defining a minimum of practice for new Gentile Christians: 'Wherefore my sentence is, that we trouble not them of the Gentiles that are turned to God, But that we write unto them, that they absteine them selves from filthiness of idoles, and fornication, and that that is strangled, and from blood' (Acts 15: 19–20; 15: 29; 21: 25). Incest as fornication violates a minimum standard of decency and ethical practice binding on non-Jews as well as Jews. The Apostolic Decree of Acts, recognizing that being in Christ does not always signify ethical seriousness, set down for Gentile converts from paganism to Christianity moral requirements whose rejection, *ipso facto*, kept one outside the pale of salvation.[89] Behind the Apostolic Decree in Acts are the Levitical laws that apply to resident aliens (vv. 17–18), indispensable according to Henry, and the rabbinic Noachide laws, binding upon every living soul, which had been given to humankind before the special revelation on Mount Sinai, laws such as those proclaimed by Sophocles in the *Antigone* 'that are not of today nor yesterday but forever'.[90]

Even so, according to the Jewish legal tradition, the specific prohibition against marrying a brother's wife, part of the plain sense of Leviticus 18, does not apply to Christians. Moreover, the gap between the plain sense of the Hebrew Bible and the rabbinic application of Torah law even as it applies to Jews is nowhere wider than in the case of levirate marriage. The talmudic tractate *Yebamot*, one of the most complex discussions anywhere of family ties, derives its name from the sister-in-law of Deuteronomy 25. In an extraordinary *halakhic* midrash on Deuteronomy 25: 6, which becomes the law, the firstborn—literally, the first child born of a levirate union—refers to the eldest sibling, upon whom the levirate devolves. It is he and not the child who will inherit the deceased brother's property. (Claudius would be pleased.) The same verse's reference to raising up a name—so that, as the Talmud has it, 'if the deceased was called Joseph, the child

---

[88] Babylonian Talmud, tractate *Sanhedrin*, 57b. One derives this interpretation both from the word itself (human being as opposed to Israelite) and from its repetition.

[89] W. D. Davies, *Paul and Rabbinic Judaism* (London: SPCK, 1955), 117.

[90] Ibid. 114. See also David Novak, *The Image of the Non-Jew in Judaism: An Historical and Constructive Study of the Noahide Laws* (New York and Toronto: Edwin Mellen Press, 1983), 26; and for a comprehensive analysis of the Noachide law governing sexual relations, pp. 199–237.

shall be called Joseph'—becomes instead justification for the transfer of inheritance to the eldest surviving brother. For this the Talmud relies on a *gezerah shawa,* an analogy between the word 'name' in Deuteronomy and in Genesis 48: 6, where it means inheritance. One need not name the child after his father. This prompts Raba to exclaim: 'Although throughout the entire Torah no text loses its ordinary meaning [that is, despite rabbinic hermeneutic ingenuity, the interpretation does not uproot completely the literal meaning of the text]—here the verbal analogy [applied to 'the firstborn . . . shall succeed in the name of his brother *who is dead'*] has come and entirely deprived the text of its ordinary meaning.'[91]

The ironies and contradictions of Hebrew scholarship applied to Henry's case mirror in miniature the ironies of canon law and theology. This is to be expected in a case where a papal dispensation is a gift that the recipient will do anything to return a generation after he has removed the tags. The irony appears at the outset, when Henry asks Pope Clement to grant Wolsey a decretal commission authorizing a judgement that could not be appealed to the Pope. (It's like asking God to create something so heavy that he can't lift it.) Both irony and the great matter reach their provisional denouement six years later, on May 23, 1533, when Thomas Cranmer, Archbishop of Canterbury, announces his judgement that the marriage between Henry VIII and Catherine of Aragon had been null and void from the very beginning (*ab initio*). Such are the ironies of her legal predicament that even Catherine's virtue works against her. As Mendoza tells Charles,

> I have reasons to believe, though the Queen herself has not said so to me, that she told the Legate [Wolsey] that she was a virgin when she married this her second husband, and that the first [Prince Arthur] had never consummated matrimony. This last declaration, however, will not, as far as I know, be adduced as a proof before the judges, lest it should appear as if some doubt was entertained respecting the validity of the dispensation.[92]

Mendoza is alluding to the impediment of *publica honestas,* which arises from a close non-sexual relationship between a man and a woman, such as betrothal. Although it is less of an impediment than affinity, Pope Julius's original dispensation failed to include it. When a couple is allowed to marry by a dispensation from the first degree of affinity, the principle of implicit dispensation removes as well the impediment of public honesty. But if a man and woman are betrothed, or if they are married but unable to consummate the union, one cannot apply the principle of public honesty, because, as J. J. Scarisbrick explains, 'there was no affinity from which the other [public honesty] could be deduced, to which it was annexed, by which it was necessarily implied. . . . In such a case the supplicant must ask explicitly for a dispensation of the impediment of public honesty. . . omitting the irrelevance of affinity.'[93]

---

[91] Babylonian Talmud, tractate *Yebamoth,* 24a.
[92] *Calendar of State Papers, Spanish,* ii. 2. 843.
[93] Scarisbrick, *Henry VIII,* 187.

Henry VIII's great matter is very far indeed from Shakespeare's *Hamlet,* whose own ironies and unresolved contradictions have been probed by generations of ingenious critics. Instead of contriving a way back, I should like to consider in the most general way what it means when, in an intolerant age, Christians rely on Jewish authority as if they themselves were Jewish, or as if the Jews were Christians, and when Jews respond to Christians with *halakha* that they know very well applies only to Jews. It is as if in a very limited way the terms Jew and Christian were mutually convertible. In the paradigmatic conversion of Paul, one becomes that which was forbidden, as the ex-pharisee, and of the strictest school, becomes one with a sect that he had persecuted. Luther, following this paradigm, describes how he reached an impasse:

The more men try to satisfy the law, the more they transgress it . . . When I was a monk, I made a great effort to live according to the requirements of the monastic rule . . . Nevertheless, my conscience could never achieve certainty but was always in doubt and said: 'You have not done this correctly. You were not contrite enough. You omitted this in your confession . . . For as Paul says, it is impossible for the conscience to find peace through the works of the Law.[94]

We need look no further than Hamlet's first soliloquy (1.2.129–59) to know that he has reached an impasse. There is no release but death from his grief and rage: 'But break, my heart, for I must hold my tongue' (l. 159). To escape requires transformation, a radical change of perspective in which some newly gained knowledge brings about a changed way of understanding. Instead of a noonday experience on the road to Damascus, the ghost provides a midnight encounter on the battlements that leaves Hamlet shaken but filled with resolve:

> Remember thee?
> Ay, thou poor ghost, while memory holds a seat
> In this distracted globe. Remember thee?
> Yea, from the table of my memory
> I'll wipe away all trivial fond records,
> All saws of books, all forms, all pressures past,
> That youth and observation copied there,
> And thy commandment all alone shall live
> Within the book and volume of my brain
> Unmixed with baser matter.   (1.5.95–104)

It might seem as if a king bound by canon law and the court at Rome, who can neither oblige that law nor evade it despite overwhelming effort, breaks the impasse and escapes from the Pope's authority by asserting his own supremacy. But in fact Henry converts with a difference. A dispensation rather than a law confines him. And an indispensable law—the severe prohibition of Leviticus 18,

---

[94] Martin Luther, 'Lectures on Galatians', in *Luther's Works,* xxvii, ed. Jaroslav Pelikan and Walter A. Hansen (St Louis: Concordia, 1963); repr. in Wayne Meeks, ed. *The Writings of St. Paul* (New York: Norton, 1972), 248.

from which he never wavered—gives him his first steps toward freedom. According to Scarisbrick, the decisive change occurred by August 1530:

Henry now became something more than an importunate subject knocking aggressively at the door of the Curia; he began to deny that he was even a subject. The Levitical argument... had always contained a latent threat to papal jurisdiction. Now, however, Henry not only challenged the pope's authority but threatened withdrawal from it; and, to do so, began to advance a new authority of his own over and against the papal.[95]

In some ways, Henry's is almost a conversion in reverse. Instead of following Paul by abandoning his former identity and dying in Christ, he exercises his own *plena potestas* against the power of the Pope. And where Augustine, once a Manichaean, becomes a Christian, Henry wields a power independent of external control that might remind us of the divided empire that God is said by heretics to share with evil.

IX

Ben Jonson, costive and splenetic, makes an unlikely but effective diplomat, mediating between the subject of the preceding section, Henry VIII's divorce, and the gender issues in this one. He also introduces us to the central figure of the book, his dear friend John Selden (1584–1654), the most learned person in seventeenth-century England and author of a half-dozen important works of post-biblical rabbinic scholarship. More capable of tact and sensitivity than we might imagine, especially if we have read his conversations with Drummond of Hawthornden, Jonson accompanied Selden to Theobalds in mid-December 1618, giving him moral support when he was ordered to appear before James I to defend his *Historie of Tithes*. Selden recounts how Jonson persuaded the king's favourite, the Marquis of Buckingham, to introduce him to the king 'in a friendly and placating manner'.[96]

The two concluding scenes of Jonson's *Epicoene* address the themes of divorce and cross-dressing, relying on an English audience's awareness of both the search for a publicly justifiable impediment to Henry VIII's marriage with Catherine and the conventions of a transvestite English theatre, in which a boy plays a woman who, in the play's denouement, is revealed to be a boy. In this 'excellent comedy of affliction',[97] Morose, 'a gentleman that loves no noise', wants to dissolve his union with a woman whom he mistakenly believed to be silent.

---

[95] Scarisbrick, *Henry VIII*, 260.

[96] G. J. Toomer, 'Selden's *Historie of Tithes*: Genesis, Publication, Aftermath', *Huntington Library Quarterly*, 65 (2002), 362. See also David Sandler Berkowitz, *John Selden's Formative Years: Politics and Society in Early Seventeenth-Century England* (Washington, DC: Folger Shakespeare Library, 1988), 23. Edward Heyward, a mutual friend, accompanied Selden and Jonson.

[97] Ben Jonson, *Epicoene*, ed. Edward Partridge (New Haven and London: Yale University Press, 1971), 74 (2.6.35). Parenthetic references are to this edition.

The final scenes are a travesty of a legal proceeding, exposing the ridiculously loose state of contemporary English divorce law and using arguments that, by virtue of association with Henry VIII's manipulation of ecclesiastical law, 'are archaic, but scarcely obsolete'.[98] Captain Otter, 'a land and sea captain' named for an amphibian, impersonates Master Parson, interpreting impediments on the bases of English Reformation principles and examples of fact, custom, or enactment ('positive divinity'; 5.3.37). Cutbeard the Barber applies the proscriptions of canon law and sounds like a medieval Catholic lawyer.

Protracting Morose's suffering beyond the limits of endurance, the two impostors discuss in Latin various impediments that have no bearing on the case at hand. An early exchange underscores the differences between the old canon law and Reformation attempts to develop a civil law that removes some of the old obstacles to marriage. Cutbeard's feigned identity might be that of a Spanish Catholic, since Otter hints at the condemnation of Spanish slavery by the English, who did not trade in slaves until 1620:

CUTBEARD. The next is *conditio*: if you thought her free born, and she prove a bond-woman, there is impediment of estate and condition.
OTTER. Ay, but Master Doctor, those servitudes are *sublatae* [removed] now, among us Christians. (5.3.95–9)

Like the two pretended antagonists, English and Spanish, the next two impediments relate not to Morose's situation but rather to Henry's, when he attempted to coerce Catherine into taking holy orders and a vow of celibacy, and when he succeeded in voiding the marriage *ab initio* on the ground of the impediment of affinity. In the discipline or ecclesiastical polity of Protestant sects, impediments protecting vows of celibacy or chastity were unnecessary, for scripture subordinates such vows to the vows of marriage. As John Witte, Jr., points out, Lutheran theologians of this period rejected impediments designed to protect the celibate, and 'canon laws prohibiting marriage to committed clerics, monks and nuns were unanimously rejected as unscriptural'.[99] The Master Doctor offers Morose *votum, cognatio,* and *ordo* as ways out of the marriage, fully aware that they don't apply:

CUTBEARD. Well, then, the third is *votum*. If either party have made a vow of chastity. But that practice, as Master Parson said of the other, is taken away among us, thanks be to discipline. The fourth is *cognatio*: if the person be of kin within the degrees.
OTTER. Do you know what the degrees are, sir?
MOROSE. No, nor care I not, sir; they offer me no comfort in the question, I am sure. (5.3.104–10)

CUTBEARD. The eighth [impediment] is *ordo*: if ever she have taken holy orders.

[98] Aurelia Henry's phrase, in her edition of *Epicoene* (New York: Henry Holt, 1906), 262.
[99] John Witte, Jr., 'The Transformation of Marriage Law in the Lutheran Reformation', in *The Weightier Matters of the Law: Essays on Law and Religion*, ed. J. Witte, Jr., and F. Alexander (Atlanta: Scholars Press, 1988), 86.

OTTER. That's superstitious, too.

MOROSE. No matter, Master Parson. Would she would go into a nunnery yet. (5.3.131–4).

Cutbeard as canon lawyer uses terms such as diriment impediment and public decency that were of some importance in Henry's case, but an impatient Morose notes their irrelevance to his:

CUTBEARD. [T]here are *duodecim impedimenta*, twelve impediments—as we call 'em—all which do not *dirimere contractum*, but *irritum reddere matrimonium*, as we say in the canon law, not take away the bond, but cause a nullity therein.

MOROSE. I understood you before; good sir, avoid your impertinency [irrelevance] of translation. (5.3.68–73)

Where Otter considers public decency to be '*affinitas orta ex sponsabilus* [relationship arising from a betrothal], and...but *leve* [slight] *impedimentum*' (5.3.140–1), Cutbeard's definition is a reminder of the problem caused by Arthur's inability to consummate his marriage to Catherine, which precludes the impediment of public decency from being annexed to the dispensation from that of affinity: 'The tenth [impediment] is *publica honestas*, which is *inchoata quaedam affinitas* [an earlier marriage which was unconsummated]' (5.3.138–9).

These scenes dwell on impotence in its various legal forms, some of which might remind us of Arthur's debility: *manifestam frigiditatem, morbus perpetuus et insanabilis* (a continual and incurable disease), *prorsus inutilis ad thorum* (utterly useless for the marriage bed), lacking *exercendi potestate* (the power of carrying out). It is the subject of a notable exchange with a hint of unimpersonated artistry, giving us a glimpse of Jonson the Latin scholar and pedant in the character of Truewit:

OTTER. That a boy, or a child, under years, is not fit for marriage, because he cannot *reddere debitum* [render his debt]. So your *omnipotentes*—

TRUEWIT [*aside to Otter*]. Your *impotentes*, you whoreson lobster.

OTTER. Your *impotentes*, I should say, are *minime apti ad contrahenda matrimonium* [least suited to contracting marriage].

TRUEWIT [*aside to Otter*]. *Matrimonium*? We shall have most unmatrimonial Latin with you: *matrimonia*, and be hanged. (5.3.167–73)

Although Morose is not impotent, he is willing to be considered so, even though it turns him into the defendant and his wife into the plaintiff: 'I am no man...Utterly unabled in nature, by reason of frigidity, to perform the duties or any the least office of a husband' (5.3.40, 42–3). But his judges still won't allow him a way out. He reaches an impasse, like Henry, which is broken by his nephew Dauphine, who first extracts from his miserly uncle a promise of money and then simply '*takes off Epicoene's peruke*', revealing him to be a boy, 'a gentleman's son that I have brought up this half year at my great charges, and for this composition which I have now made with you. What say you, Master Doctor? This is *justum impedimentum*, I hope, *error personae*?' (5.4.182–4). And both reply that it is: 'Yes sir, *in primo gradu*' [in the first degree] (l. 186).

Although *Epicoene* was probably first performed in January 1610, no quarto of independent authority has ever appeared, and the authoritative text is that of the First Folio of 1616. Selden, who owned a copy of the folio, also wrote its first commendatory poem, and thus the first ever in the collected works of a major English poet, 'Ad V[iro] CL[arissimo] BEN. Ionsonium carmen protrepticon' [To the most famous Ben Jonson an encouraging (or hortatory) poem]. Selden, the greatest legal historian of his age, would have appreciated the proceedings that conclude *Epicoene*. As we will see in a later chapter, Sir John Vaughan, in a pure expression of his teacher John Selden's legal philosophy, explains indirectly but conclusively why all the English statute law based on Leviticus 18 was enacted during the reign of Henry VIII, prohibiting absolutely what the Hebrew Bible, whose strictures have been abrogated for Christians, prohibits only conditionally.

In some of the most mature products of his rabbinic scholarship, Selden demonstrates his familiarity with details that bear upon Henry VIII's divorce, including the Italian Jewish advice to persuade the Pope to 'dispense with the King to proceed to a second marriage'. Twice he refers to his manuscript copy of *Historia de gli Riti Hebraici*, by the Venetian rabbi Leone da Modena (1571–1648), which contains a statement removed from the printed edition (Paris, 1637) by the censor, regarding the privilege of taking a second wife if one has lived with his present wife for years without issue: '*Indultu tamen Romani Pontificis impetrato*' (Yet not without procuring the indulgence or dispensation of the Pope). In his *De Successionibus ad Leges Ebraeorum in Bona Defunctorum* (1631, published by Will Stansby, who also published Jonson's First Folio), he acknowledges his reliance on an autograph copy of *Riti Hebraici* that he received from William Boswell, a fellow of Jesus College, Cambridge, who had travelled to Venice in his youth and studied there with Modena.[100]

In his *Uxor Hebraica* (1646), Selden elaborates:

Today, indeed, among the European Jews who live in Italy and Germany, with the permission of the Roman Pontiff, an additional wife was sometimes added to a barren one for purposes of procreation. I have learned this from Rabbi Leon da Modena, the Archisynagogue of Venice, in a book about Jewish customs called *Historia de gli Riti Hebraici*. This book was in manuscript form when I mentioned him before [note: '*De Successionibus ad Leges Ebraeorum in Bona Defunctorum*, cap. 14'] as an outstanding man

---

[100] Selden, *De Successionibus ad Leges Ebraeorum in Bona Defunctorum*, 60. See also Leon Modena, *The Life of Judah: The Autobiography of a Seventeenth-Century Venetian Rabbi*, ed. Mark R. Cohen (Princeton: Princeton University Press, 1988), 267. Modena proudly announces his association with Selden: 'So that it be known (although without merit) what fame I have had, in July 1634 there came to me a book printed in London in England in the year 1631, the title of which is, as will be written below here or on the facing page: "John Selden Lawyer (J. C. = Juris Consultus) *On the Succession to the Possession of the Deceased or On the Right of Inheritance According to the Laws of the Jews that were in Use at the time that their Republic was at its Height, One Book drawn from the Bible, from Both Talmuds, and from Selected Rabbinic Writings, that is, from the Sources, the Digest, and the Most Learned Teachers of the Hebrew Law*" ' (p. 170).

who has communicated with me. Since then, in a printed edition from Paris, what was said about papal permission was, it seems, deliberately censored.[101]

He concludes his reference to Modena by quoting in Italian the censored passage about taking another wife, which applies to Italians: '*e in Italia hanno usato chiederno licenza e pigliare dispensa del Papà*'.[102]

There is a record of Modena's correspondence with Selden,[103] and it is tempting to speculate that Selden may have been the recipient of a letter entirely in Hebrew, sent from Modena to an unnamed non-Jewish Englishman, explaining four terms related to tithes and offerings at the time that he was working on his *Historie of Tithes.*[104] One would hope that an intellectual atmosphere that fosters a relationship between the cosmopolitan and politically powerful Selden and the learned Venetian rabbi might have contributed at least indirectly to the eventual readmission of the Jews into England. At the very least it contrasts sharply with the stifling atmosphere created by a boorish Thomas Coryate, who attempts upon meeting a Venetian 'learned Jewish Rabbin that spake good Latin,' to convert him to Christianity. The patient rabbi answers 'that Christ forsooth was a great Prophet, and in that respect as highly to be esteemed as any Prophet amongst the Jews that ever lived before him; but derogated altogether from his divinitie.' This provokes Coryate to demand that the rabbi 'renounce his Jewish religion and to undertake the Christian faith, without which he would be eternally damned'. Although the rabbi never loses his patience with his unmannerly guest, Coryate fears for his life when a crowd of Jews gathers. A number of scholars have speculated that the rabbi is Leone da Modena.[105]

---

101 Selden, *Uxor Hebraica,* 1.9, pp. 72–3: 'Hodie vero apud Europaeos Judaeos, veluti, qui Italia ac Germania degunt, infoecundae uxori alia, prolis gratiâ, idque non sine Pontificis Romani indulto interdum superinducitur, quod R. Leonis Mutinensis [of Mutina, now Modena], Venetiis Archisy-nagogi [the priest who was the ruler of the synagogue], de moribus Ebraeorum libello seu *Historia de gli Riti Hebraici* didici. Manu scripto scilicet illo; quem [note: '*Lib. de Successionibus in Bona cap. 14.*'] alibi uti & virum praestantissimum qui mecum communicavit memoro. Nam in codice Parisiis [note: '*Anno 1637. in 8.*'] dudum impresso id quod de Pontificis Romani indulto heic habetur consulto ut videtur est dispunctum.'

102 Selden, *Uxor Hebraica,* 1.9, p. 73.

103 *List of Original Letters to and from Mr. Selden,* Harleian MSS. 7527 f. 57a: 'Leon Modena Rabi Hebreo, Italice'; cited in Cecil Roth, 'Leone da Modena and England,' *Jewish Historical Society of England, Transactions,* 11 (1924–7), 216 n. 12.

104 BL, MS Add. 27148, fo. 24. Roth's article 'Leone da Modena and England' (206–25) contains both the Hebrew original and an English translation of the letter, explicitly identified by Leone da Modena as *responsa* or *teshuvah* (תשובה), though Roth doubts that Selden is the recipient.

105 Roth, in 'Leone da Modena and England', 222; Howard Adelman, 'Leon Modena: The Autobiography and the Man', in *The Autobiography of a Seventeenth-Century Venetian Rabbi,* ed. and tr. Mark R. Cohen (Princeton: Princeton University Press, 1988); M. Lindsay Kaplan in her edition of *The Merchant of Venice: Texts and Contexts* (Boston and New York: Bedford/St Martin's, 2002), 142 n. 7. The relevant extract from *Coryats Crudities* is from Kaplan's edition, pp. 139–45. In the jacket illustration of James Shapiro's *Shakespeare and the Jews* (New York: Columbia University Press, 1996), Detail 'G' from the title-page of the 1611 edition of *Coryats Crudities* shows a turbaned rabbi with a knife pursuing a Christian. The dedicatory verse of Laurence Whitaker, sig.

Addressing the question of a second wife in his great *De Jure Naturali et Gentium juxta Disciplinam Ebraeorum* (1640), Selden reveals his philological sophistication, his extensive knowledge of rabbinic literature, and, most of all, his ability to see all sides of a question. Alongside the positive arguments and a notably sensible general opinion ('One could marry as many wives as he wished... provided that he has what suffices for them,' a proviso that could keep a man from marrying at all), Selden finds a negative position in the rabbinic commentaries on a portion of Job's answer to Eliphaz's third speech: 'He evil entreateth the barren that beareth not; and doeth not good to the widow' (24: 21). This section of Job gives contemporary scholars so much trouble that some take the drastic step of moving it 'piece by piece to other sections of the book, at the same time emending it heavily'.[106] The ultimate example that explains this verse, for both Rashi and the *Midrash Rabbah,* though not acknowledged by either, is Genesis 29: 31: 'And when the Lord saw that Leah was hated, he opened her womb: but Rachel was barren.' The midrash relates Rachel's barrenness to her favoured status. Rashi and especially the midrash play on the multiple meanings of the three-letter root עקר *ikkar* in Job 24 (principal or chief, essence, root, root-drink, barren). It is a trait of the evil generations of the flood and of Sodom to keep one wife for sex and another for children. The former, bathed and bejewelled like a bride and fed on dainties, is given a root-drink to make her infertile (כוס של עיקרין כדי שתעקר), while her rebuked companion mourns like a widow and starves. The midrash adds about the favoured one that she sits next to her husband adorned like a prostitute ('*velut meretricio ornabatur habitu*').[107] Selden's Bible manuscript from 1304, which he donated to the Bodleian Library, Oxford, in 1659, includes a Masoretic text and Rashi's commentary. Where modern editions of Rashi's commentary on Job 24: 21 begin with the unspecific כך היה מנהגם (such was their custom), the variant reading in Selden's copy is specific, connecting this behaviour with the evil generation of Noah's flood: 'כך היה דרכן של דור המבול *Ad hunc modum habuit mos sub diluvi tempora*'.[108]

To return to *Epicoene,* Erastian Selden would have appreciated Jonson's ridiculing of ecclesiastical control over causes of matrimony. The political argument of the fifth book of *De Jure Naturali* and virtually all of *Uxor Hebraica,* no less powerful for being indirect, is to reform English marriage law, including the right of divorce. For Selden, 'Marriage is nothing but a civil contract': 'Of all actions of a man's life, his marriage does least concern other people; yet of all actions of our

A3r, urges Coryate to 'fly from the Jews, lest they circumcise thee'. One need hardly add that Rabbi Modena was not the coercive figure in the actual encounter.

[106] *The Book of Job,* ed. Raymond P. Scheindlin (New York and London: W. W. Norton, 1998), 201.

[107] Selden, *De Jure Naturali et Gentium juxta Disciplinam Ebraeorum,* 5.6, pp. 564–5.

[108] Ibid. See Modena, *Life of Judah,* 266, which reports that on 28 October 1628 Leone da Modena signed a statement attesting to the authority of this Bible manuscript.

life, 'tis most meddled with by other people.'[109] Ecclesiastical law also had jurisdiction over tithes, because they were paid to men of the church, and causes testamentary, on the pretext that testaments were made *in extremis*, when churchmen were present. Selden's *Historie of Tithes* (1618) treated tithes as a matter of variable civil right and not as due to the clergy *jure divino*, and his *De Successionibus ad Leges Ebraeorum in Bona Defunctorum*, the first major work of rabbinic scholarship written after he had begun his intensive study of the Talmud, regards the law of inheritance as a civil matter.

Selden would have been amused by the constant repetition of the titles Master Doctor and Master Parson by Cutbeard and Otter as a sign of vanity. He points out that parson and person were once used indifferently: 'Though we write [parson] differently, yet 'tis but person; that is the individual person set apart for the service of such a church, and 'tis in Latin *persona*, and *personatus* is a parsonage'.[110] He would have appreciated Otter's amphibian name in a play that by its title crosses gender lines, refers to the French hermaphrodite, and features weak knights (Sir John Daw and Sir Amorous La Foole) and the aggressive members of the Ladies Collegiate (including Madam Centaure). Although the extra-grammatical meaning of *epicene* to denote partaking of the characteristics of both sexes may be incorrect, Jonson uses it anyway: 'of the epicene gender, hees, and shees'. Selden uses the figure of an otter as Jonson does, to denote an equivocal status, but also to deride pretension: 'The prior of [the Knights of] St. John of Jerusalem is said to be *primus baro Angliae*, the first baron of England; because being last of the spiritual barons, he chose to be first of the temporal. He was a kind of otter, a knight half spiritual, and half temporal'.[111]

As Blair Worden has pointed out, both Jonson and Selden probed the ridiculous excesses among the rulers of the past in order to point out dangers in the present. For Jonson, 'Tiberius's court, like Elizabeth's court, is a sink of venality and bribery'.[112] In his *Titles of Honor* (1614, rev. 1631), Selden's vast enumeration of the vanity of tyrants—including the kissing of Roman emperors' body parts by their suppliants—implicitly warns the reader to avoid servility and idolatry. Selden considers the name '*Dominus*, **Lord**, and *Signior*' as applied to human beings:

It were hard to endure such impious flatterie, as to give them the name as it is truly significant; as the dissembling and inconstant *Samaritans* did to *Antiochus Epiphanes*,

---

[109] John Selden, *Table Talk*, ed. Samuel Harvey Reynolds (Oxford: Clarendon Press, 1892), 109. All references to *Table Talk* are to this edition. Selden talks like a confirmed bachelor, although, according to Aubrey, in his later years he married the widowed Countess of Kent, whose late husband the earl was his patron: 'Marriage is a desperate thing. The frogs in Aesop were extreme wise, they had a great mind to some water, but they would not leap into the well, because they could not get out again' (p. 109).

[110] Ibid. 129.

[111] Ibid. 106.

[112] Blair Worden, 'Ben Jonson among the Historians,' in *Culture and Politics in Early Stuart England*, ed. Kevin Sharpe and Peter Lake (Stanford, Calif.: Stanford University Press, 1993), 85.

stiling him, in their Epistles, God, who had indeed to his utmost, profaned the holy Temple of the true God, most cruelly handled the Jewes, and in contempt of their law and Divinitie [marginal note: Joseph. *Archaeolog.* 12. cap. 7. & lib. 19. cap. 7. *de Herode*], compeld them eat Hogs flesh against their institution, and with the liquor straind, wherein it was boiled, daubd and abusd as many of the Bibles, as his wickednes could light on.[113]

Considering Selden's penetrating to the root of a title in order to diminish it, his section of *Titles of Honor* dealing with the crowning of poets with laurel concludes with strikingly unqualified praise. In his original but highly allusive poem to Jonson in the First Folio, Selden praises his learning most of all and deems him to be clearly deserving of so many laurel wreaths (l. 46). His praise in *Titles of Honor* is less original but more subtle and artful. Withholding judgement, he nonetheless by mere reportage and the well-placed word conveys a sense of the vanity of recent English poets, including John Skelton, who had the title of Laureate under Henry VIII; Robert Whittington, also living at that time, who called himself '*Grammaticae magister & Protovates Angliae, in florentissima Oxoniensi Academia Laureatus*'; and 'one John Kay[, who] by the title of *his humble Poet Lawreat*, dedicates to [King Edward IV] his *Siege of Rhodes* in prose'. Selden concludes by revealing that his survey fulfils a promise made to Ben Jonson:

But of the Crown of Laurell given to Poëts, hitherto. And thus have I, by no unseasonable digression, performed a promise to you my beloved BEN. IONSON. Your curious learning and judgement may correct where I have erred, and adde where my notes and memory have left me short. You are

——*omnia Carmina doctus*
Et calles Mythων plasmata & Historiam

And so you both fully know what concernes it, and your singular Excellencie in the Art most eminently deserves it.[114]

It has gone unnoticed that Selden's Latin lines are a quotation [actually a slight adaptation to reflect the shift from plural to singular] of the praise by the early fourth-century poet Ausonius, in his *Commemoratio Professorum Burdigalensium* [Poems Commemorating the Professors of Bordeaux], of the Greek and Latin grammarians Crispus and Urbicus: 'omnia carmina docti, | callentes mython plasmata et historiam [learned in all the lore of poesy, and skilled alike in mythic fictions and in history]'.[115] It is as if Jonson alone deserves the praise that Ausonius divides between two.

---

[113] Selden, *Titles of Honor*, 2nd edn. (1631), 62.
[114] Ibid. 412–13.
[115] *Commemoratio Professorum Burdigalensium*, carmen 21, v. 26, in *Ausonius*, ed. and tr. Hugh G. Evelyn White, Loeb Classical Library (London: Heinemann; New York: Putnam's, 1919), i. 130–1.

Selden's choice of Ausonius is deliberate. He traces the history of the *Agon Capitoline*, a celebration once every four years in honour of Jupiter, in which the 'Ensignes of excellencie given, by solemne judgement of the Emperor & his assistant Judges, were Crowns',[116] from its institution in the first century under the emperor Domitian to its cessation during the age of Ausonius:

And in that age of *Ausonius* the Capitolin Act ceased also, upon the same reason as their plaies of all kind did soon after. For that was dedicated to *Iupiter*, as the plaies were to the other Deities of the Gentiles, whence it is that *Tertullian*, S. *Chrysostome*, S. *Ambrosem* and some other of the Fathers so justly inveigh against them. For it could not be that either this act or the playes of those times could have been performed according to the first institution without grosse Idolatrie, which, in those times of the infancie of Christianitie, was to be feared, wheresoever any relation was but so made to the name of a false god.[117]

In his learned but leaden 'carmen protrepticon' in the First Folio, Selden had remembered Stolo's saying that the Muses would have used Plautus's Latin, and Cicero's that the son of Saturn would have used Plato's Greek, if the Muses had been speaking in Latium and Jupiter in Athens. He concludes that Jupiter and the Muses would have used Jonson's verse if they had been speaking to the people of England (ll. 26–33).[118] In *Titles of Honor*, Selden seems (or pretends) to assume that Jonson is already familiar with the arcane learning he has brought down on his behalf: 'Your curious learning and judgement may correct where I have erred, and adde where my notes and memory have left me short.' Jonson can be expected to recognize the implication of the quote from Ausonius: unlike contemporary poetasters who have appropriated the name of laureate, Jonson deserves such laurels as were bestowed in the time of Ausonius, whose own words confirm the timelessness of his poetry. He deserves to be mentioned with the ancients.

---

[116] Selden, *Titles of Honor*, 409.

[117] Ibid. 411.

[118] Selden, 'Ad V. CL. Ben. Ionsonium', repr. in *Ben Jonson*, ed. C. H. Herford, Percy and Evelyn Simpson (Oxford: Clarendon Press, 1925–52), xi. 327.

2

Selden, Jonson, and the Rabbis on Cross-Dressing and Bisexual Gods

Selden's Letter to Jonson

Selden's references in his *Titles of Honor* to Jonson's familiarity with arcana and to the early church fathers' objection to the 'grosse Idolatrie' of the theatre take us to the main subject of this chapter, Selden's letter to Jonson, on 28 February 1616, on cross-dressing, which also addresses the topic of the bisexuality of the gods. Winfried Schleiner, the letter's co-editor, calls it 'a milestone in the history of gender studies no matter how that history is conceived'.[1] Answering Jonson's query about 'the literall sense and historicall of the holy text usually brought against the counterfeiting of sexes by apparell' in Deuteronomy 22: 5, a verse cited to support the closing of a transvestite English theatre, Selden ultimately adopts a Maimonidean hermeneutic, which correctly notes that the Hebrew word כלי (*kly*) denotes not male clothing, *habitus virilis*, but only a man's armour, *instrumenta bellica*. According to Maimonides, the verse prohibits not cross-dressing *per se* but rather the ancient idolatrous rites whereby men worshipped Venus in women's clothing and women worshipped Mars, appropriately enough, in armour. Selden's answer would have been received most warmly by one of the most celebrated practitioners of a theatre founded on cross-dressing, although it never mentions the theatre. As Schleiner points out, 'Selden ends his letter with what rhetoricians call *praeteritio*, a figure of passing over with a deprecating ring: "With what ancient fathers as Cyprian & Tertullian specially have of this text, or others dealing on it as it tends to morality, I abstain to meddle." '[2] Selden's comments on the association of the theatre with idolatry 'in those times of the infancie of Christianitie' clarify the letter's true purpose, as do his remarks on conversion in *Table Talk*:

---

[1] Winfried Schleiner's phrase in 'John Selden's Letter to Ben Jonson on Cross-Dressing and Bisexual Gods [with text]', ed. Jason P. Rosenblatt and Winfried Schleiner, *English Literary Renaissance*, 29 (1999), 44. Please see Appendix for the text of Selden's letter.

[2] Ibid. 47.

I never converted but two, the one was Mr. Crashaw from writing against plays, by telling him a way how to understand that place, *of putting on women's apparel*, which has nothing to do with the business (as neither has it, that the fathers speak against plays in their time, with reason enough, for they had real idolatries mixed with their plays, having three altars perpetually upon the stage). The other was a doctor of divinity, from preaching against painting, which simply in itself is no more hurtful than putting on my clothes, or doing anything to make myself like other folks, that I may not be odious or offensive to the company.[3]

William Crashaw, scholar, minor poet, and father of the major poet Richard, was preacher at the Inner Temple, and it was in this last capacity that Selden converted him from writing against plays, pointing out that neither the biblical verse nor the objection of the church fathers has anything 'to do with the business'.[4] It is at least possible that Selden's defence of the theatre put him in mind of 'painting' (applying cosmetics), since theatres were associated with prostitution as much as with idolatry—indeed, all three were thought to work together. Clerics in the seventeenth century preached that covering one's face with cosmetics defaces the features of God, in whose image we were created, and that 'Painting was practised by Harlots, adulterated complexions well agreeing with adulterous conditions.'[5]

Selden's letter, part of a continuum of scholarly exchange with Jonson, begins as an answer to Jonson's query about cross-dressing ('I have most willingly collected what you wisht') and ends as a draft awaiting Jonson's 'instructing judgment'. The concluding hope may be more than mere courtesy, for virtually every item of information in the letter, itself a *Wunderkammer* of learning in comparative philology and mythology as well as biblical and rabbinic hermeneutics, will be elaborated in Selden's *De Diis Syris* (1617), a monumental study of the pagan gods of the Hebrew Bible. Selden adverts to the forthcoming book by distinguishing between 'the common learned reader', its intended audience, for whom the additional documentation will be new, and the uncommonly learned

---

[3] Selden, *Table Talk*, 134–5.

[4] In 'The Inner Temple and Literary London', the draft of a chapter from his work in progress, an intellectual biography of Selden, G. J. Toomer includes Crashaw among the poets, major and minor, that Selden would have known at the Inner Temple, which was 'part of the nexus of literary London'. Professor Toomer takes account of Selden's own poetic pretensions (the accompanying notes often swamped the poems themselves), including a dedicatory poem for Michael Drayton's collected *Poems* (1610), three celebratory poems for the first volume of *Britannia's Pastorals* by William Browne (1616), three poems in Greek and Latin, lamenting Prince Henry's death and celebrating Princess Elizabeth's betrothal, for Henry Peacham's *The Period of Mourning* (1613), and commendations in verse of Arthur Hopton's *Concordancy of Yeares* (1612), Samuel Purchas's *Pilgrimage* (1614), and Thomas Farnaby's edition of Lucan (1618). Toomer also discusses commendations of Selden by other, better poets, among them George Wither, who dedicated his translation of Nemesius to him, and Robert Herrick in *Hesperides*, who addresses him as '*the most learned, wise, and Arch-Antiquary, M.* John Selden', and ends, 'Live thou a Selden, that's a Demi-god' (*The Poetical Works of Robert Herrick*, ed. F. W. Moorman (Oxford: Clarendon Press, 1915), 142–3).

[5] Thomas Fuller, *A Pisgah-sight of Palestine and the confines thereof* (1650), IV.vi.116.

Jonson, for whom this letter should suffice, because his well-stocked mind, with access to a well-furnished library, can multiply examples from Greek and Latin commentaries on its own:

In the connexion of these no vulgar observations, if they had been to the common learned reader, there had been often room for divers pieces of European Theologie dispers'd in Latin & Greek autors of the Gentiles & Fathers of the church too, and often for parts of mythologie, but your own most choice & able store cannot but furnish you incidently with what ever is fit that way to be thought of in the reading.

The Jonson imagined here is like all of Selden's other readers, only more so, by virtue of his genius, and thus he is like Selden himself: sceptical, but with a humanist's respect for historical investigation and an antiquarian's interest in the documents of the past simply because they exist.

In the letter Selden relies on 'the old Scholiast' who glosses Aristophanes' *Wasps* to interpret masculine garb limitingly, as 'panoply', which accords with the Septuagint's 'trappings' or 'trappings of war', and thus with Deuteronomy's '*Celi geber*, i.e., the Armes or armor of a man.' In the Preface to the first edition of *Titles of Honor* (1614), Selden describes visiting Ben Jonson's library to consult the old Greek scholiast of Euripides' *Orestes* for evidence to counter the general assumption that crowns and diadems 'have been mongst Royall Notes [i.e. tokens] most anciently in Europe':

I presume I have sufficiently manifested the contrarie, and answerd their urged Autorities, producing also one out of Euripides his *Orestes*, seeming stranger [stronger?] against my part then anie other: which, when I was to use, and having not at hand the Scholiast (out of whom I hoped some aid) I went, for this purpose, to see it in the well-furnisht Librarie of my beloved friend that singular Poet M. Ben:Ionson, whose speciall Worth in Literature, accurat Judgment, and Performance, known only to that *Few* which are truly able to know him, hath had from me, ever since I began to learn, an increasing admiration. Having examin'd it with him, I resolvd upon my first Opinion, and found, as I ghesse, a New but more proper Interpretation of the Place.[6]

Selden loves primary sources, and in his analytic, historical account of current titles of honour, such as King, Duke, Baron, and Knight, he assures his reader: 'I vent to you nothing quoted at second hand, but ever lov'd the Fountain, and,

---

[6] Sig. D1–D1v. The passage in question describes Atreus, 'for whom Fate twined with her doom-threads a strand of strife' against his brother Thyestes. See *Orestes*, in *Euripides*, tr. Arthur S. Way, Loeb Classical Library (London: Heinemann; New York: G. P. Putnam, 1916), ii. 127. The published Latin translation consulted by Selden strangely introduces *coronam* into this passage about fate and doom. Arsenius, the old scholiast, disappointingly interprets the word in question as '*a Crown proper to Kings*' (p. 138) but inadvertently supplies Selden with the clue that allows him to read not *coronam* but rather *carminans*, the carding of wool. Arsenius 'talkes as if hee could not see the wood for trees: hee confesses that σέμματα signifies ἔρια, i. *the wooll that goes about the distaffe*, circling it as a Crown.' Having examined the scholiast together with Jonson, Selden discovers a new reading that 'well justifies the Noble Poets using and continuing the known fiction of the Destinies in their spinning out of mens Fortuns. Nay, what could be more proper in the allusion, then to suppose her first card or pull the wooll in peeces, and then make hir web of Discord?' (p. 141).

when I could come at it, usd that *Medium* only, which would not at all, or least, deceive by Refraction.'[7]

First printed in *Titles of Honor*, the verse epistle headed 'BEN:IONSON TO HIS HONORD FRIEND Mr IOHN SELDEN, HEALTH' bestows upon Selden its own title of honour, 'Monarch in Letters':

> You, that have beene
> Ever at home: yet, have all Countries seene;
> And like a Compasse keeping one foot still
> Upon your Center, doe your Circle fill
> Of generall knowledge; watch'd men, manners too,
> Heard, what times past have said; seene, what ours do;
> Which *Grace* shall I make love to first? your skill?
> Or faith in things? Or is't your wealth and will
> To informe and teach? Or your unwearied paine
> Of gath'ring? Bountie in pouring out againe?
> What *Fables* have you vex'd? what Truth redeemd!
> Antiquities search'd! Opinions dis-esteemed!
> Impostures branded! and Authorities urg'd!
> What blots and errours, have you watch'd and purg'd
> *Records* and *Authors* of! How rectified
> Times, Manners, Customes! Innovations spied!
> Sought out the Fountaines, Sources, Creekes, Paths, Wayes
> And noted the Beginnings, and Decayes.[8]

As noted already, Selden's *Titles of Honor* and *De Diis Syris* were both published by William Stansby, whose name is Latinized for the latter as Guilielmus Stansbeius, but Anglicized as (an enabling rather than competing) Will in the 1616 First Folio, '*The Works of Ben Jonson*, Imprinted at London by Will Stansby'.

Jonson begins his poem to 'my *Selden*' with the words 'I know to whom I write,' and indeed their friendship can be traced back to 1605, when Selden was newly arrived at the Inner Temple. On the day of his release from prison for mocking the king's Scottish manners and favourites in *Eastward Hoe!* Jonson banqueted his friends and names two of them, Camden, his teacher at Westminster School, and Selden, who was at the time only 20 years old.[9] Eighteen years later, in his *Execration upon Vulcan* (1623), Jonson names Selden as one of those friends who helped him to research his life of Henry V, lost in the fire: 'Wherein was oyle, beside the succour spent, | Which noble *Carew, Cotton, Selden* lent'.[10] Their long

---

[7] Sig. C4v.

[8] Sig. b1v. 'Faith in things' means 'fidelity to facts,' a gloss I owe to G. J. Toomer.

[9] Toomer, 'The Inner Temple and Literary London'. See also Worden, 'Ben Jonson Among the Historians', 67, who points out that Jonson 'seems not to have written the offending passage but rather to have given himself up to the authorities out of solidarity with his fellow authors George Chapman and John Marston.'

[10] *Ben Jonson*, ed. Herford and Simpson, viii. 207.

friendship and mutual admiration raise the question of whether Jonson's learning included at least a limited amount of Hebrew. Would Selden use Hebrew characters in his letter if he knew that his friend could not read them?

In the letter, Selden respectfully disagrees with Isaac Casaubon, the most celebrated philologist of the time, who asserts that the reason the male god Lunus is sometimes taken for male and sometimes for female 'is that in the languages of the Orient the names for Luna are taken to be of the male and female gender'.[11] Selden, at least in this instance, ranks the mythological above the philological, and he adduces a great deal of material about gendered and ungendered forms of worship of deities imagined male, or female, or both male and female:

> The most learned Casaubon supposes the worship of the two sexes in one Deity among the Eastern people to proceed from nothing but because their names are, from several roots, of both grammatical genders. . . . Clearly it was a mysterie of their theologie concluding upon the masculin-foeminin power which made both the worship & grammaticall genders, not the trifles of grammar, their ceremonies of worship.

Selden's remarks on gods of both genders, which extend even to the tetragrammaton יהוה (JHVH), bear on issues relevant to twenty-first-century forms of Christian and Jewish worship, of which the aim of a gender-neutral language in speaking of God is the best-known example. In Casaubon's *Animadversionum in Athenaeum Dipnosophistas*, (1621), the Ben Jonson-Steadfast copy at the Folger Shakespeare Library, with Jonson's autograph and motto on the title-page, partially blacked-out Hebrew words appear in the margin as well as an underlining of Hebrew in the text.[12]

Nothing can be proven from Doll Common's insane rant in *The Alchemist* except that Jonson had read the Hebraist Hugh Broughton's *A Concent of Scriptures* (1590), which cites rabbinic authorities to connect Esau, Edom, and especially the people of Kittim, descendants of Javan (Ionia, Greece), with Rome. James Kugel explains: 'The "Kittim" mentioned in Numbers 24: 24 are translated as "Rome" in *Targum Onkelos* and *Pseudo-Jonathan*, and as "Italy" (erased but still legible) in *Targum Neophiti* and the Vulgate':

---

[11] Isaac Casaubon, 'In Aelii Spartiani Antoninum Caracallum, emendationes et notae', in *Scriptores Historiae Augustae*, ed. Claudius Salmasius (Paris, 1620), 132: 'Lunae nomina et virilis et foeminei generis in linguis Orientis habeantur'. I owe this reference to Winfried Schleiner.

[12] Casaubon, *Animadversionum in Athenaeum Dipnosophistas*, cols. 263 and 910. Mark Bland directed me to this book. See David McPherson, 'Ben Jonson's Library and Marginalia: An Annotated Catalogue', *Studies in Philology, Texts and Studies*, 71 (1974), 34, who points out that it is difficult to make a judgement about the extent of Jonson's annotations since 90% of the notes (in item 34 of his catalogue) have been scratched out. He does find a reference in book 14, ch. 10 (col. 909): 'Vid. Selden, De Dis Syr.' Regarding Jonson's copy of *De Diis*, item 172 in his catalogue, which contains numerous Hebrew words, some of them marked in Jonson's red ink, McPherson asserts: 'Someone has corrected no less than fifty errata, including some not on the lengthy printed lists, and has also provided an elaborate key for the insertion of the thirteen addenda printed on sigs. T5-8. I strongly believe Jonson to be responsible for all of these marks.'

And so we may arrive by Talmud skill
And profane Greek to raise the building up
Of Heber's house, against the Ismaelite,

. . . .

                    and the force
Of King Abbadon, and the beast of Kittim,
Which Rabbi David Kimhi, Onkelos,
And Aben-Ezra do interpret Rome.[13]

Jonson's consistently dismissive opinions about others, including Shakespeare and Donne, in his conversations with Drummond, throw his unqualified praise of Selden into bold relief. In limiting his recommended books to those of only two contemporary English authors, he includes Selden's *De Diis Syris*. Drummond the Scot reports the view of one who is 'a great lover and praiser of himself, a contemner and scorner of others': 'Of their Nation, Hookers Ecclesiasticall historie (whose children are now beggars), for church matters. Seldens Titles of Honour for Antiquities here; and ane book of the Gods of the Gentiles, whose names are in the Scripture, of Seldens.'[14]

There is also, appended to the praise, the hint of a rabbinic reading that Selden had earlier shared with Jonson, who tries unsuccessfully to communicate it to Drummond: 'J. Selden liveth on his owne, is the Law book of ye Judges of England, the bravest man in all Languages, his booke titles of honour, written to his chamber fellow Heyward. . . . the Epigrame of Martial Vin Verpum he Vantes to expone.'[15] Selden had dedicated his *Titles of Honor* to his friend and chamber-fellow Edward Heyward rather than to any of the noblemen who entered the Inner Temple during his early tenure there, such as Robert Rich, later 2nd Earl of Warwick; Robert Devereux, Earl of Sussex; and Thomas Howard, Earl of Arundel.[16] This greatly impressed Jonson, who includes this fact in his commendatory poem in that book:

He thou hast given it to,
Thy learned Chamber-fellow, knowes to doe
It true respects. He will not only love,
Embrace, and cherish; but he can approve
And estimate thy Paines; as having wrought
In the same Mines of knowledge. . . .

. . . .

[13] James L. Kugel, *Traditions of the Bible* (Cambridge, Mass., and London: Harvard University Press, 1998), 366. Ben Jonson, *The Alchemist* (4.5.25–7, 29–32), ed. Gordon Campbell, Oxford World's Classics (Oxford and New York: Oxford University Press, 1995), 296.

[14] *Ben Jonson's Conversations with William Drummond of Hawthornden*, ed. R. F. Patterson (1922; repr. New York: Haskell House, 1974), 13–14. On Jonson's character, see p. 56.

[15] Ibid. 50.

[16] Toomer, 'The Inner Temple and Literary London', points out that all of them enrolled in November 1604, at the same time as Heyward, according to *Students admitted to the Inner Temple, 1547–1660* (privately printed, 1877), 167–8.

> O how I doe count
> Among my commings in, and see it mount,
> The Gaine of your two friendships! *Hayward* and
> *Selden*! two Names that so much understand!   (ll. 71–6, 79–82)

A few lines later, reports Drummond, Jonson boasts that he can interpret an epigram by Martial. Herford and Simpson's note identifies the crux:

Vin Verpum. Another of Drummond's inaccurate references: Jonson had evidently discussed Martial's Epigram XI. xciv, with the refrain 'verpe poeta'. The concluding couplet on this Jew runs:

> Ecce negas iurasque mihi per templa Tonantis
> non credo: iura, verpe, per Anchialum.

Jonson's friend, Selden, had tried his hand at an emendation: in *De Successionibus in Bona Defuncti*, Prolegomena. . . . Following up a suggestion of Joseph Scaliger that the last word was probably a corruption of a Hebrew oath, he proposed 'iura, verpe, iperan chi olam'— יפרע חי עולם—'*id est, ulciscatur, aut vindictam sumat is, qui vivit in aeternum.*' Perhaps Jonson had attempted to convey this to Drummond.[17]

Martial has accused a Jewish poet of violating his boy and refuses to believe his oath of innocence: 'There, you deny it, and swear to me by the Thunderer's temple. I don't believe you: swear, circumcised one, by Anchialus [*Anchialum*].' Selden's emendation relies on an ancient and very well-known rabbinic formula that he cites frequently and in detail, the *mi shepara*. It makes sense of the word no one can figure out, *Anchialum*, by forcing the Jew to swear not by Jupiter, in whom he does not believe, but by the living God, who will punish him if he does not keep his word. For Selden, *fides est servanda* does not mean to keep the faith in the way that the New Testament uses it. The faith that must be kept is one's word as expressed in a contract:

If two of us make a bargain, why should either of us stand to it? What need you care what you say, or what need I care what I say? Certainly because there is something about me that tells me *fides est servanda*, and if we alter our minds, and make a new bargain, there's *fides servanda* there too.

We must look to the contract; if that be rightly made, we must stand to it. If we once grant we may recede from contracts, upon any inconveniency may afterwards happen, we shall have no bargain kept. If I sell you a horse, and afterwards do not like my bargain, I will have my horse again.

Keep your contracts. So far a divine goes, but how to make our contracts is left to ourselves.[18]

In both *De Successionibus ad Leges Ebraeorum in Bona Defunctorum* and *De Jure Naturali et Gentium juxta Disciplinam Ebraeorum*, Selden devotes much

---

[17] *Ben Jonson*, i. 176.
[18] Selden, *Table Talk*, 101–2, 52. Selden's works abound in variations on this theme.

space to the fierce talmudic formula (Babylonian Talmud, tractate *Bava Metzia*, 48a), quoted in full in the original Hebrew, designed to ensure that one keep one's contract:

מי שפרע מאנשי דור המבול ומאנשי דור הפלגה ומאנשי סדום
ועמורה ששטפו ממצרים בים ,הוא עתיד ליפרע ממי שאינו עומד בדיבורו

He who punished the generations of the flood and of the dispersion [of languages at Babel] and of the inhabitants of Sodom and Gemorrah, and the Egyptians who were washed away in the sea, will exact vengeance of him who does not stand by his word [who does not keep his contract].[19]

The emendation of Martial that Selden proposes, '*iperan chi olam*' (will be punished by the Eternal), reduces the formula to its most essential elements. Other conjectures—that the Jew should swear by the name of Martial's boy or that the Romans mistook the last part of the Hebrew formula for the name of a deity—are less satisfying.[20] R. F. Patterson, editing Jonson's conversations with Drummond in 1922, before Herford and Simpson, will go to almost any lengths to avoid accepting Selden's emendation, ending with the opinion of 'Doctor Rouse, whom I consulted on the point, [and who] thinks Anchialus is "likely a man of whom we know nothing."'[21] What matters is that Selden shared this rabbinic solution to a Latin crux with Jonson.

The subject of Jonson's query to Selden, the Deuteronomic verse on cross-dressing, makes an appearance in *Bartholomew Fair*, which opened at the Hope Theatre on 31 October 1614, and was presented before James I at court on the following day. If Jonson does not explicitly defend the theatre in this play, he

---

[19] Selden, *De Jure Naturali et Gentium*, 6.5, p. 688: '*Qui vindictam sumpsit ex seculo Diluvii, & ex seculo Divisionis Linguarum, & ex hominibus Sodomae & Gomorrae, & ex Aegyptiis qui immersi sunt in mari, is sumet olim vindictam ab eo qui conventis suis non stat.*' Selden adds yet another talmudic variant reading, adding the word ששטפו [washed away] between ממצרים and בים See also 6.1 of *De Jure*, pp. 664–6, on the importance of written contracts among the Jews.

[20] See Martial, *Epigrams* (11.94), ed. and tr. Walter C. A. Ker, Loeb Classical Library (London: Heinemann; New York, Putnam's, 1930), ii. 302–3.

[21] *Jonson's Conversations with Drummond*, ed. Patterson, 51 n. Selden's reverence for rabbinic scholarship and worldly-wise toleration of the Jews might be measured against Patterson's casual remarks in his 20th-c. edition. Elizabethan and Jacobean England inherited medieval patterns of diabolization based ultimately on John 8: 44. Catholics could always convert, but, as David S. Katz has noted, 'the demonological, supernatural element in the early modern attitude to the Jews . . . renders it quite different from other forms of opposition to religious minorities and outcasts' (*Philo-Semitism and the Readmission of the Jews to England* (Oxford: Clarendon Press, 1982), 3). Jonson tells Drummond that 'Essex wrotte that Epistel or preface befor the translation of the last part of Tacitus . . . The last book the gentleman durst not translate for the evill it containes of the Jewes.' In his note on this passage, Patterson retails some of the vicious and mistaken descriptions of the Jews in the fragmentary fifth book of the *Histories*. He finds the Elizabethans too scrupulous and lacking a sense of fun: '*Jewes*. The English of Elizabeth's time were so much a nation of theologians that they would not have considered Tacitus' highly amusing and character-istic description of the Jews to be edifying reading. . . . Passages like these would have seemed blasphemous to the Elizabethans' (p. 32 n.). Patterson considers the possibility that Anchialus might be 'some Rothschild of Jerusalem' (p. 51 n.).

certainly attacks its enemies, especially the Puritan Zeal-of-the-Land Busy, who is defeated in debate by the puppet Dionysius. Busy opens the play's penultimate scene by denouncing puppet shows as the rites of Dagon and Baal: 'Down with Dagon, down with Dagon; 'tis I, will no longer endure your profanations. . . . I will remove Dagon there, that idol, that heathenish idol' (5.5.1–2, 3–4);[22] 'thy profession is damnable, and in pleading for it, thou dost plead for Baal' (ll. 18–19). Busy concludes:

> my main argument against you, is, that you are an abomination: for the male, among you, putteth on the apparel of the female, and the female of the male.
>
> PUPPET DIONYSIUS. *You lie, you lie, you lie abominably. . . . It is your old stale argument against the players, but it will not hold against the puppets; for we have neither male nor female amongst us. And that thou may'st see, if thou wilt, like a malicious purblind zeal as thou art!*
>
> *The puppet takes up his garment.*   (91–9)

In the stage direction requiring the puppet to show its sex or lack of it (99), 'his', in accordance with the grammar of the period, stands for the neuter 'its'. Jesus defeats the Sadducees by telling them that 'in the resurrection [the redeemed] neither marry, nor are given in marriage, but are as the angels of God in heaven' (Matthew 22: 30). The puppet defeats puritanical Rabbi Busy by saucily lifting its skirt and showing him that nothing is there. Although the puppet uses religious rhetoric ('we have neither male nor female amongst us'), it does not transcend sex but rather is beneath it. Jonson provides a series of correlatives to the relation between puppet shows and live theatre, including sexlessness and sex, the travesty of Hero and Leander and the story itself, told most recently by Marlowe,[23] and ventriloquism and inspiration, the puppet declaring, 'I speak by inspiration, as well as [Busy does]' (ll. 103–4). The puppet's final proof that its standing is as lawful as Busy's identifies the Puritan as a blockhead: 'I have as little to do with [L]earning as he; and do scorn her helps as much as he' (ll. 104–5).

Busy echoes Deuteronomy 22: 5 when he denounces his enemies: 'you are an abomination' (l. 91); 'I will both knock and mock down your Bartholmew-abhominations' (4.1.84–7). According to G. R. Hibbard, 'this spelling of "abomination", very common in the sixteenth century, arose from the mistaken view that the word was derived from "ab homine", meaning "inhuman". Jonson, who knew better, puts the popular etymology in Busy's mouth as a further indication of the preacher's ignorance'.[24]

---

[22] Ben Jonson, *Bartholomew Fair*, ed. E. A. Horsman, The Revels Plays (London: Methuen, 1960), 156. Parenthetical references are to this edition.

[23] For the relation of the puppet show to Marlowe's 'intensely erotic poem', as well as for provocative general reflections on gender in early modern England, see Laura Levine, *Men in Women's Clothing: Anti-theatricality and effeminization 1579–1642* (Cambridge: Cambridge University Press, 1994), esp. 89–107.

[24] Ben Jonson, *Bartholmew Fair*, New Mermaids, ed. G. R. Hibbard (London: Ernest Benn, 1977), 108.

John Selden attended a performance of *Bartholomew Fair* and remembered the scene in question: the start of the debate is a shouting match between Busy, who repeatedly calls puppets and their shows profane (5.5.61–2, 65, 67, 75), and the puppet-play presenter Lantern Leatherhead and his puppet Dionysius, who insist otherwise, '*It is not profane!*' (63, 64, 66, 68, 69). Selden's reflections on religious controversy and his response to this scene are recorded in his *Table Talk*:

> Disputes in religion will never be ended, because there wants a measure by which the business should be decided. The Puritan would be judged by the word of God: if he would speak clearly, he means himself, but that he is ashamed to say so; and he would have me believe him before a whole church, that have read the word of God as well as he. One says one thing, and another another; and there is, I say, no measure to end the controversy. 'Tis just as if two men were at bowls, and both judged by the eye: one says 'tis his cast, the other says 'tis my cast; and having no measure, the difference is eternal. Ben Jonson satirically expressed the vain disputes of divines by Rabbi Busy disputing with a puppet in his Bartholomew fair. It is so: it is not so: it is so: it is not so; crying thus one to another a quarter of an hour together.[25]

Selden in his lengthy works of scholarship and Jonson in his popular plays unmask pretension, clerical greed and ambition, and vanity. Selden must have taken delight in Jonson's mockery in *Bartholomew Fair* of the cleric Zeal-of-the-Land Busy and the magistrate Adam Overdo, just as Jonson understood very well the intent of Selden's arcane researches in *The Historie of Tithes* and *Titles of Honor*.

Perhaps the single most compelling page documenting the relationship between Selden and Jonson for a contemporary reader is the title-page of Selden's presentation copy to Ben Jonson of *De Diis Syris* (1617)—now in the Folger Shakespeare Library (call number STC 22167.2)—which Jonson annotated in the margins. The title-page contains three inscriptions in his tiny, meticulous hand: in the upper right margin is his motto '*tanquam Explorator*' (like an explorer); in the middle of the page, in ink still bright red after almost 390 years, is his autograph '*Sum Ben:Jonsonii Liber*' (I am Ben Jonson's book), and just beneath that '*Ex dono Authoris*' (gift of the author). On the reverse of the title-page in Selden's hand is his presentation:

V[iro] C[larissimo]	(To the most famous
doctiss[imo]	[and] most learned
Poetae eximio	excellent poet
Amico optime	[and] best friend
Ben. Jonsonio.	Ben Jonson.
ab autore.	From the author.)

---

[25] Selden, *Table Talk*, pp. 164–5. Reynolds lists the variant readings of the sentences dealing with *Bartholomew Fair*. He follows that of Harleian MS 1315. The Harleian MS 690 reads, 'Inigo Lanthorne disputing with his puppet in a Bartholomew Fair'. This makes Selden aware, before the split became public, of Jonson's low opinion of his theatrical collaborator Inigo Jones, whom he portrayed as the puppeteer Lanthorne Leatherhead.

Both Selden and Jonson knew real-life Busys who denounced cross-dressing from the pulpit, in sermons, biblical commentaries, anti-theatrical tracts, and other forms of prescriptive literature. Richard Rogers, a Puritan divine, predecessor at Wethersfield, Essex, of the Smectymnuuan Stephen Marshall, specifically identifies the theatre with the temple of Dagon, invokes the Deuteronomic prohibition, and veiledly refers to a recent calamity, more just than the ancient catastrophe that befell the Philistines at the hands of Samson. He condemns 'shamelesse shewes, and most dangerous stage plaies':

and some are brought on stage in womens apparell, God having commanded the contrary, and said, It shall not be so, Deut. 22.5. In the which meetings they doe not onely with the Philistims please their eye, but also strongly are incensed and provoked to lewdnes and lust, which some of them were nothing so much acquainted with before. Whom if God should shew some such strange judgements upon, as upon these here, (as we have heard that some of them have had lately faire warnings in that kinde, while they have been in the middest of their pastimes) I denie not but it were lamentable; but doubtlesse not lesse (what doe I say? nay by farre more) deserved then this.[26]

Selden in his letter and Jonson in *Bartholomew Fair* reveal their antipathy to clerical repression, though Selden does so far more indirectly. As noted already, at the end of his letter, having adopted a Maimonidean reading of the verse from Deuteronomy that would prohibit cross-dressing only as part of an idolatrous rite, Selden coolly alludes to the controversy over the transvestite London theatre: 'With what ancient fathers as Cyprian and Tertullian specially have of this text, or others dealing on it as it tends to morality, I abstain to meddle.'

Selden has a highly developed sense of irony. He loves to bury the lead, and the main intent of one of his immense scholarly books may be deliberately tucked away in a parenthesis. The real point of the letter is to provide a loophole for Jonson, a famous contributor to a theatre that had been under attack on religious grounds for the past forty years. His letter is a powerful rebuttal of its opponents' arguments, which rely heavily on Cyprian and Tertullian. His tone of scholarly detachment, diametrically opposed to the anti-theatricalists' frenzy, conveys an Olympian aloofness. In the controversy over his *Historie of Tithes* (1618), Selden notes that he describes 'what *was*', while his opponent describes 'what (*he thinks*) should have been. Why could he not have done so, and let us alone?'[27] He might have said the same to the moralistic enemies of the theatre, recognizing that his arguments would never have convinced them.

In Selden's Maimonidean reading, the prohibitions from Deuteronomy oppose 'the idolatrous customes out of ancient monuments of the Syrians', and 'in this of apparell, there was most speciall regard to the avoiding of a superstitious

[26] Richard Rogers, *A Commentary upon the Whole Booke of Judges, preached first and delivered in sundrie lectures* (London: Felix Kyngston, 1615), 780.

[27] John Selden, *Opera Omnia*, vol. iii, col. 1361; cited by Richard Tuck in *Natural Rights Theories* (Cambridge: Cambridge University Press, 1979), 85.

rite used to Mars and Venus, which was, that Men did honor and invoke Venus in women's attire, and women the like to Mars in man's armour.' But for Stephen Gosson and Phillip Stubbes there is no difference between idolatry and theatre:

Tertullian teacheth us that every part of the preparation of playes, was dedicated to some heathen god, or goddesse, as the house, stage, apparel, to Venus; . . . he calleth the Theater, Sacrarium Veneris, Venus chappell, by resorting to which we worshippe her.[28]

Seeing that playes were first invented by the devil, practised by the heathen Gentiles, and dedicat to their false ydols, goddes and goddesses, as the howse, stage, and apparell to Venus . . . it is more than manifest that they are no fit exercyses for a Christen man to follow.[29]

In later years, attacking clerical power, Selden would become an active opponent of William Prynne in matters of church government. Less well known is his role in planning an elaborate royal masque, motivated at least in part by his opposition to Prynne's *Histrio-Mastix*.[30] In that work Prynne frequently couples 'Tertullian, *De Spectac.* . . . Cyprian, *De Spect.*', particularly regarding 'these Playes, wherein men act womens parts in womans apparrell, [which] must needs be sinfull, yea, abominable unto Christians'.[31] Playing on a false etymology of the word, he says that for male actors to wear women's clothes on the stage is 'obscene':

Witnesse *Tertullian De Spectaculis, lib. c.10. p. 17.* . . . In all scenicall arts (say they) there is plainely the patronage of Bacchus and Venus which are peculiarly proper to the Stage. From the gesture and flexure of the body, they sacrifice effeminacy to Venus and Bacchus; the one of them being effeminate by her sexe, the other by his flux, & c. Witnesse *Saint Cyprian De spectaculis lib.* where he writes thus. *To this vile shamefull deed, another equall wickednesse is super-added. A man enfeebled in all his joynts, resolved into a more than womanish effeminacy, whose art it is to speake with his hands and gestures, comes forth upon the Stage: and for this one, I know not whom, neither man nor woman, the whole Citie flocke together, that so the fabulous lusts of antiquity may be acted. Yea, men . . . are unmanned on the Stage: all the honour and vigour of their sex is effeminated with the shame, the dishonesty of an unsinued body. He who is most womanish and best resembles the female sex, gives best*

---

[28] Stephen Gosson, *Plays Confuted in Five Actions* (London: Thomas Gosson, 1582), sig. D7. See also sig. B4: 'That Stage Playes are the doctrine and invention of the Devill, may bee gathered by Tertullian, who noteth verie well that the Devill forseenge the ruine of his kingdome, both invented these shewes, and inspired men with devices to set them out the better thereby to enlarge his dominion and pull us from God.' The title-page motto of the book is from Cyprian.

[29] Phillip Stubbes, *The Anatomie of Abuses* (London: Richard Jones, 1583), sig. L7.

[30] See Bulstrode Whitelock, *Memorials of the English Affairs, 1625–1660* [1682] (Oxford: Oxford University Press, 1853), i. 53–63. Whitelock describes at length a 'splendid royal mask' sponsored in 1633 by the four inns of court. Sir Edward Herbert and Mr Selden, 'one of the grandees', represented the Inner Temple. Some of the sponsors believed that this 'expression of their love and duty to their majesties . . . was the more seasonable because [it] would manifest the difference of their opinion from Mr. Prynne's new learning, and serve to confute his *Histrio Mastix* against interludes' (p. 53).

[31] William Prynne, *Histrio-Mastix. The Players Scourge, or, Actors Tragedie* (London: Michael Sparke, 1633), 179.

*content. The more criminous, the more applauded is he; and by how much the more obscene he
is, the more skilfull is he* accounted. *What cannot he perswade who is such a one?* And in
another *Epistle* of his he writes to *Eucratius* to *Excommunicate a Player, who did traine up
Boyes for the Stage, for that he taught them against the expresse instruction of God himselfe,
how a male might be effeminated into a female, how their sex might be changed by Art, that so
the divell who defiles Gods workemanship, might be pleased by the offences of a depraved and
effeminated body. I thinke it will not stand with the Majestie of God, nor the discipline of the
Gospel, that the modestie and honour of the Church should be polluted with such a filthy and
infamous contagion. For since men are prohibited in the Law to put on a womans garment,
and such who doe it are adjudged accursed. How much more greater a sinne is it, not onely to
put on a womans apparell, but likewise to expresse obscene effeminate womanish gestures, by
the skill or tutorship of an unchaste Art?*[32]

SELDEN'S RESPONSA

Selden's letter to Jonson, an important signpost on the way to his great *De Diis
Syris*, is a very early example of his research in Jewish studies, which would
become the focus of his mature scholarship.[33] Unlike the half-dozen important
rabbinical works of his later years, *De Diis Syris* refers only sparingly to the
Talmud.[34] But it does cite, among others, the Septuagint, Philo, and Josephus;
Onkelos, the proselyte who translated the Bible into Aramaic (second century
CE); the principal medieval rabbinic exegetes whose commentaries were collected
in the Great Rabbinic Bible (Heb. *Miqra'ot Gedolot*, published by the house of
Bomberg in Venice, 1524–5), including Solomon ben Isaac or Rashi (whom
Selden calls 'Solomon Jarchi or the author of the common Hebrew Gloss' of the
Torah, both written and oral), Abraham Ibn Ezra, and David Kimhi; Moses of

---

[32] William Prynne, *Histrio-Mastix*, 168–9. For the yoking of Tertullian and Cyprian to
denounce the abomination of cross-dressing according to the terms of Deuteronomy, see also
pp. 162–3, 179, 187–8.

[33] G. J. Toomer directed me to other signposts, which indicate that the 1617 edition of *De Diis
Syris* was at least four years in the making. The most important of these is a huge note by Selden to
one of his own laudatory epigrams that preface the 1613 edition of *Purchas his Pilgrimage* and
contain material on the Syrian deities that reappears in *De Diis*. The letter to Jonson remains the
longest and most important of these signposts.

[34] Jonathan R. Ziskind asserts the lack of direct reference to the Talmud in *De Diis Syriis*, in *John
Selden on Jewish Marriage Law* (Leiden: E. J. Brill, 1991), 7. But G. J. Toomer, in a characteristically
generous letter, points out that the second edition does refer to the Talmud, as in a reference to
tractate *Avodah Zarah* 44a, p. 299, on the meaning of מפלצת (*miphletzet*), the 'abominable image'
belonging to Maacah that her son the reformer King Asa burned at the Wadi Kidron, for which she
was removed as Queen Mother (2 Chron. 15: 16): 'What is the meaning of *miphletzet*? R. Judah
said, [an object which] intensifies licentiousness, as R. Joseph taught: It was a kind of phallus with
which she had daily connection.' For Selden's rabbinic scholarship, see, in addition to Ziskind,
Richard Tuck's *Natural Rights Theories* (Cambridge: Cambridge University Press, 1979), 87–97, and
his *Philosophy and Government 1572–1651* (Cambridge: Cambridge University Press, 1993), 214–
20; J. P. Sommerville, 'John Selden, the Law of Nature, and the Origins of Government', *Historical
Journal*, 28 (1984), 437–47; and Jason P. Rosenblatt, *Torah and Law in 'Paradise Lost'* (Princeton:
Princeton University Press, 1994), 79–106.

Coucy, whose compilation of the Torah's 365 negative commandments or prohibitions and 248 positive commandments, *Sefer Mitzvot Hagodol*, was part of Selden's library ('Moses Mikotzi . . . in his *Praecept. Negat.*'); and Maimonides ['I mean Moses Ben Maimon, who is also called (from the sigles of his name after the *Jewish* fashion) *Rambam*, and . . . Moses Aegyptius'], who will remain Selden's favourite authority for the rest of his life. Even as early as *De Diis Syris*, Selden will sometimes document the appearance of a single excerpt in both the *Mishneh Torah* and the *Guide for the Perplexed*, the '*Moreh Hanebochim* (i.e. as the Latin title is, *Director Dubitantium* or *Perplexorum*)'.

Not only Maimonides but contemporary Continental Hebraists with whom Selden corresponded, such as Leone da Modena, were notable contributors to responsa literature, perhaps the definitive genre of the Jewish diaspora, with hundreds of thousands of examples preserved. Responsa (Heb., *sh'elot u'teshuvot*, lit., 'queries and replies') is a rabbinic term denoting an exchange of letters in which one party consults another on a matter of practical *halakha*, or legal interpretation, with scripture as the ultimate authority. In these 'responses', already mentioned in the Talmud (*Yevamot* 105a), rabbinic authorities wrestle with the problem of applying ancient religious law to the changed circumstances of various diaspora communities.

Selden's letter is, *mutatis mutandis*, responsa, a reply to his friend Ben Jonson's query regarding the application of an element of Deuteronomic law. As an antiquarian, Selden shares with the authors of responsa a reverence for tradition. But as a scholar, he insists on accuracy and becomes impatient, even waspish, when Christian or Jewish sources disappoint him. Christians—Augustine, Jerome, Aquinas, and Eusebius—play a minor role here, and Selden rounds on Jerome for plagiarizing a mistake in his translation of Ζεὺς Ἐννάλιος, Zeus the God of War: 'A greater error about this name, is in the *Loci Ebraici* of S. Hierome, as they are publisht: where the whole translation is of that taken out of Hestiaeus (but not so acknowledged by the Father), and *Gemalij Jovis* is ridiculously for *Enyalij Jovis*.'

Selden is equally impatient with Jewish sources, presumably including even Maimonides, for what he considers an implausible etymology. Maimonides' structuralist explanation of the laws pertaining to temple worship is an elaboration of Leviticus 20: 23: 'And ye shall not walk in the manners of the nation, which I cast out before you: for they committed all these things, and therefore I abhorred them.' The manner of temple worship will be through 'difference' (20: 25). The Jewish 'priests were commanded to wear breeches' because, among the 'Idolaters neighbouring to the Jewes . . . their *Comarim* or Priests breechless (as the Jewes, not without ridiculous error think) did sacrifice to Baal-Phegor'. The 'ridiculous error' is the belief that the worship of Baal-Peor consisted of defecating in his presence, since the verb form P'r means 'to open widely' or 'to uncover oneself'. Selden elaborates, without querulousness, in *De Diis Syris*: 'So Rashi explains it well that his worship consisted in their stretching out their bare buttocks before him and making him offerings of excrement. For Peor in Hebrew means to open or stretch out; hence the name Peor.'[35] He also cites a passage from Maimonides, correctly assigning it to both his *Mishneh Torah* and the *Director Dubitantium*:

You know what the service called Peor consisted of in these times, that the man should disrobe himself [*discooperiret*] before it. And therefore the priests were ordered to make breeches to cover themselves in the house of sacrifices; and, further, not to ascend the stair to the altar, in order not to expose themselves [*ne discooperirentur*].[36]

Selden rehearses the position expressed in the Rabbinic Bible that Deuteronomy 22: 5 prohibits unchastity:

Many expositors observe the intent of this precept to be for the publique preservation of honesty in both sexes, lest, in corrupt manners, by such promiscuous use of apparel the lustfull forwardnesse of nature might take the easier advantage of opportunity. So is it noted by R.R.R. Aben Ezra, Solomon Jarchi.

According to Rashi, a woman would wear a man's clothes 'so that she would resemble a man, in order to walk freely among men, and this would only be for the purpose of adultery', and wearing a woman's garment would allow a man to go and stay unnoticed among women. Rashi adds that the Torah forbids only the wearing of clothing that leads to abomination—that is, unchastity. For a Puritan such as Gosson, who can imagine a variety of unspeakable practices and unnatural acts, Rashi's view is both limited and naive:

Some there are that thinke this commaundement of God to be restrayned to them, that goe abroade in womens attyre and use it for jugglinge, to shaddowe adulterie. These interpreters like unto narrowe mouthed vessels, will receyve nothing without losse, except it bee slenderly powred in according to the straightnes of theire owne makinge.[37]

Maimonides distinguishes between the idolatrous priest and the true one by structurally opposing *discooperiret* and *ne discooperirentur*, just as Selden implicitly opposes *Comarim* (pagan priests) and *Cohanim* (Jewish priests). Selden's rabbinic hermeneutic deconstructs the conventional reading of Deuteronomy 22: 5 by noting that 'a woman's gown, or *stola muliebris*' is not balanced by *habitus virilis* but by *kly* (or *Celi*), vessels which he reads as *instrumenta bellica*. Both Ibn Ezra and Josephus recognize the possible martial context of *kly* but do

---

[35] Selden, *De Diis Syris* (London: Guilielmus Stansbeius, 1617), 66: 'Verum nominis caussam & Numinis cultum videtur sibi bene explicasse Salomon Iarchi ad Numer. xxv. com. 3. *Ec quod distendebant coram ore illius foramen Podicus, & stercus offerebant; & hic, ait ille erat cultus eius*. Aperire n. sive distendere פער interpretatur, unde *Peor*.'

[36] *De Diis*, 66–7: 'Moses Ben Maimon in *More Nebochim*, part III. cap. XLVI' 'ita is alibi in Misnah Thorah tract. עכום cap. III': '*Tu vero scis quod servitium idoli quod vocabatur Pahor (*Peor*) in temporibus illis erat, ut discooperiret se homo versus eum. Et idcirco praeceptum est sacerdotibus ut facerent Braccas quibus cooperirent operienda in hora sacrificy: & praetera non ascendebant per gradus ad altare, ne discooperirentur.*'

[37] Gosson, *Plays Confuted in Five Actions*, sig. E4.

not develop it. Ibn Ezra notes that a woman should stay at home to raise children and not go off to wars, which would put her in the way of promiscuity. And in the letter Selden quotes Josephus: 'Watch out particularly in battles lest a woman use masculine clothing, and lest a man use feminine dress.' Still in the epistolary style, addressing the reader, Selden elaborates in *De Diis Syris*: 'What do you think of Flavius Josephus, who construed that precept as having reference to military discipline? See his *Antiquities of the Jews*, book no. 4.'[38]

Selden chooses to develop Maimonides' bolder interpretation of *kly* (vessels) by associating the *instrumenta bellica* with the god of war himself. When men worship Venus in women's clothing and women worship Mars by wearing armour, they imitate the 'community of sexes in every of the ancientest Gods'. The letter argues, and *De Diis* provides exhaustive supporting documentation, that the ancient world believed in the common sex of the gods ('communis Divum sexus').[39] In *De Diis* Selden notes that the Septuagint translation of the Bible indifferently makes Baal both masculine and feminine and that the Hebrew language has both a feminine and masculine word for the moon.[40] He cites Macrobius to prove that among the Greeks and Romans, Venus was worshipped as both armed and bearded.[41] The examples of bisexuality in the letter (Aphroditos-Aphrodite, Lunus-Luna, Adargatis-Adirdag) are extended in *De Diis* to include, among many others, Ashtar-Ashtoreth and Urania-Uranus. According to Selden, neither the holy scriptures nor the ancient mysteries of nations distinguish the sex of these gods.[42]

De Diis develops the letter's suggestion that these deities are collapsible. Venus is Astarte, Mars is Baal, but the fierce marine deity Dagon can also be associated with Aphrodite, whose name *aphros* (foam) evokes for Selden the myth of her birth. Selden notes the aptness of that association in the fecundity and promiscuity of marine animals.[43] The imitation of deific fertility and sexual completeness explains the bisexual worship that Maimonides describes.

Perhaps the most resonant passage in the entire letter is Selden's explanation of ancient cross-dressing as a bisexual imitation of a bisexual god. The thought of Venus's effeminate priests drove William Prynne into a towering rage, but Selden's reasonable scholarly tone shades into imaginative sympathy:

[38] *De Diis*, 192: 'Quid qui ad disciplinam militarem, praeceptum maxime trahat Fl. Iosephus? vide eum lib. IV.'

[39] Ibid. 176.

[40] Ibid. 150–1.

[41] See both the letter and *De Diis*, 149–50: 'Diserte Macrobius de Cypriis; *putant eandem* (Venerem) *marem ac foeminam esse*. Mitto Venerem armatam, Barbatam, Romanis & Graecis cultam . . .'

[42] *De Diis*, 149: 'Neq; n. sexum Idolorum scriptura sacra, nec prisca mysteria gentium distinguunt.'

[43] Ibid. 194: 'Quam apta autem foecundo & promiscui generis Numini huic marina illa figura Dagonis fuerit, ostendunt & priscae fabulae quae spuma ortam Venerem cantant, & Philosophorum placita queis nullum terrestre aut volatile animal tam foecundam, quam unumquodque marinorum esse memoratur.'

Neither originally, by all likelyhood, was Venus and Mars, other than the masculin-feminin or generative power supposed in the Sunne, or Sunne and Moon, which were the first creatures idolatrously worshipt. For wee must here think of these as they were Gods only, not Planets. And why may we not collect rationally in their Theologie, that in regard of the masculin-foeminin power supposed in their worshipt deity, they counterfeited themselves to be masculin-foeminin in the adoration? Which could not be better done than by a womans wearing armour, and a mans putting on a womans garment.

This extraordinary passage evokes ancient sources, most notably Aristophanes' fable in Plato's *Symposium* (190b) of the first human beings created both male and female, 'a rounded whole'. Rashi on Genesis 1: 27 cites the midrash that attempts to reconcile the singular 'in the image of God created he him' and the plural 'male and female created he them' by positing an original creature like the one in the *Symposium*, later separated.

In *De Diis*, developing the implications of this passage, Selden insists on the similarities between pagan representations of the gods and the Bible's representation of God in order to suggest that 'this community of sexes in every of the ancientest Gods' applies to JHVH as well. Selden argues that originally the names Baal and Jove denoted the 'mighty and great governor of the universe', but then, in implicit parallel with the Fall and with the myth of the dissociated sensibility, the white light of the original unified deity broke up into countless refractive gods of every colour, a spectrum of idolatrous polytheism: 'and that which at one time was so simple and single became afterwards exceedingly multifarious'.[44] Selden regards the European pronunciation of the tetragrammaton יהוה (JHVH) as a corruption of the name Jove and reads Jupiter as Jehovah pater.[45] In his enthusiasm for a favourable reading not unlike Malvolio, who similarly crushes four letters to fit his name and who frequently invokes Jove where we should naturally expect God, Selden asks, 'Who does not see, by a little change in the letters and a Latin ending, we have JHVH the same as Jove?'[46]

For Selden, 'Hosea 2:16 will demonstrate how proper Baal is for the true God':[47] 'And it shall be at that day, saith the LORD, that thou shalt call me Ishi

[44] *De Diis*, 110: 'n. Belus primo summum rerum gubernatorem Opt. Max. denotabat, ita & Iouis...idem significabat; grassante vero hominum errore ad idola transferebatur; &, quod simplicissimum & unicum inprimis erat, tam multiplex postea devenit.'

[45] Ibid. 110: 'Iouis enim ex Tetragramati Europaeorum pronuntiatione corrupta fiebat. Nec Iupiter aliud sane est quam Iouispiter, i. Ἰαὼ πατηρ, seu...Jehovah pater.' See also p. 112: When Paul, referring to the true God, tells the Athenians, 'For we are his offspring' (Acts 27: 28), it is the same as if he had said, 'We are the offspring of Jupiter', '*Jovis genus* (id est Jehovae) *sumus*.'

[46] *De Diis*, (JHVH), 111–12: 'Quantilla autem mutatione elementorum, ex Ἰαὼ seu Ἰευὼ etiam ex ipso יהוה fiat Iouis in casu recto, addita nimirum Latina terminatione, quis non videt?' For Malvolio's apostrophes to Jove, and whether or not they are related to the statute of 27 May 1606, which imposed a fine for pronouncing God's name 'in Stageplayes', see the Introduction to the Arden Shakespeare *Twelfth Night*, ed. J. M. Lothian and T. W. Craik (London: Methuen, 1975), pp. xxiii–xxiv.

[47] *De Diis*, 104: 'Et quam convenire potuerit Baal nomen DEO VERO, caput secundum Hoseae satis monstrat.'

[my husband]; and shalt call me no more Baali [my Lord].' For most readers, God in this beautiful verse at once signals an access of tenderness in his relationship with his people, substituting husband for master, and reminds perfidious Israel of its idolatrous past. According to Selden's historical reading, however, 'the people of God, with all necessary piety, called him their Baal until God himself forbade it, after the name had been used too often to designate other gods.'[48] In the letter, Selden identifies sixteen places where Baal 'is in the Greek sometimes of one, then of another gender, as if they would denote the masculin-feminin quality attributed in the worship'.

Selden's comparatist historico-philological method aims for an aesthetic of utmost inclusiveness. His lists, in both the letter to Jonson and *De Diis*, of gods who remain the same whatever they are called at different times and places, read at times like precursors and parodies of Jungian archetypes. Selden argues that the similarity of their names and offices proves that Ilethyia, Eleatho, and Lilith are the same. After quoting an inscription to Caelesti on an ancient Roman monument, he asks, 'who is Coelestis if not Urania, and who is Urania if not the queen of heaven, or Baaleth-shamaim, Luna, or Astarte?'[49] Anticipating not only trans-genderism but trans-speciesism, Selden identifies the gods Adargatis, Derce, Dagon, Atergatis, Derceto, and Oannes, among others, as both masculine and feminine and 'all one name', a variation of אדיר דג, *'Adirdag*, i.e. *piscis sublimis* or *potens*. Selden justifies the Septuagint translation of 1 Samuel 5: 4, which gives Dagon feet, by analogy with the cognate ancient myth of Oannes, at once god, human, and fish, whose feet grew from his tail. Like Captain Otter in Jonson's *Epicoene* (1.4.24), Oannes is 'an *animal amphibium*':

Ὠάννης is mentioned as a two-headed animal with human-like feet growing from his tail and the rest of him a fish. His voice was human. Emerging from the Red Sea, he came to Babylon, but he returned into the sea at sunset. He did this every day, as if he were an amphibious mammal. From him human beings learned all the various arts, letters, agriculture, the consecration of temples, architecture, political government, and whatever could possibly pertain to civilized life.[50]

This benign, numinous amphibian, connected not only to Baal and Dagon but to Venus as *Mater Deum*, might aptly personate the inclusivist ethos of Selden's letter.

---

[48] Ibid.
[49] Ibid. 159: 'Quid autem Coelestis preter Uraniam? Quid Urania, nisi coeli regina, i. Baaleth shamaim, Luna, Astarte?'
[50] See, besides the letter, *De Diis*, 174, where Selden cites Berosus, Apollodorus, and Polyhistor: 'Ὠάννης n. memoratur, biceps animal, coetera Piscis, e cuius cauda adnascebantur pedes humanis similes. Vox ei humana item; ex mari autem Erythraeo emersum Babyloniam pervenisse aiunt, occidente vero Sole in mare redijsse, moremque hunc quotidie velut αμφιβιον repetijsse; ab eo homines omnifarias artes, literas, agriculturam, aedium sacrationes, architecturam, & leges politicas didicisse, necnon quicquid ad vitam civilem pertineret possit.'

Selden's letter allows us to see examples of Renaissance poetry in another way. In Shakespeare's *Antony and Cleopatra*, 'what Venus did with Mars' is the most erotic fantasy that a eunuch can entertain (1.5.17–18). Cleopatra's own 'fierce affections' remind her of a cross-dressing experience, in which she plays Omphale to Antony's Hercules but also perhaps Venus to his Mars:

> That time– O times!–
> I laughed him out of patience, and that night
> I laughed him into patience, and next morn,
> Ere the ninth hour, I drunk him to his bed,
> Then put my tires and mantles on him, whilst
> I wore his sword Philippan.   (2.5.18–23)

Her 'tires and mantles' are kin to the σκεύη, the 'trappings' or military accoutrements of the Septuagint on Deuteronomy 22: 5, as she plays the armed Venus ('*Venerem armatam*') of Macrobius.

Undoubtedly the most magnificent adaptation of Selden's research into the gender of the pagan gods is John Milton's in Book I of *Paradise Lost*. Selden was Milton's principal source of Hebrew learning, and the catalogue of pagan deities (i. 376–521) derives mainly from *De Diis Syris*. Like Prynne, the Puritan Milton had associated theatres with bordellos. Writing almost within a year of the closing of the theatres by Parliament, he had cruelly derided amateur productions in which young divines presented themselves 'so oft upon the Stage writhing and unboning their Clergie limmes to all the antick and dishonest gestures of Trinculo's, Buffons, and Bawds; prostituting the shame of that ministery which either they had, or were nigh having, to the eyes of Courtiers and Court-Ladies, with their Groomes and *Madamoisellaes*' (*YP*, i. 887).

Milton's voice in the catalogue is even shriller in its fierce denunciation of the pagan gods who incarnated the fallen angels, demon idols who audaciously got themselves worshipped in God's holy city, 'yea, often plac'd | Within his Sanctuary itself thir Shrines, | Abominations; and with cursed things | His holy Rites, and solemn Feasts profan'd, | And with thir darkness durst affront his light' (i. 387–91).[51]

The most extraordinary passage in the catalogue is an interruption that briefly substitutes sympathy and longing for wrath. Remembering Selden on Baal and Ashtoreth, Venus and Mars, 'love or enmity', an incomplete human being contemplates the perfect sexual fluidity of the gods:

> With these came they, who from the bord'ring flood
> Of old *Euphrates* to the Brook that parts
> *Egypt* from *Syrian* ground, had general Names
> Of *Baalim* and *Ashtaroth*, those male,

---

[51] *John Milton: Complete Poems and Major Prose*, ed. Merritt Y. Hughes (New York: Odyssey Press, 1957), 221. Unless otherwise noted, parenthetic references to Milton's poetry are to this edition.

These Feminine. For Spirits, when they please
Can either Sex assume, or both; so soft
And uncompounded is thir Essence pure,
Not ti'd or manacl'd with joint or limb,
Nor founded on the brittle strength of bones,
Like cumbrous flesh; but in what shape they choose
Dilated or condens't, bright or obscure,
Can execute thir aery purposes,
And works of love or enmity fulfil.   (i. 419–31)

Besides evoking the ancient past and English Renaissance poetry, Selden's letter, addressing bisexuality and the fantasy of sexual wholeness, the fluidity of both gender and identity, and of course transvestism in the theatre, should be of interest to contemporary critics and scholars, particularly as it bears on questions of the plurality, fluidity, and cultural constructedness of gender. And because the present both illuminates and reshapes the past, contemporary contributions to gender and cultural studies and theatre history can throw into relief the most revolutionary elements of Selden's letter. Bisexual priests and priestesses incorporate both sexes in their worship of a deity known to the Egyptians as Lunus and Luna, the Mother of the World, who contains within herself the nature of each sex ('*Matrem Mundi . . . utriusque sexus naturam in se continentem*').[52] Stephen Orgel discusses Shakespeare's 'master-mistress of my passion' in Sonnet 20 and Viola/Cesario in *Twelfth Night* as 'double-gendered' figures, conceived in terms of 'equivalents of either-and-both', implying 'a world of possibilities'.[53] The polymorphousness of Selden's gods and of their worshippers is not unrelated to the polysemousness of the text, and Selden's historical approach demystifies, destabilizes, and deconstructs ancient religious texts. Laura Levine, among others, documents the hysteria of anti-theatrical Renaissance fantasies of 'monstrous androgyny, boys in delicate dresses worshipping Venuses with beards'.[54] The disordered visions of breakdown among the enemies of the theatre make Selden's letter on cross-dressing a rare and important example of calm tolerance. Contributors to gender studies have made it possible to divine the bold originality and contemporary relevance of an argument that lay hidden for centuries within a thicket of learned citations.

[52] *De Diis*, 150.
[53] Stephen Orgel, *Impersonations: The Performance of Gender in Shakespeare's England* (Cambridge: Cambridge University Press, 1996), 56.
[54] Levine, *Men in Women's Clothing*, 24.

3

Selden and Milton on Gods and Angels

Zephon and Satan

Matters of naming and identity lie at the heart of the brief but important episode in Book IV of *Paradise Lost* when the angel Zephon confronts Satan. Just as the demonic consult in Book II precedes its original, the heavenly council of Book III, so a hypocritical imitation of Zephon precedes the appearance of the legitimate one. In his 'youthful beauty' and 'grace' (iv. 845), the cherub Zephon stands as a reminder of the first time that Satan changed his identity, assuming the shape of just such an angel as he in order to mislead Uriel: 'a stripling Cherub', 'such as in his face | Youth smil'd celestial, and to every limb | Suitable grace diffus'd, so well he feign'd' (iii. 636, 637–9).

At that time, as William Empson brilliantly observes, Satan as cherub was forced to endure 'the touch of patronage which can be felt' in Uriel's remarks on the privilege of observing creation, a tone that 'cannot be distinguished from treating him as literally a young one'.[1] Zephon administers a very different sort of wound to the Satan who has returned to himself. There is in the bold moral judgement a whiff of the recently promoted young executive telling his ageing former boss that more than the locks have been changed:

> Think not, revolted Spirit, thy shape the same,
> Or undiminisht brightness, to be known
> As when thou stood'st in Heaven upright and pure;
> *That Glory then*, when thou no more wast good,
> *Departed from thee*, and thou resembl'st now
> Thy sin and place of doom obscure and foul.   (iv. 835–40; my emphasis)

An unexpected answer to Satan's magnificent question, 'Know ye not mee?' (l. 828), Zephon's rebuke undermines his antagonist's self-identification and also constitutes a bold act of naming. The biblical source of 'That Glory... Departed' is the naming of Ichabod, literally, *the Inglorious* (אי כבוד), in

---

[1] William Empson, *Milton's God* (1961; Cambridge: Cambridge University Press, 1981), p. 61. Empson also hears 'withering social contempt' in Satan's treatment of Zephon (p. 60) but ignores the cherub's decisive rejoinder.

1 Samuel 4. When her child was born and she was told that it was a son, the mother said nothing and refused to look at it: 'And she named the child Ichabod, saying, The glory is departed from Israel' (4: 21). The child has no history, for nothing more is known of him, and his name marks death and loss: the deaths of his mother in childbirth, his grandfather Eli, and his father, Eli's unworthy son Phinehas. The word translated as 'departed' actually means much more. It is an ominous word expressing 'is gone into exile'. Worse for the mother than any of these deaths and the reason for the name is the national catastrophe of the capture by the Philistines of the ark of the covenant in Shiloh: 'And she said, The glory is departed from Israel: for the ark of God is taken' (4: 22). The verses in Samuel that follow immediately tell a story that figures directly in the catalogue of pagan deities in Book I of the great epic (ll. 457–66) and, more indirectly but no less importantly, in *Samson Agonistes*: the conflict between two cult objects placed by the Philistines side by side, the ark of the covenant and the idol of Dagon, resulting in the triumph of monotheism over paganism through the mutilation of the idol.

In the thirty-five years following the publication of *Paradise Lost*, Ichabod gives its name to treatises that cross ideological boundaries and lament a lost better past. An anonymous treatise attributed to Thomas Ken, Bishop of Bath and Wells, is entitled ICHABOD: OR, *Five Groans of the Church: Prudently Foreseeing and Passionately Bewailing Her Second Fall; Threatned by these five dangerous though undiscerned Miscariages that caused her First: Viz. 1. Undue Ordination, 2. Loose Profaneness, 3. Unconscionable Symony, 4. Careless Non-Residence, 5. Encroaching Pluralities* (Cambridge, 1663). In his jeremiad *Ichabod, or a discourse shewing what cause there is to fear that the glory of the Lord is departing from New-England* (Boston, 1702), Increase Mather argues that if the Glory of God is gone out of the church, then God is gone out as well. According to an early history of English dissenters, 'The departure of the Gospel annihilated many [dissenting] congregations and left the high churchman to insult over their ruined walls, or write upon their closed doors, "a meeting house to let"; while the orthodox dissenter would inscribe, "Ichabod, the glory is departed." '[2]

---

[2] David Bogue and James Bennett, *History of Dissenters* (London, 1812), iv. 383. The authors add that 'the Scriptural name Ichabod was used, presumably with a knowledge of its derivation, with the sense of alas! regretting the good old times' (ibid.). The question of an angel's age is a vexed one, but Milton seems closer in age to Satan than to Zephon. If the name Ichabod is a shorthand lament for a better past, one can't help wondering about the possibility of the author's unacknowledged sympathy with age rather than youth. Satan's young replacements may be inferior to the rebel angels in their prime. Increase Mather's ICHABOD examines in detail the *'Declension* in the Churches of *New-England'* and asks, 'When will *Boston* see a COTTON & a NORTON, again? When will *New-England* see a HOOKER, a SHEPARD, a MITCHELL, not to mention others?' (p. 69). Even the anonymous ICHABOD (1663), spoken in the voice of the Church, laments at great length the increase of young ministers ordained too soon and the loss of older ones, 'Men *blameless, sober, just, holy, temperate; whose judgments were settled, whose passions were allayed*. . . . My young Ministers have been unstable in all their ways, unsetled in their minds, rash in their undertakings, imprudent in their carriage, weake in their discourses, unexperienced in their behaviour, not even, orderly and sta[id] in their conversation.' (p. 28).

How terrible a loss of original identity to be renamed *the Inglorious*, especially for one who aspired to equal the most high and 'to set himself in Glory above his Peers' (i. 39), and who, even when diminished, appeared no less than 'Arch-Angel ruin'd, and the excess of Glory obscur'd' (i. 593–4). Satan's reaction indicates a complete understanding of his loss:

> abasht the Devil stood,
> And felt how awful goodness is, and saw
> Virtue in her shape how lovely, saw, and pin'd
> His loss; but chiefly to find here observ'd
> His lustre visibly impair'd; yet seem'd
> Undaunted.   (iv. 846–51)

Before returning to himself and concentrating on his appearance, Satan's abashed response to Zephon's moral beauty consists of feeling, seeing, and pining. The theme of identity marks other moments in the poem that this encounter evokes, such as the parody of *kenosis* that occurs when Satan contemplates Eve's 'Heav'nly form | Angelic' (ix. 457–8): 'That space the Evil one abstracted stood | From his own evil, and for the time remain'd | Stupidly good, of enmity disarm'd, | Of guile, of hate, of envy, of revenge' (ix. 463–6). It is so important to register Satan's awareness of his loss in his reaction to Zephon's virtue that Milton picks up one last time a risky device relinquished after Book II, alleging a state of mind different from what a character's own words demonstrate, as when he describes Satan as 'Vaunting aloud, but rackt with deep despair' (i. 126). The narrator counters Satan's undaunted appearance and neutralizes his brave reply ('If I must contend... | Best with the best, the Sender not the sent'; iv. 851–2) by telling us what he is really feeling.

ZEPHON AND BAAL-ZEPHON

Milton's calling his young angel Zephon may be the boldest act of naming in the entire epic. The name is at once original and derivative, and it has been hidden in plain sight for more than three hundred years from those of Milton's editors conscientious enough to have been perplexed by it. Patrick Hume, who edited the sixth edition of *Paradise Lost* for Jacob Tonson in 1695, and who is said 'to have been the first to attempt exhaustive annotation on the works of an English poet' (*DNB*), believes that the primary meaning of the name is secrecy itself, as befits a spy in paradise: 'Zephon צפן Heb. a Secret, of צפן, to hide, whence *Joseph* had his *Egyptian* Name צפנת as a Discoverer of Dreams and secret matters, *Gen.* 41.45.'[3] Alastair Fowler dutifully refers to Numbers 26:15,

---

[3] *Notes on Milton's Paradise Lost*, part of *The Poetical Works of John Milton* (1695), p. 163. The notes were published anonymously. On the title-page of the Folger Library's copy, in an old handwriting signed H.C., is the comment, 'This Author (Hume, I suppose) should not go

where Zephon appears for the only time in the Bible, but disappointingly without addition, as a merely human name in one of its interminable genealogies: 'Of Zephon, the familie of the Zephonites'. The name Zephon also appears in a work recognized by editors as a major Miltonic source since the time of Hume, who cites it more extensively than he does any work outside of the Bible and ancient Greek and Roman literature, but not with reference to this particular angel. As we have already noted, the literary influence of Selden's *De Diis Syris* (1617), a philological inquiry into the names of the pagan gods of the Hebrew Bible as well as a pioneering study of cultural anthropology and comparative religion, extends to the work of Ben Jonson and to the list of pagan gods in Milton's *Ode on the Morning of Christ's Nativity* and Book I of *Paradise Lost*. It is likely that when Milton wrote the *Nativity Ode* in December of 1629, he drew on the augmented second edition published earlier that year.

Milton finds what he needs for the character of Zephon in the brief but complete chapter in *De Diis* that Selden devotes to Baal-Zephon, or Baal-Tzephon, named in Exodus 14: 2 as a station of the Israelites at the time of their departure from Egypt. God asks the Israelites to encamp by the sea, 'over against Baal Zephon', in order to tempt Pharaoh to pursue them: 'For Pharaoh will say of the children of Israel, they are entangled in the land, the wilderness hath shut them in' (14: 3). Selden begins by citing this verse in 'Ebraica veritas' to prove that Pharaoh wants the newly escaped Israelites to be ensnared (*irretiti*) and confused (*perplexi*). He then presents the rabbinic view of Rashi and Abraham Ibn Ezra, among others, that Baal-Zephon was an idol constructed to receive and concentrate astrological influence for the purpose of fulfilling Pharaoh's desire:

The wise men of the Hebrews say that Baal-zephon was made from formulas by the magicians of Pharaoh according to the positions of the heavenly bodies and placed near the Arabian Gulf for observing and retaining, and therefore for perplexing, the Israelites, and was given by a deity having the magical power of diverting them from their destined journey. Therefore that paraphrase of the Bible attributed to Jonathan calls it Taoth-Zephon, that is, the idol of Zephon, and the Jerusalem Targum does the same.[4]

---

unpraised.' The first part of the note is correct. The best-known example is the act of hiding the *afikomen* at the Passover Seder, which is called צפון. But the Egyptian name given by Pharaoh to Joseph, Zaphnath-paaneah, means *the god speaks and he lives*. See Gesenius's *Hebrew and English Lexicon of the Old Testament*, rev. Francis Brown, S. R. Driver, and Charles A. Briggs (Oxford: Clarendon Press, 1962), 861.

4 John Selden, *De Diis Syris* (1617), 43–4: 'Hic scribunt dicam, an somniant, Ebraeorum magistri *Baaltzephon* idolum . . . fuisse a Pharaonis Magis ad Coelestium corporum posituras fabricatum, & juxta sinum Arabicum collocatum, observandi & retinendi utique Israelitas, irretiendi, & à destinatà divinitúsque data profectione avertendi vim habens magicam. Ideò paraphrasis illa, Jonathani tributa, טעות צפון . . . id est, Idolum Tzephon vocat, atque ita Targum Hierosolymitanum.' Whenever possible, I have relied on the partial translation of *De Diis* in William Hauser's *The Fabulous Gods Denounced in the Bible* (Philadelphia: Lippincott, 1880). Jonathan ben Uzziel (1st c.) translated the Prophets but not the Pentateuch into Aramaic. Beginning in the 14th c., the Jerusalem Targum's translation of the Pentateuch was erroneously attributed to Jonathan's Targum, owing in part to their identical initials. Selden's phrasing implies some awareness of the situation.

As proof that Baal-Zephon was intended to be a sentinel looking out for the Israelites, Selden notes that the word *Zephon* derives from צפה, 'quod est *observare* seu *speculari*'.[5] He also cites the Arabic translation of Exodus 14: 2, which he reads as 'the image or likeness of Tzephon'.[6] That the likeness was human is suggested by Selden's particular reliance on the commentary of Abraham Ibn Ezra (1089–1164): 'Rabbi Abraham Ibn Ezra, a great Jewish theologian and astrologer, remarks that they [i.e. idols] were made after the human form so as to make them capable of celestial influences.'[7]

In Book IV of *Paradise Lost*, Milton daringly invents the angel Zephon as a sacred original who predates his idolatrous opposite, the Baal-Zephon of Exodus, or the northern Baal, as Selden adds ingeniously, exploiting the similarity between Baal-Zephon and Baal-Zaphon (Baal of the North). Milton's angel, of course, like his companion Ithuriel ('discovery of God'), is the sentinel charged by Gabriel to 'Search through this Garden, leave unsearcht no nook' (iv. 789). More than a spy, he must 'find, seize fast, and hither bring' (l. 796) the infernal spirit who has encamped in paradise. If there is a Baal-Zephon in the epic, 'the image or likeness of Zephon' as the Arabic translation has it, it is that stripling cherub adopted by shape-shifting Satan as his first disguise, on the first stage of his mission to spy on our first parents and to perplex and trap them. Harold Bloom and his ephebi have found examples in Milton's poetry of transumption, by means of which his classical precursors and his poetic father Spenser are discovered to be secondary imitations of his own creation.[8] Although it lacks the *frisson* of deliberate transgression, Milton's treatment of the Bible's Baal-Zephon as a profane copy, his own Zephon as the true original, already present in paradise, qualifies as a transumptive act, 'making his own belatedness into an earliness, and his tradition's priority over him into a lateness'.[9]

At the same time, Milton's Zephon is extremely derivative, since the etymologies traced by Selden in *De Diis* form his character. He is the true sentinel and snare, and Baal-Zephon is merely his idol, a simulacrum. If the idol, in human form, retains and concentrates celestial influence, the angel contains divinity. Contemplating the cherub, Satan sees 'how awful goodness is' (l. 847), 'Virtue in her shape how lovely' (l. 848):

> To strive or fly
> He held it vain; awe from above had quell'd
> His heart, not else dismay'd. (ll. 859–61)

---

[5] *De Diis*, 45.

[6] Ibid. 44: 'imago sive simulachrum Tzephon'.

[7] Ibid. 17: 'humana forma factas, ita ut coelestis influentiae essent capaces, adnotat Abraham Aben-Ezra Theologus & Astrologus Iudaeorum maximus.'

[8] See Harold Bloom, *A Map of Misreading* (New York: Oxford University Press, 1975), 128–9; David Quint, *Epic and Empire: Politics and Generic Form from Virgil to Milton* (Princeton: Princeton University Press, 1993), 42;

[9] Bloom, *Map of Misreading*, 131.

The sublime vision of the angel fills Satan with reverence, dread, and wonder, and he meekly allows two angels to arrest him and bring him to Gabriel, though in that extended encounter, which begins only twenty lines later, he regains his nerve and threatens violence that might have wrecked not only paradise 'but the Starry Cope | Of Heav'n perhaps, or all the Elements | At least' (ll. 992–4), as the epic narrator concedes. Only the infallible celestial sign of Libra, portrayed as God's 'golden Scales' (l. 997), convinces Satan to flee rather than fight.

If the name of the Hebraic angel Zephon has been hidden in plain sight, it can serve as a synecdoche of biblical Hebraic and extra-biblical rabbinic scholarship in Milton studies. To glance at Patrick Hume's early commentary on the great epic, filled with Hebrew etymologies, beginning with 'Paradise פרדס,' is to remember that the seventeenth century and not the twentieth was England's golden age of Christian Hebraism. Milton's great source for the pagan gods of the Hebrew Bible, Selden's *De Diis Syris*, meets all the criteria for Hebraism as a venerable tradition of study, summarized by Alexander Altmann: an extensive knowledge of rabbinica 'not merely as an adjunct to biblical exegesis but for its own sake', a 'tradition of respect for, and even veneration of, Maimonides', and 'the Renaissance concept of the essential unity underlying all human thought and justifying the hope in a common religion of the future'.[10] Among the scholars who greatly influenced Selden, and who similarly participated in the tradition of venerating Maimonides, are the incomparable Joseph Scaliger and Isaac Casaubon, the foremost philologist of Selden's lifetime.[11] As Altmann has noted well, in the cases of both Scaliger and Casaubon 'admiration for Maimonides and his peers goes hand in hand with ill-concealed disdain for the generality of rabbis. No praise is too high for Maimonides, but it is not infrequently coupled with some derogatory remark about the 'pettiness' (*nugae*) of the rank and file of the rabbis.'[12]

Selden and Samuel Purchas clearly have Scaliger in mind as the source of this formula, tinged with tokenism, which elevates Maimonides, whose religious rationalism makes him somehow less typically Jewish, by degrading the other rabbis, who concern themselves with either the pettiness of legal detail or the nonsense of midrashic narrative. The 1617 edition of *Purchas His Pilgrimage* lists

---

[10] Alexander Altmann, 'William Wollaston (1659–1724), English Deist and Rabbinic Scholar', *Transactions of the Jewish Historical Society of England*, 16 (1945–51), 185–211. See also Aaron L. Katchen, *Christian Hebraists and Dutch Rabbis* (Cambridge, Mass: Harvard University Press, 1984), p. x.

[11] *Joseph Scaligeri Epistolae*, Lugduni Batavorum (Leyden), Letter 62, pp. 193–7: '*Moreh Ha-Nebukin* non potest satis laudare. Ego non tantum illum librum sed etiam omnia illius Magistri opera tanti facio, ut solum illum inter Iudaeos desiisse nugari dicam.' *Isaaci Casauboni Epistolae insertis ad easdem responsibus*, Rotterdam, 1709, Letter 433 (1605), p. 231: 'Incomparabilis Rabbenu Mosis Maimonis filii *Moreh Nebukim*'. See also Letter 439 (1605) p. 234. The eulogies offered by Scaliger and Casaubon, along with those of Cunaeus, Sontagius, Drusius, Schickard, Glassius, Frischmuth, Leibniz, and others are cited in Altmann's 'William Wollaston', 205–6.

[12] Altmann, 'William Wollaston', 206.

Selden as one of the contributors of 'Manuscripts...not yet published', almost certainly the material for *De Diis*, published the same year. Purchas refers to Maimonides as 'our Rabbine (highly admired by a most admired Author)', whom he identifies in the margin: *'Jos. Scal. in Epist. ad Casaubon Omnia illius Magistri opera tanti facio, ut solum illum inter Iudaeos desiisse nugari dicam.'*[13] This helps to explain the tone of a passage in Selden's letter to Jonson, discussed in Chapter 2, consisting mainly of notes from his work in progress, *De Diis*. He introduces Jonson to 'a Rabbin of greatest worth by the estimation both of Jewes and Christians. . . . I mean Moses Ben Maimon, who is also called (from the sigles of his name after the *Jewish* fashion) *Rambam* [Rabbi Moses ben Maimon], and because his education and studies were chiefly in Egypt, he is known by the name of Moses Aegyptius, being by birth of Corduba.' Selden continues: 'Ben-Maimon liv'd about CD years since: his autority is not of the common rank; for the Jewes proverbially say of him, that *From Moses to Moses there was never any such as this Moses*, and some of great place in the state of learning speak of him, that he was *Judaeorum* (rather *Rabbinorum*) *primus qui delirare desiit* [the first rabbi to desist from nonsense].' Selden echoes his master Scaliger's quote, even as he deftly emends it parenthetically.

As noted in the preceding chapter, the astounding range of rabbinic literature on which Selden draws, even in his less mature scholarship, and his sympathy with the self-understanding of rabbinic exegesis, unequalled in seventeenth-century England, are signs of a large-mindedness at odds with the cult of Maimonides as manifested by invidious comparison.

Selden's *De Diis* is primarily a work of philology, in which classical Greek and Latin authors appear side by side with patristic and rabbinic authorities, a sign of the author's belief in the similarity underlying diverse cultures and a reminder that philology is not a value-free discipline. Embedded within *De Diis*, and impossible for Milton to ignore, are both Selden's hermeneutic of inclusion and a Maimonidean hermeneutic of exclusion. Although Milton's zeal and intransigence of judgement have their own terrible beauty, one might wish that the poet had drawn less often on Maimonides' antagonistic depiction of a pagan counter-religion and more often on Selden's calm and tolerant historicist approach to the potentially incendiary topic of idolatry. But even in its fiercest denunciations, Milton's poetry justifies the judgement of Edward Gibbon: 'For the enumeration of the Syrian and Arabian deities, it may be observed, that Milton has comprised in one hundred and thirty beautiful lines, the two large and learned syntagmas, which Selden had composed on that abstruse subject.'[14] This is a supreme example of Milton's successfully transmuting the lump.

---

[13] Samuel Purchas, *Purchas His Pilgrimage, or Relations of the World and the Religions Observed in All Ages and Places Discovered, from the Creation unto this Present* (London, 1617), 60.

[14] Edward Gibbon, *The History of the Decline and Fall of the Roman Empire*, ed. David Womersley, 3 vols. (London: Penguin, 1994), i. 449 n. 9. One can quibble about the tone if not about the judgement. Anthony Grafton has commented on the gravity of this 'comic parallel' in *The*

Taken seriously, Gibbon's use of 'comprised' (the whole comprises its parts) suggests that nothing of Selden's has been omitted from Milton's catalogue of pagan deities. In a letter to Alexander Gil, Jr., dated 2 July 1628, seventeen months before he writes the *Nativity Ode*, with its own Selden-inspired list of pagan gods, Milton deplores the ignorance of his fellow students at Cambridge, most of them prospective ministers in the church that at the time he expected to serve: 'Truly, amongst us here, as far as I know, there are hardly one or two that do not fly off unfeathered to Theology while all but rude and uninitiated in either Philology or Philosophy.' This makes him dread the possibility 'that by degrees there may break in among our clergy the priestly ignorance of a former age'. In *De Diis Syris*, Selden's philology has implications for theology and philosophy that Milton would have recognized. Many he disregarded, for reasons that will become clear, but one he adopted with spectacular results.

BAAL

As noted in Chapter 2, Selden argues that originally the names Baal and Jove denoted God, the 'mighty and great governor of the universe'. There is an ethical component to the question of whether a primeval monotheistic theology preceded idolatry, or whether monotheistic belief was the culmination of religious development that required long preparation. If monotheism precedes idolatry, then people who choose idolatry are culpable, whereas if monotheism requires long prior tradition, then primitive idolaters should not be faulted for their beliefs.[15]

Both Selden and Milton believe in an original monotheism. Selden's conception of the decline into idolatry is shaped by Maimonides, who will become his favourite authority in the half-dozen immense rabbinical works that constitute

---

Footnote: A Curious History (Cambridge, Mass.: Harvard University Press, 1997), 3. He is right, of course, but in context the remark may be less disparaging than it appears to be. Gibbon owned the 1618 edition of Selden's *The Historie of Tithes* as well as his *Opera Omnia*, ed. David Wilkins, 3 vols. in 6 (1726), and he makes use of Selden's scholarship numerous times, referring to him as 'our learned Selden' (iii. 397 n. 49) or 'the learned Selden' (iii. 86 n. 1). Gibbon's tone elsewhere in the *History*, like Grafton's in his book's subtitle, may depend on the valence given to 'curious': 'On the curious subjects of knight-hood, knights-service, nobility, arms, cry of war, banners, and tournaments, an ample fund of information may be sought in Selden' (iii. 580 n. 58). Implicitly contrasting the conspicuously erudite and prolix Latin scholarship with the more pleasing conciseness of *Table Talk*, Gibbon praises the latter: 'The learned Selden has given the history of transubstantiation in a comprehensive and pithy sentence: "This opinion is only rhetoric turned into logic." (His Works, vol. iii. p. 2073 in his Table-talk)' (iii. 86, n. 1).

[15] See Moshe Halbertal and Avishai Margalit, *Idolatry*, tr. Naomi Goldblum (Cambridge, Mass., and London: Harvard University Press, 1992), 121. In their humane and profound inquiry into the topic, they pose this and numerous other questions. They also discuss developmental theories of the 19th c., in which religious thought progressed from fetishism through animism (animals as divine objects), through hierotheism to monotheism (p. 121).

his most mature scholarship. Even as early as *De Diis Syris*, Selden sometimes documents the appearance of a single excerpt in both the *Mishneh Torah* and the *Guide for the Perplexed*. In both those works Maimonides asserts his belief in original monotheism and understands idolatry as an error of substitution.[16] In particular, the opening chapter of the *Laws of Idolatry* in his *Code of Jewish Law* describes the gradual process by which idolaters transferred their worship from God himself to representations of representations. Maimonides had no doubt that virtually all human communities believe in the existence of a supreme God.[17] Initially, worshippers thought that venerating the heavenly bodies attendant upon God increased the worship of God himself, just as honouring the king's servants is a way of honouring the king himself. The claim that God had commanded not only that the heavenly bodies themselves but also that the images of the bodies be worshipped widened the gap between God and the proper worship of him. As Moshe Halbertal and Avishai Margalit summarize Maimonides' argument, 'the masses forgot that the idols in the temples were representations of the stars and not independent forces.'[18]

Dionysius Vossius's *De Idololatria*, his brilliant Latin translation and commentary on Maimonides' *Laws of Idolatry*, was published together with the great work of comparative mythology of his father Gerardus Vossius, *De Theologia Gentili* (1641). As Jan Assmann has noted, Maimonides' commentary on the Mishnah tractate *Avodah Zarah* in book I of his *Mishneh Torah*, frequently translated into Latin, 'formed one of the basic texts of Christian apologetic literature of the seventeenth century'.[19] Turning to Baal as a point of entry into some of the key themes of *De Diis*, we can see the influence on Selden of Maimonides' conception of idolatry as 'the cultic worship accorded to the intermediaries between God and man'.[20] Selden points out that the Chaldeans boasted of worshipping the one creator for fifteen thousand years under the name Baal (Lord) or Bel or Belus:

Then, as happens when morals are corrupted and are prone to superstition, they worshipped in this name at first the sun, which the Phoenicians believed the only god in the heavens. Finally, however, the name Baal or Bel was impiously transferred even to other images, whether of stars or of kings whose memory was very dear to posterity, in order to increase, in the way that was possible, the honor either of the heavenly body or of

---

[16] See Moses Maimonides, *The Guide of the Perplexed*, tr. Shlomo Pines, introd. Leo Strauss (Chicago: University of Chicago Press, 1963), p. cxxiv; Maimonides, *De Idololatria*, tr. Dionysius Vossius, in Gerardus Vossius, *De Theologia Gentili*, 3 vols. (Amsterdam, 1641; repr.. New York and London: Garland, 1976), i. 1–175.

[17] Maimonides, *Guide of the Perplexed*, p. cxxiv.

[18] Halbertal and Margalit, *Idolatry*, 43. Maimonides, *De Idololatria*, i. 1–10.

[19] Jan Assmann, *Moses the Egyptian: The Memory of Egypt in Western Monotheism* (Cambridge, Mass., and London: Harvard University Press, 1997), 231 n. 21. On the Latin *Mishneh Torah* by the prodigiously learned Dionysius Vossius, cut down by smallpox at the age of 21, see Katchen, *Christian Hebraists and Dutch Rabbis*, 161–235.

[20] Maimonides, *Guide of the Perplexed*, p. cxxiv.

the dead man. Also various rites, ceremonies, and stated times for sacrifices were added. And so the Assyrians, the Phoenicians, and others made their ceremonies to adore Bel or Baalim.[21]

The belief that an icon incarnates the power of the god it represents turns an image as didactic sign into an idol as fetish—an idea possibly of interest to the aniconic Puritan Milton, whose anti-Catholic polemic sometimes degraded sign into fetish. The reference in the passage to 'kings whose memory became very dear to posterity' reminds us of the influence of the euhemeristic tradition, which reverses the motion, projecting human beings out into the stars.

Maimonides does not condemn the impulse behind polytheistic worship but rather the mistaken form that worship takes. In *De Diis*, Selden's powerful analogical imagination, grounded in humanist philology, collapses distinctions and emphasizes religious translatability. Augustine in his *City of God* underscores the importance of philology to theology when he summarizes the monotheistic views of Varro, who was considered the most learned person in ancient Rome. Varro believed that when people worshipped one god without the use of images, as they did in Rome for 170 years, they were worshipping Jupiter:

This same shrewd and learned author also says that in his view the only people who have apprehended what God is, are those who have believed him to be the soul which governs the universe by motion and reason. . . . If Varro could not free himself from the prejudices of inherited custom, at least he would acknowledge, and teach, that men should worship one God, who governs the universe by motion and reason.[22]

If the most basic form of idolatry is the substitution of the wrong name of God for the right name, is Varro, who worships a god without an image, a monotheist or an idolater?[23] Jan Assmann has pointed out that Varro himself, 'who knew about the Jews from Poseidonios, was unwilling to see any difference between

---

[21] *De Diis Syris*, 105: 'Deinde, ut fit corruptis moribus & in superstitionem pronis, solem fortè primò, quem . . . *solum in coelis Deum* putabant Phoenicij . . . sub hoc nomine venerabantur. postremò autem & in simulacra alia sive Astrorum sive Regum, quorum memoria posteris longe charissima, τὸ Βαὰλ sive *Bèl* ad augendum, quà fieri potuit, seu corporis Coelestis seu demortui honorem, est impiè derivatum. Varij etiam ritus, ceremoniae, stata ad sacrificia tempora sunt addita. Ita Assyrij, ita Phoenicij, alij suos fecére, coluêre Belos sive Baalim.' Selden cites Alexander Polyhistor as a source of the belief in the long-standing original monotheism of the Chaldeans. G. J. Toomer points out that since the works of that historian are lost, available only in excerpts from Syncellus, Selden is actually citing Scaliger's *Thesaurus Temporum*, which contains those excerpts. Selden identifies Baal or Bel with those whom the Europeans call Zeus and Jupiter: 'Belus enim Ζεύς & Iupiter Europaeis . . . nominabatur' (p. 114).

[22] Augustine, *City of God*, ed. David Knowles, tr. Henry Bettenson (Harmondsworth: Penguin, 1972), 4.31, pp. 174–6; 7.11–13, pp. 268–71. See also the chapter 'The Wrong God', in Halbertal and Margalit's *Idolatry*, 137–62.

[23] See Halbertal and Margalit, *Idolatry*, 137. They also discuss the opposite problem of accommodationism or 'missionary camouflage' as reflected in a controversy described by Hegel, in his lectures on religion, 'between two Catholic orders on the question of whether the Chinese, who worship a god whose name in translation is "Heaven" or "Lord," worship the right God' (p. 137). See G. W. F. Hegel, *Hegel's Lectures on the Philosophy of Religion*, ed. and tr. E. B. Spiers and J. Burdon-Sanderson (London: Routledge, 1974), iii, sixth lecture.

Jove and Yahweh *nihil interesse censens quo nomine nuncupetur, dum eadem res intelligatur* ("because he was of the opinion that it mattered little by which name he was called as long as the same thing was meant").'[24]

Selden would concur. In listing the many local varieties of the name Baal (Baal-Peor, Baal-Zebub, Baal-Moloch, among others), he cites for comparison Varro's attestation of three hundred names for Jupiter, including the Stygian Jupiter called Pluto, an Olympian Jupiter, the first in the assembly of the gods, and a Jupiter Serapis in the ancient inscriptions.[25] According to Selden, when Paul, in his Mars hill address, tells the Athenians, 'For we are also his offspring' (Acts 17: 28),

He means God. But it is the same as if he had said, 'We are of the race of God; that is, we are of the offspring of Jupiter.' . . . Zeus, Jupiter, and, in the oblique case, Dios are names which signify not so much this or that idol as they fitly designate the mighty and everlasting creator of the world. Aratus is the poet from whom he quotes, and he expressed the name of Jove as the foundation of entities.[26]

Philology and intercultural theology merge in *De Diis*, where the translatability of biblical names of God hints at a proto-Deist conception of a single divine essence that manifests itself in the totality of revelations granted to humankind. Selden's lists of ancient gods deriving from a single source attest to his great interest in the nascent field of international law and in the practice of forming treaties with other states and peoples. Assmann clarifies the point when he discusses the ancient 'explanatory list of gods' that gives divine names in Amorite, Hurritic, Elamite, and Kassite, as well as Sumerian and Akkadian: 'treaties had to be sealed by solemn oaths, and the gods that were invoked in these oaths had to be recognized by both parties.'[27] Beyond this interest in cross-cultural communication, as we noted in the preceding chapter, Selden's comparatist historico-philological method aims for an aesthetic of utmost inclusiveness.

IV SELDEN, MAIMONIDES, AND MILTON'S CATALOGUE OF PAGAN DEITIES

Milton relies heavily on the philology of *De Diis* even for the most minute details, and, like Maimonides and Selden, he believes in an original monotheism. But it would be difficult to overstate the difference between the calm of both

---

[24] Assmann, *Moses the Egyptian*, 53.

[25] *De Diis*, 109–10.

[26] Ibid. 112–13: 'i. *uti & quidam apud vos poetae dixerunt*, EIUS N. ET GENUS SUMUS. Deum Verum innuit. caeterùm idem est ac si dixisset, i. *Iouis genus* (id est Jehovae) *sumus.* . . . Ζευς, Iupiter, & in obliquo Διὸς nomina non tam hoc vel illud idolum significabat, quam rerum conditorem Opt. Max. & aeternum proprie designabant. *Aratus, secundum vulgi opinionem,* Iovis *nomen expressit, uti entium fundamentum.*'

[27] Assmann, *Moses the Egyptian*, 46.

Maimonides' rationalism and Selden's scholarly detachment and the shrillness of Milton's fierce denunciations of the pagan gods who incarnated the fallen angels. Milton's primary source for his radically anthropomorphic conception of both deity and idolatry is the Bible itself. In the catalogue of pagan deities in Book I of *Paradise Lost*, as in *Samson Agonistes*, religious worship, marriage, and politics are all exclusive relationships and all are interchangeable. God is the husband, because of the exclusivity of the marriage relationship for the woman, who can only have one husband, while he is free to have more than one wife. Idolatrous Israel is the adulterous wife. God is the king, Israel the faithless vassal whom the prophets deplore for entering into protective treaties with Egypt and Assyria, buying protection at the cost of taxation and political subjugation, thereby insulting the exclusive kingship of God.[28] As Halbertal and Margalit point out, 'the idea of exclusivity associated with the rejection of idolatry contains anarchic dynamite in that it determines theological limits to the possibility of subjugation, whether to a king of Israel who has become overly proud, or to a Gentile king who attempts to impose his authority.'[29]

There *are* translatable names in the catalogue—Tophet is Gehenna (i. 404–5), Chemos is the 'other Name' of Peor (1.412)—but they are signs of infection, of the spreading of a demonic red tide, and not of intercultural theology. In the catalogue, as in the Bible, foreign women, such as King Solomon's wives and King Ahab's wife Jezebel (ll.399–403, 444–6, 472), import alien worship, and Milton may have Henrietta Maria in mind as well.

One could write pages verifying Gibbon's insight on the relationship between Milton's poetic enumeration of the gods and Selden's learned syntagmas by listing the philological details of *De Diis* that find their way into the catalogue. Consider in the following excerpt the words 'Calf' and 'Ox', the phrase 'Grazed Ox', and the connection between the Israelite worship of the golden calf after the exodus from Egypt and the worship of the golden calves introduced by Jeroboam (1 Kings 13). The bard names the gods who 'abus'd | Fanatic *Egypt* and her Priests' (ll.479–80):

> Nor did *Israel* scape
> Th'infection when their borrowed gold compos'd
> The Calf in *Oreb*: and the Rebel King
> Doubl'd that sin in *Bethel* and in *Dan*,
> Lik'ning his Maker to the Grazèd Ox,
> *Jehovah*, who in one Night when he pass'd
> From *Egypt* marching, equall'd with one stroke
> Both her first born and all her bleating Gods.   (ll.482–9)

Selden distributes over paragraphs what Milton concentrates into phrases:

---

[28] Halbertal and Margalit, *Idolatry*, 5, 108, 214–27.
[29] Ibid. 234.

It is certain that the Israelites, defiled by an Egyptian superstition, worshipped the golden calf. You can, if you prefer, call him the golden ox. For although the correct Hebrew copy of the Bible often uses the word *egel*, which means calf, and which the Greek version translates *moschou*, also meaning a calf, and the Latin version has the word *Vitulus*, which means a male calf, in Psalm 105: 21 [106: 20] he expressly calls it 'an ox that eateth grass'. . . . In the commandments of the good and great God, in Exodus 20: 23, he says, 'You shall not make for yourselves golden gods.' And when Jeroboam ben Nabat, who for a long time dwelled in Egypt, mindful of his paternal god, formed the bullocks of molten gold, and placed them in Dan and Bethel, 'Behold,' says he, 'your gods, O Israel, who brought you from the land of Egypt.' See 1 Kings 12 and Flavius Josephus, Archaeolog. VIII.[30]

So many of the notes on the catalogue in Hume's edition incorporate the Hebrew philology of *De Diis* that it takes great effort to remember that what looks like commentary is actually the source. Hume's comments on '*Chemos*, th'obscene dread of *Moab's* Sons' (l.406) reveal at once the extent of Milton's debt to Selden and the reserves of learning behind the use of a single word ('obscene'). Hume surveys some of the opinions listed in *De Diis* regarding the 'lustful and wanton enjoyments' attendant upon the worship of Chemos:

Of the same opinion is our *Milton*, who therefore styles *Chemos* the *Obscene Dread of the Moabites*, and his Rites *Wanton*: But our Learned *Selden* disagrees, and not without sufficient Reason on his side, for Idolatry throughout the Old Testament is every where exprest, by going a Whoring after strange Gods, and by Lust and Abominations, as is sufficiently evident *Ezek*. 23. The Whoredoms, which the *Israelites* committed with the Daughters of *Moab*, cannot be proved to have been any part of the Idolatrous Rites performed in Worshipping their God, but rather the Allurements and Rewards these fair idolatresses bestow'd on their Admirers, by which they ensnared them, to bow down before their senseless Deities, and to provoke the Living God.[31]

This excerpt demonstrates Hume's great respect for the author of *De Diis* and yet his assistance in a modest act of transumption, by having Selden, who died thirteen years before the publication of the first edition of *Paradise Lost*, disagree with Milton. Most important, the nature of the disagreement is symptomatic of how seldom Selden's humane tolerance finds a place in Milton's catalogue. Hume, without acknowledging his source, plunders chapter 5 of *De Diis* for

---

[30] *De Diis*, 2nd edn. (1629), 126–7: 'Aegyptia superstitione inquinatos Israelitas Vitulum Aureum coluisse certum est. Bovem, si vis, aureum appelles licet. tametsi enim עגל *Eghel* habeat Ebraica plerunque veritas, quod μόσχου reddunt LXX. & vitulum Latini: nihilominus tam שׁוּר *schor*, id est, Bos quam עגל seu Vitulum vocatur Psalm. cv. com. 21. . . . Etiam dicto Psalmo שׁוֹר אכל עשׂב *Bos qui herbam depascitur*, expresse dicitur'; 1st edn. (1617), 51–2: 'In mandatis igitur erat Dei Opt. Max. Exod. XX. com. 23. *Deos Aureos non facietis vobis*. Et cum Ieroboam Ben Nabat, qui diu in Aegypto egisset, iuvencos illos in Dan & Bethel collocandos formaret, ex auro eos conflavit; Numinisque patrii memor, *Ecce*, inquit, *Dij tui Israel qui eduxerunt te de terra Aegypti*. vide 1 Regum cap. XII. & Fla. Ioseph. Αρχαιολογ. VIII.' Since Selden refers to '*Bos qui herbam depascitur*' only in the 1629 edition, Milton's phrase 'the grazèd ox' suggests that he was indeed using this edition.

[31] Hume, *Notes on Milton's 'Paradise Lost'*, 24–5.

associations of Chemos, also known as Peor, Baal-Peor, and Baal-Phegor, with various licentious rites and with the god Priapus. Selden, after rehearsing all of the scholarship on the subject—including opinions regarding cultic prostitution, veneration of a giant phallus, and priests defecating in the presence of the idol as an act of worship—concludes that the scatological and obscene rites are an invention, no more a part of the true worship of these gods than adultery was in Solomon's uxorious worship of the Sidonian deities:

> For these bawdy sensualities, which are recounted in the history of the Moabites, and which were punished by the vengeance of the true God, are no more part of the worship of Phegor than the adulteries of Solomon are in conformity with the rites of the Sidonians. He, on account of his affection for the Sidonian women, whom he desperately loved, also worshipped the Sidonian gods.[32]

Hume agrees with Selden, but his tone is closer to Milton's in its wrath. Perfectly consistent with that wrath, and embedded within the otherwise inclusive hermeneutic of *De Diis*, is a detailed hermeneutic of exclusion identified specifically as Maimonidean. Regarding the Hebrew Bible's cultic prescriptions and prohibitions for which there is no other explanation, Maimonides applies what Jan Assmann calls 'the principle of normative inversion', which turns another culture's obligations into abominations and vice versa.[33] Maimonides relies on '*The Nabatean Agriculture* translated by Ibn Wahshiyya' for a description of 'the doctrines, opinions, practices, and cult of the Sabians'.[34] It becomes necessary to understand idolatry because it is the mirror-image of Hebraic self-definition, what Assmann calls 'a polemical counter-construction'.[35] This narrative inversion is the utter negation of the mutual religious translatability that characterizes much of *De Diis*, but both Selden and Samuel Purchas accept Maimonides' account of the Sabians unquestioningly.[36] In fact, the Sabians are an imagined community, and Ibn Wahshiyya seems to have been the author of the work, which he passed off in the year 904 as a translation from the Chaldean.[37]

Pre-structuralist reasoning by contrast appears frequently in *De Diis*, beginning with the observation that 'the cattle which the Egyptians worship the Hebrews eat'.[38] In his letter to Ben Jonson, as we have already seen, Selden briefly summarizes Maimonides' arguments that occupy pages in *De Diis* regard-

---

[32] *De Diis*, 70: 'Foedae n. illae libidines, quae in historia Moabitidarum recensentur, & vindicta Veri DEI puniuntur, non minus sunt a Phegori cultu alienae quam Solomonis stupra a ritu Sidoniorum. Ob amorem n. Sidoniarum, quas deperibat ille, Sidoniorum Deos venerabatur.'

[33] Assmann, *Moses the Egyptian*, 31–2, 61, 216.

[34] Maimonides, *Guide of the Perplexed*, 518.

[35] Assmann, *Moses the Egyptian*, 216.

[36] See *Purchas His Pilgrimage*, 60–2.

[37] See Maimonides, *Guide of the Perplexed*, 518 n. 25. For the Sabians as an imagined pagan community, the *'ummat Sa'aba*, created by normative inversion as the counter-image of Jewish law, see Assmann, *Moses the Egyptian*, 58: 'If the Law prohibits an activity *x* there must have existed an idolatrous community practicing *x*.'

[38] *De Diis*, 61.

ing laws of the Torah that define themselves in opposition to the practice of pagans. He contrasts the Hebrew prohibition against 'the mixtion or insition of plants' with the Sabian practice as reported by Maimonides of having a beautiful woman graft the bough upon the tree while engaging in anal intercourse. He also cites a passage from Maimonides, correctly assigning it to both his *Mishneh Torah* and the *Guide*, that emphasizes contradistinctive self-definition by the use of two opposed words ('that the man should disrobe himself [*discooperiret*]' and 'in order not to expose themselves [*discooperirentur*]').[39]

Milton was familiar with the sections of *De Diis* that treat of these laws developed by a threatened minority, afraid of the contagion and infection carried by the majority culture. The exclusivist ethos of what Mary Douglas calls an 'enclave culture'[40] cháracterizes not only Maimonides' chapters on the Sabians but also Milton's catalogue of devils worshipped as gods:

> The chief were those who from the Pit of Hell
> Roaming to seek thir prey on earth, durst fix
> Thir Seats long after next the Seat of God,
> Thir Altars by his Altar, Gods ador'd
> Among the Nations round, and durst abide
> *Jehovah* thund'ring out of *Sion*, thron'd
> Between the Cherubim; yea, often placed
> Within his Sanctuary itself thir Shrines,
> Abominations; and with cursèd things
> His holy Rites, and solemn Feasts profan'd,
> And with thir darkness durst affront his light.   (i. 381–91)

The various antitheses in this passage suggest not distance but proximity and presumption. They include the opposition of verbs at the very beginning and end of a line ('Roaming... durst fix'), the fatal undercutting, by apposition, of the favourable aspect of a word ('thir Shrines, | Abominations'), and in mimetically appropriate verses, the siege of the holy by the profane ('with cursèd things | His holy Rites, and solemn Feasts profan'd'). The necessary moral distinctions between the endless variety of evil (polytheism) and the single nature of goodness (monotheism) are exposed by the opposition in number of otherwise identical terms: 'Gods' and 'God'; 'Thir Seats' and 'the Seat'; 'Thir Altars' and 'his Altar'; 'thir Shrines' and 'his Sanctuary'.

The ethos of most of Milton's catalogue is alien to Selden's own spirit of scholarly detachment and tolerance. In its negation of the surrounding cultures,

---

[39] *De Diis*, 66–7: 'Moses Ben Maimon in *More Nebochim*, part III. cap. XLVI': 'ita is alibi in Misnah Thorah tract. עבוד cap. III': '*Tu vero scis quod servitium idoli quod vocabatur Pahor* (Peor) *in temporibus illis erat, ut discooperiret se homo versus eum. Et idcirco praeceptum est sacerdotibus ut facerent Braccas quibus cooperirent operienda in hora sacrificij: & praeterea non ascendebant per gradus ad altare, ne discooperirentur.*'

[40] See Mary Douglas, *In the Wilderness: The Doctrine of Defilement in the Book of Numbers* (Sheffield: Sheffield Academic Press, 1993).

it resembles that of Maimonides as described by Selden in *De Diis*. Not least among Milton's achievements in the first half of Book I is his portrayal of Satan's separation and confinement in hell as at once pathetic and necessary for the stability of the universe. God's immutable law keeps Satan safely in hell, and every phrase of the following excerpt is another turn of the key in the lock:

> Such *place* Eternal Justice had *prepar'd*
> For those rebellious, here *thir Prison ordained*
> In utter darkness, and *thir portion set*
> As far remov'd from God and light of Heav'n
> As from the Center thrice to th' utmost *Pole*.
> O how unlike the *place* from whence they fell!   (i. 70–5; my italics)

Banked plosives and commanding predicates at the end of the line convey the impression of force easily contained. The phonetic and semantic equivalents ('place', 'Prison', 'portion') are heavily stressed to suggest pounding regularity. Here the severe antitheses require the reader to traverse again the distance separating Satan and his legions from heaven (darkness separate from light, God from those rebellious, heaven from hell, the place of line 70 from the place of line 75). Once the tight security measures have been described—the confident authority of the lines precludes any possibility of 'eruption Bold'—the narrator permits himself to be moved in Satan's own accents of lamentation. The excerpt's last line is a shocked response to the consequences of an incomprehensible error of will. It is also a compressed version of Satan's own exclamation, 'O how fall'n' (i. 84).

If the first half of Book I of *Paradise Lost* contains striking images of separation and confinement, the second half contains images of cursed union and contamination. The fusion of the devils with humankind is consistently described in terms of infection (i. 453, 483) and promiscuity (380). In this context even a neutral word such as 'borrow'd' takes on a negative moral valuation: 'Nor did *Israel* scape | Th' infection when thir borrow'd Gold compos'd | The Calf in *Oreb*' (ll.482–4). Indeed, Oreb itself, a source of inspiration in the invocation (i. 7), is emptied of its holiness and tainted by association with a sinful event.

In the catalogue one can feel the beginning of a steady upward surge—the first rush of a demonic red tide—that will lead through Chaos to paradise. Its thematic and figurative structures obliterate distinctions and portray sin as the fusion of good and evil. The narrator comes closest to compressing his images and themes—to providing an emblem of 'lust hard by hate' and the forced coupling of good and evil—in his successive accounts of an attempted homosexual gang-rape and the completed gang-rape and murder of the concubine in Gibeah:

> Witness the Streets of *Sodom*, and that night
> In *Gibeah*, when the hospitable door
> Expos'd a Matron to avoid worse rape.   (ll.503–5)

The disparate figures of the catalogue are pressed into union—as if the Israelites' 'borrow'd Gold' had composed a single monstrous idol.

In December 1629, when he turned 21, Milton attained his poetic majority with his *Ode on the Morning of Christ's Nativity*. Its account of the flight of the pagan gods bears traces of the second edition of Selden's *De Diis*, published earlier that year, transforming scholarly detachment into profound ambivalence and occasionally into sympathy, at least when compared with the catalogue published thirty-eight years later. Regarding a stanza (ll. 181–8) touched by a feeling almost nostalgic, Rosemond Tuve comments: 'the kind of allegiance he here gives to pagan myth and thought and imagery was a kind he never had to repudiate. To the end of his life he distinguishes thus between loveliness and sacredness.'[41] The stanza's plangent opening lines express the emotion that Tuve describes:

> The lonely mountains o'er
> And the resounding shore,
>   A voice of weeping heard, and loud lament   (ll.181–3)

Editors invariably cite the slaughter of the innocents (Matthew 2: 18), which echoes word for word the Hebrew Bible (Jeremiah 31: 15), where Rachel weeps for her children.[42] But since the poem is describing the waning powers of the pagan gods on the 'happy day' (l.167) for Christians of Christ's birth, an intimation of future 'bliss | Full and perfect' (ll.165–6), the true source might more likely be found in *De Diis*. There Selden speaks of the Venus of the Ascalonites, connected by water with Dagon. He quotes Macrobius, who says that 'the image of this goddess was made on Mount Lebanon, with her head veiled, with a sorrowful countenance, resting her face in one hand and the other hand inside her gown. Tears are believed to flow from her eyes at the sight of spectators.'[43]

Although there is nothing lovely about Moloch even in the ode, he is less dreadful than in the catalogue, where the narrator emphasizes the unnatural horror of child sacrifice:

> First *Moloch*, horrid King, besmear'd with blood
> Of human sacrifice, and parents' tears,
> Though for the noise of Drums and Timbrels loud
> Thir children's cries unheard, that pass'd through fire
> To his grim Idol.   (i. 392–6)

---

[41] Rosemond Tuve, *Images and Themes in Five Poems by Milton* (Cambridge, Mass.: Harvard University Press, 1957), 70.

[42] *Milton: Complete Shorter Poems*, 2nd edn., ed. John Carey (London and New York: Longman, 1997), 112; *John Milton: The Complete Poems*, ed. John Leonard (London: Penguin, 1998), 620.

[43] Selden, *De Diis*, 187: '*Simulachrum hujus Deae in monte Libano fingitur capite obnupto, specie tristi, faciem manu laeva intra amictum sustinens, lachrimae visione conspicientium manare creduntur.*'

Someone who does not already know about the rite would not learn about it
from the ode:

> And sullen *Moloch*, fled,
> Hath left in shadows dread
>   His burning Idol all of blackest hue;
> In vain with Cymbals' ring
> They call the grisly king,
>   In dismal dance about the furnace blue.   (ll.205–10)

Selden's learnedly diverse interpretations even of so obviously horrible a king
(*Moloch* means *king*) should remind us of what this book does not address in
sufficient detail: the sheer pleasure he takes in a polysemous text. In the long
chapter on Moloch, Selden identifies him as a god of the Ammonites. 'In the
worship and sacrifices in his honour they wickedly burnt their sons and daughters, with the accustomed forms and ceremonies.' But he also provides an
alternative rabbinic reading. He paraphrases Maimonides in the *Guide* ('*More
Nebochim* lib. III. cap. xxxviii') to the effect that the children were neither burnt
nor slain but rather that the priests of Moloch constructed two funeral pyres and
that they led the children between the pyres, as if to purify them:

Therefore the worshippers of fire spread abroad the opinion in those times that the
children of everyone who would not *make his son or his daughter to pass through the fire*
[Deut. 18: 10] would die. And there is no doubt that because of this absurd belief
everybody hastened to perform this action because of the strong pity and apprehension
felt with regard to children and because of the trifling character of the action and its ease,
for it simply consisted in making them pass through fire.[44]

Selden rehearses the most benign interpretations, even of fathers walking between two pyres with their children on their shoulders, presenting them cere-
monially to the priest, then receiving them and returning home with them. But
eventually he concludes that the children were not only led between the fires but
were also burnt sacrificially. Perhaps the view of Moloch in the ode is closer to the
more benign view, which nevertheless condemns the ritual as a dangerously
idolatrous practice.

  Years ago Joseph H. Summers and J. B. Broadbent found in the catalogue the
symbolic portrayal of sexual perversion.[45] Certainly the narrator lists sexual sins.
Moloch and Astarte are successful in reducing Solomon, 'that uxorious King,
whose heart though large, | Beguil'd by fair Idolatresses, fell | To idols foul'
(ll.444–6). Solomon's uxorious fall, twice mentioned in the catalogue, is expressed by the moral declension of 'fair', 'fell', and 'foul'. Although Peor has

---

[44] Ibid. 76–7.
[45] In *The Muse's Method* (Cambridge, Mass.: Harvard University Press, 1962), 90–2, Summers's
skilful disclosure of the sexual penchant of each idol terminates with Thammuz, a god of complex
necrophilic associations. J. B. Broadbent, in *Some Graver Subject* (London: Chatto & Windus,
1960), 93, finds in the mutilation of Dagon a symbol of castration.

already seduced the Israelites in Sittim, he enlarges his orgies 'Even to that Hill of scandal, by the Grove | Of *Moloch* homicide, lust hard by hate' (ll.416–17). Astarte is already famous among the Phoenicians: 'In *Sion* also not unsung, where stood | Her Temple on th'offensive Mountain, built | By that uxorious King' (ll.442–4). The wound of Thammuz allures both the Syrian damsels and Sion's daughters, 'Whose wanton passions in the sacred Porch | *Ezekiel* saw' (ll.454–5). Last comes Belial, who does not need to storm God's temple because he is its priest:

> who more oft than hee
> In Temples and at Altars, when the Priest
> Turns Atheist as did *Ely's* Sons, who fill'd
> With lust and violence the house of God.   (ll.493–6)

With Belial the worst is reached: sin enters the temple and contaminates the holy. The rape described in the passage dealing with Belial is relevant to the catalogue in general, where the devils who get themselves worshipped as idols audaciously invade Jerusalem. The city and temple must suffer the violent thrusts and withdrawals of their enemies.

I should like to conclude by quoting once again an example from the catalogue of a magnificent deviation from the norm, the same passage on Baalim and Ashtaroth that ended Chapter 2. Besides owing a great deal to Selden's analysis of bisexuality, it constitutes a positive example of the fluidity and union celebrated in many chapters of *De Diis*, as opposed to Selden's citations of passages from the *Guide* that employ contradistinctive self-definition and a hermeneutic of exclusion:

> *Baalim* and *Ashtaroth*, those male,
> These feminine. For Spirits, when they please
> Can either Sex assume, or both; so soft
> And uncompounded is thir Essence pure,
> Not ti'd or manacl'd with joint or limb,
> Nor founded on the brittle strength of bones,
> Like cumbrous flesh . . .   (i. 422–8)

The images and tone of this passage reappear in Raphael's beautiful description of angelic lovemaking at the end of Book VIII. In the rest of the catalogue, Milton, like Maimonides, envisions an embattled Israel beset on all sides by enemies seeking to infiltrate its holy places. This passage has a very different vision of the sacred. Surrounded by images of sexual pollution and perversion, it stands alone, expressing the power of sexual freedom, radiant in its beauty. Old, blind, and suffering from gout, Milton turns a fantasy of sexual perfection into unforgettable poetry. Just this once in his treatment of the pagan gods in his great epic, as in the earlier *Ode on the Morning of Christ's Nativity*, he draws on Selden's hermeneutic of inclusion as well as on his philology.

4

Samson's Sacrifice

How aptly John Milton named his tragedy *Samson Agonistes* (contestant or combatant in the public games), for almost everything about it is contested, from its date of composition to the character of its protagonist. Critics of every stripe—regenerationist or anti-regenerationist, humanist or materialist—generally agree only on one point of capital importance: their low estimation of the Mosaic law. Joseph Wittreich, who despises Samson for breaking God's law by entering the temple of Dagon, might be expected to be nomistic, since, at least according to the antinomian standards set by Norman T. Burns, his view of the tragedy is 'hopelessly "carnal"',[1] and in the Bible, at least, an enemy's enemy is a friend: 'I will be an enemy to your enemies and a foe to your foes' (Exodus 23: 22, *New Revised Standard Version*). Yet Wittreich identifies Samson's fault as 'that primitive Hebraic element which persists in Renaissance Christianity'.[2]

Certainly the law has fared no better among Samson's friends, who have turned a deaf ear to their hero's last unmediated words in the tragedy—not the dying words uttered to a hostile audience whose collective memory he intends to obliterate momentarily but rather a self-defining message intended to survive among 'certain friends and equals of his tribe' (*The Argument*) who represent posterity:

> Be of good courage, I begin to feel
> Some rousing motions in me which dispose
> To something extraordinary my thoughts.
> I with this Messenger will go along,
> Nothing to do, be sure, that may dishonor
> Our Law, or stain my vow of *Nazarite*. (ll. 1381–6)

---

[1] Norman T. Burns, '"Then Up Stood Phinehas": Milton's Antinomianism and Samson's', in *The Miltonic Samson,* ed. Albert C. Labriola, *Milton Studies*, 33 (Pittsburgh: University of Pittsburgh Press, 1996), 45 n. 16.

[2] Joseph Wittreich, *Interpreting Samson Agonistes* (Princeton: Princeton University Press, 1986), 231. Wittreich's reading of Milton's tragedy parallels post-Second World War and post-Vietnam revaluations in classical studies that led to darker, colder views of Alexander and empire and of Virgil's relationship to Augustus. Wittreich deplores Samson's betrayal of the office of judge and the 'pernicious casuistry' that would excuse his disregard of 'God's laws' (p. 69).

> nothing to comply
> Scandalous or forbidden in our Law.   (ll. 1408–9)

> Happen what may, of me expect to hear
> Nothing dishonorable, impure, unworthy
> Our God, our Law, my Nation, or myself.   (ll.1423–5)

Samson insists that he will not dishonour or transgress the law of the Hebrew Bible. But contemporary critics, like the Chorus that they patronize, equivocate where Samson and Milton will not. The Chorus had tried to excuse Samson's exogamous marriages: 'For with his own Laws [God] can best dispense' (l.314). Milton regards dispensation as a weasel word, always inferior to a law, and at its worst 'such an indulgence as the shop of Antichrist never forg'd a baser'.[3] Milton is exasperated by those who would call divorce a dispensation rather than a law: 'But surely they either know not, or attend not what a dispensation meanes. A dispensation...alwaies hath charity the end, is granted to necessities and infirmities' (*Tetrachordon*, *YP*, 2, 658). For John Guillory, who expands Samson's participation in the festival of Dagon to include his final, decidedly uncharitable act, the problem of obeying or violating God's law is 'trivial' in comparison with Samson's 'impress[ive]' dispensation from 'the *constituting prohibitions* of Hebraic culture'.[4]

Critics who regard Samson's rousing motions as merely instinctual often employ typology as a totalizing system that allows the amplitude of Milton's Hebraic poetry to shrink to the sharper focus of Christian doctrine. Submitting the Old Testament letter to the judgement of New Testament spirit, they may compare *Samson Agonistes* invidiously with *Paradise Regained*, Samson with Christ, Manoa with God (Samson's *real* father), and even Judges 13–16 (the ostensible source of the story) with Hebrews 11: 32 (the real source). A note on Samson as 'an ev'ning Dragon' (l.1692) elicited endless responses from the subscribers to the Milton e-mail discussion group, but no one questioned the description of the tragedy as 'a study in a spent and morally bankrupt ethic, abrogated by an infinitely finer Christian covenant, a play for whose exegesis Hebrews is more important than Judges'.[5]

Those friends of Samson who read his rousing motions as providential crush his parting words with a Pauline juggernaut. Even in the chapter on Christian liberty in *De Doctrina Christiana*, Milton, citing Paul himself as proof-text, insists that under the law persons who trusted in God 'were justified through their faith, but not without the works of the law, Rom. iv. 12: *the Father of the*

---

³ *The Doctrine and Discipline of Divorce*, *YP*, ii. 301.

⁴ John Guillory, 'The Father's House: *Samson Agonistes* in its Historical Moment', in *Re-Membering Milton: Essays on the Texts and Traditions*, ed. Mary Nyquist and Margaret W. Ferguson (New York and London: Methuen, 1987), 165.

⁵ Derek N. C. Wood, 9 February 1996: Mailserv@urvax.urich.edu Wood has since expanded this argument in *'Exiled from Light': Divine Law, Morality, and Violence in Milton's 'Samson Agonistes'* (Toronto: University of Toronto Press, 2001).

circumcised, etc.' (*YP*, vi. 536). Joan Bennett emphasizes instead Samson's progression to an understanding of the necessity of abrogating the moral as well as the ceremonial law, in order to be saved only by faith. When Paul asserts that 'Christ is the end of the law' (Rom. 10: 4), he brazenly identifies annulment as fulfilment. Bennett, interpreting lines 1384–6, employs the same hermeneutic to obliterate the separate identity of the Mosaic law: 'The essence of the law of Moses as well as of the Nazarite vow will not be sacrificed in their abrogation, but fulfilled.'[6] Bennett is one of the most skilful employers of a Pauline paradigm to structure the narrative of Samson's 'regeneration' to the status of elect Christian. Suppressed in these Christocentric discussions is Milton's identification of God the Father as the sole agent of regeneration, just as he is the sole agent of creation:

REGENERATED BY GOD: that is, by God the Father, for generation is an act performed only by fathers. Psal. li. 12: *God, make a clean mind for me, and renew a firm spirit within me*; Ezek. xi. 19: *I will put a new spirit within you*. . . . This *spirit* seems to mean *the divine virtue of the Father*, because the Father is a spirit and, as I have just said, no one generates except the Father. (*YP*, vi. 461)

In a work that is ironic both in itself and in its interpretative history, it is not surprising that the most strenuous antinomian argument points the way to Samson's release from his dilemma through the law that he has pledged to keep. According to Burns, in a demonstration of 'Milton's Antinomianism, and Samson's', scripture underscores the seriousness of Samson's sin in entering the temple of Dagon:

The importance of the prohibition of idolatry can scarcely be overstated. In Exodus it is the first of the commandments given to Moses. . . . God reminds the Israelites that his very name is 'Jealous' and commands them to destroy the altars and break the images of the gods of the surrounding heathens (Exod. xx, 2–5; xxxiv, 13–14).[7]

To destroy the altars and break the images requires access to the temple. A marginal note on Exodus 23: 24 in the Geneva Bible explains: 'God commandeth his not onely not to worship Idoles, but to destroye them.' Matthew Poole, the author of *Synopsis Criticorum* and an admirer of Milton, whom he cites as 'a late ingenious and learned Writer', connects God's commandment to destroy idolatry in Exodus with the story of Samson through the shared phrase 'angel of the LORD':

Either, First, a Created Angel. Or, Secondly, a Prophet or man of God, for such are sometimes called *Angels*, which signifies only *Messengers of God*; and then the following words are spoken by him in the name of God, as may easily be understood. Or, Thirdly,

---

[6] Joan S. Bennett, *Reviving Liberty: Radical Christian Humanism in Milton's Great Poems* (Cambridge, Mass.: Harvard University Press, 1989), 137.

[7] Burns, '"Then Up Stood Phinehas"', 38. See also the references to Exodus 20: 4–5 and 23: 24 to explain Samson's initial refusal to accompany the Philistine officer (ll.1319–21) in *The Poems of John Milton*, ed. John Carey and Alastair Fowler (London: Longmans, 1968), 388.

Christ the Angel of the Covenant, who is oft called *the Angel of the Lord . . . Exod.* 14.19. & 23.20 . . . *Judg.* 13.3.[8]

Samson decides to follow the Philistine messenger who has, like the angel of his birth, appeared twice. Until the moment of that decision, the Mosaic law has been for Samson, as it is for Milton, mostly negative. Besides being responsible for the regular laws applying to all Israelites against marriage to an idolater and idolatrous worship, Samson as a Nazarite cannot drink wine, cut his hair, or touch a dead body (Num. 6: 1–8). Milton's heroes are enjoined not to sip from Comus's cup, not to eat the magic fruit in paradise, and not to eat or drink at all for forty days in the wilderness. The time between Samson's threefold refusal to accompany the messenger ('I cannot come' (1321), 'I will not come' (1332, 1342)) and his threefold pledge to keep the law by changing his mind is the interval of a double take, after God's word has been understood automatically as yet one more prohibition but before it has been understood inspirationally as a positive commandment:

> I am going to send an angel in front of you, to guard you on the way and to bring you to the place that I have prepared. Be attentive to him and listen to his voice. . . . When my angel goes in front of you, and brings you to the . . . Canaanites . . . you shall not bow down to their gods, or worship them, or follow their practices, but you shall utterly demolish them and break their pillars in pieces. (Exodus 23: 20–4)[9]

Hebraic Samson wins release through the law, not, like Shakespeare's Christian Portia, by submitting to its rigour more rigorously than even Shylock thought to do, but by attending to God's commandment understood differently and by following the messenger, who brings him to the temple of the Canaanites. Samson calls Dalila 'A *Canaanite*, my faithless enemy' (l.380), and indeed the scriptural prohibition against marriage to a Philistine is inferred from verses forbidding Canaanite idolatry and idolatrous matches (Exodus 34: 13–16). As Matthew Poole explains regarding the woman of Timnah, 'the *Philistines* were . . . *Canaanites* . . . in their habitation, and concurrence with them in Wickedness, and therefore were liable to the same Censures and Judgments with them.'[10]

Far more than Samson or Milton, critics unanimously interpret the Mosaic law as narrow and monolithic, forgetting that it is broad enough to permit

---

[8] Matthew Poole, *Annotations Upon the Holy Bible* (1683; 3rd edn., London: Thomas Parkhurst, 1696), sig. Tt2. For his reliance on *Paradise Lost* in his commentary on Genesis 3, see sig. B3r.

[9] The New Revised Standard Version. See also Nahum M. Sarna, *The JPS Torah Commentary: Exodus* (Philadelphia: Jewish Publication Society, 1991), 147: 'tear [their gods] down and smash their pillars to bits.' Both the Geneva and King James Bibles read 'images' instead of 'pillars'. Hebrew *matsevah* derives from the stem *n-ts-v*, 'to stand'. It denotes stelae, cultic objects erected by the Canaanites in honor of their gods. See also Poole, *Annotations*: 'thou shalt utterly overthrow them, i.e., the People, lest thou be ensnared by their counsel or example, and quite break down their images, Or, *statues*, or *pillars*, or any thing else erected in honour to their false Gods' (sig. P2v).

[10] Poole, *Annotations*, sig. Bbb3v.

divergent responses—to take Dalila back or not, to enter the temple of Dagon or not. 'I with this Messenger will go along': the question of the messenger's identity dramatizes interpretive complexity and indeterminacy. Literally, he is simply a hostile Philistine officer. Or, more figuratively, his two appearances may constitute unwitting participation in a drama of divine providence. Like all biblical types, he would be unaware of his figural relationship with the heavenly messenger who twice descended to foretell Samson's birth. But just as Matthew Poole's commentary joined Exodus 23 and Judges 13, so perhaps the Chorus, bidding farewell to Samson, prays that the angel who announced his birth reappear as the angel who goes in front of him and brings him to the Canaanites:

> Send thee the Angel of thy Birth, to stand
> Fast by thy side, who from thy Father's field
> Rode up in flames after his message told
> Of thy conception, and be now a shield
> Of fire. (ll.1431–5)

The Bible uses the same word to denote 'angel' and 'messenger' in both the Hebrew and the Greek (*mal'akh, angelos*). Milton assumed everyone's familiarity with this identity,[11] though the memory of one's first perplexed encounter with Sonnet 19 suggests that perhaps he shouldn't have: 'Thousands at his bidding speed | And post o'er Land and Ocean without rest' (ll.12–13). Classical Jewish commentators on Exodus 23: 20 are divided on whether a heavenly or human messenger is intended by the Hebrew, and 'angel of the Lord' may simply be an idiom expressing the activity of divine providence.[12] Most Reformation commentators insist that 'this Angell is none other but Christ'. Andrew Willet polemically asserts this identity as a point of doctrine: 'Here *Moses* doth openly confesse and expresse the Divinity of Christ, which the Jewes to this day will not see or acknowledge: for this Angell is Christ, in whom the name of God is: he is called by the same names that God the Father is: as the Lord almighty, eternall... as the prophet *Isaiah* saith: *Hee shall call his name, 'Wonderfull, Counsellor, the mighty God, the everlasting Father,* &c'.[13]

---

[11] See e.g. Adam's parting benediction to Raphael as 'Ethereal Messenger'(*PL*, viii. 646), the use of messenger to mean angel in *PR*, i. 238, the 'winged Messengers | On errands of supernal Grace' (*PL*, vii. 572–3), and the indifferent use of angel and messenger in *De Doctrina Christiana* (*YP*, vi. 237).

[12] R. Samuel b. Meir, Ibn Ezra, and Nachmanides believe it denotes a heavenly messenger, while Joseph Bekhor Shor and Levi b. Gershom argue that it is a human one. For 'angel of the Lord' as an expression of divine providence, N. Sarna in *The JPS Torah Commentary* cites Gen. 24: 7, Gen. 48: 16; Exod. 14: 19; 32: 34; 33: 2; Num. 20: 16; Judg. 2: 1; 2 Sam. 24: 1; Isa. 63: 9; Dan. 6: 23' (p. 147).

[13] Andrew Willet, *Hexapla in Exodus* (London, 1633), 456, 459. See also Poole, *Annotations*, sig. Bbb3; Henry Ainsworth, *Annotations upon the second book of Moses, called Exodus* (London, 1617), sig. Tt1. Ainsworth turns rabbinic commentaries into unconscious prophecies of Christ: '*an Angel*] this is Christ, whom the Israelites are sayd to have tempted in the wildernes, *1 Cor.* 10.9....*R. Menachem* upon this place, teacheth from ancient Rabbines, that the word *I* (send) *signifieth the property of mercies and this Angel is the Angel the Redeemer* (Gen. 48.16). Also, *The holy blessed God sayd unto Moses, He that did keep the Fathers* (viz. Abraham, Isaak, and Jakob,) *shal keep the children*.'

In his heretical chapter 'OF THE SON OF GOD' in *De Doctrina Christiana*, Milton argues that there is only one God and that Christ is not him. Milton interprets Christ's names as cited by Willet in Isaiah 6: 9 in ways that emphasize his limitations. In 'the elliptical syntax of this passage', 'the everlasting Father' becomes 'the teacher of a future age' (*YP,* vi. 260–1). Although Exodus 23: 20 ff. appears in one of the blander passages of *Paradise Lost* ('at length [the children of Israel] come, | Conducted by his Angel to the Land | Promis'd to *Abraham* and his Seed'; xii. 258–60), in the chapter on the Son of God Milton engages this scriptural text passionately and polemically in a rejoinder to the common expositors. Impatient with his opponents ('no one in his senses would affirm . . .'; 'Is anyone such a fool as to think . . . ?'; 'No one in his right mind would claim . . .'; [vi. 253–4]), Milton exclaims,

I will show you where God himself declares that his name is in an angel. Exod. xxiii.20, 21: *behold, I send an angel before you, to keep you in this way* etc. *beware of him and obey his voice . . . because my name is in him.* The angel who spoke to the Israelites from that time on, and whose voice they were commanded to obey, was always called Jehovah although he was not really Jehovah. My opponents say he was Jehovah because he was Christ. . . . If . . . my opponents assert that this angel was Christ, what do they prove except that Christ was an angel. . . . (*YP,* vi. 253–4)

Milton cites Exodus 23: 20 ff. to support the argument that when God assigns his name to other beings, whether angel or Christ, that does not mean that they are one with God the Father (vi. 255), only that they are inspired by him. Milton argues in *De Doctrina* that God can inspire Christ, angels, and human beings, who do not thereby lose their separate identities. At the same time, all divinity issues from God the Father: 'it is irrelevant now whether or not [the angel of Exod. 23: 20] was Christ' (vi. 254), because the angel speaks 'not [in] his own name but [in] the name of Jehovah who is in him (see Exod. xxiii. 21)' (vi. 257). More important, God contains those whom he has inspired and through whom he has spoken: 'Therefore it is the Father whom they pierced in piercing the Son' (vi. 258). In the same textual neighbourhood, Milton cites Exodus to exclude Christ from the dispensation of the law: 'So what Jehovah is said to have spoken in Exodus was really spoken not by him but by angels in his name. No wonder, for it would have seemed unsuitable for Christ, as minister of the gospel, to be minister of the law as well' (vi. 251).

The argument that God contains those whom he loves, so that the offences against Christ are offences against himself (vi. 257), sounds like Milton's more famous argument of materialist monism in the same treatise: 'spirit . . . virtually . . . and eminently contains within itself what is clearly the inferior substance [matter]; in the same way as the spiritual and rational faculty contains the corporeal, that is, the sentient and vegetative faculty' (*YP,* vi. 309).[14] In Milton's

[14] For an admirably clear and thorough analysis of Milton's materialism, see Stephen M. Fallon, *Milton among the Philosophers: Poetry and Materialism in Seventeenth-Century England* (Ithaca, NY, and London: Cornell University Press, 1991).

tragedy, the Chorus's farewell prayer moves from God to angel to inspired human being, suggesting at once that the divine will and power manifests itself through heaven-sent messengers both angelic and human and that in ancient thought processes lines of demarcation between the sender and the sent are liable to be blurred:

> Go, and the Holy One
> Of *Israel* be thy guide
> To what may serve his glory best, and spread his name
> Great among the Heathen round:
> Send thee the Angel of thy Birth, to stand
> Fast by thy side, who from thy Father's field
> Rode up in flames after his message told
> Of thy conception, and be now a shield
> Of fire; that Spirit that first rusht on thee
> In the camp of *Dan*
> Be efficacious in thee now at need.
> For never was from Heaven imparted
> Measure of strength so great to mortal seed,
> As in thy wond'rous actions hath been seen.   (ll.1427–40)

Within the hyper-Pauline dualist context of most of *De Doctrina Christiana*, Milton employs Exodus 23: 20 ff. to assert monistic continuity of God, angel, and human being, and to exclude Christ from the dispensation of the law. But *De Doctrina* is not the doctrinal matrix of *Samson Agonistes*. William Riley Parker, contending that Milton wrote his tragedy in 1647–8, bases his argument in part on its 'severe avoidance of theology (the Fall, Original Sin, the Devil, Hell, even immortality)'.[15] Parker assumes that *Samson's* rudimentary, primitive, Hebraic theology represents an earlier, narrower, and more obscure stage in Milton's development, to be superseded by the later, ampler clarity of Christian theology in *Paradise Lost*. But if Milton's tragedy avoids the topics mentioned by Parker, it explores, in a comprehensive and nuanced way, the theological implications of God's law and of human attempts to act justly. Milton sets himself the formidable task of trying to understand on their own terms the Mosaic institution of the Nazarite, laws governing sexual relations with an unbeliever, permission to marry a beautiful captive woman (Deuteronomy 21: 10–14), religious conversion, divorce, the sin of betraying a secret and of 'prostituting holy things to Idols' (l.1358). Exodus 23: 20 ff. is only one of a series of commandments in the Hebrew Bible in which God commands his people not to assimilate and to desecrate Canaanite idols.[16] Finally, laws as disparate as Samson's relationship

---

[15] William Riley Parker, 'On the Date of *Samson Agonistes*', *Milton: A Biography* (Oxford: Clarendon Press, 1968), ii. 907.

[16] See e.g. Exodus 34: 12–13: 'Take care not to make a covenant with the inhabitants of the land . . . or it will become a snare among you. You shall tear down their altars, break their pillars, and cut down their sacred poles' (New Revised Standard Version).

with Dalila, the rules governing a 'journey of a Sabbath day' (l.149), and transgressions of 'the law of nature, law of nations' (l.891) are not only biblically Hebraic but non-biblically rabbinic. Only a narrow conception of theology leads to the conclusion that *Samson Agonistes* is almost devoid of it.

Robert Lowth set himself to the critique of Hebrew poetry in the middle of the eighteenth century, and his warning applies not only to Parker's understanding of *Samson Agonistes* but to our attempts to remove the veils of obscurity that distance in time and obliqueness in the use of metaphor have spread over both Judges 13–16 and Milton's tragedy:

if the reader be accustomed to habits of life totally different from those of the author, and be conversant only with different objects; in that case many descriptions and sentiments, which were clearly illustrated and magnificently expressed by the one, will appear to the other mean and obscure, harsh and unnatural; and this will be the case more or less, in proportion as they differ, or are more remote from each other in time, situation, customs sacred or profane, in fine, in all the forms of public and private life.[17]

To prove an early date of composition, Parker provides six pages of parallel passages matching up the tragedy with the prose tracts of the 1640s. The most compelling examples come from the divorce tracts. The manifold afflictions of unhappy marriages portrayed in Milton's prose appear newly dressed in the tragedy, in surprisingly varied contexts: in discussions of barrenness considered '[i]n wedlock a reproach' (l. 353), servitude and slavery (ll. 410–13, 416–18), accepting offered freedom rather than enduring suffering as a trial of patience (ll. 503–6, 516), despair (ll. 594–7), divine providence (ll. 668–70), the errors committed even by 'the best and wisest' (ll. 1034–40), and many others. These parallels do not prove early composition: as we have seen, the pagan gods of Selden's *De Diis Syris* (1617) stayed in Milton's mind for thirty years, from the *Götterdämmerung* of the *Nativity Ode* (1629) to the catalogue of pagan deities in Book I of *Paradise Lost*; and it is not unlikely that the great prose tracts of 1643–5—including the four treatises on divorce, *Of Education*, and the *Areopagitica*—constitute the principal doctrinal matrix of the middle books of *Paradise Lost*.[18]

---

[17] Robert Lowth, *Lectures on the Sacred Poetry of the Hebrews* (1753), tr. Richard Gregory (1787), lecture 5, rpt. in *Critics of the Bible: 1724–1873*, ed. John Drury (Cambridge: Cambridge University Press, 1989), 77. On the difficulties of historical reconstruction, see also Edgar Wind, *Pagan Mysteries in the Renaissance* (New York: W. W. Norton, 1968), 15. For a humane and lucid contemporary voice, inviting her readers to 'a complex and subtle assessment of the uses of the past' and encouraging us by example 'to make careful discriminations between one historical moment and another' (p. 247), see Barbara Kiefer Lewalski, 'Milton's *Samson* and the "New Acquist of True [Political] Experience"', *Milton Studies*, 24, ed. James D. Simmonds (Pittsburgh: University of Pittsburgh Press, 1989), 233–51.

[18] Jason P. Rosenblatt, *Torah and Law in 'Paradise Lost'* (Princeton: Princeton University Press, 1994).

Whatever the date of composition—and, according to the early life by Edward Phillips,[19] 'it cannot certainly be concluded'—Milton's most Hebraic prose has found a place in his most explicitly Hebraic poetry. In the great prose tracts of 1643–5, Milton confronts with compassion a life of mistake and the need for a second chance. Missing from these tracts are the essential tenets of Christian liberty, death to the law and redemption in Christ. In the divorce tracts Christ is a charitable interpreter who ratified the moral law of Moses and who 'never gave a judicial law' (*YP*, ii. 334). The monistic ethos of these tracts emphasizes congruity and inclusiveness. Urging Parliament to make the Mosaic law of divorce part of English civil law, these tracts shade into Erastianism. They treat as compatible all human beings' natural rights as reasonable creatures, the rights of biblical Israel as members of a holy community, and the individual privilege of the regenerate Christian saint. The higher includes the lower without any sort of turning away or disparagement and without the surrender of individuality. Regarding the relationship among pagans, Jews, and Christians, Milton emphasizes the gospel's perfect correspondence with Mosaic law 'grounded on [the] morall reason' of natural law (*YP*, ii. 264). In these tracts, as in paradise before the Fall, 'God and Nature bid the same' (*PL*, vi. 176), and Milton speaks of 'the fundamentall law book of nature; which *Moses* never thwarts but reverences' (*YP*, ii. 272).

The strongest recent arguments of literary historians have favoured a later date of the tragedy's composition, drawing parallels between Samson in prison, forced to participate in idolatrous ceremonies, and imprisoned republicans after the Restoration and Puritans ordered to attend Anglican services as a public gesture of uniformity.[20] But there are many causes of Samson's claustrophobic rage— expressed in metre that is often cramped—including his blindness: 'Myself my Sepulcher, a moving Grave' (l. 102); 'Thou art become (O worst imprisonment!) | The Dungeon of thyself' (ll. 155–6). Samson's bad marriage leaves him trapped and, worse than abandoned, betrayed, and Dalila's attempt to approach him meets with passionate denunciation:

> Not for thy life, lest fierce remembrance wake
> My sudden rage to tear thee joint by joint.
> At distance I forgive thee. (ll. 952–4)

In his great tragedy Milton transforms his own memories of marital disappointment into art. In *Colasterion* Milton answers the argument that a Christian should bear his wife's infirmities: charity, he replies, 'is contented in our peace

[19] Edward Phillips, *The Life of Mr. John Milton*, in *The Early Lives of Milton*, ed. Helen Darbishire (London: Constable, 1932), 75.

[20] See esp. Christopher Hill, *Milton and the English Revolution* (London: Faber, 1977), 432–9; Barbara K. Lewalski, *The Life of John Milton* (Oxford: Blackwell, 2000), 492–3, 522–36; Laura Lunger Knoppers, *Historicizing Milton: Spectacle, Power, and Poetry in Restoration England* (Athens, Ga.: University of Georgia Press, 1994), 142–59; Blair Worden, 'Milton, *Samson Agonistes*, and the Restoration', in Gerald Maclean, ed., *Culture and Society in the Stuart Restoration* (Cambridge: Cambridge University Press, 1995), 111–36.

with them, at a fair distance': 'I grant, infirmities, but not outrages, not perpetual defraudments of truest conjugal society, not injuries and vexations as importunat as fire' (*YP,* ii. 731). The divorce tracts are not lacking in the language of terrible imprisonment. The verse that others read as instituting marriage (Gen. 2: 24), Milton views instead as 'that greisly Porter, who having drawn men and wisest men by suttle allurement within the train of an unhappy matrimony, claps the dungeon gate upon them, as irrecoverable as the grave' (*YP,* ii. 603).

Milton's *Samson Agonistes*, like Shakespeare's *The Merchant of Venice*, taps into the roots of early modern England's powerful and contradictory social, psychological, and religious problems, but with sympathy for Judaic self-understanding. And Selden's scholarship, including but not limited to his exposition of the Jewish law of marriage and divorce, in Book V of *De Jure* and in *Uxor Ebraica*, introduces post-biblical rabbinic thought into the tragedy. Selden discusses at length, in works that we know Milton read because he quotes from them frequently and approvingly, in contexts that reveal their importance to him, 'the contracting of a marriage among Gentiles...who subsequently become proselytes and are transferred to the Jewish church or polity':

Now a convert as well as a freedman, as soon as he comes into Judaism . . . they say that he was regarded as reborn, as a 'recently born baby'; that he became Jewish and thus the things which were altogether in the past, such as blood and affinity, were poured away. Accordingly, Tacitus put it most aptly when he said of those proselytes, 'The first thing they are taught is to hold the gods in contempt and to remove themselves from their homeland, parents, children, and brothers and to hold them of no account.'[21]

When Milton's Samson reminds Dalila of her failure to remember this point, he names Selden's *De Jure Naturali et Gentium*:

> Why then
> Didst thou at first receive me for thy husband,
> Then, as since then, thy country's foe profest?
> Being once a wife, for me thou wast to leave
> Parents and country; nor was I their subject,
> Nor under their protection but my own,
> Thou mine, not theirs: if aught against my life
> Thy country sought of thee, it sought unjustly,
> Against *the law of nature, law of nations*,
> No more thy country.   (ll. 882–91; emphasis added)

---

[21] Selden, *Uxor Ebraica* (1646), 2.18, p. 207. The translation is by Jonathan Ziskind, ed. *John Selden on Jewish Marriage Law* (Leiden: Brill, 1991), 197. See also *De Jure Naturali et Gentium*, 2.4, p. 162, for a similar discussion: 'Proselytus, ex quo fit Proselytus, velut infans, qui recens nascitur, habetur.' Selden refers to 'Gemar. Babylon. Ad tit. *Iabimoth*, cap. 2. fol. 22a & cap. 11. fol. 97b. Maimon. Halach *Iebom Wechalitza* cap. 1. & *Isuri bia* cap. 14. Moses Mikotzi praec. affirm. 51. fol. 135. col. 4. *Shulcan Aruch* lib. *Aben Haezer* ca. 157.sect. 3.'

Selden's headnote to *De Jure*, v. 15 names as a subject 'Dalila Proselyta', and the chapter correctly cites numerous sources that reveal a rabbinic disbelief that a born deliverer of Israel would enter into either an exogamous marriage with a member of the oppressing nation or a sexual relationship with a harlot. Selden cites Levi Ben Gershom on both the woman of Timna in Judges 14 [v. 2] and Delilah in 16 [v. 4] (Milton cites him on 19: 2 (*YP*, ii. 336)), Moses of Coucy ('pracept Negat. 116), and 'Maimonid. Halach. *Isuri Bia* cap. 13', all of whom insist in the strongest terms ('Heaven forbid' otherwise) that Samson's wives converted to Judaism before Samson married them.[22] Selden quotes at some length in *De Synedriis*, a treatise on which Milton relied in *The First Defence of the People of England*, the passage from Maimonides' *Code* (*Isurei Bia*, the laws addressing forbidden sex acts). 'It should not enter your mind', says Maimonides, altering the literal biblical text, 'that Samson the liberator of Israel . . . would marry foreign Gentiles [i.e. idolaters].'[23] He then describes the interrogation of the proselyte, making certain that the conversion is not motivated by fear, love of a specific Israelite male, monetary concerns, or the desire for a position of authority.

Samson calls Dalila his wife and his concubine (l. 537), and in his *Commonplace Book*, under the heading 'CONCUBINAGE', Milton notes: 'That one concubine was allowed in the early Christian Church Selden proves by many statements from the Fathers, in his de jure nat et gent. Book 5. C[hapter] 7. P[age] 573' (*YP*, i. 403). In the same textual neighbourhood, Selden, suggesting the interchangeability of 'wife' and 'concubine', refers to a manuscript in 'Biblioth. Cottoniana' in which, according to the historian and theologian Paulus Orosius, after Constantine was created commander in chief of Gaul, he substituted the Anglo-Saxon 'his wyf' for the Latin 'concubine' in reference to his mother Helena, who was the concubine of his father Constantius I. Moreover, continues Selden, one can see in the old manuscript where the word 'concubine' is deleted and 'uxore' added in superscript, and not in a fresh hand.[24]

Pagan and Hebrew customs and rituals of betrothal and marriage found a place in early Christianity. Selden devotes an entire chapter of the *Uxor Ebraica* to the responsibilities of the wedding attendants ('*Paranymphi*') to lead the couple into the wedding chamber and to see to the matter of the bride's virginity. He distinguishes between the customs of ancient Judaea, where the 'comrade' or 'nuptial companion' (Aramaic: *re'uhah shushvina*) spent the entire night in the bedroom, and those of Galilee, where the paranymph would retire. In accord with the latter custom, 'St. Augustine says, "As soon as the husband begins to fondle his wife, he looks for a room that is removed from witnesses, household slaves, and even attendants, and anyone else to whom friendship might have

---

[22] Selden, *De Jure Naturali et Gentium* (1640), 5.15, p. 625.
[23] Selden, *De Synedriis*, in *Opera Omnia*, ed. David Wilkins (1726), i. 1626.
[24] Selden, *De Jure*, 5.7, p. 575.

permitted access" (*Civ. Dei.* XIV. 18).'[25] When the Bible briefly records Samson's loss of the woman of Timna, it never mentions a groomsman or paranymph: 'But Samson's wife was given to his companion, whom he had used as his friend' (Judg. 14: 20). Selden's Talmud-based discussion of the paranymph, emphasizing his intimacy with the newlyweds, introduces a note of irony and a hint of tribal night games to the chorus's taunting of Samson: 'the *Timnian* bride | . . . so soon preferr'd | Thy Paranymph, worthless to thee compar'd, | Successor in thy bed' (ll. 1019–22).

Other rabbinic laws besides those pertaining to marriage figure importantly in *Samson Agonistes*, but I will sketch them only briefly here, because they are developed at some length in later chapters. Samson's final destructive act can be read in the context of Selden's comprehensive talmudic and rabbinic chapters in *De Jure* (4.4 and 5) on the law or judgement of zealots, the *Ius Zelotarum*, which interpret many violent events in both the Hebrew and Greek Bibles as acts in accordance with the laws of normative Judaism. For Selden, this law explains why Christ, though provoking resentment, was able to act with impunity when he scourged the money-changers. Selden's central text is a *mishnah* in tractate Sanhedrin promulgating a law, with specific requirements and limitations, whereby zealots are authorized to kill one who commits an act of sacrilege.[26] The *Ius Zelotarum* would become an incendiary topic in the period of the Civil War.

A major topic of Selden's *De Jure*, universal law and its connection to international relations, is of capital importance in *Samson* because it allows for conversation between the Israelite Samson, whose ethical sense is informed by law, and Philistine tempters such as Dalila and Harapha. Samson depends on the law for both self-justification and self-condemnation. What is remarkable in the text of *Samson Agonistes* (there is nothing like it in the text of Judges) is that he agonizes over what seems to be a venial offence (revealing the source of his strength, which is not a sin traceable to scripture) but he easily shrugs off the far more serious charges that he is 'A Murderer, a Revolter, and a Robber' (l. 1180) and that he twice married a Philistine or Canaanite enemy.

Milton, like Selden's rabbis in *De Jure*, combines the topic of divine universal laws of perpetual obligation with that of the seven hostile nations who originally inhabited Canaan and whom God commands the Israelites to destroy. Samson calls Dalila 'a *Canaanite*, my faithless enemy' (l. 380). The Canaanites are included among the seven idolatrous nations subjected to the harshest biblical imperative (Exod. 34: 11; Deut. 7: 1–5, 20:17). As we will see in Chapter 7, Selden follows the biblical citation with rabbinic sources that moderate scriptural severity. The *Sifrei*, a fourth-century *halakhic* midrash, infers from the reason of the law—to remove sinful practices, idolatry in particular—that if persons from

---

[25] Selden, *Uxor Ebraica*, 2.16, p. 200.
[26] Selden, *De Jure*, 4.4, p. 487. This subject is taken up again in Ch. 5.

those nations repent, they are not killed; and Rashi adds that if they repent and become proselytes, they are received.[27]

The Philistines in Milton's tragedy violate Noachide precepts that are at the heart of *De Jure*: 'after the doings of the land of Canaan, whither I bring you, shall ye not do: neither shall ye walk in their ordinances' (Lev. 18: 3). The two most serious offences among the *praecepta Noachidarum* are those Selden places under the rubric '*inter hominem & numen sanctissimum*', idolatry and blasphemy. In the *Areopagitica*, Milton names the source of his theistic conception of natural law, the 'volume of naturall & nationall laws [*De Jure Naturali et Gentium*]' by 'the chief of learned men reputed in this Land, Mr. Selden' (*YP*, ii. 513). In that treatise and elsewhere, he makes an exception to his denunciation of civil interference in matters of religion, extending magisterial power to include the suppression of idolatry and blasphemy, which he associates with Roman Catholicism. They violate a natural law that takes precedence over both civil and ecclesiastical authority.[28] These are sins recounted in *Samson Agonistes*:

> So *Dagon* shall be magnified, and God,
> Besides whom is no God, compar'd with Idols,
> Disglorified, blasphem'd, and had in scorn
> By th'Idolatrous rout amidst their wine.   (ll. 440–3)

An influence on Milton's great tragedy less direct but more powerful than any single law is the comparative perspective adopted in the natural law discourse of Grotius's *De Jure Belli ac Pacis* (1625) and Selden's *De Jure*. Instead of exhibiting the dualistic approach of the contemporary mainstream works of systematic theology, Grotius and Selden look for connections among Greek and Roman, Jewish, and Christian laws and customs. And in seventeenth-century England only Selden places rabbinic thought at the centre of his scholarship. A Hebraic, monistic reading of *Samson Agonistes*, in accord with classical and Christian thought but insisting on the harmony between Judaic law and the spirit, would acknowledge the humanity of the Chorus, its capacity for fellow-feeling, and its considerable spiritual and intellectual development, instead of rejecting it in a spirit of Pauline dualism as a narrow, obsolete, erroneous 'chorus of enslaved Hebrews', representing 'the whole Hebrew people, bound by the law of Moses in its service to Jehovah'.[29] An ironic dualist reading presumes that 'Samson lived and died in vain',[30] because he only 'began to deliver Israel out of the hands of the Philistines' (Judges 13: 5), neither he nor his surviving countrymen completing the act. But from an ampler biblical perspective, 'he shall begin to deliver

[27] Ibid. 6.16, pp. 744–5.
[28] See Barbara K. Lewalski, 'Milton and Idolatry', *Studies in English Literature*, 43 (2003), 213–32, esp. 217.
[29] Arthur E. Barker, 'Calm Regained Through Passion Spent: The Conclusions of the Miltonic Effort', in *The Prison and the Pinnacle*, ed. Balachandra Rajan (London: Routledge & Kegan Paul, 1973), 39; Bennett, *Reviving Liberty*, p. 120.
[30] Parker, *Milton: A Biography*, ii. 909.

Israel . . . and the deliverance shall be carried on and perfected by others, as it was in part by *Eli*, and *Samuel*, and *Saul*, but especially by *David*.'[31] Instead of merely disparaging Manoa for his parental inadequacies and for a crude ethnocentricism associated with Judaism, a monistic reading would understand even from a Christian perspective the love expressed by laying out money for one's child instead of laying it up for oneself and by preparing to spend the rest of one's life nursing that child (ll. 1485–9).[32] And since the devaluing of the Chorus and of Manoa bears on their ethnicity, a monistic Christian reading would recognize Milton's employment of a positive typology (congruity rather than disparity) and his transfer of terms from one dispensation to another to emphasize God's continuous ways with all his creatures.

Is it less legitimate to read the catastrophe of the tragedy from the perspectives of the natural and Mosaic laws than from that of the gospel, as a type of the crucifixion? Perhaps Christ appears in the tragedy not as a redeemer sacrificing himself but instead as the 'angel of the Lord' who stands by Samson's side (ll. 1431–2). The theme of purification and sacrifice outside of a Christian context appears in Milton's decision to translate Aristotle's *katharsis* as *lustratio* on the title-page of the tragedy. Milton's *Elegia Sexta*, to Diodati, describes the true poet, who must live sparely:

Let only the crystal-clear water in a beechen bowl stand near him, and let him drink temperate draughts from the pure spring. More than this, his youth must be chaste and free from sin, his manners strict, and his hand without stain, even like you, O Priest, when in sacred vestment and gleaming with the waters of cleansing (Qualis veste nitens sacra, et *lustralibus* undis) you rise as augur to face the angry gods. After this manner, they say, wise Tiresias lived when the light of his eyes was gone . . . and aged Orpheus.[33]

The lustral waters and a life of abstinence connect the youthful poet who saw himself as a prophet-priest ('Diis etenim sacer est vates, divumque sacerdos'; l. 77) with the Nazarite, separate to God, whose decision to abstain from wine and to drink 'only from the liquid brook' is the subject of considerable discussion (ll. 541–57).

Manoa, rejecting 'over-just' self-condemnation (l. 514), advises Samson to repent by offering God the purificatory levitical sacrifices of the Mosaic law:

---

[31] Poole, *Annotations*, sig. Bbb3.

[32] Dayton Haskin's important book *Milton's Burden of Interpretation* (Philadelphia: University of Pennsylvania Press, 1994) asserts the complexity and indeterminacy of scriptural interpretation, and it regards Milton's poetry from an ample and generous biblical and human perspective. But even Haskin's Manoa simply can't do anything right. Instead of evoking the talents of the parable, his money is merely an index of his carnality: 'His very willingness to lay out his treasure to buy his son's release from prison suggests that he would be unlikely to appreciate the more inward conception of the locus of value that Mary has [in *Paradise Regained*]' (p. 143).

[33] *The Latin Poems of John Milton*, tr. Walter MacKellar (New Haven: Yale University Press, 1930), *Elegia Sexta*, ll. 60–70.

act not in thy own affliction, Son;
Repent the sin, but if the punishment
Thou canst avoid, self-preservation bids;

. . . .

Reject not then what offer'd means, who knows
But God hath set before us, to return thee
Home to thy country and his sacred house,
Where thou mayst bring thy off'rings, to avert
His further ire, with prayers and vows renew'd.   (ll.503–5, 516–20)

The passage does not lack ironic readings, but Milton in *Doctrine and Discipline of Divorce* uses a similar argument unironically, indicating that both Jews and Christians require the mercy of 'lawfull liberty' (*YP*, ii. 278). Where Manoa offers the prospect of the Levitical laws of atonement as a means of regaining lost peace, Milton offers the prospect of the Deuteronomic law of divorce:

If wee bee wors, or but as bad [as the Jews], which lamentable examples confirm wee are, then have wee more, or at least as much need of this permitted law, as they to whom God therfore gave it (as [the prohibitors of divorce] say) under a harsher covnant. Let not therfore the frailty of man goe on thus inventing needlesse troubles to it selfe to groan under the fals imagination of a strictnes never impos'd from above, enjoyning that for duty which is an impossible and vain supererogating: *Bee not righteous overmuch*, is the counsel of *Ecclesiastes*; *why shouldst thou destroy thy self*? (*YP*, ii. 354)

The Chorus, describing the catastrophe, twice evokes the Mosaic laws of sacrifice, first contrasting Dagon and the ceremonies of Philistine idolatry with 'our living Dread, who dwells | In *Silo* his bright Sanctuary' (1673–74), then comparing Samson with the Phoenix, a bird that 'lay erewhile a Holocaust' (1702). Birds as burnt offerings appear frequently in the Hebrew Bible ('*de avibus holocausti oblatio fuerit Domino*'; throughout Leviticus 1 and 5 in the Vulgate). This is precisely the offering required of the Nazarite if he breaks his vow by coming into contact with a dead body. The Torah devotes almost an entire chapter (Numbers 6) to the laws of the Nazarite, paying special attention to the sacrificial process initiated by corpse uncleanness:

And if any man die very suddenly by him, and he hath defiled the head of his consecration ... he shall bring two turtle[dove]s, or two young pigeons ... and the priest shall offer the one for a sin offering, and the other for a burnt offering ['*in holocaustum*', Vulgate], and make an atonement for him, for that he sinned by the dead, and shall hallow his head on that same day. (Num. 6: 9–11; AV)

Contact with a corpse defiles the locks which signify holy separation, so the vow must be initiated again. Thousands of Philistines will be dying 'very suddenly' next to Samson. Reading the catastrophe in the context of Numbers 6, Samson's death becomes a propitiatory sacrifice, and the Phoenix's rebirth becomes a correlative of the renewal of Nazarite vows.

From the beginning of the terrible interrogations, the remarkable intellectual and moral clarity of Samson's answers derives from his assured interpretations of a Torah that he experiences not as a restraint but as a path. In the Hebrew Bible the way (lit., *halakha*) is the law: 'Ye shall walk in the way which the Lord your God hath commanded you, that you may live, and that it may be well with you' (Deut. 5: 30; see also 8: 6, 10: 12, and 11: 22). Although the prejudice of Milton's entrenched Paulinism prevents him from understanding Torah as an entity entirely different from the law as Paul depicts it, *Samson Agonistes* is a heroic attempt to understand the Hebraic ethos on its own terms, as a means of living most fully according to the laws of one's best nature. Samson's final intimacy with God, love for his service, and faith in his justice are the culmination of a process that spans the drama. His faith is represented by a monistic union of thought and feeling: 'I begin to feel | Some rousing motions in me, which dispose | To something extraordinary my thoughts' (ll.1381–3). And to what extraordinary thing are this judge's thoughts disposed? To 'th'unsearchable dispose [*disponere*] | Of highest Wisdom' (ll.1746–7). In the Hebraic *Doctrine and Discipline of Divorce*, Milton asserts that the Mosaic law incarnates deity and reveals as much of God's dispose as we can know:

The hidden wayes of [God's] providence we adore & search not; but the law is his reveled will, his complete, his evident, and certain will; herein he appears to us as it were in human shape, enters into cov'nant with us, swears to keep it, binds himself like a just lawgiver to his own prescriptions, gives himself to be understood by men, judges and is judg'd, measures and is commensurat to right reason. (*YP*, ii. 292)

To regard Samson's progress specifically as regeneration is to impose a Pauline soteriology upon the story (*YP*, vi. 461–5). One might perhaps as legitimately claim that Samson's final prayer ('with head a while inclin'd | And eyes fast fixt he stood, as one who pray'd'; ll.1636–7) is the Hebrew *Shema*, traditionally the acceptance of the yoke of the kingdom of heaven: 'Hear, O Israel: the LORD our God is one LORD: and thou shalt love the LORD thy God with all thine heart, and with all thy [*nephesh*], and with all thy might' (Deut. 6: 4–5, AV). *Nephesh* is the Hebrew Bible's monistic word for a human being as both body and soul. Milton is sufficiently competent in Hebrew philology to find nine texts in *Tanakh* featuring the word *nephesh*, in which 'all properties of the body are attributed to the soul as well' (*YP*, vi. 318). The Talmud (*Berakhot* 61b) reports R. Akiva's recitation of the *Shema* just before his execution by the Romans, and in devotional manuals reciting the prayer affirms a joyous willingness to suffer martyrdom for the sanctification of God's name.

A monistic reading of Samson's purification and sacrifice would find continuities among the classical, the Hebraic, and the Christian: *lustratio* evoking pagan and Hebraic lives of abstinence and purification, *holocaust* evoking the sacrifice wholly consumed that initiates the Nazarite's renewal of his vow and, inevitably for a Christian reader, Christ the Phoenix. Certainly the tragedy progresses from initial despondent dualism to monism. Samson expresses his agony: 'O impotence of mind in body strong' (l.52); 'thy Soul | ... Imprison'd now indeed, | In real darkness of the body dwells' (ll.156, 158–9). Samson's exuberant upswing in his encounter with Harapha appears as a momentary extension of sight to touch (he threatens to 'survey' the giant with his hand (l.1230), as if his earlier wish that he might see with his body had come true (l.96)) or as a playful disparagement of sight : 'The way to know were not to see but taste.' This echoes the high spirits of Psalm 34: 8: 'O taste and see that the LORD is good', with 'taste' as direct experience or 'the revelation of the heart' (Abraham Ibn Ezra). Samson taunts Harapha as he had earlier taunted himself: '[vast] bulk without spirit' (l.1238).

Milton's great epic frequently expresses the monistic wish for an 'uncompounded essence pure' in the passionate descriptions of both good and bad angels (*Paradise Lost*, i. 423–31, vi. 344–53, viii. 622–9), and John Rogers has written insightfully of the yearning in *Samson Agonistes* for 'the animate perceptivity of the "whole body"', an 'ideal state of homogeneously diffused organic sentience'.[34] The catastrophe of this tragedy is an unparalleled monistic moment of complete attentiveness, body and soul. Until that moment, Samson had either kept or violated laws that consisted of prohibitions. At that moment, prompted by Exodus 23 as interpreted by his own holy spirit, he is given access to the temple of the enemy to uproot idolatry and tear down the pillars. His great hope had been that God might 'use him further in some great service' (l.1499), his great fear that he would sit 'Useless' (l.1501). Does it trivialize the tragedy to suggest a comparison with Milton's access to the printing press, in defiance of the Licensing Order, to advance the cause of the Reformation by uprooting the canon law prohibiting divorce? In *Eikonoklastes* he explained the title of his treatise, 'the famous Surname of many Greek Emperors, who in thir zeal to the command of God, after long tradition of Idolatry in the Church, took courage, and broke all superstitious Images to peeces' (*YP*, iii. 343).

I should like to conclude by returning to the image of the holocaust as an expression of one of Samson's and Milton's most profound desires. As noted earlier, the Nazarite who has become unclean renews his vow by bringing two birds, turtledoves or pigeons, as an offering (Num. 6: 10). But two far more exalted birds represent Samson:

> as an Eagle
> His cloudless thunder bolted on thir heads.
> So virtue giv'n for lost,
> Deprest, and overthrown, as seem'd,
> Like that self-begott'n bird
> In the *Arabian* woods embost,

[34] John Rogers, 'The Secret of *Samson Agonistes*', in *The Miltonic Samson*, ed. Albert C. Labriola, Milton Studies, 33 (1996), 118, 120.

> That no second knows or third,
> And lay erewhile a Holocaust,
> From out her ashy womb now teem'd,
> Revives, reflourishes, then vigorous most
> When most unactive deem'd   (ll.1695–1705)

Samson in his final act is not a Nazarite who asks the priest to make an offering in atonement for his violation ('facietque sacerdos unum pro peccato'; 6: 11, Vulgate), nor is he a Christian relying on the crucifixion as the ultimate sacrifice that fulfils Christ's priestly office. 'Like that self-begott'n bird', Samson has within himself the power of life and death. Attempting to transcend human nature as understood by Judaism and Christianity, Milton's Samson offers himself as a sacrifice entirely sufficient. He has suffered greatly, and he is the strongest man who ever lived: 'For never was from Heaven imparted | Measure of strength so great to mortal seed' (ll.1438–9). The Chorus, addressing God, calls Samson 'once thy glorious Champion, | The Image of thy strength and mighty minister' (ll.705–6).

Milton's Adam, under a Pauline conception of the law after the Fall, can never satisfy God's rigour. God and his Son know that he is bankrupt: 'Atonement for himself or offering meet, | Indebted and undone, hath none to bring' (*PL*, iii. 234–5). Only Christ's satisfaction through torture and death ('on mee let thine anger fall'; *PL*, iii. 237) can atone for sinful humankind. But no one tells Samson—as Adam tells Eve and the Father tells the Son—that as a mere human he lacks the ability to expiate his crime. There is a connection between the monism of the tragedy—Samson all used up, crushed like a grape offered as libation—and the desire to be oneself a 'Man . . . [who] | Shall satisfy for Man' (*PL*, iii. 294–5). As a Nazarite, Samson 'served the Lord in a more strict manner than other did',[35] and perhaps for the sake of the spiritual capital he has laid up God will forgive the rest of the debt. The cost of grace—of sacrificing a part of one's identity to live transplanted in Christ—is unaffordable to *Samson's* creator, whose strength and suffering are themselves not inconsiderable.

Samson insists that his final act will be 'of my own accord' (l.1643), and the Reformation commentators interpret this piously. For Matthew Poole, Samson remains a judge, who speaks of his own situation only to divert wrath from the nation that he represents:

And that in this Prayer he mentions only his Personal Injury, the loss of his Eyes, and not their Indignities to God and his People, must be ascribed to that prudent Care which he had, and declared upon former occasions, of deriving the Rage and Hatred of the *Philistines* upon himself alone, and diverting it from the people. For which end I conceive this Prayer was made with an audible Voice, though he knew they would

---

[35] Richard Rogers, *A Commentary upon the Whole Booke of Judges* (London: Felix Kyngston, 1615), 614.

entertain it only with Scorn and Laughter, which also he knew would quickly be turned into Mourning.[36]

But in *Samson Agonistes*, 'of my own accord', is a final assertion of independence.[37] In this tragedy, it is not Christ but Samson who is 'the end of the law', and annihilation coincides with fulfilment.

---

[36] Poole, *Annotations*, sig. Ccc1v.

[37] Peter Martyr recognizes that to act of one's own accord is to act contrary to the laws of the Nazarite. His Samson is 'bound by religion, not of hys owne accorde. . . . This man was moved by the spirite of God: neither did he these thinges of his owne wyl' (*A Commentarie upon the Book of Judges*, London: John Day, 1564), fo. 222.

5

Andrew Marvell, Samuel Parker, and the Rabbis on Zealots and Proselytes

Although they are not named—indeed, their identities are conspicuously, even teasingly withheld—John Selden and John Lightfoot, the two greatest Christian Hebraists of seventeenth-century England, stand behind the intermittent but fierce talmudic exchanges of Samuel Parker, Bishop of Oxford, and the poet Andrew Marvell. Parker is a vicious opponent, and for once the old *DNB*, which relishes the scurrilities it publishes about its clerical biographees, does not seem to exaggerate when it reports that he 'had the reputation of being a "covetous and ambitious man", who "seemed to have no other sense of religion but as a political interest and a subject of party and faction"'. The subtitle of Parker's polemic *Discourse of Ecclesiastical Politie* (1670, actually November 1669[1]) explains why he anticipates a hostile response from the nonconformists and other dissenters he would persecute: *Wherein the Authority of the Civil Magistrate Over the Conscience of Subjects in Matters of Religion is Asserted: The Mischiefs and Inconveniences of Toleration are Represented. And All Pretenses Pleaded in behalf of Liberty of Conscience are Fully Answered.* Where Milton's Christ, in *Paradise Regained*, would 'make persuasion do the work of fear' (i. 223), Parker's stated purpose is 'to force [dissenters] to that modesty and obedience by severity of Laws to which all the strength of Reason in the world can never persuade them'. The opening words of his 'Preface to the Reader' introduce the subject of zeal that will reverberate in subsequent animadversions and defences:

I cannot Imagine any thing, that our Dissenting Zealots will be able to object against this Ensuing Treatise, unless perhaps in some Places the Vehemence and Severity of its Style; for cavil I know they must: and if they can raise no Tolerable Exceptions against the Reasonableness of the Discourse it self, it shall suffice to pick quarrels with Words and Phrases.[2]

---

[1] For the actual date, see the magisterial edition of *The Prose Works of Andrew Marvell*, gen. ed. Annabel Patterson (New Haven and London: Yale University Press, 2003), i. p. xlv. This chapter is heavily indebted to both the Yale Marvell and to G. J. Toomer, the most generous and meticulous of correspondents.

[2] Samuel Parker, *A Discourse of Ecclesiastical Politie* (1669), Preface, p. i. Parenthetic page references to the *Discourse* in the body of the chapter are to this edition.

Zeal is the theme of the entire preface, which condemns the nonconformists as specifically Jewish, pharisaic fanatics, while the author initially characterizes himself by contrast as 'a Person of such a tame and softly humour, and so cold a Complexion, that he thinks himself scarce capable of hot and passionate Impressions' (p. i). If he occasionally uses invective, it is deliberate and controlled, 'and if there be any Tart and Upbraiding Expressions, they were not the Dictates of Anger and Passion, but of the Just and Pious Resentment of [the Author's] mind' (p. i). And yet, given the need to awaken authority to the dangers posed by fanatics to the welfare and security of the nation, who could 'so perfectly Charm and Stupifie his Passions, as not to be chased into some heat & briskness [?]' (p. ii); 'who I say, that loves and adores the Spirit of true Religion, can forbear to be sharp and severe to such thick and fulsome abuses?' (p. iv). Finally, he must justify his own zeal, and he knows 'but one single Instance, in which Zeal, or a high Indignation is just and warrantable; and that is when it vents it self against the Arrogance of haughty, peevish, and sullen Religionists' (p. iv).

Thus the only hot fit of Zeal we find our Saviour in, was kindled by an Indignation against the Pride and Insolence of the Jews, when he whipt the Buyers and Sellers out of the outward Court of the Temple: For though they bore a blind and superstitious Reverence towards that part of it, that was peculiar to their own Worship, yet as for the outward Court, the place where the Gentiles and Proselytes worship't, that was so unclean and unhallowed, that they thought it could not be prophaned, by being turn'd into an Exchange of Usury. Now this Insolent Contempt of the Gentiles, and impudent conceit of their own holiness, provoked the mild Spirit of our Blessed Saviour to such an height of Impatience and Indignation as made him with a seeming fury and transport of passion whip the Tradesmen thence, and overthrow the Tables. So hateful is all proud, testy, and factious Zeal to a loving and Divine Temper of mind. (p. v)

Parker had predicted in his opening sentence that his enemies would 'pick quarrels with words and phrases', and indeed he would feel the need to defend at great length in future animadversions his use of 'fury' and 'transport' in connection with Jesus Christ. But while defending himself on this very point against the chiding of John Owen in his immediate response to the *Discourse, Truth and Innocence Vindicated* (December 1669), Parker goes even farther:

the true Reason why I used these Expressions, was, because our blessed Saviour did in that Action take upon him the Person and the Priviledge of the Jewish Zelots; a sort of Men that profest to be transported by some extraordinary impulse, beyond the ordinary Rules of Law and Decency, and by consequence must be acted with a greater heat and vehemence of spirit; and therefore when our Saviour imitated their way of proceeding, it must needs carry in it a great appearance of their passionate and extatick Zeal.[3]

In both the *Rehearsal Transpros'd* (1672) and *Rehearsal Transpros'd: The Second Part* (1673), Andrew Marvell vehemently attacks Parker's depictions of Christ in

---

[3] Samuel Parker, *A Defence and Continuation of the Ecclesiastical Politie* (1671), 151–2.

both the *Discourse* and the *Defence*. At the conclusion of his first attack on Parker, he calls attention to

> that most unsafe passage of our *Saviour, being not only in an hot fit of zeal, but in a seeming fury and transport of Passion*. And striving to unhook himself hence. p. 152. of his Second Book, #he# swallows it deeper, saying, *Our blessed Saviour did in that action take upon him the Person and Priviledge of a Jewish Zelot*. Take upon him the Person, that is *Personam induere*. And what part did he play? Of a *Jewish Zelot*. The Second Person of the Trinity (may I repeat these things without offence) to take upon him the person of a Jewish Zelot, that is, of a notorious Rogue and Cut-throat. This seemed to proceed from too slight an Apprehension and knowledge of the duty we owe to our Saviour.[4]

Marvell takes up the same cudgel in the second part of the *Rehearsal Transpros'd*, which is a response to Parker's *A Reproof to the Rehearsal Transpros'd* (1673):

> You had said our Saviour in chasing the Sellers out of the Temple (Tradesmen you call them) had *put on, out of an hot fit of Zeal, a seeming fury and transport of Passion, and that he took upon him in that Action the Person and Priviledg of a Jewish Zealot*. This I found fault with in my former book . . . and with good reason, if you would but consider that you say, *A well-meaning Zealot is the worst of all Villains*. You still defend it here by the Examples of Phineas [Numbers 10–11] and Elias [1 Kings 18: 40]; and to have been *a Power, or at least a license for private persons to execute by publick authority notorious Malefactors, upon the place, without form and process of Law*. . . . This Priviledg is very far fetch'd, and long discontinued, if from the time of Phineas and Elias until our Saviour, there were no new Claim enter'd. But really it seems to me, by this and some other passages, that you do not attribute much belief to the Miracles of our Saviour, among which perhaps this was one of the most remarkable.[5]

To prove that Christ's driving the money-changers out of the temple was a miraculous act—otherwise, Christ would not have been able to carry it out with impunity—Marvell cites Grotius in his *Annotationes in Libros Evangeliorum* (Amsterdam, 1641), 'who ought to be of as much value with you as all the [other authorities] put together': Christ cleansed his father's house, the temple in Jerusalem, 'by the Majesty of his Divine Power'.[6]

More than once, Marvell accuses Parker of inconsistency when he condemns a well-meaning zealot as the worst of villains, '(even more dangerous it seems then a malicious and ill-meaning Zelot)',[7] and yet argues, in defence of his own righteous indignation, that Christ 'took upon him . . . the Person and Priviledge of a Jewish Zealot'. Marvell pokes gruesome fun at Parker for his presumption verging on blasphemy. But Henry Stubbe points out that in this instance Marvell is showing his ignorance. Stubbe (1632–76), 'the most noted Latinist and

---

[4] Andrew Marvell, *The Rehearsal Transpros'd, Prose Works*, i. 201–2. The Yale editors correct 'Zelot' to 'Zealot'.

[5] Marvell, *The Rehearsal Transpros'd: the Second Part, Prose Works*, i. 394–5.

[6] Grotius, cited in *Prose Works*, i. 395.

[7] Marvell, *Rehearsal Transpros'd, Prose Works*, i. 106

Grecian of his age' according to Anthony à Wood, raises gravamina against both Parker and Marvell in *Rosemary & Bayes: Or, Animadversions upon a Treatise Called, The Rehearsall Trans-prosed. In a letter to a Friend in the Countrey* (1672). In his play *The Rehearsal*, George Villiers, 2nd Duke of Buckingham, had satirized the conventions of heroic drama by basing his character Bayes on the poet laureate John Dryden. According to Marvell, Bayes and Dryden 'symbolize' one another. (This adds another dimension to Marvell's great lines, 'How vainly men themselves amaze | To win the palm, the oak, or bays.'). N. H. Keeble explains the relationship: 'Parker's priestcraft [at least according to Marvell] is of a piece with Bayes' stagecraft; his pronouncements on ecclesiastical policy deserve no more respect than do Bayes' pronouncements on dramatic technique.'[8] Stubbe, author of *An Essay in Defence of the Good Old Cause* (1659), criticizes Parker for his politics, but he is even more severe with Marvell (whom he calls Mr. Rosemary) for his lapses in scholarship. The name rosemary represents a falling-off from the bay laurel, the *Laurus nobilis*, just as for Stubbe Marvell's transprosed *Rehearsal* is markedly inferior to Buckingham's original.[9] After transcribing verbatim the attacks on Parker regarding Christ as Jewish zealot, Stubbe spends much of his letter pointing out Marvell's lapse in scholarship on the particular matter of zeal:

I am willing to believe that Mr. *Rosemary* did write this out of an *hearty zeal* for the honour of our blessed *Saviour*; but yet his *zeal is not according to knowledge*: Others may think that He intended to *scourge Bayes*, and cast *Him out of the Temple*, allotting unto *Him* for *changing* thus *of our Saviour* the same *doom* whereunto those were *sentenced* who *changed moneys* there. . . . After all this *blustering in Verse*, and in *Prose*: be pleased Sir to understand that *Rosemary* knows not the nature of a true *Jewish Zealot*: He had read, or heard some body tell out of *Josephus* his History of the destruction of *Jerusalem*, that there were a sort of *Zealots*, who out of a vehement and indiscreet concern for the *Mosaical Law*, begot great tumults, occasion'd much blood-shed, and were the *principal cause* of the ruine of that *State*. To compare *Christ* with *one of these*, this seemed *uncouth*, and intolerable in a *Christian*. But, behold there were another sort of *Zealots* permitted by God in the *Jewish Common-wealth*, who might *destroy their friends, kill even their sons*, if guilty of *Idolatry*: such was *Phineas*, such was *Matthias*: and in cases of great enormities & violations of the *Mosaical Law*, the actings of *Zealots* for Reformation, were approved as *Heroical*, and exempt from *judiciary censures or penalties*. Any man, of *ordinary sense*, will imagine that *our Saviour* did (since he was not *questioned* for the fact, nor *opposed* in it) assume the person of such a *Zealot*, and was secured by the *Law for Zealots*: for *it behoved*

---

[8] N. H. Keeble, 'Why Transpose *The Rehearsal?*' in *Marvell and Liberty*, ed. Warren Chernaik and Martin Dzelzainis (New York: St Martin's, 1999), 256; cited in *Prose Works of Andrew Marvell*, i. 10.

[9] Stubbe, *Rosemary & Bayes*, 5. After noting that Marvell's 'Bayes Junior' descends from Buckingham's 'Bayes Senior', 'as good Timber may by corruption produce Worms or Vermin', he adds: 'should I inlarge myself never so much in commendation of the REHEARSAL, the REHEARSAL-TRANSPROSED would derive no advantage thence.' Additionally, it was rumoured that Marvell had suffered an 'accident' in his youth—hence 'Milton the stallion, | Marvell the gelding'. Stubbe's repetition of the name 'Rosemary', frequently without the title 'Mr.', might be a sexual insult.

him to fulfill all Righteousness, at least *He came not to destroy the Law*. . . . Mr. *Selden*
[marginal note: 'Selden *de jure natur.* Heb. l. 4. c. 4, 5.'] authenticates the *Ecclesiastical
Historian*; neither is there any *just offence* in the expression.[10]

Stubbe greatly admired Selden, and his *Defence of the Good Old Cause* includes
numerous pages of directly transcribed pages from *De Jure Naturali et Gentium.
Juxta Disciplinam Ebraeorum.* The reference to *De Jure* on zeal is the only
marginal note in *Rosemary & Bayes*, but there are other places in this short
pamphlet where Selden's presence can be traced. Stubbe appeals to *Fleta* (Selden's
Dissertatio was appended to the 1647 *editio princeps*) against Parker and the
inseparability of civil and ecclesiastical power: 'if you will ask *Fleta* what power
our Kings had *antecedently* unto the Rule of Henry VIII. He had no more than
totam laicalem potestatem, a *Large power:* . . . If we look into *ancient Governments* . . . there is no such *Connexion* betwixt the CROWN and MITRE.'[11] And in
an extraordinary digression on the secret and real reasons behind certain great
events, he identifies the true cause of the English Civil War:

There was such a *conjunction of causes* which produced those dire effects, that 'tis a *fallasie*
to assign *one efficient* thereof: If I were to deduce its origine, I should fix upon the two
books, *Ignoramus*, and *Selden of Tythes*, as the occasion thereof: besides which, there were
some that wanted *white staves* [grants of arms depicting heralds holding white staves],
some that were *disappointed in their Amours*, some that were *made Cuckolds*, some that
envied the *splendour* and *magnificence* of others, which they themselves *could not*, or *would
not* imitate. These (and such like accidents) were the *true occasions*, the rest were only
coincident, or *pretences* assumed, whilst the *restless, ambitious* and *malicious Spirits*, abused
the *well-meaning Patriots*, and *Zealots*.[12]

Stubbe adds subsidiary reasons, the proliferation of lawyers and '*the property of
the Subject, Meum & Teum*', being more likely causes than '*Sibthorps* Sermon'.[13]
But he attaches great importance to Selden's treatment of tithes as a matter of
variable civil right, not due to the clergy by *jure divino*, and to a satire performed
by a body of Cambridge undergraduates before James in 1614. G. R. Toomer has
recently dismissed 'as a contemporary canard the story retailed by Thomas Fuller

---

[10] Stubbe, *Rosemary & Bayes*, pp. 13–14.

[11] Ibid. 3.

[12] Ibid. 19.

[13] Ibid. According to S. R. Gardiner, in *A History of England under the Duke of Buckingham and
Charles I. 1624–1628* (London: Longmans, 1875), ii. 173, Robert Sibthorpe's assize sermon,
Apostolical Obedience, preached on 22 February 1627, 'set forth the Royal pretensions [to irresistible
power] with irritating plainness of speech'. Sibthorp took as his text Romans 13: 7: 'Render
therefore to all their due.' Charles hoped to use it as a manifesto on behalf of a forced loan. See
also 'Archbishop Abbot, his Narrative', in John Rushworth, *Historical Colllections* (London, 1721), i.
444, which reports that Dr Worral, chaplain to the Bishop of London, assigned to review the text for
licensing, consulted Selden on the matter: 'When the chaplain entered Selden's chamber, he was
greeted with the expostulation: "What have you done? You have allowed a strange book yonder! If it
be true, there is no *meum* or *teum*; no man in England has anything of his own! If ever the tide turns,
and matters be called to a reckoning, you will be hanged for publishing such a book! . . . You must
scrape out your name. Do not suffer so much as a sign of any letter to remain in the paper." '

that Selden wrote [his *Historie of Tithes*] in revenge' for this skit that he took as an attack on himself and his common law colleagues.[14]

Although Stubbe's radical politics would have made him more sympathetic to Marvell than to Parker, he is a principled arbiter. Marvell had accused Parker of saying that Christ took 'upon him the person of a Jewish Zelot, that is, a notorious Rogue and Cut-throat'. At first Stubbe seems to suggest that Marvell, using the phrase, '*Personam induere*', might have gone even farther: 'He might also have taken notice that *personam induere* doth also signifie to put on a *perruke* and *Visor-mask*; and have with *abomination* declaimed against *Bayes*, for introducing the *Second person in the Trinity* acting a modern *Mascarade* in the *Temple*.'[15] But in fact Stubbe finds no offence in the phrase, pointing out that the risen Christ appeared to Mary Magdalene as a gardener (John 20: 15) and to disciples on the road to Emmaus as a traveller (Luke 24: 13–35). Marvell's specific attack on zeal is 'the dictate of extreme malice', and Parker's '*Personam induere*' is 'an *innocent expression* invidiously misconstrued'. And as for Parker's alleged identification of Jewish zealots with rogues and cut-throats, Stubbe concludes, 'Sir, I have examined him [Parker] strictly, but no *torture of the Rack produceth this to be his sense.*'[16]

An even stricter examination would have turned up the source of Marvell's perhaps wilful misconstruing. It is not Christ or Jewish zealots but Marvell himself whom Parker impugns as a false prophet:

though we have no Laws against counterfeit Prophets, because it is rare for any man in these Northern Climates to arrive to that degree of Impudence and Vanity, yet among the *Jewish Zealots* they were punish'd more severely than *notorious Rogues and Cut-throats.*[17]

In this exchange, Marvell had accused Parker of having 'paved a broad Causeway' to a heaven so accessible 'that one may fly thither without Grace'. Parker in response uses the term *ruach hakodesh*, which in rabbinic texts denotes divine inspiration, to ridicule Marvell as a false prophet who presumes to know the ways of God:

You know that he never intended Church-men for Ministers of State! You know what he intends! away you wretch! If you have any spark of Modesty unextinguish'd, retire into your Closet and lament and pine away for these desperate Blasphemies. The *Ruac Hakodesh* dwell in such a distemper'd and polluted mind as yours! it may as soon unite it self to a Swine. *Fatuos & hujus terrae filios quod attinet* (says a Jewish Zealot) *non magis*

---

[14] G. J. Toomer, 'Selden's *Historie of Tithes*: Genesis, Publication, Aftermath', *Huntington Library Quarterly*, 65 (2002), 346. Regarding this tradition, see also *Ioannis Seldeni ad Fletam Dissertatio*, ed. David Ogg (Cambridge: Cambridge University Press, 1925), Introduction, p. xlviii. Ogg cites Paulus Colomesius's *Vie de Jean Selden* (MS Bodley 1022, fo. 20). Professor Toomer persuasively identifies far more reasonable incentives for writing the work, although Stubbe's passage deals with secret and unadmitted motives behind public acts.

[15] Stubbe, *Rosemary & Bayes*, 11.

[16] Ibid. 12–13.

[17] Parker, *A Reproof to the Rehearsal Transpros'd* (1673), 327.

nostro judicio prophetare possunt quam asinus & rana. Asses and Tod-poles may as soon expect the Impressions of the divine Spirit as such dunces and sots as you.

Marvell's reply is brief and witty when, after repeating Parker's accusation, he adds, 'I doubt your *Ruac Hakodesh* is but at best a *Bath col.*'[18] Both John Lightfoot's text in *Horae Hebraicae et Talmudicae* and a marginal note in Selden's *De Jure* ('*Gemar. Babylon. ad tit.* Sanhedrin *cap. 1. fol. 11. & c.*') point to the Talmud's explanation for the decline from direct inspiration to mere echo (*bat kol*, Hebrew, lit. 'daughter of a voice', a lesser means of communicating with the divine): 'Our rabbis taught, Since the death of the last prophets, Haggai, Zechariah and Malachi, the Holy Spirit [the *ruach hakodesh* of prophetic inspiration] departed from Israel; yet they were still able to avail themselves of the Bath-kol.'[19]

Stubbe correctly identifies 'Selden *de jure natur.* Heb. l.4, c. 4, 5' as the source that authenticates Parker's comments on Christ as a Jewish zealot. Parker admires Selden's scholarship, though not unreservedly. Marvell demonstrates convincingly 'how civil [Parker is] to [his] friends and of consequence how generous to [his] enemies' by listing some of his censures of scholars whose general excellence he must grudgingly concede, including Galen, Pico, William Harvey, Lipsius, '*Scaliger, Selden, Bochart, Vossius, ay and Grotius*'.[20] While still in his mid-twenties, Parker had published *A Free and Impartial Censure of the Platonick Philosophie* (1666), comprising equal parts of sound scholarship and bad temper. He derides the Platonists themselves (self-styled inspired priests, 'as if they had written with a kind of *Bacchical Enthusiasme . . .* as if they were inspired at least by a *Bath-col*') as well as 'credulous' Renaissance Egyptologists such as Athanasius Kircher. He also rejects Selden's opinion that Plato and Pythagoras were familiar with Jewish scholarship, Pythagoras having received his most important ideas from Jews in Egypt, either directly or else from Egyptian priests who were conversant with 'the Mosaick writings' and the 'Oral Tradition . . . תורה שבעל פה':[21]

though *Numa Pompilius* is generally acknowledged the first *Pythagorean* (being more ancient then *Pythagorus*) yet there is not the least appearance of any commerce between him and the Jewes. And therefore when Mr. *Selden* [marginal note: '*De Jure Nat. & Gent. l.1.c.2*'] thinks that if those 7 Books of Wisdome found in the Field of *Petilius . . .* and

---

[18] Marvell, *Rehearsal Transpros'd, Prose Works*, i. 82; Parker, *Reproof,* 326; Marvell, *The Rehearsal Transpros'd: The Second Part, Prose Works*, i. 414.

[19] As will be discussed below, Marvell's source for this and almost all other talmudic scholarship is John Lightfoot's *Horae Hebraicae et Talmudicae. In Evangelium Matthaei* (Cambridge, 1658). See his commentary on Matthew 3: 17 ('and behold, a voice from heaven'). See also John Selden, *De Jure Naturali et Gentium* (1640), 1.9, p. 116. It is likely that Lightfoot borrowed from the scholar whom he called 'the great Mr. Selden, the Learnedst man upon the earth'. See his *The Harmony, Chronicle and Order of the Old Testament* (1647), sig. B3r.

[20] Marvell, *The Rehearsal Transpros'd: The Second Part, Prose Works*, i. 397–9.

[21] Parker, *A Free and Impartial Censure of the Platonick Philosophie*, 83 (on the Platonists), 104 (on Kircher), and 93 (on Plato and Pythagoras).

attributed to *Numa* by an Inscription upon the Chest in which they were, were really his, that he was probably not unacquainted with the Discipline of the *Hebrews*...the best foundation of the conjecture is the (deserved) greatness of his own *name* and *authority*, for you cannot but perceive that in it self 'tis very fond & frivolous.[22]

It is revealing of Parker's character that most of his uncritical appropriations of Selden in his later scholarship, including his extensive comments on Jewish zeal, are unacknowledged. His 'Preface to the Reader' in the *Discourse* quotes the same verses that conclude Selden's *De Jure*:

> Non monstrare vias eadem nisi sacra colenti,
> Quaesitum ad fontem solos deducere verpos.[23]

Attacking Jewish xenophobia, the verses describe the Jews 'forbidding to point out the way to any not worshipping the same rites, and conducting none but the circumcised to the desired fountain'. But where Selden identifies the source, Juvenal's '*Satyr 14*', Parker does not. And where Selden calls the accusation an example of the poet's hyperbole, Parker accepts it as an accurate picture of 'the Jewish Bigots'.

Parker's authority on all questions pertaining to zeal is Selden, whose comprehensive and ultimately Maimonidean chapters on the right of zealots, the *Ius Zelotarum*, interpret Christ's scourging of the money-changers as an act in accordance with the laws of normative Judaism. Selden discusses this law in at least three separate works, altering and developing in ways that Grotius could never have anticipated a point made in *De Jure Belli ac Pacis*: 'by the Law of *Moses*, any private Man might upon the Spot, and with his own Hands, kill a *Jew* who had forsaken GOD and his Law, or who attempted to seduce his Brother to Idolatry. The *Hebrews* call this the *Judgment of Zeal*, which was first put in Execution by *Phineas*, and afterwards passed into a Custom.'[24]

Selden fills his chapters with diverse biblical examples of zeal, including Numbers 25: 6–15 (Phineas's slaying of Zimri and Cosbi, which earns him a covenant of perpetual priesthood), 1 Maccabees 2: 23–6 (Mattathias's slaying of a Jew who was about to offer a sacrifice in public on a pagan altar), Matthew 21: 12–17 (Jesus's scourging and driving out the money-changers from the temple), John 18: 22 (one of Caiaphas's officers striking Jesus on the face), Acts 7: 57 (the

---

[22] Ibid. 103–4. For Selden on Plato and Pythagoras as learned in Jewish lore, See *De Jure Naturali*, 1.2, pp. 13 ff. On Pythagoras's circumcision, the result of Jewish persuasion, see 1.2, p. 15.

[23] Selden, *De Jure*, 846; Parker, *Discourse*, p. vi. The quotation illustrates two of the three duties toward strangers that the ancient world considered to be incumbent on everyone: showing them the way and allowing them to drink (the third is allowing them to kindle fire from yours).

[24] *The Rights of War and Peace*, tr. J. Barbeyrac (1738), 2.20.9, p. 414, cited by Selden in *De Jure*, 4.4, p. 490. Discussing zeal in *De Synedriis* 2.3, in *Joannis Selden Opera Omnia*, ed. David Wilkins (1726), i. 1529, Selden points to his earlier discussions of the topic, mainly in *De Jure*, book 4, chs. 3–5, but also in *De Successione in Pontificatum*, book 1, ch. 8. After citing his own work, he adds, 'videsis Maimon. tit. *Sanhedrin* cap. 18 [sect.] 6'.

stoning of Stephen), and Acts 23: 13 (the oath to kill Paul).[25] Despite these examples, Selden's argument is decidedly rabbinic rather than biblical. He begins with a central text to explicate, a *mishnah* from tractate Sanhedrin that he cites in both the Babylonian and Jerusalem texts of the Talmud, even noting a textual variant in the latter. The *mishnah* promulgates a law whereby zealots are to punish one who commits an act of sacrilege by stealing the service vessels of the temple, or curses by enchantment, or cohabits with an Aramean woman (i.e. a Gentile). If a priest performs the temple service while ritually unclean, his fellow priests do not charge him with this offence at a court (a *beth din*). Rather, the young priests take him out of the temple court and crush his skull with cudgels.[26]

In this instance, the different moral valences of the acts of zeal recorded in scripture are of less interest to lawyer Selden than the binding precept of the *mishnah*, an example of *halakha*, that is, a rabbinic 'legal decision regarding a matter or case for which there is no direct enactment in the Mosaic law, deduced by analogy from this law or from the scriptures' (OED). What should be emphasized, even at the risk of repetition, is the fact that where other exegetes in seventeenth-century England blame the rabbis for distorting the meaning of the Hebrew Bible with the severity of their laws, Selden recognizes that *halakha* imposes restrictions in order to prevent the enforcement of laws that authorize violence. In this case, the Talmud requires that the zealot act only at the moment the offence is being committed and that ten Israelites witness it.[27] And Maimonides, the great codifier cited more often by Selden than any other authority Christian or Jewish, goes much farther, moderating even the strictures of the rabbis. In a commentary on the *mishnah* to which Selden refers, he limits the various punishments. To be punished by a zealot, one must be an apostate who has denied the fundamental tenets of the religion ['הכופר בעקר *eo qui renuntiasset Fundamento*']. Moreover, one who cohabits with a heathen woman must do it in the presence of ten Israelites or more. After the intimate act, or if there is no assembly of Israelites present, or if she is not an idolatress, the zealot is forbidden to kill the offender. And if the transgressor killed an attacking zealot in order to save his own life, he is not liable to be executed, because the zealot was pursuing him to kill him, and the Torah does not decree the death penalty except in the manners prescribed. However, the offender is liable to extirpation by

[25] Selden, *De Jure*, 4.4, p. 490; 4.5, p. 498.
[26] Ibid. 4.4, p. 487, citing 'Tit. *Sanhedrin* cap. 9, [sect.] ult. Gemar. Babylon. ibid. fol. 81 b. & c. Hierosolymit. eod. tit. fol. 27. col. 2. [sect.] 11': '*Qui Sacrilegium commiserat* (et sacra nempe supellectili quid furatus erat;) *qui per Idolum maledixerat* (Numini) *qui coitu se miscuerat cum foemina Aramaea,* id est extera seu plane Gentili, *Zelotis fas fuit incurrere in eum* [marginal note: 'בדהן in eos *codice Hierosolymitano*']. *Sacerdotem in immunditie sua sacra obeuntem, non erat necesse ut sacerdotes caeteri in forum deducerent: sed sacerdotes qui per aetatem nondum ministerio sacro pares erant, eum extra atrium protrahebant, & cerebrum ejus fustibus elidebant.*'
[27] Ibid., where the opening words of the chapter emphasize that the zealot must act while the crime is being committed: 'in *ipso dum committebatur facinus duntaxat momento*'. For required witnesses, see p. 488, 'in Publico'.

Heaven (Hebrew: *karet*) for cohabiting with an idolatress. Even though such extirpation is not mentioned in the Torah and is not enumerated among the list of those liable to extirpation, nevertheless, it is a tradition, and its explanation is based on a scriptural phrase: 'and hath been intimate with the daughter of a strange god; the Lord will extirpate the man that doeth this' (Malachi 2: 12).[28]

In both *De Jure* and *De Synedriis* (which, as we shall see, Parker has also read) Selden cites striking pronouncements—both pagan and Jewish—on the *Ius Zelotarum* unchecked by the merciful limitations of rabbinic Judaism. He quotes extensively from Philo, whose comments on subversives who entice their fellow Israelites into the worship of other gods (Deuteronomy 13: 1–18) ignore that chapter's insistence (in verse 14) that inquiry and thorough investigation precede the bringing of charges and punishment: 'And his seductions ought to be made known to all lovers of piety, who [may be expected to] attack the wicked one without delay, having deemed it their holy duty [lit. the duty of sanctity] to kill such a man.'[29] Selden takes note of the medieval law of England's ordaining that an outlawed person be given over to the power of everyone that would kill him. Some thought that those persons who incurred a praemunire were liable to the same fate, but this was expressly guarded against by parliamentary statute, not an insignificant fact for an advocate of parliamentary rights.[30]

It is Selden's *tour de force* in *De Jure* 4.5 that draws Bishop Parker's attention, a rabbinic commentary on the cleansing of the temple (Matt. 21: 12–13, Mark 11: 15–19, Luke 19: 45–8, John 2: 13–22) that sees Jesus as a Jew acting according to the *Ius Zelotarum*. Relying on numerous talmudic texts and the commentaries of Maimonides and Obadiah of Bertinoro, among others, Selden describes in meticulous detail each of the thirteen chests, called שופרות or trumpets, with narrow mouths and wide bellies, that collected monies in the temple in Jerusalem: in the first, the money of the present year, in the second that of the year past,

---

[28] Ibid. 488: 'vide Maimonid. Halach. *Rotzach*. cap. 4. & halach. *Sanhedrin* cap. 18. & halach. *Aboda Zara* cap. 10.' See the next marginal note on the same page, which includes references to Moses of Coucy's commentary on the positive and negative laws of the Torah, which draws heavily on Maimonides' *Mishneh Torah*, and to Joseph Caro's *Code*, which relies for its decisions on Maimonides, Isaac Alfasi, and Asher b. Jehiel: 'Videsis, etiam Maimonid. halach. *Memarim* cap. 3. Mos. Mikotzi *praec. Negativ.* 163. Shulcan Aruch tit. *Iore dea* cap. 158.'

[29] Selden, *De Synedriis*, 2.3, in *Opera*, i. 1529: '*Et illecebrae ejus emittendae sunt ad omnes pietatis amatores, qui absque mora in scelestum irruant, rati sanctitatis officium talem hominem occidere.*' Philo, *De Specialibus Legibus* I, 315–16, in *Philo*, ed. F. H. Colson, Loeb Classical Library (London and Cambridge, Mass.: Heinemann and Harvard University Press, 1937), vii. 283. See also *De Specialibus Legibus*, I, 55, Loeb Edition, vii. 131. For the editor's attempt to temper Philo's brutal comments, see Appendices, *Philo*, vii. 617: 'That [Philo] should be seriously encouraging his fellow-Jews in Alexandria, where we know that the Jews had independent jurisdiction, to put apostates to death without any legal trial, seems to me almost impossible. But was it perhaps otherwise in other cities of the Dispersion, where the Jews had no such privilege and knew that the ordinary courts would not take cognizance of apostasy or heresy?'

[30] Selden, *De Synedriis*, 2.3, in *Opera* i. 1531: 'Sed sub Elizabetha regina sancito parliamentario [marginal note: 'Stat. 5. Eliz. cap. 1'] opinio abolita est.'

in the third the money that was offered to buy pigeons, etc.[31] Each person, no matter how poor, was required to pay exactly half a *sheqel*. Therefore, when he came to the exchanger to change a *sheqel* for two half-*sheqalim*, he was obliged to allow him some gain, which was called *kolbon* (Heb. קוֹלְבּוֹן, Gr. κολλυβος). And even when two paid one *sheqel* between them, each of them was obliged to allow the same gain or fee to the exchanger.[32]

Selden knows that the *kolbon* is a minute amount—one twenty-fourth of a half-*sheqel*, which Jesus paid for himself and Peter, presumably without objection (Matt. 17: 24–7)—but it still symbolizes trafficking for unholy gain. Christ's action can then be seen as a protest against the commercialization of the temple. His driving out the sheep and oxen has the practical effect of disrupting the sacrificial offerings, reminding the Christian reader of their replacement by the one unrepeatable sacrifice soon to come. What really captures Selden's imagination is John 2: 16: 'and said unto them that sold doves, Take these things hence; make not my Father's house a house of merchandise.' This immediately puts the disciples in mind of Psalm 69: 9: 'The zeal of thine house hath eaten me up.' And it dovetails in Selden's mind with a long-familiar talmudic passage that helps to explain Christ's vehemence: a *mishnah* in tractate *Sanhedrin* (24b) declares ineligible as either legal witnesses or judges gamblers with dice, 'pigeon-flyers', usurers, and traders in the produce of the sabbatical year. Selden discusses the various interpretations of the meaning of pigeon-flyers, including those who bet that their pigeon can outrace another's, and the view in Rashi's *Commentary* (the '*Glossa*') that it refers to those who train pigeons (*columbas*, pigeons or doves) to fight with each other—a form of cock-fighting.[33] As early as *De Diis Syris* (1617), before he could have been aware of the talmudic source, he notes that the Jews regarded those who handled doves as too low to give testimony and placed them on the same level as thieves, pimps, and dice-players ('fures nempe, lenones, aleatores'). This information Selden found in Philippus Ferdinandus's translation of a commentary on the 613 precepts by the obscure Abraham ben Hassan (incorrectly transcribed by Philippus as 'Kattan'), *Praecepta in Monte Sinai* (Cambridge, 1597).[34]

---

[31] Selden, *De Jure*, 4.5, pp. 492–3. It is almost certain that John Lightfoot has relied on this chapter in his commentary on Matthew 21:12. See his *Horae Hebraicae et Talmudicae. In Evangelium Matthaei*, pp. 230–32. Though he draws on some of the same rabbinic sources as Selden, he says nothing about Jesus as a Jewish zealot.

[32] Selden, *De Jure*, 492–4.

[33] Ibid. 494–95: '*columbas volare docentes*', '*excitant eas ad certamen mutuum*'. For a reminder that real doves may differ from our 'dream of a dove that saves, | Picasso's or the Pope's', see Anthony Hecht's poem 'Birdwatchers of America,' in *The Hard Hours* (New York: Atheneum, 1981), 57.

[34] Selden *De Diis Syris* (1617), 185. Regarding the source of additional information on the *venditores*, the sellers of doves, Selden notes: 'quod appendix Ferdinandi Poloni ad Abrahamum Ben-Kattun me primum docuit.' G. J. Toomer points out that Selden underlines 'Qui alunt columbas' among those barred from giving testimony in his copy of *Praecepta in Monte Sinai* at the Bodleian. For information on the author and his book, see Siegfried Stein, 'Philippus Ferdinandus Polonus', in *Essays in Honour of the Very Rev. Dr. J. H. Hertz*, ed. I. Epstein, E. Levine, and C. Roth (London:

A favourite theme, repeated in Selden's mature scholarship, and occasioned by the references to pigeons and doves in the gospels and in tractate *Sanhedrin*, is the importance of contributing to the public good. In both *De Jure* and *De Synedriis*, Selden quotes the *mishnah* in Sanhedrin 24b, the *gemara* that develops the *mishnah*, and the commentaries on the Talmud, to emphasize the importance of productivity and the moral imperative to contribute to the welfare of civilization. The four types of people enumerated in the *mishnah* have not habituated themselves to 'performing acts of charity and humane conduct'. Maimonides, in his commentary on the *mishnah*, explains further:

[such a person] is occupying himself with something that has no value for the general welfare of human society. It is a fundamental principle of Judaism that a person should occupy himself in this world with one of two things: either with Torah to perfect his soul with its wisdom, or with an occupation which contributes to the general welfare of society such as a trade or a business. It is proper to lessen the latter and increase the former as the Sages said: 'Lessen your involvement in business activities and occupy yourself with the Torah' (*Aboth*, 4: 10).[35]

This injunction must have resonated with Selden, whose torah was law and legal history, and who turned down offers of high office and additional income (he was wealthy enough already) in order to concentrate on his studies. His endorsement of the view that productivity should be a prerequisite for full citizenship is

---

Edward Goldston, 1942), 397–412. Stein notes that Philippus's book lists the seven Noachide laws, perhaps the first occasion on which Selden came across them. Abraham ben Hassan's list of the Torah's precepts was published in the Bomberg Rabbinical Bible of 1516–17, which Selden also owned. In his later scholarship Selden understandably preferred the fuller commentary on the precepts by Moses of Coucy. Philippus Ferdindandus was a converted Jew of Polish origin (hence 'Polonus'), who spent time with the Karaites in Constantinople, taught Hebrew and Arabic at Cambridge, then went to Leiden, where he taught Scaliger Hebrew. Another underscored passage in Selden's copy of Ferdinand's book, noted by Stein, is a reference to the patriotic sincerity of the Jews, not found in other early modern Christian sources. Regarding what he identifies as the Torah's sixty-fifth negative commandment, 'Thou shalt not revile judges nor curse the ruler in thy people' (Exodus 22: 27), Ferdinand comments: 'This the Jews observe, and they pray for the king under whom they live and honour him as if he had come from their own people' (Stein, 402).

[35] For Selden on what can loosely be called *tikkun olam* (repairing the world), see *De Jure*, 4.5, pp. 494–5, where he cites Obadiah of Bertinoro on the *mishnah*; and *De Synedriis, Opera*, i. 1425–6. In the latter, Selden's long list of sources may constitute a tactful way of emphasizing, in the face of Christian detraction, the consonance of biblical and talmudic negative views of usury. He makes it clear that the prohibition applies to the borrower as well as to the lender: 'Foeneratorum nomine non solum continetur hic המלוה seu *qui mutuo dat foenore*, verum etiam הלוה *qui mutuo accipit*. Nam ad utrumque interdicta sacra de foenore attinere scribunt. Ad hunc in Deuteronomio [note: 'Cap. xxiii.19']; ad illum Levitico' [note: 'Levit. xxv.37. Videsis ibid. Sal. Jarchium [Rashi], Mosem Kotzens.[Moses of Coucy] in Praecept. Negat. 193. praeter commentarios ad supra e Talmude locos indicatos']. Among the many examples in English literature of thieving, dicing, whoring, swearing, and borrowing—and thus of failing to advance public welfare—the figure of Falstaff looms large. See e.g. *1 Henry IV*, 3.3. 13–17: 'I was as virtuously given as a gentleman need to be, virtuous enough: swore little, dic'd not—above seven times a week; went to a bawdy-house not—above once in a quarter—of an hour; paid money that I borrowed—three or four times....'

reflected in his various positive formulations of the ancient passages requiring the promotion of public good.[36]

The Talmud itself objects to the profiteering from the sale of doves in the temple.[37] But according to Bishop Parker, in passages already quoted, when 'our Saviour imitated [the Jewish zealots'] way of proceeding', he was prompted less by commercial abuse than by the Jews' 'Insolent Contempt of the Gentiles, and impudent conceit of their own holiness'. What is for Selden an ancillary text in *De Jure* is the central text for Parker, Christ's citation, in Mark 11: 17, of Isaiah 56: 7, 'My house shall be called of all nations a house of prayer.' Selden discusses the universalist implications of 'all nations' ('*omnibus gentibus* seu *populis*'), which, in the context of the temple cleansing, objects primarily to the partitioning in the court of the Gentiles of non-Jews who came to the temple to offer sacrifices.[38] One wonders whether Parker's outrage over separate places of worship is related to belief in the equal sanctity of all human beings or, perhaps more likely in his case, to support of both the Act of Uniformity (1662), which 'removed from their livings any clergymen who would not subscribe to all the Thirty-Nine Articles',[39] and the Conventicle Act (1664), which prohibited more than five people (in addition to the household) from gathering to worship in separate places not officially authorized. Isaiah's vision of an ingathering of all nations might be appropriated for a scheme of coercive religious uniformity.

Although Christ's cleansing of the temple aroused the hostility of religious leaders, the *Ius Zelotarum* prevented them from arresting him immediately for disturbing the peace. Selden provides a balanced view of the law, recognizing its legitimacy for '*Homines pii*' acting within the legal framework of normative Judaism and in accordance with ancestral custom. He also knows that bad men will abuse this law, as later generations of the Hasmoneans did, whose corruptions Josephus described in '*De Bello Iudaic. lib. 4*', deeds prompted by 'close ambition varnished o'er with zeal'.[40] But he asserts that the law is ancient,

---

[36] Selden, *De Jure*, 494–5: '*incumbit rebus quae ad firmitudinem seculi*, id est ad bonum publicum seu vitae humanae commodum *spectant*'; '*quibus inest firmitudo seculi* aut *mundi*, quod vertimus, *quae bono publico utilia*.'

[37] See Mishnah, *Keritot* 1.7, Babylonian Talmud *Pesachim* 57a, and Jerusalem Talmud *Hagigah* 2.3. To correct abuses, Rabbi Simeon ben Gamaliel lowered the price of a pair of doves from a golden to a silver dinar and introduced a more lenient law regarding the number of obligatory offerings.

[38] Selden, *De Jure*, 497. On the court of the Gentiles, see tractate *Kelim*, Mishnah 1.8; and Babylonian Talmud tractate *Pesahim* 62a. The latter states that the non-Jew sends his offering—i.e. he doesn't accompany it to the altar.

[39] Introduction to *Rehearsal Transpros'd*, *Prose Works*, i. 4–5.

[40] For justification of the law while recognizing its potential for abuse, see *De Jure*, 489–90. Selden cites Josephus, '*De Bello Iudaic. lib. 4. cap. 12*' and '*lib. 7. cap. 30*'. See *Jewish War* (IV. 161, VII. 270) in *Josephus*, ed. H. St. J. Thackeray, Loeb Classical Library (London: Heinemann; Cambridge, Mass.: Harvard University Press, 1957), ii. 49, 583. Josephus's extremely derogatory remarks about the Zealots of his time are coloured by partisanship, since he himself had chosen the other side. The quote, from *Paradise Lost* (ii. 485), condemns 'specious deeds' motivated by selfishness.

established in the time of Moses to protect those who lay violent hands on others for the sake of sanctifying God, temple, and nation.

The last entry in Selden's *Table Talk*, 'Zealots', is less nuanced and more concise than the chapters in *De Jure*:

One would wonder Christ should whip the buyers and sellers out of the temple, and nobody offer to resist him, considering what opinion they had of him; but the reason was, they had a law, that whosoever did profane *sanctitatem Dei, aut templi*, the holiness of God, or the temple, before ten persons, it was lawful for any of them to kill him, or to do any thing on this side killing him, as whipping him, or the like. And hence it was, that when one struck our Saviour before a judge, (where it was not lawful to strike, as it is not with us at this day), he only replied, If I have spoken evil, bear witness of the evil; but if well, why smitest thou me? He says nothing against their smiting him, in case he had been guilty of speaking evil, that is, blasphemy, and they could have proved it against him. They that put this law in execution were called zealots; but afterwards they committed many villanies.[41]

Discussing zeal and the circumvention of due process in *De Jure*, Selden could not have known what an incendiary topic it would become in the period of the Civil War. In the very last pages of *Leviathan*, 'A Review and Conclusion', Hobbes provides an important supplement to his thirty-fifth chapter, regarding the commonwealth of the Jews: 'I have omitted to set down who were the Officers appointed to doe Execution; especially in Capitall Punishments; not then thinking it a matter of so necessary consideration, as I find it since.'[42] Where other nations leave executions to 'those, in whom want of means, contempt of honour, and hardnesse of heart, concurred, to make them sue for such an Office', the Israelites follow a divine positive law that requires the witnesses of the offence and then the rest of the people to carry them out:

Neverthelesse, this manner of proceeding being not throughly understood, hath given occasion to a dangerous opinion, that any man may kill another, in some cases, by a Right of Zeal; as if the Executions done upon Offenders in the Kingdome of God in old time, proceeded not from the Soveraign Command, but from the Authority of Private Zeal.[43]

Hobbes seems to be at pains to criticize not Selden on zeal but rather those who do not 'throughly understand' him. Hobbes considers all of the central scriptural texts that have been cited in support of the rights of the zealot, arguing that each case is an example not of 'Private Zeale, but . . . Publique Condemnation'. He also uses Selden's term for the rights of the zealot: 'Witnesses [required in executing a murderer] suppose a formall Judicature, and consequently condemn that pretence of *Ius Zelotarum*.'[44] Interestingly, Phineas the homicide, who is for

---

[41] *The Table Talk of John Selden*, ed. Samuel Harvey Reynolds (Oxford: Clarendon Press, 1892), 199–200.

[42] Thomas Hobbes, *Leviathan*, ed. Richard Tuck (Cambridge: Cambridge University Press, 1996), 487.

[43] Ibid. 487.   [44] Ibid. 488.

many revolutionaries, as he is for Milton, an exemplar of zeal, is transformed by Hobbes into a model of virtuous private counter-revolutionary action. Like Selden, Hobbes is aware of the public nature of the act and its accord with the law of Moses:

when Phinehas killed Zimri and Cosbi, it was not by right of Private Zeale: Their Crime was committed in the sight of the Assembly; there needed no Witnesse; the Law was known, and he the heir apparent to the Soveraignty; and which is the principall point, the Lawfulnesse of his Act depended wholly upon a subsequent Ratification by Moses, whereof he had no cause to doubt. And this Presumption of a future Ratification, is sometimes necessary to the safety of a Common-wealth; as in a sudden Rebellion, any man that can suppresse it by his own Power in the Countrey where it begins, without expresse Law or Commission, may lawfully doe it, and provide to have it Ratified, or Pardoned, whilest it is in doing, or after it is done.[45]

Anthony Ascham's *A Discourse: Wherein is Examined, What is Particularly Lawfull during the Confusions and Revolutions of Government* (July 1648) has been described by John M. Wallace as 'the first serious attempt to apply the principles of the *jus gentium* to the outcome of the Civil War,' 'mark[ing] the beginning of the real influence of Grotius in England'.[46] Anthony à Wood declared Ascham to be a 'great Creature of the Long Parliament', and it was in service to that parliament as ambassador to Madrid that he was murdered by royalist exiles in 1650. Despite Ascham's reworking in the *Discourse* of Grotius's arguments in *De Jure Belli*, it is clear that he is familiar with Selden's *De Jure* as well. Like Hobbes, he uses the term *Ius Zelotarum* rather than Grotius's *Judicium zeli*, the judgement of zeal:

Mr. Hobbes supposes that because a man cannot be protected from all civil injuries unless all his rights be totally and irrevocably given up to another, therefore the people are irrevocably and perpetually tied to the governor.... [S]uch a total resignation of all right and reason as Mr. Hobbes supposes is one of our moral impossibilities and directly opposite to that ancient *Ius Zelotarum* among the Jews who ... conceived they had a right of judging and punishing acts notoriously contrary to the light of nature and reason.[47]

During the period of the Parker–Marvell debate—1669 to 1673—Parliament and the bishops were more of a threat than the king to political and religious toleration,[48] and Parker was safe from everything except ridicule when he

---

[45] Hobbes, *Leviathan*.

[46] John M. Wallace, *Destiny His Choice: The Loyalism of Andrew Marvell* (Cambridge: Cambridge University Press, 1968), 32.

[47] Anthony Ascham, *A Discourse: Wherein is Examined, What is Particularly Lawfull during the Confusions and Revolutions of Government* (1648), 121. Ascham is not responding to *Leviathan*, which first appeared in 1651, but rather to Hobbes's *Elements of Law*, composed in the first half of 1640, which justifies the surrender of all rights. He might also have in mind the attacks on sedition in *De Cive* (Paris, 1642; Amsterdam, 1647), ch. 12. See *De Cive*, ed. Howard Warrender (Oxford: Clarendon Press, 1983), 145–56.

[48] See the Introduction to *Rehearsal Transpros'd*, in *Prose Works*, i. 8–9.

assumed the persona of a Jewish zealot. (At one point Marvell states that such a characterization is proof that Parker is besotted with foolishness and that this infatuation is punishment for his presumption in comparing himself to Christ.[49]) Where Parker, attacking the nonconformists, plays the role of Christ scourging the money-lenders, Marvell the tolerationist condemns Parker as the most notorious Jewish money-lender of them all. He accuses him of raising the ghost of Bishop Bramhall to vex Richard Baxter, even though the bishop himself would 'doubtless' have pardoned him at his death: 'And then, as for Extortion; who but such an Hebrew Jew as you, would, after an honest man hade made so full and voluntary Restitution, not yet have been satisfied without so many pounds of his flesh over into the bargain.'[50]

In *Rehearsal Transpros'd: The Second Part*, Marvell plays teasingly with rabbinic learning, as when he claims that he is compelled by zeal to reply to Parker's books, beginning with the *Discourse* but now including *A Reproof to the Rehearsal Transpros'd*:

of all the Books that ever I read, I must needs say I never saw a Divine guilty of so much ribaldry and prophaneness.... [I]n the whole I look'd upon it as so uncanonical and impious, that it would bear an higher and more deserved accusation then that of Onias the Son of Simeon the Just, for officiating in a Womans Zone instead of the Priestly girdle, and for the sacred Pectoral wearing his Mistresses Stomacher. I must confess that when all these things centered together upon my imagination, and I saw that none of his Superiors offer'd to interpose against an evil so great in it self, and as to me appear'd so publick in the consequence and mischief, I could hold no longer, and I, though the most unfit of many, assumed upon him the Priviledge (if any such Priviledge there be) of an English *Zelote*.[51]

Although, as Henry Stubbe recognized, Parker read *De Jure*, one cannot be at all certain that Marvell did. In what appears at first to be his most knowing talmudic response, he seems to cast a glance at the *mishnah* in tractate *Sanhedrin* that begins Selden's discussion of zeal and serves as the central text of 4.4. The story to which Marvell refers is told in some detail in the Babylonian Talmud, tractate *Menachot* 109b. Onias was tricked by his older brother Shimei, who was jealous of his succeeding to the high priesthood, into wearing a gown [Rashi: 'a leather garment', inappropriate for service in the temple] and a girdle. Shimei had clothed

[49] Ibid. 126, commenting on the Preface of Parker's *Discourse*: '[Parker] justifies his debauched way of writing by paralel to our Blessed Saviour. And I cannot but with some aw reflect how near the punishment was to the offence; when having undertaken so profane an Argument, he was in the very instant so infatuated as to say that Christ was not onely *in an hot fit of Zeal, but in a seeming Fury too, and transport of Passion*.'

[50] Ibid. 80. The character of course is Shylock in *The Merchant of Venice*, but the language is Falstaff's in *1 Henry IV*. 2.4. Falstaff is forsworn when he claims that four men set upon at least sixteen and bound them. When Peto contradicts him, he responds: 'You rogue, they were bound, every man of them, or I am a Jew else, an Hebrew Jew' (2.4.171–2). Shakespeare's audience would presumably have found the intensive pleonasm to be a source of comedy.

[51] Marvell, *Rehearsal Transpros'd: The Second Part*, *Prose Works*, i. 245–6.

him improperly while pretending to instruct him. Then Shimei placed him near the altar and said to his brother priests (אחיו הכהנים, the very same phrase used in the *mishnah*), 'See what this man promised his beloved [Rashi: "his wife"] and has now fulfilled? "On the day in which I will assume the office of high priest I will put on your gown and gird myself with your girdle." ' At this his brother priests sought to kill Onias, who fled to Alexandria. In this conspicuous display of arcane scholarship, Marvell alludes to the *Ius Zelotarum*, which authorizes the brother priests to kill their fellow who has offended while officiating at the temple service. Marvell, who is dubious about the legitimacy of the privilege ('if any such Priviledge there be'), nevertheless sees Parker as more deserving of punishment than Onias. Since Parker's offence is a public one and no one else has risen up to punish it, Marvell assumes the privilege not of a Jewish but of an 'English *Zelote*'. He has taken the story without acknowledgement not from the Talmud but from Selden's *De Successione in Pontificatum Ebraeorum* (1636), which provides references to both the *mishnah* and *gemara* in tractate *Menachot*, the complete Hebrew text of the story as found in Obadiah of Bertinoro's standard commentary on the *Mishnah*, and Selden's Latin translation.[52]

In general, Parker seems more familiar with rabbinic scholarship than Marvell, and his references are more casual and less forced, as when he complains about one of his opponents, in a passage cited by Marvell, ''*Tis an easie matter by this dancing and capering humour to perpetuate all the Controversies in the world, how plainly soever determinable, to the coming of Elias*.'[53] William Sclater, preaching at the funeral of Professor Abraham Wheelock, a Christian Hebraist and one of the contributors to the London *Polyglot Bible*, 25 September 1653, explains the last phrase, used throughout the Talmud to signify that a problem remains unresolved: 'as the Jewish rabbins, so oft as they met with texts which were ... hard to be understood, were wont to shut up all their discourse with this, *Elias cum venerit solvet dubia*, Elias shall answer this doubt, when he comes; in like sort was he as another Elias to the doubts and difficulties of many.'[54]

Marvell's most extensive, but not his most knowing, rabbinic references are in response to just such a learnedly casual remark by Parker. It all hangs on a pun that Parker knows from reading Selden but Marvell does not, though he transcribes it verbatim. To demonstrate Parker's meanness of spirit and arrogance,

[52] Selden, *De Successione in Pontificatum Ebraeorum* (1636), 1.8, pp. 158–9. Selden cites 'Misnam tit. *Menachoth*, seu *de Oblationibus Vespertinis* cap. XIII, & Gemaram Babyloniam, sub extremum capitis fol. 109a' as well as the commentary of 'Rabbi Obadias Bartenorius' (p. 158). G. J. Toomer located the reference. Regarding Marvell's knowledge of the *Ius Zelotarum*, it should be noted that this chapter of *De Successione* is one of the very few places outside of *De Jure* in which Selden discusses zealots.

[53] Marvell, *Rehearsal Transpros'd*, 140, quoting from Parker's *Defence and Continuation of the Ecclesiastical Politie*, 479.

[54] William Sclater, *The Crowne of Righteousness* (1654), 28. Sclater derives the explanation of the phrase from 'D. Lightfoot M[aste]r of Katharine Hall in Cambridge in his *Harmony*'. Selden and Lightfoot were almost the only sources for knowledge of rabbinical texts in England at this time.

Marvell quotes his criticism of the century's great philologists and scholars of comparative religion *avant la lettre*. Parker (quoted in italics) begins by censuring the work of two Englishmen, Hugh Sandford and Robert Parker, authors of *De Descensu Domini nostri Jesu Christi ad inferos* (Amsterdam, 1611), who, he claims,

first attempted to accommodate, wrongly and rashly, the Theological History of the Gentiles to the Sacred History; but whoever was the first Author, the venerable Names of Scaliger, Selden, Bochart, Vossius, ay and Grotius . . . brought it in reputation: so that every man that affects to be accounted a prime Philologer, sets up forthwith to accommodate of any fashion the Greek matters to the Hebrew; the Scabbado [scabies, scabby skin infection] *of which affectation does so break out every day*, & c. but they got the Itch it seems first of Grotius and those other Scoundrels. 'Tis to be consider'd Mr. Bayes, that you are *the wonder of this Age*, so they must all subscribe to you, and carry your books after you.[55]

For Parker, to accommodate '*the Theological History of the Gentiles to the Sacred History*' and '*the Greek matters to the Hebrew*', as those scholars do who adapt pagan thought to Jewish and Christian thought, is, figuratively speaking, to proselytize, that is, to bring a Gentile convert to the Jewish faith. Parker disapproves, and he calls this tendency '*the Scabbado*', remembering an oft-repeated talmudic pun explained by Selden in *De Synedriis*: 'A proselyte is as annoying as an abscess or scabies to an Israelite, as it is stated in scripture (Isaiah 14: 1): "and the strangers shall be joined with them, and they shall cleave, like an abscess or scabies, to the house of Jacob." '[56] There are deep reserves behind the pun, and Selden is aware of them, citing multiple references, talmudic and rabbinic. The simplest explanation of the pun is the shared three-letter root ספח in both *scabies* (ספחת) and Isaiah's *they shall cleave* (ונספחו). But Selden also knows 'the gloss,' Rashi's commentary, which gives a serious reason for the pun: the concern that proselytes will not be sufficiently careful about self-examination, which implies that one must be scrupulous about *mitzvot* (commandments), just as one has to examine oneself for scabies. There is also the concern that proselytes lack skill in performing the commandments, and that they incite acts of violence by those who resent their conversion. Selden also cites Maimonides, who compares proselytes to leprosy rather than to scabies and who notes the vexing problem of a proselyte who returns to his original religion and leads Israelites astray.[57]

[55] Marvell, *Rehearsal Transpros'd: The Second Part*, 398–9.

[56] Selden, *De Synedriis*, 3.2, in *Opera*, i. 1625. '*Molesti fuere proselyti Israelitis, etiam ut apostema seu scabies, juxta quod scriptum est* [note: 'Jesaiae cap. xiv.1'], *Et adjungatur illis advena, & sociabitur, ut apostema seu scabies domui Jacob.*'

[57] Selden quotes the talmudic passage on proselytes from tractate *Yebamot*, which he calls *Jabimoth*, but he also knows other versions. See *De Synedriis*, 3.2, in *Opera*, i. 1625: 'R. Chelbo in Gemar. Babylonia tit. *Jabimoth* cap. 4. fol. 47.2. & tit. *Kidoschin*, cap. 4. fol. 70.2 & tit. *Nidda*, cap. 2. fol. 13.2. . . . Videsis gloss. [i.e., Rashi's commentary] ad Gemar. Babylon. tit. *Nidda*, cap. 2. fol. 13.2'. See also the long quote from Maimonides' *Mishneh Torah*, 'Tract. *Isuri Bia*, cap. 13. [sections] 14, 15, & 16, 17 & 18' on cols. 1625–6. The reference to leprosy appears in 13.18.

Although Marvell's comments on the itch underscore Parker's disrespect for the achievements of these scholars, he seems to be unaware of the pun. But he knows the talmudic statement, which he picks up twenty-five pages later (in the 1673 edition). After quoting Parker on other rabbinic texts, whose hidden source frustrates him, he lashes out:

To show you, Mr. Bayes, that I too have been sometimes conversant with the Jewish Zealots, I will tell you hereupon a Story out of one of them, that shall as yours be nameless. There was among the Jews a certain kind of People that were called *Proselytes*, which you may in English interpret *Turn-coats*, concerning whom was that expression that I quoted before of our Saviour, Mat. 23.15. *Wo unto you Scribes and Pharisees, Hypocrites, for you compass Sea and Land to make a Proselyte, and when he is made, you make him two-fold more the Child of Hell than you your selves.* Now what I shall tell you of these men . . . relates particularly to your self, who, abandoning all Modesty and Christianity toward your former party, have defiled and dishonour'd the Church that has receiv'd you into protection. But concerning these *Proselytes* and Turn-Coats it was that the Jews had that Maxime; *Proselytae & Paederastae impediunt adventum Messiae* [proselytes and pederasts impede the coming of the Messiah]; and again, *Proselyti sunt sicut Scabies Israeli*; that they were like a Scab or Leprosie to Israel.[58]

It is as if Parker's learned allusion to proselytes as scabies has been festering in Marvell's imagination. Parker, like Marvell, was raised as a Puritan. After the Restoration, lacking advancement, he quickly became 'as warm a member of the Church of England as any' (*DNB*). Marvell turns Parker's joke against him, calling him a proselyte and reminding him that he must observe scrupulously all the details of the conversion process as described in the Talmud. If Marvell does not know where Parker gets his talmudic material, he will retaliate by withholding the name of his own source: 'I will tell you . . . a Story out of one of them, that shall as yours be nameless.'

Marvell's source is John Lightfoot's *Horae Hebraicae et Talmudicae. In Evangelium Matthaei* (Cambridge, 1658), whose Latin translations of talmudic and medieval rabbinic texts on the lengthy ordeal that converts must endure he cites twelve separate times word for word in one long paragraph, beginning with the two talmudic slurs against proselytes.[59] The interrogation process Marvell describes hints at Parker's likely motives for conversion to the Church of England, greed, convenience, and lust, all vices either stated or strongly implied in the biography of Parker embedded in *Rehearsal Transpros'd: The Second Part*—for example, 'he daily inlarged, not only his Conversation, but his Conscience, and was made free of some of the Town-vices; imagining . . . that by hiding himself among the Onyons, he should escape being traced by his own Perfumes.'[60] Marvell reminds Parker:

---

[58] Marvell, *Rehearsal Transpros'd: The Second Part*, 415.
[59] Lightfoot, *Horae Hebraicae et Talmudicae*, on Matthew 23: 15, p. 249.
[60] Marvell, *Rehearsal Transpros'd: The Second Part*, 262.

when a Proselyte was circumcised, they first catechized him about the sincerity of his Conversion; whether he did not do it, *ob adipiscendas Divitias* to make his Fortune; *ob Timorem*, for fear of some inconvenience; or lastly, *ob Amorem erga aliquam Israeliticam*, Whether there were not some woman in the bottom of the business. For they had a shrewd suspicion of them, *Quod non periti essent Mandatorum, quodque inducerent Vindictas, atque insuper quod forte eorum Opera imitarentur Israelitae* [that they were not skilled in the commandments, that they would bring punishment (on them), and moreover, that the Israelites perhaps might imitate their works]: and therefore it was *quod Proselyti opus habebant Triumviratu*, and they would not trust them until three men had examined and taken care that all were right.[61]

Lightfoot, a meticulous scholar, understands Christian baptism in the light of talmudic laws regarding the immersion of proselytes. He is serious about the most minute details, and he scrupulously records his sources. Thus, for example, he distinguishes among the Talmud, Rashi's commentary, and '*Maim*[onides] in *Mikvaoth*, cap. 1, & 4'. Marvell quotes from all of these sources without citation, and he takes none of them seriously. He attends to the 'scrupulous niceties in this washing' in order to ridicule both ritual immersion and Parker. When he considers the minimum amount of water in a ritual bath, he neither knows nor cares that he is misquoting Maimonides, substituting four *seah*s (large jars of water) for the forty actually required: 'They were so curious as to regulate what proportion too of water was sufficient, and the least quantity that could be allowed was, *quatuor Seae acquarum* and the dimension, *Cubitus quadratus*, & c.' Lightfoot's citation of Maimonides on *Mikvaoth* is accurate: '"*Hanc proportionem aestimârunt sapientes nostri, ad cubitum quadratum, profunditatis tricubitalis: continétque haec mensura quadraginta Seas aquarum.*" [Our wise men have esteemed this proportion to be a cubit square, and three cubits deep; and this measure contains forty *seah*s of water.]'[62]

The rabbinic sources and the contemporary Hebraists who make them accessible are invisible, their only purpose to supply Marvell with ammunition. Lightfoot once again draws on Maimonides in his commentary on Matthew 3: 6: '"*Nam si quis se totum abluat, excepto ipsissimo apice minimi digiti, ille adhuc in immunditia sua: Sique sit quispiam capillosus admodum, omnem crinem capitis abluat necesse est.*" [For if anyone washes himself all over, except for the very top of his little finger, he is still in his uncleanness. And if anyone has much hair, he must wash all the hair of his head.]' This Marvell uses to vilify Parker and to

---

[61] Marvell, *Prose Works*, i. 415; his twelve citations are taken from two sections of Lightfoot's *Horae*: Matthew 3: 6 (the baptism at the Jordan), pp. 45–7, and Matthew 23: 15 (Jesus's diatribe against proselytizing Pharisees), p. 249. Marvell's fourth quote is taken from Lightfoot's citation of Rashi's commentary: 'Glossa, *Ideo quod non essent periti mandatorum, quodque inducerent vindictas, atque insuper, quod forte eorum opera imitarentur Israelitae*, & c.' (p. 249). For the fifth quote, Marvell shifts from Matthew 23: 15 to 3: 6 and from Rashi to the Talmud (*Yebamot* 46b) : '*Proselytus opus habet triumviratu*' (p. 45).

[62] Marvell, *Prose Works*, i. 416; Lightfoot, *Horae*, 46.

suggest that the Anglican Church, represented by the Archbishop of Canterbury's palace at Lambeth, is guilty of Judaizing:

Now, Mr. Bayes, I would gladly be satisfied whether you have been rightly and duly Proselyted according to these Ceremonies (for you know that the Jewish Ceremonies are not so abrogated but that the Pro-consul may re-establish them) but particularly have been drawn cross the River to Lambeth? has not so much as the top of your little finger escaped ducking? is there not one hair of your head but has been over head and ears in the River? All this ought to have been exactly observed (especially considering how much filth you brought about you) else you are not a true Turn-coat, but remain still in your uncleanness.[63]

Bishop Parker never published a reply to the second part of the *Rehearsal Transpros'd*, but if he had, he might have counter-attacked with an argument similar to the one he used against an earlier opponent, the nonconformist John Owen:

the main design of his Assaults . . . is . . . to let us see his deep Stores of Ammunition in Jewish Learning: for some Men are mighty Rabbies at the second hand, and can furnish great Volumes with a power of Hebrew, as Brokers do their Shops with old Cloaths. And I have read a famous Writer (though he shall be nameless) that abounds with Rabbinical Quotations, all of which if you would trace them, are trivial [ordinary, commonplace] in Modern Authors. But though Men by such borrowed Gays may make the Vulgar gaze and admire them, yet they do but expose their Ignorance and Vain-glory to the Learned World.[64]

It is tempting to speculate on why Marvell would be drawn to Lightfoot, Parker to Selden, and what influence, if any, these sources had on them. Lightfoot was a Puritan who took the parliamentary side in the Civil War less reluctantly than Selden did. According to Gibbon, Lightfoot, 'by constant reading of the rabbis, became almost a rabbi himself'. In his portrait in the hall of St Catharine's College, which he served as master, he wears a skullcap and bands (a pair of strips hanging down in front), looking almost like the rabbi, in *yarmulka* and *tefillin* (phylacteries), that Gibbon compared him to. Lightfoot loves the Talmud and the rabbinic commentaries, both in themselves and for the light they shed on the New Testament and on life in first-century Palestine, but he considers the Jews to be Christ's greatest enemies. His commentary on Matthew 23: 15 suffices to explain Gibbon's use of the qualifying term. There he accuses proselytizing Jews of being motivated by hypocrisy, covetousness, and greed. They drain the purses of the new converts and, once they have caught them in their nets, allow them to perish in ignorance, superstition, atheism, and all manner of wickedness. More-over, failing to consider the inconsistency, he says all this *immediately* after quoting the two passages in which 'the talmudists truly speak very ill of pros-

---

[63] Marvell, *Prose Works*, i. 416.
[64] Parker, *Defence and Continuation of the Ecclesiastical Politie*, 153.

elytes': they impede the coming of the messiah, and they are as a scab to Israel. It is at least possible that Marvell's unremarkable prejudices would have been confirmed by his source.

Parker is nothing if not critical, and one cannot imagine him saying anything particularly charitable about Jews. To have 'the (deserved) greatness of his own *name* and *authority*' acknowledged, as Selden did, even while his argument was condemned as 'very fond & frivolous', is as much praise as one can hope for unless, like Bishop Bathurst, senior fellow of Trinity, one is in a position to advance Parker's career, in which case his praise is fulsome. Still, he does at least assume the persona of Jewish zealot, and it is instructive to contrast his source of information on Matthew 23: 12 with Marvell's. Selden quotes from Jesus's diatribe but does not develop it, and his balanced presentation could not be more different from Lightfoot's shrill accusations. The centrepiece of his discussion is a long passage from his favourite source, Maimonides' *Mishneh Torah* ['Tract. *Isuri Bia*, cap. 13. [sections] 14, 15, & 16, 17 & 18'], which discusses the difficult interrogation of one who applies to become a proselyte, including an examination of motive and an explanation of the difficulty involved in practising the religion. If the person persists and will not be discouraged, and one sees that the person is entering the religion for love of it, then finally one relents. And the proof-text is Ruth 1: 18: 'When [Naomi] saw that [Ruth] was steadfastly minded to go with her, then she left speaking to her.'[65] It may be a trivial point, but in citing R. Helbo's pronouncement in tractate *Nidah* 13b, Selden's translation preserves at least the small degree of doubt in the most literal translation, 'Proselytes and those that play with children [*ludentes cum puellis*] delay the advent of the messiah', while Lightfoot (and Marvell) assume, quite understandably, that the meaning is *Paederastae*.

One remaining question about the talmudic exchanges discussed in this chapter is whether or not Marvell knew that Selden was Parker's source. In both parts of the *Rehearsal Transpros'd*, Marvell follows his criticism of Parker's taking upon himself '*the Person and Priviledge of a Jewish Zelot*' with the accusation that such a view 'seemed to proceed from too slight an Apprehension and knowledge of the duty we owe to our Saviour': 'But really it seems to me, by this and some other passages, that you do not attribute much belief to the Miracles of our Saviour, among which perhaps this was one of the most remarkable.' If Marvell does not know about Selden and the *Ius Zelotarum*, this means nothing more than that Christ is diminished when his cleansing of the temple is seen as the act of a Jewish zealot rather than as a miracle. But if Marvell suspects that Parker has been reading Selden's *De Jure*, then there may be a hint of what the populace might think of a work that implicitly reduces the importance of Christian revelation and of Christ's redemptive mission. If the universal Noachide laws can redeem a virtuous Gentile such as Job, and if even the most

---

[65] Selden, *De Synedriis*, 3.2, in *Opera*, i. 1625–6.

minimal of Christian dogmatic beliefs are not a precondition for salvation,[66] then the question Selden poses about salvation in *Table Talk* is unanswerable: 'why should not that portion of happiness still remain to them who do not believe in Christ, so they be morally good?' To end on somewhat firmer ground, it should be noted that Parker's complaint of the modishness of 'mighty Rabbies at the second hand' displaying their 'Jewish Learning' and abounding 'with Rabbinical Quotations' attests to the currency of rabbinic scholarship in the third quarter of seventeenth-century England. Even Andrew Marvell, a reluctant Christian Hebraist, was compelled by the times to find a store of quotations. If one can purchase approval cheaply at second hand, imagine the reverence earned by 'our learned Selden', that *arbiter elegantiae* who wore his learning so well that it became in vogue.

[66] See on this point Alan Cromartie, *Sir Matthew Hale (1609–1676)* (Cambridge: Cambridge University Press, 1995), 161.

6

Natural Law and Noachide Precepts: Grotius, Selden, Milton, and Barbeyrac

The brief biography that prefaces the 1738 annotated edition by Jean Barbeyrac of Hugo Grotius's great work of natural law theory *De Jure Belli ac Pacis libri tres* (Paris, 1625) describes a dramatic escape from prison. Grotius had tied his own political fortunes to those of Johan van Oldenbarnevelt, the chief minister of the United Provinces, and when his patron fell from power and was executed at the Hague in May 1619, Grotius was sentenced to life in prison at the fortress of Loevestein in the south of Holland. There, according to his biographer,

he was severely used for above 18 months; from whence, by the Contrivance of *Mary de Regelsberg* his *Wife*, he made his Escape, who having observed that the *Guards*, being weary of searching a large *Trunk* full of Books and Linnen to be washed at *Gorcum*, a neighbouring Town, let it go without opening it as they used to do, advised her Husband to put himself into it, having made some Holes with a Wimble in the Place where the fore-part of his *Head* was, that he might not be stifled. He followed her Advice, and was in that manner carried to a *Friend* of his at *Gorcum*; from whence he went to *Antwerp* in the usual Waggon, after he had crossed the publick Place in the Disguise of a *Joyner*, with a Ruler in his Hand.[1]

There is something comic and unreal about the picture of Grotius conspicuously holding a tool to give himself an identity, the way a character in an allegorical painting might hold a compass or an anchor. The entire episode seems almost farcical, evoking both the fabliau in Ser Giovanni's collection *Il Pecorone* in which a lady conceals her lover under a pile of washing, and Shakespeare's adaptation of it in *The Merry Wives of Windsor*, in which Falstaff escapes from a jealous husband by being smuggled out of the house in a basket filled with laundry. The servants 'enter with a great buck-basket' (for dirty clothes), and their mistress Mrs Ford gives them orders:

when I suddenly call you, come forth, and without any pause or staggering take this basket on your shoulders. That done, trudge with it in all haste, and carry it among the whitsters [linen bleachers] in Datchet-mead [a meadow situated between Windsor Little

[1] Hugo Grotius, *The Rights of War and Peace* [*De Jure Belli ac Pacis*, 1625], ed. J. Barbeyrac, tr. anon. (London, 1738), p. ii. Parenthetic page references to *DJB* are to this edition.

Park and the Thames], and there empty it in the muddy ditch close by the Thames side. (3.3.8–12)

Falstaff's weight is a source of much mirth, as is the indignity of his being 'carried in a basket like a barrow of butcher's offal' and dumped by his bearers in the Thames 'with as little remorse as they would have drown'd a blind bitch's puppies, fifteen i'th' litter! And you may know by my size that I have a kind of alacrity in sinking' (3.5.4–5, 8–11).

Unlike Mrs Ford, Mary de Regelsberg represents fidelity, and the deception she practises is altogether benign. While her husband is making his escape, she is pretending that he is very sick. And when she learns that he has safely entered another country, 'she told the *Guards*, laughing at them, that the *Birds were fled*'. At first there was talk of imprisoning her in her husband's place, 'but by a Majority of Votes she was released, and praised by every Body, for having by her Wit procured her Husband's *Liberty*. Such a Wife deserved not only to have a *Statue* erected to her in the *Commonwealth of Learning*, but also to be canoniz'd; for we are indebted to her for so many excellent Works published by her Husband' (*DJB*, p. iii).

The story resonates more sombrely when one considers the fragility of cultural transmission and how, without a few breathing holes, genius might most literally have been stifled. And if the image of a fugitive lying cramped in a trunk stuffed with dirty clothes to escape persecution evokes twentieth-century memories, there is also something historically apt about Grotius having undergone such an experience. As a result of the flight of Marranos from Spain and Portugal to the Netherlands in the late sixteenth and early seventeenth centuries, the estates of Holland appointed the learned Grotius to a commission 'to amend the regulations for protecting Jews living in these lands from all scandals, anxieties, and sanctions'.[2] Tolerant for its time, Grotius's report, known as *Remonstrantie* (1615), lifted the most degrading medieval restrictions and helped to prepare the way for Dutch Jews to become recognized officially as subjects of the state (1657). Although noteworthy for providing a legal basis for Jewish settlement, not all of its recommendations would have been welcomed by those whom it affected. But alongside the expected inconveniences of compulsory registration, population quotas, and geographic restrictions were remarkably sympathetic regulations providing religious, social, and commercial freedom. Four years after aiding victims of foreign religious persecution, the genius in the trunk would enact an escape from political persecution in his homeland.

Turning from the *Life* that opens the volume to the text itself of Grotius's *De Jure Belli ac Pacis*, begun while he was imprisoned, one finds regarding specifically Jewish thought a proportion of the sympathetic to the agonistic similar to that in the *Remonstrantie*. This can occur on a small scale, as when, defending

---

[2] The phrasing from Grotius's *Remonstrantie* appears in his entry in the *Encyclopedia Judaica* (Jerusalem: Keter, 1972), vii. 939.

conventicles and assemblies, Grotius applies to Christians an ancient Jewish authority's defence of Jews: 'What Philo informs us to have been said by Augustus, of the Jewish Synagogues, is more truly and properly applicable to the Christian Congregations, That they were not Meetings for Revellings, or seditious Cabals, but pure Seminaries of Virtue.' Grotius adds that Philo 'shews elsewhere, how great a Difference there is between the Synagogues and the Mysteries of Paganism...which passage is well worth reading', and he also cites on this point Josephus, *Contra Apion*.[3] The passage reinforces a hierarchy maintained throughout the work of pagan, Hebraic, and Christian thought that corresponds to the tripartite crescendo of natural law, the Mosaic law, and the gospel.

The mix of sympathy for specifically Jewish thought and an insistence on the superiority of Christianity becomes proportionally more complex when it occurs on a larger scale. Thus, for example, in an important paragraph, Grotius distinguishes among natural law, divine positive law given to one people only, and divine, universal, positive or voluntary law that requires obedience from the moment it is promulgated:

The *Divine voluntary Law* (as may be understood from the very Name) is that which is derived only from the Will of God himself; whereby it is distinguished from the Natural Law, which in some Sense, as we have said above, may be called Divine also. And here may take Place that which *Anaxarchus* said, as *Plutarch* relates in the Life of *Alexander*, (but too generally) that GOD does not *will* a Thing because it is just; but it is just, that is, it lays one under an indispensable Obligation, because GOD *wills* it. And this Law was given either to all Mankind , or to one People only: We find that GOD gave it to all Mankind at three different Times. First, Immediately after the Creation of Man. Secondly, Upon the Restoration of Mankind after the Flood. And thirdly, Under the Gospel, in that more perfect re-establishment by CHRIST. These three Laws do certainly oblige all Mankind, as soon as they are sufficiently made known to them. (*DJB*, 16–17; my emphasis)

Grotius wants to identify as the true law of nature an extremely minimal set of rules that follow, as Richard Tuck puts it, 'as a *logical* necessity from some non-controversial assumption about the world'.[4] Theoretically, the discovery of shared moral rules in the natural, pre-civil state of humankind would provide a basis for relationships among human beings anywhere in the world. This is in part what makes the work a pioneering contribution to international relations. The benign project is to break down partition walls, but one of the problems is that distinctions threaten to break down as well, as Grotius himself recognizes in the excerpt's opening sentence. In the most famous (and subsequently most

---

[3] *De Jure Belli* (2.20.49), 448–9. See also p. 448 n. 5. Grotius cites Philo's '*De Legat. ad Cajum* (p. 1035. E. *Edit. Paris*)' as well as 'Lib. *De Sacrificant*'.
[4] Richard Tuck, 'Grotius and Selden', in *The Cambridge History of Political Thought, 1450–1700*, ed. J. H. Burns and Mark Goldie (Cambridge: Cambridge University Press, 1991), 512.

distorted) declaration of the entire work, attempting to free natural law from theology by basing its maxims on the constitution of human beings, he had concluded: '*And indeed, all we have now said would take place, though we should even grant, what without the greatest Wickedness cannot be granted, that there is no God, or that he takes no Care of human Affairs*' (*DJB*, p. xix). The immediate context of this sentence, including its own embedded denial, compromises the bold independence of the idea and collapses the distinction made in the excerpt above between natural law and the divine positive law. In the sentence following the one just quoted, before the reader has time to consider the possibility of a law based entirely on the self-sufficient power of human reason, Grotius underscores the inseparability of religion and nature:

the Law of Nature itself, whether it be that which consists in the Maintenance of Society, or that which in a looser Sense is so called, though it flows from the internal Principles of Man, may notwithstanding be justly ascribed to God, because it was his Pleasure that these Principles should be in us. And in this sense Chrysippus and the Stoicks said, that the Original of Right is to be derived from no other than Jupiter himself; from which Word *Jupiter* it is probable the Latins gave it the name *Jus*. (*DJB*, p. xix)

Although Grotius has been credited with providing a new theory of natural law that could supplant the discredited theories of the scholastics,[5] his tracing of the law of nature back to the will of God seems consistent with the thirteenth-century idea that created nature, *natura naturata*, as effect, flows from creative nature, *natura naturans*, as first cause. Instead of freeing the natural from the divine, he further blurs boundaries by developing the identification of Jupiter with *Jus*, religion with society: 'For this Reason, according to the Sentiment of MARCUS ANTONINUS, every Man, who commits an Act of Injustice, renders himself guilty of Impiety' (*DJB*, p. xix).

Grotius's editor, Jean Barbeyrac (1674–1744), attending closely to the implications of the phrase *it was his Pleasure that these Principles should be in us*, underscores the impossibility, given the terms applied to natural law, of maintaining a distinction beween that law and the arbitrariness of the divine will:

This Passage is beautiful, but ill applied.... In Reality, he is here talking of the *Voluntary Divine Law*... or of that, which, being in its own Nature indifferent, becomes just or unjust, because GOD hath commanded or forbidden it.... For he calls the will, which is the Source of this Right, a free or arbitrary *Will*; and afterwards observes, as it were occasionally, that the *Law of Nature*, of which he has been laying the Foundation, may be also considered as flowing from the Divine Will, *because it was his Pleasure to establish such interior Principles in Men*; or that his Nature should be framed in the Manner it is. (*DJB*, p. xix n. 1)

---

[5] Tuck, 'Grotius and Selden', 499.

For a reader interested in the irony, inconsistency, and ambivalence that characterize early modern Christian Hebraism, there is a special pleasure in reading Grotius in Barbeyrac's great edition. The leading eighteenth-century translator of the major writings on natural law by Grotius, Pufendorf, and Cumberland, Barbeyrac also developed his own rationalist natural law theory, equating the authority of conscience with the authority of reason.[6] Writing in the Huguenot diaspora of the 1690s, having been expelled from a religiously unified France, he had a special tolerationist reason for separating religion from society and thus a special sensitivity to Grotius's various difficulties in maintaining distinctions.

Although he never edited or translated Selden's *De Jure Naturali et Gentium*, he refers to it numerous times in his editions of Grotius and Pufendorf. And although he ridicules rabbinic exotica, it is clear that he reads all of the references to Jewish material in the scholars that he does edit with an acute awareness of Selden's scholarship. His very antipathy has the effect of highlighting the specifically Jewish nature of the material he is editing. Equally important, his general contempt for this learning is belied by the numerous specific occasions when he adopts rabbinic ideas. The contempt is never far to seek. Grotius remarks innocuously that rabbinic scholarship can be helpful: 'to understand the Sense of the Books of the Old Testament, the Hebrew Writers may afford us no little Assistance, those especially who were thoroughly acquainted with the Language and Manners of their Country.'[7] This provokes a diatribe by Barbeyrac:

But the most judicious Part of the learned World have at present but little Value for the Rabbies, and are of Opinion that those Doctors are of very little Use for understanding the Old Testament. The most antient Rabbies, whose Writings are extant, are the Authors of the *Talmud*, who lived some Centuries after JESUS CHRIST. The *Hebrew* had long been a dead Language; they had no Book in that Tongue but the Old Testament; they were very bad Criticks, and Men of little Judgment. They had no other antient Monuments of the History of their own Nation, than the Books of the Old Testament, and were unacquainted with Heathen Authors: Their Traditions must have undergone much Alteration and Corruption by Length of Time. To supply their Defects of Knowledge, and indulge their Inclination to Fables and Allegories, they have invented the most extravagant and chimerical Facts and Customs. So that they are on no account comparable to Christian Interpreters, who, like GROTIUS, have studied the Languages methodically, and had recourse to all the Monuments of Antiquity.... But the Rabbies are least to be depended on in Matters of Morality and Law. SELDEN's Treatise *De Jure Nat. ac Gent. secundum Disciplinam Hebraeorum* is a good Proof of what I advance, how advantageous an Opinion soever that learned Gentleman may have entertained for the Jewish

---

6 See Tim Hochstrasser, 'Conscience and Reason: The Natural Law Theory of Jean Barbeyrac', *Historical Journal*, 36 (1993), 289–308.

7 *De Jure Belli, Preliminary Discourse*, p. xxxiii. See also 'Prolegomena', sig. B4v in the original version (Paris, 1625): 'Ad percipiendam autem librorum ad antiquum fedus pertinentium sententiam non parum conferre nobis possunt Hebraei scriptores, ii maxime qui & sermones & mores patrios habuerunt percognita.'

Doctors.... BOECLER accuses GROTIUS of not reading the Books of the Rabbies with sufficient Care and Attention, and confining himself almost wholly to *Moses* the Son of *Maimon*. But others, perhaps, will think he allows them too much Weight, and lost too much of his Time in perusing them, though the Strength of his Judgment preserved him from the Contagion. (*DJB*, p. xxxiii n. 1)

The middle section of the paragraph in bold type is of special importance in recognizing the influence of rabbinic thought on Grotius's conception of a divine, universal, positive or voluntary law, an influence underscored in a lengthy note that relies heavily on Selden's mediation of talmudic and Maimonidean ideas and reveals Barbeyrac's profound ambivalence. According to Grotius, this universal law of perpetual obligation was first promulgated 'Immediately after the Creation of Man'. After systematically rejecting all other possibilities, such as that this is the prohibition in paradise, Barbeyrac explains that it must refer to the rabbinic idea of the *praecepta Noachidarum* or Noachide laws, at the same time insisting that Grotius is relying on 'a very uncertain Tradition'. He begins by claiming not to understand what he understands perfectly well:

I do not understand what positive Laws the Author means, which God delivered at the beginning of the World, and which are still obligatory, as soon as they are known. It is probable he understands by those Terms the several Sorts of Incest in the Collateral Line relating to the fourth of the six Commandments, which he, with the Rabbies, supposes were given to *Adam* and *Noah*, though they are only distinguished by the Name of the latter, as is also the Seventh, concerning Abstinence from Blood, which we find prescribed to *Noah*, Gen. ix.4.... SELDEN, *De Jure Nat. & Gent. juxta disciplinam Hebraeorum*, Lib. I. Cap. X. [1640 ed., pp. 118–19 in particular.] But all this is grounded only on a very uncertain Tradition, which can never have the Force of a general Law, duly promulgated ... Others ... with more Reason refer this to the Prohibition given to our first Parents in regard to *the Tree of Knowledge of Good and Evil. Gen.* ii. 16, 17. iii. 2, 3. But, tho' that positive Law would have been equally obligatory to their Posterity, had they remained in Paradise, yet as the Matter of the Prohibition was but of short Duration, and the Law could never take Place afterwards, it is to no Purpose to make it an Example of an universal positive Law. (*DJB* 16 n. 3)

Although Barbeyrac degrades rabbinic law in general and considers the Noachide precepts to be grounded in 'a very uncertain Tradition', he concedes that these must be what Grotius has in mind when he refers to a divine positive or voluntary universal law. He spends the entire long note deducing Grotius's meaning, refuting all other arguments that would place such a law directly in the Bible. Those who would 'with more Reason' identify this law with the original prohibition of the fruit of the tree of knowledge in paradise are wrong because that law, soon broken, was never renewed and is therefore obsolete. In the course of his long note, despite his belief that Grotius should inoculate himself against rabbinic 'Contagion', Barbeyrac displays a certain integrity, insisting that the first of the laws that 'certainly oblige[s] all Mankind' is rabbinic and not biblical. He considers and rejects the opinions of others who would place the divine universal law in Genesis and identify it with the Sabbath (2: 3), with the authority of a husband over his wife (3: 16), or with the use of sacrifices (4: 3). His diatribe may disparage Selden for overvaluing rabbinic learning in his magnificent study of the Noachide laws, *De Jure Naturali et Gentium juxta Disciplinam Ebraeorum*, but his own close reading of that work is evident throughout his running commentaries on Grotius and Pufendorf and probably accounts in large part for his insistence in this note that he understands Grotius's intention. Selden's scholarship, as mediated by Barbeyrac, is anachronistically at the centre of Grotius's references to rabbinic thought in this eighteenth-century edition. The inseparability of the two would have pleased the younger scholar, whose consideration of the ancient constitution of pre-Christian Britain, *Analecta Anglobritannica*, precedes and parallels Grotius's study of the early Netherlanders, *De Antiquitate Reipublicae Batavicae*; whose *Mare Clausum* was commissioned as a reply to Grotius's *Mare Liberum*; and whose *De Jure Naturali* can best be understood within the post-scholastic, anti-Aristotelian tradition of *De Jure Belli*.[8]

At the heart of this chapter is Selden's identification of natural law with the rabbinic Noachide precepts and his immense elaboration of the scattered references to those laws in the work of his strong precursor, Grotius. Barbeyrac's degradation of rabbinic learning is no match for the positive counter-evidence in Selden's lengthy paean to the ancient rabbis for their vast philological expertise and mastery of Greek philosophy and to the modern rabbis for learning wide and deep, beginning with Maimonides and ending with his own near-contemporary David Ganz, disciple of Rabbi Judah Loew, the *Maharal* of Prague, and an astronomer who knew Kepler and worked in the observatory of Tycho Brahe.[9] Although Grotius is best known for a sentence that by itself would seem to free natural law from theology, Selden's *De Jure* throws into retrospective relief Grotius's own theological approach to natural law. And while Barbeyrac has been justly cited for 'a deliberate attempt to denigrate the possible contribution of Jewish thought both to natural law and to international law',[10] his citations of Selden bring to light the rabbinic seeds of Grotius's idea of a divine universal positive law of perpetual obligation.

*

[8] For more on the relation between the two, see Tuck's 'Grotius and Selden', 499–529, and his *Philosophy and Government 1572–1651* (Cambridge: Cambridge University Press, 1993), 154–221.

[9] Selden, *De Synedriis*, in *Opera Omnia*, i. 1414–18 on the ancients; i. 1419, on thirteen moderns and their achievements in mathematics, philosophy, logic, and physics. Selden's long list of Ganz's multidisciplinary achievements suggests the importance to him of astronomy, a science that bridges gaps in Islam, Judaism, and Christianity. Selden reserves his highest praise for astronomers such as Copernicus and Galileo, and he compares Erastus to the great philosophers who have suffered for the cause of truth (*Opera*, i. 1076–7).

[10] Shabtai Rosenne, 'The Influence of Judaism on the Development of International Law', *Nederlands Tijdschrift voor International Recht*, 5 (1958), 119–49, esp. 130.

In reading Milton's prose chronologically, there is no way to prepare for the differences between the last antiprelatical tract (April 1642) and the first divorce tract (July 1643). Milton's early theological writings are marked by a Pauline absolutism that will not compound with human weakness as an inevitable condition lying within the bounds of divine forgiveness. His first published prose tract, *Of Reformation* (1641), begins by tracing the decline of the church from the perfect pattern of scripture clearly revealed, 'backslid[ing] one way into the Jewish beggery, of old cast rudiments, and stumbl[ing] forward another way into the new-vomited Paganisme of sensuall Idolatry' (*YP*, i. 520). Milton's mission in his early antiprelatical tracts is to recover the pristine original of the gospel by removing layers of ecclesiastical accretion, to rebuild the church according to the pattern stamped in religion's golden age, and to prepare for the second coming of Christ, whose distributions of reward and punishment he describes with fiery zeal. But in the great prose tracts of 1643–45—including the four treatises on divorce and the *Areopagitica*—the former absolutist confronts with compassion a life of mistake and the inseparability of good and evil in this imperfect world. Missing from these tracts are the essential tenets of Christian liberty, death to the law and redemption in Christ. In his arguments against the common expositors of the Pauline renaissance, Milton cites for the first time the opinions of the early modern natural law theorists Grotius and Selden. Such theorists, interested in universal laws, are generally less Judaeophobic than systematic theologians. Instead of a Pauline dualism that pits the carnal children of loins against the spiritual children of faith, Grotius and especially Selden look for continuities among the cultures of pagans, Jews, Muslims, and Christians. Milton's best prose is affected positively by natural law theorists who at their most progressive are humanistic, legal, and historical, rather than dogmatic, theological, and typological.

The best evidence for reading the 1644 edition of *Doctrine and Discipline of Divorce* in the context of natural law theory is found in Samuel von Pufendorf's lengthy and sympathetic discussion of it in his monumental treatise on natural law, *De jurae naturae et gentium*, or *Law of Nature and Nations* (1672), which Barbeyrac edited and annotated, and whose title of course is a homage to Selden.[11] Milton's final chapter in his divorce tract is devoted to Selden's *De Jure*, and Pufendorf follows his own discussion of Selden on divorce with six folio columns devoted to Milton's views on the subject, as if he were a natural law theorist.

It is at least worth mentioning that when Pufendorf disagrees with feminist Milton, he unintentionally judges himself, sounding like the late-middle-aged, cigar-smoking man at ease in his club chair, in a recent *New Yorker* cartoon, who confides to his friends, 'I actually prefer same sex—as long as it doesn't involve

---

[11] Samuel Pufendorf, *De jure naturae et gentium libri octo* [1672] [*On the Law of Nature and Nations in Eight Books*], ed. Jean Barbeyrac, tr. Basil Kennet (1749, 5th edn.), 6.1.24, pp. 583–6.

sex.' Pufendorf assumes that once we remove 'the Pleasures which by the Appointment of Nature sweeten and recommend', 'the Procreation of Offspring', men alone make more agreeable companions:

And thus we see, that Boys and old Men, those who have not felt the Passion of Love, and those who are past it, agree in preferring the Converse of their own Sex to all the Charms and all the Entertainments of the Fair. But Mr. *Milton* seems to dream of some more delicate and more refined Pleasures; and frames the Idea of a Wife suitable only to the Genius of a wise and learned Husband: He would have her able to be the Companion of his Studies, or to refresh him with her Wit, when he comes from severer Meditations, to compose his Cares with sweet Discourse, and charm away a melancholy Fit.[12]

Pufendorf sympathizes with the central argument of Milton's treatise, that Christ's pronouncements on divorce might 'bear another Interpretation . . . more agreeable to the Gospel Clemency and Goodness . . . than that which is at present received'—namely, that mental or spiritual unfitness should be 'a much weightier Cause of Divorce' than any physical defect.[13]

Returning to Barbeyrac's process of elimination, which ends by identifying Grotius's primordial universal law given by God with the rabbinic Adamic and Noachide precepts, we find him silently incorporating an argument from Milton's *Doctrine and Discipline of Divorce*, which he would have known from Pufendorf's commentary. Barbeyrac rejects the prohibitions of polygamy and divorce as original universal laws. Like Milton, who argues in favour of polygamy,[14] he refuses to see *unitas carnis* as the basis of monogamous marriage:

Several others . . . place the Prohibition of Polygamy and Divorce among the universal positive Laws given to *Adam*; and pretend to find it in Gen.ii. 24. . . . But, *first*, tho' MOSES says, *A Man shall leave his Father and his Mother, and shall cleave unto his Wife, and they shall be one Flesh.* Nothing can hence be concluded either for or against Polygamy or Divorce. The Expression, *Shall be one Flesh*, in itself means no more than that there shall be the strictest Union between a Man and his Wife; but it does not imply that a like tie cannot at the same Time subsist between a Husband and two or more Wives. And all that can be inferred from the same Text, in regard to the Dissolution of Marriage, is, that it ought not to be admitted rashly, and without some good Reason. The Word *Flesh*, according to the *Hebrew* Idiom, signifies all Ties, both of Affinity and Consanguinity. . . . As therefore all the Relations of a Man are *his Flesh*; so, in the same Way of Speaking, a Man may be said to be *one Flesh* with many Wives. (*DJB* 16 n. 3)

If, according to Grotius, the rabbinic Adamic and Noachide laws are the first two examples of divine universal laws ('Immediately after the Creation of Man'

---

[12] Ibid. 583.

[13] Ibid. 584.

[14] See Milton's readings of 'one flesh' in his argument for divorce in *The Doctrine and Discipline of Divorce* (*YP*, ii. 605–14), and for polygamy in *Christian Doctrine* (*YP*, vi. 355–7): 'If anyone has several wives, his relationship towards each one will be no less complete, and the husband will be no less *one flesh* with each one of them, than if he had only one wife' (p. 357). For Pufendorf's summary of Milton on 'one flesh', see *De jure naturae*, 585.

and 'Upon the Restoration of Mankind after the Flood'), the third is found 'Under the Gospel in that more perfect re-establishment by CHRIST'. Grotius argues that the gospel can be more demanding than either the law of nature or the Mosaic law, and he cites as examples of new divine and universal voluntary laws the forbidding of polygamy and divorce:

I see no Reason to allow, that the Laws of CHRIST do not oblige us to any Thing but what the Law of Nature already required of itself. And those, who are of that Opinion, are strangely embarrassed to prove, that certain Things which are forbid by the Gospel, as *Concubinage, Divorce, Polygamy,* are likewise condemned by the Law of Nature. Indeed these are such that Reason itself informs us it is more Decent to refrain from them, but yet not such as (*without* the Divine Law) would be criminal. The Christian Religion commands, that we should lay down our Lives one for another, but who will pretend to say, that we are obliged to this by the Law of Nature. *Justin Martyr says, To live only according to the Law of Nature, is to live like an Infidel. (DJB* 31)

Ignoring Christ's assurance in the sermon on the mount that he comes not to destroy the law but to fulfil it and that 'not one jot or one tittle shall . . . pass from the law,' Grotius reads Matthew 5 not as mere interpretation but as new legislation. He also uses against the Jews their own talmudic injunction to make a fence around the Torah—that is, to take preventative measures against the most serious violations by refraining from the far less harmful ones (*DJB* 201).[15] In this instance, Grotius exploits the rabbinic idea of a protective 'Barrier' (p. 201), truly a partition-wall, to emphasize the superiority of Christians over Jews. He praises the primitive Christians who voluntarily observed not only universal laws but those 'peculiarly designed for the *Hebrew* People: Nay, and extended the Bounds of their Modesty. . . that in this Virtue too, as well as in all others, they might excel the *Jews*' (p. 201). Of capital importance is Grotius's alteration of *Veteribus* to include 'to' rather than 'by' in the formula usually rendered as 'it hath been said by them of old . . . but I say unto you' (5: 21–2, 27–8, 31–2, 33–4, 38–9 43–4)—that is, Moses's legislation, delivered *to* the ancient Israelites, included provisions for divorce and permission to hate one's enemy. But more is required of Christians, and the old dispensation has been superseded. He concedes that the Hebrew Bible contains no prohibition against either polygamy or divorce, and 'where there is no Law, there can be no Transgression'. Moreover, it is certain that pagans in former ages had the liberty not only of divorce but also of marrying several wives.[16] 'But', he concludes, 'it is CHRIST who has forbid Man to put asunder that which GOD in the first Institution of Marriage had joined together; taking for the worthy Subject of a

---

[15] Mishnah, *Aboth*, 1.1. See Barbeyrac's note on p. 200 of *DJB* for a reference to this principle as found in 'Selden De Jure Nat. & Gent. & c. Lib. V. Cap. XI'.

[16] *De Jure Belli*, 191–2. For the point about pagans, see also the first edition (Paris, 1625), p. 136: 'Plerasque gentes certum est antiquitus ut divortiorum libertate, ita plurium feminarum conjugio usas.'

new Law, what was most eligible in itself, and most acceptable to GOD' (*DJB* 192).

Barbeyrac recognizes that in this passage Grotius is erecting the sort of partition-wall, with pagans and Jews on one side and Christians on the other, that his opus is intent on throwing down. Surely a tolerance for pluralistic societies would have been one of the reasons that Barbeyrac, whose family suffered religious persecution when Louis XIV revoked the Edict of Nantes in 1685, would have been drawn to Grotius's work. Another area of ideological concern, shared with other Huguenot apologists, would have been to provide a secular account of the conduct of civil societies and to demonstrate that under-lying principles of human sociability more than those of religious loyalty hold a society together.[17] Regarding Grotius's devaluation of the law of nature as fit for infidels, Barbeyrac extends that universal law, subsuming a martyr's suffering death for the gospel within the encompassing virtue of sacrificing oneself for the sake of the larger community, which applies to 'wise Pagans': 'This Instance is not altogether just . . . The Law of Nature, rightly understood, requires us in certain Cases to sacrifice our Lives for others, when a considerable Advantage may result from such an Action to the Publick. Thus we find the wise Pagans thought it their Duty to die for their Country.' Interestingly, Barbeyrac hints that the religious sacrifice may be less noble than the social one, since Christianity furnishes an additional powerful motive 'by proposing the certain Hope of a Life to come, which will make us ample Amends for the Loss of the present' (*DJB* 31 n. 2).

Milton refers favourably to Grotius's commentary, especially on Matthew 5, ten times in his divorce tracts, but his own position could not be more different. In arguing that natural law, the Mosaic law, and the gospel are entirely compat-ible and thus in agreement regarding divorce as an unabrogated law, he relies on charity as a hermeneutic principle that removes all gospel pronouncements standing in its way. Directly in opposition to Grotius, he believes that Christ introduced no new legislation, and he is not embarrassed to find that neither natural law nor the Hebrew Bible condemns polygamy and divorce. In a sense he follows Grotius's line of reasoning up to a point, arguing that, since polygamy and divorce are indeed permitted by the law of nature, they are also permitted under the gospel. Grudging as he generally is about observing the scholarly courtesies by acknowledging intellectual debts to contemporaries, he notes nonetheless, regarding his *Doctrine and Discipline of Divorce*, '*When I had almost finisht the first edition, I chanc't to read in the notes of* Hugo Grotius *upon the 5. of Matth. Whom I strait understood inclining to reasonable terms in this controversie: and something he whisper'd rather than disputed about the law of charity, and the true end of wedlock.*'[18] Grotius whispers about charity as 'the origin and consum-

---

17 See Hochstrasser, 'Conscience and Reason', 291.

18 Milton, *YP,* ii. 433–4. See p. 434 n. 11 for the text of Grotius on charity.

mation of Christ's teachings', and for him putting away a wife for whatever cause is cruel and inhuman. For Milton, however, charity dictates that a man divorce his wife rather than keep her if she is hated and thus afflicted. In *Tetrachordon*, Milton includes Grotius in a catalogue of authorities to support his position: '*Grotius* yet living, and one of prime note among learned men retires plainly from the Canon to the antient civility, yea to the Mosaic law, *as being most just and undecevable* [*sic*]. On the fifth of *Matt.* he saith, *that Christ made no civil lawes*' (*YP*, ii. 715). Indeed, no civil laws, rather universal, perpetually binding laws, issuing from the divine will, prohibiting divorce and polygamy. Rejecting Moses's teachings 'to them of old', these new gospel laws 'do certainly oblige all Mankind, as soon as they are sufficiently made known to them'.

The Mosaic laws of divorce and polygamy, according to Grotius, were replaced by a 'more perfect Rule' in the gospel (*DJB* 16, 189), and he quotes approvingly Chrysostom's assertion that '*since the coming of Christ, the way is become much narrower.... The same Degree of Virtue was not required from them* (the *Jews*) *that is expected from us.... * [T]he Gospel *contains a greater number of Precepts, and those carried to a higher Degree of Perfection*' (*DJB*, 3 n. 5 [Grotius's note]). Milton, of course, insisting in his divorce tracts on the continued relevance of the moral and judicial Mosaic laws, regards Christians as superior in faith but not in virtue: 'Wee find ... by experience that the Spirit of God in the Gospel hath been alwaies more effectual in the illumination of our minds to the gift of faith, then in the moving of our wills to any excellence of vertue, either above the *Jews* or the Heathen' (*YP*, ii. 303). Unlike Grotius, Milton in the divorce tracts sees Christians under the gospel living a less demanding life than Jews bound to the 'harsher covenant' of the Mosaic law and at least as much in need as they of the charity of the Hebrew Bible's 'permitted law' of divorce: 'If wee be wors [than the Jews], or but as bad, which lamentable examples confirm wee are, then have wee more, or at least as much need of this permitted law, as they to whom God therfore gave it under a harsher covenant' (*YP*, ii. 354).

Two rhetorical questions, similar in form, underscore differences between the thought of Grotius and Milton that transcend the subject of divorce. According to Grotius, only the gospel makes divorce a violation of the law, and to follow the undemanding law of nature is to live like an infidel. Christianity 'commands, that we should lay down our Lives one for another, but who will pretend to say, that we are obliged to this by the Law of Nature.' Milton argues instead that both prelapsarian paradise and primitive Christianity made demands on human nature that seventeenth-century Christians cannot meet. To demand perfection—for example, by prohibiting the relief of divorce—is to condemn imperfect human beings to death. All things except for Adam and Eve themselves (in the proprietorship that is the basis of marriage) were held in common in paradise, and so was money among the early Christians. Milton cites the case of Ananias and Sapphira, good and bad like all of us, donating some of their profit and holding back some, who fell down dead (Acts 5: 1–10). Natural law, the Mosaic law of divorce, and a gospel whose charity preserves that law are necessary in this fallen world: 'The Gospel indeed tending ever to that which is perfetest, aim'd at the restorement of all things, as they were in the beginning. And therefore all things were in common to those primitive Christians in the Acts, which *Ananias & Sapphira* dearly felt.... But who will be the man shall introduce this kind of common wealth, as christianity now goes?' (*YP*, ii. 665–6).

It should be noted that, despite important differences, a common interest in natural law that crosses national borders links Grotius, Selden, Milton, and Barbeyrac. Each observed at first hand the dangers of uniform religious practice, whether Catholic or Calvinist, and each in his own way defended a pluralist culture. Regarding the particular and subsidiary matter of Christian Hebraism that occupies the centre of this chapter, it should be noted that a number of post-biblical, rabbinic ideas associated with Selden originate in the early modern period with Grotius. At the same time, we should recognize that, regarding natural law, Selden's *De Jure Naturali* is the period's central text of rabbinic thought mediated by a Christian humanist, anticipated by Grotius, revered by Milton, and heavily relied upon by Barbeyrac. Historians warn us that no absolute correlation exists between a Christian scholar's knowledge and admiration of rabbinic scholarship and his attitude toward contemporary Jewish persons. Yet surely the history of the religious toleration of Jews would be incomplete without acknowledgement of the impact of the idea, disseminated by great humanists, that the rabbinic Noachide precepts are a universal, perpetually binding law issuing from the will of God.

Grotius precedes Selden in accepting the *praecepta Noachidarum* as a universal law, at once issuing from a specifically Jewish source and promulgated to all humankind, and in regarding the biblical Decalogue as binding only on the Jews, who received it at Sinai. Grotius juxtaposes the two laws in a passage inflected by Maimonides' chapter on the Noachide laws in his *Mishneh Torah*. He begins by citing various verses from the Pentateuch and Psalms attesting to the special intimacy between God and the Jews ('*What Nation is there so great who hath* GOD *so nigh unto them*') and then draws the inference that non-Jews are exempt from the Mosaic law:

For a Law obliges only those, to whom it is given. And to whom that Law is given, itself declares, *Hear O Israel*; and we read every where that the *Covenant was made with them*, and that *they were chosen to be the peculiar People of* GOD, which *Maimonides* owns to be true, and proves it from *Deut.* xxxiii.4. But among the *Hebrews* themselves there always lived some Strangers, *Pious Persons, and such as feared* GOD, as the *Syrophenician Woman*, Matt. xv.22. And *Cornelius*, Acts x.2. one ... of *the devout Greeks*, Acts xvii.4; in the *Hebrew*, חסידי אומות *the Righteous amongst the Gentiles*; as it is read in the *Talmud*, *Title of the King*; and he who is such a one is called in the Law בן נכר *a Stranger simply*, Lev. xxii.25. or גר ותושב *a Stranger and a Sojourner*, Lev. xxv.47. Where the *Chaldee* Paraphrast calls him, *an Uncircumcised Inhabitant*. These, as the *Hebrew Rabbins* say [original reads 'Hebraeorum magistri' the honorific used also by Selden] were obliged to keep the Precepts given to *Adam* and *Noah* . . . but not the Laws peculiar to the *Israelites.* (*DJB* 17–18)

When we remember Barbeyrac's diatribe against rabbinic learning, his correction of Grotius's reference to 'the *Talmud, Title of the King*' may surprise us: 'The Quotation of Tit. *De Rege* is false' (*DJB*, 18 n.) He's absolutely right. Unwittingly investing Maimonides with talmudic authority, Grotius had referred to the *Title of the King*, the section of *Mishneh Torah* dealing with the Noachide law, as if it were a talmudic tractate. Although in this instance Barbeyrac neglects to provide a source for this arcane information, it can easily be traced to Selden's *De Jure*, which quotes in full the relevant information about the pious among the Gentiles. Those who accept the seven Noachide commandments as the word of God are counted among the righteous of the nations of the world and merit a share in the world to come. Selden gives full citations to the talmudic and Maimonidean sources, including '*Halach. Melakim* [Kings] c. 8 adde eundem Halach. *Isuri Bia* cap. 14'.[19]

It is clear from Barbeyrac's fuller comment on the passage that he is reading the rabbinic sections of Grotius's book with Selden's *De Jure* at his elbow. He correctly notes various Maimonidean distinctions, as in his note on גר תושב, '*a Stranger and a Sojourner*':

Such a Stranger is distinguished from a *Proselyte*, or circumcised Stranger; as appears from NUMB, ix.14. MAIMONIDES talks much of these pious uncircumcised Persons, in his Treatise *On Idolatry*, Cap. X. Sect. 6. The same Writer, in his *Com. on Misnaioth* and elsewhere, says, that such pious Gentiles will partake of the Happiness of the World to come. (*DJB* 18 n. 6)

Following Selden's discussion of Maimonides, Barbeyrac distinguishes between '*Proselytes of the Gate*, who worshipped the one true God the creator', and '*Proselytes of Justice*, or such as were naturalized' and who therefore observed even the ceremonial laws such as circumcision and several sorts of purification. When Grotius points out that some laws were expressly declared to be given for the stranger as well as the native, Barbeyrac offers the example of 'the Prohibition of working on the Sabbath Day, Exod. xx.10' (*DJB* 19 n. 8).

Barbeyrac, in defence of Grotius's rejection of the Decalogue, records and dismisses the objection that '*Hear O Israel*' is merely the short preface ushering in the universally obligatory laws of the ten commandments. Certainly one of the commandments is a positive law of nations and therefore of limited obligation:

---

[19] John Selden, *De Jure Naturali et Gentium juxta Disciplinam Ebraeorum* (London, 1640), 832–3: '*Piis ex Gentibus Mundi pars* seu *sors est in futuro seculo.*' Hebrew typographical errors are rare in Selden's *De Jure*, despite frequent lengthy quotations. Such errors are far more frequent in Barbeyrac's edition of Grotius—the word נכר is spelled backwards—where Hebrew appears only occasionally. Could this possibly be symptomatic of a decline in Hebrew scholarship from the seventeenth to the eighteenth century?

But, beside that the fourth Commandment, relating to the Observation of the Sabbath, was only for the *Jews*, as appears from the whole Tenor of the Words in which it is drawn up.... if the *Pagans* lay under any Obligation to practise the moral Parts of the *Decalogue*, it was not as they were a Set of Laws delivered from Heaven on Mount *Sinai*, but as so many Precepts which all Men may learn from natural Reason. (*DJB* 17 n.2)

Barbeyrac may well owe this point to Selden, who makes it diffusely in *De Jure* but concisely in a comment on the Sabbath in *Table Talk*, sweeping away the Decalogue with a *sprezzatura* that belies the bitter contemporary dispute between Anglicans and Puritans over strict Sabbath observance:

Why should I think all the fourth commandment belongs to me, when all the fifth does not? What land will the Lord give me for honouring my father? It was spoken to the Jews with reference to the land of Canaan; but the meaning is, if I honour my parents, God will also bless me. We read the commandments in the church-service as we do David's Psalms; not that all there concerns us, but a great deal of them does.[20]

There are many reasons for rejecting the Decalogue as a universally binding law. Where Milton in the divorce tracts divides the Mosaic law Thomistically into a disposable ceremonial component, a permanent moral one, and a selectively applicable judicial one, in his radically Pauline chapter on Christian liberty in *De Doctrina Christiana* he insists that even the Decalogue no longer binds Christians (*YP*, vi. 531). Barbeyrac's insistence that the moral component of the Decalogue consists merely of 'Precepts which all Men may learn from natural Reason' accords with a Huguenot emphasis on individual conscience and a rationalist natural law theory. But Grotius, and after him Selden, reject it within the specifically rabbinic context of the *praecepta Noachidarum*.

Why should a Christian natural law theorist substitute a rabbinic law for a biblical one? Perhaps because at least in this instance the biblical one is exclusive, the rabbinic inclusive. Since Grotius in *De Jure Belli* attempts to identify, sometimes with sociological evidence, the minimal universal laws that cross national boundaries and underpin all human relationships, his frequent references to the partition-wall that separates Jews and Christians may have socio-political as well as legal implications. Grotius associates that partition-wall particularly with commandments that apply only to Jews. Where Paul in Ephesians (2: 11–15) tells the 'Gentiles in the flesh' that Christ has removed the 'middle wall of partition', 'the law of commandments contained in ordinances' (2: 14–15) that separated them from the Jews, Grotius argues instead that the law was not abrogated because it never applied to Christians in the first place. If this is true even of the Decalogue, it certainly applies to ceremonial laws such as circumcision and to those enumerated in Leviticus:

[20] John Selden, *Table Talk*, ed. Samuel Harvey Reynolds (Oxford: Clarendon Press, 1892), 169–70.

Hence we may conclude, that we (*who are not* Jews [not in the original]) are obliged to no Part of the *Levitical* Law, as a Law properly so called, because all Obligation beyond that, arising from the Law of Nature, is derived from the Will of the Law-giver; but it cannot be made appear, that it was the Will of GOD, that any other People, beside the *Israelites*, should be bound by that Law; for it cannot be said to be abrogated in respect to them whom it never bound.... The Advantage which we who are Strangers have obtained by the Coming of CHRIST, does not then consist in being freed from the Law of *Moses*; but, whereas before, we had only very weak Hopes in the Goodness of GOD, we are now, by an express Covenant, assured thereof; and we, together with the *Jews* (the Children of the Patriarchs) are made one Church; their Law, which as a *Partition* Wall divided us, being quite taken away, *Eph.* ii.14. (*DJB* 21)

The parenthetic reference to 'the Children of the Patriarchs' hints at a union that includes Muslims, since Grotius distinguishes the law of Moses obliging only the Israelites from the law of circumcision that 'obliged all the Posterity of *Abraham*' (*DJB* 19), a point underscored by citations of Herodotus, Strabo, Philo, Justin, Origen, Clement of Alexandria, Epiphanius, St Jerome, and Theodoret.

However Paul interprets the partition-wall in Ephesians—as the Jewish law of ordinances (*dogmata* as they are referred to pejoratively in Col. 2: 14) or even as the barrier separating heaven and earth, which Christ has removed—the image itself is suggested by the wall that separated the court of the Gentiles from the sacred areas of the temple in Jerusalem.[21] As Grotius points out, 'It was...allowed to Strangers who came from Abroad, and never submitted to the *Levitical* Law, to worship GOD in the Temple at *Jerusalem*, and to offer Sacrifices; but yet they were obliged to stand in a particular Place, separate from that of the *Israelites*' (*DJB* 19). Barbeyrac's commentary on this passage goes farther than Grotius, emphasizing a common worship among monotheists and defending the Jews from calumniators such as 'the learned Gronovius', who 'pretends that GOD allowed Strangers to pray and offer Sacrifices in the Temple of *Jerusalem*, only with a view of rendering them in some manner tributary to the *Jews*':

But this great Critick did not observe *Solomon's* Words at the Dedication of the Temple, 1 KINGS viii [which ask God to answer the prayers of the '*Stranger that is not of thy People Israel, but cometh out of a far Country for thy Name's sake*']. For which it is evident, that GOD accepted of the Homage of Strangers, when offered with pious Dispositions, as *Solomon* supposes they might be; so that GOD had a very different View on this Occasion from what our Commentator pretends: Nor is the Passage quoted from TACITUS, for proving that the *Jews* were enriched by the Offerings and Presents of the *Pagans*, well applied. (*DJB* 19 n.10)

Barbeyrac quotes a typically vicious Tacitean diatribe against '*that detestable People*' and their greed but rejects it. The source of his note may account in part for his sympathetic tone, as when he refers to a place 'where Strangers were

---

[21] See the note on Ephesians 2: 14 by Wayne Meeks in his edition of *The Writings of St Paul* (New York: W. W. Norton, 1973), 126.

allowed to enter, and perform their Devotions. See SELDEN, *De Jure Nat. & Gent. secund. Hebr.* Lib. III. Cap. VI' (*DJB* 19 n. 9).

In this chapter, Selden discusses the various enclosures of the temple, ending on a strong note of inclusiveness. He cites 'Maimonides *halach. Maighshe Korbanoth* cap. 19. & *halach. Bith habechira*, cap. 6' for the opinion that non-Jews are permitted to bring burnt offerings at whatever place and that Jews are permitted to instruct non-Jews on how to offer sacrifices to God.[22] The very last words of the chapter give the source of this opinion, the tractate '*Zebachim* cap. 14. fol. 115b'. Selden mentions that this treatise of the Babylonian Talmud addresses the freedom of non-Jews to offer sacrifices to the true God before the delivery of the Mosaic law and that it concludes, 'Furthermore, in our own times, Gentiles are permitted to do so.'[23] The reference helps to explain why a rabbinic law might be preferred over a biblical one. The discussion of non-Jews offering sacrifices includes the example of Jethro, Moses's father-in-law, a non-Jewish priest of Midian, who brought sacrifices before God. A dispute arises over whether this happened before or after the revelation of the Torah at Sinai: 'He who maintains that Jethro came before revelation holds that the children of Noah sacrificed peace offerings.'[24] The children of Noah or Noachides is a technical term denoting all people before the revelation at Sinai and all non-Jews who *ipso facto* did not accept the Levitical laws of the Torah after the revelation. The dispute over Jethro makes it clear that Jews were considered Noachides until the laws of sacrifice as stated in Leviticus became operative. Within both Christianity and Judaism, then, the Mosaic law of Leviticus is a partition-wall, and one can understand why both Grotius and Selden would view more positively the rabbinic tradition of a Noachide law that at least before the Sinai theophany provided a minimal set of moral laws that were divine and universally obligatory, uniting Christians and Jews in a way that law and gospel could not.

The rabbinic references in *De Jure Belli* highlight Grotius's influence on Selden and Selden's on Barbeyrac, despite his professed antipathy. Arguing that a just war is not contrary to the '*Voluntary Divine Law*', Grotius offers the example of 'the great *Abraham* to justify this Interpretation, who not being ignorant of the Law given to *Noah*, took up Arms against the four Kings [Gen. 6: 9], which he believed not repugnant to that Law' (*DJB* 30). Since this is not one of the seven Noachide laws, Grotius refers to

that antient Tradition among the *Hebrews*, that GOD gave more Laws to the Sons of *Noah*, which were not all recorded by *Moses*, as thinking it enough to include them afterwards in the peculiar Laws of the Hebrews. Thus it is plain from *Levit.* xviii. that there was an antient Law against incestuous Marriages, tho' not mentioned by *Moses* in its proper

---

[22] Selden *De Jure Naturali*, 3.6, p. 302: 'הגוים מותרין להקריב עולות לשם בכל מקום'. *Gentilibus licet Holocausta offere Domino quocunque locorum....At vero fas est nobis indicare illis & docere quomodo offere debeant Domino Deo Benedicto.'*

[23] Ibid.: '*Etiam & nunc Temporis Gentilibus eo uti fas est.*'

[24] Babylonian Talmud, tractate *Zebachim*, 115b–116b.

Place. Among those Commands of GOD to the Sons of Noah they say this was one, that not only Murders, but also Adulteries, Incests, and Rapines should be punished with Death, which the Words of *Job* [note: Job xxxi.11] seem to confirm. (*DJB* 30)

In spite of his particular aversion to the laws of Leviticus as a partition-wall, Grotius endorses the rabbinic manoeuvre of folding the incest prohibitions of Leviticus 18 into the Noachide laws: 'For granting, that these Prohibitions are not derived from the mere Law of Nature, yet do they plainly appear to have their Sanction from an express Order of the Divine Will: Nor is this such an Order as obliges the *Jews* only, but all Mankind' (*DJB* 197). By removing Leviticus 18 from its place in the Bible as a Mosaic law and reinscribing it as a Noachide law, Grotius is able to explain the casting out of the Canaanites for their sins (Lev. 18: 24–30) in a way that accords with his sense of divine justice. There is no transgression without law, so

if the *Canaanites*, and the People about them offended by such Actions, there must have been some Law that prohibited them, which Law not being purely natural, must needs have been given by GOD, either to them in particular, (which indeed is not very likely, nor do the Words import so much) or to all Mankind; either at the Creation or after the Flood. But now such Laws as were injoined all Mankind, seem no Ways abolished by CHRIST, but only those, which, like a Partition-Wall, separated the *Jews* from all other People. (*DJB* 197)

Grotius's discussion of marriage and incest includes a concentration of rabbinic opinion that he endorses:

Now, the *Hebrews* think that these Laws, and those that prohibit the Marriages of Brothers with sisters, were given to *Adam* at the same Time as that Injunction of serving GOD, of administering Justice, of not shedding Blood, of not worshiping false Deities, of not Robbing; but so that these matrimonial Laws should not be in Force 'till Mankind was sufficiently multiplied, which could never have been if, in the Beginning of the World, Brothers had not married their Sisters.[25]

Of special interest here are the strategies that Barbeyrac adopts in dealing with rabbinic references that make him very uneasy. His note on the passage above reads: 'But this Tradition of Precepts delivered to *Adam* or *Noah* is very uncertain, as I have already observed elsewhere' (*DJB* 199 n. 5). He objects to Grotius's rabbinic idea that the prohibitions of Leviticus 18 oblige not only the Jews 'but all Mankind', including the Canaanites. A particularly convoluted, non-instinctual marital impediment may seem to be neither divine nor universal, and if one may legitimately remove it from the list, then the validity of the list itself can be called into doubt:

---

[25] See first edition of *De Jure Belli*, p. 141: 'Has autem leges, & ne fratres sororibus miscerentur, ipsi Adamo censent datas Hebraei simul cum lege de Deo colendo, jure dicendo, non fundendo sanguine, non colendis Diis falsis, non rapienda re aliena.'

For if it be once acknowledged, that some of the Things prohibited in this Chapter of *Leviticus*, were not Sins in the *Canaanites*, tho' the general Term *all* is used, when the Question turns on such or such a Degree of Consanguinity or Affinity, if we see nothing in it that renders it unlawful by the Law of Nature, we may reasonably doubt whether it be not one of those which ought to be excepted; so that it cannot thence be inferred, that it was forbidden by a divine, positive, and universal Law; the Publication of such a Law is in itself very difficult, not to say impossible to prove. For an uncertain Tradition doth not to me seem sufficient for obliging Men to receive a Thing, as having the Force of Law. (*DJB* 197 n. 1)

Barbeyrac feels obliged to explain how the Canaanites could be justly punished according to some law more authoritative than the 'uncertain Tradition' of the *praecepta Noachidarum*:

I should rather say, that the Vices of the *Canaanites*, for which MOSES declares GOD would punish them, did not consist so much in incestuous Marriages, as in an unbridled Debauchery, which made them transgress almost every Law of Marriage, and put them on satisfying their carnal Desires with the first Persons they met, such as commonly are those with whom one has some Relation or Affinity, and with whom, on that account, one converses most. Thus the incestuous *Corinthian had his Father's Wife*, 1 Cor. V.1. not that he was married to his Mother-in-Law, which the Laws probably did not allow, but because he lived with her as if she had been his Wife, either after his Father's Death, or after she had been divorced. (*DJB* 197 n. 1)

What makes this ostensibly original interpretation both remarkable and emblematic of the ironies and ambivalences of Christian Hebraism is Grotius's explanation on the very next page of the reason for these Levitical prohibitions, an explanation that he attributes to Maimonides, even providing a reference to '*More Nebochim*, l. 3. c. 49'. According to '[t]he antient *Hebrews*, who in this Matter are no contemptible Expositors of the Divine Law, and after them *Moses Maimonides*, who has read, and with great Judgment digested all their Writings',[26] 'the Familiarity and Freedom with which some Persons daily converse together, would give Occasion to Fornications and Adulteries, if such Amours might terminate in a lawful Marriage' (*DJB* 198). Barbeyrac presents Maimonides' reason as if it were his own, although he cites his source belatedly and without acknowledgement for this particular debt, in a note on Grotius's discussion of the prohibited union of brother and sister, omitted from the Levitical prohibitions. When Grotius mentions 'an antient Tradition of a divine Law against such Marriage', the note reads: 'See Selden on this Subject, in De Jure Nat. & Gent. & c. Lib. V. Cap. XI. p. 627, 628' (*DJB* 200 n.11; see also 201 n. 7).

One finds throughout *De Jure Belli* rabbinic ideas either expressed elliptically or left inchoate that Selden will develop in *De Jure Naturali*, generally more

---

[26] See ibid. 140: 'Hebraei veteres non spernendi hac in parte juris divini interpretes, & qui omnia eorum legit summoque judicio digessit Moses Maimonides...'

sympathetically. And Barbeyrac shows the way. His cluster of references to Selden in his notes on Grotius's discussions of Jewish views of marriage reminds the reader that the subject will be developed in Book V of *De Jure Naturali* and in *Uxor Ebraica*. Grotius's observation that Jews are forbidden to make leagues of friendship only with the seven nations which originally inhabited Canaan as well as with the Ammonites, Moabites, and Amalekites (*DJB* 31, 343) is marred by a reference to 'the corrupt Interpretations of the modern Rabbins[, which] infer the contrary' and by the rehearsals of familiar charges of xenophobia leveled by Tacitus and others (p. 343). Yet Grotius also includes examples from the Hebrew Bible of hospitality toward non-Jews. And even regarding the hostile nations in Canaan, the injunction against seeking their prosperity (Deut. 23: 6) 'gives [the Israelites] no right to make War against them, without just Cause; or, perhaps, this Place may be rather understood, according to the Opinion of some of the *Hebrew* Doctors, to prohibit seeking Peace from them, but not the accepting of it when they themselves offered it' (*DJB* 343–4). And he quotes Josephus: '*For we are not inhuman in our Natures, nor are we averse to those, who are not of the same Nation and Family with ourselves.* [Note: *Antiq. Jud.* Lib. VIII. Cap. II.]' (p. 343). In *De Jure Naturali*, Selden will develop the relatively Judaeophilic implications of this idea of inhospitality and enmity authorized by God but directed only toward nations named in the Old Testament that no longer exist but not toward contemporary Gentiles. If God's giving the Jews permission to hate anyone sounds not particularly positive, one might measure the attempted damage control of Selden's argument against both the virtually universal and extreme charges of Jewish xenophobia (that continue in the twenty-first century) and the legacy in the seventeenth century of medieval patterns of diabolization based ultimately on John 8: 44. Catholics could always convert, but, as David S. Katz reminds us, 'the demonological, supernatural element in the early modern attitude to the Jews . . . renders it quite different from other forms of opposition to religious minorities and outcasts.'[27]

A concluding example that follows a thought from Grotius through Selden to Milton comes from Grotius's reference to Leviticus 18 and Job in his discussion of more than seven Noachide laws, 'which the Words of *Job* [marginal note: 'xxxi.11'] seem to confirm' (*DJB* 30). Barbeyrac has little patience with the 'very uncertain Tradition' of seven Noachide laws, and less with 'the antient Tradition among the *Hebrews* that God gave [even] more to the Sons of *Noah*, which were not all recorded by *Moses*' (p. 30). His exasperated note highlights the passage: 'I find nothing in or near these two Texts [Job 31: 11, Leviticus 18: 24–8], relating to the Subject in Hand' (p. 30 n. 13). One imagines that Grotius's marginal reference to Job 31 in the context of Noachide law caught Selden's attention, for the penultimate chapter of *De Jure Naturali* is a *tour de force* of learning and

<hr/>

[27] David S. Katz, *Philo-Semitism and the Readmission of the Jews to England* (Oxford: Clarendon Press, 1982), 3.

imagination, proving exclusively from chapter 31 and various rabbinic commentaries on it that Job was a virtuous Gentile who kept the Noachide laws.[28]

This brief chapter demonstrates both the range of Selden's rabbinic scholarship and his extraordinary philological skills. Although Rashi's commentary ('Sal. Iarch') is the source most frequently cited, there are additional references to rabbinic commentaries on verses in Job 31: 'Levi Ben Gersom', 'R. Mosem Alsheich in *Biur Iob*. fol. 74b and 75a', 'Bereshith Rabbah', 'Aben Ezra', '*Gemar. Babyl. ad tit. Baba Bathra* cap. 1, fol. 14', '*Sepher Juchasin* fol. 9b', 'R. Sem Tom', and 'Maimonid. *More Nebochim* part 3. cap. 2. & commentar'.[29] Both the headnote and the body of the chapter indicate Selden's familiarity with the talmudic emphasis on Job's pre-covenantal status. The place Selden points to in *Baba Bathra* discusses the possibility that Job was a contemporary of Abraham, Jacob, or Moses (even that Moses was the author of the book, who would, after all, have shared with his protagonist undeserved suffering and the ultimate reward of a powerful vision of God)—or that Job 'never was and never existed' except as a figure in a parable, intended presumably to teach the virtue of resignation.[30] Selden ends the chapter by quoting a beautiful passage about Job from Augustine's *City of God* (*De Civitate Dei* lib. 18. cap. 47). The rabbinic content and the Noachide context of the chapter are so strong that they transform Augustine's praise of Job as a Gentile from a slightly antagonistic answer to the Jews to an implicit equation of the dwellers of the spiritual Jerusalem with the righteous among the nations of the world:

There have been some men who belonged not by earthly but by heavenly fellowship to the company of the true Israelites, the citizens of the country that is above ... [Job] was neither a native of Israel nor a proselyte.... He traced his descent from the race of Edom; he was born in Edom; he died there.... I have no doubt that it was the design of God's

[28] Selden has succeeded in creating what sounds exactly like an ancient midrash, though none of the scholars I have queried—including specialists on the interpretative history of the Book of Job—has been able to find anything like it.

[29] Abraham ibn Ezra (1089–1164), poet, grammarian, biblical commentator, philosopher, astronomer, and physician. His commentary on Job, like that of Ben Gershom, appears in the *Biblia Rabbinica*. Levi Ben Gershom (1288–1344), acronym *RaLBaG*, known as Magister Leo Hebraeus, was celebrated for his very broad intellectual interests. His commentary on Job was one of the first printed Hebrew books (Ferrara, 1477). The commentary on Job of Moses Alshekh (16th c.; died *c*.1593), was printed in Venice in 1603. *Bereshith Rabbah* is the midrash on Genesis. The *Sefer ha-Yuhasin* is a book of genealogies by Abraham ben Samuel Zacuto (1452–*c*.1515), astronomer and historian. Joseph ibn Shem Tov was a 15th-c. Spanish rabbi and philosopher whose commentary on Maimonides is printed in many Hebrew editions of the *Guide*.

[30] Both the text of *Baba Bathra* 14b–15b and *De Jure Naturali* (pp. 834, 836) stress Job's pre-covenantal status. Selden's headnote describes the argument of the chapter: '*Capitum illustriorum Juris Naturalis seu Noachidarum vestigia expressissima in Jobi historia, ante legem Mosaicam, saltem non ubi Mosaica lex, Qua Mosaica seu Hebraica, obtinuit, conscripta* (p. 834). Amid the lengthy rabbinic disputes over when or even if Job lived, and whether or not he or his author was Jewish (Ibn Ezra believed the book was a translation from a lost original), all seem to agree that he would have lived before the promulgation of the Mosaic law. For Selden's rehearsal of various opinions from *Baba Bathra*, see p. 836.

providence that from this one instance we should know that there could be those among other nations who lived by God's standards and were pleasing to God, as belonging to the spiritual Jerusalem.[31]

Providing an original example of a rabbinic hermeneutic, though with the help of commentaries on particular verses from the *Biblia Rabbinica*, Selden amplifies Grotius's marginal note that mystified Barbeyrac, demonstrating that Job kept the Noachide laws. He cites 31: 26–8, where Job resists the seduction of the sun and moon, as proof that he does not worship strange gods. That he refrains from blasphemy is attested by his preventive daily sacrificial offerings, 'for Job said, It may be that my sons have sinned, and cursed God in their hearts' (1: 5). Selden quotes from the Hebrew original, 'וברכו האלהים בלבבם' [and blessed God in their hearts], noting that by the word ברך *Benedicere* we are given to understand that the meaning is *maledicere*. He quotes Job's oath in 31: 29–31, with a marginal cross-reference to 24: 14, to prove that he rejects homicide: 'If I rejoiced at the destruction of him that hated me, or lifted up myself when evil found him: Neither have I suffered my mouth to sin by wishing a curse to his soul.' And he reads 31: 7 ('if any blot hath cleaved to mine hands') as testimony that he has never been a thief. Regarding the establishment of civil laws, '*de Judiciis*', Selden quotes 31: 28 ('an iniquity to be punished by the judge [or judges]') and displays enormous erudition in explicating עון פלילים as '*Crimen Judicum*, id est *Judiciale, forense*', with support from Hebrew, Aramaic, Greek, and Latin sources, but especially from Rashi and Alshekh.

Most interesting of all is the reading of Job's oath regarding adultery: 'If mine heart have been deceived by a woman, or if I have laid wait at my neighbour's door; then let my wife grind unto another' (31: 9–10). Selden's extensive philological analysis of טחן (grind) emphasizes the connection between a female slave doing the heavy work of grinding between two millstones and grinding under her master as a sex slave. His citations range from Rashi and Ben Gershom to a Horation threnody, and he compares Horace's use of *permolere* (to grind thoroughly) with the dual meaning of טחן.[32] He quotes a euphemistic rabbinic reading of the word as referring to the special service that a wife performs for her husband.[33] Rashi's nine-word commentary introduces yet another word designating both activities: 'According to our rabbis, the word refers to use/sexual

---

[31] Augustine, *City of* God, ed. David Knowles (Harmondsworth: Penguin, 1972), 829. Selden, *De Jure Naturali*, 837: '*Homines quosdam non terrena sed coelesti societate ad veros Israelitas, supernae cives patriae. . . . Job . . . nec indigena, nec Proselytus . . . Sed ex gente Idumaea genus ducens, ibi ortus, ibidem mortuus est. . . . Divinitus autem provisum fuisse non dubito ut ex hoc uno sciremus etiam per alias gentes esse potuisse, qui secundum Deum vixerunt eique placuerunt, pertinentes ad spiritualem Hierusalem.*'

[32] See *De Jure Naturali*, 835, marginal note 'm': '*de* טחן *seu molendi vocabulo ad coitum (ut alienas permolere uxores ferè Horatio) designandum adhibito. Vide vulgat. vers. Thren. c.5.13. & compara cum Ebraea.*'

[33] Ibid. 835: 'מהעבדות המיוחדות אשר תעבד בהם האשה בעלה *ex ministeriis singularibus quibus marito serviebat uxor.*'

intercourse [his synonym תשמיש means both], as in Judges 16 [v. 21], "and he did grind in the prison house."' The reference, of course, is to Samson, and it is interesting to note that only in the second edition of Milton's *Doctrine and Discipline of Divorce* (1644), which introduces Selden's *De Jure Naturali et Gentium* into its argument,[34] do we find the famous anticipation of *Samson Agonistes* in the description of an unhappy marriage: 'to grind in the mill of an undelighted and servil copulation' (*YP*, ii. 258).

Grotius, Selden's strong spiritual progenitor, refers in a marginal note to Job 31 in a context of Noachide law. Rabbinic scholarship is one field in which Selden can be said unequivocally to have outdone Grotius. The chapter devoted to Job 31 is a magnificently erudite elaboration of a marginal note, just as the seven books of *De Jure Naturali et Gentium*, corresponding to the seven Noachide laws, are an immense elaboration of the scattered references to those laws in *De Jure Belli ac Pacis*. As so often happens in reading Grotius in the great edition of 1738, the very dismissiveness of Barbeyrac's note on Job 31 serves to highlight the passage for the reader. And perhaps one can be forgiven for imagining that Selden's philological analysis of a word given dual meaning by biblical and classical history lies behind Milton's powerful phrase. What is more demonstrable is that no history of early modern religious toleration is complete without reference to Grotius's *De Jure Belli ac Pacis libri tres*. The implicitly Judaeophilic context of most of its rabbinic references shades into history, affecting not only Selden, whose magnificent rabbinic learning has a definite tolerationist influence, but even a sceptic such as Barbeyrac, whose diligent study of *De Jure Naturali* as preparation for editing *De Jure Belli* complicated his attitude toward the ancient Jewish sources.

---

[34] See *YP*, ii. 350, the headnote to the last chapter (2.22): '*The last Reason why divorce is not to be restrain'd by Law, it being against the Law of nature and of Nations. The larger proof wherof referr'd to Mr.* Seldens *Book* De jure naturali & gentium.' See also the praise on the same page of 'that noble volume written by our learned *Selden*, *Of the law of nature & of Nations*, a work more useful and more worthy to be perus'd, whosoever studies to be a great man in wisdom, equity, and justice, then all those *decretals, and sumles sums*, which the *Pontifical Clerks* have doted on.'

7

Selden's *De Jure Naturali . . . Juxta Disciplinam Ebraeorum* and Religious Toleration

SELDEN AND RABBINIC SCHOLARSHIP

In 1753, during the most intense phase of the controversy surrounding the Jewish Naturalization Act or Jew Bill, the English printer William Bowyer responded with measured remarks to a speech made in Common Council against the bill. The adversary's principal argument had been that to 'collect the Jews together' would both falsify Christian prophecy, which requires that they be 'dispersed and scattered', and verify Jewish prophecies of restoration.[1] Bowyer's argument in favour of the bill is consistently humane. Where his adversary repeated the accusation that divine providence requires permanent Jewish exile, Bowyer argues instead that only providence can account for Jewish survival: 'their *preservation* through so many ages, notwithstanding their various changes and unsettled state, is what discovers the particular guidance of Heaven':

Without a singular Providence, a people disunited, and divided into an infinite number of distinct families, banished into countries whose language and customs were different from theirs, must have been mingled and confounded with other nations, and all traces of them must, these many ages, have entirely disappeared. In spite of the general aversion conceived against them, in spite of the efforts of all those nations who hate them, and who have them in their power, in spite of every human obstacle, they are preserved by a supernatural protection, which has not in like manner preserved any other nation of the earth.[2]

Bowyer ridicules his opponent's fears that Christian prophecy will be disconfirmed: 'What! to collect them all into England, and then to transplant them

---

[1] 'REMARKS on a SPEECH made in COMMON COUNCIL, on the Bill for permitting Persons professing the JEWISH Religion to be Naturalized, so far as Prophecies are supposed to be affected by it' [1753], collected in William Bowyer, *Miscellaneous Tracts*, ed. John Nichols (London, 1785), 453–5. Bowyer was a leading member of the London book trade in the eighteenth century, and major works by Defoe, Pope, Swift, and many others bear his imprint. See Keith Maslen, *An Early London Printing House at Work: Studies in the Bowyer Ledgers* (New York: Bibliographical Society of America, 1993).

[2] Bowyer, *Miscellaneous Tracts*, 457.

to Jerusalem! Not a hundred probably will be naturalized in ten years; and before we shall make a nation of them, we may trust that the "Times of the Gentiles may be fulfilled." '³ In fact, Bowyer insists on the harmony of the Jewish and Christian prophecies: 'Now I always apprehended the Jewish Prophecies are the very same in which the Christians believe; and if the latter have any which the former reject, I hope they are in no particular inconsistent.'⁴ As if to demonstrate this harmony, Bowyer cites in the same breath 'Origen, Chrysostom, and Seder Olam', who share the same opinion regarding the restoration of the Jews.⁵ Bowyer's perplexingly casual use of an obscure, midrashic, chronological work of the second century as if it were as well known as the writings of the church fathers resembles the similar and frequent use of the same work by John Selden, particularly in his study of rabbinic methods of chronological calculation, *De Anno Civili et Calendario Veteris Ecclesiae seu Reipublicae Judaicae* (1644). It turns out that Bowyer, the most learned English printer of his age, was very familiar with Selden's writings. He wrote an epitome of his study of the Sanhedrin, *De Synedriis Veterum Hebraeorum*, and that as well as 'other memoranda from that learned Writer, were the result of his superintendence of the complete edition of Selden's works in his press, 1722–1726'.⁶

Being aware of Bowyer's role as printer of the still-definitive *Joannis Selden Opera Omnia* (1726), edited by David Wilkins, helps to explain certain characteristics of the little tract: investing with equal authority ancient Christian and post-biblical, rabbinic Hebrew sources; according respect to historical documents in a style identical to Selden's; even concluding, as Selden often does, with the very same signature figure of passing over with a deprecating ring that the rhetoricians call *praeteritio*: 'I meddle not with the political reasons for or against this Bill: my design was only to shew, that Christianity is no ways affected by it.'⁷ Bowyer, like Selden, displays liberal worldly wisdom.

---

³ Ibid. 455. For 'the times of the gentiles', see Luke 21: 24.

⁴ Ibid. 453.

⁵ Ibid. 454.

⁶ John Nichols, Preface, *Miscellaneous Tracts*, pp. vii–viii. A letter from Dr Wotton, sent to Bowyer in 1726, regarding the three volumes in six of Selden's monumental *Opera Omnia*, attests to the delicate handling it received from two learned readers. Dr Wotton thanks Bowyer, 'for the trust you have reposed in me, in lending me the new *Selden*. Assure yourself it shall be particularly taken care of.' To which Mr Clarke subjoins, 'I can only add my thanks to the Doctor's, for the great treasure you have sent us. They came down safe; and I will take as much care as possible that they receive no damage. I have already put new coats upon them, that change of air and other like accidents might not affect them. I shall not think of returning them till the roads are fair again; nor shall I forget your directions about hay' (p. 39).

⁷ Bowyer, *Miscellaneous Tracts*, 458. See for comparison the conclusion of Selden's letter to Jonson in the Appendix: 'With what ancient fathers as Cyprian & Tertullian specially have of this text, or others dealing on it as it tends to morality, I abstain to meddle.' See also Selden's Apology in *Titles of Honour* (1614), sig. c4v: 'There are, which have in part handled some of my Titles, and as their Purpose. I abstain from comparison'; and *The Historie of Tithes* (1617), 486: 'But I abstain from censure.'

Acting on the belief that the stories we tell about others reveal even more about ourselves, recent and justly well-regarded studies of England and the Jews, during a period that includes Selden's lifetime, have demonstrated that a culture's representation of 'Otherness' has important consequences for its own self-imagining.[8] The often vile racist stereotypes unearthed by James Shapiro in *Shakespeare and the Jews* can only have meaning if our fantasies about others reveal our deepest fears about ourselves. The fear and loathing of Jews as child abductors, murderers, and cannibals can help to explain the confused struggles among the English in the early modern era to develop a religious and national identity in a turbulent time. Judaism as a race, nation, and religion is defined as different in every way from the English Protestantism that it threatens to contaminate.

Inevitably, Shapiro's exhaustive and valuable attempt to reconstruct a Renaissance audience's experience of *The Merchant of Venice* in the light of its preconceptions about Jews involves recourse to the most destructive myths and stereotypes. He acknowledges but understandably does not concentrate on an exception such as Selden, whose rabbinic researches, unlike those of his other great contemporary English talmudic scholar John Lightfoot, are free of Judaeophobia.[9] One might argue that Selden is precious precisely because he is uncommon, like the courageous few who throughout history have refused to be swallowed up by the mob. Generally sceptical toward harmful myths, Selden has a humanist's respect for historical investigation and an antiquarian's interest in the documents of the past simply because they exist.[10] We have already

---

[8] See esp. Michael Ragussis, *Figures of Conversion: 'The Jewish Question' & English National Identity* (Durham, NC, and London: Duke University Press, 1995), and James Shapiro, *Shakespeare and the Jews* (New York: Columbia University Press, 1996).

[9] Shapiro makes the important point that in his scholarship Selden draws upon examples from the Bible, the Talmud, and medieval Anglo-Jewish history, thus 'collapsing any simple distinction between the ancient Israelite and the modern Jewish nation' (*Shakespeare and the Jews* 174).

[10] A serious and unfortunate example of antiquarian devotion to documents overcoming scepticism would seem to be the records of Jewish ritual murder in his brief *Treatise on the Jews in England* (1617). Gerald J. Toomer, who generously read an earlier draft of this chapter, argues that Selden's position on the matter cannot be so easily determined. His history of the Jews appears in the third edition of Samuel Purchas's *Pilgrimage* (1617), and parts of it—such as a reference to 'one cruell and (to speake the properest phrase) Jewish crime . . . usuall amongst them'—sound like Purchas rather than Selden. More important, in a transcript provided by Professor Toomer of the relevant sections of William Prynne's *Short Demurrer to the Jewes Long Discontinued Remitter into England* (1656), Prynne asserts that Purchas did not print unaltered what Selden submitted to him, and Selden was angry with Purchas 'for abusing him in such a manner, and his Readers likewise' (p. 1). Selden took the stories of ritual murder from Matthew Paris, who had a virulent hatred of the Jews. A number of questions complicate the matter, including the relation of Selden's original *Treatise* to what Prynne calls 'such a poor maimed account given of [the Jews] . . . so different from that delivered [to Purchas]' (p. 1). Professor Toomer believes that Selden, reproducing his sources in a mostly straightforward narrative, 'was already too much of a skeptic to endorse the stories of Matthew Paris as is done in Purchas's rendering'. The one example in the *Treatise* that seems to derive directly from an archival source and is accompanied by one of Selden's characteristic learned notes is not of an accusation of ritual murder but rather of forced circumcision in Norwich. But 'the Jewes after procured the boy to be seene, and his member was found covered.' Selden then refers to

mentioned that Selden, a polymath, wrote a half-dozen rabbinic works, some of them immense, which respect, to an extent remarkable for the times, the self-understanding of Judaic exegesis. Selden's motto was 'περὶ παντὸς τὴν ἐλευθερίαν [liberty above all things]', and *De Synedriis et Praefecturis Juridicis Veterum Ebraeorum* (1650–5), a study of the Sanhedrin written shortly after the execution of Charles I, contains a remarkable Maimonidean discussion of whether that court could try kings not only for crimes like murder that anyone could commit but also for those which only kings could commit. Occupying 1,132 huge folio columns in the *Opera*, *De Synedriis* deals primarily with the constitution of Jewish courts, including the Sanhedrin, which, as Selden notes pointedly, was not priestly in composition. Its understated argument is thoroughly Erastian, demonstrating that matters at present under the jurisdiction of ecclesiastical courts in England were in ancient times decided by Jewish courts that could well be called secular.[11] The implicit argument is that the Sanhedrin might serve as a positive model for Parliament. Taken together, Selden's rabbinic works constitute a notable exception to those products of the English Renaissance that emphasize otherness and difference.

Selden's important contribution to political theory and international law, *De Jure Naturali et Gentium juxta Disciplinam Ebraeorum* (1640), 847 folio pages, is surely one of the most genuinely philosemitic works produced by a Christian Hebraist in early modern Europe. Selden accepts the universal validity of the non-biblical, rabbinic *praecepta Noachidarum*, the seven Noachide laws, which serve for him as the law of nature. Selden bases his theory on the Talmud, which he believes records a set of doctrines far older than classical antiquity.[12] Natural law consists not of innate rational principles that are intuitively obvious but rather of specific divine pronouncements uttered by God at a point in historical time. Selden discusses the rabbinic identification of natural law with the divinely pronounced Adamic and Noachide laws, considered by rabbinic tradition as the minimal moral duties enjoined upon all of humankind. He quotes from the *locus classicus* in tractate Sanhedrin (56a–b), which includes the traditional enumeration of the laws: the prohibitions of idolatry and blasphemy, the injunction to establish a legal system, commandments against bloodshed, sexual sins, and theft, and a seventh law, not applicable to vegetarian Adam but added after the flood

---

an ancient Hellenistic technique of 'Chirurgery, [whereby] the skinne may be drawne forth to an uncircumcision' (p. 173 of Purchas; Selden, *Opera Omnia*, iii. 1461). Does Selden believe that the Jews of medieval Norwich practised this surgical technique? There are more questions than answers. What can be asserted is that no Christian can be found in early modern England who unequivocally rejected the blood libel.

[11] See on this point Jonathan R. Ziskind's introduction to his edition, *John Selden on Jewish Marriage Law: The Uxor Hebraica* (Leiden, New York: E. J. Brill, 1991), 18.

[12] See Richard Tuck, *Philosophy and Government 1572–1651* (Cambridge: Cambridge University Press, 1993), 214. I am greatly indebted to all of Professor Tuck's writings on Selden, especially *Natural Rights Theories: Their Origin and Development* (Cambridge: Cambridge University Press, 1979).

and based on Genesis 9: 4, forbidding anyone to eat flesh cut from a living animal. Selden devotes an entire book of *De Jure* to each of the seven commandments, and he follows the order set by Maimonides, which emphasizes their decalogic nature. The first two, like the first table of the law, deal with the relations between human beings and God, while the rest govern relations among human beings.[13] While Selden accepts the authority of this post-biblical, rabbinic, universal law, he rejects the absolute authority of the biblical ten commandments on the grounds that they were given only to the Jews.

In *De Jure* Selden sets down ideas regarding the nature of Judaism and its attitude toward Gentiles that are far more charitable than those circulating in other contemporary works addressed to Christian audiences. Selden did not live to see Cromwell's Whitehall Conference, and one can never be certain that his reverence for ancient Jewish learning and toleration of contemporary Jews would have extended so far as activity on behalf of readmission. Since Menasseh Ben Israel first set foot in England in 1655, a year after Selden's death, one can assert that during Selden's lifetime no exponent of Judaism in England with a body of published scholarship equalled him in talmudic learning. Indeed, theology rather than rabbinic law was Menasseh's forte, so Selden, had he lived, might not have yielded to one whose writings he knew well and cited frequently. That would make Selden the supreme *parshan* or interpreter by default. England, after all, unlike some other European countries its size, never produced a great medieval or early modern rabbinic sage, a fact related to the expulsion of the Jews under Edward I in 1290.

The double vision explicit in the term Christian Hebraism signals the topic's profound ambivalence and inevitably raises questions of displacement and appropriation. The royalist poet John Cleveland epitomizes the problem in *The Mixt Assembly*. The chief satirist of the parliamentary cause portrays the mixed membership of the Westminster Assembly, clergy and lay, as a grotesque mismatch:

> Like Jewes and Christians in a ship together,
> With an old Neck-verse to distinguish either. (ll.45–6)[14]

The beginning of Psalm 51 that could save the neck of a condemned person claiming benefit of clergy was in black-letter Latin. For Cleveland, the biblical text distinguishes the Christian, who can save himself by his identity and his

---

[13] Selden, *De Jure Naturali et Gentium juxta Disciplinam Ebraeorum* (London, 1640), 118–19. He lists the ordinances as '*de Cultu extraneo*', '*de Maledictione Nominis sanctissimi seu Numinis*', '*de Effusione Sanguinis* seu *Homicidio*', '*de Revelatione Turpitudinum* seu *Turpitudine ex concubitu*', '*de Furto ac Rapina*', '*de Judiciis* seu *Regimine forensi ac Obedientia Civili*', and '*de Membro animalis viventis* non comedendo'. His list is based on Maimonides' distinction between those commandments that are '*inter Hominem & Numen sanctissimum*' and those that are '*inter Hominem & proximum suum*'.

[14] *The Poems of John Cleveland*, ed. Brian Morris and Eleanor Withington (Oxford: Clarendon Press, 1967), 27.

proficiency, from the Jew. The irony that *Sefer Tehillim* was written in Hebrew by a Jew is lost on him.

The central figure of the poem is the Westminster Assembly itself, portrayed as a giddy 'Antick dance' (l.67), forcing enemies to be partners, so that 'every *Gibelline* hath got his *Guelph*' (l.87):

> But *Selden*, hee's a Galliard by himself,
> And well may be; there's more divines in him
> Then in all this their Jewish *Sanhedrim*. (ll.88–90)

Selden, the only person who escapes unequivocal censure in this angry poem, is a galliard, 'a man of courage and spirit' (*OED*, which quotes line 88). Because of his unmatchable greatness, no partner can be found for him, especially from an Assembly such as this one. He is his own man, one who includes dancer, dance, and music: galliard is also 'a quick and lively dance in triple time' as well as 'the air to which the galliard is danced' (*OED*). A lay member of the Assembly, Selden is worth more than all the Anglican and Presbyterian divines who compose the clerical membership put together. Cleveland praises Selden's authentic scholarship, which, during the years that the Assembly convened, consisted almost entirely of rabbinica, and alludes perhaps to the forthcoming magisterial *De Synedriis*, a study of the *Synedrium Magnum* whose seventy-one members make up a civil court that Selden holds up as a model for Parliament. Admiring the scholarship but deploring its subject, Cleveland sneeringly brands as Jewish the Assembly that he hates almost as much as he does the Parliament whose ordinance created it. Cleveland's praise of Selden as one who contains many— and as one whose authentic Jewish learning exposes the folly of a body reviled for its resemblance to a Jewish institution—underscores the conflicting tonalities of Christian Hebraism.

If Christians in early modern England are at best ambivalent toward Jews, it should be noted that the Talmud is neither monolithic nor consistent in its attitude toward non-Jews—not surprising when one considers that the category is large enough to include the universal progenitors Adam and Noah and the Roman oppressors who destroyed the second temple. Selden's talmudic scholarship reflects the profound ambivalence of its sources. In *De Jure Naturali*, he asserts that the righteous among the Gentiles enjoy a share or portion of the world to come ('*Piis ex Gentibus Mundi pars seu sors est in futuro seculo*'), and the range of authorities he cites in support of this view includes the Talmud itself, which is the primary source, as well as his favourite commentary on the Talmud, Maimonides, and his own contemporary, Menasseh Ben Israel.[15] His learning is so wide-ranging that he can find two places in Maimonides that define the crucial

---

[15] Selden, *De Jure Naturali et Gentium*, 832. His sources include tractate Sanhedrin, 'Maimonidis tractatu *de Poenitentia*, cap. 3' and 'Manasseh Ben Israel . . . *de Resurrectione, Amstelodami, 1636*, lib. 2. cap. 8 & 9' and 'ad Deut. quaest. 163. Hispanice 2. Latine'.

term in the talmudic passage, 'the righteous among the Gentiles'—lit., 'the nations of the world':

Whoever accepts upon himself the fulfilment of these seven precepts and is precise in their observance is called one of the righteous among the gentiles and will merit a share in the world to come. This applies only when one accepts them and fulfils them because the holy one, blessed be he, commanded them and informed us through Moses our teacher that they were commanded from of old to the children of Noah. But if one decides to perform them as a result of personal preference rather than because God commanded them, then such a person is not a proselyte of the dwelling-place [i.e. a partial proselyte, who renounces idolatry for the sake of acquiring limited citizenship], nor of the righteous among the Gentiles, nor of their wise persons.[16]

Omitted are most of Selden's gap-fillings, definitions, paraphrases, synonyms, pronominal identifications, and other clarifications that are present in virtually all of his translations of ancient texts. He can discriminate legally between the partial proselyte or גר תושב, who makes a formal commitment in the presence of a court, and the righteous Gentile who accepts the Noachide precepts with the proper intent but without formalizing the acceptance. He knows that when the Talmud deprives the corrupt generation living at the time of Noah's flood from either sharing in eternal life or standing in judgment ('*judicio*'), the reference is to the day of great judgment ('*diem Judicii Magnum*').[17]

Selden is fully aware of talmudic dialogue and of opinions that either qualify or contradict one another. He knows the judgement of R. Meir that 'even a pagan who conscientiously observes the law is considered to be equal to the high priest' ['*etiam Paganum qui diligenter legem observaverit veluti Pontificem maximum habendum*'] and the equally extreme reaction of R. Yohanan that 'a non-Jew who engages in the study of Torah is liable to execution'.[18] But Selden embeds the latter view only within tractate Sanhedrin's resolution of the contradiction in its chapter on the four methods of execution: the Talmud explains that R. Meir is referring to a non-Jew who studies the seven Noachide laws that non-Jews are obligated to observe. [He indeed is worthy of praise.] But a non-Jew who keeps the rest of the laws [as an Israelite, and with the authority of an Israelite, Selden adds] is condemned to death.[19] In a prefatory statement in *De Jure*, Selden

---

[16] *De Jure*, 833: '*Quicunque susceperit in se septem Praecepta, atque monitus ea cautius observaverit... ipse est ex eis qui vocantur Pii ex Gentibus Mundi, atque ei sors est in seculo futuro. Eum vero intelligimus qui ea observaverit ideo quod praeceperit Deus O. M. ut legislator. Nam & per Mosem Magistrum nostrum nobis notum fecit, imperatam fuisse antiquitus Noachidis eorum observationem. Ceterum si sponte solum, seu ex suo potius arbitratu* (non habita imperantis Numinis sanctissimi ratione) *ea observaverit, nec pro Proselyto Domicilii, nec pro aliquo ex Piis ex Gentilibus Mundi habetur, neque in numero Sapientum eorum censendus est.*' The two cited Maimonidean texts are '*Halach. Melakim* c. 8. Adde eundem Halach. *Isuri Bia* cap. 14'.

[17] Ibid. 832.

[18] Ibid. 833.

[19] Ibid. referring to *Sanhedrin* 59a: '*Intelligendum est de septem praeceptis Paganis propriis. Nam quod ad caetera attinet; docetur in Titulo Sanhedrin capite de quatuor Poenarum capitalium*

appeals to biblical and talmudic precedent for publishing opposed points of view as a means of distinguishing more readily between truth and falsehood, with Proverbs 11: 14 and 24: 6 ('for in the multitude of counsellors there is safety') as his central text: '*Et erit salus ubi multa consilia sunt,* seu ut in Ebraeo, יועץ ברוב ותשועה *& salus in plurimis consiliariis.*'[20] The talmudic penchant for including all opinions provides the subtext of Milton's praise of Selden and his *De Jure Naturali et Gentium* ('naturall and national laws') in the *Areopagitica*. Addressing Parliament, Milton also employs this firmly established usage and points to Selden, MP for the University of Oxford, to authorize it:

> Whereof what better witnes can ye expect I should produce, then one of your own now sitting in Parlament, the chief of learned men reputed in this Land, Mr. *Selden*, whose volume of naturall & national laws proves, not only by great autorities brought together, but by exquisite reasons and theorems almost mathematically demonstrative, that all opinions, yea errors, known, read, and collated, are of main service & assistance toward the speedy attainment of what is truest. (*YP,* ii. 513)

In conversation at table, during the last year of his life, Selden recalled how his own *Historie of Tithes* (1617), which aroused so much clerical vehemence by treating tithes as a matter of civil right rather than as due by *jure divino*, was years later consulted by clerics looking to justify the institution: 'a book so much cried down by them formerly (in which, I dare boldly say, there are more arguments for them than are extant together anywhere): upon this, one [Gerard Langbaine, Provost of Queen's College, Oxford] writ me word [in a letter dated 22 August 1653] that my history of tithes was now become like *Pelias hasta*, to wound and to heal.'[21]

Selden may present opposing points of view, but it is usually not too difficult to deduce his own opinion. Regarding the Talmud's position on eternal life for righteous non-Jews, we are lucky to have a clear expression of Selden's opinion late in life as well as evidence regarding the one talmudic text, out of many on the subject, that he considered to be definitive. The *DNB,* acknowledging Selden's enormous erudition and his genius for 'direct, simple, and effective' conversation, describes his prose style in both Latin and English as digressive, prolix, and 'embarrassed'. To read Selden's scholarly prose is to recall Bizet's celebrated comment on Berlioz that he 'had genius without talent'.[22] Fortunately, his

generibus Paganum qui observaverit legem (qua Israeliticam, atque in ditione Israelitica) mortis esse reum.'

[20] Ibid. 8.

[21] *The Table Talk of John Selden,* ed. Samuel Harvey Reynolds (Oxford: Clarendon Press, 1892), 179–80. The letter is preserved in the Bodleian, MS Selden supra 109, fo. 463. The allusion is to Ovid, *Remedium Amoris,* 47, which describes the spear of Achilles, made of wood from Mt Pelion. Telephus could only be cured by the spear that inflicted the wound.

[22] Undated letter (June 1871) to Léonie Halévy: in *Lettres de Georges Bizet: Impressions de Rome; La Commune (1871)* (Paris, 1907), 322; cited by Isaiah Berlin in *Three Critics of the Enlightenment: Vico, Hamann, Herder,* ed. Henry Hardy (Princeton: Princeton University Press, 2000), 104. See

secretary Richard Milward transcribed his *Table Talk*, which, besides revealing an extraordinary talent for lucidly expressed analogy, presents his most characteristic opinions, mostly from the 1640s until the end of his life, including many of the ideas that are expressed more laboriously in *De Jure Naturali et Gentium*. The rabbinic foundation of many of those dinner-table conversations has never been recognized. His simple comment on salvation is uncommon, perhaps unique in mid-seventeenth-century England, for its religious sympathy:

We may best understand the meaning of σωτηρία, *salvation*, from the Jews, to whom the Saviour was promised. They held that themselves should have the chief place of happiness in the other world; but the gentiles that were good men, should likewise have their portion of bliss there too. Now by Christ the partition-wall is broken down, and the gentiles that believe in him, are admitted to the same place of bliss with the Jews. And why then should not that portion of happiness still remain to them who do not believe in Christ, so they be morally good. This is a charitable opinion.[23]

The source of this view is 'Gemara Babylon. Ad tit. *Aboda Zara* cap. 1. Fol. 3a', which Selden cites numerous times.[24] In the relevant passage,

R. Meir used to say, 'From where do we know that even a gentile who busies himself with Torah is equal to the high priest? It teaches, [*You shall keep my laws and rules*], *which if a man do, he shall live in them* [Leviticus 18: 5]. It does not say "Priests, Levites and Israelites" but rather "man". This teaches that even a gentile who busies himself with Torah is like a high priest.' Rather [the Gemara answers], they do not receive a reward equal to one who is commanded and fulfils, but equal to one who is not commanded and fulfils. For R. Hanina said, 'Greater is one who is commanded and fulfils than one who is not commanded and fulfils.'

Clearly, Selden knows this text, with its counter-intuitive distribution of greater rewards to one who is obliged over one who does good voluntarily. The idea underlying the passage is the contrast between the authority of the human will and the law of God. When a person acts in obedience to a Torah commandment, the merit is considered greater.

At least in *Table Talk*, as in *De Jure*, Selden views soteriology not through the lens of the proof-texts of Christian apologetics, in which Christ was given and sacrificed from the beginning of the world, but according to the Jews, whose rabbinic hermeneutic applied to Leviticus 18: 5 promises eternal life ('*shall live*') to the ethical person who performs the Torah's '*laws and rules*'. The talmudic passage addresses the question of who inherits eternal life, and the answer applies

also the invidious comparison (quoted in chapter three) of Selden's 'two large and learned syntagmas' on the idol-gods of *De Diis Syris* with Milton's 'one hundred and thirty very beautiful lines' in the catalogue of his great epic (i. 376–505), in Edward Gibbon, *The History of the Decline and Fall of the Roman Empire*, ed. David Womersley, 3 vols. (London: Penguin, 1994), i. 449 n. 9.

[23] *Table Talk*, 170–1. In the Georgetown University library's copy of the 1892 edition, there is a check beside the penultimate sentence and, in the margin, '!?!'

[24] See, e.g. *De Jure*, 117, 833.

not to the Israelite priest or Levite and not even to the Israelite layperson but rather to any human being (*ha' adam*). These are also the main elements of the Good Samaritan parable, perhaps the most beautiful in the entire New Testament, which, in the history of its interpretation, and despite its message of inclusiveness, raises disturbing questions about religious exclusivity, as does the complete text of *Avodah Zarah* 3a. The lawyer (*nomikos*) in Luke asks the question, 'What shall I do to inherit eternal life?' (10: 25). When Jesus responds with another question, 'What is written in the law? How do you read?' (10: 26), the lawyer answers with two commandments from the Hebrew Bible: 'You shall love the Lord your God...' (Deut. 6: 5) and 'You shall love your neighbor as yourself' (Lev. 19: 18). This time Jesus's response echoes Leviticus 18: 5, the central text of the talmudic passage: 'You have answered right; do this and live' (Luke 10: 28). The lawyer provides the occasion for the parable by asking further, 'And who is my neighbour?' (Luke 10: 29), and Jesus answers with the story of the man who fell among thieves, was beaten, and left for dead. The audience, hearing that a priest and Levite pass by on the other side, expects the parable to be anti-clerical and the third person to be an Israelite, but instead it is an outsider, a Samaritan, who binds the wounds, treats them with oil and wine, carries the half-dead man to the inn, leaves money with the innkeeper for further care, and promises to return.[25] The neighbour is no longer only an Israelite but includes anyone who shows mercy by loving another as himself.

Frank Kermode provides arcane and divergent readings of the parable from the church fathers as examples of 'the interminability of interpretation'. Certainly one of the interpretative constants in this parable of radical inclusiveness is a rejection of Judaism: 'The priest and Levite represent the inefficacious old dispensation'; 'the basic pattern—Christianity going on beyond the failure of Judaism'.[26] To this very day, and not only among Christian sects that would consign Jews to hell, the parable is cited as an example of Jewish xenophobia and ethnocentrism. These interpreters point out that the neighbour one is commanded to love in Leviticus 19: 18 is a fellow Jew, while Jesus broadens the definition to include everyone. Of course the same chapter in Leviticus contains the command, 'Thou shalt love [the stranger] as thyself, for ye were strangers in the land of Egypt' (19: 34).

Selden's attitude toward contemporary Jews is wittily tolerant, falling somewhat short of love:

Talk what you will of the Jews, that they are Cursed, they thrive where'er they come; they are able to oblige the Prince of their Country by lending him money; none of them beg;

---

[25] For an elegant and comprehensive reading of the parable, see Frank Kermode, *The Genesis of Secrecy* (Cambridge, Mass.: Harvard University Press, 1979), 34–9; see also John Drury, *The Parables in the Gospels* (New York: Crossroad, 1985), 132–6. Drury finds in 2 Chronicles 28: 14 ff. a source in the Hebrew Bible for good Samaritans who similarly clothe the naked, anoint, provide food and drink, and carry.

[26] Kermode, *Genesis of Secrecy*, p. 36; Drury, *Parables*, p. 134.

they keep together; and for their being hated, my life for yours, the Christians hate one another as much.[27]

Selden has a highly developed sense of irony, and this ingenious defence relies for its effectiveness on a hostile attitude toward an imaginary opponent of the Jews. That opponent represents the vast majority of his countrymen, who portray contemporary Jews as cursed and hated. As was noted, the main intent of one of Selden's immense scholarly books may be deliberately tucked away in a parenthesis, and the key phrase in this brief monologue is the casually brutal 'my life for yours'. Selden's treatise *The Duello* (1610) traces the history and set forms of single combat between appellant and defendant, who swear oaths before betting their lives. In this instance, Selden makes his point that 'Christians hate each other as much' as soon as his opponent accepts his challenge of 'my life for yours'. Both the challenge and its acceptance expose the bloody-mindedness of one Christian Englishman willing to take the life of another in order to prove that Christians hate Jews even more than they hate each other.

THE EARLY RECEPTION OF *DE JURE*

In the rest of this chapter, I want to provide a sampling of responses to the specifically rabbinical scholarship in Selden's *De Jure Naturali et Gentium*. Selden's admiration of rabbinic thought and his toleration of contemporary Jews should be measured against seventeenth-century England's legacy, mentioned in the preceding chapter, of medieval patterns of diabolization. In such a context, what would it mean to find in a magisterial work by the most learned person in the country a chapter title near the end (and in Selden important matters are always addressed near the end) on the promise of eternal life, heavenly or divine *(Coelestis, seu Divini)*, held out to the entire human race *(Noachidas seu Universum genus humanum)*, according to the opinion of the Hebrews *(ex Ebraeorum sententia)*?[28] More important, what would it mean to read a work that explicitly and consistently insists on the divine nature of the non-biblical, exclusively rabbinic *praecepta Noachidarum*? It should become clear that Selden's younger contemporaries, who used the scholarship contained in *De Jure Naturali* in the service of liberalism and inclusiveness in politics and religion, would not have been able to read the work without finding striking examples of Jewish charity toward those outside.

Selden is not the first scholar in the early modern period to treat of the Noachide laws. His intellectual hero Hugo Grotius discusses them at some length in his pioneering work *De Jure Belli et Pacis* (Paris, 1625), and Richard Hooker, in *The Lawes of Ecclesiasticall Politie* (London, 1593), believes that the Apostolic

---

[27] *Table Talk*, 79.
[28] *De Jure*, 833.

Decree in Acts 15: 28–9 contains a remnant of them. Hooker, whose remarks about Jews are contradictory and sometimes shockingly hostile, nevertheless believes in the continuity of rabbinic and Mosaic laws and the gospel. The Noachide laws are designed for all of humankind. When Christianity was in its infancy, Gentile Christians kept the Apostolic Decree, which reduces the seven Noachide laws to three; and Jewish Christians were bound to observe even the ceremonial Mosaic law, such as circumcision.[29] Selden develops hints about the Noachide laws that he would have found in Grotius. These ideas bear upon questions of the development of international law and the problem of establishing minimal conditions that enable otherwise differing persons and groups to live in peace. They also build bridges between cultures, as, for example, in the commonalities between the *praecepta Noachidarum* and the *jus gentium* of Roman law, which regard the resident alien as possessed of certain inalienable human rights.

Discussions of Noachide law in the seventeenth century that refer to Selden respectfully and often reverentially appear in the work of Isaac Newton, Henry Burton, John Lightfoot, Henry Stubbe, Henry Hammond, Jeremy Taylor, James Harrington, Edward Stillingfleet, John Toland, Samuel Pufendorf, Lancelot Addison (father of Joseph), and Sir John Vaughan, among many others. It is also clear that Selden's Hebrew scholarship influences Ben Jonson, John Milton, and Thomas Hobbes. Even so, it is not difficult to demonstrate that Selden's rabbinic influence has been neglected. The *OED* defines 'Noachic' only as 'Of or pertaining to Noah' and 'Noachian' only as 'Of or relating to the patriarch Noah or his time, esp. *Noachian deluge*, the Flood.' Its illustrative quotes mingle, apparently without recognizing the difference, references to Noah and the flood and those that speak of the connection between the Apostolic decree and the *praecepta*: 'The Noachick precepts are reduced to abstinence from blood and unclean meats' [1773]; 'Four restrictions, which belonged to what was called the Noachian dispensation' [1879]); and 'the Gentile world . . . under the Noachic covenant' [1863]. John Milton, writing on divorce in one of the non-Pauline chapters of his 'De Doctrina Christiana', follows 'Selden, [who] demonstrated particularly well in his *Uxor Hebraea*, with the help of numerous Rabbinical texts [or testimonies], [that] the word *fornication*, if it is considered in the light of the idiom of oriental languages, does not mean only adultery.' In the still definitive Columbia University Press edition of *The Complete Prose Works of John Milton*, Bishop Charles Sumner, translating '*multis Rabbinorum testimoniis*', elides the phrase's central term so that it becomes only 'numerous testimonies'.[30] Since the *OED* began with James Murray, and the Columbia Milton editors rely on the

[29] Richard Hooker, *Of the Lawes of Ecclesiasticall Politie* [1593], *The Folger Library Edition of the Works of Richard Hooker*, gen. ed. W. Speed Hill (Cambridge, Mass.: Harvard University Press, 1977), book 4, ch. 11, i. 308–19.

[30] John Milton, *De Doctrina Christiana*, in *The Works of John Milton*, gen. ed. Frank Allen Patterson (New York: Columbia University Press, 1931–8), xv. 171

first translation of *De Doctrina Christiana* by the Bishop of Winchester (1790–1874), the elision could serve as a synecdoche of the twentieth century's continuing an effacement of early modern rabbinical scholarship.

Despite Selden's ability to be friends with people of very different political and religious beliefs—it is said that the Commons came to him to learn of their rights and the Lords to learn of their privileges—it is still surprising to see how different his readers can be from one another. They include William Laud, Archbishop of Canterbury, and Jeremy Taylor, Chaplain-in-Ordinary to Charles I. Taylor gave his longest, most ambitious, and most neglected work the Maimonidean title *Ductor Dubitantium* (1660) and dedicated it to Charles II.[31] The first two chapters of Book II contain endless passages translated from *De Jure,* some of them acknowledged. Laud and Selden became friendly in 1635, and, according to Peter Heylyn, Selden became 'both a frequent and a welcome guest at Lambeth House, where he was grown into such esteem with the archbishop that he might have chose his own preferment in the court (as it was then generally believed), had he not undervalued all other employments in respect of his studies'.[32] The preacher Henry Burton, like the lawyer William Prynne and the physician John Bastwick, attacked the pompous sumptuosity of Lambeth as well as other abuses of clerical privilege. In retaliation Laud charged them with sedition, and in 1637—the year that Milton wrote *Lycidas,* that 'foretells the ruin of our corrupted clergy then in their height'—ordered that their ears be cut off. It is said that 100,000 people, most of them sympathetic to the martyrs, crowded around the scaffold to see this gruesome punishment carried out.

Where the ceremonialists of the Laudian church accepted and converted in a transformed but recognizable state the pagan, Jewish, and Catholic past, the puritans rejected it in favour of scriptural sufficiency.[33] They compared Anglican ritual with both the 'old cast rudiments' of the Jewish ceremonial law and 'the

---

[31] Taylor's *Ductor Dubitantium* embraces two encyclopedic volumes of cases of conscience. In his mature scholarship, Selden relies on the Buxtorf edition of *The Guide of the Perplexed, More Nebuchim: Doctor Perplexorum,* conversus a Johanne Buxdorfio, fil (Basel, 1629). He also uses and quotes the Hebrew version of Samuel Ibn Tibbon (Sabbioneta, 1553). In late works he sometimes quotes the Arabic original from a manuscript owned by Edward Pococke. As a young scholar, in *De Diis Syris* (1617), he cites an earlier edition of Maimonides, by the Italian orientalist and Hebraist Agostino Giustiniani, *Rabi Mossei Aegyptii Dux seu Director dubitantium aut perplexorum* (Paris, 1520).

[32] Peter Heylyn, *Life of William Laud* (London, 1671), 303. Heylyn, an apologist for Laud, may be overstating the warmth of their relationship. In correspondence, G. J. Toomer points out that Selden's first book entirely devoted to a Jewish topic, *De Successionibus,* was written in prison, 'where the government with which Laud was already associated had put him'. And the only extant letter from Laud to Selden, dated 29 Nov. 1640, when Laud was already in deep trouble with the Long Parliament, 'hardly suggests any intimacy between them . . . but only a desperate attempt by Laud, address[ing] an influential member [of Parliament], to display, too late, a spirit of compromise'.

[33] For an excellent discussion of the warring ideologies of the Laudian church and puritan Calvinism, see Achsah Guibbory, *Ceremony and Community from Herbert to Milton: Literature, Religion, and Cultural Conflict in Seventeenth-Century England* (Cambridge: Cambridge University Press, 1998).

new-vomited Paganisme of sensuall Idolatry'.[34] It is surprising, then, to find a positive reference to rabbinic scholarship derived from Selden's *De Jure* in an open letter from Burton to his fellow sufferer Prynne, published as *A Vindication of Churches Commonly Called Independent* (1644).[35] Burton, a radical Independent, rejects Prynne's idea of a national church, which he proposed on the grounds that it would resemble the national church of the Jews. Burton's attitude toward the Jews changes in the course of the treatise. He explains why the Independents cannot accept Presbyterianism:

> You require absolute obedience to the generall consent of Assembly and Parliament. Nor we dare not pin our faith upon the generalitie of mens opinions. The generalitie of the votes of the *Jewes* State carried it away, to crucifie their King. If the whole world might vote this day, the generalitie would be against Christ, as he is indeed the onely Anoynted King, Priest, and Prophet. What if the generalitie vote amisse, while yet they may *conceive* all to be right, because *consonant* to what they most affect? No.[36]

And yet Burton bases his rejection of the proposed analogy between the national church and the nation of the Jews on the inimitable superiority of the latter:

> For bring us any one Nationall, that is one intire Church, or congregation, as that of the Jewes was: or, that is of one family, as that was: or, that is a type of Christs spirituall Kingdome, as that was: or, that is the universall Church of God visible on earth, as that was: or, that is governed by the like lawes, that that was: when your selfe doe confesse, that the government of your Nationall Churches is to be regulated by humane lawes, customes, manners, and not by Gods word alone; whereas that of the Jewes was wholly governed by Gods own Law, and not at all by the Lawes of men. . . . In a word, your Nationall Churches are a mixed multitude, consisting for the greatest part of prophane persons, being as a confused lump, whereof there are nine parts of leaven to one of pure flowre, so as the whole is miserably soured, and the flowre made altogether unsavoury: But that of the Jewes, in its naturall and externall constitution, was all holy, an holy Nation, a royall Priesthood, a peculiar people, all the congregation holy, every one of them: So as in no one particular, doe your Nationall Churches hold parallell with that of the Jewes, no not in the least resemblance.[37]

The rabbinic reference comes at a crucial moment in the argument, when Burton asserts that no human law may bind the conscience. Regarding anyone's conscience, 'be it never so erroneous, as that of the Papists', one may go no further than 'to instruct and admonish, and labour to enforme and rectifie: enforce it you may not':

[34] John Milton, *Of Reformation, YP*, i. 520.
[35] Milton's second edition of *The Doctrine and Discipline of Divorce* was also published in 1644. Where the first edition of 1643 bears no trace of Selden's influence, the second reveals it everywhere: in its arguments, in its final chapter (ii. 22), whose proof is '*referr'd to Mr. Seldens Book* De jure naturali et gentium', and even in its division into books and chapters with italicized headnotes summarizing each chapter, an *hommage* to Selden found in no other prose work by Milton.
[36] Henry Burton, *A Vindication of Churches Commonly Called Independent* (London, 1644), 38.
[37] Ibid. 31.

And brother let me put it to your *Conscience*, Doe you thinke it equall, that either your conscience should be a rule of mine, or mine of yours? And if no one mans conscience may be the rule of anothers; certainly neither may all the mens consciences in the world be the Judge of any one mans. How ever we finde neither rule, example, nor reason from Scripture, to force men to religion originally; yet the Rabbins say, if man kept the seven precepts of *Noah*, he might not be forced further.[38]

The entire paragraph shows clear signs of the influence of *De Jure*, in which Selden postulates a hypothetical state of total natural freedom, upon which the laws of nature supervened. The laws were not innate but had to be learned, so that the only condition truly natural to human beings was freedom. Selden identified natural or universal law as the *praecepta Noachidarum*, uttered by God at a specific moment in historical time, when he made plain to humankind what he would punish them for.[39] There is no other universal law apart from this divine revelation. Moreover, regarding Burton's point that there is no rule, example, or reason 'to force men to religion originally', 'it is . . . remarkable, that the law of *Noah* regarding Idolatry was *Negative*, and onely told them they were not to worship *Idols*, *Angels*, *Sun* and *Moon*, and such Gods as were not the Lord *Jehovah*, but as to the positive part we find nothing expressed that they were to do necessarily.'[40] It is important to remember that when Selden speaks of the negative laws against stealing and adultery, he is thinking not of the biblical prohibitions in the ten commandments, which are binding only on the Jews, but rather of the *praecepta*, which originate in the Talmud:

I cannot fancy to myself what the law of nature means, but the law of God. How should I know I ought not to steal, I ought not to commit adultery, unless somebody had told me so. 'Tis not because I think I ought not to do them, nor because you think I ought not; if so, our minds might change: whence then comes the restraint? From a higher power; nothing else can bind. I cannot bind myself, for I may untie myself again; nor an equal cannot bind me, for we may untie one another. It must be a superior, even God Almighty.[41]

Burton continues by answering Prynne's objection that sects and divisions will multiply '*under pretence of Christian liberty*' and subvert '*all setled maintenance for the Ministery by tythes*':

as for Tithes: what Tithes, I pray you, had the Apostles? Such as be faithfull and painfull Ministers of Christ, he will certainly provide for them: as when hee sent forth his Disciples without any *purse*, or provision, he asked them, *Lacked you any thing*? They

[38] Burton, *A Vindication of Churches Commonly Called Independent*, 39–40.

[39] See the lucid and concise discussion of Selden's theory of natural law in Richard Tuck's 'The Ancient Law of Freedom: John Selden and the Civil War,' in *Reactions to the English Civil War 1642–1649*, ed. John Morrill (London: Macmillan, 1982), esp. 139–45.

[40] Henry Stubbe paraphrasing Selden's *De Jure* in *An Essay in Defence of the Good Old Cause*, or *A Discourse concerning the Rise and Extent of the power of the Civil Magistrate in reference to Spiritual Affairs* (London, 1659), 108.

[41] *Table Talk*, 101.

said, *Nothing*. Surely, *the labourer is worthy of his hire*. And as for Ministers maintenance by Tithes, I referre you to the judgment of your learned brother Mr. *Selden*.[42]

Burton's sufferings of torture and imprisonment taught him toleration, though his fellow martyr remained unmoved. Prynne's remarkable treatise opposing the readmission of the Jews not only repeats vicious slanders against them but tells horrific stories in which they are both brutally persecuted and blamed for their own victimization: 'although they were miserable, yet they were pittied by none,' he notes approvingly.[43] Burton refers to Selden as Prynne's 'learned brother' only because both were lawyers and members of the Inns of Court, Prynne of Lincoln's Inn and Selden of the Inner Temple. Certainly relations between them would not have been cordial. In 1633 Selden was one of the 'grandees' representing the Inner Temple, one of the sponsors of a 'splendid royal mask' mounted by the four Inns of Court. The purpose of presenting the masque was to 'manifest the difference of their opinion from Mr. Prynne's new learning, and serve to confute his *Histrio Mastix* against interludes'.[44]

An imprisoned voice far more in tune with Burton than with Prynne was that of William Penn, whose remarks on toleration echo *De Jure*. In a letter from the Tower dated 1 May 1669, to Lord Arlington, principal Secretary of State, 'by whose Warrant I was committed', Penn asks:

What if I differ from some Religious Apprehensions? Am I therefore incompatible with the being of Human Societies? Shall it not be remembered with what success kingdoms and common-wealths have lived under the ballance of diverse parties? And if the politicks of the most judicious and acute inquisitors after these affairs are of any worth, they are not at a stand in delivering their sense with great sharpness, 'That it is the securest prop of all Monarchical Governments.' Let it not be forgotten, that under the Jewish Constitution, the utmost they required from Strangers, to entitle them to Freedom, was an Acknow-

---

[42] Burton, *Vindication*, 56–7.

[43] William Prynne, A *Short Demurrer to the Jewes Long Discontinued Remitter into England*, Comprising, An exact *Chronological Relation* of their *first Admission into*, their *ill Deportment, Misdemeanors, Condition, Sufferings, Oppressions, Slaughters, Plunders, by popular Insurrections, and regal Exactions in*; and their *total, final Banishment by Judgment and Edict of Parliament, out of* England, *never to return again*: collected out of the best Historians. With a *Brief Collection* of such *English Laws, Scriptures*, as seem strongly to plead, and conclude against their *Readmission into England*, especially at this season, and against the *Generall calling of the Jewish Nation*. With an *Answer to the chief Allegations for their Introduction* (London, 1656). In one of many stories of small-scale persecution (he also recounts large-scale examples such as the massacre of the Jews of York), Prynne tells of a Jew who refuses to satisfy King John's exorbitant demands for cash. The king commands his tormentors that they should pull out one of his teeth every day until he pays a fine of ten thousand marks of silver: 'And when at last for 7 dayes space they had pulled out 7 of his teeth, with intollerable torment, and now on the 8 day the Tormentors had begun the like work again; this Jew, an over-slow provider for his profit, gave them the aforesaid money, that he might save the 8 tooth to himself, the other 7 being pulled out: who, with much more wisdom, and less pain, might have done so before, and have saved his 7 teeth, having but 8 in all' (p. 16). Prynne laughs at the Jew, the way Renaissance Jews would have laughed at Shylock, for his stubbornness, stupidity, and lack of self-interest.

[44] Bulstrode Whitelock, *Memorials of the English Affairs* [1682] (Oxford, 1853), i. 53.

ledgment to the Noachical Precepts, (never denied by me); nor was it better with them in latter days, than whilst the Pharisees, Scribes, Esseans, Sadducees, & c. had the free exercise of their consciences, all differing among themselves.[45]

On the occasion of Jews making application to Cromwell and 'at the request of a person of quality', Thomas Barlow (1607–91), Bishop of Lincoln, wrote a tract, 'The Toleration of the Jews in a Christian State'. Published posthumously, it was probably written not long after 1650, since Barlow refers to Selden's *De Synedriis* as having been written 'of late'. The person of quality and addressee of the opening epistle is 'the Honorable Robert Boyle, Esq.'. The hyper-systematic organization of the treatise—arranged according to numbers and lists, perhaps to please the great scientist who occasioned it—is belied by a tone so profoundly ambivalent that it verges on the schizoid. The argument itself is clear, simple, and, by the standards of the age, unusually humane. Separating himself from Erastus and his followers Selden and Hobbes, he believes it to be a manifest truth that in every Christian nation there should be two distinct powers, the sacred or spiritual and the civil or temporal. To the church belong the keys of God's kingdom and control over baptism and excommunication. Arguing for the readmission of Jewish bodies rather than souls, he reaches a conclusion to which Selden would have concurred:

That the Jews neither desiring, nor intending to be Members of our Church, but only of our Common-weal; their Admission or Exclusion depends only on the Civil Power. For the Command of the Common-weal (as it is a civil Society) being solely in the Civil Magistrate, to him only it will belong to judge whether it be fit to admit or exclude them, and to do accordingly.[46]

Barlow's general arguments are sympathetic. Citing examples from the vicious Judaeophobe Matthew Paris and others, he suggests that readmission would constitute moral reparations for past suffering:

It appears by our Story that the *Jews* (at their Expulsion, and many times before) were not only Unchristianly, but Inhumanely and Barbarously used; and then seeing Commonwealths and Societies never die (though particular Persons do) it may be a Question whether the Common-wealth of *England* now are not bound in Conscience and Equity to make some Satisfaction by real Kindness and Civility to the present *Jews* for the Injuries the same Common-wealth did to their Progenitors then?[47]

Like most others who rely heavily on Selden's Hebrew learning, Barlow both cites him and steals from him. He believes that the Christian magistrate should

---

[45] From 'The Author's Life', in *Select Works of William Penn. To Which is Prefixed a Journal of His Life* (London, 1771), p. vi.

[46] Thomas Barlow, *Analecta De Judaeis in Reipublica Christiana tolerandis, vel de novo admittendis, Several Miscellaneous and Weighty Cases of Conscience* (1692), 37.

[47] Ibid. 8.

treat the Jews as they treated the proselyte of the gate, requiring that they keep the Noachide precepts:

In the *Jewish* Church (by Gods express approbation and command) [note: 'Deut. 14.29. Exod. 20. & c.'] their . . . *Proselyti Portae*, who were neither circumcised, nor submitted to the Law of *Moses*, were permitted to live; and God expressly commands, that the *Jews* should use them kindly; provided that they abstained from Idolatry and worship't the God of *Israel*: Now if these might live in the *Jews* Church though not circumcised, nor submitting to *Moses's* Law, why may not *Jews* live in the Christian Church, though they be not baptized and submit not to the Gospel?

If the Christian Magistrate tye them to abstain from all Idolatry, Blasphemy, Murther, Adultery, and all such other Sins against the Light and Law of Nature, he tyes them to no more, then they (in their flourishing State of their Common-weal) ty'd others. For though they did not require of their Proselytes (those of the Gate I mean) to submit to the positive Law, and Precepts of *Moses* [note: '*Videsis joh. Selden de Jure naturali & Gentium apud Hebraeos.* lib. 2. cap. 2. pag. 138, 139. *& ex R. Mose Maimonide & R. Mos. Mikotzi*'], yet they did universally require of them to abstain from Blasphemy, Idolatry, and all natural Injustice, as is manifest in *Josephus*, the Sacred Text it self and their Rabbinical and Talmutical Writers.[48]

Barlow finds in *De Jure* only the most positive views on tolerating Jews, from whose margins all of his citations to works by Josephus, Strabo, Stephanus, and Ammonius derive, though he does not say so.[49]

Barlow appends to his otherwise humane argument eighteen ancient and specific legal restrictions and limitations that make Jewish admission conditional. Their enactment he leaves 'to the Piety and Prudence of the State. Yet (with Submission) I conceive such Limitations as these will be convenient, if not necessary.'[50] These include prohibitions against marriage with a Christian, building synagogues, leaving one's home on Good Friday,[51] serving as physicians, employing Christian servants, nurses, or midwives, and carrying any office or dignity in the Christian commonweal (though Barlow notes, 'it seems that sometimes even that was permitted them'). Moreover, according to canon law, 'they were not permitted to wear Garments exactly of the Christian Fashion, but were to have distinct Habits, that all might know them to be *Jews*.'[52]

Even if the law against holding public office happens to coincide with one of the Nuremberg regulations under the Nazis, the comparison would be unfair. Barlow's chief interest is not purity of blood but the flow of money: he wants the

---

[48] Ibid. 12, 42–3. See Selden *De Jure*, 2.2, p. 139, which also cites Maimonides and Moses of Coucy on *not* prosecuting idolatry outside of the land of Israel.

[49] References to these four authorities, as well as Barlow's discussion of the mass conversions to Judaism narrated in Esther 8: 17, are taken from *De Jure*, 2.2., p. 151.

[50] Barlow, *Analecta*, 66–7.

[51] Older Eastern European Jews still remember staying in the house on Good Friday for fear of being beaten. It turns out that this derives from canon law (*Can. In nonnullis* 15. [sect.] *In diebus. Extra de Judaeis*).

[52] Barlow, *Analecta*, 71.

Jews to use the tradesman's entrance when they return. From the start he points out that 'whilst the *Jews* lived in *England* it was a vast Benefit to the Crown'.[53] The last and most important law, which he praises unconditionally, enacted 'above 600 Years ago', under the reign of Edward the Confessor, and in effect until the Jews' banishment, he quotes in full in its original Latin:

Be it also known that all Jews, wherever they might be in the kingdom, are obliged to be under the liege guard and protection of the King; nor is any of them able to make himself subject to [i.e. under the protection of] any rich man, without licence of the King. For the Jews, and all that belongs to them (*omnia sua*) are the King's [property]. Whence, if anyone shall detain them or their money, the King may claim them, if he wishes, as his own property.[54]

To this law he adds, 'I wish the chief Magistrate could admit them on these Terms, for so they, and all theirs (*omnia sua*) should be *suum proprium*, which possibly might supply him with Money and so save Taxes.'[55] If someone as generally humane as Barlow provides the chief magistrate with these restrictions, one can't help wondering which of them even the most liberal of tolerationists would impose. Does Selden have legislation in mind when he praises the Jews: 'they thrive where'er they come; they are able to oblige the Prince of their Country by lending him money'?[56]

TEMPERING SCRIPTURAL SEVERITY

I should like to conclude by emphasizing two influential rabbinic ideas in Selden's *De Jure*. The first, less surprising, limits Jewish enmity against outsiders to the seven idolatrous nations inhabiting Canaan. Selden begins by citing the harsh biblical imperative to destroy those nations (Deut. 20: 18) but follows it by quoting rabbinic sources that moderate scriptural severity. The *Sifrei*, a fourth-century *halakhic* midrash, infers from the reason of the law—to remove sinful

---

[53] Barlow, *Analecta*, 7. His evidence is taken from 'My Lord Cooke *Institut.* Part 2. Pag. 506. *De Statuto Judaismi*'. He points out that during a seven-year period ('from *December* 17. *Anno* 50. *Hen* 3. Till *Shrovetide* 2. *Eduardi I*') the Jews in England contributed to the crown above 1,260,000 pounds.

[54] Barlow, *Analecta*, 74: '*Sciendum quoque quod omnes Judaei, ubicunque in Regno sunt, sub tutelâ & defensione Regis ligeâ debent esse; nec quilibet eorum alicui Diviti se potest subdere, sine Regis licentiâ. Judaei enim, & omnia sua Regis sunt. Quod si quisquis detinuerit eos, vel Pecuniam eorum, perquirat Rex si vult, tanquam suum proprium.*'

[55] Ibid. 74.

[56] The quality of obliging the prince can also be less coercive than Barlow's version. See John Toland, *Reasons for naturalizing the Jews in Great Britain and Ireland, On the same foot with other nations. Containing also, a Defence of the Jews against all vulgar Prejudices in all Countries* (1714); repr. in *Pamphlets Relating to the Jews in England in the 17th and 18th Centuries*, ed. P. Radin (San Francisco: California State Library, 1939), 56–7: 'they have deserv'd much better by their obedience and affection to the Government, towards the support of which, their purses have always been open'; p. 47: they will always be on 'the side of Liberty and the Constitution'; they owe their duty to the legal establishment in their host country.

practices—that if persons from those nations repent, they are not killed; and Rashi adds that if they repent and become proselytes, they are to be received.[57] The numerous rabbinic sources cited by Selden agree that idolaters are not to be pursued outside of the land of Israel. And according to Maimonides, the practice of offering oblations and tithes applies only within the boundaries of Israel. Even if a tribe were to go outside of those boundaries and reserve for itself a portion of the land that was promised to Abraham, it is not to offer oblations in that place. In the same chapter Selden quotes in Hebrew Elisha's response to the king of Israel on whether or not to smite their Aramean captives: 'And he answered, Thou shalt not smite them: Wouldest thou smite those whom thou hast taken captive with thy sword, and with thy bow? Set bread and water before them, that they may eate, and drinke, and go to their master' (2 Kings 6: 22).[58]

Selden believes, as does Milton in the *Areopagitica*, that truth 'may have more shapes than one', and not only is he scrupulous about citing alternate interpretations, he positively delights in them. Thus, after citing examples of humane behaviour toward idolaters, even if only for the sake of peace, he quotes a lengthy passage from Maimonides' *Mishneh Torah*, asserting that those rules apply at a time of exile when Israel has been dispersed among the nations or when the nations (Egypt, Phoenicia, Tyre) have subjugated Israel. But when Israel prevails over the nations and is restored to its homeland, no one will be tolerated in its borders, even if only passing through on business, unless that person has accepted upon himself the *praecepta Noachidarum*.[59]

The radical Independent Henry Stubbe, whose ideas about civil religion derive largely from *De Jure*, summarizes Selden's general argument:

The *Israelites* were not . . . obliged to destroy all their Neighbours that were Idolaters, they never practised such a thing, nor is the omission thereof laid to their charge . . . The Law in its letter, and as farr as man had power to execute it, was limited to the seven Nations, which God had given to the Children of Israell for a possession: Deut 12. 1. *These are the statutes, and the judgments which the Lord thy God giveth thee* [so *Exod*.34.13]. They should destroy all monuments of Idolatry in those dominions: and this is the judgment of the *Jewish* Doctors, as Mr. *Selden* reports them *de jur. natur.* l.2.c.2. It is commanded us that we destroy all foreign worship out of our land; but beyond our precincts it is not commanded us that we should persecute and destroy it. In case they made any additional conquest, that law did not reach them; yet did they by an intervenient right (as Mr. *Selden*

---

[57] Selden, *De Jure*, 6.16, pp. 744–5: 'Autor *Siphri* ad illud, *Ne doceant vos, Illinc observandum est, si poeniteant, a caede posse abstineri*. Et Salomon Jarchius ibi, *Intelligendum, si poenitentiam fecerint & proselyti fiant, fas esse etiam eos recipere*.' The *Sifrei* to Numbers and Deuteronomy, belonging to two different tannaitic schools, were printed together in Venice in 1545.

[58] On not pursuing idolatry outside of the land of Israel, see *De Jure*, 2.2, p. 139. Sources include '*Maimonides* [*Mishneh Torah*] *halach. Aboda Zara cap. 7. Mos. Mikotzi* [Moses of Coucy] *praecept. Affirm. 14. Sepher Siphri fol. 39. col. 1. Misna & Gemara tit. Aboda zara cap. 3.*' For sources prohibiting oblations and tithes outside of the boundaries, see *De Jure*, 6.16, pp. 749–50: '*Maimonides, Mishneh Torah*; Hal. Therumoth *cap. 1. Mos. Mikot Praec. Affirm. 133. Shulcan Aruch. Lib. Jore Dea cap. 331.*' For 2 Kings 6: 22, see *De Jure*, 6.16, p. 745.

[59] Selden, *De Jure*, 2.3, pp. 155–6, citing '*Halach* Aboda Zara *cap. 10*'.

phraseth it) abolish and extripate [*sic*] Idolatry in such places, *viz.* least it should become a snare unto them. Amongst the *Jews* there lived sundry other people called under the generall name of *Strangers*, which as to matters of common equity, had one and the same law or justice which an *Israelite* had: such were the *Gibeonites* and the reliques of the *Canaanites* that were undestroyed: such were those which joyned with them when they came out of *Egypt*, such were the *Proselytes* or *Strangers in the gate* who were not *Jewes*, but were all bound up (say the *Jewes*) to the seven precepts of *Noah.*[60]

Stubbe copies out many pages from *De Jure* on the seven nations and on Judaic tolerance of those who fall outside of that category. One of Stubbe's correspondents was John Locke, whose library included, among other titles by the same author, 'Selden, *De Jure Naturali juxta Disciplinam Ebraeorum*, 4to, 1665. . . . Bought in Holland'.[61] In his *Letter Concerning Toleration*, Locke's discussion of the seven nations in the context of the civil government of the Hebrews bears clear signs of the influence of Selden, a thoroughgoing Erastian:

Foreigners, and such as were strangers to the commonwealth of Israel, were not compelled by force to observe the rites of the Mosaical law: but, on the contrary, in the very same place where it is ordered that an Israelite that was an idolater should be put to death, there it is provided that strangers should not be 'vexed nor oppressed,' Exod. xxii.21. I confess that the seven nations that possessed the land which was promised to the Israelites were utterly to be cut off. But this was not singly because they were idolaters; for if that had been the reason, why were the Moabites and other nations to be spared? No; the reason is this: God being in a peculiar manner the King of the Jews, he could not suffer the adoration of any other deity, which was properly an act of high treason against himself, in the land of Canaan, which was his kingdom; for such a manifest revolt could no ways consist with his dominion, which was perfectly political, in that country. All idolatry was therefore to be rooted out of the bounds of his kingdom; because it was an acknowledgment of another God, that is to say, another king, against the laws of empire.[62]

The theorist of classical republicanism James Harrington, like Stubbe and Locke—and also like Machiavelli and the Erastian Selden—presumes that the Bible can be treated as a civil document from whose examples political precepts can be inferred. But where Selden, discussing the seven nations, emphasizes the limitations of both extra-territorial expansion and the imposition of civil law upon indigenous populations, Harrington blames the failure of the Jews to realize the ideal Hebrew commonwealth on their failure to extirpate those populations. To realize the perfect Mosaic plan through incursions on the property of others is to keep one's hands held high during battle—as Moses

---

[60] Stubbe, *An Essay in Defence of the Good Old Cause*, 106.

[61] John Locke, *Two Treatises of Government*, ed. Peter Laslett (Cambridge: Cambridge University Press, 1967). Appendix B, 'Sources of "Two Treatises" in Locke's Reading,' item 74, p. 144. See also Locke's letter to Stubbe in *The Correspondence of John Locke*, 8 vols. (Oxford, 1976–89), i. 109–12.

[62] Locke, *A Letter Concerning Toleration*, tr. William Popple [1689], ed. John Horton and Susan Mendus (London and New York: Routledge, 1991), 40.

did with the help of Aaron and Hur in the fight with Amalek (Exod. 17: 8–12)—and not to let them grow slack:

> Moses died in the wilderness; and though Joshua, bringing the people into the promised land, did what he could during his life towards the establishment of the form designed by Moses, yet the hands of the people, especially after the death of Joshua, grew slack, and they rooted not out the Canaanites, which they were so often commanded to, and without which it was impossible that their commonwealth should take any root.[63]

The second idea, the final one of this chapter, pervades Selden's most important rabbinical writings and comes closest to touching the contradictions of early modern England. It corrects the puritan distinction between the purity, clarity, and humanity of 'the Law of *Moses*' and the contamination, obscurity, and cruelty of 'the Pharisaical tradition falsly grounded upon that law' (*YP*, ii. 307). Such a distinction allows Milton at once to overthrow the statements of Christ and Paul against divorce in the New Testament while claiming to honour them. He can control the damage by explaining the statements as Christ's attempt 'to lay a bridle upon the bold abuses of those over-weening *Rabbies*; which he could not more effectually doe, then by a countersway of restraint, curbing their wild exorbitance almost into the other extreme' (*YP*, ii. 283). At the same time Milton can rely on rabbinic exegesis supporting divorce in both *De Jure* and *Uxor Ebraica* in order to reach a juridical position identical to that of the most extreme among the overweening rabbis, the Pharisees: 'this law [of divorce] bounded no man; he might put away whatever found not favour in his eyes' (*YP*, ii. 656–7).

Most Christians of the early modern period contrast the 'Hebrew truth' (*Hebraica veritas*) of the Bible with the rabbinical fables of the Talmud. Selden, throughout his writings, contrasts the severity of the literal text of the Hebrew Bible with the humaneness of rabbinic interpretations of the text and of rabbinic law. In his letter to Ben Jonson on 28 February 1616, discussed earlier, he answers a query about 'the literall sense and historicall of the holy text usually brought against the counterfeiting of sexes by apparell', namely Deuteronomy 22: 5. Selden provides an elegant loophole for his friend Jonson, who is writing for a transvestite English stage in which men take the parts of women. Following Maimonides in both his '*More Nebochim*' and '*Misnah Thorah*', he refers to Hebrew proscriptions about clothing as being in opposition to ancient practices of worshipping Mars and Venus: men invoking Venus in women's clothing and women honouring Mars in men's armour. This would prohibit cross-dressing only as part of an idolatrous rite.[64]

---

[63] *The Art of Lawgiving, The Political Works of James Harrington*, ed. J. G. A. Pocock (Cambridge: Cambridge University Press, 1977), 635. See also p. 637, where again he attributes the failure of the Israelites' foundation to their not rooting out the Canaanites. Harrington concedes that the Hebrew commonwealth 'was in parts longer lived than any other government hath yet been. . . . But that it was never established according unto the necessity of the form, or the true intent of Moses, is that which must be made further apparent' (p. 636).

[64] Introduction, 'John Selden's Letter to Ben Jonson', 46, 54.

In *De Jure*, Selden examines the *halakhic* restrictions that make it very difficult for a court to sentence a blasphemer to death—this despite numerous biblical verses (e.g. Exodus 22: 20, Leviticus 24: 15–16, Deuteronomy 17: 2 ff.) insisting on that punishment. Selden cites the rabbis, who limit blasphemy to profaning the name of God. And it must be in public. Not only that, but a court neither sentences an offender to be whipped nor to be put to death unless the act has been performed with deliberate intent and in front of witnesses, and after warning has been given.[65]

In *Table Talk*, Selden, like the great medieval rabbinic commentator Rashi, interprets the *lex talionis* of an eye for an eye (Exodus 21: 24) by the light of the talmudic tractate *Baba Kamma* 84a:

An eye for an eye, and a tooth for a tooth. That does not mean, that if I put out another man's eye, therefore I must lose one of my own, (for what is he the better for that?) though this be commonly received; but it means, that I shall give him what satisfaction an eye shall be judged to be worth.[66]

Selden's recognition of the humaneness of rabbinic law helps to account for his acceptance of the Noachide precepts and his rejection of the biblical ten commandments as an alternative dispensation intended only for the Jews. The contemporary relevance of his remarks on the Sabbath in *Table Talk* has been recognized. The right way of keeping the Sabbath was among the most bitter points of dispute between the Anglicans and the puritans, and the controversy over *The Book of Sports* has been well documented. Supporting his apparently casual pronouncement against Sabbath observance is the vast body of scholarship in *De Jure*:

Why should I think all the fourth commandment belongs to me, when all the fifth does not? What land will the Lord give me for honouring my father? It was spoken to the Jews with reference to the land of Canaan; but the meaning is, if I honour my parents, God will also bless me. We read the commandments in the church-service, as we do David's Psalms; not that all there concerns us, but a great deal of them does.[67]

Selden does not feel bound either by the ceremonial law or the conditional moral law contained in the decalogue. To conclude where we began, with the learned printer William Bowyer, the editor of his remarks on the Jew Bill notes that 'this little tract was well received by those who were superior to narrow prejudices',[68] and the same might be said of most of the readers of Selden's half-dozen rabbinical works, erudite Christians willing to cope with Selden's difficult Latin

---

[65] *De Jure*, 248–50: '*profanare Nomen Divinum dicebatur.... Et* ברבים seu publice atque בפרדהסיא, *quod ex Graeco desumtum palam ac aperte significat, id profanere dicebatur si in Ebraeorum decem praesentia commiserat.... Nimirum nullum peccatum flagra aut mors sequebatur, nisi id sponte commissum esset, adessentque testes & praecessisset admonitio legitima.*'

[66] *Table Talk*, 168.

[67] Ibid. 169–70.

[68] Nichols, *Miscellaneous Tracts*, 453.

in order to learn about Jewish laws and institutions. Of course the number of Englishmen not in thrall to narrow prejudice was considerably smaller in Selden's lifetime than in Bowyer's or in our own. It is at least worth remembering that in the first half of the seventeenth century the most learned person in England rejected the biblical decalogue as intended only for the Jews and accepted the rabbinic Noachide laws as binding upon all of humankind. On the basis of those laws and the talmudic discussions occasioned by them, he expressed hope in eternal life for those outside his own confession, rejected the myth of Jewish xenophobia, and emphasized the humaneness of rabbinic exegesis.

8

Selden and Stubbe on Idolatry, Blasphemy, and the Passion Narrative

In September 1659, as second in charge of the Bodleian Library under the Keeper Thomas Barlow, Henry Stubbe must have helped to move Selden's library of some 8,000 volumes into the Selden End of Duke Humfrey's Library.[1] The publication in that very same month of Stubbe's *An Essay in Defence of the Good Old Cause* suggests that of all the books he helped to shelve, the one he had read most carefully was Selden's own *De Jure Naturali et Gentium*. We have already touched upon Stubbe's great admiration for Selden and his transcription of whole pages from *De Jure* in his *Defence*. Stubbe embraces the idea of the seven Noachide laws, which allows him to reconcile an Erastianism as extreme as that of Hobbes with an even more radical religious Independence that would keep the operations of the holy spirit on the individual believer free from regulation by the magistrate.[2] Those seven laws, which Stubbe regarded as incumbent on all of humankind, Jewish, Muslim, and Christian, and which reduce religious doctrine to a deistic minimum, shaped his conception of a civil religion that would have entailed virtually limitless religious toleration to all but enemies of the state. He argued that no one should 'venture his soul and eternity upon the uncertain and fallible experiences of another'.[3] Stubbe would have concurred with what the Independent Henry Burton pointed out to William Prynne: 'the Rabbins say, if man kept the seven precepts of *Noah*, he might not be forced further'.[4]

Stubbe deserves to be treated in somewhat more detail than he was in earlier chapters because, reading *De Jure* as a treatise that has amassed its vast learning in defence of religious toleration, he understands that work and its implications better than most early readers. He also follows Selden into interesting and

---

[1] *The Life and Times of Anthony Wood, antiquary of Oxford*, ed. Andrew Clark (Oxford: Oxford Historical Society, 1891), 282. See also James R. Jacob, *Henry Stubbe, Radical Protestantism and the Early Enlightenment* (Cambridge: Cambridge University Press, 1983), 19, 32.

[2] See on this point Jacob, *Henry Stubbe*, 32–3.

[3] Henry Stubbe, *An Essay in Defence of the Good Old Cause* (1659), 28.

[4] Henry Burton, *A Vindication of Churches Commonly Called Independent* (1644), 40. Jacob discusses Stubbe's authorship sometime in the early 1670s of *An Account of the Rise and Progress of Mahometanism*, which finds similarities among the three religions and insists on the permanent authority of 'the seven commands of Noah' (*Henry Stubbe*, 64–7).

important byways avoided by those other readers, such as the New Testament account of the trial of Jesus as understood according to rabbinic law. It is easy to find general statements in which Stubbe sounds like both Selden and Milton. (In his *A Light Shining out of Darknes* [1659], Stubbe borrowed the translation of Dante from *Of Reformation* by 'the excellent Mr. J. Milton'.[5]) Each of them, writing on a general topic, can sound an effective alarm to freedom, as in these passages on heretics, by Selden, Stubbe, and Milton, respectively:

'Tis a vain thing to talk of an heretic, for a man for his heart can think no otherwise than he does think. In the primitive times there were several opinions; nothing scarce but some or other held: one of these opinions being embraced by some prince, and received into his kingdom, the rest were condemned as heresies; and his religion, which was but one of the several opinions first, is said to be orthodox and to have continued ever since the Apostles.

Concerning *Heresy*, the word is not alwayes taken in a bad sense: the *Sadducees* are called an *Heresy Act.* 5.17. And the *Pharisees, Act.* 15.5. and *Christianity* it self *Act.* 28.22. And as often as I hear it mentioned almost, me thinks I hear men speak as of a People that in a time of idlenesse and implicite faith dare enquire into the state of things, and imploy their judgment. Surely the case is very hard, if they who having done all that was in their power to try all things, if they misse of the truth, and hold fast not which is good, but which seems so, either thorough invincible ignorance, or such as he that made us knowes humane frailty to be lyable unto; if they I say, shall not be in as good a condition as those who received the Truth without tryall, and embraced it upon no better an account then custome, education, or interest.

Truth is compar'd in Scripture to a streaming fountain; if her waters flow not in a perpetuall progression, they sick'n into a muddy pool of conformity and tradition. A man may be a heretick in the truth; and if he beleeve things only because his Pastor sayes so, or the Assembly so determins, without knowing other reason, though his belief be true, yet the very truth he holds, becomes his heresie.[6]

Embedded in Stubbe's excerpt is the Pauline verse from 1 Thessalonians that is central to Milton's argument in the *Areopagitica* against the parliamentary licensing order: 'Try all things, hold fast to that which is good' (5: 21).[7] This verse turns up in works of systematic theology in the Pauline renaissance in chapters on 'the Holy Scriptures', with the ostensible purpose of rejecting the Roman Catholic distinction between the clergy, which is privileged to search the scriptures, and the laity, which is not. Milton appropriates the verse in order to widen the freedom to read the Bible to include the freedom to read any text.

Differences within Stubbe's multifaceted argument become clearer if the *Defence* is compared first with Selden's *De Jure* and then with Milton's political tracts, particularly those written, like the *Defence*, in the months before the

[5] *The Life Records of John Milton*, 5 vols., compiled by J. Milton French (New Brunswick, NJ: Rutgers University Press, 1949–58), iv. 281.

[6] Selden, 'Opinion', in *Table Talk*, ed. Reynolds (Oxford: Clarendon Press, 1892), 125; Stubbe, *Defence*, 122; Milton, *Areopagitica, YP,* ii. 543.

[7] See the *Areopagitica, YP,* ii. 511–12.

Restoration. Although there must always be a flexible degree of separation between different writers, direct repetition is the best evidence that the gap has been bridged, and the *Defence* crams its tolerationist argument with pages taken verbatim from *De Jure*. Stubbe relies on Selden's extensive researches in the Talmud and its rabbinic commentaries and on documents from ancient Roman history that complicate and even subvert received opinion.

Among the rabbinic passages in *De Jure* copied out by Stubbe are the *halakhic* restrictions, already touched upon, that make it very difficult for a court to sentence a blasphemer to death—this despite numerous biblical verses insisting on that punishment.[8] Stubbe also looks for limitations in the biblical verses that would make punishment unlikely in his own nation, despite the permanence of the Noachide laws against blasphemy and idolatry: Exodus 22: 20 'is directly against *Sacrificing*, which he that shall expound to be any sort of worship which is commanded not to be appayed to other Gods but *Jehovah*, speaks more then is in the Text'.[9] Deuteronomy 13: 1ff. 'is directed against *prophets* and *dreamers*, things not to be heard of in our dayes, in which those delusions as well as gifts are ceased, and that of Deut. 17.v. 2 &c. is a punishment of *corporal adorations* and service paid to the *Sun, Moon and host of Heaven*: of which I know not, nor do I hear of any among us.'[10] Stubbe cites verses that his opponents have used as weapons 'against *Paganisme* and its *toleration*', but he reads them in the context of the actual 'practise of the *Jewes*'.[11] He spends many pages transcribing biblical verses that indicate the tolerance by Israelites of idolaters. Examples include Abraham's coexisting with them on his pilgrimage, Jacob's living with Laban and marrying his daughter, 'being then, and continuing after an Idolatresse', and the Queen of Sheba's visiting Solomon in Jerusalem with a very great train. Moreover, regarding extra-biblical examples,'Will any one think that *Alexander* the great, when he and his army came to *Jerusalem*, that they became *Proselytes* to the commandements of *Noah*?'[12]

Relying entirely on Selden's quotations of ancient rescripts—the replies sent by Roman emperors to magistrates who consulted them on points of law or on actions to be taken—Stubbe echoes his source's argument: that historical documents call into question generalizations about the attitude of the Roman emperors toward the Jews. Not only were different attitudes adopted by different emperors, but even the same emperor might change his views.[13] Some of the edicts copied by Stubbe from Selden complicate the view, current today, that

---

[8] Selden, *De Jure*, 2.12, p. 263; Stubbe, *Defence*, 110–15, 125–7. Both cite rabbinic opinion that requires the blasphemer to name the tetragrammaton, in public, with deliberate intent, before witnesses, and after warning has been given.

[9] Stubbe, *Defence*, 117–18.

[10] Ibid. 118.

[11] Ibid.

[12] Ibid. 109.

[13] This opinion is also expressed in the *Encyclopedia Judaica*, under the heading 'Roman Emperors', xiv. 229.

persecutions increased steadily with the triumph of Christianity under Constantine. Stubbe, quoting Selden directly, argues instead that the pagan Romans persecuted the Jews after the destruction of the second temple. The Jews expected the imminent advent of the Messiah, who would rule the world, and this messianism would have weakened the empire. But under the Christian emperors from the time of Honorius, Arcadius, Theodosius Primus, 'and so upwards',

> though they had lost their city and Temple, yet were they in a very flourishing condition. They had several famous *Academyes*, or rather *Commonweals*, such as the *Soriana*, *Pombodithana*, *Nehardacensis*, besides their multitude of Synagogues, and great immunicyes thorough the particular indulgence of Princes. *Theodosius*, *Arcadius*, and *Honorius* AAA. made the following Rescript unto Addaeus Comes & Magister utriusque militiae; It is evident enough that the Sect of the Jewes is not prohibited by any Law. Wherefore we are very angry that their Assemblies should be interdicted anywhere. Your Excellency therefore having received these our commands, will represse with due severity the too great number of those, who under pretense of Christian religion commit all manner of licentiousness, destroying and robbing their Synagogues. Given at Constantinople 3 Kal. Octob. Theod. A. III & Abundantio Cons. that is, in the Year of our Lord, 395. [Margin: C. *Theodos.* lib. 16. tit.8. l.9. & vide l. 12. & 25.][14]

Stubbe translates various fourth- and fifth-century rescripts from *De Jure*, including the censure of any governor of a province who would impose upon the Jews a 'Moderator or President'; the insistence that the various privileges of the Jews continue to be upheld, *'For thus the holy Emperours, Constantinus, Constantius, Valentinianus and Valens by their Heavenly will and pleasure have ordained it'*; and the edict that synagogues not be destroyed or seized upon, that Jews not be obliged to any performances inconsistent with the observation of their Sabbath, and *'that none should be any way wronged, or oppressed for being a Jew'*. Moreover, the emperors Honorius and Theodosius decreed that Jews who converted to Christianity for the sake of convenience be allowed to return again, without fear of punishment, 'to their former worship and religion'.[15]

Selden speaks in several places on the pagan identification of the early Christians as Jews:

[14] Stubbe, *Defence*, 82–3; taken directly from Selden, *De Jure*, 2.9, p. 243: '"Celebres tunc eorum Academiae illae seu potius republicae clarissimae, Soriana [note: "*Videsis R. Gedaliah Ben Iechai in Shalsheleth*, fol. 35.a & c.," *i.e.* Gedaliah b. Joseph Ibn Yahya, *Sefer Shalsheleth ha-Kabbalah*, ed. Venice, 1587], Pombodithana, Nehardaiensis, id satis testantur, uti & Synagogarum Frequentia & Immunitas singularisque Principum indulgentia. Theodosii, Arcadii, & Honorii Augustorum habetur rescriptum ejusmodi ad Addeum Comitem & Magistrum utriusque militiae; *Judaeorum sectam nulla lege prohibitam satis constat. Unde graviter commovemur interdictos quibusdam locis eorum fuisse conventus. Sublimis igitur magnitudo tua hac jussione suscepta nimietatem eorum qui sub Christianae religionis nomine inlicita quaeque praesumunt & destruere synagogas atque expoliare conantur, congrua severitate cohibebit. Dat. III. Kal. Octob. Constantp. Theod. A. III. & Abundantio CONSS.* Id est, anno Christi CCCXCV." '

[15] Selden, *De Jure*, 243–4; Stubbe, *Defence*, 82–7.

In the church of Jerusalem, the Christians were but another sect of Jews, that did believe the Messias was come. To be called, was nothing else but to become a Christian, to have the name of a Christian, it being their own language; for among the Jews, when they made a doctor of law, 'twas said he was called.[16]

Stubbe's conjecture echoes Selden's argument in *De Jure* regarding the identical motive for pagan persecution of Jews and Christians:

As for the *Jews* (to give an account of them once for all) I finde them to have been persecuted under the heathen Emperours of *Rome* at the same time with the Christians, who were by the Heathens too called *Judaei*; and it hath been a conjecture of mine, that their sufferings had not a greater affinity then (possibly) the causes inducing the Heathen to such rigour were resembling. I already told you how the *Christians* did believe the personall reign of *Christ* their *Messiah*. The *Jewes* after the destruction of *Jerusalem did expect the coming of* their *Messiah*, and that he should rule the *World*. Least any danger to the Empire might arise from these opinions, which were divulged up and down by both parties, the *Romans*, I imagine, may (adding other motives and fictions against them) . . . have persecuted them; especially having fresh in their memories, how amongst other encouragements that *Vespasian* had to assume the Empire, it was none of the meanest, that *Josephus* the Historian accommodated to him the Prophecy of the *Messiah*.[17]

Stubbe explains why he has traced numerous examples from early Jewish practice, recorded in the Talmud of Babylonia, whose 'famous *Academyes*' he has named, and most of all from 'the primitive Christian Emperours' whose rescripts were issued when those academies flourished. It has all been in the service of toleration: 'If the *Jewes* have alwaies been tolerated, who deny our whole Religion, the *Trinity*, the *Messiah*, *Justification*, & c, the *new Testament*, and *Daniel* in the old; may we not *tolerate* such as differ from us in smaller cases?'[18]

The most extreme opinions on toleration Stubbe takes from Selden, such as the extension of blasphemy by Philo and by Josephus to include the reviling of pagan gods. According to Josephus, in '*Antiq.* l.4. c.8' and in his 'second book against *Appian*':

It is our custom to observe our own laws, not to accuse those of others. Our Lawgiver hath directly prohibited us to revile or blaspheme such as are reputed Gods by others, forasmuch as they bear the name of God. And *Philo* saith that *Moses* did not so much as permit the *Proselytes of justice*, or such as did entirely profess *Judaism*, to blaspheme the Gods they had renounced, least it should give occasion to others to blaspheme the true God. *Philo de Monarch lib.* 1.[19]

A closer look at Stubbe, especially when he is compared with Milton, reveals limits of toleration that are not immediately apparent. When he asks for toleration of 'such as differ from us in smaller cases', he has in mind only a

---

[16] Selden, 'Christians', in *Table Talk*, 35. See also Selden, *Opera Omnia*, i. 59, ii.10, 405, 607.
[17] Stubbe, *Defence*, 81–2. The source is Selden, *De Jure*, 2.9, p. 243.
[18] Stubbe, *Defence*, 100.
[19] Ibid. 127.

reconciliation between Lutherans and Calvinists.[20] And the *Defence* concludes with a plea on behalf of the Widdrington Catholics, who should not be made to '*suffer upon a Religious account, so neither ought they to be damnified upon a Civil*'.[21] Thomas Preston, a Benedictine writing under the name Roger Widdrington, was sent on the English mission in 1603. Imprisoned for being a priest, he wrote several works treating of the oath of allegiance proposed by James I, of which he was an upholder and apologist against the Jesuits. Stubbe shared the view of his patron and great friend, Sir Henry Vane, that 'the mystery of iniquity... is the magistrate's intermeddling with Christ's power over the judgments of men.'[22] In his extreme anti-clericalism, Stubbe assimilated Presbyterian ministers and Anglican bishops to Roman Catholic priests, and he saw all of them as a danger to the state. He would have tolerated the Widdrington Catholics as a persecuted minority with no designs on civil power. Stubbe, like Milton, insisted that religious truth is revealed only to individual believers by the operation of the holy spirit and that the magistrate should guard religious freedom from clerical intermeddling. He would have regarded royalist Episcopalians and Presbyterians as a threat to civil and spiritual liberty.

In light of the political situation in 1659, then, certain adjustments needed to be made in the application of high-sounding theory to particular cases. Neither Stubbe nor Milton could accept the republican James Harrington's theory of a genuinely equal commonwealth, because the majority of the people were rushing headlong toward the restoration of monarchy. Stubbe proposed that for the time being, true participation in the government would be 'limited to the good people which have adhered to the good old cause'.[23] Moreover, 'the Select Senate or Conservators of the liberties of England', elected for life, would be drawn from 'the several parties in the nation leagued in the establishment of a commonwealth, viz. Independents, Anabaptists, Fifth Monarchy Men, and Quakers'.[24] Similarly, in the early months of 1660, on the eve of the Restoration, Milton, in *The Readie and Easie Way to Establish a Free Commonwealth*, wanted only 'the best affected... and best principl'd of the people' to have a voice. He advocated the perpetuation of the Parliament already in power, with a membership augmented by 'men not addicted to a single person or house of lords'. Eliminating term limits for senators, he would model his Grand or General Councel after the Sanhedrin and the Areopagus:

I affirme that the Grand or General Councel being well chosen, should be perpetual; for so thir business is or may be, and oft times urgent; the opportunitie of affairs gaind or lost in a moment. The day of counsel cannot be set as the day of a festival; but must be readie

[20] Ibid. 100.

[21] Ibid. 133.

[22] Sir Henry Vane, *Retired Man's Meditations* (1656); Stubbe, *Defence*, 7–8; both cited in Jacob, *Henry Stubbe*, 31.

[23] Stubbe, *Defence*, Preface.

[24] Stubbe, *A Letter to an Officer of the Army* (1659), 60–1. See also Jacob, *Henry Stubbe*, 27–9.

alwaies to prevent or answer all occasions.... Therefor among the *Jews*, the supreme councel of seaventie, call'd the *Sanhedrim*, founded by Moses, in *Athens*, that of *Areopagus*, in *Sparta*, that of the Ancients, in *Rome*, the Senat, consisted of members chosen for term of life; and by that means remaind as it were still the same to generations.[25]

Milton may have taken some of his information from Selden's *de Synedriis*, which compares the Sanhedrin and the Areopagus, two judicial bodies that had their beginnings at about the same time and had their end nearly together.[26] And in relation to their sitting, although capital punishment could not be meted out on festival days, it was decreed in the time of Ezra that the Sanhedrin should sit on the second and fifth common days, that is, Mondays and Thursdays. This was not to exclude them from sitting on other days, but only to oblige them to sit on those two.[27]

The seven Noachide laws have always seemed to constitute a minimalist set of moral imperatives, but the similar situations of Stubbe and Milton suggest that at least one of those laws, idolatry, might be employed more repressively than the others. Although Milton would debar the civil magistrate from matters of religion and confine him to those of the natural order, in the *Areopagitica* and in his later tracts he would make an exception, extending magisterial power to include the suppression of idolatry and blasphemy, which he assumed could be recognized as evil by a natural law that takes precedence over both civil and ecclesiastical authority.[28] Libel or flagrant blasphemy, for Milton, might be identified with the Ranters on the left, but idolatry would of course be applied to Roman Catholics. Milton's specific examples of intolerance often appear within a context of general tolerance:

It is not possible for man to sever the wheat from the tares, the good fish from the other frie; that must be the Angels Ministery at the end of mortall things. Yet if all cannot be of one mind, as who looks they should be? This doubtles is more wholsome, more prudent, and more Christian that many be tolerated, rather then all compell'd. I mean not tolerated Popery, and open superstition, which as it extirpats all religions and civill supremacies, so it self should be extirpat.[29]

---

[25] Milton, *The Readie and Easie Way to Establish a Free Commonwealth, YP,* vii. 414, 433, 436.

[26] For Selden's *De Synedriis* as the source of information on the limits of royal prerogative that Milton used in his *Defence of the People of England,* see Jason P. Rosenblatt, *Torah and Law in 'Paradise Lost'* (Princeton: Princeton University Press, 1994), 90–5.

[27] Selden, *De Synedriis,* 2.16, *Opera Omnia,* i.1595, where Selden points out that by overthrowing the temple, Vespasian put an end to all capital cases in the Sanhedrin and may in great measure be said to have extinguished it. Vespasian also reduced Achaia, where the Areopagus was located, into a province, and by doing so took away the court's power. Selden discusses the session days in 2.10, i. 1433–4.

[28] See on this point Barbara K. Lewalski, 'Milton and Idolatry', *Studies in English Literature,* 43 (2003), 213–32, esp. 217; and see her magisterial *Life of John Milton* (Oxford: Blackwell, 2000), 666 n. 120.

[29] Milton, *Areopagitica, YP,* ii. 565. Lewalski cites numerous examples of Milton's association of the Laudian prelates with idolatry (*Of Reformation, Complete Prose Works,* i. 520–1, *Reason of Church Government,* i. 851) and of his identification of monarchy as 'a civil kinde of Idolatry' (*Eikonoklastes,*

Selden, in *De Jure*, distinguishes between the first two laws, idolatry and blasphemy, which are *inter hominem & numen sanctissimum*, and the other five, which are *inter hominem & proximum suum*. Milton identifies in the *Areopagitica* itself his likely source for a theistic conception of natural law, the 'volume of naturall & nationall laws [*De Jure Naturali et Gentium*]' by 'the chief of learned men reputed in this Land, Mr. Selden'.[30] The only member of Parliament to be mentioned in the treatise, and an outspoken defender of the freedom of the press, Selden was also a famous victim of censorship. In mid-December 1617, when his *Historie of Tithes* was in press and half-printed, John King, the Bishop of London, conducted a violent search that resulted in the confiscation not only of the printed sheets but also of the type that had been set up.[31]

In his *Defence*, Stubbe names the seven Noachide precepts in the order that Selden follows in *De Jure*, based on the sequence in Maimonides' *Mishneh Torah* rather than in tractate Sanhedrin. But it is clear from the many proof-texts cited that only idolatry and blasphemy interest him. In fact, he introduces the Noachide laws in the context of a discussion of texts addressing the punishment of idolaters and blasphemers: 'For the explanation of these texts I shall observe what is the opinion of the *Jewish Rabbies*, and what hath been the practice of that Nation.' After discussing in detail these seven laws, Stubbe shifts to the seven nations that originally inhabited Canaan:

> The Law in its letter, and as farr as man had power to execute it, was limited to the seven Nations, which God had given to the Children of Israell for a possession: Deut 12. 1. *These are the statutes, and the judgments which the Lord thy God giveth thee* [so *Exod.*34.13]. They should destroy all monuments of Idolatry in those dominions: and this is the judgment of the *Jewish* Doctors, as Mr. *Selden* reports them *de jur. natur.* l.2.c.2. It is commanded us that we destroy all foreign worship out of our land; but beyond our precincts it is not commanded us that we should persecute and destroy it. In case they made any additional conquest, that law did not reach them; yet did they by an intervenient right (as Mr. *Selden* phraseth it) abolish and extripate [*sic*] Idolatry in such places, *viz.* least it should become a snare unto them.[32]

After reading pages in the *Defence* filled with nothing but proof-texts on idolatry and blasphemy, one begins to realize that for Stubbe the sins of clerical idolatry might be extirpated by the irresistible imperative of natural law.

More profoundly influenced by Selden than any tract written by Milton, the *Defence*, despite its own limitations, appears to be more religiously tolerant as

---

in *Complete Prose Works*, iii. 343; *Readie and Easie Way*, vii. 425–6). He would also authorize the magistrate to prohibit Roman Catholic and Laudian idolatry in *Observations on the Articles of Peace*, iii. 316, and *Of Civil Power*, vii. 254–5.

[30] Milton, *Areopagitica*, *YP*, ii. 513.

[31] See G. J. Toomer, 'Selden's *Historie of Tithes*: Genesis, Publication, Aftermath', *Huntington Library Quarterly*, 65 (2002), 353–6, which prints Selden's bitter and detailed description of the event in a letter to Peiresc dated 6 February 1618.

[32] Stubbe, *Defence*, 106–7.

well. And Stubbe is even more religiously heterodox than Milton. In his heretical *Account of the Rise and Progress of Mahometanism*, Stubbe is forthright about his Arianism, identified as the pure faith of the early Christians, while Milton chooses not to put a label on his version of antitrinitarianism. Stubbe's lengthy discussion of blasphemy in the *Defence*, unlike Milton's,[33] may simply be the result of an appetite for scholarship. He even summarizes briefly Selden's impressive talmudic argument that understands the biblical narrative of Jesus' trial according to Jewish legal codes regarding blasphemy:

The words of the *Thalmudists* are (as Mr. *Selden* cites them *de jur. natur.* l.2. c. 12) *he is not to dye, if he expresse not the sacred name: no not though he blaspheme or curse any sacred attribute.* . . . But notwithstanding this (and much more to this purpose, which is to be seen in Mr. *Selden*) it seems evident from the condemnation of our *Saviour* in the *Gospell*, that in his dayes *blasphemy* was extended beyond the mention of that *sacred name* (of the true pronunciation whereof we are now totally ignorant, and so incapable of that blasphemy) unto the *attributes* of God.[34]

Stubbe then cites Matthew 26: 64, where Jesus replies to Caiaphas's demand, 'that thou tell us whether thou be the Christ, the Son of God': 'Hereafter shall ye see the Son of man sitting on the right hand of power.' Stubbe cites Selden on Jesus' being condemned, although he does not utter the tetragrammaton,

for blasphemy, against one of the Sacred *attributes*, which is manifestly expressed in the text in the words, *Sitting at the right hand of power,* Power *or* גבורה [*gevurah*] being by the *Jewish Rabbines* a thousand time reckoned amongst the attributes of God. I am further to observe that the *Jewes* did not reckon materiall blasphemy, such as is wickedness of life, or the profession of a religion or way inconsistent with the truth, to be the blasphemy that was to be punished with death. Thus the *blind man Joh.* 9. who avowed Christ to be *no sinner but a Prophet,* and *of God,* was not impleaded or condemned as guilty of blasphemy, and so to dye; but he was excommunicated, or excluded from the converse of the *Jewes.* And the *Disciples* in the *Acts* ch. 4. & 5. though they preached that *Jesus* was the *Christ,* and that *Salvation was to be had onely in his name,* and that *god had exalted him with his* RIGHT HAND *to be a prince and a Saviour* & c. yet were not they charged with blasphemy, or represented as guilty of death. So *Paul* in his declaration, whatever he lay down, it was not imputed to him as blasphemous: for then the people would have rent their cloaths, instead of casting them off, and have said, he was guilty of death, and not *Away with such a fellow from the earth; it is not fit that he should live. Acts* 22. v. 22, 23. from whence it may be gathered what opinion the *Jewes* had of the *Messiah,* that one might avowe himself to be, or that another was such, yet not be guilty of blasphemy, or death, for such his assertion, yet as a sower of sedition such might be punished with stripes or imprisonment.[35]

---

[33] Milton refers approvingly to the parliamentary *Act against several Atheistical, Blasphemous and Execrable Opinions* of 9 August 1650, aimed mainly at the excesses of the Ranters, in *A Treatise of Civil Power, YP,* vii. 246.

[34] Stubbe, *Defence,* 110–11.

[35] Ibid. 110–13, taken from Selden, *De Jure,* 2.12, esp. pp. 262–4. At some points Stubbe quotes Selden in the original Latin.

Before looking more closely at Selden's dispassionate inquiry into the trial of Jesus, it is worth remembering the capital importance to him of legal systems. There are sixty-three standard tractates in the Babylonian Talmud, and the text of the entire Talmud consists of some two and a half million words on 5,894 folio pages. Selden's learning is vast, ranging over a number of tractates in both the Babylonian and Jerusalem Talmud, but he chooses to place one of them, Sanhedrin, at the centre of his most important scholarship. This tractate of the Babylonian Talmud describes in exhaustive detail the moral and intellectual qualities required of a judge, the composition of the court, its days of session, its procedure and proceedings, the punishments it imposes, and a host of other matters taken up by Selden in the three vast books of *De Synedriis*. In *De Jure*, besides citing Maimonides' *Code* and numerous other sources, Selden quotes in its entirety the *locus classicus* of the Noachide law in tractate Sanhedrin (56 a–b). Although Selden in an immensely learned discussion of the Noachide laws includes R. Johanan's elaborate inference of the precepts from seven key words in Genesis 2: 16, he is well aware that the laws are talmudic rather than biblical. Significantly, he opposes R. Johanan not in his own voice but rather by citing Rabbi 'Jehuda Ben Samuel', *i.e.*, Judah ha-Levi, 'In Sepher Cozri [the Venice, 1594 edition of his *Kuzari*], part.3. sect. 73', who notes the great discrepancy between the specific commandments and the foundational text, then concludes that the verse is relied on only as a mnemonic device.[36]

Even if Selden first learned about the Noachide precepts from their codification in Maimonides' *Mishneh Torah* (*Hilkhot Melakhim*, chapter 9), eventually he turned to the primary source in tractate Sanhedrin, quoted extensively throughout *De Jure*. The entire discussion in the *gemara* of the *praecepta Noachidarum* is a commentary on a *mishnah* (55b–56a) about the punishment for blasphemy, which is itself a commentary on Numbers 15: 30 ('But the soul that doeth aught presumptuously... reproacheth the LORD'). Selden is familiar with all the relevant primary sources and with a wide range of post-talmudic rabbinic opinion on the subject of blasphemy, which is of great importance to him. Questions about the crime and its punishment, including whether or not it is meted out equally to Jews and Gentiles, generate huge unresolved disagreements. In the course of elaborating on the *mishnah*, the *gemara* mentions that non-Jews are bound by the prohibition against blasphemy, and this leads to an extensive

---

[36] Selden, *De Jure*, 1.10, p. 124. Taking the view that a single verse in the Bible dealing with permission rather than prohibition contains *in nuce* all of the Noachide precepts, R. Johanan had relied on the mode of talmudic interpretation known as *gezerah shawah*. This permits one to infer a rule from the use of a common scriptural expression in two verses; thus, the shared word 'the Lord' in the original Edenic commandment (Gen. 2: 16) and in the later verse 'he that blasphemeth the name of the Lord shall surely be put to death' (Lev. 24: 16) allows R. Johanan to infer a primordial prohibition against blasphemy. Selden adopts the more sophisticated point of view that R. Johanan merely supplies an אסמכתא (*asmakhta*), a scriptural text used as a support or mnemotechnical aid for a rabbinical enactment.

discussion regarding the legal obligations enjoined on all human beings and to the formulation of the Noachide precepts.

It is clear that for Selden the *mishnah*, which shapes his understanding of the trial of Jesus, reflects authoritative legal opinions that predate the New Testament. What interests Selden is not the divinity or humanity of Christ but rather the way both he and his interlocutor behaved according to the systematized legal precepts of *halakha*, the Jewish legal code that expands and clarifies the gospel's account of the proceedings. Although Selden considers in *De Jure* whether Jesus was guilty of blasphemy as legally defined, and in *De Synedriis* whether the court was empowered at the time to pronounce a death sentence, he approaches an emotionally fraught topic, the passion of the Christ, with a rare degree of scholarly impartiality. By citing as many opposed points of view as he does, he shakes one's confidence in the perfect followability of the events. Even the first statement of the *mishnah*, that a blasphemer is not liable to death unless he utters God's name explicitly, is contested, and by Selden's favourite source, Maimonides: 'A Noachide who curses the name of God, whether he uses the *Nomen Proprium* or tetragrammaton or another name [or attribute], that person is liable to death, which is not the case for an Israelite.'[37] The liability of Gentiles in instances where Jews are exempt is not accepted by all talmudic authorities. The great codifier R. Joseph Caro (1488–1575), in his *Kesef Mishneh* (Venice, 1574–5), a commentary on part of the *Mishneh Torah*, questions Maimonides' adoption of the more severe opinion. The *gemara* records various opinions on the matter: that both Jews and Gentiles suffer equal punishment and are liable for execution if they curse God with one of the substitute names, or that both are not liable; that a Jew is flogged, a non-Jew decapitated, for blaspheming with a substitute name; or that Jewish transgressors are put to death by stoning, while non-Jewish violators are put to death by decapitation. And against the view that a non-Jew who made an idol but did not bow down to it is in fact liable for execution, even though a Jew would not be put to death for such an offence, Rava (56b) sees the law as more lenient toward a non-Jew:

Is there really someone who says that if a non-Jew made an idol but did not bow down to it, he is liable for execution? But surely it was taught otherwise in the following *Baraita* [an external *mishnah*, a Tannaitic source outside of the *Mishnah* collected by R. Judah]: 'Regarding idolatry, transgressions for which a Jewish court would execute a Jew, a non-Jew is prohibited from doing. But transgressions for which a Jewish court would not execute a Jew, even though they are forbidden to the Jew, a non-Jew is not prohibited from doing.'[38]

---

[37] Selden, *De Jure*, 2.12, p. 263, citing 'Maimonides, *Halach. Melakim, cap. 9. & videsis Gemar. Babylon. ad tit. Sanhedrin cap. 7. fol. 56a.*': *Noachides qui maledixerit Nomini, sive id fecerit Nomine Proprio seu tetragrammato sive cognomine aliquo quocunque modo, reus est* (mortis) . . . *quod non ita obtinet in Israelita.*'

[38] For Selden's survey of various opinions, both talmudic and post-talmudic, see *De Jure*, 2.11, p. 254, and 2.12, pp. 262–4.

When one adds to the conceptual and philological complexities of the Talmud those of the gospel narratives—which provide four different perspectives—the trial becomes even more difficult to puzzle out. In Matthew 26, Caiaphas adjures Jesus 'by the living God, that thou tell us whether thou be the Christ, the Son of God'(v. 63):

Jesus saith unto him, Thou hast said: nevertheless I say unto you, Hereafter shall ye see the Son of man sitting on the right hand of power, and coming in the clouds of heaven. Then the high priest rent his clothes, saying, He hath spoken blasphemy; what further need have we of witnesses? behold, now ye have heard his blasphemy.(vv. 64–5)

Milton's Satan in *Paradise Regained* shares Caiaphas's curiosity with Milton's readers. All of them know that the term 'Son of God' 'bears no single sense' (iv. 517). Present at the baptism, Satan heard the voice from heaven pronounce Jesus 'the Son of God belov'd' (l. 513), and he kept Jesus under 'narrower Scrutiny, that I might learn | In what degree or meaning thou art call'd | The Son of God' (ll. 515–17):

> The Son of God I also am, or was,
> And if I was, I am; relation stands;
> All men are Sons of God; yet thee I thought
> In some respect far higher so declar'd.   (ll. 518–21)

Paul calls all who are led by the spirit of God Sons of God (Rom. 8: 14; Gal. 4: 4–7), and he also holds that people who have faith are Sons of God (Gal. 3: 26). The early Christians regarded the term much as Milton's Satan does, as a high designation. Only in the passage in question does the Bible invest the term with a metaphysical meaning, when Caiaphas asks Jesus if he is something more than human and follows the question by shouting blasphemy when Jesus does not deny the title.

Selden cites numerous sources on the possible meanings of 'Son of God', and, more important, he recognizes that Jesus' key word 'power' (Gr. *tēs dunameōs*, Heb. *gevurah*, Aram. *gevurta*) is used in rabbinic writings, including the Talmud, as Omnipotence, a substitute for (or attribute of) the name of God.[39] He reads Caiaphas's rending his garment in light of the conclusion of the *mishnah* on blasphemy in Sanhedrin: 'upon hearing the actual blasphemy, the judges would stand on their feet, rend their garments in mourning, and never mend them.' He even cites another *mishnah* (*Horayoth*, BT 12b) and Maimonides on the difference between the way an ordinary priest rends his garments (from the top down)

---

[39] Selden, *De Jure*, 2.12, pp. 264–5, esp. on '*Sedentem à Dextris Potestatis*' and '*Filii Dei*'. Selden even recognizes that Gentile converts to Christianity might have understood the term in light of their own mythological heroes, such as Zeus, whose union with Leda produced Helen and Polydeuces, children of god. On the many possible meanings of both son of God and of man, see E. P. Sanders, *The Historical Figure of Jesus* (London: Penguin, 1993), 239–48. On *gevurah* as an attribute of God, or substitute for the divine name, see Babylonian Talmud, tractate *Horayot* 8a, *Eruvin* 24b, and *Sifre* Num. 112.

and the way a high priest does (from the bottom up).[40] Selden understands Caiaphas's 'what further need have we of witnesses? behold, now ye have heard his blasphemy' in the context of the same *mishnah*, which requires the judges first to examine the witnesses in a case involving blasphemy by using a substitute word, *Yose*, for the divine name. The witnesses would testify that the blasphemer said 'May Yose strike Yose'. The judges would then empty the courtroom so that the blasphemy would not be repeated before the general public. Since they could not condemn the blasphemer to death without hearing his own words, they called the witnesses back in to repeat what they actually heard.[41] In this case, Caiaphas is saying that the final testimony—the blasphemy itself—has already been heard, and from the mouth of the accused.

In a passage paraphrased by Stubbe, Selden quotes at length from Maimonides on the term ביד רמה, *manu elata*, a high-handed violation of the law:

> As for *him who transgresses in a high-handed manner*, he is a *deliberate transgressor* who acts with impudence and audacity and makes his transgression known in public. Accordingly such a one does not transgress merely because of desire or because, on account of his evil character, he wishes to obtain things that are forbidden by the Law, but in order to oppose and combat the Law. Therefore it says of him: *He reviles the Lord* [Num. 15: 30]. He must indubitably be killed. Whoever acts in this manner does so only because of an opinion formed by him, in virtue of which he is opposed to the Law.[42]

The punishment for blasphemy is stoning, which is administered, according to Sanhedrin (45a–b), by having the first witness throw the guilty party down from

---

[40] Selden, *De Jure*, 2.12, pp. 266–7.

[41] Among the reasons given in the Soncino Talmud for using the word *Yose*: because it contains four letters, like the actual tetragrammaton, which must have been used by the blasphemer for him to be punished. Moreover, the numerical value of 'Yose' is the same as of Elohim (eighty-one). According to yet another view, in the statement 'May Yose strike Yose' the first stands for Jesus, the Son, and the second is an abbreviation of Joseph, the Father, by which, however, God was to be understood. The witnesses were accordingly asked whether the accused in his blasphemy had set Jesus above God the Father. (R. Joshua b. Karha, the author of this saying in the *mishnah*, lived at a time when Judaeo-Christians were thought to have ascribed more power to Jesus than to God.)

[42] Maimonides, *The Guide of the Perplexed*, 3.41, ed. Pines, p. 565; quoted by Selden in Hebrew and Latin in *De Jure*, 2.11, p. 260; paraphrased by Stubbe in *Defence*, who calls this sin 'consequentiall blasphemy (which was not to depend upon subtile consequences deduced from words or actions innocently spoken and performed, and without any evill intention, or through errour; as any man may prove out of Mr. *Selden de jur. natur.* l.2 c. 11)[;] it was accounted such, if any one without lapsing himself into idolatry, or embracing strange worships (for that was comprised by the *Jews* under the precept of Idolatry, & was also reputed a consequential blasphemy) did perswade others thereunto, or profess the lawfulness & *equity* thereof himself, and that ביד רמה *with an high hand . . . out of malepertnesse* not *ignorance*, or *mistake in judgment*. Or if any *Israelite* did in such manner violate the Law of *Moses*, or a son of *Noah*, (living among the Jews under an established politie in *Judaea*) transgress the precepts of *Noah*, not *out of weakness*, or *hasty seductions of natural concupiscence or error*, but because he *peevishly* and *malepertly* refuses to acknowledge his obligation to the contrary, or doth not reverence the *Authority, Power, Unity,* and *Verity* of God so commanding or prohibiting; that is, he denies it all *in very deed, willingly, wilfully,* and with *an high hand,* and *despises* it. This is the doctrine of the Jews, and to this doth that precept referre *Numb.* 15.30. *The soul that shall do with an high hand . . . that soul shall be cut off from among his people*' (pp. 114–15).

a height great enough to kill him, and if it does not kill him, having the second witness push a heavy stone, already there in the place of stoning, upon his chest. According to Maimonides, in his commentary on the relevant *mishnah* (45a), stoning and hurling from a great height are equal, and it does not matter if the stone falls on him or if he falls on it. Selden, in *De Synedriis*, cites Josephus [*Antiquities*]. 'Lib. 20. cap. 8' [Loeb edn. vol. 9, pp. 494–6] on Ananus's condemning of St James to be stoned. From this account arose the story of his being thrown down from the pinnacle of the temple. Selden correctly notes that casting a person headlong from some eminent place was agreeable to the Jewish manner of stoning, but not from the temple.[43]

Returning for a moment to *Paradise Regained*, and not dismissing other interpretations, one might add to Satan's challenge to Jesus to cast himself down from the pinnacle of the temple the temptation to blaspheme. If, though not entitled, he dares to claim his metaphysical Sonship without words by accepting the challenge, he will suffer the punishment to which a blasphemer is liable, dashed 'against a stone':

> Now show thy Progeny; if not to stand,
> Cast thyself down; safely if Son of God:
> For it is written, He will give command
> Concerning thee to his Angels, in thir hands
> They shall up lift thee, lest at any time
> Thou chance to dash thy foot against a stone.
>   To whom thus Jesus. Also it is written,
> Tempt not the Lord thy God; he said and stood.   (iv. 554–61)

Jesus, quoting Deuteronomy 16: 16, does not assert his divinity, just as he never, either in Milton's poem or in the New Testament, claims the title 'Son of God'. In fact, as C. H. Toy puts it, 'he means to say that he has no right to throw himself into uncommanded danger, and then expect God to deliver him.'[44] Milton would have known the work of reformation expositors such as William Ames, who identifies this sin as 'the tempting of God':

This sinne doth oft times flow from doubting or unbeliefe: because he who seekes such *triall* of God, doth not sufficiently trust the revealed word of God. . . . It flowes also from a certaine arrogancy and *pride*, whereby we refusing to subject our wills to the Will of God, doe seeke to make his will subject to our lust. But it comes most often from presumption, whereby one is confident that God will doe this, or that, which he no where promised.[45]

Selden would have known that such statements appear frequently in the Talmud, including tractate Sanhedrin, where Rav warns, 'One should never bring oneself

[43] Selden, *De Synedriis*, 2.16, *Opera*, i. 1592–3.

[44] C. H. Toy, *Quotations in the New Testament* (New York: Scribners, 1884), 22; cited by Samuel Tobias Lachs, in *A Rabbinic Commentary on the New Testament* (Hoboken, NJ: Ktav, 1987), 52 n. 16.

[45] William Ames, *The Marrow of Sacred Divinity*, tr. John St Nicholas (1642), 267.

to temptation' (107a). According to R. Yannai, 'A person should never deliberately stand in place of danger saying that God will perform a miracle for him, for perchance no miracle will be performed for him.'[46] The author of Luke would have been familiar with rabbinic statements such as these.

We have touched upon the first half of Selden's remarks in *Table Talk* on zealots, which explain Christ's driving the money-changers from the temple with impunity as an act according to *halakha*. But in the second half, Selden indicates that Christ's persecutors are also acting in accordance with the *Ius Zelotarum*:

hence it was, that when one struck our Saviour before a judge, (where it was not lawful to strike, as it is not with us at this day), he only replied, If I have spoken evil, bear witness of the evil; but if well, why smitest thou me? He says nothing against their smiting him, in case he had been guilty of speaking evil, that is, blasphemy, and they could have proved it against him.[47]

In the vast sea of *De Synedriis*, which becomes more navigable when parts of it are recognized as loosely following the order of the *mishnayot* of Sanhedrin, Selden examines in detail matters that bear on the sentencing and execution of Christ. He still finds the Jews culpable, of course, but the excess of coexisting contradictory information that he provides makes it virtually ungraspable. And the effect of the reader's incapacity is to keep important questions open. Except for Selden's reading of *gevurah*, virtually all of the specifically talmudic opinions appear, in a more orderly fashion, in John Lightfoot's commentaries on the four gospels. But Selden, unlike Lightfoot, cites relevant ancient Greek and Roman sources as well, and his sceptical humanism and impartial attitude keep him from damning the Jews, even when the subject is the passion of the Christ. Selden patiently spells out the many different opinions in detail. Lightfoot, on a single typical page, cannot resist an opportunity to condemn the Jews. Faced with the account in Matthew of the Sanhedrin spending the night judging a capital case, and on the eve of a feast day at that, both of which are forbidden, Lightfoot says that he will not trouble the reader with recounting the different legal opinions on the matter. The judges, through rancour and hatred toward Christ, seem to slight and trample underfoot their own canons ('prae odio ac virulentia erga *Christum* proprios Canones videntur nihili facere, & pedibus conculare.'). And on the same page, finding incendiary material even in Matthew's 'When the morning was come' (27: 1), Lightfoot asks why the chief priests and elders were not at prayer: But where was that religious observance of these men today? ('At ubi hodie apud hos ista religio?') And the answer is that they set prayer aside effectually to destroy Jesus ('ut *Jesum* scilicet malè perdatis').[48]

---

[46] Babylonian tractate *Shabbat* 32a. See also *Ta'anit* 20a.
[47] Selden, *Table Talk*, 199–200.
[48] John Lightfoot, *Horae Hebraicae et Talmudicae. In Evangelium Sancti Matthaei* (Cambridge, 1658), 305.

Selden's general sympathy for the Sanhedrin as a judicial institution is evident throughout *De Synedriis*. Specifically in the context of its reluctance to execute offenders, he cites, among the testimony of others, Maimonides' famous passage in the *Mishneh Torah* that concludes with the affirmation that everyone has the right to claim, 'Because of me God created the world' (*'Propter me creatus est mundus'*):

For this reason Adam was created singular in the world, to teach us that whoever removes one soul (person) from the world, it is accounted to him as if he had destroyed a complete world. And whoever saves one person, it is accounted as if that person had preserved an entire world.[49]

Some of Selden's questions about the sentencing of Jesus appear in the same textual neighbourhood as his various citations from the Talmud attesting to the superiority of the court over the king. Some of the statutes would surely have reminded him as a member of parliament of his troubles with Charles. The king may not be given a seat on the Sanhedrin, nor may he be given a position on the board for the intercalation of the year—that is, to determine whether or not to create a leap year by adding a thirteenth month, a second Adar. Besides all the other relevant sources, Selden cites the Talmud and Maimonides on the reasons for the law: others would be inclined to suppress their opinions in deference to the high office. And there is the important matter of אפסניא, *afsania*, soldiers' pay or provisions for the maintenance of the army. The king would be inclined to intercalate or not, depending on whether the army was paid by the month or by the year.[50] If the king violates the law (Deut. 17: 14–17) that prohibits him from multiplying wives, horses, silver, and gold, the Sanhedrin is authorized to scourge him.[51] And Selden explains a difficult passage in Ezra (10: 8), which appears to place the power of confiscating a subject's property in the hands of '*the princes and the elders*'. This is not to be taken as a power inherent in the king by virtue of his office but rather as a privilege flowing to him only at that particular time from the Sanhedrin.[52]

There is no qualitative difference between Selden's approach to the court's right to flog the king and Pilate's scourging of Jesus (Matt. 27: 26). Citing Josephus, Plutarch, Suetonius, Valerius Maximus, Peter Faber, and others, he proves that the Roman custom of scourging a person condemned to death was contrary to

---

[49] Selden, *De Synedriis*, 2.13, *Opera*, i. 1498: '*Idcirco etiam creatus est Adam solus in mundo, ut inde disceremus, quemlibet qui animam unam* (personam) *destrueret e mundo, censendum esse perinde ac si destruxisset mundum plenum; & quemlibet qui salvam faceret animam unam, censendum esse quasi mundum plenum salvum fecisset.*'

[50] Ibid. 2.9, *Opera*, i. 1429–30.

[51] Ibid. 2.10, *Opera*. i. 1437: '*si multiplicaret, verberandus erat*', a judgement supported by a host of sources, beginning with the Jerusalem Talmud, 'Ad. tit. *Sanhedrin*, cap. 2. fol. 19. col. 4. Halach. 1'.

[52] Selden, *De Synedriis*, 2.14, *Opera*, i. 1527.

Jewish law.[53] Selden also introduces sources that claim that Jesus was tried as a false prophet, such as is described in Deuteronomy 18: 20–2. According to this view, when Christ exclaims, 'O Jerusalem, Jerusalem, thou that killest the prophets and stonest them which are sent to thee' (Matt. 23: 37), *Jerusalem* refers to the great Sanhedrin of seventy-one members that sat in Jerusalem and was the only judicial body authorized to judge a false prophet, *killest* in the original Hebrew is the word used in rabbinic law to mean strangulation, the punishment due by law to false prophets, while *stonest* points to the punishment of those who did not pretend to prophecy, but only to lead the people into some new doctrine.[54]

Selden's wide-ranging references and comparative approach in *De Synedriis* force the reader at times to hold on tight, like a dory in a gale. Pilate's washing his hands to show non-complicity or innocence may remind Selden of the law in the Hebrew Bible for the expiation of murder where the slayer is unknown, a ritual that he believed was under the direction of the great Sanhedrin: 'and all the elders of that city, that are next unto the slain man, shall wash their hands . . . and they shall answer and say, Our hands have not shed this blood, neither have our eyes seen it' (Deut. 21: 6–7). This 'naturally' puts Selden in mind of an ancient custom among the English: when any person was found, and it was not known by what means he died, the body was reckoned as a foreigner's; and the county in which it was found was fined on account of the murder, unless the officials swore publicly in court that it was no foreigner but an Englishman that was killed. The word *murdrum* signified not only *murder* in the present sense but the fine that was the consequence of it. The proof offered to show that the victim was no foreigner was called *Englescheria*, and in Wales it was called *Wallesheria*. But this was abolished by statute in the fourteenth of Edw. III. A.D. 1339. According to Bracton, though Selden cannot locate Bracton's source, the barons of England, to provide incentive to Canute the Dane to send his army back to Denmark after his English conquest, promised him that if any of his men remaining in England should be found dead and the person accused of the death could not clear himself by ordeal, he would suffer justice; and if he were to flee, the parish where the dead soldier was found would pay sixty-six marks. This was to assure Canute that he would not suffer by sending most of his army back home.[55]

Two questions bearing on the sentencing and crucifixion Selden treats in dizzying detail: the legal problems involved in trying a capital case on the eve of a festival, and whether or not the Jerusalem Sanhedrin could have been in session when Jesus was tried. Selden cites various rabbinic statutes requiring capital cases to be completed on the day when the verdict is acquittal and on the

---

[53] Selden, *De Synedriis*, 2.13, *Opera*, i. 1516: 'Ut pro morte damnato habitus flagellabatur; quod plane contra morem Judaicum, sed Romano satis consonum.'

[54] Ibid. 3.6, *Opera*, i. 1653–4.

[55] Ibid. 3.7, *Opera*, i. 1660–2.

day afterwards when the verdict is guilty; therefore, no capital cases are considered on the eve of the Sabbath or of a festival. If a festival followed the day on which the cause was heard, the sentence could not be carried out. The matter is complicated for a variety of reasons: Jewish holidays start in the evening; the synoptics date the crucifixion on Friday, the fifteenth day of Nisan, the first day of the week-long festival of unleavened bread, while John, for whom Christ is the true paschal lamb, dates it on the one-day holiday of Passover that immediately precedes the festival—that is, on the fourteenth day of Nisan. Selden offers a possible reading of John 18: 31: 'Then said Pilate unto them, Take ye him, and judge him according to your law. The Jews hereupon said unto him, It is not lawful for us to put any man to death.' According to this reading, it is evident both from Pilate's proposal and from their reply later, 'by our law he ought to die' (John 19: 7), that the Jews had the power to inflict capital punishment. What prevented the Jews from judging Jesus was the law that forbade them to condemn anyone on a day such as Passover, when they were to prepare the paschal lamb and would need to be ritually pure.[56]

But there is of course a simpler way of reading 'It is not lawful for us to put any man to death', and Selden provides more opinions—and more contradictory ones—on whether a Jewish court could order capital punishment than on any other question in *De Synedriis*. Both ancient and contemporary scholars remain divided on the matter.[57] Recorded cases where the Jews inflicted the death penalty are termed exceptional or unusual by those who take the position reflected in John 18: 31. Among the more important sources that Selden cites—and some of these stimulate him to free-associate, as he did regarding Pilate's hand-washing—are a *baraita* (external *mishnah*) in Sanhedrin, echoed by Moses of Coucy, which states that forty years before the destruction of the second temple, the Sanhedrin moved from its permanent seat in the chamber of hewn stone within the temple compound and met thereafter in the *Hanut*, which Selden translates correctly as '*tabernis in Hierosolyma*' (an area on the temple mount of Jerusalem with stores).[58] According to Rashi and others, once the Sanhedrin moved from its permanent seat in the chamber of hewn stone, no court was fit to judge capital cases, for a verse in Deuteronomy, cited by Selden, states, 'And you shall arise, and go up to the place which the Lord your God shall choose' (17: 8), teaching that the place where the Sanhedrin sits has significance, and that when it does not sit there, capital cases may not be heard. Others argue

---

[56] See ibid. 2.10, *Opera*, i. 1433–4, where he cites 'Tit. *Sanhedrin*, cap. 4 & 5. & videsis finem capitis 3. Mos. Cotzensis praecept. aff. 98. fol. 188. col. 1' [Moses of Coucy, *Sefer Mitzvoth ha-Gadol*, ed. Bomberg, Venice, 1547].

[57] Lachs, in *A Rabbinic Commentary on the New Testament*, 429 nn. 14–15, cites numerous opposed opinions ancient and modern.

[58] Selden, *De Synedriis*, 2.15, *Opera*, i. 1553: '*Quadraginta annis ante excidium templi migravit synedrium, & sedes sibi posuit in Tabernis.*' Marginal references are to '*Sanhedrin*, cap. 5. fol. 41, a' and Moses of Coucy, 'Praecept. Affirm. 102'.

that by law the judging of capital cases does not depend upon the Sanhedrin sitting in its permanent seat in the chamber of hewn stone. Rather, the Sanhedrin decided on its own to stop judging capital cases. Selden devotes many pages to these questions, citing numerous authorities on all sides of the issue, but he is certain that the decision rested with the Sanhedrin and that the power to judge capital cases was not forcibly taken from it. And of course he recognizes an important implication of the *baraita:* the destruction of the temple occurred in the second year of Vespasian's reign and seventy years after the birth of Christ, which means that the Sanhedrin would have given up the right to judge capital cases two or three years before the crucifixion.[59] Selden cites so many different opinions that one cannot be certain of his intention. Is there the shadow of a doubt regarding the accuracy of the gospel account of the Sanhedrin's judgement of Christ? Is there reverence for *halakha* and the institution that enforces it, which makes the setting aside of those laws by individuals in a rush to judgement even more heinous? Or is there, as in the case of zealots, a sense that Christ is indeed guilty and that the Sanhedrin followed *halakha*? The sources cited by Selden, taken together, support all three positions.

Selden cites the position that if prevailing circumstances require corporal or capital punishment to be administered on a temporary basis, the court is permitted to administer those punishments as it sees fit. It is worth remarking that he cites two *tosafot* on a single page. One, on tractate *Ketubot* 30a, takes note of the Sanhedrin's self-imposed exile and also of its occasional return, according to the need of the hour, to the chamber of hewn stone. The other, on tractate *Abodah Zara*, on the statement that although the Sanhedrin ceased, the four forms of capital punishment have not, but they are administered by the hand of heaven in a manner that fits the crime—for example, someone who should have been stoned will fall from a roof.[60] For Erastian Selden, arguing for the independent jurisdiction of the Sanhedrin, there is a great deal of difference between being deprived of a power and voluntarily ceasing to exercise that power, which was the case of the Jews. The word בטל (*batel*) in the Talmud, which erroneous

---

[59] Selden, *De Synedriis*, 2.15, sect. 8, *Opera*, i. 1553: ' "Templi autem excidium illud ad annum attinet Vespasiani secundum qui Christi septuagesimo respondet." ' In sect. 10, i. 1559, Selden rejects the view of Guillaume Postel that the Jews were *driven* away, and finds Petrus Galatinus even more in error for saying that they were driven out on account of the false judgement they gave of Christ, since their migration must have happened two or three years before the crucifixion. I am indebted in this paragraph to the discussion of the *baraita* in *Sanhedrin, The Talmud: The Steinsaltz Edition*, (New York: Random House, 1998), vol. xvii, part 3, pp. 128–9.

[60] Selden, *De Synedriis*, 2.15, *Opera* i. 1563: 'Thosiphtha', ['Ad tit. *Cethuboth*, cap. 3. fol. 30, 1']: '*Dicendum est quandoque tempore opportuno rediisse synedrium in Liskath Hagazith.*' The second reference is to 'Autor Thosiphtha' ['Ad tit. *Aboda Zara*, cap. 1. fol. 8, 2'], asserting '*vindicta coelestis*'. The *tosafot*, the collective creation of Rashi's disciples and their students, are a profound and independent interpretation of the *gemara*. When we consider that Selden was essentially self-taught in reading rabbinical literature—except for the brief instruction in oriental languages (probably including Aramaic) that Ussher provided in 1609—it seems almost miraculous that he could have met the stylistic, syntactic, and conceptual challenges posed by the *tosafot*.

Christian writers translated as 'abolished' or 'permanently undone', may very well signify *intermittere*, to cause to cease temporarily. Even after the overthrow of the temple, the Sanhedrin does not seem to have been wholly extinguished but to have been of force in some parts of the Holy Land for several years after, as the *tosefta* confirmed. As proof that the Sanhedrin had the power to inflict stripes a considerable time after Christ's passion, and therefore within the forty years before the destruction of the Temple, Selden cites the example of Paul's having received 'forty stripes save one' (2 Cor. 11: 24). Although as a Roman citizen by the Portian law he could not be scourged at all, yet as a Jew he underwent the law inflicted by his countrymen.

The relinquishing of the Sanhedrin's power is of capital importance to Selden, who cites the talmudic parallel between the exilic migration in ten stages of the *Shechinah* (the indwelling divine presence), from the holy of holies to the wilderness and then to heaven, and the ten stations of the Sanhedrin's decline, from the chamber of hewn stone in the temple to Tiberias, the lowest-lying place of them all.[61] Selden consults three separate versions of Grotius's *'de Jure Belli*, lib. 3. cap. 15. sect.9' regarding the question of when the sceptre passed from Judah, which would have entailed the passing of judicial authority from the great Sanhedrin. Selden points out that both the 1625 Paris and 1631 Amsterdam editions state incorrectly that this occurred when the emperor Augustus dismissed Archelaus, the ethnarch of Judaea, confiscated his property (this occurring only a few years before the birth of Christ), annexed Judaea to the Syrian province, and placed it under a procurator responsible to the authority of the governor of Syria. In the 1642 Amsterdam edition, Grotius corrected himself, changing 'the sceptre remained until the confiscation' to 'the sceptre remained even after the confiscation'.[62]

To conclude where we began, with Henry Stubbe, we can see that one of Selden's best readers framed a humane argument based on the account of Jesus' trial in *De Jure*. In a passage followed by pages of references to Selden, Stubbe places himself and his fellow Christians in the position of the Jews and Christ in that of a brutally persecuted minority, itself accused of Judaizing due to the nature of its heresies, which it supported (as Selden supported his most provocative ideas) through the skilful use of philology. Stubbe's plea is a fitting last word on the subject:

It is very considerable how by the same law, whereby Christ was condemned for blasphemy by the *Jewes* in asserting his deity: by the same law are the *Socinians* condemned now for denying his deity. We ought then to be very tender in committing the interpretive power of such lawes to any sort of men, least analogicall blasphemy retrench upon the truth.[63]

---

[61] Selden, *De Synedriis*, 2.15, *Opera*, i. 1552.
[62] Ibid. 2.16, *Opera*, i. 1598.
[63] Stubbe, *Defence*, 113.

9

Culverwel on Selden's Rabbinica:
The Limits of a Liberal's Toleration

In *An Elegant and Learned Discourse of the Light of Nature* (1652), published posthumously, Nathanael Culverwel (1618–51), the Cambridge Platonist, becomes gradually less irenical and more polemical toward John Selden. The motto of the book, and a central text for other contemporary latitudinarians known for their positive emphasis on reason, is 'PROVERBS 20.27. נר יהוה נשמת אדם *Mens hominis lucerna Domini*, The understanding of a man is the Candle of the Lord.'[1] Culverwel, whose own candle was snuffed out early, translates the Bible's *soul* (in the King James Version) or *spirit* (the Hebrew word *neshamah*, the breath of life which God breathed into human nostrils in Genesis 2: 7) as *understanding*. Over the course of three chapters, he objects to what he considers Selden's implicit substitution in *De Jure Naturali et Gentium* of the seven Noachide laws for the innate human *understanding* that comprehends natural law, the Jews for *man*, and the שכל הפועל, the *intellectus agens* or active intellect, for *the Candle*. Culverwell's critique of three central ideas in *De Jure*—the substitution of the *praecepta Noachidarum* for innate natural laws as universal moral imperatives, the need for supernatural mediation in the exercise of reason, and a distinction between the natural and the universal that makes a limited law of nature possible—marks the limits of a mid-seventeenth-century liberal intellectual's religious toleration.

Although Culverwel translates the central text from Proverbs to accentuate the light of human reason, he faults Selden, without naming him, for failing to chide the medieval scholastics who (mis)translate Psalm 4: 6 for the same reason:

The *Schoolmen* with full and general consent understand that place of the Psalmist of this *Lumen Naturale*, and many other Authors follow them in this too securely. Nay, some *Critical* writers quote them, and yet never chide them for it. The words are these, נסה עלינו אור פניך *Eleva super nos lumen vultûs tui* [lift thou up the light of thy countenance upon us]; but yet they, very ignorantly, though very confidently render them; *Signatum est super nos lumen vultûs tui* [the light of thy countenance is imprinted

---

[1] Nathanael Culverwel, *An Elegant and Learned Discourse of the Light of Nature* (1652), 1. Parenthetic page references to the *Discourse* in the body of the chapter are to this edition.

upon us]: and they do as erroneously interpret it of the light of Reason, which (say they) is *Signaculum quoddam, & impressio increate lucis in Anima* [a certain seal and stamp of uncreated light in the soul]. So much indeed is true, but it is far from being an Exposition of this place. (p. 62)

Twice Selden quotes word for word the Vulgate translation of Psalm 4: 6 used by the schoolmen, which he then paraphrases as a light of natural reason that allows human beings to make ethical decisions and to discern the principles of natural law.[2] In this instance, Culverwel wants Selden to chide the schoolmen for an incorrect translation that expresses an opinion with which Culverwel agrees ('So much indeed is true') and from which Selden dissents. Neither proof of the stamp of the divine upon the human or of innate natural laws, both of which Culverwel believes in, 'The words are plainly put up in the forme of a Petition to heaven, for some smiles of love, for some propitious and favourable glances, for Gods gracious presence and acceptance' (p. 102). Culverwel is correct in his reading; his only error is his assumption that Selden concurs with the authorities he cites.

Although the *Discourse* is available in an excellent modern annotated edition, the occasions on which its author dresses up in plumage borrowed from Selden are more frequent than even its learned editors acknowledge.[3] Culverwel, like many others in mid-seventeenth-century England, seems to regard Selden's scholarship as a national and natural resource, whose endless bounty can be plundered with impunity. It is typical of Selden to quote extensively and initially without criticism (as he does with the schoolmen) a point of view that he will reject, allowing it to stand on its own. Culverwel's most powerful weapons against Selden are those that Selden has supplied.

In his eighth chapter, '*How the Law of Nature is discovered? Not by Tradition, nor an Intellectus Agens,*' Culverwel opposes a rational theology to Selden's sceptical anti-scholastic epistemology, which posits two external sources of the knowledge of reality: a historicized natural law identified with the tradition of the *praecepta Noachidarum*, and a divine or angelic active intellect or *intellectus agens*, derived from Averroes and expressed most frequently in *De Jure* in terms of the

---

[2] Selden, *De Jure Naturali et Gentium juxta Disciplinam Ebraeorum* (1640), 1.8, p. 102, where he also quotes the schoolmen on Psalm 4 in the context of '*participationem Legis aeternae in rationali creatura*'; and 1.9, p. 116. These quotes frame the discussion of the active intellect, which Selden believes in, to the vexation of Culverwel, and which runs counter to the medieval scholastic view.

[3] Culverwel, *An Elegant and Learned Discourse of the Light of Nature*, ed. Robert A. Greene and Hugh MacCallum (Toronto: University of Toronto Press, 1972). It feels a bit churlish to criticize the edition at all, since the editors' very helpful notes have pointed the way to numerous passages in *De Jure*. It is surprising that the editors include 'perhaps Grotius' but not Selden among the authors who contributed significantly to the argument of the *Discourse*. Some of Culverwel's citations, which the editors assume he took directly from Grotius, he found instead as marginal notes in Selden's *De Jure Naturali et Gentium*, in the very chapters to which he was responding—for example, the Maimonidean legal distinction between חוקים (statutes) and משפטים (judgments): 'Videsis [Maimonides'] *More Nebochim* part 3. cap. 26. & Hug. Grot. *de Jure Belli* lib. 1. cap. 1. par. 9' (*De Jure Naturali*, 1.10, p. 121).

Maimonidean שכל הפועל ('*aql fa 'al* in the Arabic original of the *Guide*). The only thing remarkable about Culverwel's inhospitable response to these idiosyncratic ideas, Jewish and Muslim respectively in origin and rabbinic in their formulation in *De Jure*, is that while it should be common in mid-seventeenth century England it is not. That such criticisms are not general is a sign of Selden's great reputation. Throughout the *Discourse* Culverwel hedges these criticisms and hints at his own profound ambivalence by trying to avoid naming Selden, relying instead on honorifics: 'a noble Author of our own' (p. 56) 'that learned Author, whom I mention'd not long before' (p. 57), 'that noble Author, (whom I more than once commended before)' (p. 58), and 'that worthy Author of our own in his learned book *De Jure Naturali secundum Hebraeos*' (p. 64).

It stands to reason that early modern natural law theorists are generally less Judaeophobic than systematic theologians. Instead of a Pauline dualism that pits the carnal children of loins against the spiritual children of faith, a religious rationalist such as Culverwel looks for continuities among the cultures and religions of pagans, Jews, Muslims, and Christians. Arguing that the light of reason is available to all human beings, he significantly substitutes a new final clause for Colossians 3: 11. What Paul says about evangelical light free to all, 'we may say the very same in respect of the commonnesse of natural light. Where there is neither Greek nor Jew, circumcision nor uncircumcision, Barbarian, Scythian, bound nor free, but all these are one in respect of *Nature*, and natures Law, and natures Light' (p. 68). Where Paul would heal the fundamental divisions of humankind by baptizing all nations in Christ, 'for ye are all one in Christ Jesus', Culverwel insists that all human beings already share the light of nature, a sign that the image of God in which all were created has not been lost.

Stripped of its eloquence and power, Culverwel's perplexed response to Selden's penchant for Jewish learning is what one might expect from someone who considers himself more liberal than most on the question of toleration, but whose centrist position excludes those on the margin. Developing the theme that even the darkest errors 'have some tincture of *Reason* in them', he names some of the sects that are beyond the pale:

Men love to put a plausible title, a winning frontispiece upon the foulest Errours. Thus licentiousnesse would faine be called by the name of liberty, and all dissolutenesse wold faine be countenanced and secured under the Patronage and protection of free-grace. Thus wickednesse would willingly forget its own name, and adopt it self into the family of goodnesse. Thus *Arminianisme* pleads for it self under the specious notion of Gods love to mankinde. Thus that silly Errour of *Antinomianisme* will needs stile it self an *Evangelical Honey-comb*. Thus all irregularities and anomalies in Church affairs must pride themselves in those glittering titles of a *New Light, A Gospel Way, An Heaven upon Earth*. No wonder then that some also pretend to *Reason*, who yet run out of it, and beyond it, and besides it; but must none therefore come near it? because *Socinus* has burnt his wings at this *Candle of the Lord*, must none therefore make use of it? (pp. 6–7)

Chiefly attacking Antinomianism, Culverwel also rejects Arminianism and Soci-
nianism, and he alludes to the Family of Love, which he condemns for licentiousness. He might even be glancing at Milton's divorce tracts: 'licentiousnesse
would faine be called by the name of liberty' repeats the complaint 'Licence they
mean when they cry liberty' in the sonnet 'On the Detraction which followed
upon my Writing Certain Treatises'. As Christ accused the Pharisees of abusing
the legal liberty of divorce for the sake of uncivil licence, so, perhaps, does Milton
accuse contemporary libertines who mistake promiscuity for liberty, although the
line echoes most strongly the numerous accusations against Milton for introducing licentiousness under the guise of liberty.[4] These sects, according to Culverwel, have not rejected reason so much as misused it, and they can be defeated by
it. Playing David to the Goliath of Antinomianism, he asks, 'may not the head of
an uncircumcised Philistine be cut off with his own sword?' (p. 7)

Culverwel's far less consistent response to Selden's Jewish scholarship reflects
the confusion of one who finds his sympathy for the cause being tested at every
turn. According to the Talmud and Maimonides, Selden's principal sources, the
seven Noachide laws are promulgated by God to all of humankind, but Culverwel imagines that the Jews monopolize them, doling out 'some broken beams' of
light most grudgingly:

the Jewes, who (as that worthy Author of our own in his learned book *De Jure Naturali
secundum Hebraeos* makes the report) do imagine and suppose that the light of *Nature*
shines only upon themselves originally and principally, and upon the Gentiles only by
way of Participation and dependance upon them: They all must light their candles at the
Jewish Lamp. Thus they strive as much as they can to engrosse and monopolize this
natural light to themselves; only it may be sometimes out of their great liberality they will
distribute some broken beams of it to the Gentiles. As if these מצות בני נוח these
Praecepta Noachidarum had been lockt up and cabinetted in *Noahs* Ark, and afterwards
kept from the prophane touch of a Gentile: as if they had been part of that bread, which
our Saviour said was not to be cast unto dogs; and therefore they would make them be
glad to eate of the crumbs that fall from their masters table . . . Do they think that Natures
Fountain is enclos'd, that her Well is seal'd up, that a Jew must only drink of it, and a
Gentile must die for thirst? O but they tell you they are עם סגלה . . . a Darling, and
peculiar Nation. (pp. 63–4)

As a Cambridge Platonist—albeit to a lesser extent than More, Whichcote, and
Cudworth—Culverwel would have regarded a purified and divinely inspired
human reason as both the ultimate religious authority and the basis of religious
experience.[5] He misreads the Noachide law as reported by Selden in two ways, as

---

[4] In addition to Culverwel, see Joseph Hall, *Resolutions and Decisions of Divers Cases of Conscience*
(1649); cited by William Riley Parker, *Milton's Contemporary Reputation* (Columbus: Ohio State
University Press, 1940), 79. Parker's list of printed allusions (pp. 69–119) includes numerous
Presbyterian attacks on the licentiousness promulgated in Milton's divorce tracts.
[5] See on this point Aharon Lichtenstein, *Henry More: The Rational Theology of a Cambridge
Platonist* (Cambridge, Mass.: Harvard University Press, 1962), p. vii.

a natural light instead of a divine, universal, voluntary or positive law of perpetual obligation, and as a law not only deriving from the rabbis but also hoarded by them. The references to Noah's ark and the Gentiles inadvertently remind the reader that Noah was a Gentile and that the seven precepts were promulgated to the first postdiluvians, who constituted the world's total population. As a sign of confusion, ambivalence, or both, Culverwel cites the New Testament account of the Syrophoenician woman, where Christ himself insists on Jewish exclusivity, initially refusing to heal the child of a Gentile, telling her, 'I was sent only to the lost sheep of the house of Israel' (Matthew 15: 24). Despite Culverwel's intentions, in this excerpt's proof-texts, the rabbinic precepts are handed down to everyone while the gospel is the bread intended only for the Jews, who are God's children. Since Jesus's mission is to call the Jews back to God, the Gentiles, the dogs under the table, must eat the crumbs. In this passage, as everywhere else in chapters 8 and 9 of the *Discourse*, Selden's *De Jure* lies open before Culverwel, even when he misreads it. It rankles when he reads Selden's description of the Jews as God's treasure, his special possession (Malachi 3: 17),[6] so he annexes it to an account of the Noachide precepts.

Culverwel's confusion arises not from hatred of the Jews—he is far more tolerant than most of his contemporaries in England—but from what he perceives as their insistence on their own superiority and special election. His objections would be more valid if the subject were the miraculous revelation of the Torah at Sinai rather than a law whose universality goes far toward countering the most serious and recurrent charge against the Jews, beginning in antiquity, that they hate Gentiles.[7] At times, especially early in his critique of Selden, he insists only that Gentiles, Jews, and Christians share equally in the light of nature's law. And even then, sympathetically paraphrasing Paul ('the advantage of the Jew is great'; Romans 3: 1, 2), he acknowledges the importance of priority and the advantage of the Sinai theophany and the Mosaic law:

natural light . . . doubtlesse is planted by *Nature* in the heart both of Jew and Gentile, and shines upon both with an equal and impartial beam. And yet this must not be denied, that the Jewes had even these Natural notions much clarified & refin'd from those clouds and mists which יצר הרע [lit., inclination to evil] Original sin had brought upon them, and this by means of that pure and powerful beam of heavenly truth which shined more peculiarly upon them; those Lawes which *Nature* had engraven . . . upon the tables of their hearts, sin like a moth had eaten and defaced (as in all other men it had done) but in them

---

6 Selden, *De Jure*, 1.9, p. 117: 'סגולה successionem peculiarem & populum . . . id est selectum, seu ut dicere solemus *ecclesiam visibilem*. See also 1.1, p. 10, where Selden explains that the Jews are called "עם סגולה *populum numini ipsi olim peculiarem* ac selectissimum *prae omnibus populis qui fuere super faciem terrae*.' When Culverwel objects to the opinion that Gentiles are required to fill their bottles of water at Jewish streams, '*ex fluentis Hebraicis*' (p. 65), he is quoting without attribution Selden in *De Jure* (1.1, p. 16), who cites Theodoret as the source of the phrase.

7 On Hellenistic-Roman prejudice against Jews for their perceived intolerance, see Louis H. Feldman, *Jew and Gentile in the Ancient World: Attitudes and Interactions from Alexander to Justinian* (Princeton: Princeton University Press, 1993), 123–76.

those fugitive letters were call'd home again, and those many *Lacunae* were supplyed and made good again by comparing it with that other Copy (of Gods own writing too) which *Moses* received in the Mount; and besides, they had a great number of revealed truths discovered to them, which were engraffed indeed upon the stock of *Nature*, but would never have grown out of it: so that this second Edition was *Auctior* [expanded] also, as well as *Emendatior* [corrected]; but yet for all this they have no greater a portion *of the light of Nature* then all men have. Thus Christians also are עַם סְגֻלָּה, and yet in respect of their natural condition, have no more then others. (p. 64)

And yet, in the same textual neighbourhood, he is capable of reviving the ancient canard about the Jews violating the universal duties toward strangers by not allowing them to share their water or to kindle fire from theirs. In a sort of travesty of the logical method of rabbinic exegesis known as *gezerah shavah*, the comparison of similar expressions, he joins that slander to his central text, Proverbs 20: 7:

But truly, if they were at their disposing, there be some that will question, whether they would let them sip at their fountain or no; whether they would let them light a Candle with them or no. Yes (may some say) *Pythagoras* lighted his Candle there, and *Plato* lighted his Candle at theirs. But what did they borrow common Notions of them? Did they borrow any Copies of Natures Law from them? Was this [written law] only some Jewish Manu-script, which they translated into Greek? Can *Pythagoras* know nothing, unlesse by a present metempsychosis a Jews soul come and enforme him? That *Pythagoras* should be circumcis'd by the perswasion of the Jews is not impossible, but that he could not know how to forbid Blasphemy without the Jews teachings, deserves a good argument to prove it. (p. 65)

In a wrenching of the universalist sentiment expressed in the verse (since the Hebrew Bible's *adam* refers to all of humankind), Culverwel repeats the slander against the Jews that they do not share with non-Jews. This calumny—levelled against the early Christians as well—was sufficiently widespread, even in the ancient world, to prompt Josephus to refute it: 'The duty of sharing with others was inculcated by our legislator.... We must furnish fire, water, food to all who ask for them, point out the road, not leave a corpse unburied, show consideration even to our declared enemies.'[8]

With Selden's *De Jure* open in front of him, Culverwel is familiar with the classic formulation of this charge in Juvenal's bitter *Satire 14* (103–4), which reflects hatred begotten by Jewish self-isolation.[9] Juvenal's condemnation of the Jews for not showing the way has been read as an allusion to the talmudic opinion, rejected by rabbinic arbiters of questions of *halakha*, that a Jew not

---

[8] Josephus, *Against Apion* 2.211, in Josephus, ed. H. St. J. Thackeray (London: Heinemann; Cambridge, Mass.: Harvard University Press, 1926; rpt. 1956), 379. Josephus's defence also appears generally in *Antiquitates Judaicae*, iv. 276, p. 609: 'One must point out the road to those who are ignorant of it, and not, for the pleasure of laughing oneself, impede another's business by misleading him.'

[9] Culverwel is alluding to the lines from Juvenal quoted at the very end of *De Jure* (p. 846).

teach the Torah to Gentiles. Such a reading connects with the ancient view that the Jews are keeping a terrible secret, which leads to misunderstandings and contributes even to blood libels.[10] Culverwel extends the old slander to create a new one: if natural law were indeed identical to the Noachide precepts, which it is not, the Jews would not permit others to drink from their fountain or to light their candles. Yet even as he invents this opinion, he distances himself from it ('there be some that will question'). Aside from the slander, Culverwel owes every idea in the excerpt to Selden's *De Jure*, from the question of Pythagoras's circumcision to the debt of Plato and Pythagoras to Jewish thought.[11] Culverwel's rhetorical questions are addressed to Selden, and most of two chapters of the *Discourse* are an implicit dialogue with him. It seems clear that Culverwel regards Selden as both the source of rabbinic ideas and a believer in them.

The ridiculing of 'some Jewish Manuscript' is ungrateful in light of Culverwel's own unacknowledged heavy debt to Selden's scholarship. Culverwel contrasts true natural law, found in human reason, with Selden's Noachide precepts and other arcane notions, found 'in an Oriental Tradition, in a Rabbinical dream, in a dusty Manuscript, in a Remnant of Antiquity, in a Bundle of Testimonies' (p. 72). These sources, he continues, 'tell you this story':

that these commands were proclaim'd by the voice of God himself, first to *Adam* in the first setting out of the world; and then they were repeated to *Noah* when there was to be a reprinting, and new Edition of the world after the Deluge; and thus were in way of Tradition to be propagated to all posterity. . . . O incomparable method and contrivance to finde out certainty, to rase out first Principles, to pluck down Demonstrations, to demolish the whole structure and fabrick of *Reason*, and to build upon the word of two or three Hebrew Doctors, that tell you of a voice, and that as confidently, as if they had heard it, and they are entrusted with this voice, they must report and spread it unto others, though they do it like unfaithful Ecchos with false and imperfect rebounds. (p. 72)

Culverwel precedes this account of the precepts with Selden's Latin original, which he repeats verbatim.[12] One can tell that he is looking at the page when he

---

[10] See Feldman, *Jew and Gentile in the Ancient World*, 126–9. R. Ami's opinion, in tractate *Hagigah* 13a (not to hand over the Torah to a non-Jew), has puzzled a number of rabbinic authorities, since it is not found in general even in the works of the *poskim* (lit., deciders). Various exegetes have pointed out that this would never have applied as a general law after the appearance of the Septuagint. Since R. Ami's opinion appears in the context of the rigorous qualifications that must be met by a Jew who wants to study the mystical writings connected with the throne-chariot of Ezekiel's vision (the *merkabah*), R. Samuel Eliezer ben Judah Ha-Levi Edels, known as the MaHaRSha (1555–1631), one of the Talmud's foremost commentators, argues that the statement applies not to the overt Jewish tradition of the divine message—the Bible and its understanding—but rather to the secret, covert tradition and its texts, such as the Zohar. R. Menahem ben Solomon Meiri (1249–1316) applies the statement only to those who literally worship idols, but not to Christians and Muslims, whom he considers to be ethical monotheists.

[11] For Pythagoras, including the question of his circumcision, see *De Jure*, 1.2, p. 15; for Plato lighting his candle at a Jewish source, see 1.2, p. 23. Culverwel's similar argument about Aristotle (p. 66) derives from Selden's discussion in 1.2, p. 14.

[12] Culverwel, *Discourse*, 72; Selden, *De Jure*, 1.9, p. 109.

mentions 'two or three Hebrew Doctors', since its margin contains three references: '*Zohar in* Beresith *fol. 55. editionis Mantuanae*', '*Gemar. Babylon. ad tit.*
Sanhedrin *c. 7. fol. 56.b. & c.*', and '*Maimonid. halach.* Melacim *cap. 9. & c*'. The
tone has become less irenic, and by this point in the *Discourse* it is hard to
separate Selden from the Jews as objects of attack.[13]

Culverwel's dismissive tone when he refers to 'some Jewish Manu-script'
(p. 65),' 'a dusty Manuscript', is different in degree but not in kind from the
ridicule heaped on Selden thirty years after his death by Simon Lowth (1630?–
1720), Vicar of Cosmos Blene in the diocese of Canterbury. Lowth's works
defend episcopal succession against any rite of deposition by a civil magistrate
as well as the position of the beneficed clerics who refused to take the oath of
allegiance in 1689 to William and Mary. Understandably, Lowth hates everything that Selden stands for, including his Erastianism and his support of the
parliamentary side in the Civil War, which he denounces bitterly. He grudgingly
concedes Selden's scholarship: 'his Zeal and Industry being singular, I wish his
Integrity had been so too, he seldom missing of any thing within the compass of
his designed subject, that may be any ways useful to his present Plot and
Enquiry.'[14] He inveighs against Selden's claim, based on dusty Jewish manuscripts, that 'Holy Orders has no more in it, than an imitation of that particular
School, wherein St. *Paul* was educated under *Gamaliel*; where it was usual for one
that had arrived to a degree of Eminence above others, as that of a Doctor; to
appoint and send out others under, and after, him.' Did the Holy Ghost, when it
placed overseers in that 'Church, which Christ had Purchased with his own
Blood', imitate the school of Gamaliel? And did Paul receive his apostleship from
that same school rather than from the will of God?[15]

Against Selden's eastern wisdom, Jewish and Muslim, Lowth opposes 'the
Kingdom of Christ', which he believes he considers not at all. He dwells at
some length on Selden's history of excommunication, declaiming against Selden's
assertion

that there was no Excommunication at all amongst the *Jews*, nor is therefore to be any
among Christians, because no mention of it, in an old *Jewish* Manuscript Ritual, which he
has by him, and there produces; and the courses of Penance and Repentance, are all
Innovations, because his Priest of *Mahomet* neither knew nor discovered any thing of it;

---

[13] Here I strongly disagree with Greene and MacCallum, the learned editors of the *Discourse*,
who assert, inexplicably, that 'the passage expresses a view which Selden rejects' (p. 188 n. 9), and
with Reid Barbour, in his *John Selden: Measures of the Holy Commonwealth in Seventeenth-Century
England* (Toronto: University of Toronto Press, 2003). According to Barbour, Culverwel never
acknowledges 'that Selden himself is impressed by the Jews. Rather, Selden is represented as
reporting the arrogance with which the Jews arrogate to themselves a monopoly on the universality
of nature' (p. 372).

[14] Simon Lowth, *Of the Subject of Church-Power* (London, 1685), 146.

[15] Lowth, *Church-Power*, 150–1. The section of Selden's *De Synedriis* (bk 1, ch. 14) that he
attacks is in *Opera*, i. 1098–9, on Gamaliel and Paul and סמיכת הזקנים '*per impositionem
manuum qua presbyteri creari soliti.*'

and which must be the alone Inferences from all his great Pains and Reading there shew'd to the World, if there can be any at all.[16]

Lowth's contempt for Selden, who relies for authority on 'an old *Jewish* Manuscript Ritual' instead of the Holy Spirit and the Kingdom of Christ, suggests that even Culverwel's milder remarks on Jewish manuscripts are part of a more personal attack on Selden than has been acknowledged. Perhaps more important, these references point to the widening rift in the seventeenth century between biblical philology and scripture-oriented theology. Long after the advances in biblical philology represented by Scaliger, Grotius, and Selden, which led ultimately to the separation of philology from theology effected by Spinoza, the complaints against Jewish manuscripts express resistance to the identification of *Hebraica Veritas* and the *sensus literalis* with the Jewish Bible text, complete with its exegetical tradition.

As Moshe Goshen-Gottstein has pointed out, early modern continental scholars 'broke their heads finding justification for the use of Semitic languages in biblical exegesis', while in England a scholar like Edward Pococke 'simply went ahead—as if there was no problem at all.' With 'disarming nonchalance', Pococke inquired into Syriac and Arabic equivalents of biblical terms, 'to which help the most learned Jews frequently recurre.'[17]

In *Titles of Honor* (1614), published fifteen years before he began his serious study of the Talmud, Selden appeals to the authority of medieval Jewish philological exegetes to justify relying on even the humblest of sources. Trusting his learned readers, who will know how to compare his investigation of titles of honour with those performed by others, he compares himself to the servant who inadvertently taught the rabbis how to read a key term in Isaiah 14: 23, where God promises to rise up against Babylon: 'I will sweep it with the besome [broom] of destruction' (AV):

How ere my sufficiencie be, some of them know, that the understanding of טאטא, i. Tata, in holie Writ ['Ies. cap. 14. com. 23'] is referd by the Rabbins ['Kimchi in Rad. apud Reuchlin. in vers. R. Nathanis Mordechai'] to a Chambermaid that askt hir Mistresse for a טאטא to sweep the house withall, whence one of them hearing her, before not knowing what it was, collected it was a Broom, and that the Verb was to sweep. As in hir question, so in my Discourses may occurre what many a knowing man, if ingenuous, will thank me for.[18]

---

[16] Lowth, *Church-Power*, 215.

[17] Moshe Goshen-Gottstein, 'Foundations of Biblical Philology in the Seventeenth-Century Christian and Jewish Dimensions', in *Jewish Thought in the Seventeenth Century*, ed. Isadore Twersky and Bernard Septimus (Cambridge, Mass. and London: Harvard University Press, 1987), 77–94. He quotes Pococke on p. 94.

[18] Selden, *Titles of Honor* (1614), Preface, sig. d1r. Selden's source is the translation by Antonius Reuchlinus of the concordance to the Bible by Isaac Nathan b. Kalonymos (Basel, 1556). Professor G. J. Toomer points out in correspondence that Selden's reliance on this translation, instead of directly on Kimhi's citation of the passage in his well-known ספר השרשים, *Sefer ha-Shorashim* (Venice, 1529), reveals his relative unfamiliarity with Hebrew literature in 1614.

For Culverwel, but not for Selden, reason is the imprint of the divine upon the human. Selden, more sceptically, subscribes to the idea of the *intellectus agens*, an external force, either God or a heavenly messenger, that actuates the mind's cognitive faculties. It accords with the constant emphasis in *De Jure* on an external force as the source not only of all legal obligation but of moral, intellectual, and spiritual reality. Arguably the most important word in the book is the talmudic term חייב (*chayav*), which denotes at once being guilty, obligated, and liable to punishment under the law. For Selden, no law is antecedent to its imposition. The law produces the distinction in acts between good and bad, or base and reputable. From that legal distinction arises among persons obligation and indebtedness toward the performance of a duty. In a passage cited by Richard Tuck, Selden insists that 'the idea of a law carrying obligation irrespective of any punishment annexed to the violation of it . . . is no more comprehensible to the human mind than the idea of a father without a child.'[19]

It is impossible to overstate the importance of external obligation in Selden's thought. It supports his post-sceptical defence of divine epistemology—that is, a belief, consistent with and yet in spite of anti-Aristotelian scepticism, that moral knowledge exists as a manifestation of God's will. It makes God the ultimate legislator who promulgates Noachide precepts that oblige all of humankind and operates within the human mind as *intellectus agens*, as far above mere volition as grace itself, though available not only to elect Christians but to everyone. Where Hobbes makes the human sovereign the absolute source of punitive authority, and where Grotius, though clearly religious, promulgates a natural law theoretically independent of God, Selden finds it impossible to conceive of a law of nature apart from a legislating God whose interventions enable human thought. Unlike some other natural law theorists, Selden excludes animals from the law on the grounds that only an intellectual being can grasp the idea of punishment.[20] Selden is a natural law theorist who almost certainly does not believe in natural law as it is generally conceived, as a series of imperatives innate and implanted in the human mind. His natural law is overtly religious, a universal, voluntary, divine positive law of perpetual obligation. And yet his emphasis in *De Jure* on fulfilling the precepts makes salvation possible to those outside the church. Even the most minimal of Christian dogmatic beliefs is not a necessary precondition for salvation.[21]

---

[19] Selden's starting-point for obligation is *De Jure*, 1.4, p. 46: 'Unde Ebraeis etiam חייב quod obligatum denotat, *poenae obnoxium esse* pariter significat'. What follows on pp. 46–52 develops the relationship contained in this single word between obligation and punishment. See also Richard Tuck, 'Grotius and Selden', in *The Cambridge History of Political Thought, 1450–1700*, ed. J. H. Burns and Mark Goldie (Cambridge: Cambridge University Press, 1991), 525.

[20] *De Jure*, 1.4, pp. 46–7, and especially 1.5, *passim*. Alan Cromartie makes this point in *Sir Matthew Hale (1609–1676)* (Cambridge: Cambridge University Press, 1995), 90.

[21] See Cromartie, *Sir Matthew Hale*, 160.

Just as Selden as a member of Parliament looks to the precedents set by English common law, so as a natural law theorist does he look to the talmudic and Maimonidean texts of the *praecepta Noachidarum*, which for him constitute a historical record of God's pronouncements to all human beings. Moreover, the *intellectus agens*, as a specifically external power, provides, even to antediluvian human beings and to others who lacked access to the precepts, a direct revelation of God's moral imperatives that is comparable to the one received by the original children of Noah.[22] Although Selden cites many authorities who assert the capacity of the human mind to perceive the truth, as a post-sceptical moralist he dissents from this view, emphasizing instead the necessity of constant divine intervention in the operation of the mind. God or an angel is the agent that permits the human mind to perceive, just as the sun, the fountain of light, enables the mind to see. In *De Jure*, 1.9, he cites Maimonides' formulations, including his reading of Psalm 36: 9 ('For with thee is the fountain of light; in thy light shall we see light'): 'Et de utroque pariter capiunt illud, *In lumine tuo videbimus lumen*, quod Moses Maimonides interpretatur בשפע השכל אשר ישפע ממך *per influentiam intelligentiae quae à te influit*.'[23]

One of Selden's key texts on the subject is Maimonides' commentary on the word שפע, *abundant flow*:

This term, I mean 'overflow', is sometimes also applied in Hebrew to God, may He be exalted, with a view to likening Him to an overflowing spring of water, as we have mentioned. For nothing is more fitting as a simile to the action of one that is separate from matter than this expression, I mean 'overflow'. For we are not capable of finding the true reality of a term that would correspond to the true reality of the notion. For the mental representation of the action of one who is separate from matter is very difficult, in a way similar to the difficulty of the mental representation of the existence of one who is separate from matter.[24]

Although the title of Jeremy Taylor's lengthy work of casuistry, *Ductor Dubitantium*, pays homage to Maimonides (its title compresses two Renaissance Latin translations of the *Guide*, Buxtorf's *Doctor Perplexorum* (Basel, 1629), and Agostino Giustiniani's *Dux seu Director dubitantium* (Paris, 1520)), Taylor

[22] See on this point Richard Tuck, 'Grotius and Selden', 526.

[23] Selden, *De Jure*, 1.9, p. 110. He cites in the margin specifically rabbinic sources of the idea of the *intellectus agens* as a mediating force, 'Aben Tybbon in *Ruach hachen* c. 3. et videsis R. Iehudam [Judah Ha-Levi b. Samuel] in *Sepher Cozri* [כוזרי] part 1. c. 87. part. 4. cap. 25. et 5. cap. 10. 12. et 14. Adde Mos. Maimonid. in *Moreh Nebochim* part. 2. cap. 4.' The first reference is unusually obscure. רוח חן (*Ruach Chen*) is an anonymous introduction to Maimonides' *Guide* (*Moreh Nevuchim*), attributed by Moritz Steinschneider to Jacob Anatolio b. Abba Mari, in *Catalogus Hebraeorum in Bibliotheca Bodleiana* (1852–60; repr. Hildesheim: G. Olms, 1964), no. 4036. G. J. Toomer identifies a commendatory poem by Elias Levita, prefixed to the Venice edition of 1544, as the source of the attribution of the work to Judah b. Timmon. For a reproduction of the poem, see Gérard E. Weil, *Elie Lévita, Humaniste et Massorète (1469–1549)* (Leiden: Brill, 1963), 153. Selden's attribution has stronger support than Steinschneider's.

[24] Moses Maimonides, *The Guide of the Perplexed*, ed. Shlomo Pines (Chicago: University of Chicago Press), 2.12, p. 279.

takes without acknowledgement vast sections of Selden's *De Jure*, including an almost verbatim transcription of a section on the *intellectus agens*:

In this whole affair, God is as the Sun, and the Conscience as the Eye: or else God or some Angel from him being the *intellectus agens* did inform our reason, supplying the place of Natural faculties and being a continual *Monitor* (as the Jews generally believe, and some Christians, especially about three or four ages since:) which *Adam de Marisco* was wont to call *Helias his Crow*: something flying from heaven with provisions for our needs. And the *Gloss* and *Gulielmus Parisiensis*, and before them *Maimonides*, from whom I suppose they had it, affirm this to be the meaning of *David* in the fourth *Psalm*, Offer the sacrifice of righteousness; it follows, *Quis monstrabit? Who will shew us any good?* who will tell us what is justice, and declare the measures of good and evil? He answers, *Signatum est super nos lumen vultus tui Domine*, thou hast consign'd the light of thy Countenance upon us, *ut scilicet* (as it is in another Psalm) *in lumine tuo videamus lumen, that in thy light we may see light.*[25]

This idea angers Culverwel, and in his chapter rejecting the *intellectus agens* as a Jewish idea ('a Rabbinical dream') it is very clear that he identifies Selden (ostensibly one of the 'Divers into the depths of knowledge' who should know better) as not merely a reporter but also as a subscriber. By this point, his attacks on rabbinic thought become attacks on Selden as well:

The Jews will by no means yeeld that there is light enough in the dictates of Reason to display common notions, for they look upon it as a various and unsatisfactory light mixt with much shadow and darknesse, labouring with perpetual inconstancy and uncertainty. What[,] are first Principles become so mutable and treacherous? Are Demonstrations such fortuitous and contingent things? had I met with this in a fluctuating Academick, in a Rowling Sceptique, in a *Sextus Empiricus*, in some famous Professor of doubts, I should then have lookt upon it as a tolerable expression of their trembling and shivering opinion. But how come I to finde it among those Divers into the depths of knowledge, who grant a certainty, and yet will not grant it to *Reason*? (pp. 71–2)

The Maimonidean texts on the *intellectus agens* as an overflow appear within the larger context of the limitations of divine epistemology, ways of knowing or coming to know God. Maimonides stresses the limitations of such knowledge and of the figurative language that represents the operations of the divine, as well as the impossibility of 'finding the true reality of a term that would correspond to the true reality of the notion'. In discussing those among the multitude who believe in the literal truth of their descriptions of the divine, he identifies the *yetzer hara* or evil impulse as imagination itself, 'for every deficiency of reason or character is due to the action of the imagination or consequent upon its action.'[26]

---

[25] Jeremy Taylor *Ductor Dubitantium. or The Rule of Conscience in all Her General Measures* (London, 1660; 2nd edn. 1671), 178. Taylor is quoting Selden in *De Jure*, 1.9, primarily p. 114 (where the description '*Corvus Heliae*' is applied to the '*Intellectus Agens*'), but also pp. 110–12, and p. 116, where Selden cites Averroes, Avicenna, Jacopo Zabarella, Bodin, and Cardanus as quoted by Julius Caesar Scaliger.

[26] Maimonides, *Guide*, 2.12, p. 280.

Self-conscious in his own use of figural language, Maimonides explains why he chooses the word שפע [Arabic: *fayd*], overflow, to describe the operation of the active intellect. Since the divine intellect is incorporeal, it acts neither through immediate contact nor at some particular distance:

Hence the action of the separate intellect is always designated as an overflow, being likened to a source of water that overflows in all directions and does not have one particular direction from which it draws while giving its bounty to others. For it springs forth from all directions and constantly irrigates all the directions nearby and afar.[27]

As the world derives from the overflow of God, so has He caused his knowledge to overflow to the prophets.[28] In a passage quoted in part by Selden, Maimonides closes this chapter by presenting emphatically (with his signature imperative 'Understand this') what he considers to be the Bible's own metaphors of the active intellect making possible all intellectual activity: the inexhaustible sources of light and water:

As for our remark that the books of the prophets likewise apply figuratively the notion of overflow to the action of the deity, a case in point is the dictum, *They have forsaken Me, the fountain of living waters* [Jeremiah 2: 13]—which refers to the overflow of life, that is, of being, which is life without any doubt. Similarly the dictum, *For with Thee is the fountain of life* [Psalm 36: 9], signifies the overflow of being. In the same way the remaining portion of this verse, *In thy light do we see light*, has the selfsame meaning—namely, that through the overflow of the intellect that has overflowed from Thee, we intellectually cognize, and consequently we receive correct guidance, we draw inferences, and we apprehend the intellect. Understand this.[29]

Milton's great invocation to light that opens Book III of *Paradise Lost* employs the same two metaphors: 'Bright effluence of bright essence increate, | Or, hear'st thou rather pure Ethereal stream, | Whose Fountain who shall tell?' (iii. 6–8). As Alastair Fowler has pointed out, 'the identity of the *light* addressed is debated',[30] and so many sources have been proffered that one hesitates to add another. But *De Jure* is a source that we know Milton read and admired, and the law of parsimony suggests that his sole reference to Maimonides, in *The Doctrine and Discipline of Divorce*, may derive from Selden rather than directly from the *Doctor Perplexorum*.[31] Certainly the invocation of Book III and the conclusion of 2.12 of

---

[27] Maimonides, *Guide*, 2.12, p. 279.   [28] Ibid.

[29] Ibid. 280; Selden, *De Jure*, 1.9, p. 110.

[30] See John Milton, *Paradise Lost*, ed. Alastair Fowler, 2nd edn. (London and New York: Longman, 1998), 165–7. Possible sources of the light mysticism include, besides Dante and the Bible, pseudo-Dionysius, the Cambridge Platonists, Vida's *Hymns*, the Florentine Neoplatonists, Tasso, William Drummond of Hawthornden, and numerous others. In *Paradise Lost*, ed. Scott Elledge, 2nd edn. (New York and London: W. W. Norton, 1993), 63, the editor speculates that '*Light* may carry suggestions of God, Christ . . . wisdom, and inspiration of the Holy Spirit, at the same time that it means the physical light by which men see nature.'

[31] See *Doctrine and Discipline of Divorce*, *YP*, ii. 257: 'the Rabbins and *Maimonides* famous among the rest in a Book of his set forth by *Buxtorfius*, tells us that *Divorce was permitted by Moses to preserve peace in mariage, and quiet in the family*.' See Selden on divorce in *De Jure*, 5.7, pp. 567–73.

the *Guide* have much in common: metaphors of light and water, creation of the world as the result of a divine overflow, common terms ('Bright effluence [from *ex*, "out", and *fluere*, "to flow"] of bright essence increate' and, in Selden's quotation from Maimonides, *'per influentiam intelligentiae quae a te influit'*), a self-consciousness about the limitations of divine epistemology ('May I express thee unblamed?'; 3.3), and prophetic inspiration as an extraordinary overflow of light from the divine intellect:

> So much the rather thou Celestial Light
> Shine inward, and the mind through all her powers
> Irradiate, there plant eyes, all mist from thence
> Purge and disperse, that I may see and tell
> Of things invisible to mortal sight.   (iii. 51–5)

Although, as noted, Selden cites Maimonides frequently in his discussion of the active intellect, he also finds the idea in commentaries on Aristotle by the Muslim philosophers Avicenna and Averrroes, as well as in the work of Friar Roger Bacon. In an epic embodying a myth of universal appeal, it is fitting that Milton's Muse belong to Islam, Judaism, and Christianity.

Whether Culverwel agrees or disagrees with Selden, he takes virtually all the sources cited in chapters 8 and 9 of the *Discourse*—and there are many—from *De Jure Naturali et Gentium*, though he seldom acknowledges this. It is as if Culverwel, like so many other scholars, considers Selden to be a primary rather than secondary source of rabbinic scholarship. Reading *De Jure* on Rashi, Ibn Ezra, Kimchi, or Maimonides thus becomes the equivalent of reading the *Biblia Rabbinica* or the *Guide* directly. And the same holds true of the *Uxor Ebraica* or *De Synedriis*, whether the authority cited is a major figure or one of the many lesser lights that appear in these works.

Culverwel unabashedly takes virtually every word about the *intellectus agens* from Selden, as in his reference to the angelical intelligences that emanate from the divine intellect and mediate reality to those human beings whose minds are receptive. His positive evaluation of Maimonides, like his knowledge of the *Guide*, derives entirely from *De Jure*:

The Jews indeed sometimes call every faculty an Angel, as one of the best amongst them, *Maimonides* tells us, but yet here they properly mean an Angelical being, distinct and separate from the soul.... Their own *Intellectus Agens* they call שכינה & רוח הקדש, the presence and power of God dwelling in the understanding, the influence of it they tearme שפע, as the forementioned *Maimonides* observes, that is, a copious and abundant supply of light shining upon the Minde. According to which they understand that place of the Psalmist באורך נראו אור *in lumine tuo videbimus lumen* [in thy light shall we see light]; which the Schoolmen more truly expound of the *Lumen Gloriae* in the Beatifical vision, though it may reach also to that joy and delight which Saints have in communion with God here.[32]

---

[32] Culverwel, *Discourse*, 74–5, taken from Selden, *De Jure*, 1.9, pp. 116–17.

It is significant that Culverwel relates this light to the present kingdom of grace and especially to the future kingdom of glory, both enjoyed, of course, only by Christians, while Selden relates it to the quotidian exercise of intellect among all human beings. Culverwel rails so often against Jewish exclusivity that his readers might be forgiven for forgetting that both the Noachide precepts and the active intellect are available to all human beings whatever their religion, just as his remarks on Jews as inhospitable to strangers might momentarily eclipse the obvious fact that they were not permitted to settle in the country where the *Discourse* was written.

Interestingly, although Culverwel attacks Selden, he often adopts a modified version of his ideas. The idea of the *intellectus agens* operating as the 'natural and ordinary way' of perceiving reality insults innate human understanding as the candle of the Lord; nevertheless, the idea of divine cooperation or extraordinary angelical assistance in the operations of the soul and mind is 'the only spark of Truth that lies almost buried in that heap of Errours':

That God himself as he does supply every being, the Motion of every Creature with an intimate and immediate concourse every way answerable to the measure and degree of its Entity; so he does in the same manner constantly assist the Understanding with a proportionable Co-operation. But then as for any such Irradiations upon the soul in which that shall be meerly patient; God indeed if he be pleas'd to reveal himself in a special and extraordinary manner, he may thus shine out upon it, either immediately by his own light, or else drop Angelical influence upon it. (p. 76)

It may be that Milton in *Paradise Lost* adopts a similar view of the 'special and extraordinary' operation of the active intellect on the poet-prophet of Book III, and perhaps also on fallen Adam in Book XI as the recipient of 'Angelical influence'. When Michael purges his sight to prepare him for a prophetic vision of the future, he adds to the euphrasy and rue three drops from that same source of life in Psalm 36: 9 to which Maimonides refers:

> *Michael* from *Adam's* eyes the Filme remov'd
> Which that false Fruit that promis'd clearer sight
> Had bred; then purg'd with Euphrasy and Rue
> The visual Nerve, for he had much to see;
> And from the Well of Life three drops instill'd.
> So deep the power of these Ingredients pierc'd,
> Ev'n to the inmost seat of mental sight,
> That *Adam* now enforc't to close his eyes,
> Sunk down and all his Spirits became intranst.   (ll. 412–20)

In the tenth chapter of the *Discourse*, '*Of the Consent of Nations*', Culverwel draws exclusively on sources furnished by Selden and Grotius. In this instance, he obscures the extent of his disagreement with Selden, while adapting a modified version of his position, as he did when he limited the operation of the *intellectus agens* to special and extraordinary occasions. Equating natural law with universal law, he identifies laws common among nations that have no communion, commerce, or compact with one another as the most radical and fundamental laws of nature. He offers eloquent variations on the theme of '*Vox Populi, Vox Dei*': if many touchstones agree, the gold must be pure; beauty must be transcendent if many nations are enamoured of it; and "Tis some powerful musick that sets the whole world a dancing' (pp. 80–1).

Culverwel follows his usual pattern of taking material from Selden without acknowledgment, such as his quote from Cicero that the consensus of all nations ought to be considered evidence of a law of nature. Selden, who distinguishes between the universal and the natural, rejects this view, in part because for him Noachide law is divine and positive rather than natural and innate. Perhaps equally important, and overlooked, is Selden's radical idea of the common law of England as a limited law of nature. What may have been for Selden the most attractive of the *praecepta* is דינים [*dinim*, adjudication] the injunction that every nation establish its own civil laws. Where the other six laws are examples of what the Talmud calls שב ואל תעשה (*shev v'al taaseh*, lit., *sit and do nothing*), the law of adjudication is an example of its opposite, קום עשה (*qum aseh*, lit., *get up and do*), a positive commandment whose fulfilment requires a specific action. In *De Jure*, Selden quotes the Talmud, Maimonides, and other rabbinic sources to make the point: 'Surely it has been taught: Just as the Israelites were ordered to set up law courts in every district and town [Deut. 16: 18], so were the sons of Noah likewise enjoined to set up law courts in every district and town':[33] 'How are they [the Noachides, i.e. non-Jews] commanded concerning the *dinim* [adjudication]? They are obligated to install judges and legal authorities in every district and to judge according to these six commandments and to warn the people.'[34] As Selden himself is well aware, he introduces this law belatedly and appears to devote less space to it than to the other precepts, each of which gets a whole book in *De Jure* dedicated to it.[35] But in fact it is treated at greater length than the others. The many laws of the written and oral Torah discussed throughout *De Jure* constitute for Selden the civil law of the Jews. For him, as for the rabbis, Noachide law has a double jurisdiction. It is the system of law for which non-Jews are universally obligated, and it was the system of law followed by the Jews before the revelation of the 613 commandments of the Torah at Sinai. As

---

[33] Selden, *De Jure*, 7.5, p. 805, citing '*Gem. Bab. ad. tit.* Sanhed. *cap.7. fol.* 56b': 'Traditio est, quemadmodum in praeceptis accepere Ebraei, constituere tribunalia per omnes pagos & urbes (quo referunt illud [*Deuter.* 16.18], Judices & Magistros constitues in omnibus portis tuis) *ita praeceptum est Noachidis constituere Tribunalia per omnes pagos & urbes.*'

[34] Selden, *De Jure*, 7.5, p. 805, citing 'Maimonides, *Hal.* Melakim *cap. 9*': '*Quomodo intelligendum est praeceptum Noachidarum de Judiciis?* [806] *Ex eo debent constituere Iudices & Praefectos pagatim, qui tum judicent de Sex illis praeceptis ceteris, tum populum* (de eorum observatione) *commoneant.*' On this point he also cites '*Moses Mikotzi praecept aff. 122; & videsis* [Jacob Habib's talmudic chrestomathy] Aiin Israel *part 2. fol. 111. col. 2*'.

[35] Selden, Preface, *De Jure*, sig. b3: 'Et demùm accedit ibi Caput de Judiciis seu *Regimine Forensi* atque *Obedientia Civili.*'

David Novak has pointed out, 'the correlation between these two jurisdictions is that Jews began as Noahides'.[36] According to Selden, the other six Noachide laws, repeated in the Torah, are universal, while the law of adjudication (*'de Judiciis'*) comprises all the other Torah laws that obligate only the people of Israel. Hence his view that Christians are not bound even by the Decalogue.

The view that Noachide law was original and universal, and that it was supplemented by civil laws that have the same force within a specific nation as natural laws, dovetails in Selden's mind with the view that the original natural law evolves for his own countrymen into the English common law, the highest legal authority, from which there is no appeal. As early as the *Notes on Fortescue* (1616), he called the common law of England a limited law of nature:

But in truth, and to speak without perverse affectation, all laws in generall are originally equally ancient. All were grounded upon nature, and no nation was, that out of it, took not their grounds; and nature being the same in all, the beginning of all laws must be the same. . . . [A]lthough the law of nature be truly said immutable yet it is as true, that it is limitable, and limited law of nature is the law now used in every state. All the same may be affirmed of our *British* laws, or *English*, or other whatsoever. But the divers opinions of interpreters proceeding from the weakness of man's reason, and the several conveniences of divers states, have made those limitations, which the law hath suffered, very different.[37]

This passage concludes with two images that Selden will use again in *Mare Clausum* to embody a law that despite gradual changes over time by augmentation and reduction can be called by its original name: 'a ship, that by often mending had no piece of the first materials, or as the house that's so often repaired, *ut nihil ex pristina materia supersit*, which yet, by the civil law, is to be accounted the same still.'[38] In *De Synedriis*, Selden finds a talmudic equivalent of the law that remains continuous despite accretion and loss: the idea that all future interpretations of the Torah were already revealed by God to Moses at Sinai. Selden discusses the tradition that Moses delivered the oral law (the Talmud) to the members of the first Sanhedrin, especially to Eleazer, Phineas, and Joshua. He also cites in detail the explication in both tractate *Berachot* 5a and Maimonides of Exodus 24: 12: 'And the LORD said unto Moses, Come up to me into the mount, and be there: and I will give thee tables of stone, and a law, and commandments which I have written; that thou mayest teach them.' Selden cites the opinion of Resh Lakish that all of the precepts given to Moses included their explication. 'The tables of stone' are the ten commandments; the 'law' refers to the written

[36] David Novak, *The Image of the Non-Jew in Judaism: An Historical and Constructive Study of the Noahide Laws* (New York and Toronto: Edwin Mellen Press, 1983), 53.

[37] Selden, *Opera Omnia*, ed. David Wilkins (1726), iii. 1891.

[38] Selden, *Notes on Fortescue*, *Opera Omnia*, iii. 1892. See also Selden, *Of the Dominion, or Ownership of the Sea* [*Mare Clausum*], tr. Marchamont Nedham (London, 1652), 133: 'even those things which naturally are thus flitting, do notwithstanding in a Civil sens remain ever the same; as the ship of *Theseus*, a Hous, or a Theatre, which hath been so often mended and repaired, that there is not so much as one part or plank left of the first building.'

Torah of the Pentateuch; 'commandments' signifies the *Mishnah*, which provides detailed instruction for the practical application of the written law; 'which I have written' refers to the Prophets and the Writings, written under divine inspiration; and 'teach them' refers to the *Gemara*, whose explanation of the *Mishnah* is the foundation of that instruction known as practical *halakhah*. Selden knows that this is midrashic hyperbole, but he is drawn to the conclusion 'that all these things were given to Moses at Sinai'.[39]

In *De Jure*, Selden assimilates his view of the common law as a limited law of nature to the Noachide precept of *dinim* (*de Judiciis*), a religious injunction to 'install judges and legal authorities in every district.' For Selden, whose torah is law, the English common law has an added status as a natural law ordained by God. There could then be no appeal to a higher law or to general principles outside of the law. Alan Cromartie is entirely persuasive when he notes that Selden's passionate commitment to the common law gave him an advantage 'in coping with the tactics of the crown'—particularly, with the king's attempt to appeal 'outside the common law to an inalienable prerogative'.[40] Although too young to have been a participant, Selden would have known of Bate's case (1606), which involved the king's right to levy customs without parliament's consent; later, as a close parliamentary associate of John Hampden, he would have been well aware of R. *v.* Hampden, the Ship Money case (1638), which involved the power of emergency taxation. The Five Knights' case (1626), in which Selden defended Sir Edmund Hampden, involved imprisonment of the king's opponents without revealing cause.

In both the *Notes on Fortescue* and *De Jure*, there are universal laws as well as a law of particular places, issuing from divine commandments for the children of Israel and with roots in arbitrary arrangements entered into by common consent for England and other countries. The insularity implicit in 'the several conveniences of divers states', which make the shape of the common law 'very different' for each of those states, does not bother Selden, who asserts with equanimity the view that 'the opinions, customs, constitutions and measures of all, or at least many other nations carry no weight with the Hebrews in their decisions about

---

[39] Selden, *De Synedriis, Opera Omnia*, i. 1575, citing 'Gemar. Babylon. ad tit. *Beracoth*, cap. 1. fol. 5, 1': '*Quod attinet ad illud quod scriptum est* [note: "Exod. xxiv. 12"], *Et dabo tibi tabulas lapideas, & legem, & praeceptum; quod scripsi, ut doceantur illi;* tabulae *sunt decem verba,* lex *est scriptura, &* praeceptum *est Misna;* quod scripsi, *denotat prophetas & hagiographos;* ut doceantur illi, innuit *Thalmud,* seu *Gemaricam ejus partem. Ita observandum, haec cuncta donata fuisse Mosi e Sinai.*' He also offers the similar interpretation of Exodus 24: 12 in Maimonides, ' Praefat. ad tit. Talmudic. *Zeraim* & ad *Jad Chazeka*' (1575). For related midrashic proof-texts, see Isaak Heinemann, *Darchei HaAggadah* (Jerusalem: Magnus, 1970), 11, 201. In one of the most poignant variations of the tradition (tractate *Menachot* 29a), God transports Moses to the school of R. Akiba. Sitting behind eight rows of students, Moses hears Akiba's discourses on the law without comprehension and becomes depressed (lit., becomes weak). But when they come to a certain matter, the disciples ask, 'Rabbi, how do you know this?' and Akiva answers, 'It is a law given to Moses at Sinai.' This restores Moses's spirits.

[40] Cromartie, *Sir Matthew Hale*, 31.

the nature of natural or universal law'. But this statement infuriates Culverwel, who sees it, understandably, as yet another sign of Jewish triumphalism and quotes it as an example of 'how that learned and much honoured Author of our own, does represent their minde unto you'.[41] Since all his knowledge about such matters derives from Selden, implicit in his complaint is either the question why is Selden not complaining or the assumption that he is:

Why then do the Jews look upon the גוים [*goyim*, nations, Gentiles] with such a disdaining and scornful eye, as if all the Nations in comparison with them, were no more then what the Prophet saies they are in respect of God, *as the drop of a bucket, as the dust of the Ballance* [Isaiah 40: 15], that cannot incline them one way or other.[42]

This is yet another ambivalent quotation from the Hebrew Bible, since Isaiah, offering comforting words to Zion, speaks in the voice of God, disparaging foreign nations.

Although Culverwel disagrees completely with Selden regarding the consent of nations as evidence of natural law, he sounds very much like Selden when it comes to the crucial matter of enforcement. He states emphatically 'that the obligation of *Natures* Law' does not arise 'from the consent of Nations':

That Law indeed which is peculiarly term'd ... *Jus Gentium* [the law of nations], has its vigor and validity from those mutual and reciprocal compacts, which they have made amongst themselves: but the meeting of several Nations in the observation of *Natures* Law, has no binding or engaging virtue in it any otherwise then in an exemplary way. (p. 81)

Although Culverwel is far more eloquent than Selden, he is utterly dependent on his scholarship, classical as well as rabbinic, in the chapters that register the sharpest disagreement with him. Selden's two long quotes from Cicero on the beauty of natural law are taken from '*De legibus lib. 2*' and '*De Republica lib. 3*' respectively, and these are precisely the two quotes that appear in Culverwel.[43] Perhaps it is Selden's ultimate accommodation of such a view to the external *praecepta Noachidarum* that prompts Culverwel to conclude his translation with an elaboration:

Grant, (saies [Cicero, 'that Noble Oratour']) that *Rome* were not for the present furnisht with a Positive Law able to check the lust and violence of a *Tarquin*; yet there was a Virgin-law of *Nature*, which he had also ravisht and deflour'd: there was the beaming out of an eternal Law, enough to revive a modest *Lucretia*, and to strike terror into the heart of so licentious a Prince. . . . Right Reason is a beautiful Law, a Law of a pure complexion, of

---

[41] Culverwel, *Discourse*, 82, quoting the chapter heading of *De Jure*, 1.6, p. 75: 'Gentium (saies he) *sive omnium, sive complurium opiniones, mores constitutiones, mensurae apud Hebraeos, in eo decernendo quod jus esse velint Naturale, seu universale, locum habent nullum.*'

[42] Ibid. The complaint is based entirely on Selden, including *De Jure*, 1.10, p. 119, on אומות העולם' *gentes* seu *populos mundi* atque גוים id est Gentes seu *Barbaros.*'

[43] Selden cites *De Republica* from Lactantius, since the original, as G. J. Toomer points out, was discovered in palimpsest only in the nineteenth century.

a natural colour, of a vast extent and diffusion; its colour never fades, never dies. It encourages men in obedience with a smile, it chides them and frowns them out of wickednesse. Good men heare the least whispering of its pleasant voice, they observe the least glance of its lovely eye; but wicked men sometimes will not heare it though it come to them in thunder; nor take the least notice of it, though it should flash out in lightning. None must enlarge the Phylacteries of this law, nor must any dare to prune off the least branch of it.[44]

When Culverwel adds, in the next sentence, that no 'Angel ... can absolve you from it', it is clear that he places this view in opposition to the idea of the active intellect as mediated by an angelic intelligence. His addition to Cicero, the reference to enlarging the phylacteries, is of course an attack on Pharisaism and, less obviously but no less certainly, on Selden, whose rejection of right reason as the ultimate source of legislation vexes Culverwel. It is a rejection based on reverence for rabbinic scholarship.

Culverwel alludes to Christ's words against the Pharisees, who 'make broad their phylacteries' (Matthew 23: 5)—clearly a reference to the straps of the head *tephillin*, which are visible—to 'vaunt their own righteousness'.[45] Certainly Culverwel is familiar with passages in the Talmud—all mediated by Selden— that reinforce his complaints. Selden, without a trace of hostility, reports the view that the posterity of Noah through Shem was particularly receptive to the operation of the divine light, the 'רוח הקדש *spiritum sanctum*,' the 'שכינה id est *praesentiam* seu *majestatem divinam* (verbum sonat ac si diceres *habitatio-nem* dei in homine)', and the 'סגולה successionem peculiarem & populum id est selectum, seu ut dicere solemus *ecclesiam visibilem*'. He continues with the rabbinic opinion that from the time of Moses and beyond, the *Shechinah*, the indwelling presence of the divine in the human, associated with the spirit of prophecy, no longer resided among the nations of the world.[46] It is from passages such as these that Culverwel draws his inferences, even if a specific source is lacking:

The Jews especially admire and adore the Influence of an *Intellectus Agens*, and not forgetful of their Primogeniture and priviledges, but being alwayes a conceited and a bragging generation, they would fain perswade us that God himself is their *Intellectus Agens*, but to the Gentiles he sends only an Angel to illuminate them.[47]

---

[44] Culverwel, *Discourse*, 46–7, taken from Selden, *De Jure*, 1.8, pp. 95–6.

[45] John Carey's gloss on 'Clip your phylacteries' in *On the New Forcers of Conscience*, in *Milton: Complete Shorter Poems*, 2nd edn. (London and New York: Longmans, 1997), 300.

[46] Selden, *De Jure*, 1.9, pp. 116–17.

[47] Culverwel, *Discourse*, 74. According to the learned modern editors of the *Discourse*, Greene and MacCallum, p. 190 n. 18, 'No exact source has been found for this view, but it follows logically from Maimonides' position concerning revelation: "All the prophets prophesied through the instrumentality of an angel; therefore what they saw, they saw in a parable and enigma. Not so our master Moses; for it was said of him, "Mouth to mouth will I speak with him." *De Fundamentis Legis* (Amsterdam, 1638), VII, 7."' In this passage, Maimonides is not discussing the lower status of Christians vis-à-vis Jews but rather the lower status of all other prophets, including Jewish ones, compared to Moses, who spoke to God face to face.

One might try to explain Selden's extreme sympathy, especially when contrasted with Culverwel's antipathy, by pointing to his clear recognition that the Talmud is full of unresolved legal disputes and opinions. On the same page that he records the two negative views about prophecy outside of Judaism, he also notes the talmudic opinion that 'seven prophets prophesied to the nations of the world, namely, Balaam and his father, Job, Eliphaz the Temanite, Bildad the Shuhite, Zophar the Naamathite, and Elihu the son of Barachel the Buzite.'[48] Culverwel must have read about these seven non-Jewish prophets, since they conclude the chapter that contains the negative opinions that have fuelled his resentment, but he neglects to mention them.

One can hardly blame him. Culverwel's *Discourse* is an attempt at bridge-building, and the passages which Selden cites asserting Jewish superiority distract him from his message. (Christian superiority he both assumes and asserts.) Selden's sympathy with the earliest rabbis, who saw themselves as heirs to the Pharisees, is harder to understand. After all, as a Christian he knows that the Pharisees had acquired a terrible reputation, in large part because of the intense hostility toward Pharisaism expressed in some chapters of the New Testament. Part of the answer must remain a mystery, though connected with Selden's magnificent Hebrew scholarship and a love of learning for its own sake. It is also true that the Pharisees attempted to extend holiness from the limits of the Jerusalem temple to a wider range of everyday life. Concern for ritual detail exposed them to attack by early Christians, but it also turned quotidian existence into a vast array of opportunities to fulfil divine law and thus to sanctify life.[49] According to Cromartie, Selden's priorities 'satisfied a puritan need by heightening the significance of ordinary life. The law of the Jews was established by God, but the laws that were made by the English played precisely the same role: they were in fact a duty, religious in authority and content, that a people could establish for itself.'[50]

Although they are essentially opposites, it is hard sometimes to tell the difference between an Erastian position and a theocratic one. It is impossible to read Selden's heart and to tell whether he really believes in the Noachide law or sees it merely as a set of minimum legal requirements, supported by ancient tradition, that might justify a civil religion. In Selden's rabbinic writings, the sacred and the secular become inextricably intertwined. Does he, like the Pharisees, want to extend holiness beyond the church to everyday life, or does he want to turn law into religion? According to Robert Baillie, a hostile fellow member of the Westminster Assembly, 'this man is the head of the Erastians; his glory is in

---

[48] Selden, *De Jure*, 1.9, p. 117, citing 'Gloss ad citat. tit. *Baba Bathra*, & videsis Gemaram Babylon. ad tit. *Abodah Zara*, cap. 1. fol. 3a.'

[49] This paragraph is indebted to Robert Goldenberg's chapter, 'Talmud', in *Back to the Sources: Reading the Classic Jewish Texts*, ed. Barry W. Holtz (New York: Summit Books, 1984), 129–75, esp. p. 130.

[50] Cromartie, *Sir Matthew Hale*, 161.

the Jewish learning; he avows every where that the Jewish state and church was all one, and that so in England it must be, that the parliament is the church.'[51]

It seems fitting to conclude this chapter with an especially apt possible allusion by Selden to Culverwel's *Discourse*. So many writers in seventeenth-century England happily plunder Selden's rabbinic scholarship that we cannot be certain he has only one person in mind. But the *Discourse* was published in 1652, and the comment in question can be dated fairly closely, occurring sometime between 22 August 1653 (the date of a letter from Gerard Langbaine)[52] and Selden's death in November 1654. In his *Table Talk*, Selden notes with justifiable pride and admirable restraint that thirty-six years after the publication of his *Historie of Tithes*, clerics seeking to justify their collection of tithes as a civil right could find no stronger support for their cause than the book which they had clamoured to suppress. Langbaine, Provost of Queen's College, Oxford, had written to tell Selden about this development, that the 'piece that struck deepest against the divine, will afford the strongest argument for the civil right':

They consulted in Oxford where they might find the best arguments for their tithes, setting aside the *jus divinum*; they were advised to my History of Tithes, a book so much cried down by them formerly (in which, I dare boldly say, there are more arguments for them than are extant together anywhere): upon this, one writ me word, that my history of tithes was now become like *Pelias hasta*, to wound and to heal. I told him in my answer, I thought I could fit him with a better instance. 'Twas possible it might undergo the same fate that Aristotle, Avicen, and Averroes did in France, some five hundred years ago, which was excommunicated by Stephen, bishop of Paris, (by that very name, *excommunicated*,) because that learning puzzled and troubled their divinity: but finding themselves at a loss, some forty years after (which is much about the same since I writ my history), they were called in again, and so have continued ever since.[53]

The conversations reported in *Table Talk* were probably held between 1634 and 1654, and this is the latest entry that can be dated closely. It contains an error, attributed to Selden's reporter, Richard Milward, since Selden himself wrote comprehensively and accurately in *De Jure* (1.2 and 1.9) about the matter in question, Roger Bacon's espousal of the doctrine of the *intellectus agens*. The sentence of excommunication could not have been pronounced by Stephen, who did not become bishop of Paris until 1268, some forty years after the sentence, and a year after Bacon's *Opus Tertium* was written.[54] But the entry is interesting for so many other reasons. Selden suffered for writing his *Historie of Tithes*, and knowing that his enemies could find no better ammunition for their position must have seemed almost like compensation. Langbaine's letter compared the *Historie* to '*Pelias hasta*', the spear of Achilles, made of wood from Mt Pelion.

---

[51] *Letters and Journals of Robert Baillie*, ed. D. Laing (Edinburgh, 1861), ii. 265–6.

[52] MS Selden supra 109, fo. 463.

[53] John Selden, *Table Talk*, ed. Samuel Harvey Reynolds (Oxford: Clarendon Press, 1892), 179–81.

[54] See Reynolds's note in his edition of *Table Talk*, 180–1.

Telephus could only be cured by the spear that had inflicted the wound. It is hard to imagine 'a better instance' of both wound and cure than the *Historie*, but Selden gives the example of Friar Roger Bacon's publication of the theory, derived, as we have seen, from non-Christian sources, that the active intellect was a pre-existent divine faculty distinct from human reason, infused into the mind, enabling it to discover truth. Bishop Stephen publicly condemned this theory in 1270, but a compromise was reached after objections were made to the condemnation. Bacon is one of Selden's heroes, and the parallel example of his vindication after forty years would have been yet another source of satisfaction.[55] And in both *De Jure* and *De Synedriis*, Selden had written exhaustively of clerical abuses of excommunication, which he saw as a civil rather than ecclesiastical sentence.[56] Although the editors of *Table Talk* insist that the reference to excommunication is erroneous, the emphatic parenthesis repeating the point '(by that very name, *excommunicated*)' might raise the possibility that the immensely learned Selden knew of (and would have been amused by) a sentence that excluded from the sacraments and services of the church three great non-Christian philosophers.

Finally, if this comment was made within a year of the publication of the *Discourse*, Selden might have had in the back of his mind Culverwel's attack on the *intellectus agens* as explained in *De Jure*. Attempting to hurt Selden, Culverwel could do no better than to draw on the sources provided by his attempted victim. Certainly *De Jure*, with its comprehensive survey of all sides of every crucial legal question it considers, is at least as formidable a *Pelias hasta* as the *Historie of Tithes*. This is the quality that Milton praised in the *Areopagitica* when he called on Selden to testify against pre-publication censorship:

Wherof what better witnes can ye expect I should produce, then one of your own now sitting in Parlament, the chief of learned men reputed in this Land, Mr. *Selden*, whose volume of naturall & nationall laws proves, not only by great autorities brought together, but by exquisite reasons and theorems almost mathematically demonstrative, that all opinions, yea errors, known, read, and collated, are of main service & assistance toward the speedy attainment of what is truest.[57]

---

[55] As early as the Preface of his *Historie of Tithes*, Selden notes: 'The learned Friar *Bacons* most noble Studies being out of the rode of the lazie Clergie of his time, were vehemently at first suspected for such as might prejudice the Church.' He expresses the hope that he will be vindicated by those who are worthy to judge, just as Bacon was defended, 'even while *Ignorance* yet held her declining Empire', by those who 'do wish for all light to Truth' (p. xvi).

[56] See the rabbinic writ of excommunication or *herem* in *De Jure*, 4.7, pp. 506–8. See also *De Synedriis*, 3.8, in *Opera Omnia*, i. 1669, on the right of the Synedrium, a civil body like England's Parliament, to excommunicate (he cross-lists his own 'Lib. 2 *de Success. in Pontif.* cap. 10'); and 2.15, i. 1569, where Selden, correcting what he sees as an error, insists that the excommunicated was still permitted to partake of the sacrifices in the temple at Jerusalem, though not to officiate in the priesthood. More pertinent still is *De Synedriis*, 1.7, i. 871 ff.

[57] *Areopagitica*, YP, ii. 513.

The chapters in Culverwel's *Discourse* that attack Selden's *De Jure* are in comparison with that work not a spear but a little pin that by pricking one's finger and drawing some blood makes diagnostic medical readings possible. Citing authorities brought by Selden himself to attack *De Jure*'s central ideas, primarily the Noachide precepts and the active intellect, those chapters stand in for other pages by other seventeenth-century writers that bear traces, only sometimes acknowledged, of the influence of those ideas. Intended to sting, they confirm instead the praise of Selden uttered centuries later by David Ogg: 'The most disinterested figure in an age of fierce personalities, aloof from personal motives and party prepossessions, seeking not fame but truth in an erudition more vast than was ever garnered by any other human mind.'[58]

---

[58] Introduction, *Ioannis Seldeni, Ad Fletam Dissertatio*, ed. David Ogg (Cambridge: Cambridge University Press, 1925), p. lxvi.

10

Selden's Rabbis in the Court of Common Pleas

One of the purest expressions of Selden's thought as a lawyer, political theorist, and Hebraist appears in a legal decision written fifteen years after his death by his disciple Sir John Vaughan (1603–74), Chief Justice of the Court of Common Pleas.[1] Selden inducted Vaughan into the law, made him his close friend and dedicatee of *Vindiciae Existimationis Suae*, and eventually appointed him co-legatee of his library and co-executor of his will. According to Edward Vaughan, his son, he was admitted at the age of 18 to the Inner Temple, 'where I have often heard him say, that he addicted himself to *Poetry, Mathematicks*, and such more *alluring Studies* at first, neglecting that *severer* of the *Laws* of *England*, until he became acquainted with that *incomparable Person*, Mr. *J. Selden*', one of his instructors 'in the value of *Civil Learning*'.[2]

From its first word to its last, the forty-five page decision in the very special case of Harrison versus Dr Burwell constitutes a student's homage to his teacher, demonstrating throughout Vaughan's awareness of Selden's emphasis on the historically determined character of the common law and of the rabbinic under-pinnings of his political philosophy and biblical hermeneutics. Its opening question concerns the legality of Thomas Harrison's marriage to Jane, the widow of his maternal grandfather's brother, his great-uncle Bartholomew Abbot. The incest prohibitions of Leviticus 18, cited in at least four Parliamen-tary acts,[3] are at the heart of the next two questions. Should authority reside in the 'Temporal Courts of the King', which were given judicial power concerning the lawfulness of marriages by an act of Parliament, 32 H.8 cap. 38? Or must jurisdiction rest in this case with the ecclesiastical courts,

because the unlawfulness, or lawfulness of it, by that Act, doth depend upon its being a marriage within or without the Levitical Degrees? . . . And the right knowledge of mar-riages within or without those Degrees, must arise from the right knowledge of the

---

[1] I am indebted in this chapter to Richard Tuck's discussion of Selden's influence on Vaughan as a political thinker in *Natural Rights Theories: Their Origin and Development* (Cambridge: Cambridge University Press, 1979), 113–15.

[2] Sir John Vaughan, *Reports and* Arguments, *being All of them Special Cases, & many wherein he Pronounced the Resolution of the whole Court of Common pleas*, ed. Edward Vaughan (London, 1677), sig. A2v. Parenthetic page references in the body of the text are to this edition.

[3] Vaughan cites 25 H.8. c 22, 28 H.8 c. 7, 28 H.8. c. 16, and 32. H.8. c.38.

Scriptures, of the Old Testament, specially the Interpretation of which hath been, and regularly is of Ecclesiastick Conizance [jurisdiction], and not of Lay or Temporal Conizance in regard of the Language wherein it was writ, and the receiv'd Interpretations concerning it in all succession of time. (p. 206)

In the third and final question, as in Selden's own writings, a great deal depends on a parenthetical phrase. Asking whether civil lawcourts can prohibit the questioning of the marriage by ecclesiastical courts, Vaughan notes that according to the Act of 32. H.8, cap. 38, 'no mariage shall be impeached (God's law except) without the Levitical Degrees.' It follows, then, that some marriages might be impeached according to God's law even if they fall outside of the prohibitions of Leviticus 18. In the course of his report, Vaughan will replace the biblical prohibitions of Leviticus as God's law with the rabbinic Noachide precepts in their Maimonidean formulation, just as they appear in Selden's *De Jure*. Arguing the case from first principles, he ranges very widely before delivering as chief justice the court's conclusion forbidding the ecclesiastical court from proceeding in the suit, on the ground that it is beyond that court's judicial power—a predictable decision in light of the strong flavour of Erastianism throughout the argument. Although his long philosophical discussion of the general issues involved is not always strictly relevant to the case at hand, Vaughan transforms the crabbed, pedantic Latin of *De Jure*—with its obscure phrases and remote allusions—into a model of the conciseness and clarity whose virtues Selden himself praised even when they were beyond his grasp.

It is no exaggeration to say that Vaughan wrote his report with *De Jure* open in front of him, although he also alludes to Selden's other rabbinical works simply for the pleasure it gives him to do so. Remembering both *De Successione in Pontificatum Ebraeorum* and *De Successionibus ad Leges Ebraeorum in Bona Defunctorum*, he provides as two examples of 'the Jewish Law' that apply only to Israelites 'the laws of succession and inheriting lands or goods' (p. 229). His phrase 'not now to determine' underscores the irrelevance of his introducing the Karaite Jewish sect's view of forbidden degrees, which takes up four full chapters (1.3–6) of *Uxor Ebraica*: 'Not now to determine, Whether the marriages mentioned within Leviticus 18. be only prohibited, or marriages within the degrees there mentioned. The Talmudists hold the first; the Karaits the second strongly' (p. 209).

Vaughan echoes Selden's hypothetical original state of natural freedom. Examining the sense in which any marriage and copulation can be said to be natural, he implicitly clarifies the impossibility for Selden of considering nature apart from a supervening law, since nothing is unnatural in the original amoral state:

In the first place, to speak strictly what is unnatural, it is evident that nothing which actually is, can be said to be unnatural, for Nature is but the production of effects from causes sufficient to produce them, and whatever is, had a sufficient cause to make it be, else it had never been; and whatsoever is effected by a cause sufficient to effect it, is as natural as any other thing effected by its sufficient cause. And in this sense nothing is unnatural but that which cannot be. (p. 221)

Vaughan concludes from this that 'no Copulation of any man with any woman, nor an effect of that Copulation by Generation, can be said unnatural; for if it were, it could not be, and if it be, it had a sufficient cause' (p. 221). Only copulation between creatures of different species, 'which never have appetite of Generation to each other', can be called unnatural. Pointing out that children by nature do not know their parents, he cites Selden for 'the Theban story of Oedipus and Jocasta his Mother...an obvious Example in this kind, where both ignorantly married each other, and had Issue between them. Of the marriage with the Mother, the Sister, the Step-mother, anciently permitted in Persia, Greece, Egypt, and other places of the East. *Vide*. Seld. de Jure naturali & gentium juxta disciplinam Ebraeorum l.5. c. 11 [p.599f]' (p. 224). He also cites Selden in *De Jure* on the point that 'the knowledge of our Parents is subsequent to nature, and not coequal with her, and ariseth from Civil Laws, Education, and common Reputation, not from Nature; we take those for our Parents whom the Laws denote to be so' (p. 223). He expresses with admirable clarity his teacher's view that the subjectivity of natural law as it is generally understood, separate from an imposed positive law, precludes any attempt to formulate universal principles: 'Besides, what is unnatural to man, *qua* man, must be so to all men, and at all times: But what is unnatural to this or that individual man, is unnatural only to him and only for the time it is so, and not to other men' (p. 224). Regarding differences among nations that result from custom, he gives as examples of what have been found not only '*eatable and nourishing*...but desirable as food' human flesh ('as is exampled in the *Anthropophagi*, the Cannibals or Men-eaters'), horse, dog, and cat (p. 224).

As we have seen, even someone as hostile to rabbinic thought as Jean Barbeyrac recognizes, with the help of Selden's scholarship, that when Grotius speaks of a divine, universal, positive or voluntary law, first delivered 'Immediately after the Creation of Man', requiring obedience from the moment it is promulgated, he means not the biblical prohibition in paradise but rather 'the six Commandments...given to *Adam* and *Noah*, though they are only distinguished by the Name of the latter, as is the Seventh, concerning Abstinence from Blood, which we find prescribed to *Noah*.... SELDEN, *De Jure Nat. & Gent. juxta disciplinam Hebraeorum*, Lib. I. Cap. X.'[4] As Selden knows very well, the rabbis (like the seventeenth-century English Socinians who were sometimes accused of 'Judaizing') do not believe in original sin. The Talmud is more interested in the six Adamic laws than in the forbidden fruit. These are the original '*Laws Divine* [that] *do supervene upon mans original nature with great penalty for transgressing them*' (p. 224). Vaughan, following Selden, sees law, education, custom, and

---

[4] Hugo Grotius, *The Rights of War and Peace* [*De Jure Belli ac Pacis*, 1625], ed. J. Barbeyrac, trans. anon. (London, 1738), 16 n. 3.

cultural indoctrination as second nature, but he stresses law because of the penalty attached (224). Moreover, like Selden, he identifies the divine positive '*Leges Noachidarum*' with natural law, since they are virtually coeval with the beginning of human existence:

A third way of mens acting unnaturally is, when they violate Laws coeval with their original being, though the Laws be but positive Divine, or positive Human Laws, and not of nature, primarily, nor in any other sense, intelligible to be Natural Laws. But that they bind men as soon as men can be bound, and no Law can possibly precede them.

A second reason of their being natural Laws properly, is, because mans nature must necessarily assent to receive them as soon as it is capable of assenting, and hath no power to dissent from them; for a man hath no power to dissent from, or not to assent to his own preservation, or not to dissent from his own destruction: But not to assent to the will, that is, to the Laws, of an Infinite Power, to hurt and benefit, is, to assent to his own destruction and infinite hurt, and to dissent from his own preservation and infinite benefit; for infinite power can hurt or benefit as it pleaseth. Therefore to assent to the Laws of the Deity is natural to man.

The Jews, with great constancy, speak of such Laws as given to all mankind in this particular matter of marriage, and carnal mixture, and derive them traditionally through all antiquity, as binding all Nations and People by Gods Precept, and therefore call them, among others so given, *Leges Noachidarum*, or the Laws of all the Sons of Noah, by which men were from the beginning prohibited.

1. Marriage or Copulation with their Mother.
2. With the Fathers wife.
3. With a sister by the same Mother, or with a Soror uterina.
4. With the Wife of another man.
5. Man with man.
6. Man or Woman with Beast. . . .

Of the *Natural Laws*, in this sense given to all Mankind by the Deity, from the beginning of time, concerning Marriage and bodily knowledge, See excellent matter in that incomparable Work of Mr. *Selden, De Jure Naturali & Gentium Juxta disciplinam Ebraeorum*.

And under this sense of Natural Laws hath he titled that Book, *De Jure Naturali & Gentium Juxta disciplinam Ebraeorum*; for so the Jews accounted the Laws, or *Leges Noachidarum*, given in the beginning to all Mankind, Natural Laws, though they were in truth but positive Divine Laws, because with relation to Mankind, there was no time wherein they oblig'd not. (pp. 226–7)

I quote such a long excerpt because it exemplifies the rabbinic foundation of Selden's thought as reflected in Vaughan's argument on behalf of the whole Court of Common Pleas. Richard Tuck has demonstrated admirably Selden's influence on Hobbes, as can be seen by the description of an original state of total freedom and by the emphasis on positive law, whether divine or human, as coeval with natural law and therefore in a sense identical with it.[5] Various ideas in Vaughan's

---

[5] See e.g. Tuck's *Natural Rights Theories*, 118, where he alludes to Hobbes as 'the most outrageous of Selden's followers', and 126–30, where he compares them.

report deriving from Selden sound entirely consistent with Hobbes's philosophy. Immediately following one of his frequent citations of Selden on the Noachide laws promulgated at the beginning of creation, he observes:

In this sense it is said, A man is a natural Subject when he is so born, and is bound by the Law of his Allegiance as soon as he is, and that a Prince is that Subjects natural Soveraign, because he is bound to protect him as soon as he can be protected.... For these Laws of a mans subjection as soon as he is born, being the immediate means of his preservation and good, cannot but be assented to as soon as it is possible to assent, and in that are called Natural Laws. (p. 227)

Of course, Selden's emphasis on freedom as the primal, natural condition, rather than on the nastiness, brutality, and brevity of life in a state of chaos made his argument more adaptable to radical political views. What has been less clearly understood is the centrality and consistency of rabbinic thought in Selden's political philosophy. Although every word in the long excerpt derives from Selden's writings, nowhere is the relationship between natural law and 'the Laws of the Deity' more clearly expressed than in its second paragraph, where not to assent to the laws of a power infinitely capable of preserving and destroying is to assent to one's own destruction.

Vaughan cites the rabbinic Noachide laws more often than he does the biblical Mosaic law, and, like Selden, he lists the universal incest prohibitions contained in those laws as they appear in Maimonides' *Mishneh Torah*.[6] Long before his most mature period of rabbinic scholarship, which began in 1629, when he borrowed 'the Talmud of Babylon in divers great volumes', Selden insisted on the authority and reliability of Maimonides and other medieval rabbis as recorders of the most ancient traditions. In *An Admonition to the Reader of Sir James Sempil's Appendix* (1619), which replies to the attack on the *Historie of Tithes* in the appendix of Semphill's *Sacriledge Sacredly Handled*, Selden defends himself with a wit and clarity of style that bear comparison with the language of *Table Talk*. He frequently appeals to the authority of the rabbis:

I only tell my *reader*, what the *Jewish practice* was ... and *that* I confirm by the express testimonies of the body of the *Jewish canon law*, and those three most eminent *rabbins*,

---

[6] *Mishneh Torah, Hilkhot Melakhim*, ch. 9, *halakha* 5. Maimonides derives these universal laws from Genesis 2: 24, which concludes the Torah's description of the creation of Eve and Adam's union with her, thus serving as a guide for the sexual behaviour of all of their descendants: 'Therefore shall a man leave his father and his mother, and shall cleave unto his wife: and they shall be one flesh.' 'His father' alludes to his father's wife, for otherwise, there would be no need for such a prohibition, since sexual relations with other males are explicitly forbidden. 'His mother' is to be understood simply; 'cleave to his wife'—and not another man's wife; 'wife'—and not a male; 'one flesh'—excludes a domesticated animal, beast, or fowl, for a man can never become one flesh with them. Rashi understand the last point to mean that a child can never be born from such a union. Maimonides derives the law forbidding the *soror uterina* from Genesis 20: 12, where Abraham, speaking to Abimelech, excuses his behaviour in calling Sarah his sister rather than his wife: 'She is my sister; she is the daughter of my father, but not the daughter of my mother; [thus,] she became my wife.'

Jarchi [i.e., Rashi], *Ben Maimon* and *Mikotzi* [Moses of Coucy]....The testimonies of these *Jewish* monuments furnished me with all that I have delivered, and there was never any learned man that yet doubted but they were most certain and infallible in relating to us the *practice* of that *nation*....

He offers [the apocryphal book of] *Tobit* against us...and at the best he uses here his own *fancy* and *conjecture* only, against the *express testimony* of the *Jewish* canon law, which was received by their doctors from certain *tradition*, much antienter than Sir *James* can prove that *Tobit* was written....Until he confutes the *Hebrew* doctors, and the text of the *talmud*, what I have said, remains firm and unshaken.[7]

Selden insists that even if Tobit and Josephus were contrary to his argument, which he denies utterly, 'that were nothing against the *talmud* and the *consent* of so many *Hebrew* doctors. I appeal to the learned here....We clear all by the *talmud* and the *Hebrew* doctors, and thence interpret *Tobit* by them.'[8]

Selden does not merely defend his comparative method of historical analysis; he admonishes Sir James for his neglect of history:

To be brief, Sir *James* hath written what he *thinks*, and I what I *know*: he what *should* have been, and what now *should* be, and as he *thinks* too; I what *hath* been in use and practice, and that as I *know* too, as well as the choicest *testimonies* of *Jews*, *Gentiles*, and *Christians* for all ages could instruct me.[9]

Maimonides appealed to Selden for many reasons: as a codifier of Jewish law, as a guide to the past that Selden believed could produce reliable knowledge about current institutions, and as a critic of superstition and the human imagination and their allegedly damaging effects on the life of the individual and society. The motto of *De Diis Syris*, taken from Lactantius (*Divinae Institutiones* 1.23), is '*Primus [autem] Sapientiae gradus est, falsa intelligere* [The first step of wisdom is to understand the false], and Selden's rabbinic writings refer countless times to Maimonides' '*Aboda Zara*', his *De Idololatria*. Dionysius Vos's annotated translation of the entire work, with Hebrew and Latin text side by side, constitutes a preface of almost 200 pages to Gerardus Vossius's *De Theologia Gentili* (Amsterdam, 1641), arguably the most important work of comparative mythology in the seventeenth century.

As a historian, Selden rejected the positive absolutism of the rationalist and the negative absolutism of the sceptic. It is not surprising that he is committed to a universal positive law promulgated in historical time rather than to a conception of natural law as an innate imperative of human reason. He would surely have concurred with Francis Bacon:

The formation of ideas and axioms by true induction is no doubt the proper remedy to be applied for the keeping off and clearing away of idols. To point them out, however, is of

---

[7] Selden, *An Admonition to the Reader of Sir James Sempil's Appendix* (1619), in *Opera Omnia*, iii. 1352–3, 1357.

[8] Ibid. 1356.

[9] Ibid. 1351.

great use, for the doctrine of Idols is to the interpretation of Nature what the doctrine of the refutation of Sophisms is to common Logic.[10]

Of all the idols of the mind that Bacon's scientific method intended to clear away, the idols of the theater—philosophical artificial systems that represent not the real world but their authors' own creations, received into the mind by 'the playbooks of philosophical systems'—would have seemed most damaging to Selden.[11] As he reminds Sir James Semphill, Selden examines not 'what *should* have been', which might include speculative history or the general principles of political science, but rather statute law as 'what *hath* been in use and practice'.

Richard Tuck is the first to point out that Selden's legal philosophy runs counter to another account of the common law: 'This was the view espoused *inter alia* by Coke, that the common law was the law of *reason*—that is to say, that its principles could be elucidated and (some people believed) extended in the light of general rational principles.'[12] For Selden the law is not an artificial reason. He argues that 'the same power that establishes the common law [viz. Parliament] must establish martial law, and were it established here by act of Parliament, it would be most lawful, for so it might be made death to rise before 9 a clock.'[13]

Returning to Vaughan's homage to Selden, by way of the second question posed in the report—whether knowledge of the original Hebrew of the Levitical prohibitions should invest the ecclesiastical rather than the temporal court with judicial authority—the answer is resoundingly negative. Members of Parliament cannot be deprived of ultimate authority for being insufficiently informed in the language and interpretive history of the 'Divine Law': 'it is but very lately that the Christian Churches have become knowing in the Original Tongues wherein the Scriptures were written; which is not a knowledge of obligation, and required in all, or any, but acknowledged accidental, and enjoy'd by some' (p. 208). Vaughan continues immediately with an example of Erastianism less outrageous than Selden's but almost as extreme: 'If it were enacted by Parliament, that matters of Inheritance, of Theft and Murther, should be determined in the Courts of Westminster, according to the Laws of Moses, this Objection would not stand in the way, no more can it in this particular concerning Incestuous marriages' (p. 208).

---

[10] Bacon, *The Essays* (Harmondsworth: Penguin, 1985), 277.

[11] On Bacon and idolatry, see Moshe Halbertal and Avishai Margalit, *Idolatry*, tr. Naomi Goldblum (Cambridge, Mass., and London: Harvard University Press, 1992), 242. On Selden as an admirer of Bacon's inductive scientific method, see David Sandler Berkowitz, *John Selden's Formative Years: Politics and Society in Early Seventeenth-Century England* (Washington, DC: Folger Shakespeare Library, 1988), 32–3, 72.

[12] Richard Tuck, '"The Ancient Law of Freedom": John Selden and the Civil War', in *Reactions to the English Civil War 1642–1649*, ed. John Morrill (London: Macmillan, 1982), 140.

[13] *Commons Debates, 1628*, ed. R. C. Johnson et al. (New Haven: Yale University Press, 1977), ii. 576.

Despite this example and the centrality of the Levitical prohibitions in English statute law, over the course of his report Vaughan, following Selden, will push those biblical incest laws to the margin and replace them as God's laws with the rabbinic *Leges Noachidarum*. Although we cannot trace all of the intricate reticulations of his biblical hermeneutics, arguably the most ingenious and interesting parts of the report, we should at least look at the main points regarding the central texts, all of which address forbidden sexual relations: 1 Corinthians 5: 1, Leviticus 18: 24, 27, and Acts 15. In the first example, it is clear that Vaughan accepts the universality of the Noachide precepts. Paul tells the Corinthians: 'It is reported commonly that there is fornication among you, and such fornication as is not so much as named among the Gentiles [i.e. of a kind not found even among pagans], that one should have his father's wife.' The prohibition against marrying a father's widow even if she is not his mother is, according to Maimonides, a universal law. Immediately after listing the inter-pretation of the sexual relations forbidden under the Noachide precepts as found in the *Mishneh Torah* and in *De Jure*, Vaughan cites 1 Corinthians 5: 1 as an example of Paul, an ex-Pharisee and of the strictest school, interpreting fornica-tion according to Noachide law ('this general Law') set forth in the Talmud and codified by Maimonides:

it is observed by Mr. *Selden*, That upon the Tradition of this general Law, St. Paul rebukes the Corinthians for permitting among them such a Fornication, that is, such an Incest as was not named among the Gentiles, That a man should have his Fathers wife. Some Examples of which were in Syria, as in Antiochus and Stratonice. (p. 227).

Vaughan concentrates on two verses in Leviticus 18 in order to prove that the laws of consanguinity listed in that very chapter are not universal laws. Remem-bering Paul's insistence that 'where no law is, there is no transgression' (Romans 4: 15), he insists that the inhabitants of Canaan whom God has driven out to make way for the Israelites could not have been liable under the Mosaic law, which was never delivered to them. For Vaughan, as for Selden, the Noachide precepts as codified by Maimonides really do go all the way back:

There is no colour of Argument, That the Prohibitions in the Eighteenth of Leviticus, were universal laws; but that it is said,
[Lev. 18. v. 24] *Ye shall not defile your selves in any of these things; for in all these things the Nations are defiled which I cast out before you.*
[Lev. 18. v. 27] *For all these Abominations have the men of the Land done, & c.*
How could the Land be defiled? or the men of the Land?
Or, How could they be Abominations, if not prohibited?
To the 24. and 27. Verses of the Eighteenth Chapter of Leviticus, the Answer is, That those words referr to those universal laws of the *Leges Noachidarum*, wherein *Egypt* and *Canaan* were defiled: As Incest with the Mother, *Soror uterina*, the Fathers wife; and to those horrid offences of lying with man or beast, prohibited to all mankind from the beginning. (p. 230)

Continuing to follow Maimonides as mediated by Selden, and echoing Bene-
dick's 'The world must be peopled',[14] Vaughan points out that *in primordiis
rerum*, not only the relations prohibited in Leviticus but even the most incestuous
unions were natural, necessary, and included in the command to increase and
multiply: 'For the World could not have been peopled, but by Adams Sons going
in to their Sisters, being Brothers and Sisters by the same Father and Mother, or
by a more incestuous coupling than that; and if such Carnal knowledge had been
absolutely unnatural in any sense, it had never been either lawful or necessary:
For *whatever is simply and strictly unnatural at any time, was always unnatural and
unchangeable*' (p. 222).

In his brilliant and detailed explanation of the Noachide precepts as a 'universal preceding law' (p. 236), while prohibitions against sexual sins in Leviticus
18 'are no general Law, but particular to the Israelites' (p. 228), Vaughan proves
to be as subtle as his teacher. Never actually adverting to the great matter of
Henry VIII, he nonetheless takes us back to it and explains, indirectly but
conclusively, why all of the statute law based on Leviticus was enacted during
his reign. He has no trouble understanding that biblical laws prohibiting certain
consanguineous unions can be dispensed with by Parliament. But he cannot
understand ('*This perhaps is a knot not easily untied*') how English law can be
stricter than Leviticus, prohibiting absolutely what even the Hebrew Bible, *whose
strictures have been abrogated*, prohibits only conditionally:

1. The marriage of a man with his Brothers wife, which by 28 H. 8 cap. 7. is absolutely
prohibited, and commonly receiv'd to be absolutely prohibited by the Levitical Degrees.
   But was not so by the Levitical Law, nor by the meaning of the Eighteenth Chapter of
Leviticus, but when the dead brother left Issue by his Wife.
   But if he did not, the surviving Brother was, by the Law, to marry his wife and raise
issue to his Brother....
   *This perhaps is a knot not easily untied, how the Levitical Degrees are Gods Law in
this Kingdome, but not as they were in the Common-wealth of Israel, where first given.*
(pp. 240–1)

He cites another, similar example: 'within the meaning of Leviticus, and the
constant practise of the Common-wealth of the Jews, a man was prohibited not
to marry his Wives Sister only during her life, after he might. So the Text is. *Thou
shalt not take a Wife with her Sister, during her life, to vex her, by uncovering her
shame upon her.*' And yet 'A man is prohibited by 28 H. 8. and by the receiv'd
Interpretation of the Levitical Degrees, absolutely to marry his Wives sister'
(p. 241).

If the rabbinic Noachide laws find their way unexpectedly into 1 Corinthians
5 and Leviticus 18, Vaughan reluctantly excludes them from the only one of the
central texts where interpreters often place them: the thrice-repeated Apostolic

---

[14] Shakespeare, *Much Ado About Nothing* (2.3.213–14).

Decree defining a minimum practice for new Gentile Christians to promote communion with Jewish Christians (Acts 15: 20, 15: 29, and 21: 25). The Apostolic Decree of Acts, recognizing that being in Christ does not always signify ethical seriousness, set down for Gentile converts to Christianity moral requirements whose rejection, *ipso facto*, kept one outside the pale of salvation.[15] According to contemporary scholars, behind the Apostolic Decree are both the Levitical laws that apply to resident aliens and the Noachide laws, binding upon every living soul, laws such as those proclaimed by Sophocles in the *Antigone* 'that are not of today nor yesterday but are forever'.[16]

Vaughan's reading of Acts 15: 29, deriving from Selden, is complex, but it comes down finally to the argument that the laws promoting fellowship with Jewish Christians must be a part of the Mosaic law, since Gentiles are already obligated to keep the Noachide precepts. Since his entire argument presupposes the obsolescence of the Mosaic law, Vaughan seems as reluctant as Paul must have felt to impose anything related to the ritual and ceremonial prescriptions of the Pentateuchal law, but for different reasons. Paul had hoped to unify the community of faith by destroying the ritual distinction between Jewish Christians and Gentiles. Instead, his abolition of the ceremonial law for Gentile converts to Christianity made social intercourse between them and Jewish Christians no longer possible.[17] Despite the record of Paul's intolerance of divided table fellowship, the Apostolic Decree asks pagan converts to keep three laws related to commensality by abstaining from food offered to idols, from blood, and from things strangled, and adds 'from fornication: from which if ye keep yourselves, ye shall do well'. Vaughan's reluctance stems from his belief in the absolute sufficiency and universality of the Noachide law. He blames the acceptance by Christians of the Levitical prohibitions on the Apostolic Decree:

How the rest of the Levitical Prohibitions, in the matter of marriage, came to be so generally receiv'd by Christians, as being authorized and prescribed by God, seems to have no foundation so warrantable as that Council of the Apostles in the Fifteenth of the Acts.

Where the Gentiles are directed to observe, as necessary only, four particulars of *Moses* his Law, among which they are required to abstain from Fornication, which if it had been rendred from the Septuagint, from Incest or Turpitude of Copulation, which answered the Original best; it had much facilitated the solution of this Inquiry.

For it hath no colour, That Fornication there should signifie the same with *Stuprum* [illicit sexual intercourse] and *Scortum* [prostitute], and that it should be abstained from, as a special particular of the Law of Moses, being an Offence, not only prohibited by him (yet not at all among the Prohibitions in the Eighteenth of Leviticus) but by all the Nations of the Gentiles respectively, as well as by Moses. And it is plain, the word πορνεία

---

[15] W. D. Davies, *Paul and Rabbinic Judaism* (London: SPCK, 1955), 117.

[16] For this view of the Apostolic Decree, see ibid. 114; Alan F. Segal, *Paul the Convert: The Apostolate and Apostasy of Saul the Pharisee* (New Haven: Yale University Press, 1990), 194–201 and 228–33; Novak, *The Image of the Non-Jew in Judaism*, 26.

[17] See Segal, *Paul the Convert*, 248–9.

there rendred *Fornication*, most frequently signifies in the Septuagint, both *Adultery* and *Incest;* and indeed any unlawful Copulation of man and woman. (p. 233)

Vaughan's analysis of Acts 15: 29 is the longest and most complex part of his report, and it derives entirely from the long last chapter (7.12) of *De Jure*, which Selden devotes to the Apostolic Decree and whether or not it contains a vestige of the *praecepta Noachidarum*. Vaughan points out that the dissolving of the Hebrew commonwealth has also dissolved the three laws of commensality in the Decree, which are at present of no greater sanctity for Christians than any of the other abrogated Mosaic laws. Indeed, the dissolution of the state frees the Jews from the obligations touching meats as well. If, while the 'Israelitish State' existed, 'it was against Christian Charity and Love, to give scandal and offence to an Hebrew, by eating Meat detestable to him, because God had bound him from it', so, after its destruction, 'when the Jew was equally free as the Christian Gentile, it grew a scandal to the Gentile, that the Jew should abhor or despise Meats which God had made lawful to the Gentile' (p. 236).

It is clear that Vaughan wishes that the law comprised under the heading of fornication in Acts 15 was the Noachide law. Naming Selden six times in the report, and borrowing from the scholarship of *De Jure* numerous other times, he finds occasion to list those laws yet again. Perhaps, he suggests, the sexual offences of the Gentile Christians were identical to those found odious among the Cannanites and Egyptians in Leviticus: 'Sodomy [sex between men], Buggery [intercourse of a human being with a beast], Incest with the Mother, the Fathers wife, the Soror uterina, Adultery, agreed by the Jews to be universally prohibited, which they term *Leges Noachidarum*, and which are the Offences last mentioned in the Eighteenth of Leviticus before, vers. 24. before cited' (p. 236). Vaughan provides arguments to undercut the idea that by fornication the apostles had in mind the specifically Mosaic laws of Leviticus, including the fact that marital union between the Jews and Gentiles was 'absolutely forbid' (p. 238); 'therefore their Communion by Alliance or Affinity had received no advancement by abstaining from Mosaical Incests in that respect' (p. 238).

Nevertheless, in the end, Vaughan is forced to concede that the particular laws prohibiting fornication supervening upon the universal Noachide precepts are the Levitical verses:

That the abstaining from Incestuous marriages, according to Moses his Law, was a part of the Mosaical Law, precepted to be observed by the Gentiles at that Council, I think can be little doubted, and not the abstaining from what is accounted simple Fornication, which even by Moses his Law was often satisfied by marriage of the woman, and often by mony. (p. 237)

This is precisely Selden's conclusion in *De Jure*, which brilliantly and surprisingly devotes its penultimate chapter to the presence of the *praecepta Noachidarum* in the book of Job and its last chapter to denying vestiges of those precepts in the Apostolic Decree. The very last paragraph of his immense book is, characteristically, anticlimactic, his very last words, conspicuously avoiding closure, pointing to questions that remain to be considered, and his syntax as impenetrable as it is anywhere else in the book's 847 pages:

Now it is true that the Synod did not want to impose upon Gentile converts the rest of the Mosaic rites as such; nor is it entirely surprising that it should have decided thus in those matters, lest, without the kind of abstinence that is enjoined there (which deals with basic matters, and in particular matters applying to everyday relationships between people), the Christian fellowship that should be established between Jews and Gentiles who had joined or were to join Christianity should be too difficult to get into, in the very cradle, as it were, of the church. But from what has already been said, it is sufficiently clear, that in that Synod the Noachide laws were by no means hinted at. Nor does that rule of justice, added in some texts, help to confirm the opinion of those who would say otherwise. This is not the place to discuss by what reasoning what is held there about meat that has been sacrificed to idols, and blood, and suffocated meat, was considered temporary rather than eternal (particularly in the Eastern Church), and is there to be distinguished, insofar as applies to moral law, from what is added about *porneia*—fornication or frequenting of prostitutes—and unchastity in general, and how *ta epanankes* or Necessary things, should be understood there, or how far the prohibitions of that Canon were forgivable or not forgivable, as Tertullian says; for that belongs to a different genre of writing and discussion.[18]

As noted in an earlier chapter, Grotius also asserts the universality of Leviticus 18, but he does so by removing it from its place in the Bible as a Mosaic law and reinscribing it as a Noachide law.[19] Richard Hooker, in *Of the Laws of Ecclesiastical Polity* [1593], anticipates Selden by construing the prohibitions of the Apostolic Decree specifically according to the 'lawe of the Jewes' rather than according to 'the law of nature', which he identifies as the Noachide laws. Less learned than Selden, but still immensely learned, he believes that the seventh of those laws prohibits the eating of blood, and this allows him to consider the possibility that the Apostolic Decree compresses three of the Noachide laws: idolatry, blood, and fornication. (Selden, familiar with the talmudic discussion of

---

[18] Selden, *De Jure Naturali et Gentium juxta Disciplinam Ebraerorum* (1640), 846–7: 'Cum demum cetera Jura Mosaica, qua Mosaica, nollet jam Synodus sacra Gentilibus conversis imponi; mirum non omnino est de capitibus illis ita tunc eam constituisse; ne scilicet absque ejusmodi abstinentia ibi sancita (quae circa primarias & maxime quotidianas conversationis mutuae causas versabantur) societas Christiana inter Judaeos & Gentiles pariter in Christianismum cooptatos cooptandosque contrahenda, in ipsis Ecclesiae velut incunabulis, difficilius iniretur. Sed ex jam dictis, ni fallor, non obscure liquet, in Synodo illa Jura Noachidarum neutiquam innui. Neque omnino Regula illa aequitatis in exemplaribus nonnullis subjuncta, facit ad sententiam eorum, qui aliter velint, firmandam. Qua autem ratione id quod de Idolothytis, ac Sanguine ac Suffocato ibi habetur, temporale nec perpetuum (maxime in Ecclesia Occidentali) fuerit censitum, & ab eo quod de πορνεία Fornicatione seu scortatione ac omnimodo Incestus genere adjicitur, sit ibi, quatenus hoc ad legem attineat Moralem, distinguendum, & quomodo τὰ ἐπάναγκες seu Necessaria ibi sit sumendum, seu in quantum Remissibilia seu non remissibilia, ut dixit Tertullianus Canonis ejusdem interdicta fuerint, locus hic non est disceptandi. Nam ad aliud scribendi disquirendique genus attinet.'
[19] Hugo Grotius, *Rights of War and Peace*, ed. J. Barbeyrac (London, 1738), 197.

the subject, knows that the law prohibits only the eating of flesh torn from a living animal. This is a key reason for his rejection of the view that the Decree contains vestiges of the precepts.) Hooker swerves from his original hypothesis, ending with an argument that in its general conclusion Selden and Vaughan will echo. He argues the reasonableness of the position that Gentile Christians might be obliged, according to the Apostolic Decree, to observe Jewish ordinances:

For to the Jews, who knew that their difference from other nations which were aliens and strangers from God, did especially consist in this, that Gods people had positive ordinances given to them of God himselfe, it semed marvelous hard, that the Christian Gentils should be incorporated into the same common wealth with Gods owne chosen people, and be subject to no part of his statutes, more than only the law of nature, which Heathens count themselves bound unto. It was an opinion constantly received among the Jews, [note: 'Lib qui Seder Olam inscribitur

דינין 1
ברכת השם 2
ע[בודת] א[לילים] 3
שפיכות דמים 4
גלוי עריות 5
הגזל 6
עבר מן החי] 7

that God did deliver unto the sonnes of *Noah* 7. precepts, namely 1 to live in some forme of regiment under publike lawes, 2 to serve and call upon the name of God, 3 to shun Idolatry, 4 not to suffer effusion of bloud, 5 to abhor all uncleane knowledge in the flesh, 6 to commit no rapine, 7 finallie, not to eate of any living creature whereof the bloud was not first let out. If therefore the Gentiles would be exempt from the lawe of *Moses*, yet it might seeme hard they should also cast off even those things positive which were observed before *Moses*, and which were not of the same kinde with lawes that were necessarily to cease. And peradventure hereupon the Councell sawe it expedient to determine, that the Gentiles should according unto the third, the seventh, and the fift of those precepts, abstaine from things sacrificed unto idoles, from strangled and bloud, and from fornication.[20]

What changes Hooker's mind is the prohibition in Acts against fornication, which he believes 'the Gentiles did of their owne accord observe, nature leading them thereunto'. Since the Apostolic Decree imposed new laws on the Gentile Christians, the plain sense of fornication could not have been intended. Rather, the Decree must be understood in a rabbinic context:

But verie marriage within a number of degrees being not only by the lawe of *Moses*, but also by the lawe of the sonnes of *Noah* (for so they tooke it) an unlawfull discoverie of nakednes, this discoverie of nakednes by unlawfull marriages such as *Moses* in the Lawe reckoneth up [note: 'Levit. 18'], I thinke it for mine owne part more probable to have

---

[20] Richard Hooker, *Of the Laws of Ecclesiastical Polity* [1593], in *Works: The Folger Library Edition*, gen. ed. W. Speed Hill (Cambridge, Mass.: Harvard University Press, 1977), Book IV: 11.1–11.12, i. 312–13.

bene ment in the words of that Canon, then fornication according unto the sense of the lawe of nature. Words must be taken according to the matter wherof they are uttered. The Apostles commaund to abstaine from bloud. Conster this according to the lawe of nature, and it will seeme that Homicide only is forbidden. But conster it in reference to the lawe of the Jewes about which the question was, and it shall easilie appeare to have a cleane other sense, and in any mans judgement a truer, when we expound it of eating, and not of sheading bloud. So if we speake of fornication, he that knoweth no lawe but only the law of nature, must needes make thereof a narrower construction, then he which measureth the same by a lawe, wherein sundry kindes even of conjugall copulation are prohibited as impure, uncleane, unhonest.[21]

Hooker's larger argument dramatizes the truth of his conclusion that 'the Church of Christ hath had in no one thing so manie and so contrarie occasions of dealing as about Judaisme.'[22] He respects Jewish interpreters of scripture and asserts the moral superiority of Jewish Christians, taught by the Mosaic law, over Gentile Christians. Like Selden, he knows that the first Jewish Christians observed even the ceremonial laws and that the first fifteen Christian bishops were circumcised. At the same time, assuming that the worst ceremonies of the Roman Catholic Church were picked up from the Jews and should therefore be rejected, he denounces the 'heathenish Ceremonies' of 'the *Jewes* . . . the deadliest and spitefullest enemies of Christianitie that were in the world. . . . For no enemies being so venemous against Christ as *Jewes*, they were of all other most odious, and by that meane least to be used as fit Church-paternes for imitation.'[23] Although Hooker decries the tremendous shifts in attitude toward the Jews that he systematically sets down, he himself is an example of the 'manie and so contrarie occasions of dealing' with Judaism. This radical ambivalence, echoed in Lightfoot's magnificent researches into the talmudic context of the gospels, probably derives ultimately from Paul. One need look no farther than Romans 7 to find juxtaposed an elaboration of the chapter's central idea—that in the hands of sin the Mosaic law becomes a death-producing instrument (7: 5, 10, 13)—and a less than enthusiastic protestation of the law's essential goodness: 'the law is holy, and the commandment holy, and just, and good' (7: 12). This theoretical acknowledgement of the law's divine origin and nature, added perhaps to increase Paul's credibility and persuasiveness among the Roman Jewish Christians, is eclipsed in the chapter by the devastating description of the law's actual effects. Hooker and Lightfoot, two English Christian Hebraists, throw into sharp relief what might otherwise not be noticed: the absence of vituperation in Selden's rabbinic scholarship.

Vaughan also omits negative comments about the rabbis, whose reliability he assumes. Like his mentor, speaking in a consistently level tone, he creates in what one might expect to be the extremely narrow case of Harrison *v.* Burwell regarding the legitimacy of marriage to the widow of a collateral ancestor a concise but wide-ranging epitome of books 1 and 5 of Selden's immense *De Jure*.

<hr />

[21] Ibid. 313–14.   [22] Ibid. 314.   [23] Ibid. 309.

The last chapter of *De Jure*, on the Apostolic Decree, casts a retrospective light on an obscure talmudic passage that concludes an earlier chapter of the same book (7. 3) and attests to Selden's vast erudition, exceeding even that of Grotius and Hooker. The extraordinary but neglected passage concerns a dispute over the meaning of the number thirty in Zechariah 11: 12, which will figure importantly in the passion narrative (Matthew 27: 9–10): 'So they weighed for my price thirty pieces of silver.' According to R. Judah, in tractate *Chulin* of the Babylonian Talmud (92 a–b), these are the thirty righteous people among the Gentiles (lit., nations of the world) by whose virtue the nations of the world continue to exist. But Ulla said: 'the number refers to the thirty commandments which the sons of Noah took upon themselves, but they observe only three of them. First, they do not draw up a *kethubah* [marriage contract or deed] for males; second, they do not bring the flesh of the dead to market; thirdly, they show honour to the Torah.' Selden not only quotes Ulla in the original and translates him, he also has read Rashi's commentary, the common gloss, which applies the Talmud's literal text ('they do not weigh carrion in the marketplace') to human flesh ('*hominis*'):

שלשים מצות שקבלו עליהם בני נח ואין מקיימין אלא שלשה אחת שאין
כותבין כתובה לזכרים ואחת שאין שוקלין בשר המת במקולין ואחת שמכבדין
את התורה *Triginta praeceptis quae Noachidae in se susceperunt, quorum tantum tria observarunt: Primum quod pactis dotalibus sibi Masculos non conjungerent; secundum quod non afferrent in Macellum Mortui* (hominis) *carnem; Tertium quod legi ipsi honorem exhiberent.*[24]

Rashi's commentary clarifies the outrageousness of the passage, which assumes that the Gentiles (the nations of the world) practise their vices in private. Although guilty of private acts of sodomy, they draw the line at writing a marriage deed for the purpose. And although it is assumed that they eat human flesh in private, they do not go so far as to sell it openly in the market-place. (Selden chooses this interpretation of Rashi rather than the alternative: that it refers to selling carrion rather than an animal that has been slaughtered.) It would seem that this passage is an unnoticed parody of the Apostolic Decree, focusing on sexual sins and forbidden meats, and intended to point up both the immorality of the Gentile converts to Christianity and the lax fecklessness of a Church that imagines it can curb wild exorbitance by imposing minimal laws. Selden understands that the idiomatic term קלות ראש, *qalut rosh* (lit. 'lightness of head') in Rashi's commentary means 'presumptuousness, insolence': the Gentiles are not so 'malapert' as to write deeds publicizing their homosexual unions.[25]

---

[24] Selden, *De Jure*, 7.3, p. 800.

[25] See Henry Stubbe's summary of Selden's discussion of the Chaldee paraphrase of Numbers 15: 30, '*an high hand . . . malepertnesse*', in *An Essay in Defence of the Good Old Cause*, or *A Discourse concerning the Rise and Extent of the power of the Civil Magistrate in reference to Spiritual Affairs* (1659), 115.

If not Grotius or Hooker, then Lightfoot might have had the breadth of talmudic scholarship to be familiar with this text and the skill to read Rashi's commentary. But only Selden, after duly noting the Jewish penchant for hyperbole and citing '*Sepher Juchasin* fo. 8.a' by 'R. Abraham Zacuthius', could have provided the marginal note '*Tacitus. Annal.* 15'. He then cites, only parenthetically, as an actual example of homosexual marriage, wicked Nero's becoming the wife of his catamite Pythagoras ('quemadmodum Pythagorae illi flagitio scelestissimus Nero'). Tacitus elaborates on the last orgy before the fire:

Nero himself, defiled by every natural and unnatural lust, had left no abomination in reserve with which to crown his vicious existence; except that, a few days later, he became, with the full rites of legitimate marriage, the wife of one of that herd of degenerates, who bore the name of Pythagoras.[26]

Returning to Vaughan and concluding with the only disagreement between him and Selden, we can still see the student influenced by his teacher. In *Table Talk*'s dedicatory epistle to Selden's co-executors, including Vaughan, Richard Milward points to the familiarity of the conversations he has recorded: 'you will quickly perceive them to be his by the familiar illustrations wherewith they are set off.'[27] One of the key precepts frequently illustrated is 'Keep your contracts' or '*fides est servanda*' (honour your contracts), even if poverty were to result from doing so after a reversal of fortune.[28] Selden also points out that the 'Parliament of England has no arbitrary power in point of judicature, but in point of making law'.[29] On the same page that he declares, 'every law is a contract betwixt the king and the people, and therefore to be kept,' he asserts Parliament's power in its legislative capacity but restricts it in its judicial capacity: it may 'not declare law, [that is] make law, that was never heard of before'.[30] In a Declaration or Remonstrance of the Lords and Commons (May 1642), an uncontrolled power of declaring law as they please is claimed for Parliament in direct terms. In an essay on Selden's reluctant decision to back the Parliamentary cause against the king, Tuck reminds us that 'here is the greatest jurist of his age, "the lawbook of the judges of England", as Jonson described him, throwing in his lot with illegality.'[31]

There are many reasons why the greatest lawyer of his time chose to side with Parliament, including the king's mustering of the Royal army on grounds that for

---

[26] Tacitus, *The Annals*, ed. John Jackson, Loeb Classical Library (London: Heinemann; Cambridge, Mass.: Harvard University Press, 1951), 15.37, p. 270.

[27] Selden, *Table Talk*, ed. Samuel Harvey Reynolds (Oxford: Clarendon Press, 1892), sig. B1.

[28] Ibid. 52, 100, 102, 140: 'Let them look to the making of their bargains. If I sell my lands, and when I have done, one comes and tells me I have nothing else to keep me, I and my wife and children must starve, if I part with my land: must I not therefore let them have my land that have bought it, and paid for it?' (p. 100).

[29] Ibid. 142.

[30] Ibid. 100.

[31] Tuck, 'Ancient Law of Freedom', 138.

Selden as well as Milton signalled the breakdown of law: 'So spake the Fiend, and with necessity, | The Tyrant's plea, excus'd his devilish deeds' (*Paradise Lost*, iv. 393–4). To those reasons one might add an approach to rabbinic thought serious enough to be considered constitutive rather than merely illustrative. In *De Synedriis*, Selden mentions the absolute power of the Sanhedrin, a civil body that he took as a model for Parliament, to declare war. He cites differences of opinion on the question of whether the Sanhedrin had the power of passing on the king's person. Grotius, attempting to reconcile differences among the rabbis, supposes that by 'stripes' the rabbinic authorities meant only some symbolic or voluntary penance undergone by the king for his sins, but that the court had no power of inflicting it by way of punishment. Against this view, Selden quotes Maimonides, who clearly states that flogging is the punishment for violating the prohibitions in Deuteronomy 17 against the abuse of royal power. His note following the quotation refers to 'Maimon. Hal. *Melakim*, cap. 3, section 4'.[32] The radical Henry Stubbe, relying on *De Synedriis* on the eve of the Restoration, seizes on this information when he counters William Prynne, who had defended monarchy by citing Jeremiah 17: 25: 'Then shall the Kings and the Princes enter in at the gates of the City.' For Stubbe, throwing the verse back at his opponent, a monarchy in which the legislative body has the right to punish the king is a republic, whatever Prynne chooses to call it:

THEN, that is, *after the captivity*, they had no *Monarchs* in *Israel*: such were only they that were the Descendants of *David*, as the *Jewish Rabbins* tell us; and they were subordinate to the *Sanhedrin*, and might be scourged by them in case of offence; So that this Text proves nothing... that Monarchy is best, but for the Paramount dignity of *Parliaments* over the *Kings*.... Where the *executive Power is in one person triable by a Sanhedrin by breach of Law*, it is a *Republick*, and the controversie is meerly *Grammatical*, whether this or that is duly named. So that Mr. *Prynne* here proves a *Common-wealth* to be the *best form of Government*.[33]

In a section of *De Synedriis* that Milton borrows without acknowledgement in his *Defence of the People of England* (*YP*, iv. 354), Selden treats in a number of different contexts the topic 'Rex Israelis non judicabat, nec judicabatur, Rex Judae & judicabat & judicabatur'.[34] Many times he cites both the crucial discussion in the Talmud as well as in Maimonides' *Mishneh Torah* to prove that the distinction between the kings of Israel and Judah is based on the haughtiness or violence of the former and the humility of the latter. Thus, Selden points out, Rabbi Joseph (in tractate Sanhedrin 19a) holds that the kings of Israel, violent and

---

[32] Selden, *De Synedriis*, 2.10, 3.9, *Opera*, i. 1437, 1675–8, esp. 1676.

[33] Henry Stubbe, *The Common-wealth of Israel*, or *A Brief Account of Mr. Prynne's Anatomy of the Good Old Cause* (London, 1659), 3–4. Stubbe also declares presciently: 'It is the posture of the Nation, and the disposition of the People, which makes this or that Government *best* here or there. In *France* a Monarchy at present is *best*, but an extraordinary revolution may so ordre things, that it may be as little feasible there, as amongst us' (p. 3).

[34] Selden, *De Synedriis*, 2.14, 3.9 *Opera*, i. 1524–5, 1674–5.

disobedient of the Torah, are kept from judging and being judged; and Maimonides emphasizes this point:

The kings of the House of David both judged and were judged, and it was lawful to give testimony against them. About the kings of Israel, however, the rabbis decreed that they should neither judge nor be judged, and that they should not offer testimony nor testimony be offered against them, since their hearts were proud, nor could anything spring therefrom except scandal and the abrogation of the institutes of the law. [Marginal note: 'Maimonid. Halach. *Melacim*, cap. 3. & *Sanhedrin*, cap. 2.'][35]

In Milton's *Doctrine and Discipline of Divorce,* in a passage of which Selden would have approved, the law rather than the Son incarnates deity, and by means of it God 'appears to us as it were in human shape ... binds himself like a just lawgiver to his own prescriptions, gives himself to be understood by men, judges and is judg'd' (*YP,* ii. 292). If even the heavenly king submits to human judgment, how dare Charles refuse?

Vaughan, writing his report nine years after the Restoration, may have remembered his teacher's insistence to keep one's contracts in a different way:

A man is said to act unnaturally ... when after Laws made, and Contracts civilly setled, a man shall oblige himself diametrically repugnant, and contrary to his former Obligation. As when a Subject shall by his Oath promise, or otherwise bind himself, to judge or force his King, when by his Obligation to his King, he is bound to obey him, and be judg'd by him. (p. 228)

This is the only time in the entire report that Vaughan differs from Selden; more remarkably, coming as it does in the midst of a discussion of contracts, it could be said to derive from a line of reasoning he remembered his teacher developing; so that even in disagreement Vaughan speaks in Selden's voice.

---

[35] Ibid. 3.9, *Opera*, i. 1674–5: 'Reges familiae Davidicae & judicabant & judicabantur: Etiam testimonium adversus eos praebere licuit. At vero de regibus Israel decrevere sapientes, eos nec judicare nec judicari, nec testimonium praebere nec in ipsos praeberi testimonium, quoniam corda eorum superba fuere, nec aliud inde manaret praeter scandalum atque abolitionem institutorum legis.'

11

Selden on Excommunication

If, according to Gibbon, Milton's 130 beautiful lines in Book I of *Paradise Lost* enumerate the Syrian and Arabian deities that take up 'the two large and learned syntagmas' of Selden's *De Diis Syris*, then his single line from the poem *On the New Forcers of Conscience*, 'New *Presbyter* is but old *Priest* writ large', compresses much of the scholarship distributed over three massive volumes of Selden's *De Synedriis*. In the preface of that work, Selden points out that Romanists and anti-Romanist Episcopalians have claimed a divine right of excommunication, but the Presbyterians, after inveighing against this power in papal and episcopal hands, have, as is their manner, both extended it and apportioned it among themselves, on the authority that they so confidently attribute to their own order.[1] At times in *De Synedriis*, Selden maintains that the Jews did not distinguish between ecclesiastical and secular jurisdiction, a point that could be exploited as much by theocrats as by Erastians, but at other times he insists that this single kind of jurisdiction belonged to the magistrate as represented by the Sanhedrin, a civil institution: 'There's no such thing as spiritual jurisdiction; all is civil.'[2]

Selden is seventeenth-century England's greatest Erastian, but he is also its greatest humanist scholar, and he brings his learning to bear on the subject of excommunication, which was the flash-point in the debates over clerical and secular power. People resented the meddling of the clergy in their private lives and the public shame of exclusion from the sacrament of the Lord's Supper.[3] In *De Synedriis*, Selden offers learned arguments to prove that only the ritually impure but not the morally impure were prohibited from partaking of the Passover. But not everyone will be familiar with those arguments, so elsewhere he speaks plainly and forcefully on behalf of all who would be offended if required to hold their souls open for clerical inspection:

---

[1] Selden, *Praefatio, De Synedriis, Opera Omnia*, i.762. There are valuable discussions of Selden on excommunication in Martha Ziskind's 'John Selden: Humanist Jurist' Ph.D. dissertation, University of Chicago, 1972, 206–12; and in Johann P. Sommerville's 'Hobbes, Selden, Erastianism, and the history of the Jews', in *Hobbes and History*, ed. G. A. J. Rogers and Tom Sorell (London and New York: Routledge, 2000), 160–88.

[2] Selden, 'Jurisdiction', in *Table Talk*, ed. Samuel Harvey Reynolds (Oxford: Clarendon Press, 1892), 88.

[3] See on this point Sommerville, 'Hobbes, Selden, Erastianism, and the history of the Jews', in *Hobbes and History*, ed. Rogers and Sorell (London and New York: Routledge, 2000), 162.

Christ suffered Judas to take the communion. Those ministers that keep their parishioners from it, because they will not do as they will have them, revenge, rather than reform.

No man living can tell whether I am fit to receive the sacrament; for though I were fit the day before, when he examined me, at least appeared so to him, yet how can he tell what sin I have committed the next night, or the next morning, or what impious atheistical thoughts I may have about me, when I am approaching to the very table?[4]

Selden offers another reason for resentment that goes all the way back to Chaucer's portrait of the Summoner in the *General Prologue* of *The Canterbury Tales*. The genial narrator begins, uncharacteristically, by deploring the cynical Summoner's suggestion that purse is the Archdeacon's hell, continues, as E. Talbot Donaldson puts it, 'with a fine show of righteous respect for the instruments of spiritual punishment',[5] but then, inadvertently perhaps, concludes with the neatest Chaucerian anticlimax in the *Prologue*:

> And if he foond owher a good felawe
> He wolde techen him to have noon awe
> In swich caas of the Ercedekenes curs,
> But if a mannes soule were in his purs,
> For in his purs he sholde ypunisshed be.
> 'Purs is the Ercedekenes helle,' saide he.
>
> But wel I woot he lied right in deede:
> Of cursing oughte eech gilty man him drede,
> For curs wol slee right as assoiling savith—
> And also war him of a *significavit*.[6]

The Archdeacon's sentence of excommunication can slay the soul, and absolution can save it, but it is the body's inconvenience that finally matters most: the *significat* is the writ that transfers the offender from the ecclesiastical to the civil arm for punishment.

Selden might have replied, as Chaucer's agreeable narrator did to the worldly monk, 'I saide his opinion was good' (l. 183). His own opinion is forthright: 'Men do not care for excommunication because they are shut out of the church, or delivered up to Satan, but because the law of the kingdom takes hold of them. . . . And there may be as much reason to grant it for a small fault, if there be contumacy, as for a great one'[7]—that is, even if the original offence is trivial, the clergy can excommunicate for

---

[4] Selden, 'Sacrament', in *Table Talk*, 170.

[5] E. T. Donaldson, 'Chaucer the Pilgrim,' *PMLA* 69 (1954), 933.

[6] Chaucer, *The General Prologue*, ll. 655–64, *The Canterbury Tales, The Norton Anthology of English Literature*, 7th edn., gen. ed. M. H. Abrams (New York: Norton, 2000), 230–1. Even after he had put aside contemporary poets, Selden still read Chaucer, and his manuscript of *The Canterbury Tales* contains variant readings of the beginning and end of *The Cook's Tale*—which he quotes in yet another example of scholarship for its own sake, in *De Synedriis, Opera*, i.1530.

[7] Selden, 'Excommunication', in *Table Talk*, 66.

subsequent disobedience to the order, decree, and sentence imposed. Nathanael Fiennes, in a speech in Parliament, 9 February 1640, anticipates Selden's point:

I once heard a Gentleman of the Civil Law answer... in this house, that the Excommunication was not for the thing, but for the contempt, and the less the thing was, that was commanded, the greater was the contempt: If this were so, sure the greater is the cruelty, to lay command upon so small a matter, that draweth after it so deep a censure, as to cast a man down into Hell....

Now Sir, for the ends for which this censure is executed, they are ordinarily to fetch in fees, or at the best to bring men under Canonical obedience, which is the *Ordinaries* will and pleasure, and I have sometimes seen a *Minister* pronounce an *Excommunication*, which he held in one hand, and presently after the absolution which he held in the other, so the end of the excommunication was the absolution, and the end of that was fees. (Sir) for the honour of God, for the honour of our national Church, and for the honour of the Christian Religion, let the high and great censure of the Church no longer lackey after fees, let not Christians any longer be cast to Satan, in the name of *Jesus Christ*, for the non-payment of a groat. And now Sir, we may imagine what effects are like to follow upon such premises, the great and dreadful censure of Excommunication is thereby made contemptible, and were it not for the civil restraints, and penalties that follow upon it, no man will purchase an absolution, though he may have it for a half-peny.[8]

Excommunication was a topic of capital importance in the Westminster Assembly, since it brought more sharply into focus than any other question the nature of the struggle between the Presbyterians and the Erastians. Although the Erastians, such as Selden, Lightfoot, and Coleman, were a small minority, history would eventually declare them the winners in the debate that pitted state against church, laity against clergy. Sommerville, noting the permanent reversal of 'the clericalism of the Laudian regime', goes so far as to say that 'arguably, if there was a revolution in the mid seventeenth century, it was Erastian and not puritan in nature'.[9]

Selden's treatments of this topic in both *De Jure* (4.7-8) and *De Synedriis* are, as we will see, almost exclusively rabbinic. But he conceals as much of that rabbinic context as he can when he speaks to an unsympathetic audience of Presbyterians as a lay member of the Westminster Assembly. Three of his four chief antagonists, on 20-23 February 1644, all Scottish Presbyterians, were adversaries Milton refers to in his poems: 'Galasp' (George Gillespie), Samuel 'Rutherford,' and 'Scotch What-d'ye-call' (Robert Baillie, who attacked his divorce treatises).[10] But his other antagonists include the names of Presbyterians whose initials form the first three-fifths of Smectymnuus, the party that Milton defended in both his *Animadversions upon the Remonstrants Defence against Smectymnuus* and *An*

---

[8] Nathanael Fiennes, in John Nalson's *Impartial Collection of the Great Affairs of State from the Scotch Rebellion to the King's Murther* (1682), 759–60.

[9] Sommerville, 'Hobbes, Selden, Erastianism, and the history of the Jews', 163.

[10] 'Galasp', in the sonnet 'A book was writ of late called *Tetrachordon*,' l. 9; Rutherford and Baillie in 'On the New Forcers of Conscience', ll. 8, 12.

Apology for Smectymnuus: Stephen Marshall, Edmund Calamy, and Milton's former tutor Thomas Young. Although they are all on the side of clerical power on the question of excommunication, there are differences in the degree of open- or narrow-mindedness and in their willingness to engage with Selden's formidable scholarship.

Most of them want to limit discussion to the relevant New Testament verses. The central text is Matthew 18: 15-18:

> If thy brother shall trespass against thee, go and tell him his fault between thee and him alone: if he shall hear thee, thou hast gained thy brother. But if he will not hear thee, then take with thee one or two more, that in the mouth of two or three witnesses every word may be established. And if he shall neglect to hear them, tell it unto the church [*dic ecclesiae*]: but if he neglect to hear the church, let him be unto thee as a heathen man and a publican. Verily I say unto you, Whatsoever ye shall bind on earth shall be bound in heaven; and whatsoever ye shall loose on earth shall be loosed in heaven.

Much of the discussion centres on the meaning of *ecclesia* and whether it designated an ecclesiastical or a civil body. Those disputants with limited philological skills supplied numerous senses, but all based on New Testament texts, including 'a rout of people as at Ephesus', 'an orderly meeting of judges to determine civil business', 'a congregation mixedly all together', 'all the body of Christ, visible and invisible', 'saints', and 'not the body of the people but the rulers'. Edmund Calamy names four interpretations of *ecclesia* that are tied to faction: '1. The episcopal holds it for "episcopus". 2. The Brownist, for the whole and single congregation. 3. The reformed churches, for the presbytery. 4. The Independents take it thus, "Tell the officers before the church." '[11]

Selden begins by pointing out that none of the church fathers during the first four centuries of Christianity applied Matthew 18 to jurisdiction except for Cyprian, and that text was forged. 'Then he offered these things':

1. To consider the time, place, and way of writing of this. Matthew's Gospel was first written: viz. about eight years after Christ's ascension; so is in an old copy of Greek used by Beza, and an Arabic.

2. It is conceived it was written in Hebrew. . . . Now in the Hebrew text it is עדה [*edah*] in these two editions we have, and belike in Matthew's; now in chap. xvi. [v. 18: 'on this rock I will build my church'] it is קהל [*qehal*].

Now the Acts of the Apostles, which is the first place we find 'ecclesia' in [15:4, 'And when they were come to Jerusalem, they were received of the church'], was not written of fourteen years after this of Matthew.

Now the course of admonition among the Jews was: They distinguished betwixt offences betwixt man and man, and betwixt man and God: now he that had been offended by man was to go single and desire satisfaction; and if he would not hearken,

---

[11] *The Journal of the Proceedings of the Assembly of Divines*, in *The Whole Works of the Rev. John Lightfoot, D.D.*, ed. John Rogers Pitman (1822), xiii. 164. I found a reference to *The Journal* in Martha Ziskind's informative dissertation 'John Selden: Humanist Jurist', 165–6.

they take more company, and if אינו שומע [*eyno shomaia*, he will not listen] then לביס הגד [sic: should read לב"ד הגד, tell it to the *Beth Din* or court].

Now every one of the courts was called עדה. Excommunication among the Jews might be inflicted by any of twelve years old, and so by consequence every court might do it: but the synagogue did not use it: and [the excommunicate] was not utterly outlawed from the synagogue, but some part of ordinary free conversation denied him.

Now קהל עדה 'ecclesia', & c. must be interpreted according to the occasion...as Deut. xxiii. 'an Ammonite may not enter' בקהל, id est, of women; for the Jews understand it of marrying an Israelitish woman.

He concluded that this place might very well mean a Sanhedrim. Christ was in Capernaum now when he spake this, where there was a Sanhedrim. Now his speech is so Jewish that it results to this, If an Israelite offend thee, tell the Sanhedrim.[12]

Selden is operating on an entirely different level from his interlocutors, and there are deep reserves of learning behind all of his comments. This opening salvo would surely have intimidated many members of the Assembly. And yet, if the *Journal's* transcript is reasonably accurate, Selden does not identify his sources, nor is he challenged to produce them—though Thomas Young learnedly cites both Cyprian (implying that he does not accept Selden's view that the text is a forgery) and Origen in support of independent ecclesiastical jurisdiction. Selden knows that Matthew is writing for an audience of Jewish Christians and points out that the gospel was written in Hebrew. Young concedes that this is also the opinion of Jerome and Eusebius but points out that 'Epiphanius scrupleth at it'. And Selden answers Young on the first point: '1. That Cyprian did only speak of fleeing him that would not hear the church. 2. That Origen doth as little speak of jurisdiction.'[13]

The massive *De Synedriis*, scrupulously observing the scholarly courtesies by citing its rabbinic sources, addresses the most intricate aspects of the Jewish legal system. Selden is familiar with the rabbis' unflattering proof-text for *edah* as a public assembly of ten persons: 'How long shall I bear with this evil congregation?' (Num. 14: 27), a reference to the twelve spies sent to Canaan, but excluding Caleb and Joshua, who did not murmur against God and who would be allowed to enter the promised land. He also knows the rabbinic sources—primarily *Mishnah* 8.2 in tractate *Yevamot* in the Jerusalem Talmud, but also tractate *Qiddushin* 73a in the Babylonian Talmud—that define entry into the congregation as marrying with an Israelite. Even in his earlier *De Successione in Pontificatum Ebraeorum* (sharing the covers with *De Successionibus ad Leges Ebraeorum in Bona Defunctorum* in 1636, first published separately in 1638), he says that the reading 'shall not marry a Jewish woman' for 'shall not enter into the congregation' [קהל, *qehal*] (Deut. 23: 2) is universally accepted among the Jews.[14] In *Table Talk*, as in the Assembly, he omits the specific rabbinic references:

---

[12] *Journal of the Proceedings of the Assembly of Divines*, in *Lightfoot's Works*, xiii.165–66.
[13] Ibid. 168.   [14] *De Successione in Pontificatum Ebraeorum*, in *Opera*, ii.158.

'Tis said, 23 Deuteron. 2, A bastard shall not enter into the congregation of the Lord, even to the tenth generation. *Non ingredietur ecclesiam Domini*, he shall not enter into the church. The meaning of the phrase is, he shall not marry a Jewish woman. But upon this ground, grossly mistaken, a bastard at this day in the church of Rome, cannot take orders. The thing haply well enough, where 'tis so settled: but that 'tis upon a mistake (the place having no reference to the church) appears plainly by what follows at the 3 verse: An Ammonite or Moabite shall not enter into the congregation of the Lord, even to the tenth generation. Now you know with the Jews an Ammonite or a Moabite could never be a priest; because their priests were born so, not made.[15]

Selden's reading of Matthew is perhaps best summarized by Edward Stilling-fleet in his *Irenicum*, an attempt to establish a compromise between episcopacy and the Presbyterian polity. It is not surprising that this prelate, later to become Archdeacon of London, Dean of St Pauls, and Bishop of Worcester, could not 'embrace' this reading, though otherwise his book reveals how profoundly he was influenced by both *De Jure* and *De Synedriis*, which he cites throughout. (He also cites *De Diis Syris*.) The *DNB* asserts that *Irenicum* (1st edn., 1659) 'shows clear traces of the influence of Hobbes', but in fact its theistic approach to natural law theory is frankly indebted to Selden. Although Stillingfleet disagrees with Selden on church discipline, he still praises his 'skill and learning in the Jewish Antiquities' and calls him 'our Learned Mr. Selden'.[16] He became the friend of Selden's co-executors Sir Matthew Hale and Chief Justice Vaughan, whose funeral sermon he preached. He renders an impartial exposition of Selden's argument, noting that it was 'first broached by Erastus':

The case our Saviour speaks to is that of private quarrels, wherein our Saviour layes down two directions in a way of charity, *private admonition*, and *before witnesses*; but if the party continues refractory, then it may be lawful to convent him before the Courts of Judicature among them, the *Triumvirate*, the 23. or the great *Sanhedrin*; for although the *Romans* had taken away the power of the *Jews* in capital matters, yet they allowed them liberty of judging in case of private quarrels; but if he neglected to hear the *Sanhedrin* then it may be lawful to implead him before the *Governour* of the *Province* in his Court of Judicature, by which Heathens and Publicans were to be judged; which is meant by *let him be to thee*, not as a brother Jew, *but as a Heathen and a Publican*.[17]

Selden's friend John Lightfoot, the second great Christian Hebraist of the period, spoke as a clerical member of the Assembly on 3 April 1646, though the transcript is somewhat marred. Regarding Matthew 18: 18, on the power to bind and loose, he relates it not as the Presbyterians do, to what is done with people,

---

[15] Selden, 'Bastard', in *Table Talk*, 8.

[16] Edward Stillingfleet, *Irenicum. A Weapon-Salve for the Churches Wounds. Or The Divine Right of Particular Forms of Church-Government; Discussed and examined according to the Principles of the Law of Nature, the positive Laws of God, the practice of the Apostles and the Primitive Church, and the judgement of Reformed Divines. Whereby a foundation is laid for the Churches peace, and the accommodation of our present differences* (London, 1661), 144, 148.

[17] Ibid. 225.

but rather to what is done with laws. The rabbinic terms *asar* and *hitir* mean to forbid and/or to permit some act which is determined by the application of the *halakha*. Lightfoot and Selden, both Erastians, are in complete accord on this, but Lightfoot goes farther than Selden by quoting Maimonides before the Assembly:

Where binding and loosing is spoken concerning persons? It is not whomsoever you bind, but whatsoever.... If one place in any Rabbinic author where this is taken in reference to persons, it would sway my mind.... Maimonides applies it to the permission or restriction of such a thing in the law; so in the 6th of Deut.... Whatsoever you prohibit to be used, and whatsoever you shall enlarge in the law, you shall crave the assistance of the spirit.[18]

Selden had taken a similar and riskier approach to 1 Corinthians 5: 13, applying it not to an evil person but to evil itself, though Theodoret and Augustine had also read it his way: 'That place they bring for excommunication, put away from among yourselves that wicked person, 1 Cor. v.13, is corrupted in the Greek. For it should be τὸ πονηρόν, put away *that evil* from among you, not τὸν πονηρόν, *that evil person*.'[19]

Selden, cannier than Lightfoot, knew better than to name any of the rabbinic sources that supported his readings. His intimidated opponents mainly tried to shift the ground from the unfamiliar Hebrew sources underpinning his arguments to the more familiar Greek. Thus, regarding the original language of the gospel of Matthew, 'Mr. *Herle* answered him, That ... the Greek to us is in the original, in that John that translated this gospel, had the Spirit.'[20] Most but not all of Lightfoot's Presbyterian opponents were predictably inhospitable to his learned philological argument.[21] Lightfoot spent most of his scholarly career providing rabbinic commentaries on the gospels, but William Price peremptorily dismisses the most substantial part of his argument: 'I suppose all that he spake till he came to that text in Matthew, is not to the proposition.' And Lazarus Seaman wants Lightfoot to look not at the Pentateuch, which is historical, but at the prophetic books, which are typological:

I desire he would not only look to the history of the Old Testament, but the prophecies of the Old Testament as of another kingdom.... For the New Testament, he runs upon the exposition of the Rabbins. I desire him to consider whether this be a safe principle to go upon in exposition of Scripture.

---

[18] *Minutes of the Sessions of the Westminster Assembly of Divines*, ed. Alex F. Mitchell and John Struthers (Edinburgh and London: Blackwood, 1874), 440. I owe this refererence—and the point that Lightfoot goes farther than Selden by naming a rabbinic source—to an unpublished paper by Matt Goldish, 'The Erastian Hebraism of John Lightfoot and John Selden'.

[19] Selden, 'Excommunication', in *Table Talk*, 64.

[20] *Journal of the Proceedings of the Assembly of Divines*, 166.

[21] Professor Goldish makes this point in his paper 'The Erastian Hebraism of John Lightfoot and John Selden'.

William Vines adds: 'I desire he would not tell us how he finds in Jewish authors, but what he finds in the Word of God.'[22] But Gillespie, surprisingly, is at least willing to engage Lightfoot on his own terms: 'I deny that, that is taken for granted, that there is no distinct government in the Jewish Church. . . . We will prove from the Talmudical writers an excommunication. . . . That of binding and loosing, the context carries it to persons. . . . The Jews had a binding and loosing of persons, as Buxtorf tells us.'[23]

Selden, whose approach is humanistic, legal, and historical, rather than dogmatic, theological, and typological, had his revenge even in the short run. Two days after his readings of Matthew 18 went essentially unanswered, though the Presbyterians imagined that they had defeated him with their warmed-over arguments all beside the point, he began to put basic questions to the Assembly that precipitated 'a great deal of debate':

Mr. *Selden* moved that these four things should first be agreed on. 1. That at Jerusalem there were presbyters. 2. Whether these were a presbytery. 3. Whether there were several congregations. 4. Whether these were governed by the presbytery.[24]

Selden would also have a hand in framing more unanswerable questions with serious consequences about the *jure divino* assumptions of the divines. Parliament had disappointed the Presbyterians by giving to the excommunicate the right of final appeal to a body of lay commissioners that it would appoint. When the divines petitioned against this and claimed a right to uncontrolled spiritual jurisdiction, Parliament 'in reply sent them a number of very searching queries, drawn up by a Committee of the House, touching the point of *jus divinum*, and demanding exact scriptural proof '.[25] Selden's homely analogy conveys a sense of the sheer pleasure he took at the discomfiture of the divines:

When the queries were sent to the assembly concerning the *jus divinum* of presbytery, their asking time to answer them, was a satire upon themselves. For if it were to be seen in the text, they might quickly turn to the place and shew us it. Their delaying to answer makes us think there's no such thing there. They do just as you have seen a fellow do at a tavern reckoning, when he should come to pay his share; he puts his hands into his pockets, and keeps a grabling and a fumbling and shaking, at last tells you he has left his money at home; when all the company knew at first he had no money there; for every man can quickly find his own money.[26]

---

[22] *Minutes of the Sessions of the Westminster Assembly of Divines*, 440 (Price), 441 (Seaman), 442 (Vines).

[23] Ibid. 442.

[24] *Journal of the Proceedings of the Assembly of Divines*, 172.

[25] Samuel Harvey Reynolds, note on 'Presbytery', in Selden, *Table Talk*, 156. Reynolds's edition is the best by far, and in his Appendix, Excursus E, he provides the text of the questions sent to the Assembly (pp. 208–9).

[26] Selden, 'Presbytery', in *Table Talk*, 156–7.

In *De Synedriis* (1.10), Selden demonstrates the breadth of his scholarship while arguing that the ultimate power of excommunication lay with the civil authorities, whether in the ancient *respublica* (sometimes *politia*) *Hebraeorum* or in England in an unbroken line from William I to his own day—that is, the king could annul a sentence illegally pronounced, and the state could inflict punishment on clerics who disobeyed the king's order. Selden expresses himself far more succinctly in *Table Talk* than he does in his works of formal scholarship. The divines are compared to a deadbeat who won't pay his share of the bar bill. Selden refers to the right of appeal and to the wisdom of keeping the power to excommunicate with the state. The Presbyterians are so hot for this power to excommunicate that they put Selden in mind of a bride with only one thing on her mind:

They excommunicate for three or four things, matters concerning adultery, tithes, wills, &c. which is the civil punishment the state allows for such faults. If a bishop excommunicate a man for what he ought not, the judge has power to absolve, and punish the bishop. If they had that jurisdiction from God, why does not the church excommunicate for murder, for theft? If the civil power might take away all but three things, why may they not take them away too? If this excommunication were quite taken away, the presbyters would be quiet; 'tis that they have a mind to, 'tis that they would fain be at. Like the wench that was to be married; she asked her mother when 'twas done, if she should go to bed presently? No, says her mother, you must dine first; And then to bed mother? No, you must dance after dinner; and then to bed mother? No, you must go to supper; and then to bed mother? &c.[27]

In his published investigations of ancient legal institutions and the information they provide about the origins of excommunication, Selden quotes liberally from rabbinic sources, free from anxiety about his audience's hostile reactions. The members of the Assembly, nonplussed by Selden, would have been comfortable with the terms used in Reformation debates about excommunication, such as Calvin's tripartite argument for punishing open sins:

That God may not be insulted by the name of Christians being given to those who lead shameful and flagitious lives, as if his holy Church were a combination of the wicked and abandoned. For seeing that the Church is the body of Christ, she cannot be defiled by such fetid and putrid members, without bringing some disgrace on her Head.... And here, also, regard must be had to the Lord's Supper, which might be profaned by a promiscuous admission.... A second end of discipline is, that the good may not, as usually happens, be corrupted by constant communication with the wicked.... 'A little leaven leaveneth the whole lump' (1 Cor. 5: 6).... A third end of discipline is, that the sinner may be ashamed, and begin to repent of his turpitude.[28]

---

[27] Selden, 'Excommunication', in *Table Talk*, 67–8.
[28] Summary of John Calvin, *Institutes*, 4.12.1–5, by J. Wayne Baker, 'Christian Discipline and the Early Reformed Tradition: Bullinger and Calvin', in *Calviniana: Ideas and Influence of Jean Calvin*, ed. R. V. Schnucker, Sixteenth Century Essays and Studies, 10 (Kirksville, Mo., 1988), 112.

Bullinger's contrary argument, which reached conclusions similar to Selden's, would also have been familiar to a Pauline Renaissance audience. Relying on evidence from the Old Testament, he argued against the exclusion of public sinners from the Lord's Supper: all Jews were commanded to partake of the Passover sacrifice; exclusion, when it occurred, was always temporary and based on ritual impurity, not moral impurity.[29]

Selden's approach is qualitatively different from that of the common expositors. A sceptical humanist, he brings to bear on whatever topic he is discussing vast philological and historical learning. He sees the Sanhedrin as the model of a Parliament that represents the laity, protecting it from clerical oppression by maintaining the supremacy of civil power, but also from an unrestrained monarchy: 'The pope, he challenges jurisdiction over all; the bishops, they pretend to it as well as he; the presbyterians, they would have it to themselves; but over whom is all this? The poor layman.'[30] 'The text [Render unto Caesar the things that are Caesar's] makes as much against kings as for them; for it says plainly that some things are not Caesar's.'[31] In *De Synedriis*, he recurs frequently to the Sanhedrin's power to excommunicate, noting that he has made this point in an earlier work ('Lib. 2. de Success. in Pontif. cap. 10').[32] Moreover, the Sanhedrin determined all causes against the succession to the priesthood. This reminds Selden of some cases in which the Sanhedrin had the power of judging and the king had not; and he adds the story, reported in 'Josephus, *Archaeol.* 1. 14. c. 17', of Herod's being called before the Sanhedrin, though John Hyrcanus, ethnarch and high priest of Judaea, and the most successful ruler of the Hasmonean dynasty, was strongly against it. At last Hyrcanus was forced to devise a stratagem—he proposed delaying the pronouncing of judgement until the following day—in order to save Herod from their power. They were about to sentence him to death.[33]

It would be limiting to say that Selden marshals his arguments only in the service of an Erastian agenda. Even on the limited topic of excommunication, he manages always to do more than 'de-mythologize Scriptural texts',[34] though he does that as well. He never tires of providing illustrations of biblical 'excommunication' as a civil penalty (expulsion from the day-to-day society of Jews) as opposed to a spiritual sanction.[35] He must also experience the sheer pleasure of

[29] J. Wayne Baker, *Heinrich Bullinger and the Covenant* (Athens, Ohio: Ohio University Press, 1980), 90–1.

[30] Selden, 'Jurisdiction', in *Table Talk*, 88.

[31] Selden, 'King,' in *Table Talk*, 90. See also p. 89: 'A king is a thing men have made for their own sakes, for quietness' sake.'

[32] Selden, *De Synedriis, Opera*, i. 1669.

[33] Ibid. 1670–1.

[34] Sommerville, 'Hobbes, Selden, Erastianism, and the history of the Jews', 171.

[35] Besides the frequent examples, some of them discussed below, from *De Synedriis*, see Selden's *Preface, De Anno Civili Veteris Ecclesiae, seu Reipublicae Judaicae Dissertatio* [1644], in *Opera Omnia*, i. 5:'*sed non omnino templi sacrorumve usus interdictio*'. He also develops the point that expulsion

penetrating to the meaning of difficult ancient texts in his extraordinarily clear paraphrases of the elliptical Aramaic text of the *gemara*. And Selden usually adds something in excess of what is required, as in his rabbinic commentary on Christ's attitude toward anger as expressed in the Sermon on the Mount. Since Christ uses the term *tō sunedriō*, the passage is relevant to the question of excommunication, though he almost certainly has a heavenly tribunal in mind, the *beth din shel ma'alah*, the court on high:

Yee have heard, that it was saide by them of old time, Thou shalt not kill: and, whosoever shall kill, shalbe in danger of the iudgement. But I say unto you, that whosoever is angry with his brother without a cause, shall be in danger of the Judgement: and whosoever shall say to his brother, Racha, shal be in danger of the counsell: but whosoever shall say, Thou foole, shalbe in danger of hell fire. (Matthew 5: 21–2)

Selden finds a parallel in the Babylonian Talmud, tractate *Qiddushin* 28a, which is itself a remarkable achievement, even if his paraphrase is flawed, since Christ's antithesis pits a traditional rabbinic teaching, a *shemu'ah*, what 'Yee have heard', against his individual and therefore original interpretation and application. Selden has found what resembles a precedent: 'One who calls his neighbor "slave," that is, "Canaanite slave" [presumably as a result of his liaison with a heathen bondmaid], let him be excommunicated; "mamzer" [the issue of a hateful or forbidden sexual union], he receives forty [lashes]; "rasha" ["wicked"] the sanhedrin may descend so far as his life.'[36] The apparent parallel between Christ's *Racha* and the Talmud's *rasha* is an illusion, since *Racha* (or *raqa*, רקא) is an Aramaic term transliterated in the Greek, meaning 'fool, empty-headed'. This calls the entire parallel into question, since being called a slave or a bastard is *halakhically* actionable, affecting the injured party's standing in the community, while being called a fool is not. Selden sees the end of the *baraitha* referring to the Sanhedrin, which can descend to the offender's very life. Rashi, probably on the basis of the singular 'descends', would explicitly excuse the court from responsibility in the last case, allowing the injured party, acting as an individual, to hate the offender who has called him wicked and even to descend to his very livelihood (not to his life) in an attempt to reduce his income.

One might find a comparable example in Lightfoot of a rabbinic commentary on the gospel, but Selden often provides a broader context. Where Josephus reports that Manasseh was forbidden by the elders of Jerusalem (that is, by the Sanhedrin) to come to the altar, Selden quotes in the original Hebrew the explanation of Solomon Ibn Verga 'In *Shebet Jehuda*, fol. 11.1': this is not to

---

from the synagogue is still compatible with access to the temple, with references to John 9: 22, 12: 42, and 16: 2, in *De Jure*, 4.9, pp. 518 ff.

[36] Selden, *De Synedriis, Opera*, i. 1541: '*Qui vocaverit proximum suum servum (id est, עבד כנען servum Cananaeum . . . excommunicandus erat . . . qui proximum suum vocaret Mamzerem, coitu damnato ortum verberandus erat plagis quadraginta. . . . qui vocaverit proximum suum improbum descendit* synedrium *cum eo vitam ejus.*'

be taken as if he was excommunicated from partaking of the sacrifices, but only put out from officiating in the priesthood.[37] Selden draws on the historical material compiled by Ibn Verga, but he could hardly have missed the book's central topic: the problem of the hatred of the Jews. Ibn Verga documents the persecutions undergone by the Jews from the destruction of the second temple until his own day (the 1520s).

Selden has a great ear for languages, but the most difficult challenges are posed by the Babylonian-Aramaic texts of the *gemara*. Some of his mistakes come from a text-based rather than community-based understanding of Judaism. Having never attended a circumcision ceremony, he would not know the middle term of the threefold blessing: that the infant (or proselyte, who is considered a newborn) grow up to study Torah, to stand under the wedding canopy (*khuppah*), and to perform good deeds. And yet, gifted as he is, Selden implicitly recognizes the connection between *khuppah* and the root *kh'ph'ph* (to cover, shield, protect) and reads the second blessing as one of protection.[38] In *De Synedriis*, tracing the existence of pre-Mosaic courts of law, he seriously discusses a passage in the *Midrash Rabbah* not meant to be taken literally, which speaks of the five High Court judges in Sodom over whom Lot presided as Lord Chief Justice: the names of the justices include *Rab Sheker* (Master Falsehood), *Rab Nabal* (Master Villain), and מסטידין *Maste Din* (Prevaricator, Perverter of Justice).[39]

---

[37] Ibid. 1569.

[38] Selden, *De Jure*, 2.2, on the threefold blessing of '*legem, & protectionem* seu *salutem, & bona opera*'. Six years later, in *Uxor Ebraica*, 2.13, pp. 181–7, Selden provides a flawless, detailed discussion of the various meanings of *khuppah* in rabbinic texts, specifically as they relate to marriage.

[39] See Isaac Herzog, 'John Selden and Jewish Law', *Judaism: Law and Ethics*, ed. Chaim Herzog (London: Soncino, 1974), 78, which pokes fun at this example but then more seriously believes that it reveals 'Selden's failure to appraise the relative values of his materials'. But Selden may have been working with a defective text, since instead of מסטידין *Maste Din* (Perverter of Justice), he reads מסטירין *mastirin* (secret, as in בעלי מסטירין, discreet persons), which would be a desirable quality in a judge. (There is only a tiny difference between the letter ד [*daled*] and the letter ר [*resh*].) See *De Synedriis*, 1.5, in *Opera*, i. 1123, 'Scilicet in *Bereshith Rabba* Parasch. fol. 16. col. 1.' Moreover, Herzog implicitly concedes that Selden does understand the difference between the legal sections of the Talmud, to be taken seriously, and the *asmakhtot*, the elaborate and far-fetched scriptural supports that are often adduced for mnemonic purposes. In his brief essay, first presented as a lecture at the Society for Jewish Jurisprudence, Inner Temple, London, February 1930, Rabbi Herzog, a talmudic genius, who was at the time Chief Rabbi of the Irish Free State and who later would become the first Ashkenazic Chief Rabbi of Israel, will not go so far as to call Selden a talmudist, and he thinks that the *DNB* exaggerates when it asserts that he attained a degree of proficiency in Jewish learning 'equalled by very few non-Israelites': 'I would rather say that very few non-Talmudists, Israelite or non-Israelite, have reached Selden's level of Talmudic-Rabbinic erudition. It is really uncanny that a man who certainly was not a Talmudist should have been able to produce what Selden has produced in the domain of Rabbinica' (p. 79). Herzog's standards are Olympian, and he seems to be faulting Selden, who is on his own as an interpreter of these sometimes impenetrable texts, for his defects in *sevarah* or *pilpul*—that is, in the subtle or keen rabbinical investigation or argumentation that produces truly original readings. He does not acknowledge fully the supreme difficulty of making plain sense of the text.

The last example of Selden reading the Talmud on the subject of excommunication reveals a great deal. He makes a serious but altogether excusable mistake, but he also makes available to his contemporary readers a text deleted from most editions of the Talmud, beginning, as he points out, with the Basel edition of 1578–80, and he demonstrates his philological expertise.[40] Beginning in *De Jure* and continuing in *De Synedriis*, he examines the bizarre twice-told talmudic account ('Videsis Gemar. Babylon. ad tit. *Sanhedrin*, cap. 11. fol. 107.2. & ad tit. *Sota*, cap. 9. fol. 47.1') of the excommunication of 'Jesus of Nazareth', purportedly by his teacher, the second head of the great assembly, Rabbi Joshua ben Perachiah. It is, as Selden recognizes, a rare public reference in the Talmud to 'our Lord Jesus Christ'. The story—apparently a reaction to the image of Jesus in the Christian tradition—reveals its ignorance of the historical Jesus, whom it misrepresents as a rabbinical student who has strayed from the path. Even so, the theme is the harm that can come from too severe a rejection: 'Our rabbis taught: Let the left hand repulse but the right hand always invite back: not as Elisha, who thrust Gehazi away with both hands, and not like R. Joshua b. Perachiah, who repulsed Jesus of Nazareth with both hands.'

This story, far less complex than the legal issues that Selden grapples with, still presents interpretative problems, and misinterpretation is at its very heart. According to the text, R. Joshua was a guest at an inn, where he was treated with great respect. When he exclaimed, 'What a beautiful אכסניא *akhsania* (inn)', Jesus, imagining that R. Joshua was referring to the female innkeeper (another meaning of *akhsania*), replied, ' Master, [she isn't really so beautiful, because] her eyes are *terutot* [meaning disputed: smooth and round? too long? bleared, dripping, and dim? narrow or half-closed?]. R. Joshua rebukes Jesus: 'Wicked one, is it with such thoughts that you occupy yourself [by gazing into the eyes of a married woman]? R. Joshua then excommunicates Jesus, who comes before him numerous times asking repentantly to be received, each time being rejected. The last time he appears, R. Joshua, at last ready to receive him, is reciting the *Shema* and, not permitted to interrupt his prayer with speech, makes a sign with his hand that Jesus should wait until he is finished. Jesus misunderstands, believes that he has been rejected yet again, and leaves, imagining that his master has been inexorable even in the face of repentance. It is left to the reader to imagine the harm that followed that rejection.

Selden gets the story wrong. Truly as solitary as he was in his prison cell when he first opened 'the Talmud of Babylon in diuers great volumes' borrowed from the Westminster Library, he has no one to help him with punctuation, vowel

---

[40] Selden, *De Jure*, 4.9, p. 525, mentions the censors' removal of the passage from the Basel edition and his own debt to Johannes Drusius (1550–1615), former professor of Oriental languages at Oxford, in his '*Praeterit. lib. 4. Ad D. Ioann. cap. 9. 22*'. In a copy of the great Vilna edition of the Talmud, handed down from my grandfather, Rabbi L. B. Friedlander, to my father, Rabbi M. D. Rosenblatt, to me, the account is deleted from *Sanhedrin* 107b, whose bottom margin takes up a third of the page; in *Sotah* 47a, an unidentified 'student' is substituted for Jesus.

points, or antecedents in the always elliptical text, which could read 'His master said to him' just as defensibly as 'He said, "Master".' Selden, knowing only that *akhsania* means hostess (as in the requirement that one ask after the health of one's hostess, in tractate *Bava Metzia* 87a) has Jesus praising the innkeeper's beauty ('*quam pulchra hospes haec*'). R. Joshua then replies that her eyes are smooth or round ('*oculos ei fuisse teretes* seu *rotundos*'), and Jesus rebukes him: 'Wicked one, this is the thing that you occupy yourself with, captivated by her eyes' ('*improbe, rebus ejusmodi tu occuparis*! oculis ejus caperis').

Even in this instance, a rare case of Selden getting things wrong, it is instructive to see the pains that he has taken to understand the passage. Scholars posit various etymologies for *terutot*, including the Greek δηρος 'long' or 'too long'. Steinsaltz holds that in context it is a complaint: her eyes are too narrow. But Rashi, Selden's gloss, translates it more positively as 'round' in tractate *Bekhorot* 44a, and Selden does the same, deriving the word from the Latin *teretis* (smooth), a reading that enjoys contemporary scholarly support.[41] Selden also remembers his own reading of *Qiddushin* 28a as a gloss on Matthew 5: 21–2, on the power of the Sanhedrin with regard to an offender who calls his neighbour *rasha* (*improbum*, wicked): '*vocaverit proximum suum improbum descendit* synedrium *cum eo vitam ejus*.' Selden's marginal note refers to *De Jure*, 4.8, where he lists twenty-four causes in which the court has the power to excommunicate an offender: the very first is for insulting a wise person or one's master, even after that person's death.[42] This would make Christ the offender for insulting R. Joshua. The reference to one's master's death reveals conclusively that the story is fiction. In *De Synedriis*, Selden continues to investigate the story, compiling an elaborate list of the heads of the great assembly, placing R. Joshua correctly in the second half of the second century BE. He points out that R. Simeon Ben Shatach, the disciple and successor of R. Joshua, flourished approximately one hundred and fifty years before Christ.[43] All of this in pursuit of the elusive meaning of what Milton would call a rabbinical fable. One cannot begin to imagine the labour Selden spent on the *halakha* or legal matters of the Talmud, which he almost always interprets correctly. It is no wonder that he reveres Maimonides, who many hundreds of times guides him through the labyrinth.

Selden's conspicuously learned arguments on the question of excommunication perhaps deliberately intimidated his narrow-minded Presbyterian opponents on the floor of the Assembly. But his audience also intimidated him, at least in so

---

[41] See the discussion in the Steinsaltz edition of the Talmud, with its parallel Hebrew translation of the Aramaic, in *Sanhedrin* 107a and *Sotah* 47a.

[42] Selden, *De Jure*, 4.9, p. 525: '*Vide supra cap. 7. Caus. 1*'. *De Jure*, 4.8 [not 7], p. 511: "המבזה את החכם ואפילו אחר מותו *Qui* [marginal note: '*Gemara Babylonia ad tit. Moed katon cap. 3. fol.* 17a'] *sapientem* seu *Magistrum contumeliâ affecerat, tametsi mortuum*.'

[43] See *De Synedriis*, *Opera*, i. 1590, for Selden's '*catena*' that situates R. Joshua in his proper time period. See also i. 1590, on R. Simeon flourishing 'circa annos ante Christi natales centum quinquaginta'.

far as he refrained from naming the rabbinic sources that supported his position. Those unreceptive opponents are mostly forgotten, except as names castigated by Milton. We can imagine what Selden thought of them. According to a report by Anthony Wood: 'The house of parlament once making a question whether they had best admit bishop <James> Ussher to the Assembly of Divines Mr. Selden said "they had as good inquire whether they had best admit Inigo Jones the king's architect to the Company of moustrap-makers."'[44] More seriously, in a letter from Selden to Francis Tayler, dated 25 June 1646, which Tayler prefixed to his 1649 edition of the Jerusalem Targum, Selden attacks the wilful ignorance of Christians who reject Jewish scholarship:

Without eastern learning the triumphs celebrated by the pretentious and otherwise learned ignorance of many are either ridiculous or dangerous to us in the west: these, through utter lack of knowledge of the origins and primal sources of things and practices which are found in the Bible, boldly manufacture dreams for themselves, but dreams which are to their own advantage among men, and cunningly impose these as burdens on others.[45]

The preceding chapters, unlike this one, have addressed Selden's cultural influence on figures whose names we remember. Many were sympathetic to his arguments, but all were patient readers of his published Latin works of rabbinic scholarship, in which he spoke his mind freely, although with a scholarly detachment that often required them to draw their own inferences. In light of that dominant mood and of a scholarship so multifaceted that none of his readers could see him whole, any conclusions must inevitably be somewhat tentative and limited.

---

[44] *The Life and Times of Anthony Wood, antiquary, of Oxford, 1632–1695, described by Himself*, ed. Andrew Clark (Oxford: Clarendon Press, for Oxford Historical Society, 1891), 425.

[45] *Memoirs of the Life and Writings of the Right Rev. Brian Walton*, ed. Rev. Henry John Todd (1821), i. 41: 'Certè sine ea triumphos agit nunc ridiculos, nunc perniciosos nimìs in Occidente, pomposa et alioquin docta multorum ignorantia; quae dum origines primosque rerum morumque in sacris literis occurentium fontes nimiùm nescit, somnia sibi, sed quae è re inter homines suâ fuerint, audacissimè fingit, aliisque vaferrimè, ut sarcinas, imponit.' Todd adds: 'It appears, that Tayler was one of the Assembly of Divines; probably through the means of Selden.' The translation, by Gerald J. Toomer, is taken from his paper 'Ussher and Selden: Two Views of Scholarship', which he presented at an international conference in Marsh's Library, Dublin, on James Ussher and the Republic of Letters, 19 November 2004.

Conclusion

In offering some tentative conclusions, I should like to introduce some other figures besides those addressed in the preceding chapters, who—unlike most of Selden's Presbyterian opponents in the Westminster Assembly—took the time to read his mature rabbinic scholarship. Had a separate chapter been devoted to each of them, this study of his cultural influence would still be merely partial rather than exhaustive.

It is tempting to read Selden's great works only in terms of their political agendas: *De Jure*'s seven Noachide laws in the service of a civil religion, reducing religious doctrine to a deistic minimum; *Uxor Ebraica*'s researches into ancient laws of marriage and divorce revealing at once their corruption over time by clerical greed and the illogic of Reformation England in thrall to canon law; and *De Synedriis*'s use of Jewish history to undermine clerical claims to political power. Selden's major works of rabbinica *do* contain thoroughgoing Erastian arguments, but they also reveal an extraordinary love of the sources for their own sake. These works taken together form a sort of treasure-house of rare verbal artefacts, comparable to the more material collections of Thomas Howard, Earl of Arundel, and Sir Robert Cotton. They include an actual writ of excommunication in *De Jure*;[1] the texts of a marriage contract, blessings under the marriage canopy, and a divorce decree in *Uxor Ebraica*; and prayers from the liturgy of Chanukah that are so comprehensive that they include a little-known hymn to be sung only on those years when there is a second Sabbath in that eight-day holiday (from '*Machzor*, Jud. Germanensium part. 1. fol. 105.2': '*poema* seu *hymnum sabbati secundi dedicationis*'), and a transcript of *Megillat Taanit*, a calendar used by Buxtorf but not acknowledged, all in *De Synedriis*.[2]

Selden's vastly inclusive style is not limited to rabbinic material. He shares with his readers illustrations of ancient coins as well as Arabic manuscripts—some of them translations from the Greek via Syriac—on topics including mathematics and philosophy, that were part of the great revival of scholarship sometimes referred to as the twelfth-century Renaissance. His own *Mare Clausum* (1635) was the first book in which Arabic movable types appeared in England, and

---

[1] Selden, *De Jure*, 4.7, pp. 506–8.
[2] Selden, *De Synedriis, Opera*, i.1734–35 (Chanukah liturgy), and i.1747–57 (the calendar).

Selden was the dedicatee of Edward Pococke's great work of scholarship *Specimen Historiae Arabum*.[3] As G. J. Toomer has noted, Selden knew the Arabic Pentateuch not only in the printed text of Erpenius but in a manuscript version in the library of Thomas Howard. In *De Jure*, he quotes from the tenth-century Arabic ecclesiastical history of Eutychius, Patriarch of Alexandria, and his publication in 1642 of a long extract, with translation and commentary, 'is notable as the first Arabic text (as distinct from isolated quotations) printed in England'.[4] Besides the relevance of Eutychius's annals to contemporary controversies regarding the status of presbyter and bishop in early Christianity, Selden's achievements in Arabic, like his rabbinic scholarship, reveal a voracious appetite for knowledge that far transcends partisan politics of Church or State. As Toomer has demonstrated, Selden discusses Eastern titles as early as the first edition of *Titles of Honor* (1614), but his more extensive use of Arabic coincides with the beginning of his serious talmudic study. In 1629, at the request of the Elzevirs in Leiden, who had access to Erpenius's Arabic types, he prepared a second and augmented edition of *De Diis Syris*, with long Arabic quotations.[5]

The breadth of learning in *De Jure Naturali et Gentium* appealed to Giambattista Vico (1688–1744), who saw Selden, Grotius, and Pufendorf as a triumvirate, the 'three princes of the doctrine of the natural law of the gentes'.[6] It was more than the cultivated obscurity of the erudite style that influenced Vico. Nonnarrative history, founded on a revival of antiquarian scholarship, is connected to the rise of profound scepticism about the reliability of narrative history, which bias or ignorance might mar. Isaiah Berlin's description of the historical jurists favoured by Vico applies to Selden:

Gifted scholars . . . antiquarian and legal, began to arrive at their conclusions by careful scientific techniques . . . basing themselves on monuments—literary documents, inscriptions, coins, medals, monuments of art and architecture, laws, rites, continuing or remembered traditions—'objective' entities, *realia*, which, it was maintained, could not be corrupt or unscrupulous or tell lies.[7]

Vico ultimately rejects the three princes, despite finding them all attractive. His disagreement with Selden begins with the theory of the phases that individuals and cultures pass through—birth, development, maturity, decline, and

---

[3] The very first book printed in England to include Hebrew and Arabic letters is Robert Wakefield's *Oratio de laudibus trium linguarum* (London: Wynkyn de Worde, 1524). The third language is Aramaic, which he calls Chaldaic.

[4] G. J. Toomer, *Eastern Wisedome and Learning: The Study of Arabic in Seventeenth-Century England* (Oxford: Clarendon, 1996), 65–6.

[5] Ibid. 64.

[6] Giambattista Vico, *The Third New Science [CXIV]*, in *Vico: Selected Writings*, ed. Leon Pompa (Cambridge: Cambridge University Press, 1982), 197, 207, 218; *The New Science of Giambattista Vico*, rev. trans. of the 3rd edn (1744), ed. Thomas Goddard Bergin and Max Harold Fisch (Ithaca, NY: Cornell University Press, 1968), 94.

[7] Isaiah Berlin, *Three Critics of the Enlightenment: Vico, Hamann, Herder*, ed. Henry Hardy (Princeton and Oxford: Princeton University Press, 2000), 153.

fall—which is at odds with the notion of the *praecepta Noachidarum*. Vico derides the idea of 'the matchless wisdom of the ancients', recognizing instead the barbaric origins of ancient thought:

Are we seriously to suppose that the 'first men, stupid, insensate and horrible beasts,' the impious progeny of Noah, wandering in the great forest of the earth—that these creatures found not the slightest difficulty in conceiving a set of eternal, unalterable, universal principles (quod ubique, quod semper, quod ab omnibus creditum est) [what is believed everywhere, always, by all], binding on all men at all times, and laying down once and for all both what men do, and what they ought to do: principles concerning which the most profound philosophers and the most learned jurists notoriously do not agree, but which, nevertheless, are said to be engraved on the hearts of all men from all eternity?[8]

Vico's demonstrations of ontogeny recapitulating phylogeny apply only to the Gentile nations, and he insists that the Jews, taught by God, were the privileged recipients of revelation. He sees Selden's very inclusiveness as a fatal error. When Vico considers the postlapsarian wandering of the Gentiles in bestial liberty, he also reflects on 'which first necessities or utilities common to the nature of such wild and brutish men must have been felt in order for them to be received into human society. Selden failed to consider this, for he proposed origins common to the gentile and Jewish nations, without distinguishing between a divinely assisted people and others completely lost.'[9]

Vico concedes that divine providence plays an important role in Selden's thought, as it does in his own, which distinguishes both of them from Grotius and Pufendorf. But his emphasis falls on the difference between Selden's belief in an original universal Noachide law that united all of humankind and his own belief in the perpetual enmity between Jews, who received that law along with God's favour, and Gentiles, who remained benighted:

Next Selden, who accepts providence, but pays no attention whatsoever to the inhospitality of the first peoples or to the division which the people of God made of the whole world of nations at that time into Hebrews and gentiles.... And his claim, that the Hebrews afterwards taught the natural law to the gentiles, turns out to be impossible for him to prove, because of Josephus' magnanimous confession, which is supported by the important reflection of Lactantius [his denial that Pythagoras was a pupil of Isaiah] ... and by the enmity ... which the Hebrews have always displayed towards the gentiles, an enmity which, diffused as they are through all nations, they maintain to this day.[10]

As has been mentioned already, Selden, throughout his mature scholarship, and more informally in *Table Talk*, implicitly but unmistakably contrasts the severity

[8] G. B. Vico, *Scienza nuova, Opera*, ed. Benedetto Croce, Giovanni Gentile, and Fausto Nicolini, 8 vols. in 11 (Bari: Laterza, 1911–41), 374; cited by Berlin, *Three Critics of the Enlightenment*, 59.
[9] Vico, *Third Science*, ed. Pompa, 105–6.
[10] Ibid. 219.

of the Hebrew Bible with the humaneness of normative Judaism as shaped by the rabbis of the Talmud and the great medieval codifiers of the law. As a partisan of the oral law, he maintains the cultic strictures and specifications of Leviticus but transforms through merciful rabbinic interpretation the Bible's brutal and implacable laws of capital punishment and the programmes of annihilation of the seven nations. Vico, like almost all of the other Christians mentioned in the preceding chapters, prefers before all rabbinic attempts to temper scriptural severity the unadorned text of the Old Testament, even with its flashes of a tribal God's ferocity. Vico calls the Jews of Old Testament times the people of God, who received the truth by direct revelation from God, while contemporary Jews are dispersed among the nations and marked by enmity toward their hosts.

Without minimizing these differences between Selden and Vico, some important similarities are worth mentioning. According to Isaiah Berlin, although Vico asserts the force of divine providence, he honours 'the defenders of local custom, ancient ways, individual traditions that varied from place to place with roots too remote and tangled to be rationalized and fitted into any universal system'.[11] Selden balances a belief in a divine, universal law of minimal obligation with a commitment to an evolving native English common law that protects its citizens from those who would appeal to timeless and universal truths to support claims to overriding authority. In his early legal writings, he conceives of the laws 'now used in every state' as limited laws of nature, splitting off in different directions from a uniform universal natural law as a result of 'divers opinions of interpreters . . . and the several conveniences of divers states'. Years later, as a result of his immersion in rabbinica, Selden substitutes Noachide law— a divine, universal, positive law of perpetual obligation—for the universal law of nature. English common law is then assimilated to the Noachide precept of *dinim* (*de Judiciis*), the talmudic injunction to 'install judges and legal authorities in every district'. This gives English common law added status as a law ultimately ordained by God, like the judicial Mosaic law, which both augments and evolves from the original Noachide law. In a pioneering essay on Selden and Milton, Eivion Owen asserts that Milton, in his *Doctrine and Discipline of Divorce*, misleads his readers when he claims that Selden, in *De Jure*, concerns himself with 'the divine testimonies of God himself lawgiving in person to a sanctified people'. For Owen, it is precisely with 'unsanctified peoples that Selden is here primarily interested'—that is to say, with Gentiles under Noachide law rather than with Jews under the Mosaic law.[12] Owen believes that Milton is confused when he speaks of the Mosaic law as a law of nature and of nations. But in fact Milton, familiar with the extensive discussions of laws applying only to Jews in a book whose subject is the Noachide precepts, understands the Mosaic law as a

---

[11] Berlin, *Three Critics of the Enlightenment*, 159.
[12] Eivion Owen, 'Milton and Selden on Divorce', *Studies in Philology*, 43 (1946), 238.

divine but limited natural law deriving from the divine universal law to establish civil courts.

Vico's balance between providence and historical laws may owe something to Selden's balance of immediate and mediate or remote and proximate causes. There is a useful and flexible degree of separation between those causes. At moments of integration, Selden looks across the gap between the universal divine law and English common law, as when he insists that there is no appeal from the latter. And at moments of wide and profound difference, he gazes down into it and finds it unbridgeable. Thus, for example, Selden opposes *jus divinum* (divine right), whether applied to the king or to the Presbyterian system of church government. Yet in *Table Talk*, in an emphatically uncontroversial tone, he claims, 'All things are held by *jus divinum*, either immediately or mediately.'[13] And on the very next page, he asserts, 'A king is a thing men have made for their own sakes, for quietness' sake. Just as in a family one man is appointed to buy the meat.'[14] Of course the crucial distinction is between immediate or mediate divine right. Even the fiercest opponent of royal or clerical pretension to divine right would not deny that all power derives ultimately from God. To say that all is held mediately by *jus divinum* is to say nothing more than that God has created human beings, who in turn create institutions.[15] And, as Victoria Kahn reminds us, 'if God is the remote cause of binding contracts, by virtue of his power to punish, convention is the proximate cause, not least of all the conventions of legal language'.[16] The practical effect of such a distinction between causes is to free both human discretion and the common law from coercion by external authorities enforcing uniformity:

Keep your contracts. So far a divine goes, but how to make our contracts is left to ourselves; and as we agree about the conveying of this house, or that land, so it must be. If you offer me a hundred pounds for my glove, I tell you what my glove is, a plain glove, pretend no virtue in it, the glove is my own, I profess not to sell gloves, and we agree for a hundred pounds; I do not know why I may not with a safe conscience take it. The want of that common obvious distinction between *jus praeceptivum*, and *jus permissivum*, does much trouble men.[17]

For Selden, the universal obligation *fides est servanda* is at the heart of the divine, primal civil law of *dinim* (*Judiciis*), though specific contractual negotiations will vary with the times and the contracting parties. Selden describes contingencies in

---

[13] Selden, '*Jus Divinum*', in *Table Talk*, ed. Samuel Harvey Reynolds (Oxford: Clarendon Press, 1892), 88.

[14] Selden, 'King', in *Table Talk*, 89.

[15] See on this point J. P. Sommerville, 'English and European Political Ideas in the Early Seventeenth Century: Revisionism and the Case of Absolutism', *Journal of British Studies*, 35 (1996), 168–94, esp. 187.

[16] Victoria Kahn, *Wayward Contracts: The Crisis of Political Obligation in England 1640–1674* (Princeton: Princeton University Press, 2004), 32.

[17] Selden, 'Contracts', in *Table Talk*, 52.

the contract between the mistress of his house, Lady Kent, and the eminent lawyer Sir Edward Herbert, whose services she sought to retain at an annual salary:

Lady Kent articled with Sir Edward Herbert, that he should come to her when she sent for him, and stay with her as long as she would have him; to which he set his hand: then he articled with her, that he should go away when he pleased, and stay away as long as he pleased; to which she set her hand. This is the epitome of all the contracts in the world, betwixt man and man, betwixt prince and subject; they keep them as long as they like them, and no longer.[18]

The profound implications of Selden's homely example would not have been lost on a republican reader. Acknowledging that human beings can change their minds, it applies to the relationship between the Long Parliament and Charles, and it is tempting to read it as a description of Selden's own relationship with the Countess of Kent, his mistress with whom he lived openly after her husband's death—a relationship of serial monogamy that accorded precisely with an offshoot of the divine universal Noachide law forbidding sexual sins, the pre-Mosaic civil law of the Jews, as described at length in *De Jure*. Before the promulgation of the Mosaic law, if a man met a woman in the marketplace, and they wanted to marry, they retreated to a private place in his residence and had sex, and she was his wife. Selden correctly identifies the common root בעל (*baal*) of the words 'husband' and 'sexual intercourse' and the rabbinic law that one acquires a wife through intercourse. And either party had the right to dissolve the marriage at will.[19]

Selden's philological skill, evident in most of the preceding chapters, is another reason that Vico would have been drawn to him. According to Isaiah Berlin, Vico's 'grasp of the peculiar use of symbols, especially of language, which belong uniquely to their own time and place, their own stage of social growth... marks the beginning of comparative cultural history, indeed of a cluster of new historical disciplines', including comparative anthropology and sociology, comparative law, linguistics, ethnology, and the history of ideas, of institutions, of civilizations—what is called the social sciences.[20] For Selden, who predates Vico and may lay claim to some of those disciplines, language is the most important of the conventions that illustrate the succession or simultaneous existence of autonomous cultures that cannot be wholly assimilated to one another. Every language categorizes reality differently. And even within the English language, words change their meaning: 'sometimes we put a new signification to an old word, as when we call a piece, a gun. The word gun was in use in England for an engine to cast a thing from a man, long before there was any gunpowder found out.'[21]

---

[18] Selden, 'Contracts', in *Table Talk*, 89.
[19] Selden, *De Jure*, 5.4, pp. 551–5. He cites, among numerous others, 'Maimonides, *Halach Ishoth*, cap. 1. & vide in Gemara Hierosolymit. Ad tit. *Kidoschim* cap. 1 fol. 58. col. 2. verba Rabbi Iona nomine R. Samuelis' (p. 551).
[20] Berlin, *Three Critics of the Enlightenment*, 11.
[21] Selden, 'Language', in *Table Talk*, 98.

Just as metaphor cloaks to reveal, the cloak that is the English language reveals cultural change:

If you look upon the language spoken in the Saxon time, and the language spoken now, you will find the difference to be just as if a man had a cloak that he wore plain in queen Elizabeth's days, and since has put in here a piece of red, and there a piece of blue, here a piece of green, and there a piece of orange tawny. We borrow words from the French, Italian, Latin, as every pedantic man pleases.[22]

Selden's discussion of pre-Mosaic sexual relations, noted above, includes the episode of Judah and Tamar (Genesis 38) and hints at the difference between the discourse of natural lawyers and that of the common expositors of the Pauline Renaissance. Where the Torah punishes with stripes one who has violated the prohibition of having sex with a prostitute, Selden, relying mainly on Maimonides, concentrates instead on the difference between pre- and post-Mosaic dispensations and on the contractual legality of the relationship, as exemplified by Judah's handing over to his disguised daughter-in-law the major tokens of his identity, his signet, bracelets, and staff (Gen. 38: 18). It is not sin but contract that interests Pufendorf, who cites approvingly both Grotius and Selden:

Grotius, in Favour of his Opinion [that after a person has committed a crime in accordance with an obligation, the other party is obliged to pay the price agreed on], urges the Example of the Patriarch *Judah* in the Scripture, who appear'd very earnest and solicitous to send *Thamar* the Price of her playing the Harlot. To this Mr. *Selden* answers: 'That in the Judgment of those Times, it pass'd for lawful, for a Woman, free from Marriage and other Restraints, to bestow herself upon a Man, without any Condition of living together; and this either *gratis*, or for a Reward. And that, therefore, this Agreement was able to produce a good and valid Obligation, being made about a Matter, which . . . was *civilly* lawful, or according to the Opinion of States and People in those Days.[23]

In both *De Jure* and *Uxor Ebraica*, Selden develops the connection, derived from David Kimhi's great twelfth-century lexicon *Sefer ha-Shorashim*, printed in Venice in 1529, between פרה (*parah*), the root of the word 'fruitful' in Gen. 1: 28 ('be fruitful and multiply'), and אפריון (*aperion*), the conjugal bed of Solomon (Song of Solomon 3: 9). An entire chapter of *Uxor Ebraica* discusses entry into the *huppah* or nuptial bower ('*introductionem in chuppam, id est, in thalamum nuptialem*') and rehearses the rabbinic argument that leading a betrothed woman into the bower rather than pronouncing matrimonial blessings effects matrimony: '*Non benedictio sponsorum facit seu perficit nuptias, sed deductio in thalamum.*'[24] Milton, who married Katherine Woodcock in a civil ceremony performed by an alderman and a justice of the peace,[25] appeals to 'Selden . . . in

---

[22] Ibid.

[23] Samuel Pufendorf, *Of the Law of Nature and Nations* [*De Jure Naturae et Gentium* (1672)], tr. Basil Kennett, 5th edn. (1749), 301.

[24] Selden, *De Jure*, 5.3, pp. 545–51, esp. 545; *Uxor Ebraica*, 2.12, pp. 182–7.

[25] David Masson, *The Life of John Milton* (Cambridge: Macmillan, 1859–94), v.281; William Riley Parker, *Milton: A Biography* (Oxford: Clarendon Press, 1968), i.480, ii.1052–3.

his Uxor Heb. Book 2. C[hapter] 28, all of it, and [chapter] 29' for evidence 'that the ministers of the Church had no right, among the earliest Christians, to share in the celebration of either contracts or nuptials'.[26] By the time he wrote *The Likeliest Means to Remove Hirelings*, his anti-clericalism had become even more extreme, and again he appeals to Selden:

As for marriages that ministers should meddle with them, as not sanctifi'd or legitimat without their celebration, I finde no ground in scripture either of precept or example. Likeliest it is (which our *Selden* hath well observd, *l.*2, *c.* 28, *ux. Eb.*) that in imitation of heathen priests who were wont at nuptials to use many rites and ceremonies, and especially, judging it would be profitable, and the increase of thir autoritie, not to be spectators only in busines of such concernment to the life of man, they insinuated that marriage was not holy without their benediction, and for the better colour, made it a sacrament; being of it self a civil ordinance, a houshold contract, a thing indifferent and free to the whole race of mankinde, not as religious, but as men: best, indeed, undertaken to religious ends.... Yet not therefor invalid or unholy without a minister and his pretended necessary hallowing, more then any other act, enterprise or contract of civil life, which ought all to be don also in the Lord and to his glorie.[27]

'To the Nuptial Bow'r | I led her blushing like the morn' (*Paradise Lost*, viii. 510–11), Adam recounts, and perhaps this silent act solemnized his marriage to his blushing bride.[28] Excepting the Bible itself, Selden's books provide the fullest commentary on the nuptials of our first parents and on their unpriestly 'Rites | Mysterious of connubial Love', which 'God declares | Pure, and commands to some, leaves free to all' (iv. 742–3). Typically inclusive, Selden crams the margins with rabbinic and classical sources, cheek by jowl, including Varro on the urging of matrimony in ancient Rome and the ritual humiliation of bachelors. He cites both the midrash *Genesis Rabbah* and Rashi, who proclaim that one who brings a soul into the world builds a world. And he discourses learnedly on such related topics as the *halakhic* obligation to reproduce (and exemptions from that obligation) and the celibacy of the Essenes.[29] There is a qualitative difference between Selden's non-judgemental, humanist rabbinic scholarship applied to the Hebrew Bible and the emphasis on the literal and tropological levels of meaning in the early modern Protestant tradition. It is hard to imagine what contemporary Milton scholars have in mind when they speak not merely assertively but aggressively of Selden's 'scriptural Protestantism' qualifying the 'Hebraic influence'.[30]

*

---

[26] Milton, *Commonplace Book*, *YP*, i.402.

[27] Milton, *The Likeliest Means to Remove Hirelings*, *YP*, vii.299.

[28] For additional discussion of the bower as the principal emblem of the wedding in Milton's great epic, see my *Torah and Law in 'Paradise Lost'* (Princeton: Princeton University Press, 1994), 95–7.

[29] Selden, *De Jure*, 5.3, pp. 545–51.

[30] Victoria Silver, *Imperfect Sense: The Predicament of Milton's Irony* (Princeton: Princeton University Press, 2001), 380 n. 7.

Students of Selden are greatly indebted to the valuable scholarship of Richard Tuck and J. P. Sommerville, who have focused on the natural law and universalist political theory that occupied his last twenty-three years, and of David Sandler Berkowitz and Paul Christianson, who have shed light on his parliamentary career, his defence of English common law, and his contribution to a new genre, the history of a practice, custom, or institution, such as his *Titles of Honor* and *Historie of Tithes*.[31] Selden develops this genre in his rabbinic scholarship, which begins with histories of the laws of priestly succession and inheritance and ends with an unfinished yet vast study of places of assembly, including the synagogue and the Sanhedrin. It is not the least of Selden's historical and philological achievements in *De Synedriis* that he can represent the synagogue as a positive model of church institutions and the Sanhedrin as a civil court that the English Parliament would do well to imitate. Even in the twenty-first century, those two cold Greek words respectively connote Jewish inferiority and cruelty: *synagoga*, the decrepit old woman vanquished by a vital and young *ecclesia*, and *Sanhedrin*, the tribunal that handed Christ over to the Romans to be crucified. Where other Christian writers used *synagoga* in a general sense, as a Jewish analogue or negative type of *ecclesia*, Selden attends to the historicity of individual houses of worship and study. Both Edward Stillingfleet's *Irenicum* and Sir Isaac Newton's *Of the Church* repeat an argument frequently expressed in *De Synedriis*:

Now from this constitution of Synagogues the form of Church government among the Christians had its rise: the Christian Jews who first preached the Gospel forming their disciples into Synagogues. For the First Christians being Jews had a Jewish form of government.[32]

---

[31] See esp. Richard Tuck, *Natural Rights Theories: Their Origin and Development* (Cambridge: Cambridge University Press, 1979); id., ' "The Ancient Law of Freedom": John Selden and the Civil War', in *Reactions to the English Civil War 1642–1649*, ed. John Morrill (London: Macmillan, 1982), 137–61; id., 'Grotius and Selden', in *The Cambridge History of Political Thought, 1450–1700*, ed. J. H. Burns and Mark Goldie (Cambridge: Cambridge University Press, 1991), 499–529; and id., *Philosophy and Government, 1572–1651* (Cambridge: Cambridge University Press, 1993); J. P. Sommerville, 'John Selden, the Law of Nature, and the Origins of Government', *Historical Journal*, 27 (1984), 437–47; id., *Royalists & Patriots: Politics and Ideology in England, 1603–1640*, 2nd edn. (London and New York: Longmans, 1999); and id., 'Selden, Grotius, and the Seventeenth-Century Intellectual Revolution in Moral and Political Theory', in *Rhetoric & Law in Early Modern Europe*, ed. Victoria Kahn and Lorna Hutson (New Haven and London: Yale University Press, 2001), 318–44; David Sandler Berkowitz, *John Selden's Formative Years: Politics and Society in Early Seventeenth-Century England* (Washington, DC: Folger Shakespeare Library, 1988); Paul Christianson, *Discourse on History, Law, and Governance in the Public Career of John Selden, 1610–1635* (Toronto: University of Toronto Press, 1996).

[32] Sir Isaac Newton, *Of the Church* (MS Bodmer), Appendix B in Matt Goldish's *Judaism in the Theology of Sir Isaac Newton* (Dordrecht: Kluwer, 1998), 172. Goldish devotes a chapter to 'Judaism in Newton's Church History' (pp. 109–40). See also Stillingfleet, *Irenicum* (London, 1661), 239–90. Newton owned the works of Selden and Stillingfleet. See John Harrison, *The Library of Isaac Newton* (Cambridge: Cambridge University Press, 1997), nos. 1481–4 (Selden) and 1561–5 (Stillingfleet).

Although not all political theorists would agree with Richard Tuck regarding the nature and extent of Selden's influence on Hobbes, he has demonstrated unarguably their strong intellectual kinship. Despite their common opposition to autonomous ecclesiastical authority over the laity, enlightened Episcopalians could read them with approval. Clear traces of the influence of Hobbes have been found in Bishop Stillingfleet's *Irenicum*, which explicitly regards the particular form of church government as immaterial and as left undecided by the Apostles. But, as with some other seventeenth-century works identified as Hobbesian in outlook, it becomes difficult to unravel the separate strands of Selden's and Hobbes's ideas, especially since Stillingfleet cites those on which they are in perfect accord. Even so, one can begin by identifying explicitly rabbinic elements mediated by Selden, which Stillingfleet sometimes extends or modifies. Just as Selden devotes part of *De Jure* to talmudic discussions of supplements to the seven Noachide laws,[33] Stillingfleet believes that the requirement to devote one day in seven to the worship of God is a law of nature 'or at least a tradition received from the sons of *Noah*'.[34] And he regards the sacrifices brought by Cain and Abel as the fulfilment of a divine command, a pre-Mosaic institution enshrined in the Talmud but not in the Pentateuch: '*Moses* his silence in reference to a command, is no argument there was none, it not being his design to write at large all the particular precepts of the *orall* Law.'[35] As in the rabbinic commentaries on the New Testament by Selden and Lightfoot, Stillingfleet reads αἰών or עולם (*olam*) in Matthew 24: 3 as *world*, 'the Disciples speaking in the sense of the Jews.'[36]

Stillingfleet refers in his notes to Selden's major works, and his arguments betray their influence. Just after citing *De Diis*, he offers a sympathetic view of idolatry as the expression of a natural instinct to worship the divine, 'so that in the most prodigious Idolatry, we have an argument for religion, and in the strange diversities of the wayes of worship, we have an evidence how naturall a society for worship is.'[37] His references to Selden's rabbinic scholarship in *De Jure* are so pervasive that even when they drop away from the discussion, they leave unmistakable traces behind. Clearly the *leges Noachidarum* shape his view of the divinity of natural law:

It is not bare reason which binds men to the doing of those things commanded in that Law, but as it is expressive of an eternall Law, and deduceth its obligation from thence.

---

[33] See e.g. Selden, *De Jure*, 7.2, pp. 792–3, a comprehensive discussion of the reverence due a parent as a Noachide law, including the passage in tractate *Baba Kamma* on a son's making restitution for what his father has stolen. Selden quotes verbatim a son's proper response to a sinning parent: 'He shouldn't say to him, "Abba or Father, you have transgressed the words of the Torah", but rather he should say to him, "Father, such and such is written in the Torah", as if he is consulting or asking him rather than admonishing him' (p. 793).

[34] Stillingfleet, *Irenicum*, 18.

[35] Ibid. 37.

[36] Ibid. 165.

[37] Ibid. 76.

And so this Law, if we respect the rise, extent, and immutability of it, may be call'd deservedly the Law of Nature; but if we look at the emanation, efflux, and originall of it, it is a divine Law.... For the sanction of this Law of Nature, as well as others, depends upon the will of God, and therefore the obligation must come from him, it being in the power of no other to punish for the breach of a Law, but those who had the Legislative power to cause the obligation to it.[38]

Stillingfleet's Erastian citations of Selden and Hobbes blur distinctions between civil and church government. His own rough correlative of remote and proximate, mediate and immediate causes is general or universal and particular. There is a universal natural law that civil government be established, but the particular form it takes—monarchy, aristocracy, democracy—is a matter of positive law only. Similarly, rejecting *jure divino* Episcopal or Presbyterian church government, Stillingfleet concludes that '*no one Form is determined as necessary for the Church of God in all ages of the World*': 'those things in Church Government . . . have no other foundation but the Principles of *humane prudence* guided by the Scriptures; and it were well if that were observed still.'[39] This in turn resembles Selden's own view of adjudication as the single positive Noachide law: there is a universal divine commandment to set up law courts, but the particular form that the law takes within a given community is left up to its human legislators. To violate a particular civil law is to violate a limited natural law that has evolved from a universal law of adjudication. The one major difference is that by assimilating his original view of English common law as a limited law of nature to the Noachide precept of *dinim* (*de Judiciis*), Selden assumes that his own country's civil laws are authorized by God and are thus ultimately no less divine than the civil laws of the Jews enumerated in the Pentateuch.

Stillingfleet cites Hobbes in *De Cive*, who resembles Selden in *De Jure* on the principle *fides est servanda*, which is 'that Original and fundamental Law of societies, *viz.* Standing to Covenants once made':[40]

Men entring upon societies by mutual compacts, things thereby become good and evil which were not so before. Thus he who was free before to do what and how he pleased, is now bound to obey what Laws he hath consented to; or else he breaks not only a positive Law, but that Law of nature which commands man to stand to Covenants once made, though he be free to make them.[41]

In light of the many citations of *De Jure* in *Irenicum*, especially regarding the law of nature as a divine universal voluntary law of perpetual obligation, Stillingfleet's position on government resembles Selden on *dinim* (*de Judiciis*), especially in its deliberate mix of the divine and the human, Church and State:

38 Stillingfleet, *Irenicum*, 15.
39 Ibid. 87 (on civil government), 385, 416–17 (on church government).
40 Ibid. 33.
41 Ibid. 33. He cites 'Hobs *de Cive* cap. 1. Fol. 11' (p. 32).

the manner of investing Church-Governours in their authority, is not determin'd by the Law of Nature; but that there should be a power Governing, is (supposing a society) of the immutable Law of Nature, because it is that without which no society can be maintained. And this is one of those things which are of the Law of Nature, not in an absolute state of liberty, but supposing some acts of men (which once supposed) become immutable and indispensable. As supposing propriety, every man is bound to abstain from what is in anothers possession, without his consent, by an immutable Law of Nature; which yet supposeth some act of man, *viz*, the voluntary introducing of propriety by consent.[42]

The irenic purpose of Stillingfleet's book is to reconcile the Episcopal and Presbyterian churches, though the 1659 publication date combined with an Erastian blurring of distinctions between the religious and the secular might inadvertently have contributed to a subversive connection between covenant and contract. Whether the topic is the prohibition in paradise, the ceremonial Mosaic law, or the Apostolic Decree in Acts, Stillingfleet insists that despite their divine origin all were temporary and are at present obsolete, since laws cease to bind once the reason for them ceases: 'no command doth bind against the reason of the command.'[43]

The spirit of inclusiveness and reconciliation informs the *Irenicum* in large ways and small, as in various tripartite crescendo movements from universal natural law to Hebraic Mosaic law to Christian gospel. Stillingfleet paraphrases the Schoolmen regarding the Sabbath: 'Nature dictates that God should be worshipped, the Law informs what day and time to spend in his worship, Grace must enable us to perform that worship on that day in a right manner.'[44] In their theological treatises, most of Selden's Presbyterian enemies in the Westminster Assembly contrast inferior Old Testament types with the Christian antitypes that supersede or even reverse them, to emphasize discontinuity, changes in the decorum governing a particular dispensation, and differences in God's relationship with his creatures. The learned Stillingfleet, who was on good terms with nonconformists, emphasizes God's continuous ways with his faithful throughout history.

Inclusiveness is at the heart of Selden's *De Jure*, in his organization of the Noachide laws into two essential parts, individuals' relationship with God and with their neighbour;[45] in the confluence of ideas from his Greek, Latin, Arabic, and Hebrew sources; and of course in his choice of subject, the Jewish conception of universal moral imperatives. Isaac Newton's *Irenicum*, its title an explicit

---

[42] Stillingfleet, *Irenicum*, 87.

[43] Ibid. 20.

[44] Ibid. 18: '*Cultus est a natura, modus a lege, virtus a Gratia.*'

[45] Selden, *De Jure*, 1.10, p. 118: '*inter Hominem & Numen sanctissimum*', '*inter Hominem & proximum suum*'. See also Selden's mordantly witty comment on 'Preaching' in *Table Talk*, 146: 'The things between God and man are but a few, and those, forsooth, we must be told often of; but the things between man and man are many; those I hear not of above twice a year, at the assizes, or once a quarter at sessions; but few come then, nor does the minister ever exhort the people to go at these times to learn their duty towards their neighbour.'

hommage to Stillingfleet and its rabbinic ideas an implicit one to Selden, refers to the Noachide precepts and to the two essential religious commandments, first promulgated in paradise and never superseded, though corrupted by the confusion of metaphysics, love of God and of one's neighbour:

All nations were originally of the Religion comprehended in the Precepts of the sons of Noah, the chief of wch were to have one God, & not to alienate his worship, nor prophane his name; to abstein from murder, theft, fornication, & all injuries; not to feed on the flesh or drink the blood of a living animal, but to be mercifull even to bruit beasts; & to set up Courts of justice in all cities & societies for putting these laws in execution.[46]

The religion of God's people in all ages, except the ceremonial part, has been one & the same. Thou shalt love the Lord thy God with all thy heart & with all thy soul & with all thy mind. This is the first & great commandment & the second is like unto it. Thou shalt love thy neighbour as thy selfe. On these two commandments, saith Christ, hang all the law & the Prophets, Matth. 22.37. And on these two also depend all the Gospel. For these are the laws of nature, the essential part of religion which ever was & ever will be binding to all nations.[47]

Milton's commitment to the principle whereby love of God and of one's neighbour is transposed into different keys may derive in part from Selden's comparatist historico-philological method of interpretation of history, jurisprudence, and religion. As I have tried to demonstrate elsewhere,[48] Milton refers in *De Doctrina Christiana* to the tree of knowledge, a pledge of the relationship between humankind and God, and marriage, a pledge of the relationship between human beings, as the two divine universal positive laws of paradise.[49] In a passage in Plato's *Symposium* that Milton knows well, Socrates distinguishes between those people whose creative instinct is physical and those whose creative desire is of the soul. The latter 'long to beget spiritually, not physically, the progeny which it is the nature of the soul to create and bring to birth. If you ask what that progeny is, it is wisdom and virtue in general.'[50] Writing in *An Apology* of happiness both individual and communal, Milton places these remarks in a framework of Platonic idealism and ethical doctrine: 'the first and chiefest office of love, begins and ends in the soule, producing those happy twins of her divine generation knowledge and vertue.'[51] Under the Mosaic law, the counterparts of the two pledges in paradise and the twin progeny of the soul under natural law are the two tables of the Decalogue. Moreover, the chronology of *Paradise Lost* begins with the metaphorical begetting of the Son as ruler over the angels, which

[46] Isaac Newton, *Irenicum* (Keynes MS 3), in Goldish, *Judaism in the Theology of Sir Isaac Newton*, app. A, p. 167.

[47] Newton, *Of the Church* (MS Bodmer), in Goldish, *Judaism in the Theology of Sir Isaac Newton*, app. D, p. 182.

[48] This paragraph and the next are taken from my *Torah and Law in 'Paradise Lost'*, 18, 131–2.

[49] Milton, *Christian Doctrine*, *YP*, vi. 353.

[50] Plato, *Symposium* (209A), trans. Walter Hamilton (Harmondsworth: Penguin, 1951), 90.

[51] Milton, *An Apology against a Pamphlet*, *YP*, i. 892. See also *Animadversions*, i. 719.

Raphael narrates as Sinai theophany. God's emphatically legal declaration ('Hear my Decree, which unrevok'd shall stand') compresses into just two lines the two tables of the law, the love of God ('Under his great Vice-gerent Reign'; v. 609) and of our neighbour ('abide | United as one individual Soul'; v. 609–10).

Milton asserts that the law and the gospel, correctly understood, are entirely compatible: 'The works of the faithful are the works of the Holy Spirit itself. These never run contrary to the love of God and of our neighbor... which is the sum of the law.'[52] For Milton, Stillingfleet, and Newton, but not evidently for Selden, whose central subject is rabbinic law, the advent of Christ transposes the two tables of the law into the highest key. To begin the second book of *De Doctrina Christiana*, Milton defines the two parts of Christian theology: 'The first book dealt with FAITH and THE KNOWLEDGE OF GOD. This second book is about THE WORSHIP OF GOD and CHARITY.'[53] The aesthetic counterpart of this theological principle of transposition—from natural law to Mosaic law to Gospel—is the inclusively tripartite crescendo movement in Milton's poetry.[54]

Both Selden and Milton influence the works of the deist and tolerationist John Toland. In his biography of Milton, Toland considers the chief design of *Paradise Lost* to be the 'display [of] the different Effects of Liberty and Tyranny', and he also praises 'particularly... those excellent Volumes [Milton] wrote on the behalf of Civil, Religious, and Domestic Liberty'.[55] His major work *Nazarenus* attempts to reconcile Jewish and Gentile Christians by demonstrating that the Mosaic law was never abrogated for the former and that its continued observance 'throughout all generations' was 'designed in THE ORIGINAL PLAN OF CHRISTIANITY'.[56] Toland cites criticisms of Paul, including his ambitious striving for power and his not having learned his gospel from those who were immediately taught by Christ himself. Besides, Paul taught only the Gentile Christians and never the Jewish to abstain from circumcision and the rest of the law.[57] Toland draws on Selden's historical scholarship to support his consistently sympathetic view of the Jewish Christians, whom he calls Nazarenes or Ebionites (from *evion*, 'poor'), who worshipped Christ properly even when the first Gentile converts 'gave their bare

[52] Milton, *Christian Doctrine*, YP, vi. 640.

[53] Ibid. 637.

[54] See e.g. the analysis of the crescendo arrangement in Sonnet 23 by Leo Spitzer, 'Understanding Milton', in his *Essays on English and American Literature*, ed. Anna Hatcher (Princeton: Princeton University Press, 1962), 116–31. One can find this arrangement in other Miltonic works, including *Lycidas*, *Paradise Lost*, and, most extensively, in the 1644 edition of *Doctrine and Discipline of Divorce* and *Tetrachordon*. It is, I think, no accident that the inclusive spirit of this arrangement informs Milton's best poetry and prose, while the spirit of rejection informs his less successful work: Books XI and XII of *Paradise Lost*, which employ the negative typology of Hebrews, emphasizing disparity rather than congruity (xii. 285–314), and the Pauline distinction between children of loins and children of faith (xii. 446–50); and some of the antiprelatical tracts of the early 1640s, with their denunciation of Jewish/ Catholic institutions and ceremonies.

[55] John Toland, *The Life of John Milton* (1699), 133, 5–6.

[56] Toland, *Nazarenus* (1718), Preface, p. iv.

[57] Ibid. 30–1.

names to CHRIST, but reserv'd their Idolatrous hearts for their native super-stitions. . . . So inveterate was their hatred of the Jews (tho indebted to them for the Gospel) that their observing of any thing, however reasonable or necessary, was a sufficient motive for these Gentile converts to reject it.' Moreover,

Mr. SELDEN, never to be mentioned without honor, shows, that at least for the space of seven years after the death of CHRIST, none of the Gentiles embrac'd his doctrine; all his followers, till the conversion of CORNELIUS the Centurion, who was a proselyte of the gate, having been of the Jewish nation and religion.' [note: 'De Synedriis, l. 1. n. 8']⁵⁸

Numerous ideas in *Nazarenus* derive from Selden's work, including references to 'a Noachic precept, equally binding all the world upon a moral account', and the view that the first Christians were reckoned as Jewish heretics: 'nor is SELDEN the only person, that, in later times, has asserted CHRISTIANITY to be no more than A REFORMED JUDAISM. [note: '*De Syned.* l[ib]. 1. c. 8.']; the true religion being one and the same in substance from the beginning.' ⁵⁹ Toland, like Selden in *De Synedriis*, stresses continuity between Jewish and Christian houses of worship, and he censures Jerome for 'blasphemously' referring to the Jews' house of prayer as *synagogues of Satan* ('*synagogis Satanae*').⁶⁰ He states forthrightly the ultimate purpose of his book:

Toleration . . . (in *Scripture*, among other names, call'd *Long-suffering* and *Forbearance*) is no less plainly a duty of the *Gospel*, than it is self-evident according to the Law of Nature: so that they who persecute others in their reputations, rights, properties, or persons, for merely speculative opinions, or for things in their own nature indifferent, are so farr equally divested both of Humanity and Christianity.⁶¹

In preparing to conclude, it is impossible not to be struck by the vast amount even of *known* material on Selden's cultural influence that has been omitted, more than has been included. A parallel study might have been written, substituting Cowley for Milton, since the epic *Davideis* contains many pages of acknowledged—and even more of unacknowledged—ideas taken from *De Diis Syris*; Jeremy Taylor or Sir Matthew Hale for Sir John Vaughan, since the opening chapters of the second book of Taylor's *Ductor Dubitantium*, often direct though unacknowledged translations of *De Jure*, are an expression of Selden's thought as pure as Vaughan's considerably briefer legal decision in the case of Harrison versus Dr Burwell; and Hale, like Vaughan a disciple of Selden and co-executor of his will, drafted a tolerationist comprehension bill in 1688 that relaxed the requirements for conformity to the Church of England; Hobbes or Pufendorf for Grotius on natural law theory; Spinoza for Vico, especially since, as Richard Tuck conjectures, Selden's *De Jure Naturali et Gentium juxta disciplinam Ebraeorum* 'was likely to be particularly attractive to a Jew' like Spinoza;⁶² and the Cambridge Platonist Henry More for Nathanael Culverwel,

---

⁵⁸ Toland, 25. ⁵⁹ Ibid. 46 (on Noachide law), 29 (on early Christians).
⁶⁰ Ibid. 59. ⁶¹ Ibid. 40. ⁶² Tuck, *Natural Rights Theories*, 142.

with an entirely different set of criticisms of Selden. In *An Explanation of the Grand Mystery of Godliness*, in the course of his rejection of paganism, More must disprove those sources, like Selden's *De Diis*, that implicitly connect it with Christian mysteries, such as expiatory sacrifice, apotheosis, and mediating spirits. More betrays his own anxiety over the similarities between paganism and Christianity in his parallel lives of Apollonius and Christ as well as in his use of 'onely-begotten son' in an account taken from 'Selden . . . out of *Porphyrius*'. More refers to the *akedah*, the binding of Isaac, but he is thinking of the crucifixion:

Porphyrius out of the *Phoenician* Chronicles tells us that this *Saturn* the *Phoenicians* call *Israel*, who was their ancient King, and sacrificed his onely-begotten son to deliver his Kingdome from a present danger of warre. His sons name also, he saith, was *Jeoud*, which has near affinity with the Hebrew יחיד . . . and the whole narration seems to some a deprav'd story of *Abraham's* sacrifice.[63]

Selden, named often by More, is clearly one of those whom he has in mind as overly sympathetic to polytheistic worship, who aver 'that the *various Rites* done to *Particular Deities* were meant to *One Supreme Cause of all things*'. This idea provokes More into coining the word *monotheism*, used for the first time to condemn Egyptian priests who worship certain spheres or globes, information taken from 'Mr. *Selden*':

But that *This One Object of Worship* was not the true God, but the *Material World*, the very figure they make use of does most naturally intimate; and I have noted above that *Mundus* and *Jupiter* in the Pagan Philosophy is one and the same. . . . Thus to make the *World* God, is to make no God at all; and therefore this Kinde of *Monotheisme* of the Heathen is as rank *Atheisme* as their *Polytheisme* was proved to be before.[64]

More's condemnations extend to the carnal worship of God by the Jews, who care only about '*the Gratifications of the Animal life, as appears in all their Festivals*', and to the Quakers and 'Apostate Spirits' in the '*New-found World*' of America, who are under the dominion of Satan.[65]

It would be unfair to abandon More without remembering that a different and more elevated spirit animates his greatest works, including, among many others, the *Conjectura Cabbalistica* (1653), the *Divine Dialogues* (1688), and the *Enchiridion ethicum* (1666). More, like Selden, declined academic preferments and devoted himself to a life of study, and his relationship with Lady Conway, whom he visited at Ragley in Warwickshire, was not compromised by gossip, as Selden's was with the Countess of Kent.[66] But Selden, unlike More, was averse to partisan

---

[63] Henry More, *An Explanation of the Grand Mystery of Godliness* (1660), 88.

[64] Ibid. 61–2.

[65] Ibid. 74, 77.

[66] See *Aubrey's Brief Lives*, ed. Oliver Lawson Dick (London: Secker and Warburg, 1949), 271, for a vulgar account of Selden's sexual prowess and of his relationship with the Countess, who 'would let him lie with her and her husband knew it. After the earl's death he married her.' The modern editor's list of Selden's major publications omits all of the rabbinic scholarship.

disputation and, unlike Milton at his worst, indifferent to dogma and an enemy to fanaticism. Even Aubrey, the gossip, ends his life of Selden with the words of 'a learned man': '*if Learning could have kept a man alive our Brother had not dyed.*'[67]

In his love of scholarship and the law, Selden lived a life of rare integrity. During the 1640s, when Sir Thomas Cotton was suspected of being a royalist, Selden used his influence with the Parliamentarians to protect the London property of the Cottons, including the great library, from confiscation and damage.[68] A letter from Meric Casaubon, dated 21 October 1650, which brings 'the illustrious *Selden*... before our eyes in the most amiable point of view', attests to Selden's generosity in relieving the poverty of the correspondent, the son of the eminent philologist Isaac Casaubon.[69] H. J. Todd, in his life of Brian Walton, declares that Selden, 'this great friend, or dictator, (as he has been sometimes called) of learning of the English nation', 'was, from the first, a promoter' of the Polyglot Bible, having co-signed with James Archbishop of Armagh an endorsement of the project, loaned 'at least one Arabic manuscript', and been himself a pioneer in eastern learning in England and a patron of some of the project's most active participants.[70]

There are many examples of Selden's parliamentary labours on behalf of individual rights and in opposition to constitutional violations by King Charles and Archbishop Laud. When the printers and booksellers of London petitioned against Laud's restraint of certain publications, Selden's speech *At the Committee for Religion*, 11 February 1629, is the only recorded response:

MR. SELDEN.... There is no law to prevent the printing of any book in England, only a decree in Star Chamber. Therefore that a man should be fined [alt. version 'sued'] and imprisoned, and his goods [alt. version 'books'] taken from him, is a great invasion on the liberty of the subject. Therefore he moved that a law may be made on this. This is referred to a select committee to be examined.[71]

Less than three weeks later, after Parliament challenged the king's claim that necessity compelled him to collect tunnage and poundage without authorization (a claim echoed by Milton's Satan, who 'with necessity, | The tyrant's plea, excused his devilish deeds'; *PL*, iv.393–4), Charles dissolved the Parliament, no longer even pretending to care for either the liberties of the subject or the immunities of parliamentary privilege. Selden was one of nine members of parliament for whom the Privy Council issued warrants on 3 March 1629.

---

[67] Ibid. 273.
[68] Colin G. C. Tite, *The Manuscript Library of Sir Robert Cotton* (London: British Library, 1994), 63.
[69] *Memoirs of the Life and Writings of the Right Rev. Brian Walton*, ed. Rev. Henry John Todd (1821), i. 315.
[70] Todd, in *Memoirs of Walton*; G. J. Toomer (on Selden as pioneer and patron), in 'Ussher and Selden' (ch. 11 n. 45), 1–2.
[71] 'True Relation', in Wallace Notestein and Frances H. Relf, *Commons Debates for 1629*, University of Minnesota Studies in Social Sciences, 10 (Minneapolis, 1921), 58–9.

His study was sealed, and he was committed to the Tower, 'without any cause expressed and simply on the order of the king'.[72]

Professor Berkowitz has documented clearly and thoroughly Selden's parliamentary struggles and his imprisonments on matters of principle.[73] Two apparently unrelated matters may bear upon Selden's love of rabbinic scholarship and the absence in his work of the central tenets of Christian liberty, abrogation of the Mosaic law and redemption in Christ as a gift of divine grace. During his imprisonment, Selden was given only nineteen sheets of paper, each signed with the initials of the governor, 'nor did I dare use any other'. More than two decades later, as Berkowitz reports, 'Selden proudly wrote that he still possessed these initialed sheets, now bound together, as a souvenir of his tower studies.'[74] Selden used one of these sheets, then, to write to Sir Robert Cotton, on 4 July 1629, asking him to procure from the Westminster Library 'the Talmud of Babylon in divers great volumes', the beginning of a vast scholarly project that would occupy him for the rest of his life. I would suggest that Selden's love of *halakha* (lit., *path*, the legal decisions of normative Judaism, included as binding precepts in the Mishnah) developed during the next twenty-five years as a result of his immersion in those complex ancient texts. In the dedication of the first of those talmudic researches, *De Successionibus in Bona Defuncti, Ad Leges Ebraeorum, Liber Singularis* (1631; rpt. 1636), embedded in a discussion of the contributions made by Judaism to Christianity, Selden contrasts scholars with 'idler men' in a tone of deliberate understatement:

Nor are they able to allow (as idler men of disdainful temper do) that the Commentaries and Traditions of that most Noble nation to which the most ancient and unique privilege of Divine prophecies once belonged to such an extent should be entirely disregarded.[75]

Selden's letter to Francis Tayler, written more than fifteen years later, is far more passionate about both the importance of the 'origins and primal sources of things and practices which are found in the Bible' and about the dangerous ignorance of those who lack the knowledge of 'eastern learning'.

To step into the realm of speculation, it is tempting to find a connection in Selden's Erastian thought, which merges religious and civil law, between his avoidance of the topic of divine grace and his explicit refusal of the king's grace. In 1626–7, the Five Knights case (or Darnel's Case, named after one of the defendants, Sir Thomas Darnel) revolved around the writ of *habeas corpus*.

---

[72] This is noted in *Ioannes Seldeni vindiciae secundum integritatem existimationis suae....* (London, 1653); see also Berkowitz, *John Selden's Formative Years*, 226–30.

[73] Berkowitz, *John Selden's Formative Years*, 84–292.

[74] Selden, *Vindiciae...Maris Clausi, Opera Omnia*, ii. 1428; cited by Berkowitz, *Selden's Formative Years*, 233–4.

[75] Selden, *De Successionibus in Bona Defuncti, Ad Leges Ebraeorum, Liber Singularis* (1636 edn.), p. ii: 'nec admittere queunt (quemadmodum fastidientis stomachi ignaviores) ut Commentarii & Traditiones gentis Nobilissimae cui antiquissima & singularis oraculorum Divinorum praerogativa olim adeo competiit, plane negligantur.'

The defendants had refused to pay the forced loan and were languishing in prison. They refused to petition the king for the grace and favour of release, because that would have been an admission of wrongdoing. Others on their behalf petitioned for counsel, and Selden was appointed to represent Sir Edmund Hampden. His proof-text, asserting that no free man shall be imprisoned without due process of the law, was a statute of the Magna Carta. During Selden's own imprisonment in 1629, along with other members of parliament, King Charles wanted to 'present bail' but as a matter of grace rather than of right and to provide sureties for good behaviour, and either condition was enough to make Selden and most of the other prisoners decline the offer. Selden the lawyer held out for unavailable due process instead of availing himself of a petition of grace. As Berkowitz points out, regarding Selden's 1634 petition to the king for release from bail: 'Selden, who had earlier proclaimed "not by grace but by right," had consistently refused to go that route and Charles with equal stubbornness had insisted it was the only way.'[76]

I should like to end on somewhat firmer ground by returning to the topic of an earlier chapter, Selden and religious toleration, but this time keeping in mind its complete accord with Selden's acts of personal charity, support of scholarship, advocacy of constitutional rights, and humanist scholarship. S. R. Gardiner records the discussion in the House of Commons on 13 October 1647, regarding Cromwell's compromise with the Parliamentary Presbyterians, according to which Presbyterian government was to be established in the Church for three years, while others, 'with certain exceptions', who desired to worship in any other way were at liberty to do so, provided that they did not disturb the peace. Among the exceptions were those who professed 'the Popish religion'. According to Gardiner, 'Selden ... pleaded hard for the Catholics, as believers in Jesus Christ', and when he met with the usual response that Catholics were idolaters, discoursed at length on 'the well-known distinction between idolatry and prayers for the intercession of the saints'. Selden failed, 'and the House without a division persisted in refusing toleration to the Catholics'.[77] His pleas on the floor of the Commons came despite the negative comments in his scholarship about the 'Pontificii' (adherents of the Papacy).

As has been noted already, in his rabbinic scholarship, and especially in *De Jure*, Selden sets down ideas regarding the nature of Judaism and its attitude toward Gentiles that are far more charitable than those circulating in other contemporary works addressed to Christian audiences. His comments on contemporary Jews in *Table Talk* are also uncommonly generous, especially those under the heading 'Salvation'. Selden did not live to see Cromwell's Whitehall Conference, and he died before Menasseh ben Israel set foot on English soil, so

---

[76] Berkowitz, *Selden's Formative Years*, 289; for petitions of grace, see also pp. 129, 261.

[77] Samuel R. Gardiner, *History of the Great Civil War 1642–1649* (London, New York, Bombay: Longmans, Green, 1901), iii. 375–7.

one can never be certain that his reverence for ancient Jewish learning and toleration of contemporary Jews would have extended so far as activity on behalf of readmission. It is clear, however, that his writings had a positive influence on both the readmission question, in a treatise by Thomas Barlow, and, in the next century, on the Jewish Naturalization Act, or Jew Bill of 1753, in an essay by William Bowyer. If readers of Selden in the twenty-first century can remove the overlay of prejudice that begrimes not only the words *synagogue* and *Sanhedrin* but also *Pharisee* (whose negative connotations Selden, a partisan of the oral law, did much to expunge), then his cultural influence will not have ended.

APPENDIX

Selden's Letter to Jonson

Edited by Jason P. Rosenblatt and Winfried Schleiner

A NOTE ON THE TEXT

The text is printed from a draft of the letter to Jonson in Selden's own hand at the Bodleian Library, Oxford University (Selden supra 108 fos. 64–5 Bodl. L.). Since Selden invariably reckons the year according to the English custom at that time of reckoning the new year from 25 March or Lady Day,[1] his letter sent 'From the Inner Temple this XXVIII of Feb. CIƆ.DC.XV' (1615) was actually composed in 1616. Selden bequeathed the letter to his close friend, executor, and disciple in matters of liberal culture and English law, Sir Matthew Hale, judge, of Alderley, Gloucestershire. A copy of the letter, made when it was in Hale's possession, appears in Selden's *Opera Omnia*, vol. ii, part 2, cols. 1690–6. In our edition, substantive variant readings—not differences in spelling—are given in endnotes, cued by superior letters, with the draft manuscript text bracketed and the less reliable *Opera* variant beside it.

To my honor'd and truly worthy freind[a]
Mr. Ben Jonson.[b]

Thus ambitious am I of your love, but of your iudgment too. I have most willingly collected what you wisht, my notes, touching the literall sense and historicall of the holy text usually brought against the counterfeiting of sexes by apparell. To omit varietie of translations, the text it self is thus out of the Originall, word for word: *A mans armor shall not be upon a womans, and a man shall not put on a womans garment*. In *Deut*. XXII. 5. so is it, and not as the Vulgar hath it, that *a woman shall not wear a mans garment, nor a man a womans*. That which the woman is forbidden is called כְלִי־גֶבֶר *Celi-geber*, i.[e.] the Armes or armor of a man, that which the man may not wear is שִׂמְלַת אִשָּׁה *Shimlath Isha*, i.[e.] a woman's gown, or *stola muliebris*. The Greeks, whom they call the Septuagint, follow[c] the Ebrew truth. οὐκ ἔσται, say they, σκευὴ ἀνδρὸς ἐπὶ

---

[1] See Selden, *Opera Omnia*, vol. ii, part 2, 'Epistolae Variae', col. 1707, a letter to Edward, Lord Herbert of Cherbury, dated '*Londini*. Feb. 3. 1619. *Juliano*', and col. 1709, where Selden explains the English custom to the German orientalist Christian Ravis: '*Londini* 15 Februar. 1641. sc. more Anglico qui in Martio demum incipiunt 1642. non in Januario.'

γυναικί, οὐδὲ μὴ ἐνδύσηται ἀνὴρ στολὴν γυναικείαν. [There will not be the clothing of a man on a woman, nor will a man put on feminine dress.] So I read in them; rather σκευὴ than σκεύη as the publisht books have,[2] although σκεύη plurally signify the same which *Celi* doth in another notion, that is vessels or instruments. But the reason why I would alter that in the publisht Septuagint is, besides the self matter, because Fl. Josephus *Judaic. Archaeolog.*[d] IV. *cap.*8 remembers that negative commandment with the same word. Beware, saith he, least the woman use ἀνδρικῇ σκευῇ [masculine garb], and for the woman's garment there he uses the self same as the LXX, that is στολῇ γυναικείᾳ [feminine dress].[3] I know ἀνδρικὴ σκευή may be interpreted *virilis apparatus* generally, or *habitus virilis*; but it best here signifies as in Aristophanes his Σφῆκες [*Wasps*], where the old scholiast interprets it by πανοπλία [panoply],[4] and if you retain σκεύη in the LXX, yet then too it stands for σκεύη πολεμικὰ [trappings of war] or *instrumenta bellica*. So that the text by its words alone hath not so much reference to the sexes using each others clothes, as to the forbidding the Man the womans habite, but the woman the mans armor. Although I know the Canon law out of ancient authority prohibits a woman the man's clothes calling them ἀνδρεῖον ἀμφίεσμα [masculine garb]. But that I ghesse proceeded rather from prevention of indecency than persuasion of this text. You may see Gratian's Decree, Dist. XXX. Cap. VI. which is taken out of the Councill of Gangra in Paphlagonia held in the year CCC.XXV,[5] & the originall of it is in the *Codex Canonum can. LXXII.* whereto Photius also in his *Nomocanon* tit. XI. cap. XIV. hath reference.[6] Agreeing to the Greek, is the Chaldee paraphrase of Onkelos, *Let not ther be a mans ornaments of armes upon a woman, and let not a man adorne himself with a woman's ornaments.*[7] Many expositors observe the intent of this precept to be for the publique preservation of honesty in both sexes, lest, in corrupt manners, by such promiscuous use of apparell the lustfull[e] forwardnesse of nature might take the easier advantage of oportunity. So is it noted by R.R.R. Aben Ezra, Solomon Jarchi or the autor of the common Ebrew glosse, & Moses Mikotzi, by the first two on this place,[8] by Mikotzi in his *Praecept. Negativ.*

---

[2] Feminine singular, from σκευή, 'equipment, attire, apparel', rather than nominative plural, from σκεύος, 'vessel or implement of any kind'.

[3] Josephus, *Jewish Antiquities*, iv. 301, ed. H. St. J. Thackerary, Loeb Classical Library (London: William Heinemann; New York: G. P. Putnam, 1926), iv. 621.

[4] Aristophanes, *Wasps*, ed. Douglas M. MacDowell (Oxford: Clarendon Press, 1971), l. 615, p. 77, on σκευὴν, in a phrase meaning 'equipment which is a protection against missiles'.

[5] *Decretum Gratiani* (Venice, 1605), Distinctio XXX, C. VI, p. 136: 'If a woman out of her fancy finds it convenient to put on a piece of male clothing and therefore imitates male attire, she should be execrated.'

[6] Photius of Constantinople, *Nomocanon, Canones S.S. Apostolorum Conciliorum* (Paris, 1620), Tit. XI, Cap. XIV, p. 171: 'Therefore women of religion should not be tonsured.'

[7] Onkelos (second century CE), in his Aramaic *targum* on the verse, renders the key term as *zayin*, 'armour'.

[8] Like the *targum* of Onkelos, the literal scriptural commentaries of Abraham Ibn Ezra (1089–1164) and Solomon ben Isaac or Rashi (1040–1105) appear in the Great Rabbinic Bible, on Deuteronomy 22: 5. The rabbis regard the prohibition as prophylactic. Ibn Ezra notes its

LIX.[9] Philo the Jew understands it in his περὶ ἀνδρείας [*Peri Andreias*] , as if men were forbidden there, even in the least kind to incline to the quality of the weaker sex. Fl. Josephus chiefly appropriats it to the warre and thus expresses it: φυλάσσετε δὲ μάλιστα ἐν ταῖς μάχαις ὥστε μήτε γυναῖκα ἀνδρικῇ σκευῇ χρῆσθαι μήτε ἄνδρα στολῇ γυναικείᾳ.[10] But a Rabbin of greatest worth by the estimation both of Jewes and Christians, hath a very different exposition. I mean Moses Ben Maimon, who is also called (from the sigles[f] of his name after the *Jewish* fashion) *Rambam* [Rabbi Moses ben Maimon], and because his education and studies were chiefly in Egypt, he is known by the name of Moses Aegyptius, being by birth of Corduba. This Moses in his *More Hanebochim* Part. III. cap. XXXVI. makes a division of the precepts of the old Testament into XIV. kindes of them; the second is touching such things as were to prevent Idolatry, and in it he puts those negatives against sacrifices to Moloch, against witchcraft, the consulting with *Ob, Jideoni*,[11][g] the superstitious part of Astrologie with divers more such like;[h] but amongst them specially he refers that of Apparell and armor to an Idolatrous use. Supposing, that, as in the Temple, adoration was constituted toward the West, hewed stones were not allowed, sacrifices of Beasts were ordained, the Priests were commanded to wear breeches, and the mixtion or insition of plants of severall kindes were forbidden, because Idolaters, neighbouring to the Jewes, worshipt towards the East (as you well know) & had their Temples of hewed stone, and gave divine honor to Beasts (especially the Egyp-

---

proximity to laws concerning warfare (Deut. 21: 10 ff.), a sign that women should not fight alongside men, in men's garb, lest they be led to lewdness. Rashi holds that a woman should not wear man's apparel in order to look like a man, to consort with men, for this can only be for the purpose of unchastity. Neither should a man put on a woman's garment in order to go and stay unnoticed among women. According to Ibn Ezra, the verse also implies that a man who shaves his beard will mingle more easily among women for purposes of adultery. Rashi sees an implication that a man should not shave either pubic or armpit hair.

[9] The *Sefer Mitzvot Gadol* of Moses of Coucy (13th c.), first published before 1480, and subsequently published three times by 1547, in Italy, is a supplement to the *Mishneh Torah* of Maimonides, which is cited word by word on every page. It arranges rabbinic law into positive and negative precepts.

[10] Josephus, *Jewish Antiquities*, iv. 301, on Deuteronomy 22: 5: 'Beware, above all in battle, that no woman assume the accoutrements of a man nor a man the apparel of a woman.' According to the editor, Thackeray, 'R. Eliezer ben Jacob ... based upon this verse ... the rule that a woman might not bear arms' (p. 621).

[11] 'Necromancer, wizard', prohibited in Leviticus 20: 27 and Deuteronomy 18: 11. For these laws emphasizing Israel's difference from its idolatrous neighbours, see Maimonides, *The Guide of the Perplexed*, tr. Shlomo Pines (Chicago: University of Chicago Press, 1963), 3.37, pp. 540–50. Selden's *Guide* is a Latin translation by the Italian orientalist and Hebraist Agostino Giustiniani, *Rabi Mossei Aegyptii Dux seu Director dubitantium aut perplexorum* (Paris,1520). Produced with the aid of Jacob Mantino, whom we may remember as having stood with the Pope in the matter of Henry's divorce, this translation relies on the faulty manuscript of an anonymous 13th-c. translation entitled *Dux Neutrorum*. Both these faulty Latin texts are based on the Hebrew translation by Judah Al-Harizi (1170–1235) of Maimonides' original Arabic text, *Dalalat al-Hairin* . The better-known Latin edition by Johannes Buxtorf the younger, *Doctor Perplexorum* (Basel, 1629), is based on the more reliable Hebrew translation of Samuel Ibn Tibbon (1160–1230).

tians), and their Comarim[12i] or Priests breechlesse (as the Jewes, not without ridiculous error think[13]) did sacrifice to Baal-Phegor, and that when of one kind insition was to be into another, the bestial ceremonie was *ut ramus inserendus sit in manu* (so are the Latin words of my autor) *alicuius mulieris pulchra, & quod vir aliquis cognoscat eam praeter morem naturalem, & dixerunt quod in tempore illius actus, debet mulier inserere ramum in arbore.*[14] Supposing that, as in these and divers more such like related by him, producing the idolatrous customes out of ancient monuments of the Syrians, so in this of apparell, there was most speciall regard to the avoiding of a superstitious rite used to Mars and Venus, which was, that Men did honor and invoke Venus in womens attire, and women the like to Mars in mans armor, as out of an old Magician, one Centir, he recites. His words are, in my Latin copy: *Istud autem est propter quod scriptura dicit, Non accipiat mulier arma viri, neque vir induatur veste muliebri. Invenies autem in libro artis magicae, quem composuit Centir; quia dicitur ibi, ut vir induat vestem muliebrem pictam, cum steterit coram stella, quae vocatur Venus & mulier assumet Loricam & arma bellica cum steterit ante stellam quae dicitur Mars. Est etiam hic alia ratio, quoniam opus istud, suscitat concupiscentiam, & inducit genera fornicationum.*[15]

---

[12] Pagan priests, in implicit contrast to *Cohanim*, Jewish priests.

[13] For the 'ridiculous error', see Ch. 2; BT Sanhedrin 60b, 63a; and Selden's lengthy discussion in *De Diis Syris*, 66–70, which quotes Maimonides on the subject in both the *Guide* ('Moreh Nebochim, part III, cap. XXXVI') and in 'Misnah Torah tract. עכום cap. 3'. Selden quotes Rashi approvingly on the etymology of *Peor* (to open or stretch out): 'Verum nominis caussam & Numinis cultum videtur sibi bene explicasse Salomon Iarchi ad Numer. xxv. com. 3. לפני פי הטבעת ומרציאין רעיי על שם שפורעין *Ec quod distendebant coram ore illius foramen Podicus & stercus offerebant; & Aperire n. sive distendere פער interpretatur, unde Peor.'*

[14] Maimonides, *Dux seu Director dubitantium*, Book III, fo. 97. *Guide*, tr. Pines, p. 548: '[They mention that] the bough that is meant to be grafted ought to be held in the hand of a beautiful girl and of a man who has come into her in a disgraceful manner that they describe and that the woman must graft the bough upon the tree while the two are performing this act.'

[15] *Dux seu Director dubitantium*, bk. 3, fo. 96a: 'that is the reason the scripture declares that a woman should not take the warlike arms of a man, nor should the man put on the garments of a woman. But you will find the instructions in the book of magical arts, which Centir composed, that the man should put on the female embroidered garments when he stands before the star called Venus, and the woman should wear the coat of mail and warlike implements of the man when she stands before the star called Mars. In my opinion there is another reason for this [prohibition against cross-dressing], namely, that it arouses lust and brings about various kinds of debauchery.' In *De Diis*, 190–2, Selden repeats the Maimonidean quotation in a long chapter on Venus, adding that 'the star called Mars must be understood to be none other than the masculine Venus' (p. 192). Centir the magician is the unique creation of Giustiniani's corrupt text. He does not appear in the *Dux*'s primary source, the Al-Harizi translation. 'The Book of Tumtum' ('Libros טומטום,' Buxtorf), cited four times by Maimonides in the *Guide*, is inexplicably rendered three different ways by Giustiniani, twice as 'libro de Zenzir' (bk. 3, fos. 99, 103), once as 'liber Reitar' (bk. 3, fo. 92a), and once, in the passage cited, as 'libro . . . quem composuit Centir'. Fifteen years later, in his *De Successionibus in Bona Defuncti* (1631), Selden discusses at some length Tumtum or 'Gentalibus Obstructi', pointing out correctly that in rabbinic writings a *Tumtum* is what you call someone whose genitalia are occluded and one can't determine whether the person is male or female: 'hinc... est quod vocant eum genitalia ita obstructa, ut mas an foemina sit non constet, Tumtum' (p. 41). More important, Selden records his access to Ibn Tibbon's Hebrew translation of Maimonides' original Arabic ('R. Samueli Aben Tybbon debetur, qui ex autoris Arabico transtulit') and substitutes for the earlier, corrupt text ('*libro artis Magicae quem composuit Centir*') Ibn Tibbon's correct reading

These are in the chap. XXXVIII. What the originall of the autor is, I know not. I could never see the Arabique or Ebrew copy, as Buxtorf on the other side saies he could never meet with the Latine one.[16] For it was first written in Arabique by that Moses, and turned in Ebrew by *R.* Samuel Aben Tybbon, the Latin translation also being enough ancient. Ben-Maimon liv'd about CD years since: his autority is not of the common rank; for the Jewes proverbially say of him, that *From Moses to Moses there was never any such as this Moses*, and some of great place in the state of learning speak of him, that he was *Judaeorum* (rather *Rabbinorum*) *primus qui delirare desiit.*[17] He wrote other things, but this work of his *Moreh Hanebochim* (i.[e.] as the Latin title is *Director*[j] *Dubitantium* or *Perplexorum*) in his ripest years about fifty, & made it as the draught of his last hand in medling with holy philosophy. What words he uses for Venus and Mars, I certainly know not. But I know that it's certain that those two deities, though under other names, or at least, two every way like them, were adored in those Eastern parts, and that most anciently. The whole consent of European writers allow, the originall of Aphrodite or Venus out of Syria, as she is for a goddesse, and I doubt not but that she was worshipt in the Palestine Dagon, or Astaroth, or both. You know that of Cicero III. *de Nat. Deorum. Quarta Venus Syria Tyroque concepta quae Astarte* (that is *Astaroth*) *vocatur, quam Adonidi nupsisse traditum est.*[18] Ovid, Manilius, Hyginus, others have as much in substance.[19] & whencesoever the Latin Venus is derived (which very name might with little difficulty be with her rites thence traduced) it's certain that the Chaldeans called her by a word even almost interpreting Aphrodite. You know that is usually fetcht from ἄφρός

---

of the phrase in question: '*Liber Tomtom*, id est, de dubio eiusmodi sexu, antiquitùs scriptus, citatur Mosi Maimonidi in More Nebochim lib. III, cap. XXXVII, ubi legem (Deut. XXII, 5) de habitu sexum ementito explicat' (pp. 41–2).

[16] Johannes Buxtorf the elder (1564–1629) published several dictionaries and grammars of Hebrew as well as a four-volume Great Rabbinic Bible (Basel, 1618–19). His son, Johannes Buxtorf the younger (1599–1664), also a distinguished Hebraist, mentions in the introduction to his Latin translation of Maimonides' *Guide* (dated 1629) that he had seen Giustiniani's *Dux* six years before and had found it inadequate. One can therefore assume that the older Latin version was not available in the Buxtorf household at the time of Selden's letter. By the time of his *De Diis Syris* (1617), Selden will also be able to cite the Hebrew copy.

[17] 'The first rabbi to desist from nonsense.' See also *De Diis*, 191: 'R. Mose Ben-Maimon (qui primus Rabbinorum delirare desiit, & de quo, est apud Judaeos diverbium, a Mose usque ad Mosem, nequaquam fuisse hactenus talem Mosem).' The scholar 'of great place in the state of learning' is Joseph Scaliger. See Samuel Purchas in *Purchas His Pilgrimage, or Relations of the World and the Religions Observed in All Ages and Places Discovered, from the Creation unto this Present* (London, 1617). Purchas refers to Maimonides as 'our Rabbine (highly admired by a most admired Author)', whom he identifies in the margin: '*Jos. Scal. in Epist. ad Casaubon Omnia illius Magistri opera tanti facio, ut solum illum inter Iudaeos desiisse nugari dicam*' (p. 60).

[18] See Cicero, *De nat. deor.*, trans. H. Rackham (Cambridge, Mass.: Harvard University Press; London: Heinemann, 1979), 342. 'Syria Tyroque' probably should be 'Syria Cyproque': 'The fourth Venus was conceived of Syria and Cyprus, and is called Astarte. It is recorded that she married Adonis.'

[19] See *De Diis*, 178–9, which quotes Manilius, *Astronomicon*, bk. IV, on Venus's watery adventures, including her transformation into a fish.

[foam]. & they called her *Delephat*, derived, as it seems, from *Deleph* דלף i.[e.] *Stillatio*, which hath affinity enough with her shorter name ἀφρώ in Nicander.[20] Hesychius: Δελέφατ ὁ τῆς Ἀφροδίτης ἀστέρ,ᵏ ὑπὸ Χαλδαίων.[21] Her antiquity cannot be doubted of, seeing indeed she was truly the *Mater Deum* in Mythologie, and somewhere the old Scholiast on Apollonius, you may remember, delivers it from a Greek tradition, that she was the eldest of Deities. For Mars; he is affirmd the same with Baal or Belus, the most known & most ancient by name in any memorie of idolatrie, and that by authority of holy writ. He is remembered in *Numer.* XXII. *com. Ultimo.*[22] Both Cedren and the autor of the *Fasti* Siculi, out of ancient monuments, now lost, deliver, that in the Assyrian Empire, Thurus succeeded Ninus and that his father Zamis brother to Rhea nam'd him Ἄρης or Mars; & that he was the first to whom that nation erected columnes (columnes were at first the statues for Deities) and that they named him Baal, which say those autors, interprets Ἄρης πολέμου θεὸς [Ares the god of war]. They missed of the interpretation; for *Baal* signifies Lord or *Dominus*: But in the matter they were right, and doubtlesse well directed by some Asiatique autority. For the same Belus or Baal is by a most ancient historian, Hestiaeus, cited by Eusebius in his IX. *Proparasc. Evangel;* and in his Chronicle that's only in Greek, called Ζεὺς Ἐννάλιος [Zeus the god of war] or *Jupiter belli praeses*, where he speaks of his Temple, priests, and reliques of about the time of the confusion of Languages.[23] What is Ζεὺς Ἐννάλιος but Mars in the very particulars of fiction? Josephus *Orig. Judaic.ˡ I.* cap. VI. cites the same place of Hestiaeus, but it's misprinted Ἐννέλιος; it's some fault, but every one sees what it should be.[24] A greater errorᵐ about this name, is in the *Loci Ebraici* of S. Hierome, as they are

---

[20] *De Diis*, 193–4: 'Quod autem habet Hesychius, Chaldaeis & Assyriis Venerem Δελεφὰτ dictam, etiam iis quae Graeci & Latini de Venere tradunt satis est congruum. Delphah n. id est דלפה venereos amplexus denotare sive concubitum lingua Babylonica potest; nisi mauelis a דלפא Dilpha, i. gutta, seu stilla ita dictam, uti apud Graecos . . . ' Ἀφρώ appellatur. . . . '[But that according to Hesychius among the Chaldeans and Assyrians Venus is called Delephat is quite congruent with what Greeks and Latins say of her. For Delephat, in the Babylonian tongue, can denote venereal embraces, or intercourse, unless it is preferred to call her so from the word Dilpha, which means a little or a drop. Among the Greeks she is called Aphrodite, from Ἀφρώ, foam.] See also Nicander, *Alexipharmaca*, l. 406, in *Nicander: The Poems and Poetical Fragments*, ed. A. S. F. Gow and A. F. Schoolfield (Cambridge: Cambridge University Press, 1953), 120. This is the only place where the name Ἀφρώ is used for Aphrodite.

[21] *Hesychii Alexandrini Lexicon*, ed. Kurt Latte (Hauniae [Copenhagen]: E. Munksgaard, 1953), i. 416, δ590, a gloss on 'Delephat': 'The star of Aphrodite as called by the Chaldeans.'

[22] Numbers 22: 41: 'And it came to pass on the morrow, that Balak took Balaam, and brought him up into the high places of Baal.'

[23] Eusebius, *Preparation for the Gospel*, 416d, tr. Edwin Hamilton Gifford (Oxford: Clarendon Press, 1903; rpt. Grand Rapids: Baker, 1981), i. 448: 'Hestiaeus . . . speaks thus: "But those of the priests who escaped took the sacred things of Zeus Enyalios, and came to Sennaar in Babylonia: afterwards they were scattered thence, and everywhere formed their communities from speaking the same language. . . . "'

[24] Josephus, *Jewish Antiquities*, i. 119, in the Loeb edition, IV, 57, cites the same passage from Hestiaeus as Eusebius. The editor notes: 'the warlike (Enyo = Lat. Bellona), in Homer an epithet of Ares, here only applied to Mars.'

publisht; where the whole translation is of that[n] taken out of Hestiaeus (but not so acknowledged by the Father) & *Gemalij Jovis* is ridiculously for *Enyalij Jovis*[25] This by the way. & so much for the antiquity of these deities; which, being not made clear, hinders the autority of that historicall exposition out of Centir & Ben Maimon. Lesse doubt need be made of that kind of worship, by change of apparell. The self same was in Europe, where nothing of that kind was, if not traduced out of Asia. You best know that of Philochorus, an old Greek, in Macrobius *Saturnal.3. cap.* VIII.[26] He° makes Venus the same with the Moon (such confusion of names is frequent) & reports *ei² sacrificium facere viros cum veste muliebri, mulieres cum virili, quod eadem & mas aestimatur & femina.*[27] A masculin & feminin Venus differs not in the Gentiles['] Theologie[q] from Mars and Venus. For every deity was of both sexes and ἀρρηνόθηλυς [masculine and feminine], as the Egyptians held the Moon to be, which Plutarch reports, & as the old Hermes saies, in his *Poimander*, of the true GOD; well agreeing with that of the Schoolmen, *Masculinitas consignificata hoc nomine Deus, non ponitur circa Deum*, as Aquinas's words are.[28] And this very goddesse so distinguisht by that sex, whereof she was president, that they stiled her the feminin goddesse or θεάν γυναικείαν, & at whose sacrifices no kind of male creature was to be endured in the temple (for θεὰ γυναικεία was nothing but the *Bona Dea*; & *Bona Dea* is the same with Venus, which, beside other testimonies, is justified out of an old inscription on the Portal of her temple, the fragment whereof remains among others now in Arundel house;[29] thus conceived BONAE DEAE VENERI

---

[25] In the edition of St Jerome published by Migne in 1845, Jerome does refer to the historian Hestiaeus. Jerome's misreading of *enyalius* ('warlike') as *gemalius* is acknowledged with shame by the editor (*dicere erubesco* = I blush to say) and corrected. See *Liber de situ et nominibus locorum Hebraicorum* in Jerome, *Opera*, iii, no. 266 (Migne, *Pat. Lat.*, xxii, col. 1918).

[26] In Macrobius, *Saturnalia* 3.8.3, Aterianus claims to have read with Calvus of a powerful God Venus, not a goddess. He further reports the poet Laevius (or Laevinius) to venerate a masculine Venus, and finally gives the view of Philochorus quoted next.

[27] *Saturnalia* 3.8.3: 'That men sacrifice to her/it [*ei* is gender neutral] in female clothes, women in male attire, since one and the same is considered both male and female.'

[28] The presumed narrator Hermes Trismegistus reports that Poimander in a vision revealed to him the genesis of nature in this way: 'The mind who is god, being androgyne and existing as life and light, by speaking, gave birth to a second mind, a craftsman, who as god of fire and spirit, crafted seven governors ... [Man] is androgyne because he comes from an androgyne father.' *Hermetica*, ed. and trans. Brian Copenhaver (Cambridge: Cambridge University Press, 1992), 2–3. As to the Latin phrase quoted by Selden, 'The maleness connoted by the name *deus* is not [to be] applied to God,' Selden may be quoting it from some compendium, rather than directly from Aquinas (who does not use the word *masculinitas*). However, discussing the Trinity and particularly whether the Son is different (*alius* or *aliud*) from the Father, Aquinas makes the distinction between *significatio* (signification) and *consignificatio* (connotation) in his *Summa*: 'Praeterea, Alius & aliud idem significant; sed sola generis consignificatione differunt. Si ergo Filius est alius a Patre videtur sequi quod Filuius sid aliud a Patre.' He denies that the masculine gender connoted by *alius* is relevant with respect to God: 'Hoc autem nomen alius masculine sumptum, non importat nisi distinctione suppositi.'

[29] House of the Howards in the Strand. It passed to Philip Howard, 1st Earl of Arundel, in 1580; to Thomas Howard in 1607 (upon his restoration to the Earldom of Arundel), who stored in it his collection of marbles. Later in the century it was the meeting place of the Royal Society. The

CNIDIAE[30]) this goddesse so much nothing but Woman[r], was yet, of both sexes, mystically. *Pollentemque Deum Venerem*, saith Calvus in Macrobius; & there Laevius:[s] *Venerem igitur almum adorans sive femina sive mas est, ita ut alma noctiluca est.*[31] And in Rome was an armed, and in Cyprus a Bearded Venus.[32] Neither originally, by all likelyhood, was Venus & Mars other then the masculin-feminin or generative power supposed in the Sunne, or Sunne & Moon, which were the first creatures idolatrously worshipt. For wee must here think of these as they were Gods only, not Planets. And why may not we collect rationally in their Theologie, that, in regard of the masculin-foeminin power supposed in their worship deity, they counterfeited themselves to be masculin-foeminin in the adoration? Which could not be better done than by a woman's wearing armor, and a man's putting on a woman's garment. The more willingly I here note this community of sexes in every of the ancientest Gods, because also the Seventy interpreters conferred with the Ebrew, & with profane story, do most specially shew that community, & that not without reference, as it's[t] probably to be thought, to those very rites spoke of in *Ben Maimon*. No man has not heard of the name of Astarte or Astaroth, whom Cicero, Suidas, [and] others make but a Venus; Lucian & Achilles Tatius the moon; Philo of Byblus, in his Phoenician theologie out of Sanchoniathon, both Moon & Venus;[33] S. Augustin upon Judges & Plutarch in Crassus, Juno or Venus or what els is in that[u] kind feminin, the Greek interpreters in both numbers have her only feminin. And an old inscription is with ΘΕΑΣ ΣΙΔΩΝΟΣ [of the goddess of Sidon], for her questionlesse. Yet in the originall of I *Reg.* xi. *com.* 5. she is called אֱלֹהֵי צִדֹנִים Elohi Zidonim, i.[e.] Deus Zidoniorum; the Ebrew indeed having no word in the holy book expressing a Goddesse as *Dea* in Latin. So, that frequent name of Baal or in the plurall Baalim (not at all distinguisht by gender, in the originall scripture, saving that it is taken for masculin, as it signifies Lord, although the idolaters had their Baaleth or Beeleth for the feminin of Baal, which in Megasthenes, cited by Josephus & elsewhere, is Βῆλτις) is in the Greek sometimes of one and then of another gender, as if they would denote the masculin-foeminin quality attributed in the worship, as in *Numer. cap.* xxii.

house was demolished in 1678. See *The London Encyclopedia*, ed. Ben Weinreb and Christopher Hibbert.

[30] 'To the good godddess Venus of Cnidos.' The city of Cnidos was reputed to have the famous statue of Aphrodite made by Praxiteles.

[31] Again Macrobius, *Saturnalia*, 3.8.3 (see n. 26). 'The powerful god Venus' [both noun and adjective are masculine], says Calvus in Macrobius, and then Laevius is quoted 'to worship the gracious Venus [*Venerem almum*, where *almum* signals masc. gender] who is male or female according to how she shines by night'.

[32] In *De Diis* (p. 149), after citing Macrobius's view that for the Cypriots Venus was both male and female, Selden says: 'I submit that among the Greeks and Romans Venus was worshipped as both armed and bearded.'

[33] In *De Diis*, 151, Selden cites Philo of Byblus in greater detail to connect Astarte with the moon. Astarte is said to have placed the head of a bull on her head as the insignia of her royalty. After wandering over the earth, she found a star fallen from the air, which she consecrated to Tyrus, her

comm. ult. τοῦ Βαάλ [i. e., genitive] for Baal-Phegor. So is it in 4 *Reg.* cap. x, xi, and xvii. & in *Hos.* xi. tmemate 2 τοῖς Βααλεὶμ ἔθνον [they were sacrificing to Baal gods]. In *Jerem.* L,ᵛ for Bel (differing from Baal, but by dialect) Βῆλος ὁ ἀπτόητος [Bel the undaunted]³⁴ & divers other such places, are all for the masculin. Yet in mention of the same in *Hos.ii.comm.*8. is τῇ Βαάλ [to Baal, using feminine article]. So in *Jerem.ii.comm.* 23 (where the LXX exceedes the Ebrew by a few words³⁵) & *Zephan.* cap. i. *tmemate* 4. and in I *Samuel. cap.* vii. *com.* 13. τὰς Βαλεὶμ [also feminine].³⁶ So is the Ammonites Moloch, although usually known for a masculin Deity, yet nam'd for a Goddesse in the Greek. *Jerem. cap.*xix. *com.*5. the words are ᾠκοδόμησαν ὑψηλὰ τῇ Βαάλ τοῦ κατακαίειν τοὺς υἱοὺς αὐτῶν ἐν πυρί [They have built the high places to Baal (fem.), for whom they burnt their sons in fire] and in *cap.* xxxii. *tmem.* 35 they turne the text. *They built altars* ἐν τῇ Βαάλ (where ἐν [in], I think, abounds) *in the valley of the sonne of Ennom that they might offer their sonnes & their daughters* τῷ Μολόχ βασιλεῖ [to Moloch the king]. Are not here τῇ Βαάλ [to Baal, fem.] & τῷ Μολόχ [to Moloch, masc.] for the same? That which they call altars to Baal is in the originall the hie places of Baal. As here, so in 1 *Reg. cap.* xix. *comm.* 18. *And I will keep in Israel seven thousand all which have not bowed the knee* τῇ Βαὰλ, καὶ πᾶν σόμα ὅ οὐ προσεκύνησαν αὐτῷ [to Baal (fem.), and have not prostrated their whole body to him]. In these two places, you see, in the same verse they change the sex. This last is in part and more near the Ebrew truth alleged by St. Paule to the Romans, *cap* xi. *comm.* 4. where he hath also τῇ Βαάλ [i. e., feminine], yet follows not the LXX in the rest.³⁷ I know some would have εἰκόνι or δυνάμει [image or power, both fem. nouns in the dative] understood with τῇ [fem. dative sing. article] io[i]ned to Baal, & so save the diversity of gender. But under their favor the scriptures use will not enough justify it, although it be true too, that in *Tobit cap.*i.*com.*5. you have ἔθυον τοῦ Βαάλ τῇ δυνάμει [They used to sacrifice to the power of Baal], as some copies are; others beingʷ τῇ δαμάλει [to the calf (fem.)] in that place. To this purpose is it, that the Syrian God Dagon remembered as masculin in the holy text, is feminin to all European writers. What the Greeks & Latins have of Adargatis, Derceto, Atargata, Derce (all one name) & the like,³⁸ you best know being most conversant in the recondit parts of humane

sacred island. The passage connects the bull's head, the lambent flames that seemed to play and curve around her forehead, and the image of the moon that she carried before her.

³⁴ Jeremiah. 50: 2: 'say Babylon is taken, Bel is confounded'.

³⁵ In *De Diis* (p. 151), Selden explains what he means by the parenthesis: the shifting gender of the deity is recognized by the Septuagint, 'for they do not always make [Baal] feminine, but at one time masculine and at another feminine'. Jeremiah 2: 23: 'How canst thou say, I am not polluted, I have not gone after Baalim?'

³⁶ Zephaniah 1: 4: 'I will cut off the remant of Baal from this place'; and 1 Sam. 7: 4 (not 7: 13): 'Then the children of Israel did put away Baalim, and Ashtaroth, and served the Lord only.'

³⁷ Romans 11: 4: 'I have reserved to myself seven thousand men, who have not bowed the knee to the image of Baal.'

³⁸ On Ádir dag, Adargatis, Derceto, Derce, etc., see Ch. 2.

learning. That Adargatis or Atergatis (the Syrian Deity) was nothing else in origination of her name but אַדִיר דָג *Adirdag*, i.[e.] *Piscis sublimis* or *potens* [an imposingly tall or powerful fish]. And as profane story shewes that Adargatis was *mulier formosa supernè* [a good-looking woman above] ending in a fish (Lucian, Diodore, others iustify it) so in that text in I *Sam.cap.v.*4. where Dagon fell before the ark, & his head and hands were broken of[f], it is added, that only the forme of a fish, or so much as was fish was left of him.[39] So doth D. Cimchi & others understand it;[40] & well, against such as have with error fetcht the name from another word signifying wheat, & took Dagon for Jupiter frumentarius. Dagon then & Atergatis or Artaga (as Phurnutus calls it, somewhat nearer to Adirdag; the other names being varied rather by transposition of letters than ought else) will fall out to be all one, yet of both sexes. The Septuagint make it masculin, & above what is in the Ebrew, say that by the fall both the feet of it were broken of[f], which yet makes nothing against the being of it partly in forme of a fish.[x] For although neither the Ebrew speak of any feet it had, nor that[y] European writers, by their own testimonie, give their Atergatis more than a fish taile, yet upon examination of some Chaldean monuments, left by Berosus a Priest of Belus (I mean the true Berosus) it will appear both that the LXX, or who ever were the autors, did not add that of the feet without ground, and also that the ancientest goddesse or God worshipt by idolatrie in those parts was half of human forme, half fish, but so that out of the fish taile leggs of human shape came[z] as out of a mans body. For he (that is Berosus),[aa] out of reliques of antiquity left from the eldest of time in Babylon, reports that when in the beginning of things the Babylonians or Assyrians were altogether ignorant of what instruction might furnish them with, there came amongst them out of the red sea a creature called Oannes having a body of a fish & two heads, one of a fish, another human; & feet like a man growing out of the taile, that it had a voice like a man, that it taught the Assyrians all arts, laws, & what els fit for civil society;[41] & that to his time (he lived under Alexander) the statue

[39] 1 Samuel 5: 4: 'And when they arose early on the morrow morning, behold, Dagon was fallen upon his face to the ground, before the Arke of the Lord: and the head of Dagon, and both the palmes of his hands were cut off upon the threshold, only the stumpe of Dagon was left of him.'

[40] In *De Diis* (pp. 172–3), Selden explains that 'in Azotus or Asdodus, a renowned city of Palestine, there was a celebrated temple of Dagon, in which the inhabitants kept the ark of the covenant in presence of that idol'. Then he quotes 1 Samuel 5: 4 on how its head and both palms were cut off upon the threshold, until 'only the form of a fish was left of him, *uti R. D. Cimchi explicatur*' [as R. David Kimhi explains it]. Selden continues: 'He takes *Dag* and *Dagah* as fish, therefore he is called Dagon.' David Kimhi (1160–1235) of Narbonne, Provence, was a celebrated grammarian and exegete, whose writings were among the first Hebrew books to be printed, the earliest being the Psalms commentary (Bologna, 1477). His commentary on Samuel appeared with the first printing of the Hebrew Bible (Soncino, 1485).

[41] In his prologue to his *Babyloniaca*, Berossus, who identified himself as a priest of Bel during the time of Alexander, reports how the beast Oannes, shaped like a fish, but with a human head, revealed to people knowledge of letters and sciences. It said there had been a time when humans were born with two wings, two heads and a bisexual body, that is, both male and female. See Berossus, *Babyloniaca*, ed. Stanley Mayer Burstein (Malibu, Calif.: Undena, 1978), 13–14.

of it was kept, with divers other most portentous pieces of relation touching Belus & Omorca, which, although they be all fabulous, yet do enough prove both the antique forme supposed by the Septuagint in giving Dagon feet, & also their opinion of that marine Deity which in truth was nothing but Venus. *Scilicet in piscem sese Cytherea novavit*, saies Manilius.[42] Neither doubt I but that this Oannes, Dagon & Artaga were originally all one. You see Baal, Dagon, Moloch, Astargatis,[bb] the greatest names in the Eastern theologie of the Gentiles, were expressly noted by both sexes, & according to that mysterie of community of sexes, were worshipt. So had the Greeks Ἀφρόδιτος & Ἀφροδίτη [Aphroditos, masc., and Aphrodite], the Latins Lunus & Luna, which two were so had in divine honor in Mesopotamia as Spartian reports in his *Caracalla*, where, while the most learned Casaubon supposes the worship of the two sexes in one Deity among the Eastern people to proceed from nothing but because their names are, from severall roots, of both grammaticall genders, he doth not with tolerable performance second his own worth.[43] Clearly it was a mysterie of their theologie concluding upon the masculin-foeminin power which made both the worship, & grammaticall genders, not the trifles of grammar, their ceremonies of worship. But thus much of the truth or likelyhood of that reported rite in change of apparell, which whether it be well applied to the holy text, I will not affirm. In the connexion of these no vulgar observations, if they had been to the common learned reader, there had been often room for divers pieces of European Theologie disperst in Latin & Greek autors of the Gentiles & Fathers of the church too, and often for parts of mythologie, but your own most choise & able store cannot but furnish you incidently with whatever is fit that way to be thought of in the reading. With what ancient fathers as Cyprian & Tertullian specially have of this text, or others dealing on it as it tends to morality, I abstain to meddle. What ever this is which I have collected, I consecrate to your Love, & end with hope of your instructing iudgement.

From the Inner Temple this XXVIII. of Feb. CIƆ.DC.XV [1615].[44]

Endnotes: Variant Readings

a. freind] Friend
b. Jonson] Johnson

---

[42] Marcus Manilius, *Astronomica* 4. 579: 'Certain it is that the goddess of Cytharea changed herself into a fish' [when she plunged into the waters of Babylon to escape from snake-footed Typhon]. Tr. G. P. Goold (Cambridge, Mass., and London: Heinemann, 1977), 267–9.

[43] The famous philologist had commented on a reference by Aelianus Spartanus to a male god Lunus in his account of Antoninus Caracalla: 'Frivolous stuff aside, the reason why some should have taken this god for male and others for female and why some have used the name as masculine while others as feminine, we think, is that in the languages of the orient the names for Luna are taken to be of the male and female gender'. Isaac Casaubon, 'In Aeliani Spartiani Antonimum Caracalum, emendationes et notae', in *Scriptores Historiae Augustae*, ed. Claudius Salmasius (Paris, 1620), 132 (Casaubon's footnote to line 9).

[44] In the new style, this is 1616.

c. Greeks...follow] Greek...followeth
d. *Judaic. Archaeolog.*] *Archaeol.*
e. lustfull] least
f. sigles] six letters
g. *Yideoni*] [nothing]
h. with divers more such like] & c.
i. Comarim] *Cohanim*
j. *Director*] *Ductor*
k. ἀστέρ star (of Aphrodite)] ἀνὴρ husband (of Aphrodite)
l. *Judaic.*] *Jud.*
m. error] originally *fault* (crossed out in MS)
n. is of that] of that is
o. He] he
p. *ei*] in
q. Gentiles['] Theologie]*Gentilis Theologus*
r. Woman] a woman
s. Laevius] Laevinius
t. it's] its
u. that] the
v. L = 50] I
w. being] bring
x. in forme of a fish] in form of fish
y. that] your
z. originally *came forth* in MS, *forth* crossed out
aa. (that is Berosus)] not in MS
bb. Astargatis] Atargatis

Select Bibliography

PRIMARY SOURCES

AINSWORTH, HENRY, *Annotations Upon the Fifth Booke of Moses, called Deuteronomy* (1619; repr. London, 1639).

—— *Annotations upon the second book of Moses, called Exodus* (London, 1617).

AMES, WILLIAM, *The Marrow of Sacred Divinity*, tr. John St Nicholas (1642).

ARISTOPHANES, *Wasps*, ed. Douglas M. MacDowell (Oxford: Clarendon Press, 1971).

ASCHAM, ANTHONY, *A Discourse: Wherein is Examined, What is Particularly Lawfull during the Confusions and Revolutions of Government* (1648).

AUBREY, JOHN, *Aubrey's Brief Lives*, ed. Oliver Lawson Dick (London: Secker and Warburg, 1949).

AUGUSTINE, *City of God*, ed. David Knowles, tr. Henry Bettenson (Harmondsworth: Penguin, 1972).

AUSONIUS, ed. and trans. Hugh G. Evelyn White, Loeb Classical Library, 2 vols. (London: Heinemann; New York: Putnam, 1919).

BABINGTON, GERVASE, *Comfortable Notes upon the Five Bookes of Moses*, in *Works* (1622).

BACON, FRANCIS, *The Essays* (Harmondsworth: Penguin, 1985).

BAILLIE, ROBERT, *Letters and Journals of Robert Baillie*, ed. D. Laing (Edinburgh, 1861).

BARLOW, THOMAS, *Analecta De Judaeis in Reipublica Christiana tolerandis, vel de novo admittendis, Several Miscellaneous and Weighty Cases of Conscience* (1692).

BEARD, THOMAS, *The Theater of Gods Judgements* (London, 1597).

BEROSSUS, *Babyloniaca*, ed. Stanley Mayer Burstein (Malibu, Calif.: Undena, 1978).

BIBLE, *The Book of Job*, ed. Raymond P. Scheindlin (New York and London: W. W. Norton, 1998).

—— *The Five Books of Moses*, ed. and tr. Robert Alter (New York and London: W. W. Norton, 2004).

—— *The Holy Bible* Geneva (1560).

—— *The Holy Bible* (London, 1611).

—— *Miqraot Gedolot* [Biblia Rabbinica], 15 vols. (Lublin, n.d.).

—— The New Revised Standard Version, *The New Oxford Annotated Bible*, ed. Bruce Metzger and Roland E. Murphy (New York: Oxford University Press, 1991).

—— *The New Testament*, tr. the English college then resident in Rheims (Antwerp, 1600).

—— *Torat Chaim Chumash*, Pentateuch with rabbinic commentaries, 6 vols. (Jerusalem: Mossad Harav Kook, 1986).

BORDE, ANDREW, *The Fyrst Boke of the Introduction of Knowledge* (*c.* 1560).

BOWYER, WILLIAM, 'REMARKS on a SPEECH made in COMMON COUNCIL, on the Bill for permitting Persons professing the JEWISH Religion to be Naturalized, so far as Prophecies are supposed to be affected by it' [1753], collected in William Bowyer, *Miscellaneous Tracts*, ed. John Nichols (London, 1785), 453–55.

BULLOUGH, GEOFFREY (ed.), *Narrative and Dramatic Sources of Shakespeare*, 8 vols. (New York: Columbia University Press, 1973).

BURTON, HENRY, *A Vindication of Churches Commonly Called Independent* (1644).

Cajetan Responds: A Reader in Reformation Controversy, ed. Jared Wicks, SJ (Washington, DC: Catholic University of America Press, 1978).

Calendar of . . . State Papers . . . Relating to the Negotiations between England and Spain (1485–1509), 13 vols. in 18 (London: Longman, 1862–1954): vols. i and ii ed. G. A. Bergenroth; vols. iii–vii ed. Pascual de Gayangos.

CALVIN, JOHN, *Institutes of the Christian Religion*, ed. John T. McNeill and Ford Lewis Battles (Philadelphia: Westminster Press, 1960).

—— *Commentaries on the Four Last Books of Moses*, tr. C. W. Bingham (1850; rpt. Grand Rapids: Eerdmans, 1950).

CASAUBON, ISAAC, *Animadversionum in Athenaeum Dipnosophistas* (1621).

—— *Epistolae insertis ad easdem responsibus* (Rotterdam, 1709).

—— 'In Aelii Spartiani Antoninum Caracallum, emendationes et notae', in *Scriptores Historiae Augustae*, ed. Claudius Salmasius (Paris, 1620).

CICERO, MARCUS TULLIUS, *De natura deorum*, trans. H. Rackham (Cambridge, Mass.: Harvard University Press; London: Heinemann, 1979).

CLEVELAND, JOHN, *Poems*, ed. Brian Morris and Eleanor Withington (Oxford: Clarendon Press, 1967).

Commons Debates, 1628, ed. R. C. Johnson et al., 6 vols. (New Haven: Yale University Press, 1977–83).

Commons Debates for 1629, ed. Wallace Notestein and Frances H. Relf, University of Minnesota Studies in Social Sciences, 10 (Minneapolis, 1921).

CULVERWEL, NATHANAEL, *An Elegant and Learned Discourse of the Light of Nature* (1652).

—— *An Elegant and Learned Discourse of the Light of Nature*, ed. Robert A. Greene and Hugh MacCallum (Toronto: University of Toronto Press, 1972).

DARBISHIRE, HELEN (ed.) *The Early Lives of Milton* (London: Constable, 1932).

DIODATI, JOHN, *Pious and Learned Annotations upon the Holy Bible* (London, 1651).

The Divorce Tracts of Henry VIII [1531], ed. Edward Surtz, SJ, and Virginia Murphy (Angers: Moreana, 1988).

ELLIS, SIR HENRY (ed.), *Original Letters of Eminent Literary Men of the Sixteenth, Seventeenth, and Eighteenth Centuries* (London: Camden Society, 1843).

Encyclopedia Judaica (Jerusalem: Keter, 1972).

EURIPIDES, trans. Arthur S. Way, Loeb Classical Library, 4 vols. (London: Heinemann; New York: G. P. Putnam, 1916).

EUSEBIUS OF CAESAREA, *Preparation for the Gospel*, tr. Edwin Hamilton Gifford, 2 vols. (Oxford: Clarendon Press, 1903; rpt. Grand Rapids: Baker, 1981).

FISHER, JOHN, *De Causa Matrimonii Serenissimi regis Angliae liber* (Alcalá, 1530).

FORREST, WILLIAM, *The History of Grisild the Second: A Narrative, in Verse, of the Divorce of Queen Katherine of Aragon*, ed. W. D. Macray (London: Whittingham and Wilkins, 1875).

FOXE, JOHN, *Actes and Monuments of these Latter and Perillous Days* (1563; rpt. Stationers' Company, 1684).

FRAZER, Sir JAMES GEORGE, *Totemism and Exogamy* (London: Macmillan, 1910).

FREUD, SIGMUND, *The Origins of Psychoanalysis*, ed. Marie Bonaparte, Anna Freud, and Ernst Kris (New York: Basic Books, 1954).

FULLER, THOMAS, *A Pisgah-sight of Palestine and the confines thereof* (1650).

GIBBON, EDWARD, *The History of the Decline and Fall of the Roman Empire*, ed. David Womersley, 3 vols. (London: Penguin, 1994).

GOSSON, STEPHEN, *Plays Confuted in Five Actions* (London: Thomas Gosson, 1582).

GOUGE, WILLIAM, *Of Domesticall Duties* (London, 1622).

GRATIAN, *Decretum Gratiani* (Venice, 1605).

GROTIUS, HUGO, *The Rights of War and Peace* [*De Jure Belli ac Pacis*, 1625], ed. J. Barbeyrac, trans. anon. (London, 1738). [*DJB*]

HARPSFIELD, NICHOLAS, *A Treatise on the Pretended Divorce between Henry VIII and Catherine of Aragon* [1556], ed. Nicholas Pocock (Westminster: Camden Society, 1878).

HARRINGTON, JAMES, *The Political Works of James Harrington*, ed. J. G. A. Pocock (Cambridge: Cambridge University Press, 1977).

HEGEL, G. W. F., *Hegel's Lectures on the Philosophy of Religion*, ed. and trans. E. B. Spiers and J. Burdon-Sanderson (London: Routledge, 1974).

Hermetica, ed. and trans. Brian P. Copenhaver (Cambridge: Cambridge University Press, 1992).

HERRICK, ROBERT, *Poetical Works*, ed. F. W. Moorman (Oxford: Clarendon Press, 1915).

HESYCHIUS OF ALEXANDRIA, *Hesychii Alexandrini Lexicon*, ed. Kurt Latte, 2 vols. (Hauniae [Copentagen]: E. Munksgaard, 1953).

HEYLYN, PETER, *Life of William Laud* (London, 1671).

HOBBES, THOMAS, *De Cive* (Paris, 1642; Amsterdam, 1647).

—— *De Cive*, ed. Howard Warrender (Oxford: Clarendon Press, 1983).

—— *Leviathan*, ed. Richard Tuck (Cambridge: Cambridge University Press, 1996).

HOLINSHED, RAPHAEL, *Chronicles of England, Scotland, and Ireland*, 6 vols. (1587; rpt. London: J. Johnson, 1808).

HOOKER, RICHARD, *Works: The Folger Library Edition*, gen. ed. W. Speed Hill, 7 vols. (Cambridge, Mass.: Harvard University Press, 1977).

JONSON, BEN, *The Alchemist*, ed. Gordon Campbell, Oxford World's Classics (Oxford and New York: Oxford University Press, 1995).

—— *Bartholomew Fair*, ed. G. R. Hibbard, New Mermaid (London: Ernest Benn, 1977).

—— *Bartholomew Fair*, ed. E. A. Horsman, The Revels Plays (London: Methuen, 1960).

—— *Ben Jonson*, ed. C. H. Herford, Percy Simpson, and Evelyn Simpson, 11 vols. (Oxford: Clarendon Press, 1925–52).

—— *Ben Jonson's Conversations with William Drummond of Hawthornden*, ed. R. F. Patterson (1922; rpt. New York: Haskell House, 1974).

—— *Epicoene*, ed. Aurelia Henry (New York: Henry Holt, 1906).

—— *Epicoene*, ed. Edward Partridge (New Haven and London: Yale University Press, 1971).

JOSEPHUS, ed. H. St J. Thackeray, R. Marcus, and L. Feldman, Loeb Classical Library, 10 vols. (London: Heinemann; Cambridge, Mass.: Harvard University Press, 1926–81).

[KEN, THOMAS], ICHABOD: OR, *Five Groans of the Church* (Cambridge, 1663).

LATIMER, HUGH, *Sermons and Remains*, ed. George Elwes Corrie, Parker Society (Cambridge: Cambridge University Press, 1845).

Letters and Papers, Foreign and Domestic, of the Reign of Henry VIII, ed. J. S. Brewer (London: Longman, 1876).

LIGHTFOOT, JOHN, *The Harmony, Chronicle and Order of the Old Testament* (1647).

—— *Horae Hebraicae et Talmudicae. In Evangelium Matthaei* (Cambridge, 1658).

—— *The Journal of the Proceedings of the Assembly of Divines*, vol. xiii in *The Whole Works of the Rev. John Lightfoot, D.D.*, ed. John Rogers Pitman (1822).

LOCKE, JOHN, *Correspondence*, ed. E. S. de Beer, 8 vols. (Oxford: Clarendon Press, 1976–89).

—— *A Letter Concerning Toleration, tr. William Popple [1689]*, ed. John Horton and Susan Mendus (London and New York: Routledge, 1991).

—— *Two Treatises of Government*, ed. Peter Laslett (Cambridge: Cambridge University Press, 1967).

LOWTH, ROBERT, *Lectures on the Sacred Poetry of the Hebrews* (1753), tr. Richard Gregory (1787); rpt. in John Drury, ed., *Critics of the Bible: 1724–1873* (Cambridge: Cambridge University Press, 1989), 69–102.

LOWTH, SIMON, *Of the Subject of Church-Power* (London, 1685).

LUTHER, MARTIN, *Works*, gen. ed. Jaroslav Pelikan, 55 vols. (St Louis: Concordia, 1955–86).

MACROBIUS, AMBROSIUS AURELIUS THEODOSIUS, *The Saturnalia*, tr. Percival Vaughan Davies (New York: Columbia University Press, 1969).

MAIMONIDES, MOSES, *De Idololatria*, tr. Dionysius Vossius, in Gerardus Vossius, *De Theologia Gentili*, 3 vols. (Amsterdam, 1641; rpt. New York and London: Garland, 1976).

—— *Dux sive director dubitantium . . . aut perplexorum*, tr. Agostino Giustiniani (Paris, 1520).

—— *The Guide of the Perplexed, More Nebuchim: Doctor Perplexorum*, tr. Johann Buxtorf (the Younger) (Basel, 1629).

—— *The Guide of the Perplexed*, tr. Slomo Pines, introd. Leo Strauss (Chicago: University of Chicago Press, 1963).

—— *Mishneh Torah*, 6 vols. (Vilna: Rosencranz and Schriftsetzer, 1900).

MANILIUS, MARCUS, *Astronomica*, trans G. P. Goold (Cambridge, Mass., and London: Heinemann, 1977).

MARTIAL, *Epigrams*, ed. and trans. Walter C. A. Ker, Loeb Classical Library, 2 vols. (London: Heinemann; New York: Putnam's, 1930).

MARVELL, ANDREW, *The Prose Works of Andrew Marvell*, gen. ed. Annabel Patterson, 2 vols. (New Haven and London: Yale University Press, 2003).

MATHER, INCREASE, *Ichabod, or a discourse shewing what cause there is to fear that the glory of the Lord is departing from New-England* (Boston, 1702).

MILTON, JOHN, *Complete Poems and Major Prose*, ed. Merritt Y. Hughes (New York: Odyssey Press, 1957).

—— *The Complete Prose Works of John Milton*, gen. ed. Don M. Wolfe, 8 vols. (New Haven: Yale University Press, 1953–82). [*YP*]

—— *The Latin Poems of John Milton*, tr. Walter MacKellar (New Haven: Yale University Press, 1930).

—— *The Life Records of John Milton*, compiled by J. Milton French, 5 vols. (New Brunswick, NJ: Rutgers University Press, 1949–58).

—— *Paradise Lost*, ed. Scott Elledge (New York and London: W. W. Norton, 1993).

—— *The Poems of John Milton*, ed. John Carey and Alastair Fowler (London: Longmans, 1968; 2nd edn. 1998).

—— *Works*, gen. ed. Frank Allen Patterson, 18 vols. in 21 (New York: Columbia University Press, 1931–8).

Minutes of the Sessions of the Westminster Assembly of Divines, ed. Alex F. Mitchell and John Struthers (Edinburgh and London: Blackwood, 1874).

MODENA, LEON [Leone da Modena], *The Life of Judah: The Autobiography of a Seventeenth-Century Venetian Rabbi*, ed. Mark R. Cohen (Princeton: Princeton University Press, 1988).

MORE, HENRY, *An Explanation of the Grand Mystery of Godliness* (1660).

NALSON, JOHN, ed., *Impartial Collection of the Great Affairs of State from the Scotch Rebellion to the King's Murther*, 2 vols. (1682–3).

NICANDER of COLOPHON, *Nicander: The Poems and Poetical Fragments*, ed. A. S. F. Gow and A. F. Schoolfield (Cambridge: Cambridge University Press, 1953).

NICOLSON, MARJORIE HOPE (ed.), *The Correspondence of Anne, Viscountess Conway, Henry More, and their Friends, 1642–1684* (New Haven: Yale University Press, 1930).

PARKER, SAMUEL, *A Defence and Continuation of the Ecclesiastical Politie* (1671).

—— *A Discourse of Ecclesiastical Politie* (1669).

—— *A Free and Impartial Censure of the Platonick Philosophie* (1666).

—— *A Reproof to the Rehearsal Transpros'd* (1673).

Patrologia Latina, ed. J.-P. Migne, 221 vols. (1844–55, 1862–5).

PAUL, *The Writings of St. Paul*, ed. Wayne A. Meeks (New York: W. W. Norton, 1972).

PENN, WILLIAM, *Select Works. To Which is Prefixed a Journal of His Life* (London, 1771).

PETER MARTYR *A Commentarie upon the Book of Judges* (London: John Day, 1564).

PHILO, ed. F. H. Colson, George Herbert Whitaker, and Ralph Marcus, Loeb Classical Library, 10 vols. (London: Heinemann; Cambridge, Mass.: Harvard University Press, 1929–62).

PHOTIUS OF CONSTANTINOPLE, *Nomocanon, Canones S.S. Apostolorum Conciliorum* (Paris, 1620).

PLATO, *Symposium*, trans. Walter Hamilton (Harmondsworth: Penguin, 1951).

POOLE, MATTHEW, *Annotations Upon the Holy Bible* (1683; 3rd edn., 1696).

PRYNNE, WILLIAM, *Historio-Mastix. The Players Scourge, or, Actors Tragedie* (London: Michael Sparke, 1633).

—— *A Short Demurrer to the Jewes Long Discontinued Remitter into England* (London, 1656).

PUFENDORF, SAMUEL, *De jure naturae et gentium libri octo* [1672] [*On the Law of Nature and Nations in Eight Books*], ed. Jean Barbeyrac, trans. Basil Kennet, 5th edn. (1749).

PURCHAS, SAMUEL, *Purchas His Pilgrimage, or Relations of the World and the Religions Observed in All Ages and Places Discovered, from the Creation unto this Present* (London, 1617).

RADIN P. (ed.), *Pamphlets Relating to the Jews in England in the 17th and 18th Centuries* (San Francisco: California State Library, 1939).

Records of the Reformation: The Divorce 1527–1533, ed. Nicholas Pocock, 2 vols. (Oxford: Clarendon Press, 1870).

ROGERS, RICHARD, *A Commentary upon the Whole Booke of Judges, preached first and delivered in sundrie lectures* (London: Felix Kyngston, 1615).

RUBENS, PETER PAUL, *Letters*, ed. Ruth Saunders Magurn (Evanston: Northwestern University Press, 1955).

—— *Correspondance de Rubens et documents épistolaires concernant sa vie et ses œuvres*, ed. Charles Ruelens and Max Rooses (Antwerp: Veuve de Backer, 1887–1909).

RUSHWORTH, JOHN, *Historical Collections*, 8 vols. (1721).

SCALIGER, JOSEPH, *Epistolae* (Lugduni Batavorum [Leiden], 1627).

SCLATER, WILLIAM, *The Crowne of Righteousness* (1654).

SELDEN, JOHN, *Ad Fletam Dissertatio*, ed. David Ogg (Cambridge: Cambridge University Press, 1925).

—— Bodleian Library MSS, supra 108 and 123.

—— *De Anno Civili et Calendario Veteris Ecclesiae seu Reipublicae Judaicae* (1644).

—— *De Diis Syris* (1st edn. 1617; 2nd edn. 1629).

—— *De Diis Syris*, partial tr. by William Hauser under title *The Fabulous Gods Denounced in the Bible* (Philadelphia: Lippincott, 1880).

—— *The Duello Or Single Combat: From Antiquitie derived into this Kingdome of England* (1610).

—— *Historie of Tithes* (1618).

—— *De Jure Naturali et Gentium juxta Disciplinam Ebraeorum* (1640).

—— *De Successione in Pontificatum Ebraeorum* (1636).

—— *De Successionibus ad Leges Ebraeorum in Bona Defunctorum* (1631, 1636).

—— *De Synedriis et Praefecturis Juridicis Veterum Ebraeorum* (1650–5).

—— *Ioannes Seldeni vindiciae secundum integritatem existimationis suae*...(London, 1653).

—— *Of the Dominion, or Ownership of the Sea* [*Mare Clausum*], tr. Marchamont Nedham (London, 1652).

—— *Opera Omnia*, ed. David Wilkins, 3 vols. in 6 (1726).

—— *Table Talk*, ed. Sir Frederick Pollock (London: Quaritch, 1927).

—— *Table Talk*, ed. Samuel Harvey Reynolds (Oxford: Clarendon Press, 1892).

—— *Titles of Honor* (1614, rev. 1631).

—— *Uxor Ebraica* (1646)

—— *Uxor Ebraica*, tr. Jonathan R. Ziskind as *John Selden on Jewish Marriage Law* (Leiden and New York: E. J. Brill, 1991).

—— 'John Selden's Letter to Ben Jonson on Cross-Dressing and Bisexual Gods [with text']', ed. Jason P. Rosenblatt and Winfried Schleiner, *English Literary Renaissance*, 29 (1999), 44–74.

SHAKESPEARE, WILLIAM, *Hamlet*, ed. Joseph Quincy Adams (Cambridge, Mass.: Riverside, 1929).

—— *King Henry VIII, or All is True*, ed. Jay Halio (Oxford: Oxford University Press, 1999).

—— *The Merchant of Venice: Text and Context*, ed. M. Lindsay Kaplan (Boston and New York: Bedford/St Martin's, 2002).

—— *The Norton Shakespeare Based on the Oxford Edition*, gen. ed. Stephen Greenblatt (New York and London: W. W. Norton, 1997).

—— *Twelfth Night*, ed. J. M. Lothian and T. W. Craik, Arden Shakespeare (London: Methuen, 1975).

STEINSCHNEIDER, MORITZ (ed.), *Catalogus Hebraeorum in Bibliotheca Bodleiana* (1852–60; rept. Hildesheim: G. Olms, 1964).

STILLINGFLEET, EDWARD, *Irenicum. A Weapon-Salve for the Churches Wounds. Or The Divine Right of Particular Forms of Church-Government; Discussed and examined according to the Principles of the Law of Nature, the positive Laws of God, the practice of the Apostles and the Primitive Church, and the judgement of Reformed Divines. Whereby a foundation is laid for the Churches peace, and the accommodation of our present differences* (London, 1661)

STUBBE, HENRY, *The Common-wealth of Israel, or A Brief Account of Mr. Prynne's Anatomy of the Good Old Cause* (London, 1659).

—— *An Essay in Defence of the Good Old Cause or A Discourse concerning the Rise and Extent of the power of the Civil Magistrate in reference to Spiritual Affairs* (1659).

—— *Rosemary & Bayes: Or, Animadversions upon a Treatise Called, The Rehearsall Transprosed. In a letter to a Friend in the Countrey* (1672).

STUBBES, PHILIP, *The Anatomie of Abuses* (London: Richard Jones, 1583).

Students admitted to the Inner Temple, 1547–1660 (privately printed, 1877).

TACITUS, CORNELIUS, *The Histories and the Annals*, ed. Clifford H. Moore and John Jackson, Loeb Classical Library, 4 vols. (London: Heinemann; Cambridge, Mass.: Harvard University Press, 1951–2).

TALMUD, BABYLONIAN, *Der babylonische Talmud . . . nach der ersten, zensurfreien bombergschen ausg. (Venedig, 1520–23)*, 9 vols. (Berlin: S. Calvary, 1897–1935).

—— (Vilna: Romm, 1866).

——, with translation and commentary in modern Hebrew, ed. Adin Steinsaltz, 35 vols. completed so far (Jerusalem: Institute for Talmudic Publications, 1976–).

The Talmud [English], gen. ed. I. Epstein, 18 vols. (London: Soncino, 1978).

TAYLOR, JEREMY, *Ductor Dubitantium, or The Rule of Conscience in all Her General Measures* (London, 1660; 2d ed. 1671).

TERTULLIAN, *Treatises on Marriage and Remarriage* (Westminster, Md.: Newman Press, 1951).

TOLAND, JOHN, *Nazarenus: Or, Jewish, Gentile, and Mahometan Christianity* (London, 1718).

—— *Reasons for naturalizing the Jews in Great Britain and Ireland, On the same foot with other nations. Containing also, a Defence of the Jews against all vulgar Prejudices in all Countries* (1714).

TYNDALE, WILLIAM, *The Practice of Prelates* [1530], ed. Henry Walter for the Parker Society (Cambridge: Cambridge University Press, 1849).

VAUGHAN, Sir JOHN, *Reports and* Arguments, *being All of them Special Cases, & many wherein he Pronounced the Resolution of the whole Court of Common pleas*, ed. Edward Vaughan (London, 1677),

VANE, Sir HENRY, *Retired Man's Meditations* (1656).

VICO, GIAMBATTISTA, *The New Science of Giambattista Vico*, rev. trans. of the 3rd edn. (1744), ed. Thomas Goddard Bergin and Max Harold Fisch (Ithaca, NY: Cornell University Press, 1968).

—— *Opera*, ed. Benedetto Croce, Giovanni Gentile, and Fausto Nicolini, 8 vols. in 11 (Bari: Laterza, 1911–41).

VICO, GIAMBATTISTA, *Vico: Selected Writings*, ed. Leon Pompa (Cambridge: Cambridge University Press, 1982).

VIVES, JUAN LUIS, *Apologia sive Confutation*...(1531).

—— *The Instruction of a Christian Woman*, trans. Richard Hyrde (1529; rpt. London, 1592).

WAKEFIELD, ROBERT, *On the Three Languages* [London, 1524], ed. and trans. G. Lloyd Jones (Binghamton, NY: Medieval and Renaissance Texts and Studies, 1989).

WALTON, BRIAN, *Memoirs of the Life and Writings of the Right Rev. Brian Walton*, ed. Rev. Henry John Todd (1821).

WEEMSE, JOHN, *An Exposition of the Lawes of Moses* (London, 1632).

WHITELOCK, BULSTRODE, *Memorials of the English Affairs, 1625–1660* [1682], 4 vols. (Oxford, 1853).

WILLET, ANDREW, *Hexapla in Exodus* (London, 1633).

—— *Hexapla in Leviticum* (London, 1631).

—— *Synopsis in Papismi* (London, 1594).

WOOD, ANTHONY à, *Athenae Oxonienses*, ed. Philip Bliss, 6 vols. (London: F. C. & J. Rivington, 1891–1900).

—— *The Life and Times of Anthony Wood, antiquary of Oxford*, ed. Andrew Clark, 5 vols. (Oxford: Clarendon Press, for Oxford Historical Society, 1891).

SECONDARY SOURCES

ADELMAN, JANET, *Suffocating Mothers: Fantasies of Maternal Origin in Shakespeare's Plays, 'Hamlet' to 'The Tempest'* (London and New York: Routledge, 1992).

ALTMANN, ALEXANDER, 'William Wollaston (1659–1724), English Deist and Rabbinic Scholar', *Transactions of the Jewish Historical Society of England*, 16 (1945–51), 185–211.

ASSMANN, JAN, *Moses the Egyptian: The Memory of Egypt in Western Monotheism* (Cambridge, Mass., and London: Harvard University Press, 1997).

BAKER, J. WAYNE, *Heinrich Bullinger and the Covenant* (Athens, Ohio: Ohio University Press, 1980).

BARBOUR, REID, *John Selden: Measures of the Holy Commonwealth in Seventeenth-Century England* (Toronto: University of Toronto Press, 2003).

BARKER, ARTHUR E., 'Calm Regained Through Passion Spent: The Conclusions of the Miltonic Effort', in *The Prison and the Pinnacle*, ed. Balachandra Rajan (London: Routledge & Kegan Paul, 1973), 3–48.

BENNETT, JOAN S., *Reviving Liberty: Radical Christian Humanism in Milton's Great Poems* (Cambridge, Mass.: Harvard University Press, 1989).

BERKOWITZ, DAVID SANDLER, *John Selden's Formative Years: Politics and Society in Early Seventeenth-Century England* (Washington, DC: Folger Shakespeare Library, 1988).

BERLIN, ISAIAH, *The Crooked Timber of Humanity*, ed. Henry Hardy (Princeton: Princeton University Press, 1990).

—— *Three Critics of the Enlightenment: Vico, Hamann, Herder*, ed. Henry Hardy (Princeton: Princeton University Press, 2000).

BLOOM, HAROLD, *A Map of Misreading* (New York: Oxford University Press, 1975).

BOOTH, STEPHEN, 'On the Value of *Hamlet*', in Norman Rabkin, ed., *Reinterpretations of Elizabethan Drama*, Selected papers of the English Institute (New York and London: Columbia University Press, 1969), 137–76.

BOGUE, DAVID, and BENNETT, JAMES, *History of Dissenters* (London, 1812).

BURNS, NORMAN T., '"Then Up Stood Phinehas": Milton's Antinomianism and Samson's', in Albert C. Labriola, ed., *The Miltonic Samson, Milton Studies*, 33 (Pittsburgh: University of Pittsburgh Press, 1996), 27–46.

CHERNAIK, WARREN, and DZELZAINIS, MARTIN, eds. *Marvell and Liberty* (New York: St Martin's, 1999).

COHEN, JEREMY, *Living Letters of the Law: Ideas of the Jew in Medieval Christianity* (Berkeley: University of California Press, 1999).

CHRISTIANSON, PAUL, *Discourse on History, Law, and Governance in the Public Career of John Selden, 1610–1635* (Toronto: University of Toronto Press, 1996).

CROMARTIE, ALAN, *Sir Matthew Hale (1609–1676)* (Cambridge: Cambridge University Press, 1995).

DAVIES, W. D., *Paul and Rabbinic Judaism* (London: SPCK, 1955).

DONALDSON, E. T., 'Chaucer the Pilgrim', *PMLA* 69 (1954), 928–36.

DOUGLAS, MARY, *In the Wilderness: The Doctrine of Defilement in the Book of Numbers* (Sheffield: Sheffield Academic Press, 1993).

DRAPER, JOHN W., *The Hamlet of Shakespeare's Audience* (Durham, NC: Duke University Press, 1938).

DRIVER, S. R., PLUMMER, ALFRED, BRIGGS, C. A., gen. eds. *Deuteronomy: The International Critical Commentary* (Edinburgh: T. & T. Clark, 1895).

DRURY, JOHN, *The Parables in the Gospels* (New York: Crossroad, 1985).

EMPSON, WILLIAM, '*Hamlet* When New', *Sewanee Review*, 61 (1953), 15–42, 185–205.

—— *Milton's God* (Cambridge: Cambridge University Press, 1961; repr. 1981).

EPSTEIN, I., LEVINE, E., ROTH, C., eds., *Essays in Honour of the Very Rev. Dr. J. H. Hertz* (London: Edward Goldston, 1942).

ERLICH, AVI, *Hamlet's Absent Father* (Princeton: Princeton University Press, 1977).

FALLON, STEPHEN M., *Milton among the Philosophers: Poetry and Materialism in Seventeenth-Century England* (Ithaca, NY, and London: Cornell University Press, 1991).

FELDMAN, LOUIS H., *Jew and Gentile in the Ancient World: Attitudes and Interactions from Alexander to Justinian* (Princeton: Princeton University Press, 1993).

FLATTER, RICHARD, *Hamlet's Father* (London: Heinemann, 1949).

FORDE, DARYLL, and RADCLIFFE-BROWN, A. R., eds., *African Kinship and Marriage* (London: Oxford University Press, 1950).

GARDINER, S. R., in *A History of England under the Duke of Buckingham and Charles I. 1624–1628*, 2 vols. (London: Longmans, 1875).

—— *History of the Great Civil War 1642–1649*, 4 vols. (London, New York, Bombay: Longmans, Green, 1901).

GESENIUS, WILLIAM, *Hebrew and English Lexicon of the Old Testament*, tr. Edward Robinson, rev. Francis Brown, S. R. Driver, and Charles A. Briggs (Oxford: Clarendon Press, 1962).

GOLDENBERG, ROBERT, 'Talmud', in Barry W. Holtz, ed., *Back to the Sources: Reading the Classic Jewish Texts* (New York: Summit Books, 1984), 129–75.

GOLDISH, MATT, *Judaism in the Theology of Sir Isaac Newton* (Dordrecht: Kluwer, 1998).

GOODY, JACK, ed., *The Character of Kinship* (Cambridge: Cambridge University Press, 1973).

GOSHEN-GOTTSTEIN, MOSHE, 'Foundations of Biblical Philology in the Seventeenth-Century Christian and Jewish Dimensions', in Isadore Twersky and Bernard Septimus, eds., *Jewish Thought in the Seventeenth Century* (Cambridge, Mass., and London: Harvard University Press, 1987), 77–94.

GRAFTON, ANTHONY, *The Footnote: A Curious History* (Cambridge, Mass.: Harvard University Press, 1997).

——*Joseph Scaliger: A Study in the History of Classical Scholarship*, 2 vols. (Oxford: Clarendon Press, 1983).

GUIBBORY, ACHSAH, *Ceremony and Community from Herbert to Milton: Literature, Religion, and Cultural Conflict in Seventeenth-Century England* (Cambridge: Cambridge University Press, 1998).

GUILLORY, JOHN, 'The Father's House: *Samson Agonistes* in its Historical Moment', in Mary Nyquist and Margaret W. Ferguson, eds., *Re-Membering Milton: Essays on the Texts and Traditions* (New York and London: Methuen, 1987), 148–76.

HAAKONSSEN, KNUD, ed., *Grotius, Pufendorf and Natural Law* (Aldershot: Ashgate, 1999).

HALBERTAL, MOSHE, and MARGALIT, AVISHAI, *Idolatry*, tr. Naomi Goldblum (Cambridge, Mass.: Harvard University Press, 1992).

HARRISON, JOHN, *The Library of Isaac Newton* (Cambridge: Cambridge University Press, 1997).

HASKIN, DAYTON, *Milton's Burden of Interpretation* (Philadelphia: University of Pennsylvania Press, 1994).

HECHT, ANTHONY, *The Hard Hours* (New York: Atheneum, 1981).

HEINEMANN, ISAAK, *Darchei HaAggadah* (Jerusalem: Magnus, 1970).

HELLER, MARVIN J., *The Sixteenth Century Hebrew Book: An Abridged Thesaurus*, 2 vols. (Leiden and Boston: Brill, 2004).

HERZOG, ISAAC, 'John Selden and Jewish Law', in Chaim Herzog, ed., *Judaism: Law and Ethics* (London: Soncino, 1974), 67–79.

HILL, CHRISTOPHER, *Milton and the English Revolution* (London: Faber, 1977).

HOCHSTRASSER, TIM, 'Conscience and Reason: The Natural Law Theory of Jean Barbeyrac', *Historical Journal*, 36 (1993), 289–308.

HONIGMANN, E. A. J., 'The Politics in *Hamlet* and "The World of the Play",' in John Russell Brown and Bernard Harris, eds., *Hamlet*, Stratford-upon-Avon Studies, 5 (London: Edward Arnold, 1963), 129–47.

HUME, PATRICK, *Notes on Milton's 'Paradise Lost'*, in *The Poetical Works of Milton* (1695).

JACOB, JAMES R., *Henry Stubbe, Radical Protestantism and the Early Enlightenment* (Cambridge: Cambridge University Press, 1983).

JOSEPH, BERTRAM, *Conscience and the King* (London: Chatto & Windus, 1953).

JOYCE, GEORGE HAYWARD, SJ, *Christian Marriage: An Historical and Doctrinal Study* (London and New York: Sheed and Ward, 1933).

KAHN, VICTORIA, *Wayward Contracts: The Crisis of Political Obligation in England 1640–1674* (Princeton: Princeton University Press, 2004).

KATCHEN, AARON, *Christian Hebraists and Dutch Rabbis* (Cambridge, Mass: Harvard University Press, 1984).

KATZ, DAVID S., *The History of the Jews in England 1485–1850* (Oxford: Clarendon Press, 1996).

—— *Philo-Semitism and the Readmission of the Jews to England* (Oxford: Clarendon Press, 1982).

KERMODE, FRANK, *The Genesis of Secrecy* (Cambridge, Mass.: Harvard University Press, 1979).

—— 'What is Shakespeare's *Henry VIII* About?', *Durham University Journal*, NS 9 (1947–8), 48–55.

KERRIGAN, WILLIAM, *Hamlet's Perfection* (Baltimore and London: Johns Hopkins University Press, 1994).

KNOPPERS, LAURA LUNGER, *Historicizing Milton: Spectacle, Power, and Poetry in Restoration England* (Athens, Ga.: University of Georgia Press, 1994).

KUGEL, JAMES L., *Traditions of the Bible: A Guide to the Bible as It Was at the Start of the Common Era* (Cambridge, Mass., and London: Harvard University Press, 1998).

LACHS, SAMUEL TOBIAS, *A Rabbinic Commentary on the New Testament* (Hoboken, NJ: Ktav, 1987).

LEVIN, HARRY, *The Question of Hamlet* (New York: Oxford University Press, 1959).

LEVINE, LAURA, *Men in Women's Clothing: Anti-theatricality and Effeminization 1579–1642* (Cambridge: Cambridge University Press, 1994).

LEWALSKI, BARBARA K., *The Life of John Milton* (Oxford: Blackwell, 2000).

—— 'Milton and Idolatry', *Studies in English Literature*, 43 (2003), 213–32.

—— 'Milton's *Samson* and the "New Acquist of True [Political] Experience"', *Milton Studies* 24, ed. James D. Simmonds (Pittsburgh: University of Pittsburgh Press, 1989), 233–51.

LICHTENSTEIN, AHARON, *Henry More: The Rational Theology of a Cambridge Platonist* (Cambridge, Mass.: Harvard University Press, 1962).

LLOYD JONES, G., *The Discovery of Hebrew in Tudor England: A Third Language* (Manchester: Manchester University Press, 1983).

McPHERSON, DAVID, 'Ben Jonson's Library and Marginalia: An Annotated Catalogue', *Studies in Philology*, 71 (1974), 1–106.

MASLEN, KEITH, *An Early London Printing House at Work: Studies in the Bowyer Ledgers* (New York: Bibliographical Society of America, 1993).

MASSON, DAVID, *Life of John Milton: Narrated in Connection with the Political, Ecclesiastical, and Literary History of his Time*, 7 vols. (Cambridge: Macmillan, 1859–94).

MILLER, PETER N., *Peiresc's Europe: Learning and Virtue in the Seventeenth Century* (New Haven and London: Yale University Press, 2000).

NOTH, MARTIN, *Leviticus: A Commentary* (London: SCM, 1965).

NOVAK, DAVID, *The Image of the Non-Jew in Judaism: An Historical and Constructive Study of the Noahide Laws* (New York and Toronto: Edwin Mellen Press, 1983).

ORGEL, STEPHEN, *Impersonations: The Performance of Gender in Shakespeare's England* (Cambridge: Cambridge University Press, 1996).

OWEN, EIVION, 'Milton and Selden on Divorce', *Studies in Philology*, 43 (1946), 233–57.

PARKER, WILLIAM RILEY, *Milton: A Biography*, 2 vols. (Oxford: Clarendon Press, 1968).

PARKER, WILLIAM RILEY, *Milton's Contemporary Reputation* (Columbus: Ohio State University Press, 1940).

QUINT, DAVID, *Epic and Empire: Politics and Generic Form from Virgil to Milton* (Princeton: Princeton University Press, 1993).

RAGUSSIS, MICHAEL, *Figures of Conversion: 'The Jewish Question' & English National Identity* (Durham, NC, and London: Duke University Press, 1995).

ROGERS, JOHN, *The Matter of Revolution: Science, Poetry, and Politics in the Age of Milton* (Ithaca, NY, and London: Cornell University Press, 1996).

—— 'The Secret of *Samson Agonistes*', in Albert C. Labriola, ed., *The Miltonic Samson*, Milton Studies 33 (Pittsburgh: University of Pittsburgh Press, 1996), 111–32.

ROSENBLATT, JASON P., *Torah and Law in 'Paradise Lost'* (Princeton: Princeton University Press, 1994).

ROTH, CECIL, *A History of the Jews in England*, 3rd edn. (Oxford: Clarendon Press, 1985).

—— 'Leone da Modena and England', *Jewish Historical Society of England, Transactions*, 11 (1924–7), 206–25; ibid. 17 (1951–2), 39–41.

SANDERS, E. P., *The Historical Figure of Jesus* (London: Penguin, 1993).

SARNA, NAHUM, *The JPS Torah Commentary: Exodus* (Philadelphia: Jewish Publication Society, 1991).

SCARISBRICK, J. J., *Henry VIII* (Berkeley and Los Angeles: University of California Press, 1968).

SCHNUCKER, R. V., ed., *Calviniana: Ideas and Influence of Jean Calvin*, Sixteenth-Century Essays and Studies, 10 (Kirksville, Mo; 1988).

SEGAL, ALAN F., *Paul the Convert: The Apostolate and Apostasy of Saul the Pharisee* (New Haven: Yale University Press, 1990).

SELLIN, PAUL R., 'The Reference to John Milton's *Tetrachordon* in *De Doctrina Christiana*', *Studies in English Literature*, 37 (1997), 137–49.

SHAHEEN, NASEEB, *Biblical References in Shakespeare's Plays* (Newark, Del.: University of Delaware Press, 1999).

SHAPIRO, JAMES, *Shakespeare and the Jews* (New York: Columbia University Press, 1996).

SHAWCROSS, JOHN T., 'The Dating of Certain Poems, Letters, and Prolusions Written by Milton', *English Language Notes*, 2 (1965), 251–62.

—— *John Milton: The Self and the World* (Lexington, Ky.: University Press of Kentucky, 1993).

SHOULSON, JEFFREY S., *Milton and the Rabbis: Hebraism, Hellenism, & Christianity* (New York: Columbia University Press, 2001).

SILVER, VICTORIA, *Imperfect Sense: The Predicament of Milton's Irony* (Princeton: Princeton University Press, 2001).

SOMMERVILLE, J. P., 'English and European Political Ideas in the Early Seventeenth Century: Revisionism and the Case of Absolutism', *Journal of British Studies*, 35 (1996), 168–94.

—— 'Hobbes, Selden, Erastianism, and the History of the Jews', in G. A. J. Rogers and Tom Sorell, eds., *Hobbes and History* (London and New York: Routledge, 2000), 160–88.

—— 'John Selden, the Law of Nature, and the Origins of Government', *Historical Journal*, 27 (1984), 437–47.

—— *Royalists & Patriots: Politics and Ideology in England, 1603–1640,* 2nd edn. (London and New York: Longmans, 1999).

—— 'Selden, Grotius, and the Seventeenth-Century Intellectual Revolution in Moral and Political Theory', in Victoria Kahn and Lorna Hutson, eds., *Rhetoric & Law in Early Modern Europe* (New Haven and London: Yale University Press, 2001), 318–44.

SPITZER, LEO, 'Understanding Milton', in his *Essays on English and American Literature,* ed. Anna Hatcher (Princeton: Princeton University Press, 1962), 116–31.

STEINMETZ, DAVID C., ed. *The Bible in the Sixteenth Century* (Durham, NC, and London: Duke University Press, 1990).

TITE, COLIN G. C., *The Manuscript Library of Sir Robert Cotton* (London: British Library, 1994).

TOLAND, JOHN, *The Life of John Milton* (1699).

TOOMER, G. J., *Eastern Wisedome and Learning: The Study of Arabic in Seventeenth-Century England* (Oxford: Clarendon Press, 1996).

—— 'Selden's *Historie of Tithes*: Genesis, Publication, Aftermath', *Huntington Library Quarterly,* 65 (2002), 345–78.

TOY, C. H., *Quotations in the New Testament* (New York: Scribners, 1884).

TUCK, RICHARD, ' "The Ancient Law of Freedom": John Selden and the Civil War', in John Morrill, ed., *Reactions to the English Civil War 1642–1649* (London: Macmillan, 1982), 137–61.

—— 'Grotius and Selden', in J. H. Burns and Mark Goldie, eds., *The Cambridge History of Political Thought, 1450–1700* (Cambridge: Cambridge University Press, 1991), 499–529.

—— 'The "Modern" School of Natural Law', in Anthony Pagden, ed., *The Languages of Political Theory in Early-Modern Europe.* (Cambridge: Cambridge University Press, 1987), 99–122.

—— *Natural Rights Theories: Their Origin and Development* (Cambridge: Cambridge University Press, 1979).

—— *Philosophy and Government 1572–1651* (Cambridge: Cambridge University Press, 1993).

WALLACE, JOHN M., *Destiny His Choice: The Loyalism of Andrew Marvell* (Cambridge: Cambridge University Press, 1968).

WEIL, GÉRARD E., *Elie Lévita, Humaniste et Massorète (1469–1549)* (Leiden: Brill, 1963).

WEINREB, BEN, and HIBBERT, CHRISTOPHER, eds., *The London Encyclopedia* (London: Macmillan, 1983).

WELLS, STANLEY, *Shakespeare: A Life in Drama* (New York: W. W. Norton, 1995).

WILSON, JOHN DOVER, *What Happens in Hamlet* (Cambridge: Cambridge University Press, 1937).

WIND, EDGAR, *Pagan Mysteries in the Renaissance* (New York: W. W. Norton, 1968).

WITTE, JOHN, Jr., and F. ALEXANDER, gen. eds. *The Weightier Matters of the Law: Essays on Law and Religion* (Atlanta: Scholars Press, 1988).

WITTREICH, JOSEPH, *Interpreting Samson Agonistes* (Princeton: Princeton University Press, 1986).

WOOD, DEREK N. C., *'Exiled from Light': Divine Law, Morality, and Violence in Milton's 'Samson Agonistes'* (Toronto: University of Toronto Press, 2001).

WORDEN, BLAIR, 'Ben Jonson among the Historians', in Kevin Sharpe and Peter Lake, eds., *Culture and Politics in Early Stuart England* (Stanford, Calif.: Stanford University Press, 1993), 67–89.

—— 'Milton, *Samson Agonistes*, and the Restoration', in Gerald Maclean, ed., *Culture and Society in the Stuart Restoration* (Cambridge: Cambridge University Press, 1995), 111–36.

—— *The Rump Parliament 1648–1653* (Cambridge: Cambridge University Press, 1974).

ZISKIND, MARTHA, 'John Selden: Humanist Jurist', Ph.D. dissertation (University of Chicago, 1972).

Index

Abraham ibn Ezra 155 n. 29
  astrological interpretation of
    Baal-Zephon 77
  on the Book of Job 155 n. 30
  on messenger/angel of
    Judges (13) 97 n. 12
  opposing women warriors 68–9
  on Psalm (34) 109
  one of Selden's early rabbinic
    sources 78
Adelman, Janet 14 n. 3
Ainsworth, Henry 19 n. 21,
  20, 97 n. 13
Altmann, Alexander 79
Ames, William 195
Andrewes, Lancelot 3
Aquinas, St Thomas 36, 67, 149
Aristophanes 56, 70
Ascham, Anthony 126
Assmann, Jan 82–4, 87
Aubrey, John 51, 109, 274 n. 66,
  275
Augustine, St 16, 20, 25 n. 33, 83, 103,
  155, 156 n. 31, 250
Ausonius 52–3

Babington, Gervase 25 n. 35
Bacon, Sir Francis 231–2
Bacon, Roger 215, 223–4
Baillie, Robert 222–3, 246
Baker, J. Wayne 252–3 nn. 28–9
Barbeyrac, Jean
  diatribe against rabbinic
    thought 139–42
  family suffered religious
    persecution 145
  on Gentiles offering sacrifices 150
  Grotius's editor 135, 145
  on identity of divine and natural
    law 138
  and Maimonides 153

on Noachide precepts 140–1, 143,
    152, 154, 228
  profound debt to Selden's rabbinic
    scholarship 141, 144 n. 15, 147, 154
  rationalist natural law theory of 139
  translator of major writings on natural
    law 139
Barbour, Reid 209 n. 13
Barker, Arthur 105 n. 29
Barlow, Thomas 174–6, 182, 278
Bastwick, John 170
Beard, Thomas 25
Bedouelle, Guy 36 n. 67, 39 n. 80
Bennett, James 75 n. 2
Bennett, Joan S. 95, 105 n. 29
Berkowitz, David 10, 45 n. 96, 232 n.
    11, 267, 276–7
Berlin, Isaiah 165 n. 22, 260–2, 264
Bible
  on the active intellect 214
  Christian reliance on Jewish
    translators 39
  creation of humans in 202
  on cross-dressing 68, 179
  on destroying tokens of
    idolatry 95, 99, 104
  Elohim as human judges 11
  on forbidden sexual unions 42, 48,
    152, 234, 237
  and Gentiles 220
  on hospitality toward strangers 154,
    166–7
  on levirate marriage 21, 33, 35–6
  London Polyglot 128, 275
  on messenger/angel 97
  mixing genders in 69–70
  monism of 108
  moral law of 36
  on pagan gods 1, 79, 85–90
  passion narrative in 193
  permitting divorce 146

Bible (*cont.*):
  on Samson 96, 104, 107–8
  Selden's copies of 50, 66,
    68, 123 n. 34
  Selden's hermeneutic skill 276
  variant English translations of 23–4,
    36, 96 n. 9
  on zeal 104, 119–20
  and Zephon 77
Bloom, Harold 78
Bodin, Jean 213 n. 25
Bogue, David 75 n. 2
Boleyn, Ann 8, 23, 28–9
Bomberg, Daniel 3, 66, 123 n. 34,
  199 n. 56
Booth, Stephen 19
Borde, Andrew 32 n. 55
Bowyer, William 158–9, 180–1, 278
Boyle, Robert 174
Brahe, Tycho 141
Broadbent, J. B. 91
Browne, William 55 n. 4
Burns, Norman 93, 95
Burton, Henry 171–3, 182

Calamy, Edmund 247
Calvin, Jean 15, 24 n. 32, 27, 187,
  252
Campeggio, Lorenzo 37–8
Carey, John 3 n. 5, 221 n. 45
Caro, R. Joseph 35, 121, 192
Casaubon, Isaac 58, 79, 275
Casaubon, Meric 1, 275
Catherine of Aragon
  childless widow of Prince Arthur 18
  divorced by Henry VIII 23, 29, 43
  heroine of *Grisild the Second* 27
  and the impediment of public
    decency 47
  and levirate marriage 23 n. 30, 29
  portrayed sympathetically in *The Life
    of King Henry the Eighth* 26–8
  and Spain 25
  victim of Henry's dirty tricks 37–9, 46
Chapuys, Eustace 33–7
Chaucer, Geoffrey 245
Chernaik, Warren 115 n. 8

Christian Hebraists
  behind exchanges of Marvell and
    Parker 112–34
  differences between Lightfoot and
    Selden 132–3, 160, 196, 239, 241
  differences between Rittangel and
    Selden 4
  and Henry VIII's great matter 34–6
  irony, contradiction, and double vision
    among 8, 32, 139, 153, 162–3
  and Selden's equivocal status 9
  and Selden's philosemitism 161, 239
  veneration of Maimonides 79–80
Christianson, Paul 10, 267
Cicero, Marcus Tullius 53, 217, 220
Cleveland, John 162–3
Coryate, Thomas 49–50
Cotton, Sir Robert 2, 57, 103, 259, 276
Cotton, Sir Thomas 275
Crashaw, William 55
Cromartie, Alan 11, 134 n. 66, 211 nn.
  20–1, 219, 222
Cromwell, Oliver 162, 174, 277
cross-dressing 45, 54–5, 64, 69, 72–3,
  179, 279 ff.
Culverwel, Nathanael
  as Cambridge Platonist 202–5
  critique of Selden 203–5, 220
  debt to Selden 203, 215, 217, 221
  Discourse of the Light of Nature 202–25
  and the *intellectus agens* 215–17
  and the Jews 206–9, 213
  rational theology of 203, 205, 213,
    217
Cyprian, St 54, 64–6, 159 n. 7, 247–8

Darnel, Sir Thomas 276
Davies, W. D. 42 n. 89, 235 n. 15
Digby, Sir Kenelm 5–6
Diodati, John 21 n. 25, 106
Donaldson, E. Talbot 245
Douglas, Mary 88
Draper, John 29 n. 50
Drummond, William 45, 59, 61,
  214 n. 30
Drury, John 100 n. 17, 167 nn. 25–6
Dryden, John 115

Drayton, Michael 9, 55 n. 4
Dzelzainis, Martin 115 n. 8

Empson, William 23 n. 29, 74
Erastianism
  Bishop Stillingfleet's 269–70
  and *Epicoene* 50
  Harrington's 6, 178–9
  Henry Stubbe's 182
  Lightfoot's 250
  in Milton's prose tracts (1643–5) 101
  and Sanhedrin as secular court 161, 200
  Selden as head of in England 209, 222,
    244, 246, 259, 276–7
  and Westminster Assembly debates on
    excommunication 246–53
Euripides 56
Eusebius 67, 248, 284

Fallon, Stephen 98 n. 14
Farnaby, Thomas 55 n. 4
Feldman, Louis 206 n. 7, 208 n. 10
fides est servanda (keep the faith)
  as honouring the terms of a
    contract 60, 241, 263, 269
Fiennes, Nathanael 246
Finch, Henry 8
Fisher, John 24 n. 32, 27
Forrest, William 27
Fowler, Alastair 76–7, 214
Foxe, John 25 n. 36, 29 n. 51
Frazer, Sir James George 19 n. 20
Freud, Sigmund 14, 29
Fuller, Thomas 55 n. 5, 116–17

Ganz, David 141
Gardiner, S. R. 116 n. 13, 277
Gibbon, Edward 80–1, 85, 132, 244
Gil, Alexander, Jr. 81
Gillespie, George 246, 251
Goldenberg, Robert 222 n. 49
Goshen-Gottstein, Moshe 210
Gosson, Stephen 65, 68
Gouge, William 17 n. 13
Grafton, Anthony 80–1 n. 14
Greene, Robert A. 203 n. 3, 209 n. 13,
    221 n. 47

Grotius, Hugo
  on Christ's scourging the money-
    changers 114
  on divorce 146
  escape from prison 135–6
  on Jews and Christians 136–7, 142,
    146, 154
  on Leviticus (18) 149–50, 152–3
  on Matthew (5) 144–6
  and Milton 146
  on natural law 105, 137–54
  on Noachide law 141–4, 147–8, 152,
    154–5, 168–9, 228
  as pioneer in international relations 10
  on the Sanhedrin 201
  and Selden 141, 147, 149, 151, 153
  on zeal 119, 126
Guillory, John 94

Halbertal, Moshe 81 n. 15, 82, 83 nn.
    22–3, 85, 232 n. 11
Hale, Sir Matthew 249, 273, 279
Halfan, Elijah Menahem 39
Hall, Joseph 205 n. 4
Hampden, Sir Edmund 219, 277
Hampden, John 4, 219
Harpsfield, Nicholas 26, 37–8, 43
Harrington, James 6–7, 178–9, 187
Haskin, Dayton 106 n. 32
Hauser, William 77 n. 4
Hecht, Anthony 122 n. 33
Hegel, G. W. F. 83 n. 23
Henry VIII 18, 23–8, 32–45, 46–8,
    116, 234
heresy 121 n. 29, 183
Herrick, Robert 55 n. 4
Herzog, Isaac 255 n. 39
Hesychius 24 n. 32, 283
Heylyn, Peter 170
Hibbard, G. R. 62
Hill, Christopher 101 n. 20
Hochstrasser, Tim 139 n. 6, 145 n. 17
Hobbes, Thomas 169, 174, 211, 229–30,
    249, 273
  De Cive 126 n. 47, 268–9
  Leviathan 125
Holinshed, Raphael 25 n. 34

Honigmann, E. A. J. 23 n. 29
Hooker, Richard 168–9, 237–9
Hopton, Arthur 55 n. 4
Howard, Thomas, earl of Arundel 59,
   259, 260
Hume, Patrick 76–7, 79, 86–7

Jacob, James 182 nn. 1, 2, 4, 187 nn.
   22, 24
Jerome, St 67, 150, 248, 273
Jew Bill 158, 180, 278
Job
   answer to Eliphaz 50
   observer of the Noachide laws 154–7
   prophet 222
   virtuous Gentile 133
Jones, Ernest 14
Jonson, Ben
   The Alchemist 58–9
   Bartholomew Fair 61–3
   Conversations with Drummond 59–61
   Epicoene 45–7, 71
   friendship with Selden 45, 48, 50–3,
     54–61, 63
   Selden's letter to 66–7, 71, 80, 87,
     159 n. 7, 179, 241, 279 ff.
Joseph, Bertram 29
Josephus
   Against Apion 137, 207
   Antiquities 68–9, 86, 154, 186,
     195, 253
   History of the Jews 115, 186
   Jewish War 124
Joyce, George 27 n. 41

Kahn, Victoria 263, 267 n. 31
Karaites 2, 4–5, 123 n. 34, 227
Katchen, Aaron 79 n. 10, 82 n. 19
Katz, David 32 n. 54, 33, 36 n. 66, 37 n.
   69, 39, 61 n. 21, 154
Kay, John 52
Keeble, N. H. 115
Ken, Thomas 75
Kermode, Frank 28, 167
Kerrigan, William 14 n. 3
Kimchi, David
   cited by Jonson 59

   cited by Milton 5
   cited by Selden 66
   on Isaiah (14: 23) 210
   on Song of Solomon (3: 9) 265
Knoppers, Laura 101 n. 20
Kugel, James 58–9

Lachs, Samuel 195 n. 44, 199 n. 57
Lactantius 220 n. 43, 231, 261
Langbaine, Gerard 1, 165, 223
Lasker, Daniel 3
Latimer, Hugh 26
Laud, William, Archbishop of
   Canterbury 170, 188 n. 29, 246, 275
Levi ben Gershom 5, 156
Lévi-Strauss, Claude 31
Levin, Harry 16 n. 10
Levine, Laura 62 n. 23, 73
Leviticus (18) incest prohibitions
   and the Apostolic Decree 234–7
   as additional Noachide laws 151–2
   cultic strictures and specifications 262
   a decalogical code 21
   and the dispensability of God's word 26
   and ecclesiastical vs. temporal
     courts 232
   and eternal life 166
   and Jesus's response to the lawyer in
     Luke (10) 167
   and Job 154
   and marriage to a deceased brother's
     widow 16–21, 26, 29, 30–5, 234
   as moral and perpetual 36
   as not binding on the Christian
     conscience 41–2
   opposed to deuteronomic levirate
     marriage 21–5
   as a partition-wall 151
   Sir John Vaughan's interpretation
     of 226–7
   superseded by Noachide precepts
     233–4
   whether Canaanites punished for not
     observing 152–3
Lewalski, Barbara 100 n. 17, 101 n. 20,
   105 n. 28, 188 nn. 28–9
Lichtenstein, Aharon 205 n. 5

Lightfoot, John 112, 128 n. 54, 132–3, 160, 239, 241
  Horae Hebraicae et Talmudicae 118, 131, 196
  Journal, Proceedings, Assembly of Divines 246–51
Lloyd-Jones, G. 32 n. 55
Locke, John 178
Lowth, Robert 100
Lowth, Simon 209–10
Luther, Martin 20 n. 24, 36, 44

MacCallum, Hugh, *see* Greene, Robert A.
McPherson, David 58 n. 12
Macrobius 69, 72, 90
Maimonides, Moses
  on blasphemy 193–5
  Christian Hebraists' veneration of 79
  on cross-dressing 54, 69, 179, 279 ff.
  on Gentiles 151, 163
  humanely reinterpreting legal severity 120, 177
  on idolatry 81–3, 91
  on incest 41, 153, 230, 233
  on the *intellectus agens* 212–15
  on levirate marriage 24 n. 32, 25
  on Noachide laws 147–8, 162, 189, 191–2, 205, 217, 233–4
  and normative inversion 67–8, 87–9
  on preserving a life 197
  on proselytes 129, 131, 133, 148
  on public welfare 123
  on punishing a king 242–3
  as Selden's favourite source 67, 80, 120, 133, 231, 257
  on Samson 103
  on statutes and judgments 203 n. 3
  structuralism in 67–8, 88
Mantino, Jacob 39
Margalit, Avishai, *see* Halbertal
marriage
  as a contract 259
  in *De Jure* 154
  in *Der Bestrafte Bruder-mord* 26
  a divine law in paradise 271
  exogamous 94, 103, 175

  forbidden degrees in Leviticus (18) 234–5
  free from clerical interference 266
  in *Hamlet* 17–21, 29–30
  and Henry VIII's great matter 25, 32–45
  with an idolater 96
  impediments in *Epicoene* 45–8
  and incest 22, 152, 226, 236
  in Jewish law and custom 2, 33–6, 40, 42
  levirate 16–17, 23, 42
  in *The Life of King Henry VIII* 26–8
  and natural law 227–8
  and Noachide law 229
  papal bull of dispensation 23
  rituals 103
  in *Samson Agonistes* 101
  second 31, 36–7, 48
  Selden on 50–1
  at will 264
Martial
  Epigrams 59–61
Marvell, Andrew
  on inspiration 118
  and Lightfoot's rabbis 130–3
  on proselytes 128–34
  and Selden's rabbis 127–8
  on zeal 113–15, 117, 127
Maslen, Keith 158 n. 1
Masson, David 266 n. 25
Mather, Increase 75
Mede, Joseph 8
Mendoza, Inigo de 37 n. 41, 43
Menasseh ben Israel 4, 162–3, 277
Miller, Peter 1 n. 1
Milton, John
  De Doctrina Christiana 3, 94, 98–9, 149, 169–70, 271–2
  On the Morning of Christ's Nativity 77, 93–111, 157
  Paradise Lost: on bisexuality 72–3; on catalogues of pagan deities 77, 85–92; on Exodus (23: 20) 96–9; on inspiration 214–16; on marriage 266; on monism 109; on naming and identity 74–9; on transposition 271–2;

Milton, John (*cont.*):
  on zeal 124 n. 40; on Zephon 74–9
  Paradise Regained 94, 106 n. 32, 112,
    193–5
  *The Readie and Easie Way to Establish a
    Free Commonwealth* 187–8
  Samson Agonistes: angels in 97–8, 106;
    antinomian readings of 93–5; and
    Canaanite idolatry 96, 99, 104–5;
    date of composition 101; divergent
    interpretations of 93; fidelity to the
    Mosaic law 93–4, 95–6, 99–100;
    Hebraic Samson 96, 108; and
    Judaic self-understanding 102; and
    Milton's divorce tracts 100–1;
    monism in 101, 105–6, 108–9;
    monotheism vs. paganism in 75; and
    laws of the Nazarite 96, 107;
    regeneration in 95, 108; Samson's
    bad marriages 101, 103–4;
    Samson's death 107–9; and Selden's
    De Jure 102–5; and *Uxor
    Ebraica* 103–4
Milward, Richard 166, 223, 241
Modena, Leone da 8, 48–50, 67
More, Henry 6 n. 9, 205, 273–4
Moses of Coucy
  commentary on Maimonides' *Mishneh
    Torah* 121 n. 28, 123 n. 34
  on the Sanhedrin's leaving the temple
    compound 199
  one of Selden's three favourite rabbinic
    sources 231
  tolerant regarding prosecution of
    idolatry 175 n. 48
  on usury 123 n. 35

Newton, Sir Isaac 10, 169, 267, 270–2
Nĩno, Rodrigo 40
Noachide laws
  on acquiring a wife through
    intercourse 264
  adjudication in 218
  and the Apostolic Decree 234–7
  blasphemy and idolatry in 184,
    188–9
  Culverwel's critique of 205

in Grotius's *De Jure Belli* 140, 143, 151
in Hooker's *Lawes of Ecclesiasticall
    Politie* 168–9, 237–9
Job's observance of 133, 154–7
and the law of nature 262
and Levitical incest prohibitions 152
in Maimonides' *Mishneh Torah* 147–8,
    233
minimal moral duties 10
observance guarantees eternal life 41
organized into two parts 270
rabbinic in origin 2
locus classicus in tractate Sanhedrin 191
in Selden's *De Jure Naturali* 141, 161,
    164, 191, 202, 217
in Sir John Vaughan's legal decisions
    226–43
six of the laws originate in paradise
    10 n. 14
in Stubbe's *Defence of the Good Old
    Cause* 182
supplemented by civil laws 11, 218–19
in the work of Phillipus Ferdinandus
    Polonus 122–3 n. 34
in the work of seventeenth-century
    British intellectuals 10
universal divine laws of perpetual
    obligation 9, 42
see also Selden, WORKS, *De Jure Naturali
    et Gentium*
Novak, David 42 n. 90,
    218, 235 n. 16

Ogg, David 10, 13, 117 n. 14, 225
Orgel, Stephen 73
Owen, Eivion 262
Owen, John 113, 132

parable
  Good Samaritan 167
  Job as figure in 155
  of the talents 106 n. 32
Paris, Matthew 160 n. 10, 174
Parker, Samuel
  on proselytes 129
  and Selden's rabbis 113, 118–25, 129
  on zeal 112–24

Parker, William Riley 99, 205 n. 4,
  266 n. 25
Patterson, Annabel 112 n. 1
Peacham, Henry 55 n. 4
Peiresc, Nicolas-Claude Fabri 1, 187 n. 3
Penn, William 173–4
Peter Martyr 111 n. 37
Phillips, Edward 101
Philo
  on blasphemy 186
  on synagogues 137
  on zeal 121
Pocock, J. G. A. 6, 179
Pococke, Edward 1, 170 n. 31,
  210, 260
Polonus, Philippus Ferdinandus
  122–3 n. 34
Poole, Matthew 95–7, 106 n. 31,
  110–11
Preston, Thomas 187
Price, William 250
proselytes
  as annoying as an abscess 129–30
  among the seven Canaanite
    nations 177
  and Christ's denunciation of
    Pharisees 130
  of the gate 148, 164, 175, 178, 273
  interpreted by Marvell as
    turncoats 130–2
  interrogation of motives 103, 130
  of justice 148, 164, 186
  as newly born 102, 255
  and pederasts 130, 133
Prynne, William 65, 72, 160 n. 10,
  170–3, 242
Pufendorf, Samuel 10, 139, 142–3,
  169, 265
Purchas, Samuel
  Purchas His Pilgrimage 55 n. 4, 66 n.
    33, 79–80, 87, 160–1 n. 10

Quint, David 78 n. 8

Ragussis, Michael 160 n. 8
Raphael, Marco 34–6
Rashi (Solomon ben Isaac)

on the androgynous first human
  being 70
on Baal-Zephon 77
on the barren wife of Job (24: 21) 50
on conversion 131
on cross-dressing 68
on excommunication 254, 257
and humaneness of rabbinic law 180
on Job's righteousness 155–6
on laws prohibiting usury 123 n. 35
on matrimony 266
on 'one flesh' 230 n. 6
on Onias's offence 127–8
on a parody of the Apostolic
  Decree 240–1
on pigeon-flyers 122
on proselytes 105, 129, 177
on the Sanhedrin's powers 199
as Selden's 'common Hebrew Gloss' 66,
  231, 257
on the worship of Baal-Peor 67–8
variant readings in the *Commentary* 50
Regelsberg, Mary de 135–6
religious toleration 7, 10, 61 n. 21,
  126–7, 139, 147, 158–81, 182, 184,
  186, 202, 272–3, 277–8
responsa 49 n. 104, 66–7
Reynolds, Samuel Harvey 51 n. 109,
  63 n. 25, 223 n. 54, 251 n. 25
Rittangel, Joannes Stephanus 3–5
Rogers, John 109
Rogers, Richard 64, 110 n. 35
Rosenblatt, Jason 66 n. 34, 100 n. 18,
  188 n. 26, 266 n. 88, 271 n. 48
Rosenne, Shabtai 141 n. 10
Roth, Cecil 33 n. 57, 49 n. 103,
  122 n. 34
Rubens, Peter-Paul 1–2
Rutherford, Samuel 246

Sanders, E. P. 193 n. 39
Sanhedrin (court)
  and the Areopagus 187–8
  authority exceeding that of the
    king 197, 242
  and capital cases 4 n. 6, 188 n. 27,
    196

Sanhedrin (*cont.*):
  and the chamber of hewn stones 4,
    199–201
  as a civil body 161, 244, 267
  and excommunication 249,
    253–4, 256
  and Noachide law 11–12
  punishing blasphemy 191–6
  and ritual expiation 198
  sessions of 188
  as Selden's model for Parliament 4, 6,
    161, 224 n. 56, 242, 253
  the subject of Selden's *De Synedriis* 2,
    161, 197, 218
  and the trial of Jesus 198
Sanhedrin (tractate), *see* Talmud
Sarna, Nahum 96 n. 9, 97 n. 12
Scaliger, Joseph
  admired Maimonides 79–80
  advances in biblical philology 210
  an important source of Selden's early
    scholarship 83 n. 21
  knew Hebrew 123 n. 34
  offered grudging praise by Parker
    118
Scarisbrick, J. J. 15 n. 9, 25 n. 33,
    32 n. 54, 33, 43, 45
Schleiner, Winfried 8, 54,
    58 n. 11, 279
Sclater, William 128
Seaman, Lazarus 250
Segal, Alan 235 nn. 16–17
Selden, John
  addressed as Rabbi 4
  on behalf of Roman Catholics 277
  defending freedom of the press
    275
  and the Five Knights' Case 219,
    276–7
  on the importance of 'eastern
    learning' 258, 276
  imprisonment 1–2, 276–7
  language education 58–9, 61, 200,
    220, 255
  and the Petition of Right 1
  relieving poverty 275
  tolerant toward Jews 166–7

WORKS
  *An Admonition to the Reader
    of Sir James Sempill's
    Appendix* 230–1
  De Anno Civili 2, 159, 253 n. 35
  De Diis Syris 63, 66–71, 77–81,
    83–92, 273–4
  *De Jure Naturali et Gentium juxta
    Disciplinam Ebraeorum* 1–11,
    104–5, 119–25, 139–41, 154–7,
    161–81, 183–94, 211–22,
    228–41, 256–7
  *De Successione in Pontificatum
    Ebraeorum* 8, 119 n. 24,
    128, 227, 248
  *De Successionibus ad Leges Ebraeorum
    in Bona Defunctorum* 48–9, 51, 60,
    170 n. 32, 227, 276
  *De Synedriis et Praefecturis Juridicis
    Veterum Ebraeorum* 6–7, 103, 123,
    129, 133 n. 65, 141, 188 nn. 26–7,
    192, 195–201, 224 n. 56, 242–3,
    252–7
  Dissertatio ad Fletam 9, 116, 117 n. 14,
    225 n. 58
  The Duello 168
  Historie of Tithes 4–5, 45, 51, 64,
    116–17, 165, 189, 223–4, 267
  letter to Ben Jonson on
    cross-dressing and bisexual
    gods 54–73, 159 n. 7, 279 ff.
  Mare Clausum 9, 141, 218, 259
  Notes on Fortescue 11, 218–19
  Table Talk 60, 63, 125, 134, 149,
    165–8, 172, 180, 196, 223–4,
    244–5, 251–3, 263–5
  Titles of Honor 51–3, 56–7, 59, 210,
    260
  Uxor Ebraica 2–3, 48–50, 102–4, 154,
    169, 179, 227, 265–6
Sellin, Paul 3 n. 5
Sforno, Obadiah 40
Shaheen, Naseeb 15 n. 5
Shakespeare, William
  All's Well That Ends Well 38
  Antony and Cleopatra 72
  Hamlet 14–32, 44–5

1 Henry IV 123 n. 35, 127 n. 50
The Life of King Henry the Eighth, or All is True 26–8, 34
Merchant of Venice 102, 127 n. 50, 160
The Merry Wives of Windsor 135–6
The Tempest 6
Twelfth Night 70 n. 46, 73
The Winter's Tale 27
Shapiro, James 32 n. 55, 49 n. 105, 160
Shoulson, Jeffrey 12 n. 18
Silver, Victoria 266 n. 30
Skelton, John 52
Socinians 201, 204–5, 228
Sommerville, J. P. 9–10, 66 n. 34, 244 n. 1, 246, 253 n. 34, 267
Spitzer, Leo 272
Stansby, William 48, 57
Steinsaltz, Adin 257
Stillingfleet, Edward 249, 267–71
Stubbe, Henry
    on the crucifixion 190, 201
    and heresy 183, 190, 240 n. 25
    on Noachide law 169, 172, 182, 189
    republicanism of 242
    and Selden's ancient rescripts 184–6
    and Selden's rabbinica 115–18, 177–8, 184–7, 190, 194
    on toleration 186–7
    on zeal 114
Stubbes, Philip 65
Summers, Joseph 91

Tacitus
    hostile descriptions of Jews 61 n. 21, 150, 154
    on Nero's homosexual marriage 241
    on proselytes 102
Talmud
    Barbeyrac's diatribe against 139–40
    on blasphemy 190, 193–4
    Bomberg edition 3, 8, 191
    on contracts 60–1
    on contributing to public welfare 123–4
    on courts of law 191, 200–1, 217, 262
    on the death penalty 6
    and excommunication 253–5

    on Gentiles offering temple sacrifices 151
    incest laws in 42
    on inspiration 118, 221–2
    laws of inheritance in 2, 42–3, 51
    limiting royal prerogative 197
    levirate marriage in 42–3
    moderating scriptural severity 120–1, 179–81
    negative view of usury in 123 n. 35
    and Noachide law 9–12, 161 ff., 172, 191, 217, 228, 237–8, 268
    on obligation and liability 211
    parody of the Apostolic Decree in 240–1
    paranymph in 104
    on proselytes 129–31
    publishing opposed points of view 165
    responsa in 67
    on righteous Gentiles 155, 163–7
    and Selden's interpretative errors 255–7
    and Selden's linguistic skill 4, 6–7, 61, 162, 231
    as Selden's prison reading 2
    on succession in the priesthood 2
    on tempting God 195–6
    on zealots 104, 120–2, 127–8
Tayler, Francis 258, 276
Taylor, Jeremy 10, 169–70, 212–13, 273
Tertullian 25 n. 33, 53–4, 64–6, 159 n. 7, 237
Tite, Colin 275 n. 68
Toland, John 169, 176 n. 56, 272–3
Toomer, G. J. 2 n. 2, 45 n. 96, 55, 57, 59, 66, 83 n. 21, 112 n. 1, 116, 122 n. 34, 128 n. 52, 160 n. 10, 170 n. 32, 210 n. 18, 258 n. 45, 260
Toy, C. H. 195
Tuck, Richard 137, 141 n. 8, 161 n. 12, 172 n. 41, 211–12, 226, 229, 232, 241, 273
Tyndale, William 23 n. 30, 36

Vane, Sir Henry 187
Varro, Marcus Terentius 83–4, 266

Vaughan, Sir John 48, 169
  on forbidden sexual relations 227,
    232–6
  homage to Selden 226–43
  on Noachide laws 227, 229, 234, 239
  on obedience to the king 243
  on state of nature 227–30
Venus
  armed and bearded 69, 72, 73
  attacked by enemies of the
    theatre 69, 73
  as bisexual generative power 70
  identified with other deities 69
  Mater Deum 71
  in Milton's *Nativity Ode* 90
  worshipped by men in women's
    clothing 54, 65, 69, 179, 279 ff.
Vico, Giambattista 260–4, 273
Villiers, George, 2nd Duke of
  Buckingham 115
Vines, William 251
Vives, Juan Luis 25 n. 33, 31
Vossius, Dionysius 82, 231

Wallace, John 126
Walton, Brian 275
Weemse, John 17 n. 13, 20
Wells, Stanley 26 n. 40
Westminster Assembly 162–3, 222,
  246–51, 270
Wheelock, Abraham 128
Whitelock, Bulstrode 65 n. 30, 173 n. 44

Whittington, Robert 52
Widdrington Catholics 187
Wilkins, David 159
Willet, Andrew 17 n. 13, 18 n. 18, 21,
  25 n. 37, 27–8, 97–8
Wilson, John Dover 14
Wind, Edgar 100 n. 17
Witte, John, Jr. 46
Wittreich, Joseph 93
Wood, Anthony à 115, 126, 182 n. 1, 258
Wood, Derek 94 n. 5
Worden, Blair 51, 57 n. 9, 101 n. 20

Young, Thomas 247–8

zealots, right of (*Ius Zelotarum*)
  Anthony Ascham on 125
  and Christ's persecutors striking
    him 196
  and Christ's scourging of the money-
    changers 119, 124, 133
  Hobbes on 125–6
  an incendiary topic in the Civil War
    period 104
  and laws of normative Judaism 104
  Marvell's talmudic reference to
    127–8
  Philo's extreme position on 121
  rabbinic mitigation of 120
Ziskind, Jonathan 66 n. 34, 102 n. 21,
  161 n. 11
Ziskind, Martha 244 n. 1, 247 n. 11